PSYCHOLOGY OF ADOLESCENCE

Books by Luella Cole

The Elementary School Subjects

A History of Education

The Improvement of Reading

Teaching in the Elementary School

Psychology of Adolescence

Workbook in Psychology of Adolescence
(with F. S. Hamilton and R. L. Marquis)

Students' Guide to Efficient Study
(with J. M. Ferguson)

Psychology of Childhood and Adolescence
(with John J. B. Morgan)

Psychology

of

Adolescence

FOURTH EDITION

by Luella Cole, Ph.D

Rinehart and Company, Inc.

PUBLISHERS   NEW YORK

To Florence Gertrude Jenney

Teacher and Friend

of My Own Adolescent Years

Preface

In writing the original form of this book and in preparing the three revisions, I have been guided by three general principles that have determined the selection and presentation of materials.

First, I have tried to present a balanced and comprehensive picture of adolescent growth along all lines—physical, emotional, social, moral, and intellectual. Naturally, the published reports of research in these various phases of adolescent development are not equal in number, scope, or value, but within the limits imposed by the available studies, I have given equal emphasis to growth in each field.

Second, I have considered the usefulness of each study for prospective teachers, teachers in service, parents of adolescents, and the adolescents themselves—many of whom read the book and write me letters about their problems—in order that the material may be of the greatest value to these various groups of readers. Special emphasis has been given to those research studies that contribute most to the problems of daily life in the school, the home, and the community.

Third, I have used many case histories, anecdotes, personal reminiscences, figures, and other illustrative materials, not only to make the text of greater interest to the student but to facilitate the application of what is learned to the daily life of adolescent boys and girls.

The present revision differs from its predecessors in the substitution of more recent or more complete studies for such reports as have become outdated, in the inclusion of more interpretation of the data—and especially of a more psychoanalytic interpretation—and in the emphasis upon material from recent studies in personality and sociometry. In response to the modern interest in personality, I have added a chapter on this topic.

The list of novels illustrating problems of growth and possible solutions—good and bad—to these problems has been revised and brought up-to-date. The references to the periodical literature at the end of the chapters have been grouped into topics instead of being listed alphabetically, in order that the lists may provide more guidance than before and may also be used for the initial readings needed for term papers or reports.

I trust that adherence to the basic principles of selection and presentation, together with the modernizing changes introduced in this revision, has produced a text that will be of value to those who deal with adolescent boys and girls.

LUELLA COLE

Berkeley, California*
June, 1953.

---

* Since the Post Office can rarely find me under my maiden name, unless the street and house number are included, I append my address, for those who wish to write me: 2521 Benvenue Avenue, Berkeley 4, California.

One hundred and eighty-eight multiple-choice examination items based on this text are available to instructors at a nominal cost.

Table of Contents

Introduction

List of Illustrations

List of Tables

Introduction

CHAPTER ONE

Adolescence as a Period
of Human Growth

Adolescence as a phenomenon among the young of all social classes is largely a product of modern culture and civilization. Puberty, to be sure, is as old as the human race, and some recognition of the physiological changes that constitute puberty is very ancient indeeed. But until recently, except for a few male children of well-to-do families, there has never been time for ten years of adolescence. The great-grandparents of present-day Americans finished their schooling by the age of twelve or thirteen, went to work shortly thereafter, married any time after sixteen, and were maintaining themselves economically by the age of eighteen. It is only recently that education has been extended and marriage delayed until a true period of adolescence has become an almost universal phenomenon in American life. High schools are still at a loss as to what the crowds of adolescents should be taught, because the development of public secondary education is so recent. For instance, less than fifty years ago there was not a single public high school in the borough of Manhattan in New York City, and the College of the City of New York maintained a subfreshman year for those who —like the writer's husband—entered college direct from the eighth grade, because they lived in a borough that had no high school. In 1952, in the same borough there were twenty-five high schools—eleven academic or commercial, and fourteen vocational—enrolling 217,031 pupils. The same mushroom development has taken place all over the country. This period of adolescence for everyone is new in the world's history. It remains to be seen what constructive use can be made of it.

I. Relation of Adolescence to Other Age Levels

Before taking up the problems that are thrust upon the growing boy or girl, it might be well to state briefly just what years in the life of an individual fall into the various periods of growth that will be referred to frequently throughout this book.

People have long been aware of the fact that an individual progresses from one period to another in an orderly series of stages throughout his entire existence. Perhaps the best-known expression of this theme is contained in the lines quoted on the following page.

All the world's a stage,
And all the men and women merely players:
They have their exits and their entrances;
And one man in his time plays many parts,
His acts being seven ages. At first the infant,
Mewling and puking in the nurse's arms.
And then the whining school-boy, with his satchel
And shining morning face, creeping like snail
Unwillingly to school. And then the lover,
Sighing like furnace, with a woeful ballad
Made to his mistress' eyebrow. Then a soldier,
Full of strange oaths, and bearded like the pard,
Jealous in honour, sudden and quick in quarrel,
Seeking the bubble reputation
Even in the cannon's mouth. And then the justice,
In fair round belly with good capon lined,
With eyes severe and beard of formal cut,
Full of wise saws and modern instances;
And so he plays his part. The sixth age shifts
Into the lean and slipper'd pantaloon,
With spectacles on nose and pouch on side,
His youthful hose, well saved, a world too wide
For his shrunk shank; and his big manly voice,
Turning again toward childish treble, pipes
And whistles in his sound. Last scene of all,
That ends this strange eventful history,
Is second childishness and mere oblivion,
Sans teeth, sans eyes, sans taste, sans everything.[1]

The modern psychologist has broken down these stages of growth into smaller units and has studied each more or less intensively—infancy the most and middle age the least. The entire range of ages from birth to death may now be divided as follows:

Infancy	birth to 2 years
Early childhood	2 to 6 years
Middle childhood	6 to 11 years (girls); 6 to 13 years (boys)
Preadolescence or late childhood	11 to 13 years (girls); 13 to 15 years (boys)
Early adolescence	13 to 15 years (girls); 15 to 17 years (boys)
Middle adolescence	15 to 18 years (girls); 17 to 19 years (boys)
Late adolescence	18 to 21 years (girls); 19 to 21 years (boys)
Early adulthood	21 to 35 years
Middle adulthood	35 to 50 years
Late adulthood	50 to 65 years
Early senescence	65 to 75 years
Senescence	75 years, onward

It should be understood clearly that one does not automatically pass from one of these periods to another on a given birthday. One level of

---

[1] Shakespeare, *As You Like It*, II, vii, 139–166.

development shades gradually into the next; indeed, the earlier stages are so short that each is hardly established before premonitory signs of the following one appear. For the adolescent years, the age limits differ for the two sexes because girls mature on an average two years earlier than boys, who do not catch up with them until the last years of adolescence. It will be noticed that the main divisions of the school system correspond roughly to the developmental levels of the years before adulthood.

Each of the periods has its own problems which must be solved if the individuals are to enter the next period without handicap. Adolescence is perhaps no more important a stage of development than any other, but it is the last stage before adulthood, and it therefore offers to both parents and teachers the last opportunity to educate a child for his adult responsibilities.

II. Specific Problems of Adolescence

Near the beginning of the adolescent period the boy or girl achieves sexual maturity and, in some specific capacities, intellectual maturity as well. By the end of adolescence, physical growth is complete and intellectual growth very nearly so. Only severe deprivation can prevent a human organism from reaching adult size, shape, and function, or from growing into its expected mental maturity. In short, Nature will provide for these two types of growth, unless some catastrophe intervenes. The real problems of adolescence are therefore emotional, social, moral, and economic.

Most adolescents solve their problems by slow degrees during the ages from twelve to twenty-one. The adolescent with severe conflicts and violent reactions is so much more dramatic than the boy or girl who develops slowly and without fireworks, that one is likely to overemphasize the storm and stress of the period. In the normal growth of a normal individual, childhood fades, adolescence advances, and adulthood arrives in a gradual, smooth series of small changes and with only temporary and incidental difficulties and disturbances.

The boy or girl enters adolescence with a child's adjustment to the world. No matter how perfect his emotional and social adaptation may be, it is not suitable for adult life. A child is normally dependent upon others, has little or no interest in members of the opposite sex, expects to be supported both emotionally and financially by his family, takes his judgments ready-made from those he admires, and has neither the interest nor the ability to deal with generalized principles. At the end of his adolescence he should be ready to leave his home—emotionally and actually—to maintain himself economically, to manage his own social contacts, to make up his own mind, to establish his own home, and to concern himself with the general principles behind surface phenomena.

In the change from dependent childhood to independent adulthood an individual has to find a satisfactory answer to many problems, the more important of which are to be discussed shortly. These problems have been grouped, for the sake of convenience, into eight areas of human interest and activity: emotional maturity, establishment of heterosexual interests, social maturity, emancipation from home control, intellectual maturity, the beginnings of economic independence, adult uses of leisure, and the establishment of an interest in general principles of conduct. Table 1 provides a brief overview of the problems, which will be taken up in detail later on. Naturally, no adolescent is likely in a few short years to attain maturity in all phases. The child that he was will remain with him to the end of his days, popping up from time to time with childish if not infantile solutions. However, an adolescent must make a beginning in the process of meeting the new requirements of life.

Table 1

OBJECTIVES OF THE ADOLESCENT PERIOD

A. *General Emotional Maturity*

From
1. Destructive expressions of emotion
2. Subjective interpretation of situations
3. Childish fears and motives
4. Habits of escaping from conflicts

to
1. Harmless or constructive expressions
2. Objective interpretations of situations
3. Adult stimuli to emotions
4. Habits of facing and solving conflicts

B. *Establishment of Heterosexual Interests*

From
1. Interest in members of same sex
2. Experience with many possible mates
3. Acute awareness of sexual development

to
1. Interest in members of opposite sex
2. Selection of one mate
3. Casual acceptance of sexual maturity

C. *General Social Maturity*

From
1. Feelings of uncertainty of acceptance by peers
2. Social awkwardness
3. Social intolerance
4. Slavish imitation of peers

to
1. Feelings of acceptance by peers
2. Social poise
3. Social tolerance
4. Freedom from slavish imitation

D. *Emancipation from Home Control*

From
1. Close parental control
2. Reliance upon parents for security
3. Identification with parents as models

to
1. Self-control
2. Reliance upon self for security
3. Attitude toward parents as friends

E. *Intellectual Maturity*

From
1. Acceptance of truth from authority
2. Desire for facts
3. Many temporary interests

to
1. Demand for evidence before acceptance
2. Desire for explanations
3. Few, stable interests

F. *Selection of an Occupation*

From
1. Interest in glamorous occupations
2. Interest in many occupations
3. Over- or underestimation of ability
4. Irrelevance of interests to ability

to

1. Interest in practical occupations
2. Interest in few occupations
3. Accurate estimate of ability
4. Reconciliation of ability and interests

G. *Uses of Leisure*

From
1. Interest in vigorous unorganized games
2. Interest in individual prowess
3. Participation in games
4. Interest in many hobbies
5. Membership in many clubs

to

1. Interest in team games
2. Interest in success of team
3. Spectator interest in games
4. Interest in few hobbies
5. Membership in a few clubs

H. *Philosophy of Life*

From
1. Indifference toward general principles
2. Specific moral habits
3. Behavior based upon achievement of pleasure and avoidance of pain

to

1. Interest in general principles
2. Generalized moral principles
3. Behavior based upon conscience and duty

The first set of problems centers around the attainment of emotional control. Children have little power to inhibit their responses, they have many fears, they are self-centered, and they run away from what is disagreeable. It is, then, one task of adolescence to emerge from childish into adult forms of emotional expression, to substitute intellectual for emotional reactions at least in recurring situations, and to learn that one cannot escape reality.

The second set of problems centers around the attainment of adult attitudes toward sex. The centering of one's emotional attention upon members of one's own sex or upon older people is a typically childish reaction. Neither of these love interests is an adequate cornerstone for an adult adjustment. The pubertal changes usually arouse a great interest in sex, which may find expression in an exaggerated awareness of one's own bodily development or that of other people. During the period both boys and girls do a great deal of experimenting in emotional—not necessarily sexual—relationships. The interest of a boy in *all* girls merely because they are girls, and of a girl in *all* boys merely because they are boys, is strong in early adolescence but should disappear by the end of the period. It should be replaced by a concentration upon a single person as a mate. The adolescent has, then, to develop first an acute interest in possible future mates and then to recover from the incidental effects of this acute interest. During the years when these changes are in progress, a boy or girl gets into more or less serious difficulties, but no trouble can possibly be as serious as the failure of the normal developments to take place.

A third group of problems concerns general social maturity. Until boys and girls establish themselves securely in their social milieu they have little attention for other problems. Adolescent boys and girls tend to show a slavish dependence upon and imitation of their friends. This attitude is definitely helpful during the years it should last, but its continuance makes adult life unduly difficult. Many adolescents are also intolerant—a trait that marks them off from both the child and the adult. The child has the tolerance of ignorance and insensitivity to social stimuli, while the true adult has the tolerance of knowledge and understanding.

A fourth set of problems clusters about the establishment of independence from home supervision. Emancipation from home ties is necessary because the adolescent will never become a real adult as long as his parents make his decisions for him, protect him from unpleasantness, and plan his daily life. In most homes the children grow gradually away from the parents, but in some they are either pushed out too fast or kept under restraint too long.

In the intellectual field there are certain objectives to be achieved. Some individuals never develop sufficient mental ability to reach these objectives, but the majority of adolescents could, with training, make more progress toward them than they sometimes do. As people grow older they should become more and more unwilling to accept statements on the basis of authority alone and should want to see the evidence. They want also to know why things are as they are. In early adolescence many interests arise, too many for all of them to continue; later on, there is commonly a narrowing of interests to a few that become permanent. Persistence of intellectual dependence upon authority or of too widely scattered interests is an indication that adolescence has not yet been left behind.

No one is truly an adult until he earns his own living. One set of problems therefore concerns the development of economic adulthood. A child concerns himself only incidentally and quite unrealistically with future occupations; an adolescent tends to overemphasize glamour and to suppose that interest is all one needs for success; an adult has reached a compromise based upon his abilities, his interests, and his opportunities.

In the world of today people have more leisure than they ever had before. It is only recently that educators have realized how necessary it is for an adolescent to learn how to make wise use of his leisure time. One of the important contributions of the high school's extracurricular program to adolescent adjustment lies in its training for the use of leisure. Games and hobbies contribute greatly to the enjoyment of life, but if they demand too much time, energy, or money, the adult has to forsake them. As boys and girls grow older they develop a spectator interest in the more active games, and they begin to substitute the less strenuous amusements of adult life for the rough-and-tumble of childhood.

Finally, an adolescent should make a beginning in the development of a point of view concerning the world about him. Sometimes such an integrating attitude toward life has its basis in religion, and sometimes not. Children have neither the intellectual capacity nor the experience in living to make sound abstractions and are therefore unable to develop ideals. The adolescent, however, is almost certain to adopt general principles of conduct, whether or not these principles lead to socially approved behavior. Naturally, it is only the most precocious of adolescents who enter adulthood with a coherent philosophy of life or with a complete set of ideals. A beginning is all one can expect, but as an adolescent nears adulthood he should start to select whatever values he can find to give life a meaning for him.

III. Summary

In modern society a long period of adolescence has replaced the short period of puberty that was recognized as important from early times. Just as primitive peoples utilized the few months of puberty as a period for special preparation of boys and girls for their future participation in the life of the tribe, so modern educators want to utilize the longer period of adolescence for special preparation in meeting the manifold problems of present-day society.

In order to pass from childhood to adulthood the adolescent must solve a number of problems. He must develop heterosexual interests, become free from home supervision, make new emotional and social adjustments to reality, begin to evolve a philosophy of life, achieve economic and intellectual independence, and learn how to use his leisure time profitably. If he fails in any of these achievements, he fails to gain full maturity. To put the matter in a nutshell, the main business of the adolescent is to stop being one!

IV. Suggestions for Further Reading and Study

This text contains four sets of references or other additional materials. There are (1) those in the footnotes, which indicate the source of a table, figure, or statement. Some of these appear in other lists, and some do not. At the end of each chapter there is (2) a list of references, divided into two main groups. The first group contains only books—whenever possible, widely used books that should be available even in small libraries. The book lists are purposely long, so as to contain several alternative assignments. A student would rarely be expected to read more than one of the book references. Some of the assignments cover specific chapters that parallel roughly those of the present text; other references are to books in which some matter treated briefly in the text is presented in a comprehensive survey. The second group includes titles from monographs, proceedings, reports, yearbooks, and articles in periodicals, each giving results from a definite piece of research. They are grouped under topics, partly for convenience and partly for use in helping students begin work on special topics or term papers. These lists are not to be regarded as adequate bibliographies but only as springboards for getting a student started. The full bibliographical citation appears the first time a reference is quoted, but not subsequently.

In addition to the readings for each chapter, there is (3) a list of novels beginning on page 679ff. Each novel exemplifies at least one problem of adolescence. Some books carry a single group of characters from birth or early childhood into adult years; others describe a cross section of life during adolescence; still others show how environment may influence growth; some are primarily about adults, whose behavior is explained in terms of their personal history; a few deal with abnormal developments. The course will provide a better understanding if each student reads at least three novels, and then writes not a summary of the plot but a brief statement concerning the problems of adolescence illustrated by each novel.

On the last few pages of the book, the student will find (4) a list of problems and projects, grouped by chapter. Many different topics have been included in the hope that each student will be able to find at least one that intrigues him.

REFERENCES FOR FURTHER READING

BOOKS

1. Breckenridge, M. E., and E. L. Vincent, *Child Development: Physical and Psychological Growth through the School Years,* W. B. Saunders Company, rev. ed., 1949, 622 pp. (Chap. 1.)
2. Corey, S. M., and V. E. Herrick, "The Developmental Tasks of Children and Young People," in F. Henne, A. Brooks, and R. Ersted, *Motion Pictures, Communication, and Youth,* American Library Association, 1949, 233 pp. (Pp. 3–13.)
3. Fleming, C. M., *Adolescence: Its Social Psychology, with an Introduction to Recent Findings from the Fields of Anthropology, Physiology, Medicine, Psychosomatics, and Sociometry,* International Universities Press, 1949, 262 pp. (Chap. 1.)
4. Garrison, K. C., *Growth and Development,* Longmans, Green & Co., 1952, 559 pp. (Chap. 17.)
5. Garrison, K. C., *Psychology of Adolescence,* Prentice-Hall Inc., rev. ed., 1951, 510 pp. (Chap. 12.)
6. Havighurst, R. J., *Developmental Tasks of Education,* Longmans, Green & Co., 1948, 86 pp.
7. Hurlock, E. B., *Adolescent Development,* McGraw-Hill Book Company, 1949, 566 pp. (Chap. 1.)
8. Kuhlen, R. G., *The Psychology of Adolescent Development,* Harper & Brothers, 1952, 675 pp. (Chap. 1.)
9. Landis, P. H., *Adolescence and Youth,* McGraw-Hill Book Company, 1947, 470 pp. (Chap. 2.)
10. Malm, M., and O. G. Jamison, *Adolescence,* McGraw-Hill Book Company, 1952, 512 pp. (Chap. 1.)

11. Merry, F. K., and R. V. Merry, *The First Two Decades of Life* (a revision and extension of *Human Infancy to Adolescence*), Harper & Brothers, 1950, 600 pp. (Chaps. 4, 5.)
12. Sadler, W. F., *Adolescence Problems: A Handbook for Physicians, Parents, and Teachers*, C. V. Mosby Co., 1948, 466 pp. (Chap. 1.)
13. Schnell, D. M., *Characteristics of Adolescence*, Burgess Publishing Company, 1947, 68 pp.
14. Warters, J., *Achieving Maturity*, McGraw-Hill Book Company, 1949, 349 pp. (Chap. 1.)

MONOGRAPHS, BULLETINS, PROCEEDINGS, YEARBOOKS, ARTICLES

1. Cline, E. C., "Social Implications of Modern Adolescent Problems," *School Review*, 49:511–514, 1941.
2. Frank, L. K., "This Is the Adolescent," *Understanding the Child*, 18:65–69, 1949.
3. Lorge, I., and R. Kushner, "Characteristics of Adults Basic to Education," *Review of Educational Research*, 20:171–184, 1950.
4. Zachry, C. B., "Customary Stresses and Strains of Adolescence," in *Annals of the American Academy of Political and Social Science*, 236:136–144, 1944.

PART ONE

Physical Development

presentation of all systems at once—aside from being impossible—would be confusing in the extreme. It is hard enough for most students to master, one at a time, the main facts of physical growth in the various systems of the body. In any case, an exposition has to start with a given topic and then proceed to others; and to be orderly, it has to proceed according to some plan. The writer has elected a logical rather than psychological plan of presentation, namely, the description of one type of change after another. A child grows in every system simultaneously and continuously, but his growth in all systems cannot be simultaneously described. In the interests of clarity, one has to begin *somewhere* and proceed from the point of departure by logical steps. However, the student should never forget that these serially described developments are all taking place at the same time within each individual's body.

I. Height and Weight

1. General Curves: Until the last two or three decades, growth curves were based upon results obtained by measuring many children of each age from birth or early childhood to maturity. The children were, however, different children at each successive age. The more recent results are based upon measurement of the same children year after year. By this technique one gets a more accurate picture of growth in general and of individual development in particular. Such measurements are often termed "longitudinal." The curves to be given in this and in later chapters are based, whenever possible, upon continuous measurement of the same children. Results for boys and girls are given separately in the figures that record growth, because members of the two sexes develop at different rates and in different ways. Since the facts about adolescence should be related to similar data from the preceding years, the curves shown in Figures 1 and 2 on pages 17 and 19 extend from birth to maturity. The various periods have been marked off.

The curves bring out, especially, two points that are of importance in nditioning the attitudes of adolescents. In the first place, it is clear that wth is rapid just before and during the early adolescent years. Among s, the curves for height and weight rise steeply from ages 13 to 15, additional smaller gains until 20, when adult height is reached, gh weight still continues to increase. Among girls, growth is rapid in lescence but slower during the adolescent period. A second point s the relative growth rates for the two sexes. Girls show the same ins as boys during childhood, although they average about a half er and a pound and a half lighter. However, because girls develop ects faster than boys, their preadolescent growth spurt comes between the ages of 11 and 13 they average about an inch from 12 to 14, about six pounds heavier. Final adult size for

CHAPTER TWO

Growth in Tissue,
Muscle, and Bone

Adolescence is fundamentally a period of physical and physiological change. To be sure, it is characterized by emotional, social, moral, and intellectual changes also, but these cannot be correctly assessed unless seen in relation to the underlying physical developments which, in a few short years, write finis to childhood and thrust the individual into the world of adults.

So far as teachers are concerned, the facts about growth are mainly important, not in themselves, but in their relation to the personalities and capacities of adolescent boys and girls. The body, the mind, the emotions, and the total personality are so interdependent that any consideration of one away from the others is dangerous. The teacher's main job is to bring about learning and adjustment to life. But the learner is a living, growing, changing, developing organism. If the teacher does not have at least a rudimentary knowledge of the organism she is trying to teach, she may not be successful.

Growth thus furnishes the physical basis for emotional, social, intellectual, and economic maturity. If a child did not increase in statu his muscles did not become strong, if his sex organs did not grow brain did not mature, if his internal organs did not increase i efficiency to meet the requirements of an enlarged body, the never become an adult. He could never achieve mature idea he could never support himself economically, he could nev in adult society. Because of these all-pervasive effects it seems desirable to begin the survey of adolescence picture of the physical manifestations of the peri consideration of what these changes mean to a adolescent reactions to them.

This chapter and the next contain mate ous kinds: increase in height and weight body, changes in bone structure, varia of various internal organs, changes in pubertal alterations of the body—b The typical reactions of adolescen Naturally, growth occurs simultaneou women, however, is approximately five inches shorter and twenty-seven pounds lighter than for men.

The curves for weight show parallel phenomena, but the shapes of the curves are different. The curves in Figure 1 are convex, and those in Figure 2 are somewhat concave; in extreme form, the difference is between ⌐ and this ⌡ . For a year after birth the gains in weight parallel those for height, but then the yearly increment becomes less for several years. Whereas a child acquires half his twenty-year height by the time he is three years old, or she is two and one half, he does not gain half his

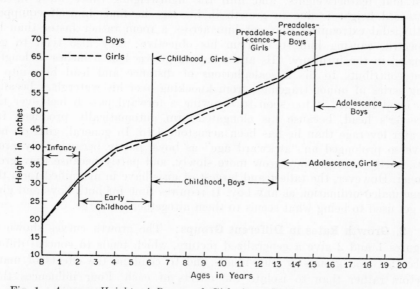

Fig. 1. *Average Height of Boys and Girls from Birth to Maturity*

From age 6 to age 19 these results are based upon F. K. Shuttleworth, "Physical and Mental Growth of Boys and Girls Ages Six through Nineteen in Relation to Age of Maximum Growth," *Monographs of the Society for Research in Child Development*, IV, No. 3 (1939), 248, 249. Below age 6, the curves are averages of several studies, most of which are not longitudinal.

twenty-year weight until he is eleven and one half, or until she is ten. The preadolescent growth spurt in weight for both boys and girls is considerably more marked than that in height. Throughout childhood girls average a pound lighter than boys, at age 13 they average twelve pounds heavier, and after age 16, from twenty to twenty-five pounds lighter.

The curves for both height and weight reflect the different effect upon growth produced by masculine and feminine sexual maturity. In girls the beginning of menstruation almost at once causes a retardation in both height and weight. In boys, however, sexual maturity has an exactly opposite effect. During pubescence, while boys are beginning to acquire adult sexual characteristics, they grow rapidly; and for two or three years after becoming mature, they grow even faster. This difference in the effect of sex hormones upon growth is the fundamental cause of the differences in adult size between the sexes, since up until the age of maturity for girls the differences, while measurable, are either trifling or only temporary. It is adolescent growth that produces the typical differences between the sexes.

For many boys and girls, the rapid increase in size is somewhat disconcerting. A boy may gain as much as 6 inches and 25 pounds in a single year. Such a child starts the year at, say, 112 pounds and ends it at 137; he has progressed in twelve months out of the flyweights, through the bantam and featherweights, and into the lightweights. Since most of his increased height is due to growth in his legs he finds himself equipped with pedal extremities that get him across a room rather faster than he expected, causing him to overrun his objective; they also tend to get tangled in the furniture. His arms, having grown 4 or 5 inches in length, also contribute to his miscalculations of distance and lead him into a long series of minor tragedies, from knocking over his waterglass because his hand reached it too soon to throwing a forward pass 6 feet over the receiver's head, because his elongated arm automatically produced far greater leverage than he has been accustomed to. In general, girls do not have so prolonged an "awkward age" as boys, partly because they grow less, partly because they grow more slowly, and partly because they grow sooner. However, the tallest and largest of girls have in magnified form the same malco-ordination as any boy. It requires time for both boys and girls to get used to being what seems to them altogether too large.

2. Growth Rates in Different Groups: The growth curves shown in Figures 1 and 2 give a generalized picture, which tends to conceal differences between groups or individuals and to combine the effects of many factors rather than to isolate the effects of each. Four influences that hasten or retard growth and have an effect upon final adult height are (1) the age level at which an individual child grows fastest, (2) the nearness of a child to puberty, (3) his remote (racial) and immediate (familial) inheritance, and (4) the environment in which he lives, especially his degree of freedom from disease and the adequacy of his diet. In general, those whose period of maximal growth comes earliest and those who are going to mature early tend to grow faster than other children. These facts are especially true of boys. In Figure 3 on page 20 there are growth curves in height and weight for three groups of boys: members of Group A experienced their period of maximal growth between the ages of eleven and thirteen; Group B made its greatest gains two years later, between thirteen and fifteen; and Group C, four years later, between fifteen and seventeen. These periods are indicated on the curves by small circles. It will be seen at once that the three curves for height are all of the same general shape, but that the steepness of the rise depends upon how early a boy passed through the period of most rapid growth. The same is true of the three curves for weight. At age 18 the three groups show a difference of only 4 inches in height and 28 pounds in weight. At age 15, however, the differences are $6\frac{1}{2}$ inches and 57 pounds. Similar results have been obtained from parallel groups of girls.

As will become increasingly clear in the following pages, the nearness of a child to his or her maturity exerts an influence upon various phases of growth. Those who are going to mature earliest grow faster almost from

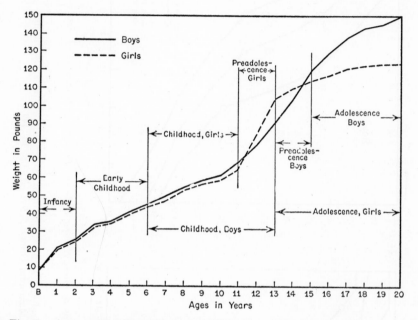

Fig. 2. *Average Weight of Boys and Girls from Birth to Maturity*

These results are from the same sources as those in Figure 1.

birth than those who are going to mature late. One investigator[1] summarized his results from the 1,406 boys by classifying them into four groups: A, those who were already mature at $12\frac{1}{2}$; B, those who were already pubescent at $12\frac{1}{2}$ and became mature by $13\frac{1}{2}$; C, those who were prepubescent at $12\frac{1}{2}$, pubescent at $13\frac{1}{2}$, and mature between $13\frac{1}{2}$ and $14\frac{1}{2}$; D, those who were still immature at $14\frac{1}{2}$. The heights and weights of these four groups are shown in Figure 4, on page 21. The relationship between maturity and growth was already evident at $12\frac{1}{2}$, with a difference of 5 inches in height and 25 pounds in weight. Two years later, these differences had become $6\frac{1}{2}$ inches and 45 pounds.

The relation between faster than average growth during childhood and an early onset of maturity is brought out somewhat differently in another way. The same investigator followed the development of the 17 tallest, the 17 heaviest, the 18 shortest, and 18 lightest boys in a total of 1,406 who were first measured at age 12. Of the 17 heaviest boys, 71 per cent reached

[1] H. S. Dimock, *Rediscovering the Adolescent*, Association Press, 1937, 287 pp.

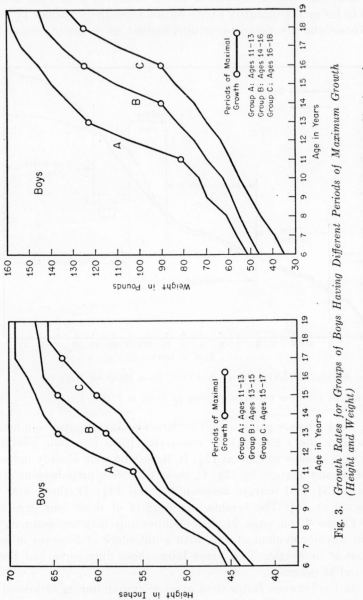
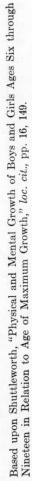

Fig. 3. *Growth Rates for Groups of Boys Having Different Periods of Maximum Growth
(Height and Weight).*

Based upon Shuttleworth, "Physical and Mental Growth of Boys and Girls Ages Six through
Nineteen in Relation to Age of Maximum Growth," *loc. cit.,* pp. 16, 149.

puberty within a year of the measurement, as did 65 per cent of the tallest boys.[2] There was some overlapping between these two groups, also between those at the other extreme, since height and weight have a fairly high cor-

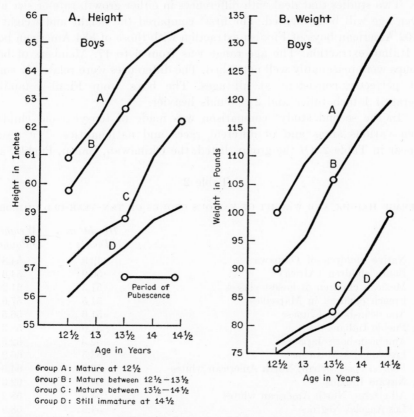

Group A : Mature at 12½
Group B : Mature between 12½—13½
Group C : Mature between 13½—14½
Group D : Still immature at 14½

Fig. 4. *Maturity and Growth Rates for Adolescent Boys*

Based on H. S. Dimock, *Rediscovering the Adolescent*, Association Press, 1937, p. 258.

relation with each other. Only 17 per cent of the 18 shortest and 6 per cent of the 18 lightest boys reached puberty within a year after the initial measurement.

3. Racial and Environmental Differences: Racial and family stock also have an effect upon growth, especially upon the determination of adult stature. Most Oriental groups tend to be short; even those who grow up under the best of conditions are not as tall as the average for members of the white or black races. The tallest and the shortest peoples in the world—the Shilluk of the Upper Nile and the Pygmies of the Congo—both belong to the Negro race, but the former are about two feet taller than the latter. The differences cannot be attributed to diet or climate, since

[2] *Ibid.*, p. 219.

both groups have an inadequate diet and live in the tropics. Different groups of the white race show heights varying from that of the taller Negroes to the average for Orientals (when the latter are adequately fed).

Two studies that deal with differences in either growth rate or size at a given age will be presented. The first[3] compared the height and weight of 1,102 American boys of Finnish extraction with those of 884 American boys of Italian extraction. The age range was from 6 to 17. Members of both groups were reasonably well nourished. The differences were relatively small but perfectly consistent at all ages. The boys from Finnish families averaged 1 inch taller and 2½ pounds heavier.

In the second study[4] comparison was made of ten-year-old children from various areas and of different races and nationalities. The results appear in Table 2. Of the groups listed, the Okinawan, Bantu, Pueblo, and

Table 2

AVERAGE HEIGHT AND WEIGHT OF VARIOUS GROUPS OF TEN-YEAR-OLD CHILDREN

	Height in Inches	Weight in Pounds
1. Native children of Okinawa	49.9	54.8
2. Bantu children (Africa)	50.9	54.6
3. Mexican children of lowest classes	51.3	61.2
4. French children in Marseilles	51.5	57.6
5. American-born Chinese	51.6	56.5
6. Pueblo Indians	51.6	58.3
7. American-born Japanese	52.3	62.5
8. Los Angeles Mexicans	53.5	66.2
9. Poorest class, urban, North American whites	53.7	64.0
10. Navajo Indians	54.0	62.3
11. All classes, North American whites	54.6	68.2
12. Los Angeles Negroes	54.9	68.9
13. Children of American business and professional men	55.7	72.2

Based on H. V. Meredith, "Body Size in Infancy and Childhood: A Comparative Study of Data from Okinawa, France, South Africa, and North America," *Child Development*, 19:179–195, 1948.

lower-class Mexican children lived on markedly inadequate diets, which doubtless operated to reduce the size that inheritance alone would have caused. The difference in averages between the lowest and highest is nearly 6 inches and almost 18 pounds. These children were only ten years old at the time of measurement, so presumably none had begun his preadolescent or adolescent spurt. Since the taller a child is at ten, the more he is likely to grow during this spurt—a most unfair arrangement—the adult heights

---

[3] W. D. Matheny and H. V. Meredith, "Mean Body Size of Minnesota School Boys of Finnish and Italian Ancestry," *American Journal of Physical Anthropology*, n.s., 5:343–355, 1947.

[4] H. V. Meredith, "Body Size in Infancy and Childhood: A Comparative Study of Data from Okinawa, France, South Africa, and North America," *Child Development*, 19:179–195, 1948.

and weights of the above groups would probably show differences nearly twice as great.

Environmental factors influence growth primarily by furnishing or withholding necessary food materials and by preventing or permitting the spread of disease and infection. Statistical studies have demonstrated a general world tendency toward an increase in stature. Measurements of recruits in countries that have had universal military service for many decades show increases of both height and weight from the earliest to the most recent generations in the same population. In the United States, the men who were drafted in World War II were $\frac{6}{10}$ inch taller and $9\frac{1}{2}$ pounds heavier than their counterparts in World War I.

One especially valuable investigation[5] contains reports on the measurement of all school children between ages 6 and 14 in the city of Toronto in the years 1892 and 1939. At the latter date, the six-year-olds averaged 2 inches taller than was the case 47 years earlier, and the fourteen-year-olds 3 inches taller. There had been no change of any moment in the constitution of the population in Toronto during the half century between the measurements. The increase cannot therefore be attributed to variation in racial or family stock but must be regarded as due to better nutrition and greater freedom from disease.

Thus far, the discussion has concerned groups of children of various ages. Only incidental reference has been made to differences among individuals. It seems desirable, therefore, to present a few curves for individuals and to emphasize the differences thus revealed by pictures of children who were all of the same chronological age but showed contrasts in size.

4. Individual Differences in Growth: Curves for four girls and five boys are shown in Figure 5 on page 24. Girl A was as tall at 10 as Girl D at 17; Girl B grew rapidly between 12 and 14, while Girl C grew slowly between these ages; Girl D grew at an almost uniform rate and was still growing at 17. The differences in height from the tallest to the shortest were 5 inches at age 6, and 14 inches at age 17. Boy A grew rapidly from the start, increased his rate after 15, and was still growing at 17; Boy D grew very slowly at first, gradually increased his rate, and then at 15 entered a brief period of acceleration. Boy C grew so rapidly between 13 and 14 that he overtook Boy B, who exceeded him at all other ages. By the end of their seventeenth year two of the five boys had almost stopped growing, one was slowing down, and two were accelerating. No two children show identical curves.

Any teacher notices differences in size among pupils of the same age, but few people realize the extent of such variations. The pictures in Figures 6 and 7 on page 25 will demonstrate this point. The first shows the size of five boys at age 14. The shortest boy is about 8 inches shorter than the tallest, and the lightest is some 60 pounds lighter than the heaviest; parallel

---

[5] H. V. Meredith and E. M. Meredith, "The Stature of Toronto Children Half a Century Ago and Today," *Human Biology,* 16:126–131, 1944.

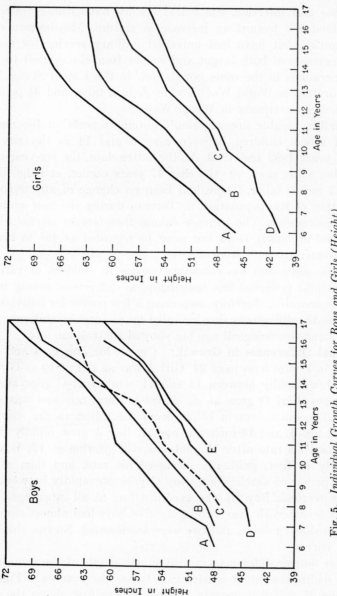

Fig. 5. *Individual Growth Curves for Boys and Girls (Height)*

Based upon figures in W. F. Dearborn, J. W. N. Rothney, and F. K. Shuttleworth, "Data on the Growth of Public School Children," *Monographs of the Society for Research in Child Development*, III, No. 1 (1938), Nos. 513 M, 941 M, 1062 M, 1091 M; 909 F, 1272 F, 1875 F, 1885 F.

differences for the five fifteen-year-old girls are 9 inches and 38 pounds. Variations in build make these differences seem even greater. The largest

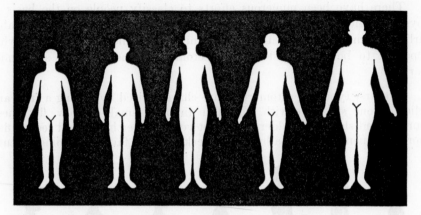

Fig. 6. *Variations in Size among Fourteen-Year-Old Boys*

From W. W. Greulich, *et al.*, "Somatic and Endocrine Studies of Pubertal and Adolescent Boys," *Monographs of the Society for Research in Child Development*, Vol. VII, No. 3 (1942), Plates 9 and 10. Used by permission of the publisher.

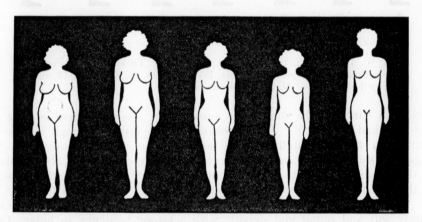

Fig. 7. *Variations in Size among Fifteen-Year-Old Girls*

From F. K. Shuttleworth, "The Adolescent Period: A Graphic and Pictorial Atlas," *Monographs of the Society for Research in Child Development*, Vol. III, No. 3 (1938) Figs. 90–93. Used by permission of the publisher.

of the boys and girls have already reached almost their adult size and shape, whereas the smallest are still children in height and weight, and the smallest boy retains markedly his childish contours.

II. Bodily Types

There have been numerous efforts to classify people on the basis of physical traits ever since the days of the ancient Greeks, and probably earlier. A modern study that was limited to college men found what appeared to be three basic types: ectomorphs, mesomorphs, and endomorphs.[6]

The first type, the ectomorphs, are characterized by having a frail and delicate bone structure with long, thin limbs, a small, narrow, flat chest, rounded and sloping shoulders, long but very slender hands and feet, a flat, short abdomen, thin legs, a long, thin neck, a small face, a stooping posture,

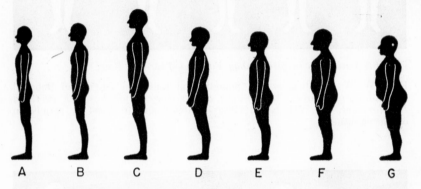

A   B   C   D   E   F   G

Fig. 8. *Differences in Body Build among Boys*

From W. H. Sheldon, S. S. Stevens, and W. B. Tucker, *The Varieties of Human Physique,* Harper & Brothers, 1947, Figs. 18, 24, 32, 66, 65, 72, and 57. Used by permission of Harper & Brothers.

and an S curve in the spine. The musculature is slight, there is little if any fat, and the outline of the bones is often visible through the flesh. Growth of hair is usually profuse all over the body. Silhouette A, in Figure 8, shown above, is an extreme type of ectomorph; B also belongs to this classification, although he is not so extreme as A. Not all members of this group are tall, but they rather tend to be.

At the other extreme are the endomorphs. Their bodies are predominantly soft and round and smooth, with a strong tendency to bulge. The trunk is large, round, and very thick; the abdomen is especially large and usually protrudes; the head is round and big, it sits atop a short, thick neck, and it contains a face that suggests a full moon; the upper arms and upper legs are extraordinarily wide and heavy, both arms and legs are short, and the hands and feet are much too small for the rest of the body. The fingers are short and pudgy. Endomorphs in youth have fairly strong muscles, although these are of the smooth feminine type. The bodily weight

[6] W. H. Sheldon, S. S. Stevens, and W. B. Tucker, *The Varieties of Human Physique,* Harper & Brothers, 1940, 347 pp.

of endomorphs gives them more power than one would expect. At all ages their skeletons are well covered with a smooth layer of fat which prevents the bony structure from showing through. As they grow older they usually acquire several layers of fat, especially around the abdomen and hips and on the upper arms and upper legs. Their skin is usually quite fine, as is their hair, which is likely to be rather sparse. Silhouettes F and G of Figure 8 show young endomorphs.

Between these two extremes and partaking of some of the characteristics of both, but fusing them into a distinct physical type, are the mesomorphs. These people have a square, strong, tough, hard, firm body, with a long, straight trunk, heavy ribs, broad shoulders, a fairly large but muscular abdomen, a slender, low waistline, and fairly broad hips. The shoulders are, however, usually so wide that by comparison the hips seem nar-

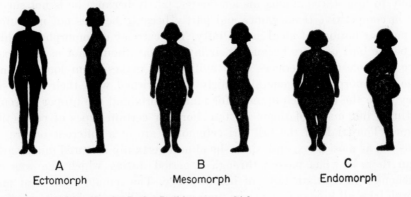

| A | B | C |
| Ectomorph | Mesomorph | Endomorph |

Fig. 9. *Differences in Body Build among Girls*

From Sheldon, *et al., The Varieties of Human Physique,* pp. 290–299. Used by permission of Harper & Brothers.

row. The neck is long but thickish, and the facial bones are quite prominent. The arms and legs are neither unduly long nor unduly short, but they are powerfully muscled, and the muscles are of the type that form protruding lumps. The forearms, wrists, calves, and ankles are large and thick, with squarish fingers and toes. The skin is thick and the hair coarse. Silhouette D of Figure 8 is that of a typical young male mesomorph.

Of course, the majority of people are not pure types. They partake of the characteristics of more than one kind of body structure. Mixtures may be seen in silhouettes B, C, and E of Figure 8. It should be noted that the various builds here illustrated form an unbroken series from the extreme ectomorph to the extreme endomorph. The modern theory is that everyone has at least a little of three elements—ectomorphy, endomorphy, and mesomorphy—in his structure, but that the exact mixture differs from one person to another. The "pure" types are those of the two ends and in the exact middle of the entire distribution. The majority of the population occupy positions at some intermediate point.

Girls show the same variety in their types of body, but since no one has yet measured a comparably large feminine population, there are no available photographs of the many possible gradations from one extreme to another. Only three pairs of silhouettes are therefore given in Figure 9 on page 000 to illustrate the three types already discussed as they appear when one makes allowances for feminine curves and proportions. A is a slender ectomorph, C is a well-rounded endomorph, and B is a square, sturdy mesomorph (minus the protruding muscles, since feminine muscles remain smooth, even when they are just as strong as their bulging masculine counterparts). A characteristic of the female mesomorph is that her shoulders are as wide as and sometimes wider than her hips.

2. **Indirect Results of Differences in Size and Build:** Size and shape have a profound influence upon the individual who dwells within the body. In American culture, the boy who is short or weak or lightly muscled is likely to lose status among his age-mates, partly because he is not successful in competitive team games and partly because he does not measure up to popular notions of ideal masculinity. The extreme endomorphs are likely to be the butt of jokes because their layer of fat, though not usually excessive in adolescence, reduces their agility and makes them look feminine. The mesomorphs are generally fairly well satisfied with their build since they have the native equipment for many sports and the proper masculine outlines, but many of them are too short for certain types of competitive games. The trials of the tall girl ectomorph are of a different nature. She is as tall as most boys, and, since she almost certainly matured much earlier, than they, she has passed through a period during which she was conspicuously taller than boys of her own age. The female adolescent endomorph tries all kinds of diets and may exercise diligently, but she continues to be too round and too dumpy looking for her taste. She never has what is regarded as proper adolescent chic because she cannot make herself flat enough and especially because her main protuberances are in the wrong places. The feminine mesomorph is likely to be a tomboy in childhood and a competitor of boys in her adolescence. She outplays boys up until the time when they begin their final growth spurt. Subsequently, their long arms and legs give them such leverage and speed that she can no longer compete. Other girls may look down on the mesomorph because she is not "feminine"; boys often actively dislike her because she is a competitor, not an admirer; and she is almost certain to pass through a period of stress during adolescence because the tomboy habits of her childhood are no longer useful in maintaining prestige and may become actual menaces to her position among either boys or girls.

Adolescents often make quite extreme reactions to compensate for their size. For instance, a tall girl may never go to dances because she is certain to be taller than most of the boys she dances with. Or a large girl may go in for athletics, politics, masculine clothes, and a career because she cannot be "cute" and feminine. Or a small-sized boy may become a "grind" largely because he cannot compete on equal terms physically with other boys—

and may, if he attempts games, even be beaten by girls. Very tall boys also have difficulties of adjustment.[7] Chairs, desks, beds, driving seats of cars, and even doorways are too small for them. Whenever they are on their feet, they cannot help feeling conspicuous, and they are constantly being reminded of their height by inquiries about the condition of the atmosphere up where they are, and by similar pleasantries. The writer knows one girl of six feet two who was so miserable in American schools that she went to Sweden for her education, where her excessive height would be less conspicuous and where she would not be forced every week into three hours of gymnasium work and four hours of participation in some game—all of which made her acutely miserable. Fat girls and boys are among the unhappiest of adolescents and are almost always maladjusted. Usually, their obesity is basically due to glandular dysfunction, which can often be helped to some extent by proper medicine and diet. This matter of the pervasive effect of physical condition in influencing both personality and social prestige will be discussed further in later sections.

Anyone who doubts the importance of variations in height, weight, or appearance from the average should listen to adolescent nicknames: Shrimp, Skeeter, Beanpole, Bug, Spider, Butch, Fatty, Big Boy, Shorty, Baldy, Whitey, Spike, Whale, Swede, Machine Gun, Blubber, Foxy, Squeaky, Piggy, Barrel, Dopey, Stinky, Bull, Cotton, Slim, or Tiny—generally used ironically. Other nicknames are derived from places of residence—Texas, or Boston—from distortions of real names—Gus, Sambo, or Marge—or from defects of personality—Show-off or Sissy. Usually a nickname is a sign of affection, admiration, and popularity among adolescents,[8] although a few of the derogatory ones are not.

III. Motor Co-ordination, Strength, and Athletic Skills

1. Co-ordination and Agility: The development of motor co-ordination, balance, and general agility during childhood, preadolescence, and adolescence has been shown by four sets of results, each indicative of a different phase of growth. One investigator measured the ability of children to keep their balance when walking on a rail.[9] For this measurement the investigator used three rails: one 4 inches wide and 9 feet long, one 2 inches wide and 9 feet long, and one 1 inch wide and 6 feet long. Each child made three trials on each rail. His total raw score was the total number of feet that he remained on each rail at each of his nine trials. Since, however, the rails were of different widths and the balancing task therefore of varying difficulty, the distance that a child made on his three trials on Rail I was left as it stood, that on Rail II was multiplied by 2,

---

[7] F. B. Briggs, *Tall Men Have Their Problems, Too* (The Author, 21 Coolidge Hill Road, Cambridge, Mass.), 1943, 147 pp.

[8] E. S. Dexter, "Three Items Related to Personality: Popularity, Nicknames, and Homesickness," *Journal of Social Psychology*, 30:155–158, 1949.

[9] S. R. Heath, "Preliminary Maturational Norms for Boys and Girls," *Motor Skills Research Exchange*, 1:34–36, 1949, and S. R. Heath, "Clinical Significance of Motor Development with Military Implications," *American Journal of Psychology*, 57:482–499, 1944.

and that on Rail III by 4. If a child walked the full length of all three rails, his score would be 153. It is the composite score that appears in Figure 10, shown below. Boys are at most ages superior to girls and become increasingly so during adolescence, not because their rate of improvement increases markedly but because the girls almost stop improving.

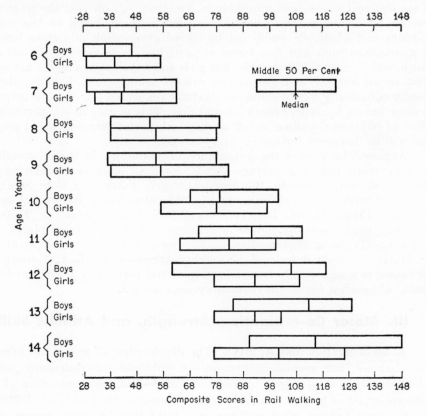

Fig. 10. *Growth in Balance*

Based on S. R. Heath, "Preliminary Maturational Norms for Boys and Girls," *Motor Skills Research Exchange,* 1:34–36, 1949.

A second investigator measured the accuracy of aiming and of rapidly passing a basketball. The scores on the two tests appear in Figure 11 on page 31. The results are given in terms of the per cent that the score at each age was of the average for seventeen-year-old boys. This group scored the highest on most of the tests and was therefore used as the standard. In aiming, the girls excelled the boys at all ages. They reached the average for seventeen-year-old boys at thirteen and one half and from then on scored appreciably above it. Aiming is a skill which requires relatively little strength, but it does take patience, a trait in which girls excel because they soon learn that only by patience and accuracy can they overcome the handicap imposed upon them by their slight build, shortness, and inferior strength. Also, girls do relatively more things requiring small, accurate eye-hand adjustments than do boys. And they are more mature in all ways,

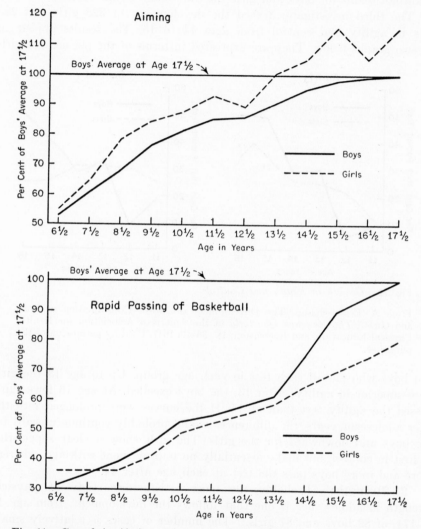

Fig. 11. *Growth in Aiming and Handling a Basketball*

From J. E. Anderson, *The Psychology of Development and Personal Adjustment*, Henry Holt and Company, 1949, pp. 138, 139. Used by permission of the publisher.

including their eyesight. The boys were slightly superior to girls during middle and late childhood in their ability to handle a basketball, but after the girls entered puberty their rate of improvement became slow while that of the boys increased markedly. Since relatively little strength is involved, the difference is due in large measure to a greater familiarity with handling basketballs on the part of the boys, to better leverage, and to greater interest. It is probable that if one compared the members of the basketball teams for boys and girls the differences would be small.

The third investigator traced the development of 325 girls and 285 boys in agility and control from ages 11 to 16. The results appear in the two graphs below. They are expressed in terms of the per cent of girls

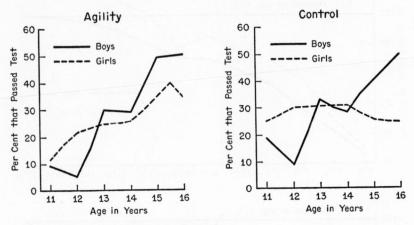

Fig. 12. *Growth in Agility and Control*

From A. Espenschade, "The Development of Motor Co-ordination in Boys and Girls," *The Research Quarterly* of the American Association for Health, Physical Education, and Recreation, 18: 36–40, 1947. Used by permission of the publisher.

and boys who passed each test in each age group. Up to age 13 the girls were superior in agility; after 13, the boys excelled. At age 16 fewer girls passed the agility test than at 15. If the curves were prolonged into the later adolescent years, the differences would probably continue upward for the boys and downward for the girls. The girls show a clear superiority at first in control, but make essentially no improvement with age, whereas more and more boys pass the test at each age after 14.

2. Strength: Probably the most satisfactory study of physical strength in adolescence is one that follows the development, from age 11 to 17½, of 89 boys and 87 girls.[10] The number of cases is relatively small, but the same children were measured every six months, with the result that one gets a picture of longitudinal growth. Results are given in Figure 13, page 33, for (a) strength of grip, for (b) exerting a pull when the arms are held at shoulder level with the elbows slightly bent and the registering instrument grasped by both hands at chest level, and for (c) exerting a thrust in the same position. In strength of grip boys are

---

[10] H. E. Jones, "Motor Performance and Growth: A Developmental Study of Static Dynamometric Strength," *University of California Publications in Child Development*, Vol. I, No. 1, 1949, 181 pp.

superior to girls at all ages, but the significant differences do not appear until the boys begin to mature. The difference between boys and girls at age 11 was 4 pounds of pressure; at 17 it was 20 pounds.

In the pull and thrust tests girls were superior to boys at age 11 by 2 and 7 pounds, respectively. For these tests leverage is especially important, and girls of 11 or 12 have outgrown boys in length of arm, width of

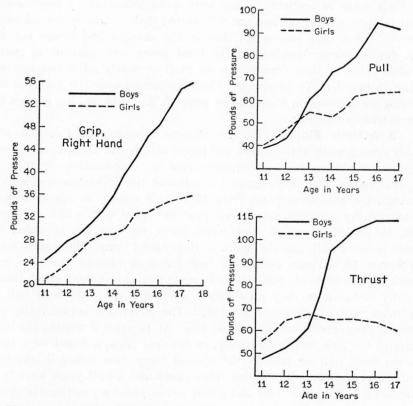

Fig. 13. *Growth in Strength*

From H. E. Jones, "Motor Performance and Growth," *University of California Publications in Child Development*, 1949, I, 35, 36. Used by permission of the University of California Press, publishers.

shoulder, and weight because they are already preadolescent while boys are not. Their ability to thrust is very nearly as good at 11 as it is at 17. Boys, however, make enormous gains in both tests after the age of 13. In all cases the great increase in strength occurs during the years when the largest proportion of boys become mature. Actually, the muscles of girls become longer and heavier during adolescence than in childhood, but these changes are far more marked among boys, who sometimes double their strength in three or four years.

The effects of the age of maturity upon strength have been especially well shown by two investigators. Early maturing boys, as shown in Figure 14, on page 35, were at all ages stronger than boys who matured late. The same is true of girls, but to a much smaller degree.

The second investigator gave a number of strength tests and totaled the scores. The higher this total is, the greater the strength. The boys in the investigation were grouped, at each age from 12 through 16, according to their stage of maturity. Some were quite immature or prepubescent; that is, their sex organs had not yet started their characteristic adolescent growth. Some were pubescent; that is, the changes had begun but were not yet complete. Members of the third group were mature, or postpubescent; that is, their organs were of adult or nearly adult size and were adult in function. To present the clearest contrast only the first and third groups are included in Figure 15 on page 35. At every age the mature boys are markedly superior.

3. Athletic Skills:　The development of athletic skill depends obviously upon growth in the length and power of legs and arms, upon increases in muscular strength, upon improvements in co-ordination, balance, and general agility. One investigator has followed the development of children through the adolescent years from 12 years 9 months of age to 16 years 9 months, by measuring each half year the speed with which they could run, the height to which they could jump, the distance to which they could throw a ball, and the width of their broad jump. The results appear in Figure 16 on page 36. In all four forms of exercise the boys made marked improvement, but the girls ran more slowly and could jump a shorter distance as they grew older. Their ability to throw a ball and to jump upward increased a little.[11] The difference between the sexes became greater with the passage of time. At 12 years 9 months the inferiority of the girls was, respectively, on the four tests, a fourth of a second in the dash, half an inch in the upward jump, two inches in the broad jump, and forty feet in the ball throw; four and a half years later it was one and a half seconds, four and a half inches, two feet, and nearly seventy feet, respectively. With each passing year after age 13, the girls showed an actual loss in some abilities, presumably because their interests had become social, and they were far more anxious to attract boys than to compete with them.

It is only recently that people have realized the extreme importance of size, strength, and athletic ability, especially for boys, in the determination of social status among children and adolescents.[12] American culture

---

[11] The "jump-and-reach" test was as follows: a child stood facing a wall; with a piece of chalk he made a mark as high up as he could reach with his heels still on the floor; then he jumped and reached, making another mark at the height of his leap. The upward jump was measured by the distance between marks.

[12] See, for instance, H. E. Jones, "Physical Ability as a Factor in Social Adjustment in Adolescence," *Journal of Educational Research*, 40:287–301, 1946, and W. A. Schonfeld, "Inadequate Masculine Physique as a Factor in Personality Development of Adolescent Boys," *Psychosomatic Medicine*, 12:49–54, 1950.

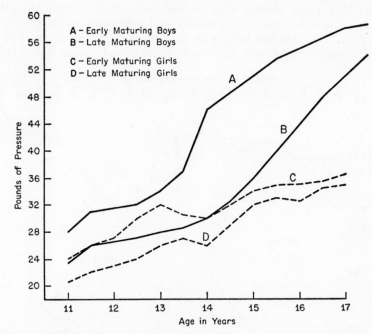

Fig. 14. *Maturity and Strength (1)*

From Jones, "Motor Performance and Growth," *loc. cit.,* p. 63. Used by permission of the University of California Press.

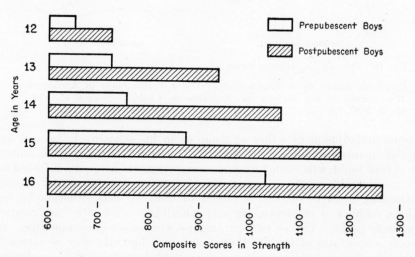

Fig. 15. *Maturity and Strength (2)*

Based on figures in Dimock, *Rediscovering the Adolescent,* p. 238.

puts a high premium upon sheer physical superiority. It is not surprising, therefore, that a big, strong, athletic boy feels satisfied with himself and finds himself able to achieve popularity and admiration without any particular effort. The race has been won for him, and he can relax. The path to social success is therefore smoothed for him and, unless there is some

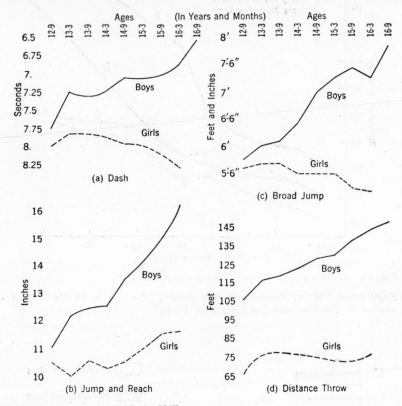

Fig. 16. *Increase in Athletic Skills*

Based on figures in A. Espenschade, "Motor Performance in Adolescence," *Monographs of the Society for Research in Child Development*, Vol. V, No. 2, 1940, 126 pp.

extreme maladjustment either at home or in his schoolwork, he will be a popular member of adolescent society. The short, slender, weak-muscled boy of frail build, who cannot meet the competition of his peers, is forced into an uncomfortable position because the clearest road to popularity, through outstanding athletic success, is closed to him. To this situation he may make a number of responses. He may withdraw completely from competition, form perhaps one or two friendships with other noncompetitors, and become a spectator of the life that rushes past him. He may so resent his inferiority that he becomes bitter and as verbally aggressive as he dares to be. Or he may seek a compensation by becoming a buffoon—which gets him attention and sometimes admiration; by gaining academic success— which gets him occasional admiration and very little attention from his age-mates; or by fawning upon the bigger boys, trying to pick up a few pale rays of reflected glory as a hanger-on. He may become sufficiently absorbed and sufficiently successful in the school chorus, on the school newspaper, or in school politics to almost forget that he will never be a football hero.

Sometimes a restricted kind of athletic success can be achieved by a frail, underdeveloped boy, or even by a tubby, fat one, if the school's athletic program is wide enough. Thus, anyone can learn to swim, and both the slender and the overweight lad, or lassie for that matter, have natural buoyancy as compared to the heavily muscled mesomorph who cannot float. The small, slight boy can gain admiration as a diver, especially as the springboard will throw his 100 pounds much higher than it will throw the 180 pounds of a big boy and will thus give him more chance to do something spectacular and attention getting. The plunge gives the overweight boy his chance, because the distance an individual can go is directly proportional to weight, once he has mastered the technique of hitting the water at the right angle. If a boy is not too small there is a chance that he can play shortstop on the baseball team; to be sure, a long reach is desirable but at the high school level of performance, its lack can be compensated for by extra agility. If a boy is tall but too slender for the rougher sports, he may succeed either in tennis, in which his extra leverage will offset his lack of strength, or in fencing, because he has an abnormally long reach and lunge but presents an abnormally narrow target for his opponent to hit. The one sport in which one small boy in a school is definitely in demand is rowing—and the smaller the coxswain is, the better. Unless a boy has some crippled condition or a heart deficiency that prevents even mild exercise, he can find something in which he excels, provided the offerings of the school are sufficiently varied. A step in the right direction has been made by having separate school teams in basketball, football, and baseball on the basis of weight. A boy can therefore become a star quarterback on the hundred-pound team, have the fun of playing, and achieve a moderate amount of respect. Of course, he would rather be on the A squad with the biggest boys, but success on the E squad provides a not-too-unsatisfying compromise. What has been said of boys may equally well be applied to girls in case they wish to achieve athletic success. It is no accident that most outstanding feminine divers are small; they cannot race against long-limbed girls, but they have excellent success in diving. However, many small, weak girls need no compensation, because "weakness" is an accepted and even admired feminine characteristic. All a girl has to do is to play up being "helpless" and she can achieve popularity among boys—provided she is a likable person; in short, her lack of strength makes her boy friends feel bigger and stronger than they are and flatters their masculine ego because they have someone to "protect." The small, weak boy has no such comfortable retreat open to him.

One investigator of strength during adolescence compared numerous estimates and measures of emotional adjustment, personality, and social status for the ten strongest boys and the ten weakest.[13] Five of the former occupied positions of popularity and high prestige among their age-mates, four showed a satisfactory status, and only one was unpopular. Six of the

[13] Jones, "Motor Performance and Growth," *loc. cit.*

ten showed excellent emotional adjustment, three were about average, and one had several emotional problems. They were all in good health and all successful athletes. The ten weakest boys present a marked contrast. They had relatively poor health and no memberships on athletic teams. Six of the ten weakest boys were so shy and unsure of themselves that they were practically isolated from their fellows and had no social status at all. Four of the ten were a bit more assertive but did not succeed in achieving more than a slight degree of prestige, which they were unable to maintain as they grew older. Over the six years of the study, only one of the ten showed a consistently good emotional adjustment, three were about average but with evidence of some tension, and the remaining six were markedly maladjusted emotionally.

There is thus evidence that mere size and strength form one important basis for adequate social and emotional adjustment. Naturally, as in any comparative situation, some individuals must occupy positions at the bottom of the series, but if teachers and parents are aware of this possible source of difficulty, they may be able to minimize the effects upon personality and to guide the smaller boys away from destructive expressions of aggression on the one hand, and on the other into such compensatory activities as may be open to them, so that they too may find a place in the sun of their age-mates' admiration.

Changes in the bones and muscles of the body are among the clearest indications of oncoming puberty. When a boy starts cutting his second molars, when his chest grows deep, his shoulders broad, his hands and feet big, his arms and legs long, his features large, and his muscles strong, he is clearly an adolescent. When a girl shows the same changes—though the shoulder and chest developments are less marked—and in addition reveals a widening of the hips, she too has entered her adolescent years.

IV. Skeletal Growth

The bones of the body change not only in length and size from birth to maturity but also in density and in hardness. Also, they change their shape. Some of the smaller bones are not present at birth, and some of the larger ones are mostly cartilage. If a baby's bones were not soft, he could never be born, because no rigid body of six to eight pounds could pass down the mother's birth canal.

1. Bones of Hand and Wrist: The most usual method for determining the growth of the skeleton is to make X-ray photographs of the bones in the hand and wrist, and then to estimate general skeletal age from this sample. The bones that show in such pictures have their own method of growth, which must be understood before the X-ray pictures, shortly to be presented, will be intelligible.

Each finger is composed of three small straight bones which are aligned with a fourth and longer bone in the back of the hand. The thumb has only two short bones instead of three, plus a long one from the base of the thumb to the wrist. The arm is composed of two long bones, one considerably thicker than the other, the ends of which appear in the pictures. In the wrist there are at maturity no less than 8 small bones marvelously fitted together and shaped to the nearer ends of the long bones which underlie the back of the hand and to the wrist end of the arm bones. There are also two tiny bones that develop during early adolescence on the first joint of the thumb. There is, then, a total of 31 small bones: 3 in each finger = 12; plus 3 long and 2 little round ones in the thumb = 17; plus 2 in the arm = 19; plus 4 in the hand = 23; plus 8 in the wrist = 31. Although there are minor variations from bone to bone, all the long bones of the fingers follow the same general pattern of growth. They become longer and the cartilage slowly changes to bone; that is, the cartilage "ossifies." As a result, the X-ray pictures show a sharper definition, because a hardened bone throws a more clearly outlined shadow than a soft cartilage. In addition to ossifying, the finger bones (called phalanges[14]) and the bones in the back of the hand (called metacarpals) acquire a sort of appendage called an epiphysis, which they subsequently absorb. Each epiphysis grows into a shape that fits the bone to which it becomes attached. Figure 17 on page 40 records the growth in length and shape of five bones and of the epiphyses that eventually fuse with three of them. In Column 1 are the outlines as they appear at birth of (A) the first phalanx of the middle finger—the phalanx nearest the body— (B) the corresponding metacarpal, (C) one of the bones in the wrist, and (E) the end of the larger of the two bones in the forearm—the radius. It will be noted that there are wide spaces between each two bones in this series.

The epiphysis of the phalanx first appears as a small dot. Then it flattens out into an oval disc which gradually becomes as wide as the end of the phalanx (Column 5) and then develops curved edges that permit it to "cap" the end of the bone (Column 6), at the same time fitting itself perfectly over its entire surface. Finally, it grows on to the phalanx. For a little while, a thin line shows along the edge of the union (Column 7), but presently phalanx and epiphysis fuse into a single, solid bone (Column 8). The epiphysis of the metatarsal also first appears as a dot of cartilage, but it continues to be round, gradually becoming larger (Columns 2–5). It then broadens where it will attach itself to the bones, assumes a shape to fit the bone surface (Columns 6–7), and finally becomes a knob. It should be noted that the adjoining surfaces of the two epiphyses have also shaped themselves to each other (Column 8). The epiphysis of the radius begins as a tiny disc (Column 2), becomes an elongated oval (Columns 3–4), grows thicker at one extreme than at the other, and becomes shaped on one surface to fit the end of the radius and on another to fit the nearest wristbone (Columns 5–8).

The wristbones follow a different pattern of growth. They begin as small round or oval lumps of cartilage and grow, not only by becoming bigger and by ossifying, but by changing their shape. Each bone grows as many distinct "faces" as may be necessary to fit it to other wristbones and to the base of whatever long bones it will move upon. Since each bone in the wrist has a different position and function from those of any other, each has its own pattern of growth. Two samples appear in C and D of

---

[14] The singular is phalanx.

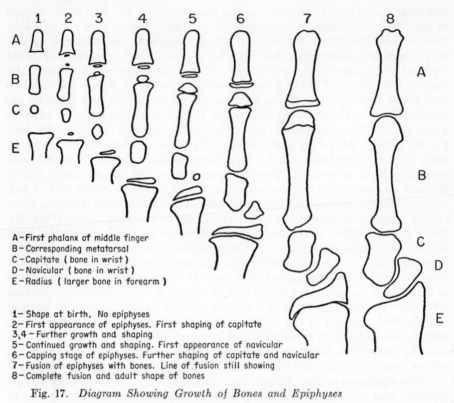

A – First phalanx of middle finger
B – Corresponding metatarsal
C – Capitate (bone in wrist)
D – Navicular (bone in wrist)
E – Radius (larger bone in forearm)

1 – Shape at birth. No epiphyses
2 – First appearance of epiphyses. First shaping of capitate
3,4 – Further growth and shaping
5 – Continued growth and shaping. First appearance of navicular
6 – Capping stage of epiphyses. Further shaping of capitate and navicular
7 – Fusion of epiphyses with bones. Line of fusion still showing
8 – Complete fusion and adult shape of bones

Fig. 17. *Diagram Showing Growth of Bones and Epiphyses*

Drawing made from X rays in T. W. Todd, *Atlas of Skeletal Maturation,* C. V. Mosby Co., 1937, 203 pp.

Figure 17. Bone C begins as a dot of cartilage, becomes round and then oval, elongates, and gradually assumes an irregular shape, with a depression in one face into which a curved end of the second bone (D) fits when both are mature. The nearer end of the metatarsal and the farther face of the bone also develop so as to fit each other. Bone D does not appear until a child is between four and six years old. It goes through the same initial stages as Bone C, then becomes a triangle (Column 6), and finally a sort of crescent (Columns 7–8), the curves and points of which fit the shapes of adjacent bone structures. When the five bones shown in Figure 17 attain adult shape and size—normally at age 17 for girls and age 19 for boys—they articulate upon each other to form a series. At maturity the long bones (A, B, and E) with their fused epiphyses are several times longer than at birth, as indicated by the increasing space they occupy in the diagram.

In X-ray photographs, which are presented in Figures 18 to 27 on pages 41 to 45, one can trace the developments already briefly outlined and can see what is meant by "skeletal age." The first series of photographs shows the average development for girls at the following age levels: 3 months, 2 years 3 months, 6 years 9 months, 12 years 9 months, 14 years

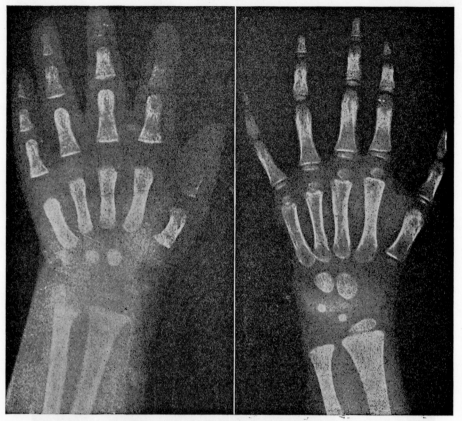

FIG. 18   FIG. 19

Fig. 18. *X Ray of a Girl's Hand, Age Three Months*
Fig. 19. *X Ray of a Girl's Hand, Age Two Years, Three Months*

These pictures and those that follow in the series are from T. W. Todd, *Atlas of Skeletal Maturation*, C. V. Mosby Co., 1937. These are from pp. 135, 147. The pictures are used by permission of C. V. Mosby Co.

9 months, and 16 years 3 months. The series for boys gives averages for the same years except for the two extremes. The picture for the three-month-old boy has been omitted since the two sexes show no significant differences at that age and that for the mature male hand has been omitted because the only differences between it and a girl's mature hand is the size of the bones. The baby's picture (Figure 18) shows soft, indistinct shadows for the 19 long bones that make up the fingers and hand, and for the ends of the two bones in the forearm; there are also two smallish dots that will develop into wristbones. This picture explains why one cannot push a small baby's arm into a sleeve but must reach two fingers through the lower end of the sleeve, grasp the baby's hand, and back out of the opening, pulling the infant's hand through after one's own; the baby's bones are not yet jointed, and his hand, when pushed toward a sleeve, simply folds back on the arm.

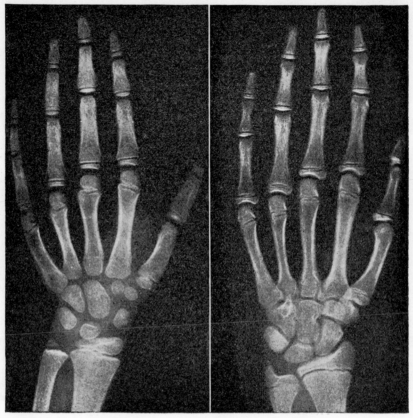

FIG. 20   FIG. 21

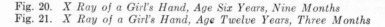

Fig. 20. *X Ray of a Girl's Hand, Age Six Years, Nine Months*
Fig. 21. *X Ray of a Girl's Hand, Age Twelve Years, Three Months*

From Todd, *op. cit.*, pp. 165, 189.

At 2 years 3 months the average girl (Figure 19) has developed disc-shaped epiphyses at the base of the phalanges, ball-shaped ones for the metatarsals, and an epiphysis on the radius. The two wristbones that were present at birth have reached the oval stage, and two more have appeared. At 6 years 9 months (Figure 20) the girl has epiphyses that are as wide or almost as wide as the bones they will fuse with, and they have begun to shape themselves to provide a close fit. The wrist now contains 7 bones. The increase in ossification is shown by the increased sharpness and clearness of all the shadows. At 12 years 9 months (Figure 21) the girl's epiphyses are in the capping stage and are ready to fuse with the bones. She has no new bones in the wrist, but the seven have grown larger and have changed their shapes. By the end of her fourteenth year (Figure 22) much fusion has taken place, although one can still see in many places the thin line between epiphysis and bone. The last picture in this series (Figure 23) shows a practically adult hand and wrist.

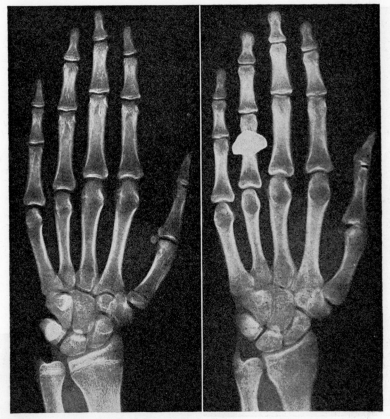

FIG. 22   FIG. 23

Fig. 22. *X Ray of a Girl's Hand, Age Fourteen Years, Nine Months*
Fig. 23. *X Ray of a Girl's Hand, Age Sixteen Years, Three Months*

From Todd, *op. cit.*, pp. 197, 203.

Figures 24 to 27 give a similar series for boys. Figure 24 should be compared with Figure 19. At least five epiphyses in the boy's hand are lacking and another five are mere dots. The earliest two wristbones are not yet quite oval, and no others have developed. The bones are appreciably less dense than those of the two-year-old girl. At 6 years 9 months (Figure 25) the epiphyses of the phalanges are neither as long nor as shaped as those of the girl (Figure 20) and the metatarsal epiphyses are rounder; there is also more unossified area in the boy's wrist than in the girl's. The boy's bones are, however, already a bit bigger than the girl's. This difference in size becomes steadily more marked with age. Comparison of Figure 26 with Figure 21 shows the boy to be still less mature than the girl, since there is less capping, less fusion, and less shaping. The bones of the hand in Figure 27 show some fusion of the metatarsals with their epiphyses, but very little elsewhere. This hand is hardly more mature than that shown in Figure 21, although there is two years' difference in chronological age. The

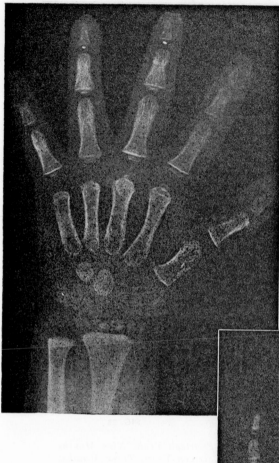

Fig. 24 (left). *X Ray of a Boy's Hand, Age Two Years, Three Months*

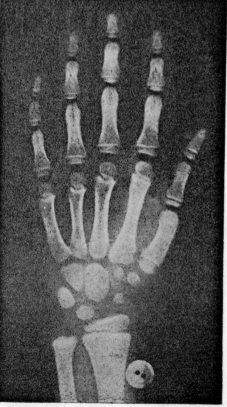

Fig. 25 (right). *X Ray of a Boy's Hand, Age Six Years, Nine Months*

These X rays are from Todd, *op. cit.,* pp. 67, 85.

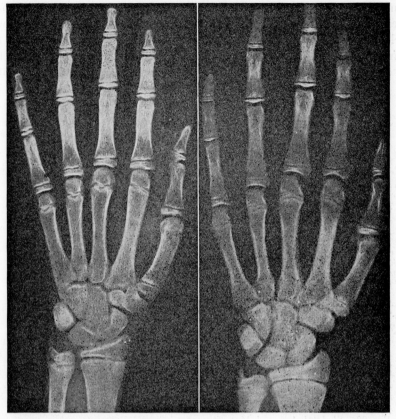

FIG. 26   FIG. 27

Fig. 26. *X Ray of a Boy's Hand, Age Twelve Years, Nine Months*
Fig. 27. *X Ray of a Boy's Hand, Age Fourteen Years, Nine Months*

From Todd, *op. cit.*, pp. 109, 117.

average boy reaches the mature stage, such as appears in Figure 23, about two years later than the average girl. At maturity there is almost no empty space left in the wrist, and the bones have become dense enough to throw a clearly defined shadow on the X-ray plate.

There is a marked relationship between the age of puberty and the skeletal age. Figure 28 on page 46 shows results for three groups of girls who matured at different ages. At age 7 the girls who—as later proved— matured early already had a skeletal age of over eight, and they remained consistently in skeletal age from one and a half to two years ahead of their chronological age. All three groups maintained their relative positions to each other during the entire decade covered by the measurements.

There are large individual variations in skeletal growth. A few individual curves for girls, based upon consecutive measurement of the same individuals, are shown in Figure 29 on page 47. The measures are in terms of the calcified area in the bones of the wrist. The norms for this measurement are ind cated by lines drawn across the figure. At age 8, Girl B had a calcified area in her wrist above that of the average girl of age $9\frac{1}{2}$, while Girl F's wrist area at the same age was well below that of a normal five-year-old. At age 14 the corresponding variation for these two girls was from the average of age $8\frac{1}{2}$ to well beyond the average of age $15\frac{1}{2}$. Girl A reached

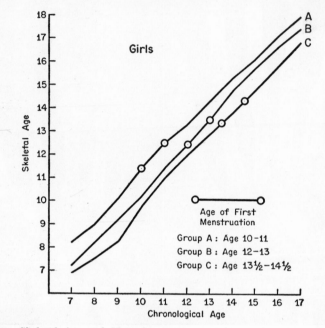

Fig. 28. *Skeletal Age and Maturity*

From F. K. Shuttleworth, "Sexual Maturity and the Skeletal Development of Girls Ages 6 to 19," *Monographs of the Society for Research in Child Development,* III, No. 5 (1938), 2. Used by permission of the publisher.

what appears to be her maximum development between ages 12 and 13. Girls E and F were still growing at sixteen, but Girls C and D showed signs of stopping growth between fourteen and fifteen. Girl F at all ages was extremely retarded. At $14\frac{1}{2}$, the last measurement made, she had the skeletal age of $8\frac{1}{2}$ years.

2. Growth of the Teeth: The teeth also have characteristic growth rates. The permanent teeth begin pushing out the baby teeth when a child is five or six years of age. From that time on until the early years of adolescence a child acquires 1 or 2 teeth each year. The thirteen-year-old has 26 or 27 of his 32 teeth. As in all kinds of physical development, the girls are in advance of the boys; their teeth erupt earlier, so that at all ages they have a larger number.[15] The second molars usually erupt at the beginning of adolescence. Their appearance is one of the surest signs that

[15] P. Cattell, "Dentition as a Measure of Skeletal Growth," *Harvard Monographs in Education,* No. 9, 1938, 91 pp.

puberty is close. The third molars, or wisdom teeth, erupt at some time after seventeen years of age. The cutting of these molars is often a painful process, and they may cause both dental trouble and emotional distress when they arrive.

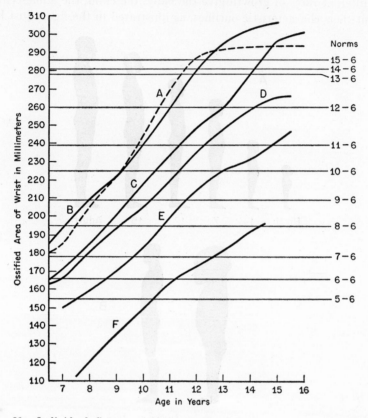

Fig. 29. *Individual Curves of Skeletal Growth*

From P. Cattell, "Preliminary Report on the Measurement of Ossification of the Hand and Wrist," *Human Biology,* 6:461. 1934. Used by permission of the publisher.

3. Proportional Growth: The various parts of the body grow at different rates and reach their maximal development at different times. The head, for instance, does the major part of its growing before birth, and most of the rest soon after. At birth it equals one fourth of the baby's total length. At age 6, it is already 90 per cent of its adult size and equals one sixth of child's height. In adulthood, the head is one eighth of the body's length. contrast, the long bones of the arms and legs are extremely short at bi remain comparatively short during childhood, and then lengthen qui just before or during adolescence. At puberty they are four times as lo they were at birth, and at maturity five times as long. Adult legs m

half the total height as compared to less than a third at birth. The trunk is relatively long at birth but doubles its length by age 6; it grows little from then till the later years of adolescence. At maturity the trunk is three times as long and wide as it was at birth, and two and one half times as thick. These different rates of growth give the baby, the child, the adolescent, and the adult their characteristic outlines, as illustrated in the figure just below.

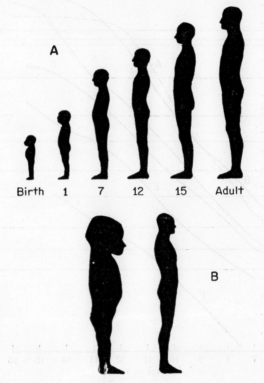

Fig. 30. *Characteristic Proportions at Different Ages*

Based on J. P. Schaefer (ed.), *Morris' Human Anatomy* (10th ed.), 1942, pp. 25, 44. Used by permission of The Blakiston Company, publisher.

Part A of the diagram shows both proportions and size at intervals from birth to maturity. The two silhouettes of Part B show the typical adult outline and the outline an adult would have if he retained, without alteration, the proportions of a newborn baby and merely grew larger.

In a profile view, the waistline does not show much, if at all. If the silhouettes were drawn from the front or the back view, it would be evident that the child had no waistline. A small girl's shorts and slacks will stay sufficiently "up" for purposes of modesty because her hips are a little wider than her superstructure, and her buttocks protrude a trifle, but keeping a small boy's shorts on him presents a real problem, because he is the same width from shoulder to knee and perfectly flat; he has constantly to "hitch" them, since there are no protuberances in his shape to prevent gravity from

pulling them down until they come to rest somewhat precariously on the lower edge of his buttocks. In early adolescence the waistline appears, but it is very high because the trunk has not yet grown proportionally as much as the legs. Toward the end of adolescence the lowering of the waistline adds the last development needed for the achievement of adult proportions.

The growth of the muscles and the depositing of fat just below the skin have their own pattern and rhythm of development, which is affected only slightly by exercise or by diets unless they are of extremely high or low caloric intake. At birth the muscles make up 27 per cent of the total body weight. At age 15, they have become 32 per cent and at age 16, 44 per cent— or nearly half the weight of the body. The weight of the muscles may be estimated most directly and easily by measuring the amount of creatinine excreted in a child's urine during a 24-hour period, since it has been already determined that one gram of urinary creatinine represents 17.84 grams of muscle weight.[16] For both boys and girls the increases up to nine years of age are small, although even in childhood the boys excreted 10 to 20 per cent more at each age than girls, indicating that their muscles were already somewhat heavier. The amounts from ages 10 to 13 are larger, and those from ages 13 to 16 very much larger for both sexes, but especially so for boys.

During childhood girls often have a slight deposit of fat on their arms, legs, chests, and abdomen—just enough to give them a curved rather than a flat appearance. Boys have much less. Members of both sexes begin to put on larger quantities of fat under the skin at about the period of pubescence. The tendency is especially noticeable in girls, most of whom now have a layer of fatty tissue over almost the entire body. The comparative growth of fat and muscle in the two sexes has been studied in great detail from birth to maturity. The muscles selected for intensive study were those in the calf of the leg.[17] Boys exceeded girls almost from infancy in the breadth of the muscle, while girls exceeded boys in the depth of fatty tissue between muscle and skin. The proportion of fat, muscle, and bone at five different age levels is shown in Figure 31 on page 50. For boys the proportion of fat is never quite as high as for girls. By the time adulthood has been reached a man's leg contains only 8 per cent fat, while a woman's contains 18 per cent, but his bones and muscles are both bigger and heavier. These differences became more pronounced with age and continued into adulthood.

It is this characteristic development and the distribution of fat and muscle that prevent a boy from swimming more than a few minutes in cold water in which his twin sister can swim in comfort for an hour. After the beginning of adolescence a boy's increased arm and leg length and strength

---

[16] N. B. Talbot, from a personal communication quoted in H. C. Stuart, "Normal Growth and Development during Adolescence," *New England Journal of Medicine,* 234:666–672, 732–738, 1946.

[17] E. L. Reynolds and P. Grote, "Sex Differences in the Distribution of Tissue Components in the Human Leg from Birth to Maturity," *Anatomical Record,* 102:45–53, 1948.

permit him to swim short distances faster than most girls, but almost any girl can remain in the water as long as she wants to without getting muscle cramps, because her muscles are well insulated by fatty tissue. Moreover,

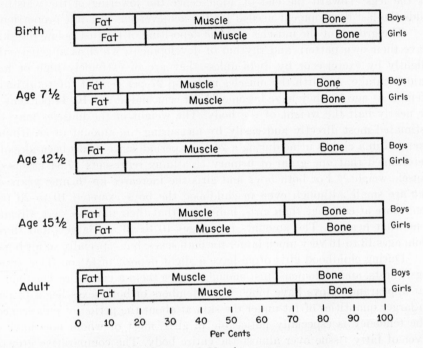

Fig. 31. *Growth in Fat, Bone, and Muscle*

Based on E. L. Reynolds and P. Grote, "Sex Differences in the Distribution of Tissue Components in the Human Leg from Birth to Maturity," *Anatomical Record,* 102:45–53, 1948.

this same tissue allows her to float whenever she gets tired. It is no accident that more women than men finish distance swims, although only a very small proportion of girl swimmers ever attempt them.

4. Growth in Facial Bones and Features: An individual's face also grows, slowly in childhood and then more rapidly in the early years of adolescence. The nose and mouth widen, the nose becomes longer and more prominent, and the jaw juts out farther.[18] The upper part of the face usually grows faster than the lower, the jaw being commonly the last feature to attain its adult size and angle. While some faces grow in a symmetrical fashion, most do not. Adolescents typically have unbalanced and unsymmetrical faces—a situation that is a source of much embarrassment to them. Since the nose generally begins to grow before the other parts, the thirteen-

[18] The statements in this paragraph and the following ones are based upon measurements by A. Bjork, *The Face in Profile,* Berlingska Boktryckerist, Lund, Sweden, 1947, 180 pp., and M. S. Goldstein, "Development of the Head in the Same Individuals," *Human Biology,* 10:197–219, 1939.

or fourteen-year-old child seems destined for a while to imitate Cyrano de Bergerac. Matters are not helped by increases in the height of the forehead, since these changes make the upper part of the face too heavy. They also

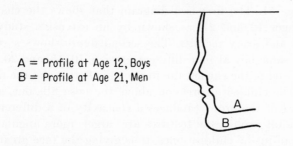

A = Profile at Age 12, Boys
B = Profile at Age 21, Men

Fig. 32. *Diagram of Facial Growth*

Based on A. Bjork, *The Face in Profile,* Berlingska Boktryckerist, Lund, Sweden, 1947, pp. 127, 130.

make the eyes seem to have become smaller, although actually they do not change in size at all. In an infant's face, they look enormous; in a child's

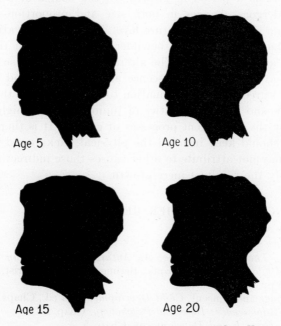

Age 5   Age 10

Age 15   Age 20

Fig. 33. *Profile of the Same Child at 5, 10, 15, and 20 Years of Age*

face, they seem large; in an adolescent's face, they have merely assumed their adult relation to the rest of the face. It is usually a year or two and sometimes longer before the chin develops and nicely balances the already-mature nose, giving the face the underlying bone structure of maturity. Another source of asymmetry of the face during adolescence is its tendency to grow in length before it grows in width.

The differences in facial proportion are well shown in Figures 32 and 33 on page 51. The first is a diagram that shows the changes in profile between ages 12 and 21, as shown by an extensive study of twelve-year-old boys and army recruits. The second figure shows a series of four profiles of the same boy at four different ages: 5, 10, 15, and 20. At the later ages, as compared to the earlier, the forehead is flatter and the nose is longer and thicker. The childish depression above the nose fills out, and then the jutting forward of the brows produces a concavity of a different shape and type. In the adult profile, the features are larger, more angular, and stand out farther than in the childish ones, thus giving the face greater depth. In early childhood the lips are flat, and they do not become full and curved until fairly late in the development of the face. The chin is the last feature to change from youthful to adult size and shape.

V. Summary

Adolescence is a period of growth. In the course of a few years the individual undergoes changes in both size and proportion—changes that take him from a childish to a mature level. The rapidity, variety, and force of these developments are alike bewildering, even though they are sometimes exciting and satisfactory. The alterations are indeed so extensive that some people have regarded adolescence as a sort of second birth. Usually there is some degree of malco-ordination to be seen during the period. Both the schoolwork and the personalities of junior high and high school pupils are affected by the concurrent processes of growth. It is therefore essential that teachers should keep in mind the physical background of adolescence so that they may not attribute to other causes those indirect manifestations that are mainly the result of mere growth.

REFERENCES FOR FURTHER READING

BOOKS

1. Bjork, A., *The Face in Profile: An Anthropological X-Ray Investigation of Swedish Children and Conscripts,* Berlingska Boktryckerist, Lund, Sweden, 1947, 180 pp.
2. Breckenridge and Vincent, *Child Development,* 2d ed., Chaps. 7, 8.
3. Fleming, *Adolescence: Its Social Psychology,* Chap. 2.
4. Garrison, *Growth and Development,* Chap. 5.
5. Garrison, *Psychology of Adolescence,* Chap. 3.
6. Greulich, W. W., and S. I. Pyle, *Radiographic Atlas of Skeletal Development of the Hand and Wrist,* Stanford University Press, 1950, 190 pp. (Pp. 1–29.)
7. Hurlock, *Adolescent Development,* Chap. 3.
8. Jones, H. E., *Development in Adolescence: Approaches to the Study of the Individual,* Appleton-Century-Crofts, Inc., 1943, 161 pp. (Chap. 5.)

9. Keliher, A. V., *Life and Growth*, Appleton-Century-Crofts, Inc., 1941, 245 pp. (Chaps. 6, 7, 8.)
10. Kuhlen, *The Psychology of Adolescent Development*, Chap. 2.
11. Landis, *Adolescence and Youth*, Chap. 3.
12. Malm and Jamison, *Adolescence*, Chap. 4.
13. Scheinfeld, A., *Women and Men*, Harcourt, Brace and Company, 1943, 453 pp. (Chaps. 10, 11.)
14. Sheldon, W. H., *et al.*, *The Varieties of Human Physique*, Harper & Brothers, 1940, 347 pp. (Chaps. 3, 6.)
15. Stolz, H. R., and L. M. Stolz, *Somatic Development of Adolescent Boys*, The Macmillan Company, 1951, 551 pp. (Chaps. 3, 5, 13, 14.)
16. Thompson, H., "Physical Growth," in L. Carmichael, *Manual of Child Psychology*, John Wiley & Sons, Inc., 1946, 1068 pp. (Pp. 255–294.)
17. Wile, I. S., *The Challenge of Adolescence*, Appleton-Century-Crofts, Inc., 1939, 484 pp. (Chaps. 3, 4.)
18. Zachry, C. B., and M. Lighty, *Emotions and Conduct in Adolescence*, Appleton-Century-Crofts, Inc., 1940, 563 pp. (Chaps. 2–4.)

MONOGRAPHS, BULLETINS, PROCEEDINGS, YEARBOOKS, ARTICLES

A. *General Growth (Summaries)*

1. Jensen, K., "Physical Growth and Physiological Aspects of Development," *Review of Educational Research*, 20:390–410, 1950.
2. Jones, H. E., and N. Bayley, "Growth, Development, and Decline," *Annual Review of Psychology*, 1:1–8, 1950.
3. Stuart, H. G., "Normal Growth and Development during Adolescence," *New England Journal of Medicine*, 234:666–672, 1950.

B. *General Growth (Studies)*

1. Meredith, H. V., "The Rhythm of Physical Growth," *University of Iowa Studies in Child Welfare*, Vol. II, No. 3, 1935, 128 pp.
2. Richey, H. G., "The Relation of Accelerated, Normal, and Retarded Puberty to the Height and Weight of School Children," *Monographs of the Society for Research in Child Development*, II, No. 1 (1937), 1–67.
3. Shuttleworth, F. K., "Physical and Mental Growth of Boys and Girls Ages Six through Nineteen in Relation to Age of Maximum Growth," *Monographs of the Society for Research in Child Development*, Vol. IV, No. 3, 1939, 291 pp.
4. Symonds, K., "The Brush Foundation Study of Child Growth and Development: II. Physical Growth and Development," *Monographs of the Society for Research in Child Development*, IX, No. 1 (1944), 1–87.

C. *General Growth (Appraisal)*

1. Krogman, W. M., "A Handbook of the Measurement and Interpretation of the Height and Weight of the Growing Child," *Monographs of the Society for Research in Child Development*, Vol. XIII, No. 3, 1950, 68 pp.
2. Wetzel, N. C., "Grid for Evaluating Physical Fitness: A Guide of Individual Progress from Infancy to Maturity," NEA Service, Inc., 1948.

D. *Factors Affecting Growth*

1. Matheny, D., and H. V. Meredith, "Mean Body Size of Minnesota Boys of Finnish and Italian Ancestry," *American Journal of Physical Anthropology*, n.s., 5:343–355, 1947.
2. Meredith, H. V., "Body Size in Infancy and Childhood: A Comparative Study

of Data from Okinawa, France, South Africa, and North America," *Child Development*, 19:179–195, 1948.
3. Meredith, H. V., "Stature and Weight of Children of the United States," *American Journal of Diseases of Children*, 62:909–932, 1941.
4. Meredith, H. V., and E. M. Meredith, "The Stature of Toronto Children Half a Century Ago and Today," *Human Biology*, 16:126–131, 1944.
5. Reynolds, E. L., and G. Schoen, "Growth Patterns of Identical Triplets from Eight through Eighteen Years," *Child Development*, 18:130–151, 1947.
6. Wilde, E., "Health and Growth of Aleut Children," *Journal of Pediatrics*, 36:149–159, 1950.

E. *Motor Development*

1. Bayley, N., and A. Espenschade, "Motor Development from Two Years to Maturity," *Review of Educational Research*, 14:367–374, 1944.
2. Espenschade, A., "The Development of Motor Co-ordination in Boys and Girls," *Research Quarterly* of the American Association for Health, Physical Education, and Recreation, 18:30–43, 1947.
3. Espenschade, A., "Motor Performance in Adolescence," *Monographs of the Society for Research in Child Development*, Vol. V, No. 2, 1940, 126 pp.
4. Heath, S. R., "Preliminary Maturational Norms for Boys and Girls," *Motor Skills Research Exchange*, 1:34–36, 1949.
5. Seashore, H. G., "The Development of a Beam Walking Test and Its Use in Measuring Development of Balance in Children," *Research Quarterly* of the American Association for Health, Physical Education, and Recreation, 18:246–260, 1947.
6. Seashore, R. H., "The Development of Fine Motor and Mechanical Abilities," *Forty-third Yearbook of the National Society for the Study of Education*, 1944, Pt. I, pp. 123–125.

F. *Muscular Development*

1. Jones, H. E., "The Development of Physical Abilities," *Forty-third Yearbook of the National Society for the Study of Education*, 1944, Pt. I, pp. 100–122.
2. Jones, H. E., "Motor Performance and Growth," *University of California Publications in Child Development*, Vol. I, No. 1, 1949, 181 pp. (Chaps. 1, 3, 4, 7.)
3. Reynolds, E. L., and L. C. Clark, "Creatinine Excretion, Growth Progress, and Body Structure in Normal Children," *Child Development*, 18:155–168, 1947.
4. Reynolds, E. L., and P. Grote, "Sex Differences in the Distribution of Tissue Components in the Human Leg from Birth to Maturity," *Anatomical Record*, 102:45–53, 1948.

G. *Skeletal Growth*

1. Allen, L., "Facial Growth in Children of Five to Eight Years of Age," *Human Biology*, 20:109–145, 1948.
2. Cattell, P., "Dentition as a Measure of Maturity," *Harvard Monographs in Education*, No. 9, 1938, 91 pp.
3. Goldstein, M. S., "Changes in the Dimensions and Form of the Face and Head with Age," *American Journal of Physical Anthropology*, 22:37–90, 1936.
4. Goldstein, M. S., "Development of the Head in the Same Individuals," *Human Biology*, 10:197–219, 1939.
5. Hurme, V. O., "Ranges of Normalcy in the Eruption of Permanent Teeth," *Journal of Dentistry for Children*, 16:11–15, 1949.

H. *Body Build*

1. Bayley, N., and L. M. Bayer, "The Assessment of Somatic Androgyny," *American Journal of Physical Anthropology*, 4:433–462, 1946.
2. Bayley, N., and R. Tuddenham, "Adolescent Changes in Body Build," *Forty-third Yearbook of the National Society for the Study of Education*, 1944, Pt. I, pp. 33–35.
3. Bruch, H., "Psychological Aspects of Obesity," *Bulletin of the New York Academy of Science*, 24:73–86, 1948.
4. Stolz, H. R., and L. M. Stolz, "Adolescent Problems as Related to Somatic Variations," *Forty-third Yearbook of the National Society for the Study of Education*, 1944, Pt. I, pp. 80–99.

I. *Reactions to Bodily Development*

1. Jones, H. E., "Physical Ability as a Factor in Social Adjustment in Adolescence," *Journal of Educational Research*, 40:287–301, 1946.
2. Jones, M. C., and N. Bayley, "Physical Maturing among Boys as Related to Behavior," *Journal of Educational Psychology*, 41:129–148, 1950.
3. Schonfeld, W. A., "Inadequate Masculine Physique as a Factor in Personality Development of Adolescent Boys," *Psychosomatic Medicine*, 12:49–54, 1950.

CHAPTER THREE

Physiological Growth

While the numerous changes already described in bone and muscles are in progress, other developments are taking place in the circulatory, digestive, respiratory, neural, and glandular systems of the body. Many of these changes are of vital importance in conditioning the behavior of the individual boy or girl.

I. Growth in Circulatory, Respiratory, Digestive, and Neural Systems

1. Circulatory System: The heart has its own growth rate, as do the other organs of the body. At age 6, it is four to five times as heavy as at birth; at 12, it is seven times as heavy; and at 18, it is twelve times as heavy. During the years of adolescence, the weight of the heart nearly doubles. The size of the transverse diameter of the heart is shown in Figure 34 on page 57. In childhood, boys' hearts are a little larger than girls'; from age 9 to 13, girls' are larger; from 13 on, boys' hearts grow rapidly, while girls' grow very slowly and not much more. The veins and arteries do not increase in size at the same rate that the heart does. Before adolescence, they have already reached a more nearly adult size than has the heart; and they grow more slowly than it does during the early years of adolescence. Thus, during childhood a small heart pumps blood through relatively large arteries and veins, but during adolescence, a large heart pumps blood through relatively small blood vessels. This condition may impose strain upon the pump for a few years, especially among rapidly growing boys.

Changes in both the size and the tension of the arteries are reflected in measures of blood pressure. From childhood to late adolescence the blood pressure rises steadily from 80 to 85 millimeters at age 6 to age 17, when it levels off at 110–115 for boys and 100–105 for girls, as indicated in Figure 35 on page 57. Sex differences up to age 10 are not significant. From age 10 to 13, girls show a slightly higher average than boys. After age 13, however, the average blood pressure for boys tends to rise above that for girls; and after 16 there is quite a difference, because the boys continue to show an increase, while the pressure of the girls decreases until about age 20, when both sexes have reached their normal adult level.

In contrast to blood pressure, the average pulse rate decreases with age for both sexes, but the average for girls is at all ages several beats above that of boys. This development is shown in Figure 36 (a) on page 58. The

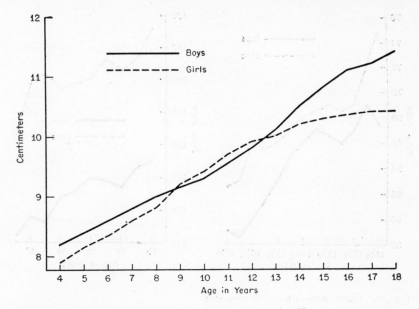

Fig. 34. *Growth in the Transverse Diameter of the Heart*

Based on figures in M. M. Maresh, "Growth of the Heart Related to Bodily Growth during Childhood and Adolescence," *Journal of Pediatrics*, 2:382–404, 1948.

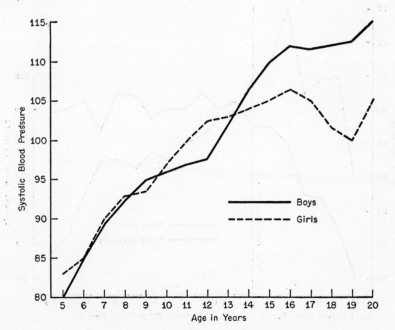

Fig. 35. *Blood Pressure from Age 5 to Age 20*

Based on figures in H. G. Richey, "The Blood Pressure in Boys and Girls before and after Puberty," *American Journal of Diseases of Children*, 42:1281–1330, 1931.

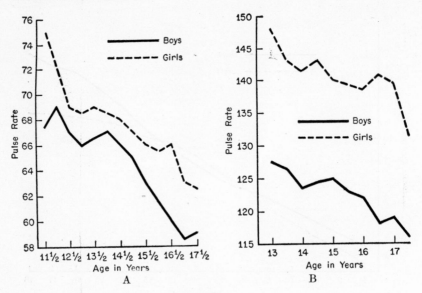

Fig. 36. *Pulse Rate during Adolescence*

N. W. Shock, "Physiological Changes in Adolescence," *Forty-third Yearbook of the National Society for the Study of Education,* 1944, I, 56–79. Used by permission of the publishers.

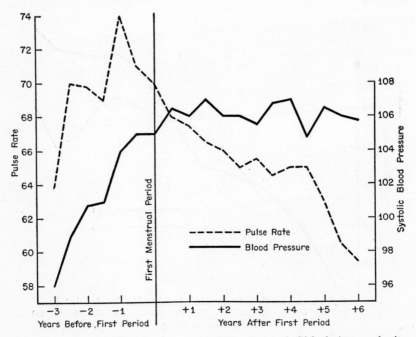

Fig. 37. *Systolic Blood Pressure and Pulse Rate of Girls before and after Puberty.*

N. W. Shock, "Physiological Changes in Adolescence," *loc. cit.* Used by permission of the publishers.

difference between the two sexes becomes even more marked if the pulse rate is taken one minute after a prescribed unit of exercise (Figure 36 [b]). In this second comparison, the girls' hearts are consistently about 20 beats above the boys'.

Physiological maturity has a marked effect upon both blood pressure and pulse rate. The changes may be seen most easily in girls, since their first menstrual period affords conclusive evidence of maturity at a particular time, whereas there is no such single criterion for boys. Figure 37 on page 58 shows the results for fifty girls, tested every six months for many years, for both blood pressure and pulse rate. The scale for reading the former curve is at the right of the figure; that for the latter is at the left. When the data are tabulated with reference to each girl's first period and without respect to chronological age, it can be seen at once that blood pressure rose sharply during the three years before puberty and for six months thereafter, and then settled to a new level at about 106. In contrast, the pulse rate, which had been climbing irregularly but rapidly for the years just preceding the first menstrual period, fell off sharply and steadily for the next six years. Physiological maturity thus operated to stabilize the upward trend of blood pressure and to reverse that of pulse rate.

2. Respiratory System: During childhood and adolescence the lungs grow, keeping pace with the increased width and depth of the chest. This development can be traced by measurement of vital capacity. To obtain this measurement, a child draws as much air into his lungs as he can and then expels it into a tube that is connected with a finely balanced drum, which rises as the expelled air enters below it. The examiner can read off the vital capacity from figures on the surface of the drum. Sample results appear in Figure 38 on page 60. At all childhood ages, boys have a slightly greater vital capacity than girls. There is a marked increase for both sexes between ages 10 and 14. This acceleration continues into adulthood for boys, but for girls it soon slows down; girls therefore fall farther and farther below boys in vital capacity at each successive age. Some of the difference is doubtless due to the failure of girls to participate as freely as boys in strenuous games after puberty, but differences in total size are probably more important. Individual results indicate a considerable amount of variation. Thus, some girls are superior to the average of all boys, and an occasional boy measures considerably below the average for girls of his age.

In general, adolescent lungs are quite capable of handling any burden that is likely to be put upon them. Although they have not yet reached adult volume, they will develop in proportion to the demands of the organism. Except for actual disease (mainly tuberculosis) they are not likely to become abnormal.

Results from recent studies on the reaction of lungs and heart to strenuous exercise indicate that immediately after exercise the amount of oxygen breathed is increased to seven or eight times the amount required for maintaining normal vital processes when the individual is in a state of complete relaxation. Recovery of normal breathing for boys of fourteen took only fifteen to twenty minutes. Some adults, however, needed as long as three hours to reach the same degree of recovery after the same amount of exercise. These results reflect the great vitality of adolescence.[1]

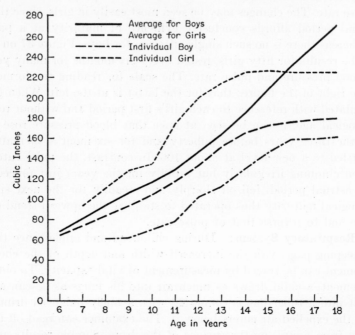

Fig. 38. *Measures of Vital Capacity*

Based on B. Baldwin, "The Physical Growth of School Children," *University of Iowa Studies in Child Welfare,* I, No. 1 (1926), 28ff., and B. Boynton, "A Study of the Rhythm of Physical Growth," *University of Iowa Studies in Child Welfare,* XII, No. 4 (1936), 40ff.

3. Digestive System: During adolescence the organs of digestion undergo considerable growth. The stomach becomes longer and increases in capacity. Because of the rapid growth rate in the size of the body, the adolescent needs more nourishment than formerly, and because of the enlarged capacity of his stomach, he craves more food. The net result is usually a tremendous appetite for three or four years. The daily intake may run as high as 5,000 calories and is rarely less than 3,000. In some adolescents the perpetually hungry condition is so marked that it seems practically impossible for them ever to get enough to eat, although they consume more food in twenty-four hours than adults need in twice that time. These youngsters are described—in New England, at least—as having a "hollow leg," where presumably all the food they eat is cached.

---

[1] N. W. Shock, "Physiological Changes in Adolescence," *Forty-third Yearbook of the National Society for the Study of Education,* 1944, Pt. I, pp. 64, 67.

Digestive difficulties during adolescence are doubtless due partly to mere overloading of the stomach but partly to actual deficiencies of vitamins or calcium. Furthermore, the boy or girl usually begins to eat meals away from home during this period. Adolescents can be trusted to make a lunch of hot dogs, chili con carne, or hamburgers and French fries, washed down with Coca-Colas or milk shakes, and followed by banana splits or strawberry waffles. The ubiquitous bakery truck contributes its share of digestive discomfort. It requires the entire period of adolescence for most people to learn to eat a reasonably balanced meal on their own initiative—if they ever do learn. In many adolescent groups, it is considered a social virtue to eat absurd combinations of food at highly unconventional and irregular hours. Such reactions may contribute to emancipation from home control and to status among one's peers, but they also contribute to stomach aches and other digestive disturbances.

The skin eruptions that plague adolescents are incidental by-products of the many changes in the chemistry of the body during the adolescent period; the usual diet of high school boys and girls doubtless helps in the production of the pimples that are the bane of an adolescent's life, although diet is not the only cause, as will be pointed out on page 62. A sallow skin, relatively large pores, and skin blemishes are normal accompaniments of adolescence. Any teacher who expects undivided attention from a girl with a cold sore on her lip or a boy with a small boil on his nose is doomed to disappointment. Adolescents will fuss interminably about these facial blemishes, making themselves and everyone else completely miserable. They are the most gullible users of any and all ointments or other medicaments. In the course of time, however, most adolescents do outgrow their troubles, and their skins become clear. Recovery is important because adolescents tend to ostracize a boy or girl whose acne is repulsive to them. For social as well as physical reasons, therefore, a reasonably clear skin is highly desirable.[2]

4. Nervous System: The number of different fibers in the nervous system is practically complete at birth, but not all neural functions are present at that time. So far as gross size is concerned, the nervous system develops very little during adolescence. There is almost no increase in the length, width, capacity, or weight of the brain during these years, because the brain has achieved its adult size by the end of childhood. What growth there is, then, is confined to further development of the fibers, in both length and thickness, and to further contacts among them. It is probable that the complexity of the brain—that is, the total number of contacts between fibers —is greatly increased during the early years of adolescence.

The facts in regard to neural growth are, in any case, not as important to the teacher as the effects. The increased ability to think and, in particular, to generalize is probably the result of the increased complexity of the brain. To be sure, part of the ability to think and reason comes from the individual experiences each person has as he grows older. It is, moreover, not true that children are completely without ability to reason. Their capacities are doubt-

---

[2] Adolescents with seriously affected skin should see a dermatologist, who can almost certainly help them.

less underestimated because they sometimes reach erroneous results through their lack of knowledge. The impulse to think in more general terms is perhaps due also to the need for such thinking; the physical, emotional, and social changes during adolescence precipitate problems to which the boy or girl wants an answer. Presumably, the further development of the brain furnishes the physiological basis for the more complex forms of thinking in which the adolescent indulges. Indeed, an outstanding characteristic of adolescent boys and girls is their spontaneous joy in mental activity—even if the topics thought about are not always those presented in the curriculum.

II. The Glandular System

1. The Duct Glands: The human body contains both duct and ductless—or endocrine—glands. The former are of relatively little importance for the present discussion, although important enough in the total economy of the organism, since their action has few psychological concomitants. The only points that will be noted in regard to them are the increase at adolescence in the activity of the sweat glands and the frequent failure of the oil glands to drain properly. The oil glands, although sometimes discharging altogether too much oil and producing a greasy appearance, more often fail to drain adequately because for a few years the ducts are too small. The normal discharge therefore hardens, a speck of dirt gets into it during the hardening, and a blackhead appears. The sweat glands also produce distressing symptoms, both directly through perspiration and indirectly through the development of body odors. The boy is upset because his shirt sticks to him at the slightest provocation and is acutely embarrassed when the perspiration on his hands stains the dress of the girl he dances with. With the aid of salves and all manner of deodorants, the adolescent girl carries on a constant fight against perspiration, and especially during her menstrual periods against body odor as well. Neither sex is altogether successful because the glands are both active and sensitive. Not only warmth and exercise produce undesired amounts of perspiration; any emotional disturbance is equally fatal. When a teacher sees a luckless student begin to perspire, she would do well to release him temporarily from whatever academic effort he is involved in. If his attention is being divided between the telltale moisture on his forehead and the intricacies of an imperfect subjunctive, he might as well sit down.

2. The Ductless Glands: The endocrine, or ductless, glands merit discussion because of their effects, direct and indirect, upon both physical condition and emotional life. The position of these glands is shown in Figure 39 on page 63. Their names are the pituitary, the thyroid, the parathyroids, the suprarenals, the pineal, the endocrine tissues in the pancreas, the thymus, the ovaries, and the testes. Each gland has its own rhythm of growth, some of which are illustrated in Figure 40 on page 64. In each case the figures show the per cent the gland is at each age of its size at age 20. The thymus develops rapidly in childhood; at thirteen it is 250 per cent heavier than at birth and 150 per cent heavier than in adult life. The thyroid, para-thyroids, and pituitary develop at a fairly regular rate from birth to maturity. The pineal gland grows rapidly and reaches 90 per cent of its adult weight before a child is ten years old. The suprarenals lose weight during the first year of life and do not regain their size at birth until the middle years of adolescence; thereafter, they grow quickly to their adult weight.

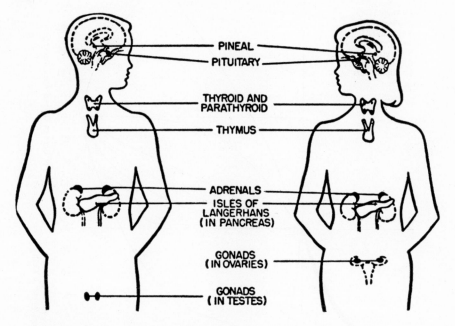

Fig. 39. *Position of the Endocrine Glands*

By permission from *Health Observations of School Children*, by G. M. Wheatley and G. T. Hallock, p. 93. Copyright, 1951, McGraw-Hill Book Company, Inc.

Each of these glands has its specific function in the chemistry of the body. Thus the pituitary controls growth in general, and the increased ac-tivity of its anterior lobe is the trigger that sets off the great physical changes of adolescence. It also has some influence in stimulating the appear-ance of the secondary sexual characteristics. If the pituitary is overactive from birth it will produce a giant; if underactive from birth, a dwarf. When the gland becomes abnormal during childhood or adolescence the person affected develops huge hands, big feet, and coarse features. Puberty is sometimes advanced—that is, it occurs before age 9 in girls or 11 in boys— or retarded until after age 17 in either sex, because the pituitary has be-come hyperactive sooner or later than usual, although there may be other reasons. There is at least one recorded case of a girl who began to men-struate at 7 months of age. By the time she was six years old she had a skeletal age of $13\frac{1}{2}$ and the figure of an adolescent girl.[3] Either advanced or

[3] W. W. Greulich and S. I. Pyle, *Radiographic Atlas of Skeletal Development of the Hand and Wrist*, Stanford University Press, 1950, p. 9.

retarded puberty presents problems to both parents and teachers. A nine-year-old girl or an eleven-year-old boy is not yet ready intellectually, socially, or emotionally to become an adolescent, and the child's associates are not yet ready to understand what has happened to him. Nor can the maturity be kept secret, even if this were wholly desirable, because the girl's

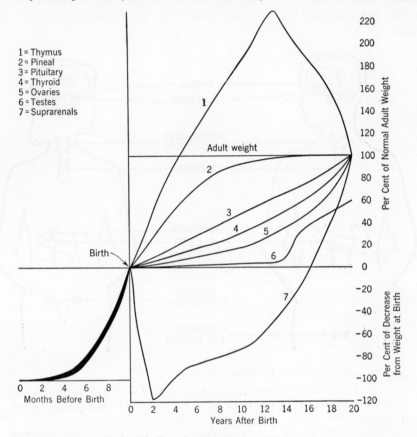

1 = Thymus
2 = Pineal
3 = Pituitary
4 = Thyroid
5 = Ovaries
6 = Testes
7 = Suprarenals

Fig. 40. *Growth Rates for Certain Glands*

The curve for prenatal growth is to be found on p. 263 of C. M. Jackson, "Some Aspects of Form and Growth," in L. Carmichael (ed.), *Manual of Child Psychology,* John Wiley & Sons, Inc., 1946.
The separate curves for growth after birth come from J. H. Harris, *et al., The Measurement of Man,* University of Minnesota Press, 1930, p. 200. Used by permission of the respective publishers.

breasts will soon develop, as will the boy's genitalia, and their voices will become lower, especially the boy's. These children then become objects of great curiosity and possible ridicule among their peers. A delayed adolescence is almost as bad, although the problems are different. The child fails to keep up with his group in any respect, except intellectually. In his schoolwork he may be successful, but outside the classroom he is as a pygmy among giants, and his social maladjustment is practically inevitable.

The suprarenal glands produce two secretions. One affects the development of masculine secondary sexual characteristics, while the other acts in times of emotional stress as a chemical whip on all the nerve centers of the body. The action of this second secretion will be described in more detail in another chapter.

The parathyroids control the absorption of calcium, a chemical necessary for the development of bone, for the nourishment of nerves, and for the clotting of the blood. These glands are tiny but absolutely essential to life. If they are accidentally removed during a goiter operation, the patient dies within a few days. The thymus and pineal glands and the pancreas also contribute to growth, to the assimilation of chemical materials, and to the regulation of various bodily functions, but their work has few if any mental or emotional accompaniments.

The thyroid gland regulates the rate at which metabolism takes place within the body. If the gland is not sufficiently active, an individual is slow, lethargic, and listless because all his bodily processes are retarded. His hair and nails are coarse and brittle, and his skin is thick and leathery. Usually, he is overweight and is likely to suffer from a chronic constipation. If medication by a simple taking of sheep's thyroid to compensate for the internal deficiency is begun soon enough, the individual usually becomes nearly, if not entirely, normal. An overactive thyroid causes the bodily functions to proceed too quickly. The heart beats too fast, the digestion is too rapid, and the nerves are overstimulated. The individual is too easily excited, too emotional, too quickly fatigued, too irritable. Usually he is underweight. The thyroid is a chronic troublemaker for adolescent girls, especially in the Middle West. In some sections, if iodine is not put into the drinking water, the percentage of girls with a thyroid enlargement, usually a "puberty goiter," runs as high as 30.[4]

Since the thyroid is mainly responsible for the rate at which an organism is functioning, one can estimate the adequacy of thyroid action by measuring the rate at which some fundamental bodily activity is progressing. The commonest approach to the problem is to determine the amount of oxygen used by the lungs in a given amount of time, under carefully controlled conditions.[5] If more than an average amount of oxygen is needed, the organism is running too fast, chiefly because it is being overstimulated by too much secretion from the thyroid; if less than an average amount of oxygen is needed, the organism is running too slowly. The average consumption of oxygen decreases from age 2 onward, the decrease being rapid at first but becoming slower during adolescence, with the boys maintaining a higher metabolic rate than girls at all ages.

Some interesting results appear in Figure 41 on page 66. The heavy lines give the curves for metabolic rate among 50 boys and 50 girls tested at six-month intervals from eleven and a half to eighteen years of age; the two broken lines show the record for two individuals in the group. The individual curves show marked rises just before or at puberty, followed by conspicuous decreases, with a subsequent recovery and establishment at an adult level. The irregular development shown by the individual curves

---

[4] J. S. Richardson, "The Endocrines in Adolescence," *Practitioner,* 162:280–296, 1949.

[5] The individual is supposed to have been lying down and to have eaten nothing for twelve hours. Usually the test is made about 7 A.M. while the person is still in bed.

almost always takes place for both boys and girls, but since puberty begins at different times for different individuals, the sudden increases and decreases cancel themselves out in the construction of a group curve, because when one thirteen-year-old, prepubertal child's curve is rising sharply another thirteen-year-old, postpubertal's is falling rapidly. Therefore, when results from a number of cases are combined, the group curves appear smooth.

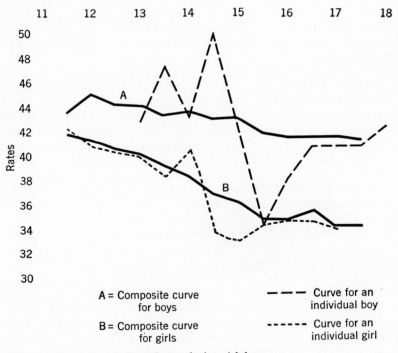

A = Composite curve for boys

B = Composite curve for girls

— — — Curve for an individual boy

------ Curve for an individual girl

Fig. 41. *Basal Metabolism Rates during Adolescence*

From Shock, "Physiological Changes in Adolescence," *loc. cit.*, pp. 62, 63. Used by permission of the National Society for the Study of Education.

The teacher who is alert to the situation will find in her classes many children who need medical attention because of glandular malfunctioning. Sluggishness, sleepiness, overweight, leathery skin, failure to grow, early appearance of secondary sex characteristics, irritability, excitability, jumpiness, inattention, fainting, painful menstruation, fast pulse, and protuberant eyeballs are all danger signals that suggest glandular involvement. Children showing such symptoms should be sent at once to the school doctor.

III. Sexual Maturity

The maturing of the sex glands is the most important single development of the adolescent years. Indeed, puberty consists essentially in this maturation. The mere physical ability to produce offspring is, however, not nearly as significant at the moment as the added depths and nuances of emotional and social life that develop along with puberty. These emotional developments will be discussed at length in a later chapter. The present discussion will be limited to a description of the physiological changes and the reaction of adolescents to them.

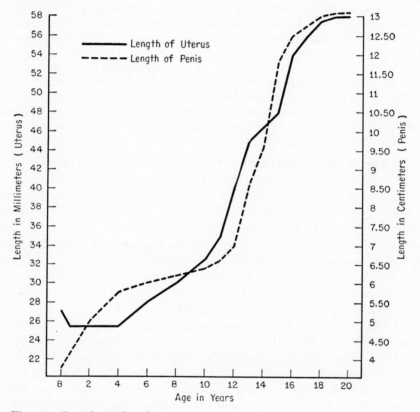

Fig. 42. *Growth of Sex Organs*

Based on figures in Morris, *Human Anatomy* (P. Schaefer, ed.), The Blakiston Company, 10th ed., 1942, p. 196, and W. A. Schonfeld and G. W. Beeke, "Normal Growth and Variability of the Male Genitalia from Birth to Maturity." *Journal of Urology*, 48:755–777, 1942.

1. The Sex Organs: Before beginning this discussion it seems advisable to present a brief statement concerning normal growth of the organs from birth to maturity.

During infancy and early childhood, the ovaries grow a little but very slowly, reaching about 10 per cent of their adult weight by age 8. They then begin to grow a bit more rapidly and gain half their final size by age 16. The other half is added during the next four years. (See Figure 40.)

The sperm cells are developed by the testicles (testes), which grow extremely slowly at first. At birth they are about 3 per cent of their adult weight, and at age 10 they have increased to only 6 per cent. The curve is definitely concave. Between ages 12 and 15 the testes begin to grow rapidly, achieving about 41 per cent of their final weight by the latter age. Development then becomes slower and even at 20 the glands are only 60 per cent of their adult weight and size.

Figure 42 traces the growth of the uterus and the penis.[6] The uterus at birth is over 45 per cent of its adult length. Almost at once, however, it shrinks and does not recover its size at birth until the girl is five years old. It grows slowly during childhood and then rapidly in preadolescence and adolescence, reaching its adult weight by age 20. The penis grows quite rapidly during the first four years of life, increasing from less than a third of its eventual length to nearly a half. It then grows slowly during childhood. At age 11 it has reached only half of its adult length. Growth then accelerates, especially from ages 14 to 17, after which the rate becomes slower, continuing until a boy has become a young man. Its growth is not quite complete at age 20.

2. Age of Sexual Maturity: Girls show normally a variation in the age of first menstruation from 10 to 17. Those who mature before age 12 are considered precocious and those who mature at or after age 15 as more or less retarded. Over 75 per cent of girls have their first period at twelve, thirteen, or fourteen years of age. The total distribution of menstrual ages, based upon a combination of many studies, appears in Figure 43 on page 69. The percentage of girls who menstruated for the first time at or before nine was so small as to be nearer to zero than to one; only 2 per cent became mature at age 10 and 8 per cent at 11. Thereafter, the proportion increased rapidly. The cumulative per cent of sexually mature girls at the end of the twelfth, thirteenth, and fourteenth years was, respectively, 31, 65, and 88. At ages 15 or 16 the remaining 12 per cent had their first period.

Since boys do not have any single, easily determined evidence of sexual maturity, such as girls do, and since they normally take at least six months and often as long as two years to pass from a clearly immature to a clearly mature level, it seems best to group them into three levels at each age: prepubescence, pubescence, and postpubescence. The percentages in each of these groups from ages 10 to 18 are shown in Figure 44 on page 70. Those in the first group are still children; their organs are small, there is no pubic hair, and their voices are still high. Boys in the second group show some but not all of the signs of maturity; they are in the process of becoming mature. Those in the third group show all the indications of male sexual adulthood, although their organs will continue to grow in size until about twenty-five years of age. An onset of pubescence before age 12 in boys may be considered precocious. Twelve, thirteen, and fourteen are the ages at which 70 per cent of boys become pubescent. Few boys reach the postpubescent stage before thirteen and only 30 per cent before fourteen. The

---

[6] Students who need diagrams of the male or female genitalia in order to follow the discussions will find excellent ones in A. Scheinfeld, *Women and Men,* Harcourt, Brace and Company, 1943, pp. 111 and 133.

commonest ages are fourteen and fifteen, during which another 54 per cent reach full maturity. The last 16 per cent arrive at that stage by the end of their seventeenth year. In Figure 44, 15 per cent show an early pubescence and 15 per cent a delayed one.

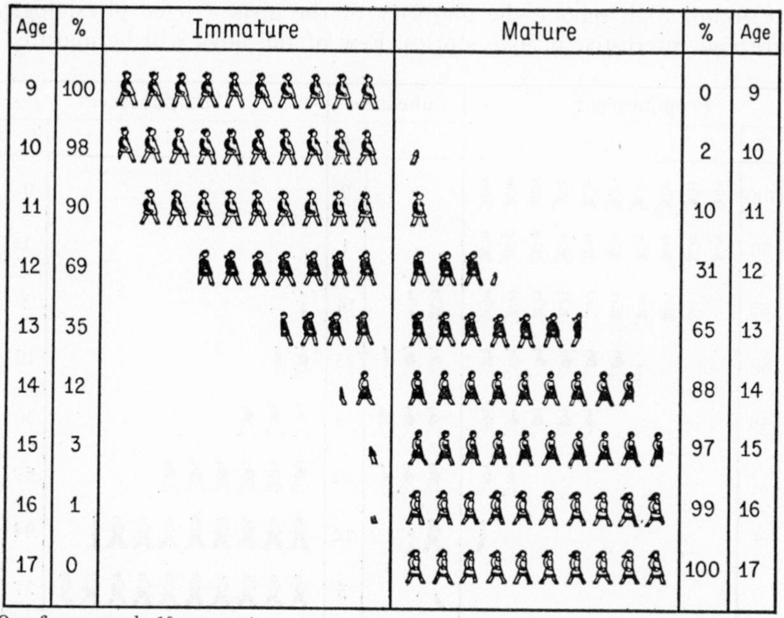

Age	%	Immature	Mature	%	Age
9	100	𝖆𝖆𝖆𝖆𝖆𝖆𝖆𝖆𝖆𝖆		0	9
10	98	𝖆𝖆𝖆𝖆𝖆𝖆𝖆𝖆𝖆	𝖆	2	10
11	90	𝖆𝖆𝖆𝖆𝖆𝖆𝖆𝖆𝖆	𝖆	10	11
12	69	𝖆𝖆𝖆𝖆𝖆𝖆𝖆	𝖆𝖆𝖆	31	12
13	35	𝖆𝖆𝖆𝖆	𝖆𝖆𝖆𝖆𝖆𝖆	65	13
14	12	𝖆	𝖆𝖆𝖆𝖆𝖆𝖆𝖆𝖆	88	14
15	3		𝖆𝖆𝖆𝖆𝖆𝖆𝖆𝖆𝖆	97	15
16	1		𝖆𝖆𝖆𝖆𝖆𝖆𝖆𝖆𝖆	99	16
17	0		𝖆𝖆𝖆𝖆𝖆𝖆𝖆𝖆𝖆𝖆	100	17

One figure equals 10 per cent.

Fig. 43. *Age of Maturity for Girls*

Based on data in R. G. Barker and C. P. Stone, "On the Relation between Menarcheal Age and Certain Aspects of Personality, Interests, and Physique in College Women," *Journal of Genetic Psychology and Pedagogical Seminary*, 45:121–135, 1934, and "Physical Development in Relation to Menarcheal Age in College Women," *Human Biology*, 8:198–222, 1936, E. T. Engle and M. C. Shelesmyak, "First Menstruation and Subsequent Menstrual Cycles of Pubertal Girls," *Human Biology*, 6:431–453, 1934; H. N. Gould and M. R. Gould, "Age at First Menstruation in Mothers and Daughters," *Journal of the American Medical Association*, 98:1349–1352, 1932 (material for daughters only was used); M. L. Reymert, "Relationships between Menarcheal Age, Behavior Disorders, and Intelligence," *Character and Personality*, 8:292–300, 1940.

It will be noted that boys reach maturity about two years later than girls. Consequently, there is a period during which a far larger proportion of girls are mature than of boys. As a result, girls are more sex-conscious than boys of their own age. There is some basis for the popular observation that a girl of thirteen is already a young lady, while a lad of thirteen is still a little boy.

In a hypothetical school containing 200 thirteen-year-old children, of whom one half were boys and one half girls, there would be the following situation: 65 girls would be physically mature and 35 immature, while 30 of the boys would be mature, 24 just entering pubescence, and 46 still children. This mixture would be extremely hard to teach, because of the differences in emotional attitudes and interests. The actual school situation is even more complex than this illustration because in any one class the range of chronological ages is at least three years, with the children in each age group showing varying degrees of maturity. Thus, in a literature class in the junior high school, the majority of the girls will be physiologically mature and interested in love stories. Few of the boys will be mature, and

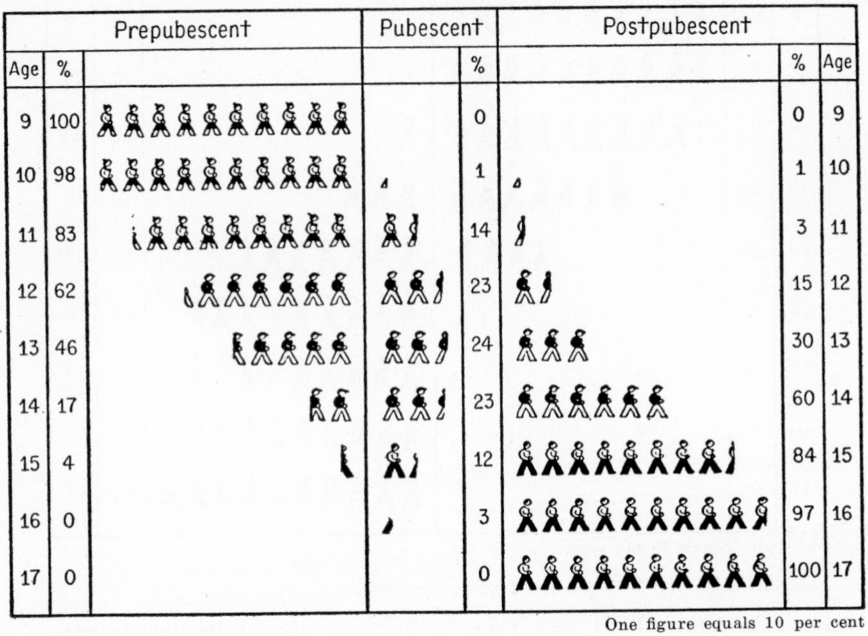

		Prepubescent			Pubescent		Postpubescent			
Age	%					%			%	Age
9	100						0		0	9
10	98						1		1	10
11	83						14		3	11
12	62						23		15	12
13	46						24		30	13
14	17						23		60	14
15	4						12		84	15
16	0						3		97	16
17	0						0		100	17

One figure equals 10 per cent

Fig. 44. *Age of Maturity for Boys*

Based on data in H. G. Richey, "The Relation of Accelerated, Normal, and Retarded Puberty to the Height and Weight of School Children," *Monographs of the Society for Research in Child Development*, Vol. II, No. 1, 1937, 67 pp.; and H. S. Dimock, *Rediscovering the Adolescent*, Association Press, 1937, pp. 209–211.

fewer still of them will have developed romantic interests; as a group they will be interested primarily in stories of adventure. As the years continue, more and more of them begin to show the interests and emotional attitudes characteristic of physiological maturity. This fact of variability between sexes is not therefore of mere academic interest to the teacher. Because of it, for the early years of adolescence at least, she needs to furnish a wide choice of instructional materials. In fact, in any class until the middle of high school, this matter of varying degrees of maturity is sure to create problems of interest and discipline.

The age of sexual maturity is related to height, weight, and skeletal development. Those who mature earliest are, from the age of six, taller, heavier, and more advanced in skeletal development than those who mature later. Figure 45 shows some illustrative results in weight for groups of boys

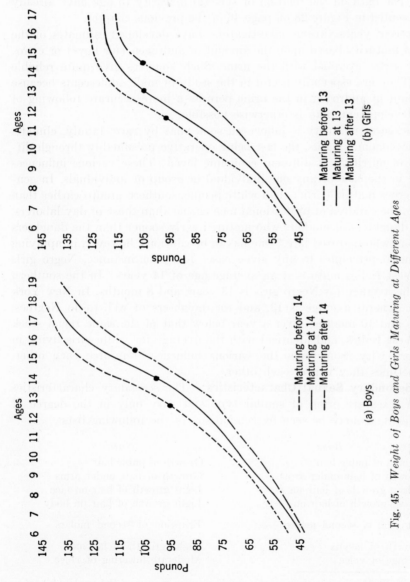

Fig. 45. *Weight of Boys and Girls Maturing at Different Ages*

From H. G. Richey, "The Relation of Accelerated, Normal, and Retarded Puberty to the Height and Weight of School Children," *Monographs of the Society for Research in Child Development*, II, No. 1 (1937), 22, 30. Used by permission of the National Research Council.

and girls who matured at different ages. On the chart a dot has been placed to indicate the approximate age of puberty for each group. Among boys the advent of puberty seems to accelerate growth. For the girls, however, the onset of menstruation marks the end rather than the beginning of rapid growth. The data on the relation of skeletal maturity to age have already been presented in Figure 28 on page 46 of the previous chapter.

In recent years various investigators[7] have developed estimates of the degree of maturity based upon the amount of androgen (for boys) or estrogen (for girls) excreted with the urine. Such analyses give quite reliable results. They are especially useful in the study of male adolescents because the amount of androgen in the urine permits a more accurate following of sexual development than is otherwise possible.

The age of maturity is influenced somewhat by race, family, climate, and socioeconomic status, the last being operative presumably through differences in nutrition at different economic levels. These various influences combine in the case of any one individual or group of individuals. In general, Negroes mature earlier than white people, southern groups earlier than northern, the children of professional men earlier than those of day laborers, and the daughters of mothers who matured early sooner than the daughters of mothers who matured late.[8] One has to be cautious, however, in applying such general principles to any given case. Thus, for instance, Negro girls in the West Indies mature at an average age of 14 years.[9] In the southern states, the average for Negro girls is 13 years and 8 months. In New York City the general average is 13, and for daughters of well-to-do Negroes, 12 years and 10 months—over a year below that of the same racial stock in the West Indies, and identical with the average for white girls living in New York City. Sometimes the various influences reinforce each other, but sometimes they cancel each other.

3. Secondary Sexual Characteristics: The secondary characteristics for both sexes are often of similar type and vary only in the degree of development, as may be seen by comparison of the following lists:

Boys	Girls
Growth of pubic hair	Growth of pubic hair
Growth of hair under arms	Growth of hair under arms
Heavy growth of hair on face	Light growth of hair on face
Heavy growth of hair on body	Light growth of hair on body
Eruption of second molars	Eruption of second molars
Growth of larynx	Slight growth of larynx
Change of voice	Moderate lowering of voice

[7] See W. W. Greulich *et al.*, "Somatic and Endocrine Studies of Pubertal and Adolescent Boys," *Monographs of the Society for Research in Child Development,* Vol. VII, No. 3, 1942, 65 pp.

[8] H. N. Gould and M. R. Gould, "Age of First Menstruation in Mothers and Daughters," *Journal of the American Medical Association,* 98:1349–1352, 1932.

[9] N. Michelson, "Studies in Physical Development of Negroes: Onset of Puberty," *American Journal of Physical Anthropology,* 2:151–166, 1949.

Boys	Girls
Widening of shoulders	Widening of hips
Thickening of muscles	Slight thickening of muscles
Increase in perspiration	Increase in perspiration
Sometimes slight and temporary development around breast nipples	Development of breasts

The growth of pubic hair and of hair under the arms is about the same for both sexes. Facial and body hair are much heavier for boys, but the same developments appear in reduced form among girls as a light down upon the upper lip and on the forearms and lower leg. The voices of children are of much the same pitch, without respect to sex. Thus, in a study[10] of seven- and eight-year-old children, the pitch for both boys and girls averaged close to middle C, about an octave above the average for adult males. A curious fact which emerged from this study was the appearance of "breaks" in the voices of both boys and girls, and of the same average number for members of both sexes. Change of voice usually begins during the fourteenth or fifteenth year with huskiness and lack of control in volume as the first symptoms. The larynx enlarges, and the boy's voice eventually becomes about an octave lower.[11] Many boys experience no marked "breaks." Their voices gradually become lower and heavier without loss of control.[12] One boy of the writer's acquaintance sang soprano in a church choir until he was fourteen, then alto for two years, then tenor, and finally bass by the time he was twenty-one, but at no time did he lack the necessary control for singing. Only about half the boys studied have reported "breaks." The girl's voice shows only a moderate degree of lowering, but the childish treble disappears, and the timbre of the voice becomes heavier and richer.

Members of both sexes show a lengthening and thickening of the muscles, but this development is so marked in boys that it is often overlooked in girls. Boys become markedly broader in the shoulders, while girls become definitely wider in the hips. These changes contribute much to the characteristic outline of men and women. Some boys develop a temporary swelling under their nipples during their period of pubescence, but the condition does not last.

For girls the development of the breasts is the most important of the secondary changes. In one study of the rate of growth of the breasts, semi-

---

[10] G. Fairbanks, J. H. Wiley, and F. M. Lassman, "An Acoustical Study of Vocal Pitch in Seven- and Eight-Year-Old Boys," *Child Development*, 20:63–69, 1949; and G. Fairbanks, E. L. Herbert, and M. Hammond, "An Acoustical Study of Vocal Pitch in Seven- and Eight-Year-Old Girls," *Child Development*, 20:71–78, 1949.

[11] E. T. Curry, "Voice Changes in Male Adolescence," *Laryngoscope*, 56:795–805, 1946.

[12] C. P. Pedrey, "A Study of Voice Changes in Boys between the Ages of Eleven and Sixteen," *Speech Monographs*, 12:30–36, 1945.

annual examinations were made of girls between ages 8 and 15.[13] The breasts developed from a bud to mature size in about three years, between ages 11 and 14. Thirty-eight per cent of the girls had small breasts, 28 per cent had large ones, and 34 per cent had breasts of medium size. In shape, 20 per cent were flat, 20 per cent were conical, and 60 per cent were hemispherical. The various outlines and percentage distributions are represented below in Figure 46. In 54 per cent of the girls, the breasts began to develop

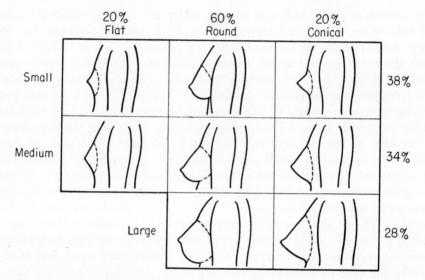

Fig. 46. *Growth of the Breasts*

Based on E. L. Reynolds and J. V. Wines, "Individual Differences in Physical Changes Associated with Adolescent Girls," *American Journal of Diseases of Children,* 75:329–350, 1948.

before the pubic hair started to grow, in 32 per cent the hair appeared first, and in the remaining 14 per cent the two secondary characteristics appeared and developed together.

4. Reactions to Sexual Maturity: The achievement of sexual maturity is of great importance to the boy or girl. It is also the source of some embarrassment. The boy's organs not only grow rapidly in size until he suspects they may show through his clothing, but they seem to react without his volition. At night the boy is often distressed by dreams that seem to him highly indecent. He is practically certain to masturbate more or less; even if he does not, his nocturnal emissions may embarrass and frighten him. If he does not have frequent discharges, he may become uncomfortable from tension. Most boys require physical relief, which is usually obtained by a combination of masturbation and daydreams of

[13] E. L. Reynolds and J. V. Wines, "Individual Differences in Physical Changes Associated with Adolescence in Girls," *American Journal of Diseases of Children,* 75:329–350, 1948.

girls.[14] At the beginning of the genital period, the physical stimulation is the more important element, but gradually the intellectual and emotional elements become sufficient for stimulation and fuse with the physical. Girls do not experience nearly as much need for release as boys do.

A boy experiences erections as a reaction to a wide variety of stimuli, some of which are not of obviously sexual character, such as sentimental music, riding in a car or on a train, swinging, or becoming generally excited, as at a football game, or frightened, as when on the way to battle. The commonest stimuli are conversations on sexual matters with either other boys or girls, pictures of female nudity, pornographic pictures or books, daydreams, love scenes in moving pictures or in books, and dancing.[15] Boys are much more easily stimulated than girls, in part because their organs are external, and in part because their mechanism has a hair-trigger reaction quite missing in girls. An erection, while sometimes disturbing to a boy, is also a source of pride as a sure sign of masculinity.

The secondary sex changes are also important. An excessive growth of pubic hair or lack of it is sure to arouse remarks in the common dressing room of the gymnasium, even though these comments may be complimentary. Indeed, as puberty approaches, boys watch each change with great anxiety, because the acquisition of masculinity has such prestige value among age-mates. The appearance of hair on the face and the resulting introduction to shaving, while generating a feeling of manly development, may be uncomfortable. Especially to be pitied is the boy who has needed for some time to shave but has been prevented from doing so by his parents.

Single manifestations of masculinity may appear at any age from middle childhood to late adolescence—that is, from the end of elementary school till toward the end of high school. Evidence accumulated from personal interviews with 291 adolescent boys is summarized in Figure 47. The results show that a boy's voice may change, his nocturnal emissions begin, his ability to ejaculate develop, and his pubic hair appear as early as seven, eight, or nine years of age and as late as some age after sixteen. The percentage of boys having nocturnal emissions increases fairly regularly from ages 13 through 17, but some boys have not shown any emissions until 18 or 19.

Masturbation may begin in infancy and is practiced by a fourth of the boys by the time they are eight years old. By age 12, over three fourths of the boys masturbated, and by age 16, all of them. Since this sexual practice is so widespread, it cannot be called abnormal. So far as known the physiological results are either harmless or beneficial; the damage, if any, is emotional. Many boys suffer from feelings of shame and guilt, which often accompany the act, and are frightened half out of their wits by horrible predictions of insanity or impotence in later life. Unless the masturbation is excessive it does no harm provided a boy does not get the idea

---

[14] F. B. Strain, *The Normal Sex Interests of Children*, Appleton-Century-Crofts, Inc., 1948, 210 pp.

[15] G. V. Ramsey, "The Sex Development of Boys," *American Journal of Psychology*, 56:217–233, 1943.

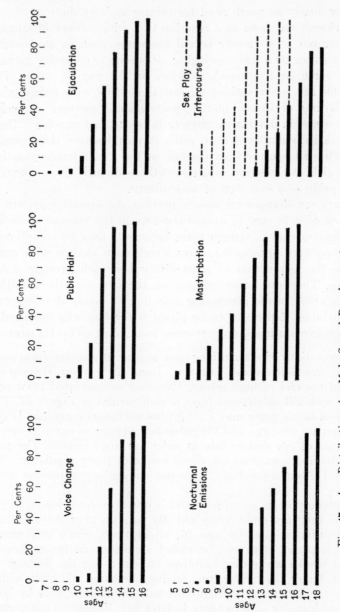

Fig. 47. *Age Distributions for Male Sexual Development*

Based on G. V. Ramsey, "The Sex Development of Boys," *American Journal of Psychology,* 56:217–233, and "The Sex Information of Younger Boys," *American Journal of Orthopsychiatry,* 13:347–352, 1943; and for one distribution only, A. C. Kinsey, W. B. Pomeroy, and C. E. Martin, *Sexual Behavior in the Human Male,* W. B. Saunders Company, 1948, p. 175.

that he is abnormal. If the boy is not scolded or threatened or made to feel ashamed, he will outgrow the habit. The best single method of either prevention or cure is to keep a boy's life so full of so many interesting things that he has relatively little time for daydreaming and relatively little attention left over from other interests to become absorbed in any form of sexual activity. Sex play is common.[16] It begins as early as four, and the percentage of boys indulging in some form of sex play increases with every year. By ten years, 45 per cent have had such experiences, and by fourteen the per cent has reached 100. The earliest reported attempts at intercourse were at age 12. By fifteen years of age, 45 per cent had at least tried to have intercourse. The percentage increased to 60 at sixteen and, in the sample studied, at least one such attempt had been made by 82 per cent of the boys before they were 19. Visits to prostitutes were reported as early as fifteen, and at least one such visit had been made by 40 per cent of the boys before their twentieth year. Adults are often shocked by the figures on sex play and sex experience among children and adolescents, but this attitude stems partly from a failure to realize that sexual interests are a normal part of life at all ages and partly from a conviction that these interests are "dirty." Each new study of the subject points more and more clearly to the natural spontaneity of such interests and activities and to their widespread occurrence at all ages.

Boys differ greatly from each other also in the extent of their knowledge about sexual phenomena and in their sexual practices. Results are summarized in Figure 48 on page 78. Some boys know about the origin of babies as early as five years of age, but others do not learn until age 13 or 14. Knowledge of menstruation is acquired as early as age 8, but as many as half the boys are not aware of it until after age 15. Since most girls are already mature at this age, there would seem to be a need for an earlier imparting of this item of information; otherwise boys are likely to be puzzled and curious about the behavior of girls during their monthly periods. Knowledge of prostitution may be acquired at a very early age; the fact that prostitutes exist is known to all or practically all boys by the time they are fifteen years old. Knowledge of venereal disease does not reach half the boys until they are fourteen, and even at eighteen it is not universal. In view of their experiences, this information should surely be provided in early adolescence. Information about contraceptives has been acquired by over half the boys of twelve, and by all of them at eighteen.

Failure to mature as early as other boys or the development of feminine characteristics is a source of great emotional disturbance.[17] Mere delay— with resulting small organs, high-pitched voice, and small stature—is deeply distressing and leads to difficulties of both social and emotional adjustment. Physical manifestations that are listed as being disturbing to boys include lack of sufficient height or weight, uneven growth of facial features, lack

---

[16] The facts in the rest of this paragraph are taken from A. C. Kinsey, W. B. Pomeroy, and C. E. Martin, *The Sexual Behavior of the Human Male*, W. B. Saunders Company, 1945, pp. 137, 141, and 175.

[17] W. A. Schonfeld, "Inadequate Masculine Physique as a Factor in Personality Development of Adolescent Boys," *Psychosomatic Medicine*, 12:49–50, 1950.

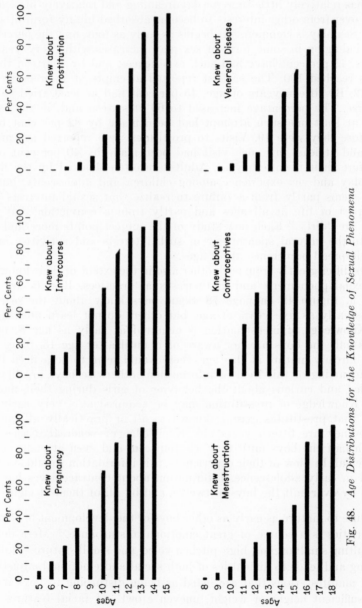

Fig. 48. *Age Distributions for the Knowledge of Sexual Phenomena* Based on Ramsey, "The Sex Information of Younger Boys," *loc. cit.*

of muscle, lack of shoulder breadth, unusually small or unusually large genitals, development of the nipples, fatness, breadth in the hips, feminine roundness of entire body, and sundry types of skin blemish—especially acne.[18] About a third of the boys in one group showed concern over one or more such conditions as those just listed.

As a boy becomes physiologically mature his interests and attitudes undergo changes. Emotional reactions are so clearly dependent upon physical developments that the relation between the two can be measured. In one study,[19] attitudes were first determined by means of a scale for measuring emotional age. Then his urine was analyzed for hormones. The more hormones a boy passed, the higher was his score on the test of attitudes and interests. The relation held in general among all boys included in the study and also for the development of the individual boys from year to year, although the degree of correlation was higher in some cases than in others.

The average boy has perhaps a more pronounced emotional reaction to his maturity than the average girl, because he is more acutely and constantly aware of it. His organs are external. They are subject to the incidental pressure of such external objects as wearing apparel or bedclothes. He is forced to touch himself several times a day when he urinates. To himself, his sexual development seems obvious and uncontrollable. If he consults his friends about his difficulties, he receives chiefly smutty stories and misinformation; if he asks his father, he is often met with embarrassment and evasiveness; if he consults an older man, he is lucky if he is not sent to prostitutes; if, in desperation, he visits some quack, he gets frightened out of his wits. He cannot consult most of his teachers because they are unmarried women. Even his mother can tell him very little; she was never a boy, and by now she has reached a conservative, feminine middle age that is as likely to be horrified as to be helpful.

A girl's adolescence involves quite different kinds of strain and difficulty from those experienced by boys. A girl may receive a considerable emotional shock from her first menstruation, whether or not she has been warned of its arrival, since there is something understandably terrifying in a hemorrhage that cannot be stopped. Bleeding is so associated with unpleasantness that many girls can never dissociate this emotional tone from their menstrual periods, even though the total amount of blood lost averages about three tablespoonfuls. There are even a few girls who are so disturbed emotionally during their periods that they are quite unlike themselves. Even after the periods are established, their recurrence taken for granted, and any initial discomfort forgotten, girls may experience what boys do not—

[18] H. R. Stolz and L. M. Stolz, "Adolescent Problems as Related to Somatic Variations," *Forty-third Yearbook of the National Society for the Study of Education,* 1944, pp. 80–99.

[19] R. T. Sollenberger, "Some Relationships between the Urinary Excretion of Male Hormones by Maturing Boys and Their Expressed Interests and Attitudes," *Journal of Psychology,* 9:179–189, 1940.

actual pain from sexual functioning. The relatively few girls with some abnormal condition have undoubted pain. For the others—the great majority—the pain is slight if it exists at all, although there may be a general lassitude, some digestive disturbance, and an unusual degree of emotionality and nervousness. Some girls make a practice of spending the first day of each period in bed—and a day's relaxation once a month in comparative isolation from social pressures is not a bad idea—but few girls require such treatment merely because of the menstrual period. Mothers are likely to be indulgent on this point, so it is probable that a first day in comfortable semi-invalidism will retain its popularity. One can hardly help noticing, however, that when a girl has something she really wants to do, she usually gets up and does it, whether or not she is menstruating. There are, in every school generation, a few girls who never have any sensations at all from their periods.

The matter of how much exercise a girl should take during her periods is one that is perennially open to discussion. Actual practice varies from rest in bed to exercise as usual. There is perhaps no general rule that will hold in even the majority of cases. Each girl has to find out for herself what she can comfortably do during her periods and what makes her too tired. Thus she may find that she can play a leisurely game of tennis with her little brother without any but beneficial results, but that she cannot play a tournament match without fatigue and strain. Often it is not the amount of exercise that exhausts a menstruating girl as much as the emotional tension involved in competition. If there is no pressure to sacrifice herself for the good of her team, an adolescent girl will stop a form of exercise that makes her uncomfortable before she has done herself any damage.

Almost all girls are more or less embarrassed by or during their periods. They wonder if the pad they are wearing is showing; they wonder if the blood has soaked through their dresses; they wonder if boys can tell if they are menstruating; they wonder if their body odor may have become offensive. They get upset because they have to explain to others why they are not going swimming or why they are not playing hockey. None of these sources of embarrassment form any part of menstrual physiology but are superimposed upon it by adolescent social life. Of all the worries, the concern about a possible stain on her dress is a girl's most constantly recurring dread. Some girls have this fear in such exaggerated form that they will not stand up in class. Since most teachers of adolescent youth are women, they should have no difficulty in recognizing and evaluating this behavior.

Sometimes the beginning of menstruation intensifies a maladjustment that has been in existence for some time but in a subacute form, or the development may give a new turn to an old difficulty. Occasionally, it precipitates a brand-new conflict of some sort, but not often.

The girls who mature earliest have a temporary position of prestige among other girls and are often called upon to guide their less mature friends through the first few menstrual periods. A late-maturing girl has the same lack of status experienced by the late-maturing boy, but the situation is not complicated by small stature, partly because there is no general prejudice against short women, partly because success in competitive sports is not so important to her as to a boy, and partly because her growth spurt—being a feature of preadolescence—has already taken place. In fact, if her puberty is delayed long enough, she may do a little extra growing. A girl who tends toward a masculine type of body is also in a somewhat less precarious social position than a boy whose body tends to be feminine. Such a girl may feel that she is altogether too flat and lacking in proper curves, but she will be actually admired by other girls because clothes hang well on her. Also she can gain prominence, if she wishes to do so, in sports and games. In any case, she rarely meets the scorn and ostracism that are often the lot of the too-feminine boy.

When one compares mature and immature girls of the same age, one finds quite marked differences among them in attitudes and interests.[20] A mature girl is interested in boys, in all forms of social life—especially in dances and parties—in personal appearance and adornment, and in sentimental love stories in both books and movies. Her interest in games decreases. She does a good deal of daydreaming and becomes quite introspective. The noisy, athletic, objective, energetic young hoyden who does not care how she looks, who still competes with boys, and who regards love stories as silly has not yet reached her maturity.

The three girls described below were all profoundly affected by their menstrual periods, although only one of them had any marked physical discomfort.

Anna, who did not begin to menstruate until she was sixteen, completely refused to admit she had any periods. After the first three or four she had her hair cut like a man's, wore men's clothes, smoked a pipe, and really appeared to be a man. She was not homosexual, or at least there was never any evidence to that effect. In fact, she appeared to be sexually frigid. She moved to a new place, got a job in an office, passed as a man, and remained there for about three years. Then she decided to change from men's clothes to feminine slacks and to let her hair grow to the length of a normal bob. She had developed a pleasant acquaintanceship with several boys and men in the town where she worked, and many of these friendships continued unbroken for another three years, during which she was really neutral rather than either masculine or feminine. Gradually, she resumed women's clothes, married, and has lived a normal life since. It is probable that Anna would have had some form of maladjustment during her adolescent years, as her home situation was poor and she was not popular in school, but the form her escape from life took was induced by the shock of her first menstrual periods, her conviction that she could not bear a monthly recurrence, and her determination to deny the whole thing by becoming a man.

Louise's first period came when she was fourteen, after she had entered high school and had become quite popular. She had been told by her mother well in advance of the phenomenon and had not seemed at all concerned or worried over the prospect. After the periods were established, however, she began to refuse in-

[20] C. P. Stone and R. G. Barker, "The Attitudes and Interests of Premenarcheal and Postmenarcheal Girls," *Journal of Genetic Psychology and Pedagogical Seminary,* 54:27–71, 1939.

vitations to parties—not always, but for the days before, during, and after her periods. She gave up swimming and other sports altogether. After about six months of this behavior, she refused to leave the house while she was menstruating, on the grounds that everyone would know her condition and she would be too embarrassed to face people. Her parents tried to talk her out of this attitude, but without success. Louise had gotten the idea firmly fixed in her mind that she was "unclean" during her periods and must stay away from others. This state of affairs continued throughout high school. On the advice of the family doctor, Louise was sent to a girls' college at some distance from home. In this feminine environment, she soon lost her phobia. She is still a bit shy and easily embarrassed, but she is gradually regaining the social poise that was hers before she began to menstruate.

Madelaine's first periods, at the age of thirteen, were quite painful and she had bouts of nausea during them. After about six months there was no more pain or nausea, only a feeling of heaviness and an occasional cramp or a headache. The physical symptoms were mild, and since Madelaine had perfectly normal organs, her doctor assured her that even these minor discomforts would not continue for long. Actually, they did soon disappear. Madelaine, however, continued to dread her periods and to react emotionally to them. About three days before a period was due she became moody, irritable, and nervous. The symptoms increased as the period came nearer. For about forty-eight hours after the menstrual flow began Madelaine was so bad-tempered, unreasonable, and violent that members of her family learned to leave her alone. After the first two days of the period, she began to regain her usual pleasant disposition and by the end, she was herself again. Madelaine tried to control her outbursts, and as she grew older succeeded to some degree, although she continued to stay alone as much as she could for at least twenty-four hours after each menstrual flow began. To her family, teachers, and friends, Madelaine seemed to be two people: one that was cheerful, lovable, and normal and one that was moody, sullen, suspicious, irritable, and explosive. This Jekyll and Hyde transformation continued until after Madelaine was married and had had her first child. The long absence of menstrual periods during her pregnancy, plus the complete absence of discomfort after they reappeared, seemed to have broken the cycle, and the sunny, happy Madelaine has been the only one in evidence since.

The first girl described above had had little security in her childhood, had always been a tomboy, and was not given any proper information about sex before her first period. It is probable that menstruation influenced the form of her maladjustment but was only an additional and final cause of it. The second girl made in exaggerated form the withdrawing reaction that is common and normal. Most girls fear that some odor or the appearance of a blood stain will betray their condition, but the vast majority manage to overcome this fear. The notion that a menstruating woman was unclean is widespread and common among primitive peoples and was the basis of many taboos. The second girl showed no abnormal behavior but rather a too extreme form of a normal attitude. The third girl's condition is not easily explained and was probably due to glandular involvement. She had been a remarkably stable child, and she is now a remarkably stable woman. Had there been a history of a moody disposition, and especially of sudden swings from one extreme to another, one would assume that the menstrual period merely acted as a trigger to precipitate a mood that would have appeared sooner or later, anyway. As it was, the black mood was linked definitely with menstruation and never occurred at any other time. There may have been a deep-seated, unresolved conflict at the bottom of the phenomenon, but it seems more probable that the causes were mainly physical and that they operated through the effect of ovarian secretions upon other glands.

Adolescent girls have other worries that are based upon physical characteristics. Girls who are unusually tall or fat become extremely self-conscious. So also do girls with unusually large hands or feet or legs. They are even more upset than boys by any irregularities in facial growth. A skin blemish is a source of profound concern, and hair that for some reason cannot be persuaded to lie properly in the accepted mode of the moment is almost as bad. Girls are worried if their breasts are too small and even more upset if they are too large. Many a girl is deterred from games in which she would love to participate because her breasts obviously move when she runs or jumps. Even though the development of the breasts gives prestige value to a girl, she is not altogether easy in her mind about their conspicuousness. The widening of the hips is likely to inspire an attack of rigid dieting, on the assumption that fat rather than bone is the cause. Most adolescents are much too hungry to continue their dieting for long, but an occasional strong-minded damsel needs a sane explanation of the change which has suddenly precipitated her from a size fourteen to a size eighteen dress. Most modern girls are annoyed but not unduly alarmed by the appearance of hair on the arms or face, because the ubiquitous beauty parlor will attend to the matter, but there are still a few girls who are made miserable by facial hair and do not know what to do about it. Of the secondary changes, however, the breasts give rise to the most frequent embarrassment. Like the boy's sex organs, they are external, they move, and they show through the clothing. In one study, over 40 per cent of the girls complained of discomfiture over such manifestations as have just been enumerated.[21] Two studies which illustrate the pervasive social and emotional effects of having a definite physical handicap are presented below:

As a little child Louisa was spontaneously gay and happy, with a great feeling of security in her mother's devotion. She was in kindergarten before her age-mates began to tell her that her face was "funny" or "dirty" or "all purple." Louisa's house contained no mirror, and she had therefore not known that she had a large, dark birthmark across her nose, half her forehead, one cheek, one ear, and her upper lip. Her mother had concealed the condition as long as she could and had almost smothered the child with love to compensate for the defect. The affection had in it an element of compulsion, which made one feel that the mother had been originally repulsed by the birthmark and was now overcompensating as a means of escape from what she considered an abnormal attitude of rejection. During her childhood Louisa often forgot for hours or even days at a time that she had a birthmark. Once in a while some age-mate made fun of her, but most children accepted her without more than an initial period of inspection prompted mostly by curiosity. With the approach of adolescence, however, and with the development of a quicker perception on Louisa's part, the social situation underwent a marked change for the worse. Louisa discovered that people did not want to look at her because her appearance made them feel ill, and she realized that her childhood chums, now become highly sensitive to social pressures, found her a handicap to their prestige. After a few rebuffs Louisa withdrew from more than casual contacts with age-mates. Louisa went to high school, with the intention of becoming eventually a cataloguer in some library, not because the work attracted her but because it involved working behind the scenes where social contacts would be few. Rebuffed, isolated, and withdrawn,

---

[21] Stolz and Stolz, "Adolescent Problems as Related to Somatic Variations," *loc. cit.*

Louisa had reached the stage of asking only for peace and shelter. Then the miracle happened. One day she read a newspaper article about a new make-up cream that hid scars or birthmarks. Secretly and without more than a faint hope of relief, she bought some, and on an afternoon when her mother was caring for a sick friend she tremblingly followed the directions and was completely stunned by the face that looked back at her from the mirror. It was not only free of blemish, it was pretty— except for its petulant expression. Louisa and her mother experimented with the compound for some days, and then, convinced of its effectiveness, the girl changed her plans. She and her mother moved to another city and Louisa went to college, where she eventually became a teacher. Her social success was beyond her wildest dreams, and her personality developed along what were probably its normal lines. She had as many friends and dates as any other girl, and even filled a few minor roles of leadership. Louisa is now a happy young teacher who is understandably successful with "problem" children. She has almost forgotten that she has a birthmark.

Nancy was the youngest daughter of a wealthy family. Her two older sisters were pretty children and grew up to be attractive adolescents. Both attended a socially first-class boarding school where they did mediocre work but were popular and had a good time. Both girls had expensive debuts, and both are now married. Nancy was a homely and awkward child. By the time she was four or five years old, her socialite mother had completely rejected her. Her father, a successful trial lawyer, was sorry for his ugly duckling and was kind enough to her when he remembered her existence, but he also neglected her, largely because he spent relatively little time with his family and left the upbringing of the three girls to his wife.

When Nancy became old enough to enter school, her father wanted her to be sent to public school, but the mother was unwilling to do so and equally unwilling to enter the child in the fashionable day school attended by the children of her friends. She therefore hired a combination teacher, companion, housekeeper, and watchdog to act as governess to Nancy, sent the two away to the country, and circulated the rumor that her youngest daughter had a tendency to tuberculosis and could not attend school. Nancy and her governess lived in almost complete seclusion until the girl was fourteen. The father saw her about once a month, but the mother not more than two or three times a year. At this point, the governess died, and some new disposition had to be made of a homely, awkward, isolated, sensitive girl. After much discussion, some of which Nancy overheard, the mother entered the girl in a small, obscure, distant boarding school, using the girl's middle name as a last name.

By this time Nancy knew very well that she was a disgrace to the family, that her mother was bitterly ashamed of her, and that her sisters did not wish her to speak to them if she should meet them in any public place. She was also convinced that their estimate of her was quite correct. At fourteen, Nancy was a tall, thin, awkward, homely girl who shuffled along the school corridors looking at her own feet and avoiding as many contacts as possible. At mealtime she sat where she was told to sit, passed the bread or the butter as requested, kept her eyes on her plate, spoke to no one, and answered only in monosyllables if spoken to. In class her work was brilliant, but she recited with her eyes on the floor and she often stammered when called upon. At this school every girl was required to take part in some sport. At the time of her registration Nancy had been assigned to tennis, at which she turned out to be extraordinarily good at net playing, a talent which she herself did not know she possessed. She made the school tennis team at the end of her first year. Thus encouraged, she went in for various sports and was reasonably successful in several. Because of her superior work in school she was often asked by her teachers to help girls who were having difficulties, and these tutoring sessions brought her in contact with a number of girls who eventually not only admired but liked her.

Although Nancy came from an excellent family, she had been given little or no help in those skills that her mother could most readily have taught her. She did not know how to select clothes, to use make-up, to maintain a conversation, or even to be gracious. During her first two years in boarding school Nancy had to acquire the simple, basic, social skills that she badly needed. Her schoolwork remained excellent, she had reasonable success in school athletics, and she had many acquaintances although no close friends. She continued to wear any clothes that were bought for her by her mother and to throw them on without effort to make herself attractive, although she was always clean and neat. During her third year she was called upon to tutor the most popular girl in the school. The school idol was not long in seeing Nancy's true worth and in becoming her loyal friend. Since Nancy had plenty of money, her new friend simply sent Nancy's clothes to the Salvation Army, spent over $400 in buying new ones, turned Nancy over for a day to an expert beautician, and convinced Nancy that attention to appearances was really necessary.

What emerged from the week-end spree of buying and self-improvement was an extraordinarily handsome girl, who was not conventionally pretty but was certainly striking. Never again could Nancy be overlooked. With the handicap of her ugliness removed both publicly and in her own mind, Nancy became both happy and moderately popular. Because of her abilities she was encouraged to go on to college. There, in a new environment among people who did not know she had ever been homely, she attained outstanding success. She is now happily married to a man of excellent background. In her leisure time she continues to tutor high school youngsters and works voluntarily with a social agency, taking neglected and rejected children into her own home, where she gives them such understanding and affection that many of them recover. As an ironical corollary, Nancy's social status is appreciably higher than that of either sister and she is, at forty, the best looking one of the three.

The extremely fat adolescent girl is a very unhappy creature. She is commonly rejected by her age-mates, who are at a stage of development during which they set great store by appearances, and she makes little appeal to boys. Some overweight girls become motherly in their effort to find some possible relationship with boys, and others become frankly immoral, thus obtaining attention of a kind even though it is only a substitute for what they really want. The fat girl needs help from her family, her doctor, and her teachers if she is to find happiness and a normal adjustment.[22] One basic point about overweight should be firmly grasped: That for some reason food has become a weapon against tension and anxiety. The obese girl therefore eats to relieve strain. She comforts herself with sodas, sundaes, cakes, and cookies because she is unhappy, and the more she comforts herself the more she has to comfort herself about! Medical treatment is not the teacher's business, but she can give a good deal of support, without which the best of medication may prove of little avail. The following study may help illustrate the many problems that beset the fat girl or boy.

Mary Lou came of a family in which every member overate and every member

---

[22] H. Bruch, "Psychological Aspects of Obesity," *Bulletin of the New York Academy of Science,* 24:73–86, 1948.

was fat. By the time she was four years old she was already overweight, clumsy, and slow on her feet. She had a normal amount of energy, but she tired quickly, and she was often too rough with her age-mates—not intentionally but because she was bigger and heavier than they and her co-ordination was poor. During her childhood she got along well enough, although she was never popular. Her schoolwork was good, and on a Binet examination she earned an IQ of 132. As the years went by she grew rapidly, both vertically and horizontally, and was always the largest child in the classroom.

Mary Lou started to menstruate during her year in the sixth grade. As soon as the periods were well established she began to take on weight at an alarming rate. At entrance to high school two years later she was nearly six feet tall and weighed 212 pounds. During her freshman year she developed what was, even for her, an enormous appetite and gained another 40 pounds. She was too big and clumsy to play any games, and she did not know how to keep herself clean. As a result of her physical condition she became an outcast. Her reaction to her unpopularity was to read sentimental novels by the dozen, munching candy the while. Early in her sophomore year in high school she ran upstairs one day because she was late to class and collapsed in the corridor. The school doctor found her heart to be in a bad condition and called her parents in for a conference, at which he told them that Mary Lou must go on a strict diet and lose at least 75 pounds.

Probably the parents did their best, but there was always a lot of food on the table at mealtimes and the other members of the family ate heartily. There was therefore little help from the family and much temptation. Mary Lou did substitute celery for candy while she read, and she did eat a little less at mealtimes. For the first time in her life a month passed without any gain in weight, but the doctor was not satisfied. It was suggested that Mary Lou be boarded out with someone who was a light eater and would not constantly if unintentionally tempt Mary Lou to eat more than her regime called for. It happened that the art teacher in the high school wanted a girl to live with her and do some of the housework, and she agreed to take Mary Lou home with her for a month on trial.

The new plan worked well. Mary Lou made herself useful in the small ménage and really stuck to her diet. Mary Lou remained with the teacher, making only an occasional visit to her parents and never eating a meal at home, for a semester, during which she lost 30 pounds. In her junior and senior years Mary Lou continued to live with the teacher on week days, but she spent week ends and holidays at home. By this time she had gained enough self-control and maturity to stick to her diet voluntarily even in the face of temptation. She entered her senior year weighing 170 pounds. It is unlikely that she will ever weigh less, but she is so tall that she looks slender. At the present time Mary Lou is planning to enter college and study to be a dietitian in a hospital. She has both the ability and the interest, and it is probable that she will succeed.

A great improvement in social and emotional adjustment has kept pace with the physical rehabilitation. At the end of her freshman year Mary Lou was an object of avoidance among her classmates. Her reaction was to isolate herself still further, to feel abused, and to derive her main pleasures in life from eating—thus indulging in the customary reaction of fat people who use food as a defense and as a substitute for other types of enjoyment. She was a problem for several teachers and for many of the more prominent students because she developed hectic crushes on them and made a nuisance of herself. At the end of her senior year she had to some extent compensated for her earlier indiscretions and had found a few friends, mostly younger than she. It is probable that at the college she plans to attend in an adjoining state, where the other students will have no recollection of her as an objectionable young adolescent, she will be able to develop normal and satisfactory social relationships.

5. The School and Adjustment to Sexual Growth: In one re
adolescence in American high schools is made relatively easy for girls
relatively hard for boys. When a girl has a problem she can go to her fav
ite teacher and ask questions without much if any embarrassment and
with good prospects of getting a sensible answer. Thus a girl can, in emergencies, find an adult woman of whom she is fond, in whom she has confidence, and to whom she is not related. A boy has no such wide choice of
personalities, since so few of his teachers are men. He cannot, without
deep and perhaps lasting embarrassment on both sides, talk of sexual problems with his women teachers. There remain the coaches of various sports,
and to them he goes in times of stress. Much of his schooltime adolescence
is inevitably spent in a predominantly feminine atmosphere, which intensifies his problems and offers little aid in their solution.

From the above account one can see that boys and girls reach puberty
at different ages, that their sexual maturing has different manifestations,
and that they have different problems. Because American boys and girls
go through school together and because promotion in American schools is
based more upon age than upon scholastic achievement, children of both
sexes and similar ages reach junior high school at just about the time
when girls begin to mature in large numbers. The period from ages 12 or
13 to ages 14 or 15 is the worst possible time for boys and girls to be
educated together, because they are too dissimilar in their size, physiological
age, interests, and attitudes. The number of problems in the average classroom would be appreciably reduced if in junior high school the boys were
taught by men and the girls by women, if the sexes were kept separate in
classes and in games, and if only at school social events was there more
than casual, voluntary contact between them. The first steps toward maturity are easier for the individual if the situation is not complicated by the
presence of girls among boys or boys among girls. Once functions and
attitudes are established, members of the two sexes are probably better off
together. Separation from late childhood onward raises more problems than
it solves, but separation from twelve to fifteen has proven beneficial where
it has been tried.

IV. Summary

Adolescence is a period of internal change and development as well
as of skeletal and muscular growth. Every system of the body is altered to
some degree. The outstanding change is the establishment of sexual maturity, which is evidenced by both primary and secondary changes. The process
takes some time in both boys and girls. The former need about two years
for the development from childhood to early maturity. Girls begin to
develop two years earlier than boys and reach their adult stage more
quickly. Members of both sexes display a variety of attitudes toward the
changes in their bodily functions, and these attitudes influence their personalities, their schoolwork, and their general adjustment to life. Of all

the developments that take place during adolescence the coming of sexual maturity is the most profound and the most significant in its influence upon the behavior and interests of boys and girls.

REFERENCES FOR FURTHER READING

BOOKS

1. Breckenridge and Vincent, *Child Development*, Chap. 2.
2. Cureton, T. K., *Physical Fitness Appraisal*, C. V. Mosby Co., 1947, 566 pp. (Chaps. 9, 10.)
3. Dimock, H. S., *Rediscovering the Adolescent*, Association Press, 1937, 287 pp. (Chaps. 11, 12.)
4. Fleming, *Adolescence: Its Social Psychology*, Chap. 3.
5. Garrison, *Growth and Development*, Chap. 6.
6. Garrison, *Psychology of Adolescence*, Chap. 4.
7. Hurlock, *Adolescent Development*, Chaps. 2, 12, 13.
8. Merry and Merry, *The First Two Decades of Life*, Chaps. 4, 5.
9. Sadler, *Adolescence Problems*, Chap. 21.

MONOGRAPHS, BULLETINS, PROCEEDINGS, YEARBOOKS, ARTICLES

A. *Measures of Bodily Functions and Organs*

1. Greulich, W. W., "Physical Changes in Adolescence," *Forty-third Yearbook of the National Society for the Study of Education*, 1944, Pt. I, pp. 8–32.
2. Greulich, W. W., *et al.*, "Somatic and Endocrine Studies of Pubertal and Adolescent Boys," *Monographs of the Society for Research in Child Development*, Vol. VII, No. 3, 1937, 65 pp.
3. Lewis, R. C., *et al.*, "Standards for the Basal Metabolism of Children from 2 to 15 Years of Age Inclusive," *Journal of Pediatrics*, 23:1–18, 1943.
4. Maresh, M. M., "Growth of the Heart Related to Bodily Growth during Childhood and Adolescence," *Journal of Pediatrics*, 2:383–404, 1948.
5. Shock, N. W., "Basal Blood Pressure and Pulse Rate in Adolescence," *American Journal of Diseases of Children*, 68:16–22, 1944.
6. Shock, N. W., "Physiological Changes in Adolescence," *Forty-third Yearbook of the National Society for the Study of Education*, 1944, Pt. I, pp. 56–79.
7. Shock, N. W., "Standard Values for Basal Oxygen Consumption in Adolescence," *American Journal of Diseases of Children*, 64:19–32, 1942.
8. Shuttleworth, F. K., "Sexual Maturity and the Skeletal Growth of Girls," *Monographs of the Society for Research in Child Development*, Vol. III, No. 5, 1938, 56 pp.

B. *The Endocrines*

1. Ellis, R. W. B., "Puberty Growth of Boys," *Archives of Diseases of Children*, 23:17–26, 1948.
2. Engle, E. T., and M. C. Sheleszyak, "First Menstruation and Subsequent Menstrual Cycles in Pubertal Girls," *Human Biology*, 6:431–453, 1934.
3. Michaelson, N., "Studies in Physical Development of Negroes: Onset of Puberty," *American Journal of Physical Anthropology*, 2:151–166, 1949.
4. Reymert, M. L., "Relation between Menarcheal Age, Behavior Disorders, and Intelligence," *Character and Personality*, 8:292–300, 1940.
5. Richardson, J. S., "The Endocrines in Adolescence," *Practitioner*, 162:280–296, 1949.
6. Richey, H. G., "Relation of Accelerated, Normal, and Retarded Puberty to the

Height and Weight of School Children," *Monographs of the Society for Research in Child Development*, Vol. II, No. 1, 1937, 67 pp.

7. Simpson, M. E., C. W. Asling, and H. M. Evans, "Some Endocrine Influences on Skeletal Growth and Differentiation," *Journal of Biology and Medicine*, 23:1–27, 1950.

C. *Secondary Sex Characteristics*

1. Curry, E. T., "Voice Changes in Adolescence," *Laryngoscope*, 56:795–805, 1946.
2. Kubitschek, P. E., "Sex Development of Boys with Special Reference to the Appearance of Secondary Sex Characteristics and Their Relation to Structure and Personality Types," *Journal of Mental and Nervous Diseases*, 76:425–451, 1932.
3. Pedry, C. P., "A Study of Voice Changes in Boys between the Ages of Eleven and Sixteen," *Speech Monographs*, 12:30–36, 1945.
4. Reynolds, E. L., and J. V. Wines, "Individual Differences in Physical Changes Associated with Adolescent Girls," *American Journal of Diseases of Children*, 75:329–350, 1948.

D. *Attitudes, Information, and Interests*

1. Barker, R., and C. P. Stone, "The Interests of Pre-menarcheal and Post-menarcheal Girls," *Journal of Psychology*, 54:27–71, 1939.
2. Ramsey, G. V., "The Sex Development of Boys," *American Journal of Psychology*, 56:217–233, 1943.
3. Ramsey, G. V., "The Sex Information of Younger Boys," *American Journal of Orthopsychiatry*, 13:347–352, 1943.
4. Sollenberger, R. T., "Some Relationships between the Urinary Excretion of Male Hormones in Maturing Boys and Their Expressed Interests and Attitudes," *Journal of Psychology*, 9:179–189, 1940.

CHAPTER FOUR

Health and Hygiene

A chapter on health during the adolescent period does not need to be long because health is, in general, so good. The vitality of the secondary school group is high; over half of the individuals at each adolescent age are not sick at all during any given year, and not over a very small proportion of them are sufficiently sick often enough to call a doctor three times or more during the same period. The main problem of health during this period consists in helping adolescents to stay well.

In spite of the generally high vitality and resistance to disease, there are, however, some chronic defects and diseased conditions that affect some of the high school population. Although the number of pupils concerned is not large, the conditions may be serious for those involved. The present chapter will consist of two main sections, one on chronic conditions—such as inadequate vision, defects of hearing, defects of speech, nasal abnormalities, infected tonsils, malnutrition, obesity, skin eruptions, decayed teeth, and defects of posture—and one containing some suggestions for the content of a hygiene course for adolescents.

I. Chronic Conditions

From 10 to 15 per cent of school pupils have more or less incorrect posture, a similar proportion have infected tonsils, and nearly one fourth show nasal abnormalities—mostly adenoids, deviated septum, or catarrh. According to one city survey, from one to two thirds have uncared-for dental decay.[1] The average for elementary school was 33 per cent, for junior high it was 58 per cent, and for senior high, 62 per cent. The degree varied also with social and economic status. In a high school serving the "best" district in a city, 39 per cent of the children had uncared-for dental decay; in the vocational school located in one of the city's "poor" districts, the percentage was 83. A similar degree of difference existed between the children of men in professional or managerial positions and the children of unskilled laborers. Eighteen per cent of high school pupils were malnourished, 1 per cent had defective hearing, 9 per cent had postural defects or flat feet, 6 per cent had an abnormal condition of the nose or throat, and

---

[1] F. H. Lund, E. R. Yeomans, and E. A. Geiger, "Health Indices in Relation to Age, Sex, Race, and Socio-Economic Status," *Journal of Social Psychology*, 24:111–117, 1946.

1 per cent showed heart disease. Except for dental decay, the incidence of these defects was lower in high school than during childhood. All of these conditions are serious, not only because of their effect upon health, but also because of their indirect effect upon both personality and progress in school.

1. Inadequate Eyesight for Schoolwork: Defective vision is so obvious a handicap and so common as to merit special consideration. The proportion of children who have defective vision, according to an average of

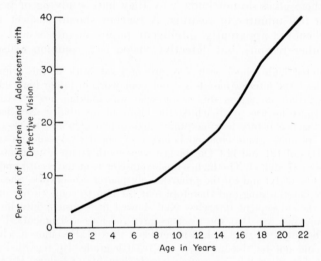

Fig. 49. *Effect of Age and Strain upon Eyesight*

Based on figures in L. H. Brownlee, "A Threat to Healthy Eyesight," *Hygeia,* 20:77–79, 1942.

three independent studies, is represented in Figure 49, above. It rises steadily during the school years. These percentages reflect the increasing demands made by schoolwork upon those who remain in school. Any teacher can easily observe the fact that as pupils continue through school, more and more of them have to wear glasses. In the lower grades children can learn much by ear and thus avoid eyestrain, but each successive year demands more and more reading, both in school and out. In a study of 5,000 pupils, only 18 per cent of those in elementary school and 12 per cent of those in high school were found to have perfect vision.[2] The above figures refer only to those who remain in school. Among those who do not, the percentage of visual defects is lower, presumably because they read less.

School pupils show their visual defects clearly enough, but teachers do not always recognize the symptoms: holding the book too close to the eyes, going to the board to read what is on it, going to stand under the clock in order to read the time, squinting, rubbing the eyes, shading them from light, complaining of pain after reading, becoming irritable after or

[2] M. M. Dalton, "A Visual Survey of 5,000 School Children," *Journal of Educational Research,* 37:81–94, 1943.

clearly uncomfortable while reading or doing other close work, and so on. If a pupil with defective vision really wants to study, he will strain his eyes, complain of discomfort, and be treated. Many pupils, however, do not have a passionate desire for learning, so they build up the defensive habit of neglecting their work, as a means of saving their eyesight. They do not complain of eyestrain because they rarely do enough reading to feel any. Their main symptom is not pain, but abstinence from study. The fundamental defect is often so covered by emotional attitudes about schoolwork that they themselves do not know why they hate studying or become restless after a few minutes of reading. A teacher should suspect inadequate eyesight whenever apparently intelligent pupils do not study. Naturally, there are other reasons, but defective vision is a common cause.

Neil entered high school with a record of good work in the primary grades, average work at the intermediate level, and poor work in junior high school. It had been assumed that he was a dull pupil who was making heavy weather of his schooling because he was approaching the limits of his ability. Neil had had four tests of intelligence before leaving junior high school. On the first—a group test for use with primary grade children before they could read—and on the Binet he had earned IQ's of 121 and 113. On the last two—both group tests involving reading —his IQ's were 87 and 84. The high school counselor read the record and was struck both by the loss of IQ and by the progressively poorer schoolwork. She wondered if the boy were deteriorating and therefore sent for him to come to her office.

During the subsequent interview Neil showed little insight into his difficulties. His chief complaint was that the teachers gave too long assignments. Upon further questioning he admitted that he had never liked to read. He enjoyed school but was afraid he would not be able to finish the twelfth grade. He regarded failure as a disgrace and seemed unduly preoccupied with thoughts of failure. He had recently begun to fancy that other pupils were calling him stupid behind his back. In spite of his evident discouragement, the counselor felt that the earlier IQ's were more accurate than the later ones, but if they were correct then there must be some block, defect, frustration, or handicap that was interfering with normal progress. Neil's dislike of reading was especially curious, assuming that he was fundamentally bright rather than dull. The counselor decided to watch the boy read and see what she could deduce from his procedure, so she pretended to be busy with finishing a report and asked him to read his history assignment until she was free again to continue the interview. As she shifted papers about on her desk, she covertly watched him. Neil read about three minutes and then began to wiggle and twist. At the end of five minutes he was glancing out the window, closing his eyes for several seconds at a time, and becoming more and more restless. Presently he went out to get a drink, then to go to the toilet, then to look at something on the bulletin board, and then to make a telephone call. At the end of thirty-five minutes he had completed barely five pages of reading. His behavior had impressed the counselor as being much like that shown by small children who see just well enough to read a little but not well enough to read comfortably. She therefore asked Neil about his eyesight; as far as he knew, it was normal. He was clearly not nearsighted, and he said he had never been troubled with headaches. Nevertheless, the counselor sent him to an oculist, who found a slight astigmatism and a slight muscular imbalance. Both conditions were mild, but together they made reading an uncomfortable procedure. In the first three grades Neil had learned to recognize the commonest words but had followed the stories by guesswork and had learned other subjects largely by ear. He was able to read for only two or three minutes without discomfort, and he simply stopped reading before the discomfort developed into pain. Being a bright child he got along well enough at first, but in the intermediate grades the reading load became heavier and not everything in his books was discussed in class. However, he picked up enough by listening carefully and by reading in short snatches to keep up with the class average. In junior high school his failure to read became too great a handicap, even for a bright mind. Two of his teachers had evidently suspected a reading deficiency and had independently given him tests, but Neil could always pull himself together for the few minutes that were necessary for a test, so he made good scores on both occasions, although he was a little slow. The boy's defect was hidden even from himself, but it had influenced both his progress in school and his emotional attitudes.

The wearing of glasses made consecutive reading possible for Neil, and he no longer had to protect himself by neglecting his work. Incidentally, the boy's behavior was evidence of his fundamental intelligence. Dull children go on trying to read and get first headaches and then attention; it takes a bright child to neglect work in order to stay comfortable! For a semester Neil attended a class in study methods, since he had to learn how to work efficiently and to break the habits formed during eight school years of stopping after every few lines to rest his eyes. By the end of his freshman year Neil was doing good work. During the following summer he read from morning till night. The world of books suddenly burst upon him, and he was fascinated with the ideas he found. His parents had to chase him out of the house to play for a while each day. Neil is now a successful and well-adjusted college sophomore.

2. Defects of Hearing: The actual number of school children with defective hearing in the entire country can only be estimated from sample surveys in which all the children in a given district have been tested. In one such survey,[3] 20,273 children out of a total of 20,663 enrolled in the schools of a single county were tested by group tests on a single day; the 390 absentees were not measured, but there is no reason to suppose that the addition of results from this accidentally missing half of 1 per cent would make any difference in the figures. The tests indicated defects of sufficient degree to interfere with schoolwork in 1,646 cases. Of these, however, 82 were found upon individual testing to be normal, their previous low score on the group test having been presumably due to mere inattention. Removal of wax from another 129 pairs of ears raised the hearing of these children to a satisfactory level, leaving a final total of 1,435 children, or approximately 7 per cent of the total enrollment whose defect was established beyond doubt by the individual examinations. At this rate, there would be seven such children in every hundred. It should be remembered that in the case of both vision and hearing, the results here quoted do not include the blind, nearly blind, deaf, or nearly deaf children, since they are not in the public schools. At the high school level it is probable that five pupils in every hundred do not hear perfectly what is said to them.

The symptoms of hearing defect are usually quite obvious: frequent asking to have questions repeated, indifference to noise or the whispering of other children, failure to look up from work at some sound that is sufficient to attract others, cocking the head sidewise to listen, failing to catch

---

[3] A. A. Grossman and R. E. Marcus, "Otolaryngological Experience in a Hearing Survey," *Journal of Speech and Hearing Disorders,* 14:240–246, 1949.

directions given orally, speaking in a "flat" voice, and putting fingers into the ears to rub the canal or eardrum. Such items of behavior are sometimes regarded as mere personal idiosyncrasies and therefore ignored.

The many incidental results of deafness are shown in the following narrative:

It would be difficult to exaggerate the annoyances, discomforts, embarrassments, and emotional strain that are produced by the affliction of deafness. The victim is considered dull, stupid, disinterested, indifferent, and queer, all because he cannot apprehend the voice vibrations around him. He is in the world but not a part of it.

I became slightly deaf the year of my graduation from normal school. . . . As a result of my impaired hearing I gradually developed an inferiority complex. I became sensitive, retiring, and sullen, and spent most of my time brooding and moping. As time passed, I shrank more and more from social contacts; I accepted few invitations, avoided people in general, and constantly tried to conceal my defect.

Having decided early in life to teach, I could not easily switch to another field. The realization that I would probably not be given a diploma if the faculty members discovered my predicament, started my tactics of concealment. I devised all sorts of little tricks for "getting by" the instructors without exposing my deafness. Although I made good grades, it was at the cost of great nerve strain. All went fairly well until I reached the stage of practice teaching. There was no sidestepping this apparently hopeless and impossible task. Yet you may be surprised to learn that the critic teacher rated me high and did not even discover my handicap. The fact that the section was small was in my favor, but the secret of success in this task lay in my ability to work and plan. I arranged my lessons so as to avoid discussions and confusions. This is one of the little arts that the deaf acquire.

After graduation I was recommended as an elementary teacher in a large city school system. I cannot express to you my feeling of despair upon arriving in that city, nor describe the many heartaches experienced during my first year of teaching. Besides classroom problems, there were teachers, supervisors, and parents to be faced. I wanted to shrink from them all, and resorted to the old trick of concealment. Becoming desperate, I finally took a course in lip reading. While the course did me very little good, my association with the hard-of-hearing was a real inspiration. I found that they thought nothing of their affliction, but joked about it as if it were any ordinary physical ailment. It was during this period that I decided to admit that I was deaf, to face the issue squarely, and to take the consequences. To my surprise, I grew much happier. I began to realize that by trying to deceive others, I had merely deceived myself, and had built up a barrier which shut me off from people. This discovery made me feel more at ease. My fear of being found out was gone, and that gave me courage.

Having assumed a more wholesome attitude toward deafness, my philosophy of life changed. I cultivated attitudes of optimism, confidence, helpfulness, sincerity, and intellectual and emotional poise. . . . My efforts were not without success.[4]

3. **Defects of Speech:** Many investigators of speech difficulties do not distinguish between stuttering and stammering. In actual practice, both are often called stuttering, and in some instances the same child shows the two defects simultaneously or at different times. It seems, however, worth while to describe both types of defect. Stuttering consists of a repetition

---

[4] J. E. W. Wallin, *Minor Mental Maladjustments in Normal People*, Duke University Press, 1939, pp. 231–232. Used by permission of the publisher.

of a sound, as in the song: "K-k-k-k-k-Katy, B-b-beautiful K-k-Katy . . ." The difficulty may occur with any consonant. If one child in a school stutters, the others will imitate him, and at least one or two may fall victims to their own mockery and find themselves unable to stop when they want to. Stammering is quite different. The stammerer does not repeat sounds; he is unable to make any coherent noise at all. His mouth opens, his jaws move, and he tries hard—but nothing happens. The accompanying facial contortions are painful to watch. Sometimes the stammerer finally breaks through a "block," and sometimes he does not.

Other types of speech defect that are common in the first grade are lisping, the substitution of one sound for another (such as "w" for "r"), and baby talk ("ittie" for "little," for instance). The last two have virtually disappeared by the time pupils reach high school, but an occasional lisper is still heard.

The number of pupils with speech defects has to be estimated from samples, as in the case of both hearing and vision. The number found in a given survey depends in some measure upon what the investigator includes among defects that are less obvious than those already mentioned and upon how he classifies his results. Thus, from a study of 13,500 children, one investigator reports 13 cases of cleft palate,[5] 77 stammerers, and 175 instances of defective articulation.[6] These figures give a total of approximately 2 per cent. Other estimates are higher, but they include more types of defect. For instance, the total in another study[7] comes to 700 disorders per 10,000 school children, or 7 per cent. Of each 700 defects, 550 are classed as faulty articulation (with or without impairment of hearing), 60 as stammering, 50 as retardations of speech development, 15 as voice disorders (harshness, nasality, breathiness, loudness), and 25 as cases having some clearly physical basis for the disorder (such as cerebral palsy, other nervous diseases, or cleft palate). The commonest single type consists of those whose articulation is indistinct, jerky, too rapid, breathy, or inaccurate as to the sounds of letters; children who substituted one letter for another are presumably included here, also. The two studies do not differ materially in the number of stammerers found; in the first, 0.5 per cent stammered, and in the second, 0.6 per cent—that is, 5 or 6 children in every 1,000.

Of all defects that are without physical basis, stammering is the most serious because of its pervasive effect upon a child's emotional and social life. It proves itself to be of emotional origin by its capricious appearances and disappearances. There are, for instance, concert singers who stammer when they talk, ministers who preach fluently but stammer in talking with parishioners, students who stammer in their native English but speak acquired French or German or Spanish without defect, businessmen who

[5] A condition that exists at birth. After proper surgery and with, or without, an artificial palate, the child can learn to speak. This defect is due to purely physical causes.

[6] P. Henderson, "The Incidence of Stammering and Speech Defects in School Children," *Bulletin of the Minnesota Public Health Laboratory Service*, 6:102–105, 1947.

[7] W. Johnson, "To Help the Child with a Speech Handicap," *Child*, 15:12–14, 1950.

conduct as much business as possible on the telephone because they stammer only when face to face with another person, children who recite aloud to themselves in their rooms without hesitation but cannot say identically the same words in class, actors who are tense and hesitant in speech off the stage but relaxed and fluent on it (even when they have to invent a few lines to cover an unexpected pause), teachers who often stammer in one class and never in another, and so on. The writer knows one young man who teaches his college classes with not more than two or three attacks of stammering in a year, but he is as likely as not to come to grief in asking his best friend for a match. In order to reach any understanding of such odd phenomena, one must go back to the early days of the stammerer and trace the development of his difficulties.

Either stuttering or stammering begins in an utterly commonplace sort of way. The small child merely hesitates, breaks his rhythm, repeats a letter or word, or mispronounces a sound. Practically all children go through this stage, at some age between two and five, when their ideas flow more rapidly than their words. If no one pays any attention to such symptoms, no harm is done, and the maturing speech mechanism soon becomes adequate, even though some errors of articulation or pronunciation may remain. The stage of hesitation and broken rhythm is called primary stuttering. Unfortunately, some parents are not willing to let nature take its course and merely wait while their child grows up. They begin to correct him, to interrupt him, to make him go back and repeat, to scold him, to compare him unfavorably with his siblings, to fuss at him, to be ashamed of him, and generally to make talking an unpleasant and thoroughly exasperating experience.[8] Johnny dashes into the house to tell his mother about a little boy who has just moved in next door, but before he gets out his first sentence she has interrupted him four times. He is unable to communicate to her his excitement because she keeps on correcting him until what should have been a pleasurable sharing of an episode has deteriorated into a rejection of Johnny's story and incidentally of Johnny himself. Telling his mother about the new little boy *should* have been fun, but the experience was spoiled by criticism. Naturally, one has to correct a child's speech but not when he is in the full flood of narrative. If enough such disappointing experiences pile up in a child's life, he becomes torn between his natural desire to speak and a contrary desire not to speak, between an urge to outshout his mother and an urge to please her, between a hostility toward her and a love for her. During this period Johnny is not so much acquiring a stammer as acquiring an attitude of deep concern over the hesitations he already has.

At this point the child has reached a parting of the ways, and the path he follows will depend in large measure upon the attitude of his parents. If the parents are overprotective, oversolicitous, and overanxious, if they have high standards for their child, if they demand perfection from him, if they bewail his defect and beg him to correct it, they will succeed in

---

[8] C. Van Riper, *Stuttering*, National Society for Crippled Children and Adults, 1948, 60 pp.

transferring to him their own anxiety, their own tension, their own fears. In extreme cases, they may reject him because of his failure to reach their standards.[9] The child responds to his parents' concern by trying harder and getting worse, or by outbursts of irritation, or by withdrawing from the whole problem and not talking at all. As the weeks roll by, the act of talking becomes more and more closely associated with struggle, tension, frustration, failure, disappointment, discomfort, displeasure, and perhaps punishment. A child's early efforts are so painful to him that he emerges from them with a fixed fear of words and a feeling of panic toward the whole matter of speech. It is not long before he discovers that his fear of words and his inability to speak them are ruinous handicaps in his efforts to attain status among his age-mates, or to make progress in school. Times without number he experiences the frustration of knowing the answer but being totally unable to give it after his teacher has noticed his wildly waving hand and called upon him.

Most healthy, vigorous children now start to fight back in earnest, a step that precipitates them into the class of secondary stutterers and stammerers. They notice that if they take a deep breath, they don't stammer; so they take a deep breath before every third word—thus interrupting their rhythm still further—and in a week's time they have achieved an inseparable fusion of stammering and deep breathing. Or perhaps they notice that balling their fists up tight will reduce the difficulty; in this case, they fuse muscular rigidity with their stammer. Others bat their eyelids together five times, or twitch their shoulders, or pat their stomachs, or open and close their mouths; whatever the mannerism, it is soon tacked on and becomes part of the stammer. The initial effect of such efforts is almost always so good that most stutterers experiment with and acquire several mannerisms before abandoning this mode of approach. The good result comes, not from the gesture or other form of preparation, but from the diversion of attention. For a few days the child must remember to complete the gesture before speaking, and he is so busy patting his stomach that he starts to speak without thinking about it, and therefore loses his defect. Presently, however, the patting gesture becomes so automatic that his attention returns to his speech, and then he is worse off than before, because now he has both a stammer and a mannerism. Moreover, they are so fused together that without the mannerism he cannot speak at all. He now begins what is likely to be years and maybe a lifetime of the same unpleasant experience repeated ad infinitum: before he speaks he becomes obsessed with a fear of the words themselves, while he speaks he feels utterly helpless and deeply frustrated, and after he is again silent he suffers from his social inadequacy, from a fear of ridicule, from acute self-consciousness and embarrassment, and from a hopeless sense of permanent inferiority. At the onset of adolescence, with its powerful social and emotional drives, the stammerer has fresh troubles. He cannot have "dates," or go to dances,

[9] D. Meltzer, "Personality Differences between Stutterers and Non-Stuttering Children as Indicated by the Rorschach," *Journal of Psychology,* 17:35–39, 1944; B. C. Meyer, "On the Nature of Stuttering," *Medical Clinic of North America,* 32:617–622, 1948; L. E. Richardson, "A Personality Study of Stutterers and Non-Stutterers," *Journal of Speech and Hearing Disorders,* 9:152–160, 1944; L. Stein, "The Emotional Background of Stammering," *British Journal of Medical Psychology,* 22:189–193, 1949.

or even talk to girls in the school corridors. He is usually too self-conscious to play games well, he cannot recite in class, he is rarely asked to join clubs, and, if he has a bosom friend, it is likely to be another outcast like himself.

There is not much that a teacher can do directly for children with speech defects, but she can help them indirectly by bringing about a change of attitude in the other pupils toward them. She can also give them the little extra attentions that children crave, so that they will feel accepted and wanted. If the teacher is able to provide in her room a place where the afflicted child can relax in safety, without fear of ridicule from his age-mates or impatience from herself, he may improve greatly without special aid. Perhaps the saddest thing about the stutterer's history is that the entire development is so unnecessary. There seems good evidence that children do not begin to show a real defect until some well-intentioned but quite misguided and often misinformed adult diagnoses the condition. Up until then they were just ordinary children making the ordinary progress in learning to speak; after that they were "labeled" as abnormal and dragged from one specialist to another, getting worse constantly because they spend more and more of their time thinking about their troubles.

It is not surprising that stammerers grow up with personalities that, while within the normal range, differ from those of other people. In general, their personality structure is of the obsessive-compulsive type. They want to talk, they have a great pressure of words inside them, and they experience a constant compulsion to speak; but at the same time they have an obsessive fear of words (which they nurse assiduously and refuse to let go); they still believe, despite much proof to the contrary, in the magic power of particular gestures, and they dread the attitudes of other people toward them.

In general, a stammerer develops one of three different sets of traits, depending upon what kind of reaction he makes after he has become aware that other children avoid him because of his handicap: (1) He may make an aggressive, fighting response, try to domineer over others, show great hostility toward his brothers and sisters, indulge in outbursts of temper, and become destructive in a frantic, disorganized effort to overcome the aversion he has encountered. (2) He may collapse within himself under the continued pressure, withdraw from human contacts, become mute, and trust no one. Or (3) he may continue to hover on the edges of his social group, picking up such crumbs of contact as may fall to him and developing into a shy, dependent, overanxious, unstable person who is both desirous of social contacts and afraid of them, and cursed with a bitter sense of his own inferiority. Stutterers and stammerers of all types tend to have psychosomatic disorders in addition to their speech difficulties.[10]

---

[10] J. L. Despert, "Psychosomatic Studies of Fifty Stuttering Children," *American Journal of Orthopsychiatry,* 16:100–113, 1946, and B. C. Meyer, "Psychosomatic Aspects of Stuttering," *Journal of Nervous and Mental Diseases,* 101:127, 1945.

Since stuttering and stammering arise largely because a child is expected to reach a high standard in speech at too early an age, and are subject to much parental pressure if they do not, it is not surprising that boys, who develop more slowly than girls, furnish the bulk of the stammerers, at a ratio of eight boys to one girl.[11] A particularly likely victim is the boy with two or three older sisters, a perfectionist mother, and an indifferent father. Such a mother would probably fuss at him more or less anyway, but her standard has been set by the girls, and she expects her son to speak as well at each successive age as they did. If he is a normal boy developing at a normal rate, he cannot maintain the linguistic speed of his sisters, with whom he is likely to be compared to his own disadvantage. If his father is too indifferent to interfere, the boy has an excellent chance of developing a speech defect. The two case histories given below illustrate the types of home background that produce stammerers:

Recently, the writer had to tell a mother and father that their only son's hope of recovering from his stammering was to leave his home and live with foster parents or with relatives. There is not too good a chance that little Jimmie will recover even then, but at home there is no chance at all. The family group consists of Jimmie, aged eight, an older sister of twelve years, an aunt, the parents, and a housekeeper. The aunt is the mother's twin sister. The two women still resemble each other so closely that the children have great difficulty in telling them apart—a situation regarded by the adults as uproariously funny but found to be highly disturbing to the children. The mother is a self-willed, self-assertive, aggressive woman, who has always dominated her twin and now rules her husband and children. She is rigid in her thinking, conventional in her behavior, unable to relax her hold on anything or anyone she regards as hers, meticulous about her housekeeping, and obsessively perfectionistic toward her children. Both children have been rigidly trained to be neat, to keep their possessions in order, to hang up their clothes, to be unobtrusive, and to do as they are told. In her own way, the mother is intensely proud of both children. The father is an overanxious, well-meaning, childish, and futile individual. He overprotects both his children and tries to compensate for their mother's stern handling by coddling them as much as he dares to. The daughter has worked out her own compromise. She conforms on the surface to her mother's requirements, but she dislikes her mother and adores her father. She is sly, deceitful, self-centered, and—aside from her affection for her father—as cold as her mother. Young Jimmie is a confused, dependent, shy, anxious, fearful, frustrated child. Both his parents demand more of him than he can give. He strains himself to the utmost to meet their expectations, but he knows that he will never succeed. As a result, he feels inferior and insecure. The aunt is a source of confusion to the children, partly because of her physical identity with their mother, partly because there is tension between her and the father, and partly because she has little to do and occupies herself with hectoring the children. The housekeeper is a naturally sympathetic woman, but she has refused to become involved emotionally in the situation. She sees better than anyone else what is happening, and when Jimmie has one of his screaming nightmares she is the only one who can quiet him. At such times he violently rejects his mother.

Jimmie's difficulties with speech began as soon as he tried to talk. Both parents were so eager to have him reach perfection that they pushed him. Jimmie has a

---

[11] H. Schuell, "Sex Differences in Relation to Stuttering, Part I," *Journal of Speech and Hearing Disorders*, 11:277–298, 1946.

normal degree of general intelligence, but his linguistic ability is definitely low and his vocabulary small. His first reaction to being high-pressured into speech was to become mute for hours on end. These periods drove his father frantic with worry and the mother frantic with frustration. Moreover, he was punished for them. Since his first solution met with so bad a reception, Jimmie took refuge in a stammer. Even his mother reluctantly admits that discipline and punishment are of no avail in controlling the stammer, but she does not know any other method of approach. The father tried rewarding his son for each perfectly spoken sentence, but this method backfired, because Jimmie worked so hard to get the reward and his father's approval that he stammered worse than ever. His sister adds to his troubles by furnishing a contrast in fluency and by giving him many a sly dig that passes unnoticed by his parents. She regards him as a competitor for the father's love and has no intention of letting him trespass on her preserves.

Jimmie has recently shown a tendency to remain in the kitchen with the housekeeper, playing quietly and wordlessly in a corner. It is probable that he feels secure there, since she asks him no questions and makes no demands upon him. The woman has a friendly attitude toward Jimmie, but she also has a genius for minding her own business. It seems to the writer that the boy's one hope for recovery is to go away from home, preferably with the housekeeper, for a trial period of at least a year, as a means of finding out what mere relief from pressure will do for him. During the trial year he should not see his parents. If an arrangement with the housekeeper is impracticable or if the parents are unwilling to let her and him alone, he could be sent, young as he is, to a boarding school at a considerable distance from home, but unless the school is selected with great care, he is likely to get worse rather than better. He needs a permissive atmosphere, careful guidance, an absence of pressure, freedom to develop his excellent mechanical ability, and general emotional security. If left to themselves his parents would be likely to choose a military school with strict discipline and conventional methods of instruction, thus perpetuating the worst features of the home. It remains to be seen what action will be taken. The father is deeply concerned about his son and is willing to sacrifice his own pleasure in seeing the boy every day to the lad's present and future development. The mother, however, cannot admit failure; like other dictators, she has to be right all the time. If she can think out a rationalization that absolves her from blame, she may agree to a separation. If Jimmie remains within his present family group he is not likely to stop stammering.

Maurice is now about twenty years old and is working as a plumber, a type of labor that is below his mental capacity but does not require more talking than he is able to do without too much strain. He has stammered since he was five years old.

His severe emotional disturbances began when he was four and old enough to be affected by the constant quarreling of his parents. When he was five, they were divorced and he was given into the care of his mother, who promptly bundled him off to her parents because he interfered too much with her activities. His grandparents lived on an isolated farm and were elderly, chronically ill people. The child was continually repressed in both his speech and his activities. His grandmother was especially intolerant of "mess" and noise. Maurice remained in this sheltered atmosphere for about three years. At this time his mother remarried and he went to live with her and his stepfather, neither of whom wanted him. This marriage also ended in divorce, after a good deal of emotional strain and outbursts of violent quarreling. The boy was then placed in a foster home and was beginning to relax in a kindly and permissive atmosphere, when his mother again married and took him to her new home. The third husband was a ne'er-do-well and a drunkard, from whom the mother soon separated, without a divorce. Subsequently, she lived with two other men without benefit of a marriage ceremony. Maurice never had any security except during his year in the foster home. He still goes to see his foster mother fairly frequently, and it is significant that he stammers little while there.

Maurice's school life was also interrupted with every change of address, and he was constantly under the necessity of adjusting himself to a new group of age-mates. He got along a little better in school than elsewhere, but his speech defect sometimes aroused amusement and made him feel insecure and unhappy. As adolescence approached he withdrew more and more from social relationships at school, although he always did reasonably well in his work. His IQ on several different tests has not been lower than 120. He has never had a girl friend and has avoided even casual contacts with girls whenever possible. He is understandably suspicious of marriage as a social institution.

The seriousness of the stammering varies a good deal with the circumstances. With strangers, to whom he has to talk in the course of business, he stammers relatively little. His boss has never heard him stammer at all, after the first week or so. Maurice is his best workman and is well aware of that fact. He can therefore relax because he feels competent and successful. In all purely social relationships Maurice stammers, sometimes badly. He is least able to talk with his mother, with whom he still lives although he has no affection for her; but he is isolated and immature in his emotional development, he has no other place to go, and he still feels a little safer with her than he would if he lived entirely alone.[12]

Any treatment for stammering requires a long time and usually a change in a child's entire mode of life. The first step is to take off the pressure. One should encourage the child to talk when he feels like it, should protect him from teasing or bullying from other children, should show affection for him, and should provide a place where he can relax and feel safe. It rarely does any good to attack the speech difficulty directly. However, the parent-teacher association can make a positive contribution by getting before all parents the facts about the genesis of speech defects. An individual teacher can also adapt for her own procedure in the classroom the following set of suggestions intended for parents, who should

1. Plan a definite activity each week for the child to share with them, in order to develop a feeling of companionship. It may be going out for a supper of hamburgers and malted milk, going to town, visiting the zoo, going fishing or hunting, playing checkers, or making a birdhouse. The only requirement is that it involve time spent pleasantly together.

2. Plan a definite time during the day when the child can have an hour or two with one or both parents, and receive their full attention.

3. Plan a program which will help the child to develop confidence in his ability to do something. This should be something the child wants to do, and from which the child, and not primarily the parents, derives satisfaction. It may be learning to skate, to swim, to take care of rabbits, a dog, or a canary, having a paper route, or being a boy scout, as long as it is something the child really wants to do and not beyond his ability to accomplish adequately. He should select the activity for himself, because parents often have a way of expecting too much, or sometimes too little, from their children. The parents should be encouraged to show interest in the child's progress but should refrain from too zealous an expression of it, lest they inadvertently exert too much pressure, making the activity theirs and not the child's, thereby destroying the child's pleasure in it.

[12] Based upon L. P. Thorpe, *The Psychology of Abnormal Behavior,* The Ronald Press, 1948, p. 261.

4. Plan situations which will help the child to build confidence in his ability to talk. He should be encouraged to go to the door, to answer the telephone, to perform errands, to tell jokes and stories and riddles, and even to make puns. He needs to find out that he can do these things, and if the way in which he does them is accepted in a matter-of-fact manner, he will begin to enjoy them and to learn that talking can be fun.[13]

The essence of this treatment is the reacceptance of the child by his parents and the association of pleasant experiences with speech. A teacher can follow the same advice in her treatment of a stammerer.

II. Hygiene for Adolescents

It is assuredly not the writer's purpose to outline a course in hygiene; it is merely to call attention to certain problems of adolescents, to the solving of which the work in hygiene could contribute. Since it is the modern objective of schoolwork to help pupils understand themselves and their immediate problems, certain topics in the required hygiene course should contribute directly to a better adjustment of students to life, both in and out of the classroom. On the basis of the presentation thus far of physical growth and health, there would appear to be at least four topics that should be included in the required course in hygiene.

First, the teacher of the course might do well to emphasize the causes, symptoms, and seriousness of defects in the eyes, nose, and teeth, since such defects make up a large proportion of chronic physical handicaps. High school pupils who have these defects have probably had them for years; if these conditions are to be treated, the pupil himself may have to take the initiative. If the teacher shows an objective attitude in the matter and makes it clear that these conditions, while serious in the long run, are not going to be immediately fatal, the reaction of most pupils is an intelligent and unemotional consideration of their own handicaps.

Second, the course should certainly contain material about diet, especially about the food requirements of the adolescent years. An average boy from ages 13 to 16 needs more calories than the average man: 3,200 as compared with 3,000 per day. From 16 to 20 his requirements are even higher—3,800 calories. Girls from 13 to 15 need more than the average woman: 2,800 calories as compared to 2,500, but from 16 to 18 the needs decrease and 2,400 calories are enough.

An investigation of the diets for one week of 43 boys and 81 girls in the junior and senior high schools of two cities and two consolidated schools showed that only 4 of the 124 adolescents had had an adequate intake of food materials during the week studied.[14] The amount of meat and eggs came fairly close to being enough, but almost all diets were low on minerals, because the boys and girls did not eat enough fruit and

[13] H. Schuell, "Work with Parents of Stuttering Children," *Journal of Speech and Hearing Disorders,* 14:251–254, 1949. Used by permission of the publishers.

[14] C. E. Gray and N. R. Blackman, "More High School Students' Diets Evaluated," *Journal of Home Economics,* 39:505–506, 1947.

vegetables. In addition, a great many pupils missed one or two meals during the week. About a third missed at least one breakfast, and a few did not eat breakfast at any time. Over the week end the nourishment was not as adequate as it was during the week, largely because many pupils either worked or played so much that they failed to eat more than two meals on Saturday or Sunday, or both.

The elements that are most frequently deficient in a diet are the minerals—calcium and iron—and the vitamins. Many pupils who are nervous and irritable have a deficiency in calcium, a mineral needed also for bone growth and dental development. Both minerals and vitamins come chiefly from fresh vegetables and fresh fruit. Since these foods are expensive, they are the first to be omitted when funds are low. During the depression years, the effects of such deprivations were measurable. Children from families that were in comfortable circumstances at the beginning of the depression but poor at the end changed from being above average in weight to being almost as far below average as children from families that were poor throughout the period. At the same time the really poor made a slight gain in weight, perhaps because these children were better fed by relief agencies than they were by their parents in normal times.[15]

A third topic that is almost certain to be included in the average hygiene course relates to the maintenance of regularity in all physiological habits. Most high school pupils already know that they ought to get eight hours of sleep, to eat their meals at regular hours, to have at least one bowel movement each day, to exercise an hour a day, and to have occasional periods of rest and relaxation. What they need is not so much knowledge as aid in applying their knowledge to themselves. They have reached the age at which they are taking over from their parents the responsibility for personal health and efficiency. During the years of transition they fail to apply what they know.

A fourth matter, about which there may be some difference of opinion, is the giving of sex education. The facts are probably best presented in a course in biological science, provided that the course is taken by everyone. If the hygiene course is the only required one in biology, then the facts about sex have to be presented there, if anywhere.

A glance at the usual sources of information about sex should convince one that the school would do well to include sex instruction in some required course. Results from one study are summarized in Figure 50 on page 104. Of the girls, 55 per cent had received sex information from their mothers, but only 21 per cent of the boys in this study had received such help from their fathers. An average of 10 per cent got information from high school classes; 20 per cent of the boys and 45 per cent of the girls obtained further illumination on the subject from classes in college. About two thirds had read books dealing with sexual phenomena. Doctors, ministers, and

15 C. E. Palmer, "Height and Weight of the Depression Poor," *United States Public Health Reports,* 50:1106–1113, 1935.

representatives of youth organizations had contributed little. The common-est course of information for both sexes was the "bull session." It should be noted in passing that the usual method of enlightenment by classmates may be adequate for acquisition of the basic facts, but they are inadequate either for learning the proper words and phrases or for developing a frank

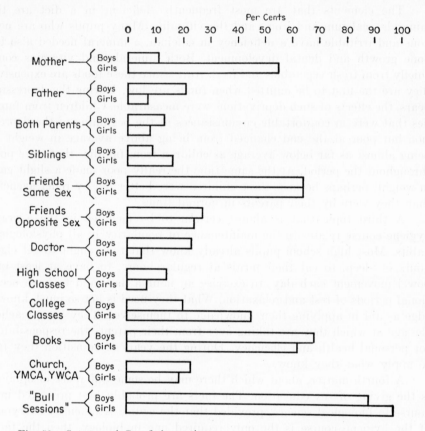

Fig. 50. *Sources of Sex Information*

Based on figures in L. D. Rockwood and M. E. N. Ford, *Youth, Marriage, and Parenthood,* John Wiley & Sons, 1945, pp. 26, 29.

and open attitude. Parents and other older people generally do not con-tribute enough. Books form the main source of reliable information, but these were not read by all the boys and girls included in the study.

Most people feel that sex education is best given by the parents. Prob-ably it should be, but it often is not. For instance, among 500 college girls, only 7 per cent felt that their parental instruction had been adequate, an-other 20 per cent had received a fair amount of instruction, 21 per cent had been given some help but not enough, and the remaining 52 per cent felt the information to have been totally inadequate.[16] From such testimony it would seem that the school would have to take over the responsibility; otherwise, pupils are dependent upon what they can find out from unreliable sources.

Further indication of the inadequacy of sex education, in school or out, is given by a consideration of the statistics about venereal diseases. During World War II there was a marked increase in the frequency of venereal infection in the adolescent population, but one must remember that such statistics give only a partial picture of the true situation because they include only those cases reported to health officers. From sample surveys of communities it seems clear that not more than one case in three or four is reported. However, the age distribution of the unreported cases does not perhaps vary much from that of known cases. One summary of 3,241 primary infections reports the average number as 5 cases a year per 1,000 up to age 10, with a steady increase thereafter, from 6 at age 12 to 52 at age 15; ages 17 and 18 are the highest, with 111 and 136 primary infections, respectively.[17] Ages in the next decade showed an average of 107 a year; for early adulthood it was 103, and for middle age, 21. In twenty quarantine stations for women with venereal disease, half were below 18 and a third were below 17.[18] Army physicians estimated that about one third of all venereal infections among soldiers were acquired from girls of 13 to 19 years of age.[19] A more recent report shows a decline of 50 per cent in the number of new cases of syphilis reported between 1947 and 1951 and a decrease of 36 per cent for gonorrhea.[20] From such data, it would seem that schools should include in some required course all facts concerning sex that pupils are likely to need, otherwise many will not learn them.

In addition to the presentation of facts about sex, a school should do everything it can to build up a healthy attitude toward all matters pertaining to sex. The many problems faced by adolescents can perhaps best be discussed in the mental hygiene class, if there is one and if all pupils take it. Otherwise these questions also become material for the hygiene course. Sex is so important to adolescents that they need, in self-defense, to develop a sane attitude. The results of misinformation and of unhealthy emotional attitudes are shown in the following story:

Jack was a senior in high school. He had had a fairly good record for the first three years, but his work had been getting poorer and poorer since the beginning of his last year, and he had been unaccountably absent from school a few times. His teachers had noted a change of personality also. He seemed to be brooding about

[16] A. Ellis, "Love and Family Relationships of American College Girls," *American Journal of Sociology*, 55:550–558, 1950.

[17] "Proceedings of the Conference on Venereal Disease Control Work," *Venereal Disease Information Supplement*, United States Government Printing Office, 1947.

[18] T. Parran, "Fitness for Freedom," *Venereal Disease Information*, 24:185, 1943.

[19] E. W. Norris, A. F. Doyle, and A. P. Iskrant, "Venereal Disease Epidemiology in the Army Third Service Command; Progress Report for January through June, 1943," *Venereal Disease Information*, 24:282, 1943.

[20] Reported in *Time*, 59:51, 1952.

something, and he was becoming more and more isolated from his former friends. Although there was a feeling that Jack was under tension, neither his teachers nor his parents nor his friends were prepared for his attempt at suicide by slashing his wrists with a safety razor blade. After he had been taken to the hospital and given treatment, he agreed to talk over his difficulties with one of the doctors. At the subsequent interview, he gave the all-too-familiar story summarized below:

During his late childhood he had developed the habit of masturbating but had not been especially worried about the matter until he reached adolescence. His indulgence became rather excessive for a few months, and he developed feelings of shame. He made several efforts to break the habit; with each relapse he became more and more deeply convinced of his worthlessness. At a "bull session" some misinformed friend convinced him that only insanity lay in wait for the chronic masturbator and offered to introduce him to girls who would relieve his tension. Jack began therefore to visit prostitutes. For a few weeks he felt better, but soon he was plagued by doubts as to the possibly greater sinfulness of his present conduct and fears as to the possibility of venereal disease. About two months before his attempt at suicide he had gone to a quack to be cured of what he thought was gonorrhea. He resolved to stay away from prostitutes, but was unable to keep his promise to himself. After each visit he developed an acute panic, which, however, he had until recently been able to control. His suicide attempt had been made after such a visit while he was at the bottom of the slough of despair, reproach, and helplessness.

The doctor talked long and earnestly with Jack. He advised him to return to his former habit of masturbation until such time as he should marry—and to marry as early as he could. In the meantime he should keep himself busy with school, athletics, and clubs, so as to have little time left for sexual indulgence. He told the boy flatly that there was no danger of his going insane as a result of masturbation. He also went with Jack for a talk with the school doctor, who promised to keep an eye on the lad and to be available for counsel if the boy should again find himself in deep emotional waters.

III. Summary

Teachers are only too well aware of a bursting vitality on the part of their pupils. To the forty- or fifty-year-old teacher the average high school boy or girl is a dynamo going at top speed and unable to slow down. Most adolescents have so much energy that they get into the habit of burning it up recklessly. Fatigue, overstrain—whether physical or emotional—and overexertion are the enemies that adolescents have to learn to combat. A course in hygiene should therefore stress the avoidance of overstrain, from either emotional or physical causes. Pupils may best be persuaded to incorporate these cautions into their lives if they plan their days and nights so as to assure themselves of enough rest, relaxation, and sleep to maintain their vitality at its high level.

Good sexual hygiene is extremely important to keep boys and girls comfortable, normal, and well adjusted. They cannot be expected to understand the changes that have taken place in their bodies or to acquire sensible attitudes toward them without help from adults. Presumably the relevant information and training are best given by parents, but since many parents do not seem able sufficiently to overcome their own somewhat guilty attitudes toward sexual matters to discuss the situation with their children it becomes necessary for the school to provide both the information and the training in attitudes. Adolescents will almost certainly obtain the facts they need from some other and less desirable source, in case both parents and school fail them, but the sources are likely to supply a feeling of shame and secrecy along with the information. These feelings may color the entire subsequent life of the adolescents, especially their early heterosexual adjustments, and to make it difficult from them in turn to educate their children. It is therefore the duty of the school to step in and break the transfer of undesirable attitudes from one generation to the next.

REFERENCES FOR FURTHER READING

BOOKS

1. Breckenridge and Vincent, *Child Development*, Chaps. 4, 14.
2. Cureton, *Physical Fitness Appraisal*, Chaps. 5, 6, 7.
3. Diehl, H. S., *Textbook of Healthful Living*, McGraw-Hill Book Company, 3d ed., 1949, 699 pp. (Chaps. 7, 9, 14, 17, 20.)
4. Garrison, *Psychology of Adolescence*, Chap. 17.
5. Garrison, K. C., *The Psychology of Exceptional Children*, The Ronald Press, rev. ed., 1950, 517 pp. (Chap. 4.)
6. Keliher, *Life and Growth*, Chap. 9.
7. Louttit, C. M., *Clinical Psychology of Children's Behavior*, Harper & Brothers, rev. ed., 1947, 661 pp. (Chaps. 5, 12, 14.)
8. Sanford, R. N., *et al.*, *Physique, Personality, and Scholarship: A Co-operative Study of School Children*, National Research Council, 1943, 705 pp. (Pp. 28–43.)
9. Strain, F. B., *New Patterns in Sex Teaching*, Appleton-Century-Crofts, Inc., 1934, 242 pp. (Chaps. 2, 6, 9, 10.)
10. Turner, C. E., *School Health and Health Education*, C. V. Mosby Co., 1952, 471 pp. (Chaps. 4, 5, 18.)
11. Van Riper, C., *Stuttering*, National Society for Crippled Children and Adults, 1948, 60 pp.
12. Wheatley, G. M., and G. T. Hallock, *Health Observations of School Children*, McGraw-Hill Book Company, 1951, 491 pp. (Chap. 8.)
13. Wile, *The Challenge of Adolescence*, Chaps. 3, 4.
14. Williams, J. F., and C. L. Brownell, *The Administration of Health Education and Physical Education*, W. B. Saunders Company, 1951, 438 pp. (Chaps. 8–10.)
15. Zachry and Lighty, *Emotion and Conduct in Adolescence*, Chap. 7.

MONOGRAPHS, BULLETINS, PROCEEDINGS, YEARBOOKS, ARTICLES

A. *Physical Handicaps*

1. Barker, R. G., B. A. Wright, and M. R. Gonick, "Adjustment to Physical Handicaps and Illness: A Survey of Physique and Disability," *Social Science Research Council Bulletin*, No. 55, 1946, 372 pp. (Chaps. 2, 3, 5.)
2. Brownlee, L. H., "A Threat to Healthy Eyesight," *Hygeia*, 20:77–79, 1942.
3. Dalton, M. M., "A Visual Survey of 5,000 School Children," *Journal of Educational Research*, 37:81–94, 1943.
4. Grossman, A. A., and R. E. Marcus, "Otolaryngological Experience in a Hearing Survey," *Journal of Speech and Hearing Disorders*, 14:240–246, 1949.

5. Martin, M., "The Hard-of-Hearing Child at Home and in School," *Understanding the Child*, 18:111–113, 1949.

B. *General Health*

1. Blair, R., L. Roberts, and M. Greider, "Results of Providing a Liberally Adequate Diet to Children in an Institution," *Journal of Pediatrics*, 27:410–417, 1945.
2. Lund, F. H., E. R. Yeomans, and E. A. Geiger, "Health Indices in Relation to Age, Sex, Race, and Socio-Economic Status," *Journal of Social Psychology*, 24:111–117, 1946.
3. Rogers, J. M., "What Every Teacher Should Know about the Physical Condition of Her Pupils," *Pamphlet No. 68*, United States Office of Education, rev. ed., 1945, 23 pp.

C. *Speech Defects*

1. Capehart, R., "Survey of Speech Defects in Illinois High Schools," *Journal of Speech and Hearing Disorders*, 4:61–70, 1939.
2. Despert, J. L., "Psychosomatic Studies of Fifty Stuttering Children: I. Social, Physiological, and Psychiatric Findings," *American Journal of Orthopsychiatry*, 16:100–113, 1946.
3. Duncan, M. H., "Home Adjustment of Stutterers *versus* Nonstutterers," *Journal of Speech and Hearing Disorders*, 14:255–259, 1949.
4. Glassner, P. I., "Personal Characteristics and Emotional Problems in Stutterers under the Age of Five," *Journal of Speech and Hearing Disorders*, 14:135–138, 1949.
5. Henderson, P., "The Incidence of Stammering and Speech Defects in School Children," *Bulletin of the Minnesota Public Health Laboratory Service*, 6:102–105, 1947.
6. Johnson, W., "An Open Letter to Mothers of Stuttering Children," *Journal of Speech and Hearing Disorders*, 14:3–8, 1949.
7. Johnson, W., "To Help the Child with a Speech Handicap," *Child*, 15:12–14, 1950.
8. Lassers, L., "How Parents and Teachers Can Help Prevent Stuttering and Stammering," *Oregon State Department of Education Bulletin*, 1945, 41 pp.
9. Lemmert, E. M., and C. Van Riper, "The Use of Psychodrama in the Treatment of Speech Defects," *Sociometry*, 7:190–195, 1944.
10. Meyer, B. C., "Psychosomatic Aspects of Stuttering," *Journal of Nervous and Mental Diseases*, 101:127–157, 1945.
11. Richardson, L. H., "The Personality of Stutterers," *Psychological Monographs*, Vol. LVI, No. 7, 41 pp.
12. Schuell, H., "Sex Differences in Relation to Stuttering," *Journal of Speech and Hearing Disorders*, 11:277–298, 1946.
13. Schuell, H., "Work with Parents of Stuttering Children," *Journal of Speech and Hearing Disorders*, 14:251–254, 1949.

D. *Sex Attitudes and Information*

1. Brown, F., "What American Men Want to Know about Sex," *Journal of Social Psychology*, 27:119–125, 1948.
2. Whitehorn, J. C., "Sex Behavior and Sex Attitudes in Relation to Emotional Health," *Stanford Medical Bulletin*, 2:45–60, 1947.

Emotional
Development

PART TWO

Emotional
Development

CHAPTER FIVE

Emotional
Growth

There is a wealth of information in regard to emotional development, both normal and abnormal, from infancy to old age. Obviously not all of this material is of value to the secondary school teacher. It is the author's intention to summarize in the present section those points which are relevant to everyday association with adolescents. With this object in view, theoretical discussion may be almost entirely omitted. The present section will contain chapters on (1) the general nature of emotions and their normal growth, (2) the part of the school in influencing emotional development, (3) the nature of conflicts and their possible solutions, (4) the development and measurement of personality, and (5) the description of abnormal emotional states with which a teacher sometimes has to deal.

I. Nature of Emotions

1. Human Needs: Various psychologists and others have made lists of the basic human needs, basic human urges, or basic human drives. All three phrases refer to the same phenomena. The difference is that a "need" is a static condition, whereas a "drive" is a dynamic tendency to action and an "urge" is the feeling that is derived from the need and precipitates the drive. The use of one word or the other depends upon what phase of the total phenomenon one wishes to emphasize. Many people use them interchangeably, and perhaps the nuances of meaning are hardly worth preserving. What is important to remember is that each individual carries within himself, from birth to death, certain inner springs of feeling that may be aroused by any of a number of stimuli, and certain desires that are of such fundamental importance to him that he constantly seeks gratification for them.

The list presented in Table 3 is a combination of several lists by a number of writers. One can see at once that the fundamental needs are of several sorts. Some are clearly physical, such as the drive to secure food when hungry, to obtain shelter when cold, to mate when stimulated, or to recover when ill. Others have a less obvious physical basis, if any. Urges of this latter type are often called the "drives for ego satisfaction," such as the desires for approval, for self-expression, for love, or for security. Others arise because man is a social animal and must therefore maintain some kind

Table 3

THE BASIC HUMAN NEEDS

A. *Bodily needs*

1. Need to go on living
2. Need to avoid danger
3. Need to relax
4. Need to recover when ill or injured
5. Need to overcome handicaps

B. *Personal needs*

6. Need to grow
7. Need to be normal
8. Need to have and keep possessions
9. Need to overcome difficulties
10. Need to be loved
11. Need to feel secure
12. Need to escape blame
13. Need to express oneself
14. Need to seek thrills and excitement
15. Need to seek some form of sexual expression
16. Need for independence

C. *Social needs*

17. Need to have friends
18. Need to be popular
19. Need to be a leader
20. Need to follow a leader
21. Need to control others
22. Need to protect others
23. Need to imitate others
24. Need to have prestige
25. Need to seek praise
26. Need to resist coercion
27. Need to oppose others

D. *Intellectual needs*

28. Need to think
29. Need to acquire facts
30. Need to think out explanations
31. Need to relate and interpret facts
32. Need to organize
33. Need to work toward a goal
34. Need to believe in something outside oneself

Modified and rearranged from a list given in R. N. Sanford, *et al., Physique, Personality, and Scholarship; A Co-operative Study of School Children*, National Research Council, 1943, 235; from a questionnaire based upon a selection of needs, in L. Raths and L. Metcalf, "An Instrument for Identifying Some Needs of Children," *Educational Research Bulletin*, 24:169–185, 1945; and from H. Schacter, *How Personalities Grow*, McKnight & McKnight, 1949, Chap. 3.

of social relationship with his neighbors. He desires friends, praise, loyalty, prestige, and leadership. Man also has intellectual needs; he wants to know, to understand, to organize, and to interpret. Above all he likes to think, even though the subject of his thoughts may not always be socially approved.

Even a casual inspection of the list in Table 3 should convince a reader that different people, while sharing to some extent in all these needs, differ enormously among themselves as to the relative strength of the various drives. To one person the mere need to go on living is so strong, and the social drives so weak, that he arranges his life to satisfy this one need and eventually becomes a recluse and a hypochondriac. In another the need to be admired is the most powerful of the lot, while a third is ruled by his need for self-expression. The miser and the millionaire have a strong need to get and keep material possessions; the nun has profound needs to believe in some power outside herself, to follow where others lead, and to protect those weaker than herself; the demagogue's deepest desire is to control others, to lead them, to be worshiped by them; and so on for everyone in the world. Some needs tend to go together harmoniously, but a given person may show a most inharmonious combination of simultaneous desires. Thus, a desire for a hero's prestige may exist beside an intense desire to avoid danger. Most of the reactions one makes between being born and dying are made because they contribute directly or indirectly to the satisfaction of some need or to a restoration of equilibrium after a need has had no adequate outlet for some time, or a drive has long been frustrated.

All drives are not equally important at all ages. In one study the strength at different age levels was rated by teachers, and these ratings were checked by testing and other means. The drives showed individual development as indicated in Figure 51 on page 114: for instance, the desire to seek care and protection (B, 3) was seventh from the top at ages 5 and 6, but decreased to the twenty-fourth position by ages 13 and 14. The desire to know about things (B, 2) decreased, but the urge to know and understand the reasons for things increased (B, 1). Need for play as a release from tension (A, 3) grew from one age level to the next. The desire to make friends (A, 1) was high at all ages. The urge to enjoy sensuous experiences (B, 4) first waxed then waned, probably because social stimuli became of greater importance. The need to avoid blame (A, 2) became stronger with the passing of time, presumably because children learned of the social ostracism and punishment that may be meted out to those who admit their guilt. Desire to attack others (B, 5) was relatively high in early childhood but fell off abruptly as soon as children learned other and more acceptable methods of assertion and protest. Needs to surrender oneself, to be independent, and to work toward a goal (A, 5, 6, and 4) all started low and increased with age. Desire to organize (B, 6) was relatively low at all ages.

As these drives develop, they produce more or less tension, which mounts until it becomes so uncomfortable that it has to be discharged in some kind of reaction. Thus when a child who is accustomed to being the focus of parental affection sees his parents pay attention to his newly born brother or sister, he begins to feel uncomfortable because his own ego drives are thwarted, and he pushes himself forward in some way in an effort to recapture his former position. If his behavior brings about the desired results, the tension disappears. Similarly, a young man who has fallen in love generates a good deal of inner tension, which finds normal expression if the object of his affection falls in love with him.

However, life is not so arranged that drives can always be satisfied, either within a short time, or, in some cases, at all. Therefore the tension, instead of being discharged, becomes greater. As long as it continues, the

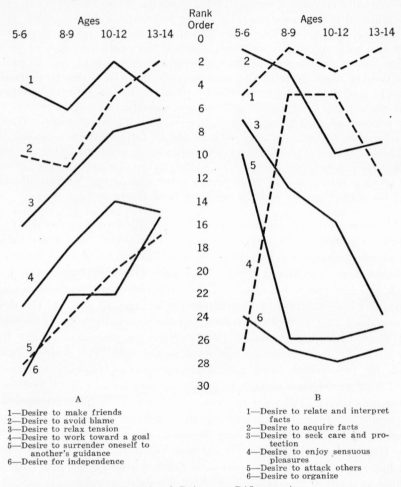

A

1—Desire to make friends
2—Desire to avoid blame
3—Desire to relax tension
4—Desire to work toward a goal
5—Desire to surrender oneself to
    another's guidance
6—Desire for independence

B

1—Desire to relate and interpret
    facts
2—Desire to acquire facts
3—Desire to seek care and pro-
    tection
4—Desire to enjoy sensuous
    pleasures
5—Desire to attack others
6—Desire to organize

Fig. 51. *Strength of Emotional Drives at Different Ages*

Based upon R. N. Sanford, *et al., Physique, Personality, and Scholarship,*
National Research Council, 1943, 705 pp.

individual is in an emotional state. His ego desires a satisfaction that his environment prevents him from obtaining. Eventually the urge will find some form of expression that satisfies him more or less and gives relief from strain. For instance, a high school boy who has the normal desire for social recognition from his age-mates may find his urge blocked by the poverty and low social standing of his parents, by the inferior school records of older siblings, and by his own small, undernourished body. As day after day goes by without satisfaction of his drive for recognition, his frustration increases. He may get relief by becoming a member of a delinquent group, in which his misdeeds bring him satisfaction for the fundamental urge that is in itself perfectly normal.

This general discussion may perhaps be made clearer by the analysis of an individual case. For this purpose the writer has selected a middle-aged woman whose personal history shows unusually well the interplay of drives, tensions, frustrations, and substitute responses, with a final solution.

Miss X came from a quite comfortable but not socially prominent home, in which she was an only child. She was an undersized, unattractive girl whose mental level was slightly below average. During her childhood Miss X played normally enough with children in the neighborhood, although she was never popular and was often forced to take some inferior part in games. The other children picked on her more or less, ran away from her when they were tired of her dullness, and generally snubbed her, but she was willing to put up with such treatment for the sake of company. With the coming of adolescence she developed unusually strong drives for dominance and attention. She was the first girl of the neighborhood to wear silk stockings, evening dresses, and white kid gloves. She hung around the street corners to waylay boys. She invited other girls into the drugstore and bought them all the ice cream they could eat, for the sheer pleasure of being seen with them. In all ways she tried to find satisfaction for her urges by pushing herself forward among her age-mates. Other girls usually rejected her offers and considered her a bore. Between the ages of sixteen and twenty-one she entered three different boarding schools but was forced to leave each one in turn, partly because she was too dull to pass the work and partly because she soon stirred up trouble among the girls. During these episodes of schooling she vacillated between two types of behavior. Sometimes she would sidle up to the most prominent girls in the school and ask them to come to her room or to go some place with her; at other times she would burst into their rooms and cry for an hour because no one liked her and she was miserably unhappy. Her frustration thus often showed directly, but was almost as evident during her more usual behavior of soliciting attention in spite of continued snubs.

For some years after leaving the third boarding school she remained at home, in a desultory and generally unsatisfactory manner doing volunteer work of various sorts as a means of gaining recognition. Committee chairmen dreaded having her put in their groups because of her constant importunities and her striving to dominate other members. During this time she developed a number of mannerisms that made · her even more unpopular than before, and she seemed headed for a serious breakdown as one after another of her efforts met with rebuff. Presently she was reduced to attending public lectures and concerts as her only means of contact with people; she would settle herself for the evening with some mere acquaintance and then buttonhole people for days thereafter to tell them she had attended the function with such and such a family or person.

When Miss X was about thirty years old her parents died within a few weeks of each other, leaving her a modest income. During their illness Miss X hired a pleasant, quite ordinary, uneducated Negro girl to help her with the housework. This girl stayed on after the parents' deaths and became the first person who ever had given Miss X the genuine affection and admiration that she had craved all her life. Over this girl Miss X could dominate. The two became good friends and continued to live together, Miss X willingly paying the bills. This strangely assorted pair settled down in great contentment. The girl had never known anyone as kind as Miss X, and the latter had never known anyone as appreciative of her. The Negro girl brought friends of her own race to the house, where Miss X made them welcome. Few of these friends had completed grammar school and Miss X's attendance at fashionable boarding schools seemed to them remarkable. Instead of being an outcast, Miss X found herself suddenly popular. Her native ability was probably greater than that of her new acquaintances and her social position was certainly superior. During the years that have elapsed since this change in her circumstances she has lost her mannerisms and has become a well-adjusted person. She lives modestly, uses her extra funds for helping Negro families, is an adviser for several Negro charities, and is living a happy and useful life. Her drives for domination and attention are now satisfied and her substitute reactions have disappeared. She no longer pesters her former acquaintances. She has an abundant social life, and she is a leader.

In this woman's history one can see the working out of the fundamental human drives. She was born with handicaps, mental and physical. She was so driven by her desires that she was not content with a moderately good adaptation to lower middle-class society—a position she might have achieved —but pushed herself into social groups in which she was hopelessly out-classed. The first thirty years of her life were spent in a state of continual frustration. Then by accident she found herself in a social group in which she could be a leader. Having found that she could not compete in one circle she has finally been successful in another. Her ego is satisfied, and she has become, within the limits set by her social group, a success.

2. Nature of an Emotional Experience: An emotion may be defined for the specialist in many technical words, but for the layman the familiar, simple definition of an emotion as a "stirred-up state of the entire organism" is probably more understandable. Or, if further definitions make the matter any clearer, an emotion may be called "a response of the entire human being to a stimulus" or an "integrated reaction of the total organism." It should be remembered that an emotion, however defined, is not the same thing as a basic drive or a basic need; it is the reaction that accompanies either the satisfaction of or the frustration of a basic need. Thus, an individual has a need to be accepted by his age-mates, to be loved by his intimates, or to express himself in some way. If these drives are fulfilled, he is happy, joyful, contented, or in love. If the drives are frustrated, he is angry, frightened, worried, jealous, anxious, or full of sorrow. The emotions are thus related to the basic drives but they are not identical with them.

All emotions have a physical basis or accompaniment, and the curious thing about this physical reaction is that it is almost the same for all emotions, although such states as fear, anger, horror, sorrow, joy, excitement, jealousy, or love certainly "feel" different to the individual who experiences them. The only differences from one emotion to another are in intensity; that is, one can be annoyed, irritated, angered, or infuriated, or one can be apprehensive, worried, frightened, or in mortal terror. The changes become more profound, more widespread, and more exhausting with each increase in intensity, but they are identical for the same degree of intensity for fear, anger, love, or jealousy. The following description will therefore serve for all.

The entire body participates in the reactions that furnish the basis for or accompaniment to an emotional experience. These physical changes are produced through the action of the autonomic nervous system. This is *not* the central nervous system. The two systems exist alongside each other, with little interrelation between them. The nerves of the central nervous system run from the sense organs—eyes, ears, nose, tongue, and skin—to the spinal cord, cerebellum, or brain, whence other nerves run to the skeletal muscles. This system is under voluntary control. It is the system by means of which, for instance, one eats a bowl of cereal, or hits a tennis ball, or pounds a nail, or puts on lipstick. The nerves of the autonomic system run mostly to and from the internal organs, and they are not under voluntary control. Indeed, so long as this system functions normally, the individual does not even know he has it inside himself. It is the autonomic system that keeps the heart going, the lungs breathing, the stomach and intestines digesting, the kidneys excreting, and the glands of the body manufacturing and delivering their chemicals. Its main distributions are to the following organs, taking them in order from the head downward: the eyes (not to open or close them, but to dilate the pupil), the tear glands, the mucous membrane of the nose and mouth, the salivary glands in the mouth, the parotid glands, the larynx, the heart, the lungs, the stomach, the liver, the pancreas, the intestines, the kidneys, the adrenal glands, the bladder, the colon, and the genitals; there are connections also with the main blood vessels and with the sweat glands in the skin.

A diagram of these connections appears in Figure 52 on page 118. As indicated, the system has three main divisions, the cranial (shown in the figure by the nerves at the left and top), the sympathetic (shown at the right), and the sacral (shown at the left and bottom). The first and the last work together in direct opposition to the sympathetic branch and are therefore usually called, collectively, the parasympathetic branch. Nerves from both sympathetic and parasympathetic branches run to all the vital organs enumerated above. The function of the sympathetic branch of the autonomic system is to inhibit digestion, to constrict the blood vessels, to dilate the pupil of the eye and the bronchioles of the lungs, to make the hair stand erect, to release blood sugar from the liver, to stimulate the secretion of sweat, to release adrenalin from the suprarenal glands, to increase the blood pressure and pulse, and to check the flow of saliva. The action of the parasympathetic branch is exactly the opposite. These nerves make the heart beat more slowly, constrict the pupil of the eye, increase salivation, increase stomach and intestinal action, dilate the blood vessels, reduce the blood pressure, and stop the secretions from the suprarenal and sweat glands. During normal periods the two divisions are evenly balanced, but when an emotion develops, the sympathetic branch is in the ascendancy; then, as the emotion subsides, the parasympathetic branch becomes the stronger, until the normal balance is restored.

This arrangement of nerves that operate during an emotion explains some of the characteristics of an emotional experience. For instance, when one is insulted, he cannot help *feeling* angry, because the emotion is served by nerves not under his control, although he can refrain from answering or from fighting, because the nerves that run to his speech mechanism and the muscles in his arms and legs are under his control. It is a fertile source of maladjustment that people can thus refuse an emotion its normal outlet; the feeling is so powerful that, if one outlet is blocked, it will find another

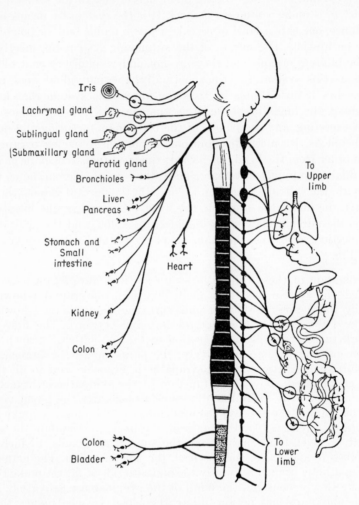

Fig. 52. *The Autonomic Nervous System*

C. H. Best and N. B. Taylor, *The Physiological Basis of Medical Practice*, The William Wilkins Co., 1939, p. 1520. Used by permission of the publisher.

and perhaps even less desirable one. A strong emotion often precipitates incidental physical symptoms, such as the nausea and diarrhea that many athletes experience for hours before a competition, or the dead faint of a person who is terribly frightened, or the breathlessness, blushing, and perspiration of a young man trying to propose. After an emotion has passed, the individual is suddenly exhausted because of the upheaval within his fundamental processes and is likely to drop off to sleep wherever he is, as is dramatically shown in the pictures of soldiers released from duty who go instantly to sleep before they have time enough to move themselves out of danger.

As soon as one begins to experience an emotion, the physiological changes start. An almost immediate effect is the secretion of adrenalin by the suprarenal glands. The adrenalin is discharged by the glands into the blood stream, by which it is carried over the entire body within a few seconds. Its action upon different bodily structures is varied. It acts upon the stomach to retard the normal digestive processes. In extreme cases the peristalsis of the stomach and intestines completely ceases. During an emotion only about 15 per cent of the normal amount of gastric juice is secreted by the stomach. The salivary glands cease functioning almost entirely. It acts upon the liver, causing this organ to discharge into the blood stream the sugar that is normally stored in it.[1] This sugar is carried by the blood stream to the muscles. It is the "food" which the muscles require for their contractions. The adrenalin further acts upon the small muscles controlling the amount of air that can be taken into the lungs. These muscles become relaxed so that the person who is angry breathes in more oxygen and discharges more carbon dioxide than is normally the case. The breathing of the person becomes more rapid and somewhat irregular. The adrenalin also acts upon the blood vessels which supply the abdominal organs, driving the blood from the abdomen into the muscles, nervous system, and lungs. Another effect is upon the composition of the blood, by the increase of those chemicals that make it coagulate more quickly. The adrenalin directly affects the heart muscles, and causes the heart to beat more rapidly and with more power. As a result of this change, the blood pressure rises for the duration of the emotion. It is the driving of the blood from the viscera into the muscles and to the surface of the body generally that produces the redness of the angry person's face and the general feeling of warmth that he experiences. The adrenalin also causes the sweat glands in the skin to function, thus producing dampness in the palms of the hands and on the face. Tears, sometimes quite inappropriate to the emotion, often flow because of the stimulation of the lachrymal glands. There may be loss of bladder or colon control, and, in the case of men and boys, sudden erections that have no sensible relation to the emotion being felt. The muscles which control the skeleton, because they are supplied with an extra allowance of blood sugar, often contract until they quiver with sheer tenseness. During an emotion the individual has actually a greater strength and a greater endurance than during his usual calm state, but he does not have the control over his muscles that he has when he is not emotionally disturbed. Thus in an actual fight between two people of normally equal muscular development, one of whom is extremely angry and the other of whom is quite calm, the angry fighter has the greater strength and is likely to damage the other seriously if he ever succeeds in landing a blow, but his muscular control is often so poor

---

[1] W. B. Cannon, *Bodily Changes in Pain, Hunger, Fear, and Rage,* Appleton-Century-Crofts, Inc., 1915, 311 pp.

that he cannot hit his opponent at all, while the unemotional opponent continues to land much lighter blows whenever he wishes to do so.

It should be clear that the internal changes are preparation for some kind of violent action, such as running away or fighting. If the excess adrenalin and sugar are not used, if the generated readiness to act is not discharged in some way, pathological developments may follow. It is not necessary that the "natural" form of discharge be used. Any activity that uses up the excess glucose in the muscles is as good as any other. The discharge may also take the form of words or even thoughts. If the individual's emotional steam is not released, however, it will perpetuate the seething inside him, will precipitate conflicts, and will eventually discharge itself through abnormal channels.

II. The Life History of Three Major Emotions

Emotions appear early in life. From birth, babies show a general state of excitement when they are stimulated. Their main response is an undifferentiated howling and thrashing about. Presently, however, the onlooker can tell whether the baby finds a given stimulation pleasant or unpleasant. Further differentiation soon occurs, and the emotions of fear, rage, excitement, and joy become recognizable. The child of two has added jealousy, love, and hate to his repertoire. By the time he enters school, he has a full emotional equipment. The differentiation of the generalized excitement seen in infancy into a number of emotional states thus takes place long before adolescence.

At different ages, individuals are susceptible to different stimuli. At any one age they fail to notice some to which they have previously reacted, and they become aware of others to which they have heretofore been indifferent. It may, for instance, suddenly strike a third-grade child that schoolwork is competitive, and this new idea may generate in him a feeling of shame because he has thus far puttered happily about at the bottom of the class. Other stimuli, once powerful, may lose their meaning or may arouse a different emotion. Thus the ten-year-old boy thinks it is funny to pull out someone's chair just as the person is about to sit down in it, the adolescent scorns such behavior as a "kid trick," and the adult is fearful of possible injuries to the coccyx. The expression of the emotion also varies with age, the change being mostly away from direct, obvious, violent behavior and toward subtlety. The jealous four-year-old openly pushes his rival out of the way and seizes the center of the stage, but the jealous woman of forty leaves the spotlight on her rival while she indirectly and with seeming innocence makes her appear ridiculous.

The type of treatment to be given in this section has been used to bring into relief the effect of age and experience upon emotional behavior. The general background against which emotions develop has already been discussed, but the particular situations that thwart the drives and thus produce frustration differ from one age level to another. In most recent work on the emotions the tendency has been to synthesis rather than to analysis. However, it seems to the writer that the study of single emotions has certain values in helping a student to see the underlying mechanisms and to understand why the frustration of a basic drive should be disrupting. Naturally, one should not become so intent upon specific stimuli and reactions that he loses sight of the total individual or the total environment. For purposes of clarity and emphasis, therefore, the analytical approach has been preserved, with the expectation that the insertion of many case studies and the later discussions of frustrations, conflicts, and problems will afford the material necessary for an adequate synthesis and application of the treatment to life situations.

An emotional experience may be divided for convenience into three parts. First, there is the stimulus which causes the emotion. Second, there is the internal adjustment already described. And third, there is the response made. The second of these parts, the internal adjustment, appears to vary only with the capacity of the body to react. These changes have been studied by the physiologist and do not constitute a psychological problem. The teacher should understand their nature, but there is nothing that she or anybody else can do about them. There are, however, great changes from birth to old age in the stimuli which produce emotions and the responses that are made. The biography of an emotion must, then, concern itself with the causes and effects of the emotional upheaval. Moreover, the school can do something about the matter by introducing or removing stimuli and by directing the expression of emotions into channels of social acceptability.

A "life history" of each possible emotion would result in far too long a discussion, even if there were adequate data for such a treatment. Moreover, there is no accepted list of emotions. Some psychologists list three, four, or five emotions; others admit about a dozen, and there are a few who enumerate even more. It seems undesirable to introduce moot problems into this text; in any case, the exact number of emotions need not be determined so far as the forthcoming treatment is concerned. The writer would be inclined to group the emotions into three types, depending upon the kind of behavior they lead to, and to list the emotions as follows: (1) anger, jealousy, hatred, and hostility as emotional states of an aggressive character; (2) fear, worry, dread, sorrow, embarrassment, regret, and disgust as inhibitory states; and (3) love, affection, happiness, excitement, and pleasure as joyous states. One emotion from each group has been selected for discussion in some detail. The treatment given could, however, be extended to any other emotion concerning which sufficient evidence was available. The main thing for teachers to realize is that, although internal changes during an emotion vary only in intensity, the stimuli for and reactions to emotional stimulation have typical stages of development that can be traced just as surely as the stages of intellectual growth. Illustrative material from three emotions should make this point sufficiently clear.

1. Emotional States Leading to Aggressive Behavior: In this group of emotions, anger is the one selected for discussion, partly because it is more frequently and easily aroused than the others and partly because there is a considerable literature about it. The situations that produce anger will first be considered.

The baby becomes angry if he is not fed when hungry, if his soiled clothes are not replaced by dry ones, or if his freedom of movement is restricted. In the largest number of instances, the small children who have been studied became angry because someone tried to take a plaything away from them. The next most important category includes conflicts arising over dressing and going to the toilet. In fact, these two types of situation contribute approximately three fourths of all the stimuli causing outbursts of annoyance in preschool children.[2] Most of the remaining situations consist of some interruption of the child's activities by others. In short, children become annoyed at the necessary routine of life and at the thwarting of an activity either by interference from others or by the sudden loss of a treasured possession.

For adolescents the causes of anger were quite different. They have been studied by means of "anger diaries"—records kept over a period of time concerning the causes of anger, the reactions made, and sometimes the duration of the emotion. A sample page from such a diary appears in Table 4.

Most of the causes here enumerated are concerned with schoolwork. A few other typical stimuli that aroused anger in adolescents are listed, in their own words, below:

1. My mother makes me get home before midnight.
2. My boy friend ran his fingers through my hair and made me look a mess.
3. My father's fraternity turned me down after giving me a big rush.
4. My girl said she'd go to the movies with me, but when I called for her she'd already gone with someone else.
5. My math teacher calls on me by saying "Now let's hear from our football hero." She knows I can't answer her silly questions.
6. I postponed a date to oblige a girl friend who had two men coming on the same evening, and she hung on to the really nice guy all the time and left me with a poor stick.
7. I paid $70 for my dress and the shop assured me it was an exclusive model, but when I got to the dance, there was another girl with a dress just like mine.
8. A girl from my home town brought back a baby picture of me that she had stolen from our family album, showing me lying on a rug with nothing on, and she's been showing it to people.
9. I tripped over the last hurdle and everyone in the stands just laughed.
10. My French teacher makes me try to pronounce words with nasals in them and when I do the kids laugh, and when I won't he bawls me out.
11. My brother took the new sweater I was going to wear to the school picnic, and I had to go in my old one.

Another investigator asked a group of college women to keep both

---

[2] A. F. Ricketts, "A Study of the Behavior of Young Children in Anger," *University of Iowa Studies in Child Welfare*, 9:159–171, 1934, and F. L. Goodenough, *Anger in Young Children*, University of Minnesota Press, 1931, 278 pp.

Table 4

ANGER CHART OF THE BRIGHTEST MALE STUDENT

Cause	Impulse controlled	Impulse yielded to	Effect
Large assignment in Vocational Education course	To make sarcastic remark to teacher		Defiance toward the course
Editorial in Stanford paper		Commented about it to colleague	Laughed about the incident
Examination	Tear up question	Sigh of anguish	Nervousness
Recalled forgotten appointment	Call up and apologize	Slight feeling of fear	Decision to try to remember better
Poor grade on examination	Razz instructor on type of exam	Made alibi	Rationalized
Awakened by noise	To throw vacuum sweeper downstairs	Cursed slightly, moved cover over head	Wished I could go some place and never be disturbed
Assignment of 140 pages discovered	To beat up an instructor	Swore	Trembling and excited feeling
More work than could complete	To throw book away		Feeling of hopelessness of studying any more
Argument	To sit on him or trample	Raised voice and put up defense	Nervousness and inability to study
Phone call	To cut wire	"Damn that phone"	
First whistle	To miss class and sleep	Reminded that I would miss breakfast	Realized I would be uncomfortable all morning

From H. Meltzer, "Anger Adjustments in Relation to Intelligence and Achievement," *Journal of Genetic Psychology*, 50:63–82, 1937. Used by permission of the Journal and the author.

anger and fear diaries for a week, writing down emotional episodes as soon as possible after their occurrence.[3] The students also indicated in each instance whether the precipitating situations were actually present or were something recalled from the past or anticipated for the future. The average number of anger reactions a week per student was 16, with a range from a completely pacific 0 to a bellicose 42. The fears—to be discussed further in the next section—averaged 12, with a range from 2 to 36. The number of episodes of each type correlated with each other with a coefficient of 0.72, suggesting that there is an underlying degree of emotionality that affects all reactions; that is, those who were most often angry or afraid were also most frequently excited, happy, in love, jealous, or melancholy, while those

---

[3] A. Anastasi, N. Cohen, and D. Spatz, "A Study of Fear and Anger in College Students through the Controlled Diary Method," *Journal of Genetic Psychology*, 73:243–249, 1948.

who lacked fear or anger also lacked strong expressions of other emotions. The situations precipitating fear or anger differed in one important respect from each other. Feared situations were mostly in the future, a few in the present, and almost none in the past—70, 27, and 3 per cent, respectively. Almost all situations precipitating anger were in the present—94 per cent of them—with 3 per cent in the past and 3 per cent in anticipated situations. For anger, the situations may be classified as follows:

	Per cent
Those arising from thwarted plans	52
Those leading to loss of prestige	21
Those arising from schoolwork	13
Those arising from family relationships	10
Those arising from abstract problems	4

The thwarted plan and the loss of status contribute nearly three fourths of the situations that led to anger. When plans were frustrated, the agent was a person in 46 per cent of the episodes, an institutional factor—such as rules and regulations, red tape, or "schedules"—in 23 per cent, personal inadequacy in 16 per cent, and the perversity of things, accident, or chance in 15 per cent.

Causes of adult anger have hardly been investigated, but what evidence there is suggests some continuance of childish irritation at objects that refuse to function and adolescent sensitivity to social slights, real or imagined. A new type of stimulus is, however, fairly frequent. Adults become angry over such matters as the failure of an able man to be promoted or the interference of government agencies in their business enterprises.

The three levels of development may be summarized as follows: In early childhood, anger comes most frequently from conflicts over playthings or daily routine. There are also outbursts of anger if an absorbing activity is interrupted or if the desire to do some interesting thing is thwarted. In adolescence, the causes of anger are primarily social. The individual gets into a situation in which he feels himself embarrassed, ridiculous, offended, or annoyed, and forthwith develops tension. The adult also becomes angry if his work or leisure is too much interfered with, and he is inclined to feel concerned over abstract justice or social conditions. It is small wonder that the child, the adolescent, and the adult sometimes fail to understand one another's reaction to the same situation.

The writer is reminded of an episode at a neighbor's house during her childhood. The sixteen-year-old boy of the family had asked his history teacher—a man of about fifty—to the house for dinner. As the hour for the teacher's arrival grew near, the boy called his ten-year-old sister, saw that she put on a clean dress, lectured her on being a lady, parked her in the swing on the front porch, and ordered her to sit there and stay clean—if she could. The lad was in his room putting the finishing touches on his own toilet, when his small sister spied the teacher approaching the house. Being on her good behavior, the child went to meet him and —because she wanted to be especially nice—asked him to come in through the back door and kitchen, on the principle that this method of entrance was more informal and friendly. Both the mother of the family and the teacher were a bit surprised to come face to face in a small back hall generously cluttered with overcoats and rubbers, but neither was especially disturbed. The adolescent boy, however, was furious. For him the evening was ruined because the mores had been so outraged. He scolded his sister until she dissolved in tears and his mother intervened. The two children were finally separated, but the boy remained angry and sullen, especially after the mother refused to punish her small daughter when the latter had had only the best of intentions. The little girl, who adored her big brother, was too brokenhearted to eat, so she sat at the table, alternately sniveling and bursting out with angry words of self-defense. The adults tried to act as if nothing had happened, but without conspicuous success. As the dinner party continued, the parents became greatly annoyed at their children's behavior, and the teacher became embarrassed at their annoyance. By the end of the meal the teacher was angry at the parents for making him uncomfortable, the parents were angry at the children, and the children were angry at each other.

The reactions made when one is angry also show a development. The small baby becomes quite rigid; he screams and beats the air with his arms and legs. This is his only reaction, probably because his mental and muscular development is so slight that other reactions are not possible. The preschool child also cries, screams, and becomes stiff; in addition, he kicks, strikes, bites, scratches, stamps his feet, jumps up and down or throws himself on the floor.[4] To a slight extent he scolds and talks back, but in this reaction he is inhibited by his undeveloped articulation and his limited vocabulary. By adolescence the response of talking has become by far the most important.[5] Actual violence is reported in only a few instances, although there is frequent reference to the suppression of such behavior. Instead, the boy or girl tends to substitute the reactions of pacing the room, being generally restless, going out for a walk, or indulging in some violent exercise as a means of working off emotion. Some slight degree of subtlety is shown by those who refuse to speak to the people who have made them angry or hurt their feelings. Finally, there is a persistence of infantile behavior in the form of stamping the feet, or kicking things, on the part of the boys, and of crying, on the part of the girls. Among adults, the verbal responses have almost completely taken the place of all other forms, although women still cry and men still kick things. It should also be noted that the younger the individual, the more immediate is the release of emotional tension. Direct release is perhaps best physiologically for the person who is under tension, indirect release the next best, and suppression—with its storing up of tensions—quite undesirable at any age.

The duration of the anger also varies somewhat with the age of the individual. Among preschool children, the outbursts lasted less than five minutes in 90 per cent of the cases.[6] For college students the average period was fifteen minutes, and the total range from one minute to forty-eight

----

[4] Ricketts, *op. cit.*
[5] H. Meltzer, "Anger Adjustments in Relation to Intelligence and Achievement," *Journal of Genetic Psychology*, 50:63–82; and Anastasi, *et al.*, "A Study of Fear and Anger in College Students through the Controlled Diary Method," *loc. cit.*
[6] Ricketts, *op. cit.*

hours.[7] The number of anger experiences per week does not seem to vary greatly with age; the main differences are to be found in the situations causing anger, in the responses made, and in the duration of the responses.

Jealousy has been studied less than anger, but a few recent investigations have brought out certain points about its nature and causation. One writer classifies the types of jealousy as being intellectual, possessive, and sexual.[8] The emotion seems in general to arise whenever an individual feels himself threatened by an actual or supposed loss of affection or prestige. The reactions into which one is driven may be positive and consist either of aggression toward or competition with the person causing the emotion, or they may be negative and consist of withdrawal from competition, hero worship, repression, or masochism.[9] The former is seen in the child who strikes his baby brother, and the latter in the adolescent who attaches himself to more successful people by making heroes of them, thus avoiding competition, since one does not even try to compete with one's heroes.

2. Emotions Leading to Inhibitory or Defensive Behavior: The second of the three most powerful emotions is fear, which seems to be present from birth. The typical reactions are paling, trembling, perspiring, becoming rigid, panting, and—subsequently or coincidentally—running away. These reactions may become attached to practically any stimulus and are not necessarily attached to more than a few. Most of the things a human being fears he has learned to be afraid of.

Clinical histories show children, adolescents, and adults to be afraid of many objects, situations, and relationships. One may fear sharp knives, snakes, elevators, water, dogs, fountain pens, or practically anything else. One may fear people who are big, clever, sarcastic, cruel, overbearing, humorous, sly, and so on. One may be afraid to meet people, to be alone, to be in a crowd, to give a speech, to recite in class, to write an examination, or to go to a dance. The number of social situations causing agitation seems almost infinite. One may also have relatively remote or generalized anxieties such as fear of poverty in old age, of death, of disease, of drowning, of becoming blind, of failure, of being separated from one's family, of losing one's job.

In recent decades various efforts have been made, through the use of questionnaires and tests, to obtain information as to the fears and other emotional attitudes of normal children and adolescents. The results to be presented come from several different studies,[10] the outstanding points of

---

[7] Meltzer, *op. cit.*, and Anastasi, *et al.*, *op. cit.*

[8] B. Sokoloff, *Jealousy: A Psychiatric Study,* Howell, Soskin, Publishers, Inc., 1947, p. 54.

[9] H. Vollmer, "Jealousy in Children," *American Journal of Orthopsychiatry,* 16:660–671, 1946.

[10] R. Pintner and J. Lev, "Worries of School Children," *Journal of General Psychology,* 56:67–76, 1940; A. T. Jersild and A. M. Holmes, "Children's Fears," *Child Development Monographs,* No. 20, 1935, 358 pp.; K. C. Pratt, "A Study of the 'Fears' of Rural Children," *Journal of Genetic Psychology,* 67:179–194, 1945; R. Zeligs, "Children's Worries," *Sociology and Social Research,* 24:22–32, 1939; R. Zeligs, "Social

which have been combined in the interests of brevity. Below is a list of the worries mentioned most frequently by fifth- and sixth-grade children, whose ages would be roughly from ten to thirteen. They were afraid of or worried about such things as these:

> Failing a test in school
> Father or mother being sick
> Father or mother working too hard
> Getting a bad report card
> Father losing his job
> Being late to school
> Being hurt by knives, guns, poison, fire, floods
> Being in an accident, holdup, burglary, or fight
> Being hurt by animals
> Being sick, suffering, choking, dying
> Losing money while doing an errand
> Losing one's fountain pen
> Losing one's friends

Most high school pupils continue to show a number of typical childish fears, but new sources of worry appear[11] because they are subject to many new pressures and drives. Adolescents concentrate upon such anxieties as the following: fear of school examinations, automobile accidents, and disease; worry over inadequate funds, lack of ability, getting a job, loss of work by parents, or appearance of the home; fear of being sinful, of being led astray by bad companions; worry over being unpopular or unsuccessful, over hurting other people's feelings, over being shy, self-conscious, dull, or lonely, over being tempted to cheat, over losing one's religious beliefs, over making a bad impression upon others, over being unable to concentrate; fear of growing up, of blushing, of being socially incompetent, of having sexual experiences, of masturbating, of daydreaming, of having crushes, of disappointing one's parents; concern over having pretty clothes and lots of friends; anxiety about being different from others, being teased or scolded, being treated unfairly, being too closely watched, being laughed at, or being a failure. These myriad anxieties may be grouped under six main heads: worries related to the problem of emancipation from home, those related to maintenance of social status, those concerned with educational adjustment, those concerned with vocational selection, those related to problems of sex, and those that offer a threat to existence.[12]

In the "fear" diaries referred to on pages 122–124, the situation that precipitated the reaction in 40 per cent of the cases was the likelihood of failure (or of a low mark) in schoolwork, the prospect of a loss of status in 31 per cent, the possibility of illness or accident in 17 per cent, and the

---

Factors Annoying to Children," *Journal of Applied Psychology,* 29:75–82, 1945; J. B. Winker, "Age Trends and Sex Differences in the Wishes, Identifications, Activities, and Fears of Children," *Child Development,* 20:191–200, 1949.

[11] R. Lunger and J. D. Page, "The Worries of College Freshmen," *Pedagogical Seminary and Journal of Genetic Psychology,* 54:457–460, 1939; A. F. Bronner, "Adolescent Anxieties," *Child Development,* 13:206–208, 1936; C. J. Marsh, "Worries of College Women," *Journal of Social Psychology,* 15:335–339, 1942; A. H. Martin, "A Worry Inventory," *Journal of Applied Psychology,* 29:68–74, 1945.

[12] Bronner, "Adolescent Anxieties," *loc. cit.*

probability of conflict with the family in 6 per cent. Perhaps some worry about schoolwork is inevitable, but the above figures seem a little high.

Some fears that develop during childhood and adolescence disappear by the time an individual becomes an adult, although a few linger on to the brink of the grave, and a small number of highly acute anxieties arise to take their places. These are connected primarily with one's job or family, and to a lesser extent with one's own physical and mental health. There is also increasing anxiety concerning old age, especially if, as senescence approaches, it becomes evident that there may not be enough money for self-support.

Fears are created by the physical and social world as it exists. Certain typical adult worries could be greatly reduced if not eliminated by a different organization of society that would provide for more even distribution of wealth, a lessening of class consciousness, a relief from prejudice, a better guarantee of steady work, and a greater security against a destitute old age. The universality of such fears is shown by the readiness with which people accept any government that they hope will relieve them of these anxieties. Man is well on his way to conquering the physical forces in the world, but it remains to be seen whether or not he can control those that are social or emotional.

The reactions to fear are not varied. The main behavior is a rigidity of the entire body and an intense pallor. The running-away behavior is usually secondary to the immobility. The reactions shown by persons of all ages are in large measure variations, more or less subtle, upon these two central patterns. The baby grows rigid and pale; he is helpless to do anything else. Small children often run away, preferably toward a protector. As children grow older and their intellectual abilities mature, they discover that the mores do not approve of cowardice, so they learn to do their running away before the stimulus appears; that is, they learn to avoid situations that may cause anxiety. Thus the pupil who is afraid to address the class in his oral English work develops a spurious toothache on the day he expects his turn to come. He is running away just as clearly as if he had fled from the classroom, only in a less conspicuous manner. The adult who is afraid has usually better control than the child or adolescent, but a protracted strain will break him down to the childish levels of rigidity, crying, and running away. Thus many a man collapses from anxiety while his young wife is enduring a twenty-four-hour labor at the birth of their first child. Fear reactions are rarely converted into secondary forms, as anger responses are. They are controlled better as a person grows older, and they are avoided whenever possible; but they are always lurking behind the individual's defenses, presumably because of their close relation to the most fundamental of all needs—the need to stay alive.

Specific fears show a development with age. Some wax and some wane. Figure 53 on page 129 shows the responses toward a few specific fears by boys and girls from the sixth grade through the senior year of college. In general, fears of things or of controllable or unlikely circumstances tend to become less, while fears of failure and of inadequacy tend to increase. Thus, the fear of being kidnaped disappears among boys, partly because they grow big enough to defend themselves and partly because they sense its improbability. Among girls this fear persists longer, presumably because of reports in the papers of incidents that involve the kidnaping of girls for sexual purposes. Fear of fire also becomes markedly less with age.

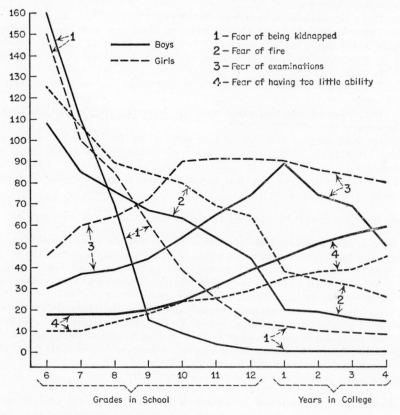

Fig. 53. *Specific Fears at Different Ages*

Based on detailed data in the Ph.D. thesis of O. R. Chambers, Ohio State University, 1930.

The typical scholastic fear of examinations is already present in the sixth grade, and mounts steadily through the freshman year of college; thereafter it decreases, perhaps because it has already eliminated those who are most fearful, and the survivors are sufficiently toughened to resist it. Worries about having enough ability and about possible failure increase with age.

Recent wars have demonstrated the universality of fear. Even young, healthy, vigorous men who in civilian life would have been ashamed to admit their fright spoke simply and honestly to one another of their panic. Modern warfare is so frightful that the human spirit cannot find in it enough uplift to cover the agonizing fear that gripped every man sometimes and some men frequently. In order to keep normal men as free as possible from panic, the Army during World War II emphasized the treatment of fear as one topic in its indoctrination. The principles set forth boiled down to a number of simple rules that are as useful in peace as in war:

1. Learn to recognize the early symptoms of fear, so that you know when you are becoming frightened.
2. Don't be ashamed of your fear. Better men than you have known it.
3. Think objectively about the situations in which you may become frightened and plan in advance what you can do. If you have work to do, keep your mind on it; if the time must be spent in waiting, decide what you will do or think about to fill the time.
4. Talk to your friends sometimes about your anxieties. Don't try to keep your fears a secret.
5. Remember always that other men are depending on you. If you blow up, they're sunk.
6. Have all the fun you can, as long as you can, up to the last split second. Nothing keeps panic away from you and your buddies as successfully as a sense of humor.
7. Although you admit your fear to your intimates, try not to show it publicly, because it is so contagious.[13]

These rules may well be applied to situations in ordinary civilian life.

Suppose, for instance, that you are a thirty-year-old woman with two small children and that you are desperately afraid of thunderstorms. You talk the situation over with your husband, instead of trying to suppress it; you ask him to help you, if he is at home when a storm comes, and you plan activities to keep yourself busy. One afternoon the thunder begins to roll and the lightning to crackle, but you are prepared. You set about making a complicated cake—the chore decided upon in advance—that requires your full attention. You carefully suppress the evidences of your fear because you do not want to pass this agony on to your children. Your husband does his bit by telling funny stories, exchanging banter with you, lighting your cigarettes, distracting the children's attention at critical moments—and suddenly the storm is over, and you have been only mildly alarmed.

Fears have a tendency to entrench themselves firmly and to spread over an individual's entire life, distorting and circumscribing it, as in the story below:

Dorcus was a girl of eighteen who had been sick during much of her childhood. She had not been able to go to school although she sometimes played quiet games with other children after school hours or on rainy Saturdays. In the course of her first fifteen years of life Dorcus had to have several operations, for all of which she was given ether. With each successive operation it became harder and harder for her to take the anesthetic, and on the last occasion she had to be held down on the table by main force. As long as Dorcus continued to live quietly at home there seemed to be no aftereffects of the trauma she suffered at each operation. Soon after her entrance to high school, however, she began to show some odd reactions. She would not take the subway from her home to the school—the quickest means of

---

[13] Condensed and adapted from J. Dollard, *Victory over Fear*, Yale University Press, 1944, 64 pp.

transportation; she would not ride in the school elevators; she would not use the locker assigned to her; and she fought frantically against any hand put upon her either during her physical examination or in games. Her fear of being compelled into a situation in which she might be hurt was so intense that she shook off, in obvious terror, even such slight contacts as a guiding touch on her arm, and her claustrophobia was so intense that she could not bear to put even inanimate objects such as books and papers into a locker where they would be unable to get out. Elevators and subways raised the claustrophobia to an unbearable pitch. After a short time in high school, Dorcus was sent to the school psychologist, who was not long in discovering the connection between the girl's history of operations and her fear. Dorcus explained readily that when she went under ether she had always dreamed that she was in a coffin and buried alive. She had always awakened in panic which presently transferred itself to the moment at which the dream began as she went under ether, and caused her to fight madly from the first whiff until she was completely unconscious. Her revolt against physical restraint was, of course, a reaction to a stimulus that recurred, although in greatly attenuated form, whenever the slightest force was used to push her into a course of action, or whenever she found herself in a small, enclosed space. This girl's fear was hard to cure because it had a basis in a series of severe and repeated emotional shocks. Dorcus eventually made a fair recovery, largely because she was a very intelligent girl and was able to develop a good understanding of the situation. She has learned to ride in subway trains and elevators without more than an occasional qualm, and she can even go through tunnels under rivers, although she still has to grit her teeth to remain quiet. Two or three rather torrid love affairs have taught her to like being touched. Once in a while, in the office of a dentist or doctor, she still shows a tendency to hysteria if the nurse tries to hold her hands or to restrain her in any way while the doctor is giving her a treatment, but the outbursts are relatively rare and are not nearly as severe as they were earlier. This girl's history is instructive in showing how a fear can condition an individual's entire adjustment to society. Dorcus was rapidly becoming an outcast among her age-mates because of her peculiarities, which seemed to them to be merely silly. If she had not been helped she could easily have become the most unpopular girl in the school.

Fear is destructive. Its only value is to prevent one from doing something that is dangerous or unwise. It is therefore useful for survival in moments of actual physical danger under primitive conditions. In a modern environment, however, the reactions may lead to unnecessary injury or death, as in a theater fire when the running-away response may be the only cause of fatalities. In general, worry only interferes with accomplishment and leads to maladjustment. The conquest of unnecessary fear has become an important problem of mental hygiene.

3. Emotions Leading to Joyous Behavior: The third of the fundamental emotions is love. As in the case of both fear and anger, there is a definite development from infancy to adulthood in the stimuli which cause this emotion. It is probable that the bodily background also changes with age, since children are undeveloped sexually and since individuals beyond middle age have more or less lost their sexual vigor. Because of the physiological changes at puberty, the bodily turmoil into which love precipitates the adolescent is both profound and unexpected. He has already experienced the emotion which in childhood passes for love, but he has not had the same internal adjustment as now becomes possible. Whereas a small child may be just as angry as an adolescent, he is not normally in love in just the same way.

In the Freudian literature one finds much concerning the development of erotic interest, with special emphasis upon the importance of the earliest stages of growth. Five more or less distinct stages are recognized: the oral, the anal, the Oedipal, the latent, and the genital. The earliest period continues from birth till the time the child stops nursing. It is a period of dependence, during which the satisfaction of all the baby's needs comes from his mother. When she nurses or fondles him, he reacts by laughing and crowing. Since hunger is his chief driving force, nursing is his chief joy, and his mouth is the chief area through which pleasure comes—hence the name of this stage. During the second and third years of life, the child is being trained to use the toilet, and his erotic interests become attached to these activities. Most children get pleasure from their eliminative processes and show a desire to play with the products. This anal stage is of relatively short duration. During both of the two earliest periods the child's interest is focused on himself. Between, roughly, the ages of four and six, he passes through the Oedipal state. The name is derived from a Greek myth of a boy who unknowingly killed his father and married his mother. During this period the little girl "falls in love" with her father and becomes hostile toward her mother, and the little boy "falls in love" with his mother and becomes jealous of his father. The resulting Oedipus complex is normally resolved before or soon after the entrance to school, partly by the interest in age-mates and partly by association with a greater number of adults. The child who has emerged from these three lowest levels now enters a period of latency during which his love life is quiescent and he is concerned chiefly with working out a satisfactory relationship with his peers and with gaining control over his immediate environment and over himself. With adolescence the genital stage begins.[14]

It should be pointed out that thus far there is relatively little objective proof of the above theory of development. For instance, breast-fed babies, who should derive more satisfaction than bottle-fed babies, do not seem to be any better adjusted in later life than the latter.[15] Premature or delayed toilet training has not been shown to have a measurable effect upon subsequent personality. All one can say at the present time is that the existence of these levels, as based upon observations, may be taken for granted, but that their significance cannot be; nor can one assume that they form a *proven* series of the expression taken by an underlying sexual drive. The concept has, however, been of value in clinical work and in understanding certain intergroup relationships. It has also permeated modern thought and speech. To date, however, no one can offer objective proof of its accuracy, and perhaps such proof will never be possible, even though the theory be entirely correct. In any case, one should know what the Freudian ideas in this respect are and should use the concepts whenever they seem to shed light upon human problems.

---

[14] F. B. Strain, *The Normal Sex Interests of Children*, Appleton-Century-Crofts, Inc., 1948, 210 pp.

[15] H. Orlansky, "Infant Care and Personality," *Psychological Bulletin*, 46:1–48, 1949.

In psychological literature the person or thing that inspires the emotion of love has been termed the "love-object." The love-objects that are most powerful in arousing the emotion vary with age, just as the situations arousing either fear or anger also vary. The first love-object for babies of either sex is undoubtedly the mother, or the person who looks after them. The mother usually remains the exclusive love-object during the first year of life. Later on, she may be displaced by the father or she and the father may be about equally potent in arousing the child's affections. A mother is not usually displaced in the affection of her sons although she is quite often superseded by the father in the affection of her daughter. The reason for this situation appears to be partly that many women are actually more attached to their sons than to their daughters and partly that many men are unwilling to display their affection toward their sons for fear the boys will become sissies. By the time a boy is perhaps two years old the average man is unwilling to fondle or kiss him or otherwise display a love which may be quite as deep as that which he feels toward his daughter. However, there are no social inhibitions operating against his caressing his little daughter as much as he wants to. Consequently, girls in the second or third years of life often transfer their deepest love to their fathers, whereas boys are less likely to do so. In any case, throughout the child's early years of life, the parents, or older persons functioning as parents, remain the chief objects able to bring about the emotion of love. As soon as the child goes to school, a particular teacher may displace one or both of the parents, but the teacher belongs in the same category as an adult and is not therefore a new type of love-object—though she may arouse the jealousy and antagonism of the parents.

A person of approximately the same age as one's parents is thus an infantile type of love-object. Some children, however, are allowed or even encouraged to continue fixations on parents, older friends, or teachers. If this situation persists into the years of adolescence the child is far too dependent upon older people for his emotional satisfaction, and he is usually abnormally attached to his own home. If the situation goes on into adult life, it becomes truly serious, because the individual falls in love with people much too old. A young man of twenty-five is rarely happy for long with a woman of forty-five; nor is a young woman likely to remain in love with a man who is a great many years her senior. Middle age and youth are approximately adjusted as parent and child or as teacher and pupil, but not as husband and wife. Dependence for emotional satisfaction upon older generations is a symptom of persistent infantilism.

This fixation upon adults, often adults of the opposite sex, continues normally through the early years of childhood—that is, till about the sixth or seventh year. From this time, for a few years, children are usually more deeply attached to some other child of their own age and sex than to anyone else. Parents sometimes resent this situation and try to discourage the attachments. This second period of development, in which the love-object is another person of the same sex and approximately the same age (sometimes a little older) has been referred to as the "homosexual" stage. It is the same as the Freudian "latent" stage. These childish attachments are

INFANCY—BABYHOOD
Boy and girl interested only in themselves
•
EARLY CHILDHOOD
Seek companionship of other children regardless of sex
•
ABOUT AGE EIGHT
Boys prefer to play with boys, girls with girls
•
AGES 10 to 12
Antagonism shown between sex groups
•
AGES 13 to 14
Girls become interested in boys, try to attract their attention; boys aloof
•
AGES 14 to 16
Boy group also shows interest in girls; some individuals begin to pair off
•
AGES 16 to 17, ON
"Going out in couples" becomes general

Fig. 54. *The Seven Stages of Boy-and-Girl Relationships*

From *Women and Men*, p. 133, copyright, 1943, 1944, by Amram Scheinfeld. Reproduced by permission of Harcourt, Brace and Company, Inc.

perfectly normal and are a necessary step in the gradual emancipation of a child from the emotional ties which bind him to his home. The period of devotion of boys to boys and girls to girls continues, usually becoming more intense, up to the years of adolescence. The attachments are so strong that boys and girls eleven or twelve years of age will have nothing more to do with each other than is absolutely necessary.

The various stages in the relationships of boys and girls are pictured in Figure 54 on page 134. Little children of both sexes play happily together. In middle childhood the activities become different, and a tendency to separation of the sexes appears. In the preadolescent years the separation not only increases but is characterized by dislike of members of each sex for members of the other. Because girls mature earlier, there is a period during which they are interested in boys, who, however, are still hostile to them. In early adolescence the interest become mutual, but for a year or two boys and girls tend to go about in small groups, the adjustments apparently being easier under such circumstances than in isolated pairs. Sometime during middle or late adolescence the "pairing-off" stage appears.

There is evidence that homosexual interests continue, especially in girls, for a long time. The attitude may be shown only by excessive affection for girl friends, but often it appears as a "crush"—that is, an intense devotion to an older woman. Most women teachers in high school have to contend, at one time or another, with a crush. The type of girl who develops a crush is usually a somewhat isolated individual who has had only superficial ties with her feminine age-mates and very little contact with boys. She may be afraid of boys, or quite indifferent to them, or friendly with them in an objective way, but for one reason or another they have never aroused her affections. Or it may be that she has never aroused theirs. Such a girl has to fixate her affections upon someone, and since her normal development is temporarily blocked, she reverts to an infantile pattern and attaches herself to an adult, continuing, however, the interest in her own sex that has occupied her during the later years of childhood. If a somewhat isolated girl has a quick mind and a real enthusiasm for her work, she is likely to be dreadfully bored by other girls and attracted to her teachers because their conversation seems to her worth listening to. Moreover, her superior work in class attracts her teachers to her. Most of these attachments are of relatively short duration, while they help to tide a girl over a crisis.

A number of situations tend to condition a girl in such a way as to make an attachment to an older woman seem to her a natural solution to her difficulties. A few of the more common conditioning situations are listed below:

A. RELATIONSHIP TO MOTHER
  1. Recent loss of her mother
  2. First absence from a home in which the mother has been the central figure
  3. Rejection by mother, coupled with envy of the relationship of other girls to their mothers
  4. Absence of mother from home, through divorce or death, with the result that the girl has never before known affection from an older woman

B. RELATIONSHIP TO AGE-MATES
  5. Nonacceptance by other girls

C. RELATIONSHIP TO BOYS

6. Lack of opportunity to make normal contacts with boys and rejection by such boys as are available
7. Fear of boys and men
8. Any recent unpleasant experience with boys, especially if it has been disillusioning
9. Image of an ideal man of so godlike a character that all living boys and men seem not worth bothering about

Perhaps no one of these background factors is potent enough to push an adolescent girl into developing crushes, but a combination of them is likely to do so.

The homosexual type of love-object, regardless of comparative ages, is obviously not desirable as a permanent stimulus. In some instances, however, an individual remains in this stage of development and becomes permanently attached to other members of his or her own sex. Usually such adults are considered definitely beyond the pale and may be quite ostracized. If the public would stop regarding childish attachments as "abnormal" and would look upon them rather as a sign of immaturity, a great deal of despair could be eliminated.

During adolescence a third stage usually emerges, in which the love-object is another individual of approximately the same age but of the opposite sex. For the majority of individuals this adult and socially approved type of love-object completely takes the place of the two previous types as far as the deepest emotions are concerned. Naturally, girls still love their mothers and fathers, and they still love their girl friends and teachers, but their deepest emotions are centered upon boys as love-objects rather than upon either parents or friends. Usually the transfer from friends of one's own sex to members of the opposite sex is easy and natural. All that seems to be needed for normally adjusted youngsters is the presence in the environment of a large number of possible love-objects. If a girl goes to a high school in which five hundred boys are enrolled, she is presented with five hundred potential love-objects, among which she will discover at least a dozen suited to her particular personality. All she needs is enough boys to choose from. Similarly, all a boy normally needs to distract his emotion from friends of his own sex is a sufficient assortment of girls.

As the transfer is being made, boys and girls present types of behavior that are rather baffling to adults. The boys hector and tease the girls, hide their books, catcall to them, and hang about on street corners waiting for them to pass. One has to remember that throughout childhood boys who are chums constantly pummel and shout names at each other; physical or verbal attack is a boy's commonest expression of affection. It takes some lads quite a while to discover that this familiar mode of behavior, even in its mildest forms, will not do for expressing their interest in girls. On occasion the boys, being young and having little judgment, may go too far, but as long as their behavior is within bounds it should not be punished, and, if reproved, only on the basis of bad manners, not bad intentions. Girls are quite capable of preventing most excesses themselves, and they are well aware that they have often deliberately precipitated a boy's reactions. The girl whose books are snatched, whose hair is pulled, or whose appearance is greeted by catcalls is convinced of her popularity. These early hetero-sexual manifestations are very trying to adults, but they seem satisfactory to the participants.

An excellent summary is given below of the typical behavior of both boys and girls during the period of transition. Especially to be noted is the relation between the behavior shown and a pupil's sense of security within his group. As already mentioned in other connections, girls mature emo- tionally and socially at an earlier age than boys.

As for their interest in the opposite sex, the girls were at first not particular whose attention they attracted. Any susceptible boy in the group might become a temporary target. As they grew older they became more and more discriminating and also more disdainful of boys of their own chronological age. The boys were thus often inducted into the social life of the girls before they were ready for it and were then dropped suddenly from it as the girls found more mature boy friends. Some-times they were successful in resisting the attentions of the girls, later becoming themselves interested in younger girls. When left to their own devices, the boys frequently first became interested in rather boyish girls and girls who were kindly and tolerant of their rather awkward social techniques. The transition to the more demanding and sophisticated "feminine" type sometimes occurred rapidly. There were some girls in the group who were regularly turned to by boys just venturing upon social contact with the opposite sex. At this period, parties and appearance were the chief subjects of conversation among the girls. The boys, although usually older when they showed this interest, showed it just as intensely. They did not go in couples to parties at first, though the effort was always made to have an equal number of boys and girls. Later, a few of the more mature would go in couples, the others going in groups of boys or girls and sometimes mixing to go home after the party. As they grew older, it was not acceptable to go to a party (now a "dance") except in couples. At the "dance" there would be almost no interchange of partners unless couples had gone as a foursome. At that period social security was gained by "going steady" so that it was the thing to do to stick to the same companion not only all evening but for a period ranging from a week to several years.[16]

Toward the end of adolescence or early in adult life there should be a narrowing of the field to one person of the opposite sex and of approximately the same age. Out of possible love-stimuli the young man or woman should select one as a permanent mate. The man about town and the career girl who continue for years to "play the field" have not taken this last step. Their frequent change of love-object classes them not as sophisticates but as sixteen-year-olds.

The relatively few people who do not succeed in becoming attached to an adult love-object are those who are prevented either by environment or

16 J. Chaffey in H. Meek, *The Personal-Social Development of Boys and Girls, with Implications for Secondary Education,* Progressive Education Association, 1940, p. 614. Used by permission of the author and the Association.

by their own nature from making the necessary social contacts. In this case development is usually only retarded, but it may be permanently blocked. There are also a few people whose development is retarded or warped because of personal traits that prevent normal social relationships. They may be too shy or too easily embarrassed to make the necessary social contacts with members of the opposite sex. They may be homely or have an actual deformity—or something they regard as a deformity—and so feel themselves unattractive, and are unwilling to make an effort at heterosexual adjustment. Other causes may be found in the life history of those who cannot react to adult stimuli. Sometimes girls develop early in childhood such strong feelings of rivalry with and jealousy toward boys and men that they cannot ever fall in love with them. They remain competitors with men all their lives. Other girls have experienced some profound shock concerning sexual matters and are too inhibited by fear to react normally to men. Boys sometimes have such a deep mother-fixation that they are not emotionally free to fall in love until after the mother dies—and perhaps not then. Other boys are afraid of girls—for any number of reasons—and are too suspicious to love any of them. Two cases whose histories are adequately known to the writer illustrate certain of these background conditions.

Many of Phil's acquaintances have wondered why he did not marry. He is a most personable and pleasant man who has many women friends, but he never seems to fall in love with any of them. He shows no signs whatever of homosexual interests. Phil's mother died when he was a boy, and he and his father lived together until the father died when Phil was twenty-one. Since then he has been in some college, either as a student or as a teacher. At present he is a professor in a state university, where he has plenty of chances to meet all kinds of girls and women. In fact, he is with women a good deal, but he does not want more than companionship from them.

The fundamental trouble is that Phil idealizes the type of woman that he might marry, but at the same time he visits prostitutes whenever he needs to. These two attitudes simply will not fuse. The idealistic attitude came in part from hearing his father talk in reverent terms of the dead mother, in part from reading much romantic literature—his father had few examples of modern realism in his library— and in part from sheer ignorance of girls during his adolescent years. When he was about thirteen he began to admire girls, especially one damsel of fifteen whom he saw in church. For nearly two years the high spot of the week was Sunday morning when he could sit in church and watch her for nearly two hours, but he never spoke to her. This sort of worship from afar is a more or less continuous performance with him, and he still does not care about meeting his idols more than casually. In the later years of adolescence he began to visit prostitutes. As a matter of convenience to himself, he visits the same one at intervals for years, and pays her for services rendered with no more emotion than he would pay a laundress for ironing his shirts. His sex life and his friendships with women are completely separate. Women graduate students and teachers find Phil a charming companion with whom they feel safe—as they certainly are. He would never insult them by attempting the slightest physical intimacy. He has often passed through the preliminary courting stages of interest and friendship, but he does not get any farther. He has learned, to his sorrow, that unattached women sometimes fall in love with him, so he usually restricts his friendships to women who are already firmly attached to some other man. He keeps many faculty wives harmlessly thrilled by his attentions, and he squires other men's fiancées whenever the men happen to be out of town. He loves women, but he will probably never be in love with any one woman, because his sexual drives are to him so shameful and degrading that he could never center them upon the idealized woman of his dreams.

Ernestine is now a woman of forty. She is still unmarried and likely to remain so. Ernestine was the child of unusually tall parents, and she began early to tower over other girls of her own age and to be rejected by them because she was too rough. As a result of her size and of her rejection she turned to the company of boys. She was a good deal bigger than most of them, but they admired strength, size, and agility, all of which she possessed in abundance. During her preadolescent years she was the idol of almost every small boy in the neighborhood because of her prowess in games and sports. As the boys became adolescent, they overtook her in strength and some of them in size, but none of them in athletic skill. In high school she played on the school baseball and basketball teams. The male members had to accept some razzing from opponents, but they liked Ernestine and defended her. In her uniform she looked so like a boy and she acted so like one that even her opponents soon forgot about her sex and accepted her. Throughout high school and college Ernestine continued to be with boys most of the time. She studied with them, went to shows with them, swam, rode, and hunted with them.

At present Ernestine is a buyer for a large department store. She sometimes buys coats and sport clothes for women but most of her work is with men's clothes, and she is extraordinarily successful. Almost all her friends are men. When social or business engagements require contact with girls or women Ernestine is amiable enough, and they seem to accept her as an odd fish though harmless, but as a general thing she simply forgets their existence. Since most of her men friends are married she sees them only at lunchtime or at parties; they all are fond of her. Two or three years ago she took the Terman masculine-feminine test and scored at the 95th percentile for men; that is, only 5 per cent of men expressed attitudes more characteristically masculine than hers.

Ernestine has never shown the slightest emotional interest in any girl or woman, and she has repulsed vigorously any effort on the part of homosexual women to attach themselves to her. A few men have been attracted by her fine physique, but she does not respond to their advances, and as they know her better they change from would-be lovers into good friends. Ernestine seems satisfied with both her professional and her private life. It is an interesting commentary upon her emotional change of sex that she does not arouse jealousy in the wives of her male friends. In all except physiological details Ernestine is a man, but because she has a woman's body there is no clear path for her to follow in reaching sexual maturity. She might, however, marry an effeminate man.

The normal development shown by stimuli giving rise to the emotion of love may be summarized as follows: The first love-objects are adults of the same or opposite sex; the second love-objects are normally persons of about the same age and the same sex; and the third are persons of about the same age and the opposite sex. During the years of infancy and early childhood, when the child's chief need is for care and security, he loves most those who give him these elements. When he begins to strike out for himself, he loves most those people who best recognize him as an individual —his friends, who incidentally serve to break his early bonds with his home. Finally, he reacts to a type of love-object which, sooner or later, will lead to marriage and will permanently end his infantile attachment to his parents.

III. Objective Measures of Emotional Maturity

Within the past three decades, investigators have been working on tests for measuring emotional attitudes and emotional maturity. The results are expressed in terms of "emotional age," a concept exactly paralleling that of "mental age." Thus a fifteen-year-old girl with an emotional age of twelve shows the emotional reactions expected of twelve-year-olds; she has a retardation of three years, and an "emotional quotient" of 80.[17]

The tests used to determine emotional age consist actually of the measurement of attitudes, opinions, and interests. One such scale contains four subtests which investigate what a pupil thinks is wrong, what he worries about, what he is interested in, and what traits he admires. Children think many actions to be wrong, they are afraid of many things, they have wide interests, and they admire a large assortment of traits. Adults are far more lenient in their judgment of right and wrong, they have lost many of their fears, they have fewer interests, and they admire only a limited number of human characteristics. The scores for this test are therefore high for children and low for adults.

Another test covers mainly interest in material objects, in careers, in ownership of various articles, in activities, and so on. Items of this sort reflect maturity because interests of all kinds change with age. The little boy wants a toy wagon to play with, he wants to be a cowboy or a bandit or a G–man when he grows up, and his favorite activity is "just running." As he grows older his interests change; at sixteen his most urgent wish is for a tuxedo, and he hopes to become a member of a jazz orchestra.

Results from the two tests just described appear in Figure 55 on page 141. In one case the curves descend and in the other they ascend, but this difference is due to the technique of test construction and is of no importance. In both cases, the girls show a slightly greater degree of maturity than boys; in (a) of the diagram their scores are lower, and in (b) they are higher. In Figure 56 on page 142 are four sample curves based on single items from the first of the tests, results of which were given in the previous figure. Even on single items the girls tend to mature in their opinions earlier than the boys—the one exception being "bribery," which is a predominantly masculine form of sinfulness. Most children thought smoking to be wrong; emancipation from this attitude comes earlier for boys but is more complete for girls, most of whom are not inhibited in their own smoking by the desire to be athletes. The idea that card playing is wrong follows a similar but more gradual course. In the meantime, the idea that conceit is not only tiresome but wrong has been growing. So also has the notion that bribery is a sin; the curve for boys is still rising at the end of the last year of measurement, although the girls show an increasing lack of concern in this matter with age.[18]

---

[17] See pp. 483–488.

[18] A second, but less extensive, investigation made twenty years after the one upon which the above figures were based showed the expected change toward more lenient

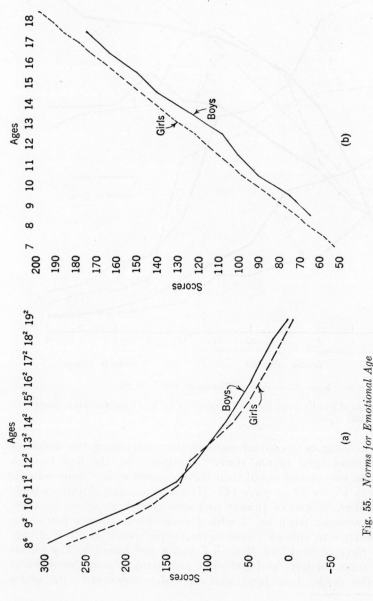

Fig. 55. *Norms for Emotional Age*

(a) Based upon S. L. Pressey and L. C. Pressey, "Development of the Interest-Attitude Tests," *Journal of Applied Psychology*, 17:1–16, 1933.

(b) Based upon P. H. Furfey, "A Revised Scale for Measuring Developmental Age in Boys," *Child Development Monographs*, Vol. II, No. 2, 1931; and Sister Celestine Sullivan, "A Scale for Measuring Developmental Age in Girls," *Studies in Psychology and Psychiatry*, Catholic University, Vol. III, No. 4, 1934, 65 pp.

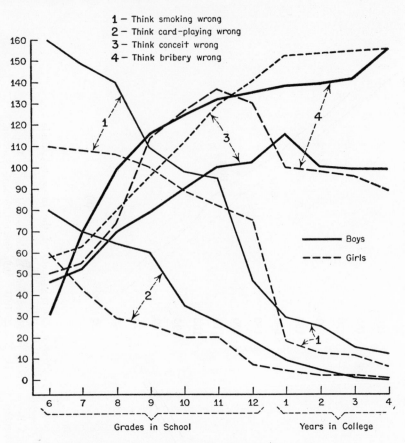

Fig. 56. *Specific Things Regarded as Wrong at Different Ages*

Based on detailed results from the Ph.D. thesis of O. R. Chambers, Ohio State University, 1930.

One may investigate emotional maturity by determining the wishes of children of different ages. In one study[19] children from the first through the twelfth grade were asked to tell their three deepest wishes. Some sample results appear in Figure 57 on page 143. Most of the small children wished for material things. Wishes of juniors and seniors in high school centered upon self-improvement (such as "I wish I could learn algebra better" or "I wish I could go to college") and upon people (such as "I wish my mother didn't have to work" or "I wish I had a girl friend"). The trends are much the same for boys and girls, but girls tend to show increases or decreases a little earlier than boys, and on wishes concerned with sports

standards with the passage of time. Somewhat fewer children thought smoking wrong, and girls reached an emancipated stage somewhat earlier. (See S. L. Pressey, "Changes from 1923 to 1943 in the Attitudes of Public School Children," *Journal of Psychology*, 21:173–188, 1946.)

[19] A. T. Jersild and R. J. Tasch, *Children's Interests and What They Suggest for Education*, Columbia University Press, 1949, 173 pp.

the two sexes differ a good deal. It is clear from this sampling that a developmental scale could be made on the basis of what children wished for most passionately.

The measurement of emotional maturity gives a clue to the behavior of sundry social misfits. Certain delinquents, for instance, are found to have relatively high mental ages, but low emotional ages. The intractable children in school, who precipitate a goodly proportion of the situations requiring discipline, are also characterized by retarded emotional development. The "problem" employee in industry and the "problem" professor in college have also been shown to have the interests, drives, attitudes, and reactions

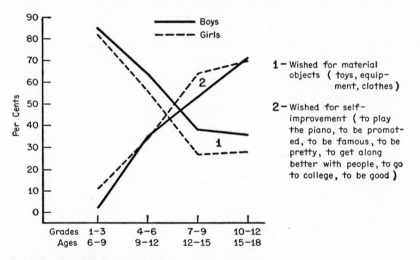

Fig. 57. *The Wishes of Children and Adolescents*

Based on A. T. Jersild and R. J. Tasch, *Children's Interests and What They Suggest for Education,* Columbia University Press, 1949, pp. 108, 116.

of children or adolescents, and therefore to be unemployable in work demanding adult behavior. The Army and Navy were not long in discovering that measurements of emotional age were useful in indicating men who would have difficulty in adjusting themselves to military life. Of all the conditions that prevented men from becoming soldiers, mere childishness, in one form or another, was the commonest. Some of the men could be educated into maturity quickly but others could not.

Measures of emotional age are now being used widely to supplement results with tests of intelligence. Thirty years ago bright children were accelerated in school as far as their intelligence permitted, without respect to their social or emotional competence. The results of rapid advancement on the basis of ability alone are shown in the study below:

Oscar is at present a college professor of great erudition. He has a fine mind and has become fairly well adjusted to life during the last two decades, although a few oddities still cling to him.

When the writer first knew him, he was nine years old and in the eighth grade. The work there was far too easy for him, and his father wanted him to enter high school. The principal refused to accept him because of his youth. The father then asked to have "one of these new mental tests" given to his son, as a means of showing that the boy was quite capable of doing work in high school. The writer was called in to give the Binet test. Oscar's IQ, on the basis of several testings, varied from 173 to 191, giving him a mental age between 16 years 4 months and 17 years 3 months. Oscar was tall and heavy for his age, but he was 7 inches shorter and 40 pounds lighter than the average sophomore in high school, where his mental age would place him. His social adjustment to the group he was already in was poor, and there seemed no likelihood that it would improve any by being advanced among adolescents. The high school principal continued in his refusal to accept Oscar, in spite of the demonstrably high IQ, so the father removed his son from school and sent him to a private tutor. This move put an end to such tenuous social contacts as Oscar had with his public school mates, and he became a complete isolate. Even when he tried to play with other children, he was usually rejected, except by those well below his own chronological age, among whom he functioned as a kind and resourceful adult mind in a child's body. Oscar spent 90 per cent of his waking time studying Latin, Greek, geometry, and algebra and the remaining 10 per cent in being a supernursemaid to a group of five- to seven-year-old children.

Oscar was ready to enter college when he was twelve years old, but he was not accepted for another three years, during which he acquired a reading knowledge of French and German, a fair mastery of world history, and a working knowledge of archaeology. In due course he entered college, completed the requirements in two and a half years, and graduated at eighteen. Again he had to wait before he could continue his education, because the graduate school would not accept him until he was twenty. He spent the two years in Egypt as an unpaid young assistant of an archaeological party. He had collected the material for his Ph.D. thesis and had finished a first draft of his thesis before he was allowed to enter the graduate school. He received his Ph.D. when he was twenty-two. Since then he has become an outstanding classical archaeologist, but he has never been popular with either his co-workers or his students. Oscar retained his childishness well into middle age, but he has finally shown signs of social and emotional maturity in recent years. When he was nearing fifty, he had a sort of "nervous breakdown" accompanied by a profound melancholia. He voluntarily entered a rest home for the summer. While there, he was looked after by a pleasant, even-tempered, competent woman of about his own age. She made him so comfortable and gave him such a sense of security that he married her. She had been an orphan and had had such a hard time in life that the prospect of looking after only one wealthy and pliable man instead of a succession of complaining patients seemed like heaven to her. She is an uneducated but basically intelligent woman, who is glad to care for Oscar in return for security, present and future. She has no idea what his erudiate monologues are about, but she listens pleasantly, says "Yes" or "No" or "Well, now!" at intervals, and darns socks or hems towels "so as not to waste the evening." For Oscar she is ideal. Her commonplaceness has provided just the rock he needed for emotional security.

Oscar is not yet and probably never will be a normal individual, but he is gradually mastering the simple social skills that he should have acquired as an adolescent. He is beginning to see dimly what other people are like. His more advanced students and he are meeting together in class with understanding and even a mild feeling of affection. Among his colleagues Oscar has lost most of his earlier habits of alternately pushing himself into and dominating conversation and of retiring into a silent isolation. His overcompensatory behavior was both aggressive and unpleasant and it had often brought him ridicule and overt rejection, but at least it resulted in human contacts, whereas his alternate behavior gave him safety at the cost of isolation. This brilliant mind is gradually emerging from the maladjustment of an improper education.

If this boy's emotional age had been measured and taken into consideration, he would presumably not have been so drastically accelerated. At present the approved procedure is to measure a child physically, mentally, socially, and emotionally, and then to consider all these factors in determining his grade placement.

IV. Frustration, Tension, Conflict, Adjustment, and Escape

1. The Nature of Conflict: Everyone experiences frustration at times, and everyone develops, sooner or later, one or more types of reaction that make the frustration easier to bear. What is commonly known as "adjustment" is primarily a reaction to frustration, by means of which an individual tries to avoid or dissipate unpleasantness, so that he can live with his difficulties without wearing himself out in useless emotional turmoil.

Frustration is the feeling of helplessness, disappointment, inadequacy, and anxiety that is produced by the blocking of any drive. This complex feeling, plus the consciousness of uncertainty as to what one should do next, produces a general tightening of the whole body, generally referred to as "tension." Thus, the blocking of a drive leads to frustration, which leads to tension, which leads to reaction and adjustment. This series of phenomena unfolds itself thousands of times in everyone's life. It works almost, if not quite, automatically. It is the human safety valve, by means of which self-destroying emotions may be discharged, for the most part rather harmlessly.

The trigger that sets off the series is the thwarting of a drive which has its roots in a basic human need. The blocking may be due to any number of causes or any combination of them. For instance, an adolescent boy who feels a need for friendship with girls may be blocked because he is in a boys' boarding school where he has few chances to meet girls, or he may be thwarted at home by the presence of a possessive mother who effectively keeps girls away from him and him away from them. Such conditions act as external privations over which he has little control. Or, his desire may be blocked by internal difficulties, such as fear of appearing ridiculous, a feeling of shyness, or a certainty that he would be unable to talk to a girl. Some such internal blocks are only temporary, and some are entirely imaginary, but others are likely to be permanent, such as self-consciousness because one is crippled or homely or from the wrong side of the tracks. In still other instances, a drive is thwarted because it is not as strong as some competing drive. The boy who wants more girl friends may also want to become both the high school football hero of the year, and, ultimately, a famous surgeon. As a result he has to spend many hours practicing and studying and has no time for social life. His first urge is blocked, therefore, by his own competing desires. Sometimes an individual even has two directly opposing urges at the same time—such as a desire to learn and a desire to throw a given textbook in the wastebasket, or an urge to go on campaigning for a certain office and a strong desire to go home and sleep. As can readily be appreciated, any given drive has a moderately good chance of being either partly or wholly blocked before it can be completely satisfied. People differ greatly in their capacity for and tolerance of frustration—their willingness to "endure and wait." They differ also in the readiness with which they can find and enjoy substitute means of satisfaction when the more direct ones are blocked.

Before going on to discuss the various types of escape, it might be well to present certain features of the Freudian viewpoint that contribute to an understanding of conflicts, especially in the case of a conflict that is largely if not wholly unconscious. The sum total of drives that derive their force from bodily pleasure and purely selfish satisfaction the Freudians refer to as the "id." The id consists mainly of those drives that human beings share with animals, drives that impel one to satisfy bodily needs and to be comfortable, without respect to what effect the satisfaction or comfort may have upon anyone else. The id thus acts wholly upon the pleasure principle—the I-want-what-I-want-when-I-want-it idea—without any more sense of guilt than a cat has when she settles herself comfortably in the sunshine on a perishable *objet d'art*. It also appears to be much the same as the "devil" that the Puritans tried to drive out of their children, and its behavior is strangely like that attributed to the seven deadly sins. The id seems to carry on a subterranean existence in the unconscious, reminding one somewhat of a submarine with a schnorkel. The second level of consciousness is the "ego." Its main task is to make adjustments and compromises between the id and a third entity called the "superego." This last is easily identified as one's conscience, or source of values, or awareness of right and wrong, or realization of what ought to be. Since many of the impulses from the id run counter to the principles of the superego, the ego is constantly under two kinds of pressure and must continually reconcile opposing demands. It must give some satisfaction to the drives of the id, but must do so without arousing the opposition of the superego, and at the same time must see to it that the solution does not clash with reality. The ego operates mostly upon the principle of social acceptance. Under the domination of this principle it learns sufficient control of selfish desires to permit of a social life.

2. Escapes from Conflict: All people are faced with the reality of the physical world, the reality of other people's interests and activities, the reality of their own bodies, and the reality of their own drives. The solutions that are possible for finding comfort, avoiding disaster, releasing tension when it does accumulate, or escaping from conflict are of various types. In theory such an escape or solution should lead to a better relationship to other people, should be conducive to mental health, should make future adjustments easier, should benefit society, and should not divert one from one's goals in life. Unfortunately, there are no perfect solutions. They are all forms of compromise between the good of the individual and the good of society. However, it is often helpful to check against the above criteria any given compromise or escape in order to estimate its values and to recognize its defects.

Some forms of escape occur more frequently than others, and all of them —if used in moderation—are normal and relatively harmless. They are also highly useful because they permit the ego to solve its problems, to reconcile conflicts, and to shed its feelings of guilt. Or, in non-Freudian language, they bring possible solutions to the emotional conflicts of daily life, with a resulting peace of mind and a forgetting of emotional episodes. It is only when one method of escape becomes a fixed method of dealing with all reality that it becomes dangerous.

The adjustments or escape mechanisms are classifiable into five different types. Two sets of terminology are given because both phrases are frequently used in the literature. The various mechanisms within each group appear in Table 5.

1. Most people at some time try simple repression as a mode of reaction, and a few persist in its use. At best it brings only partial escape. It consists essentially of convincing oneself that a given impulse is wrong and of thenceforth denying its existence. It is the sort of reaction made by an

Table 5

ESCAPES AND ADJUSTMENTS

1. Escape by denying reality (adjustment by repression)
2. Escape by distorting reality (adjustment by deception)
   a. Rationalization
   b. Projection
   c. Segregation
   d. Sour grapes
   e. Displacement

3. Escape by retreating from reality (adjustment through surrender)
   a. Regression
   b. Fantasy
   c. Conversion

4. Escape by attacking reality (adjustment through attack)
   a. Physical aggression (delinquency)
   b. Verbal aggression

5. Escape by compromising with reality (adjustment through compromise)
   a. Compensation
   b. Sublimation
   c. Identification

Adapted and modified from N. Cameron, *The Psychology of Behavior Disorders*, Houghton Mifflin Company, 1947, pp. 142–186; J. M. Josselyn, *Psychosocial Development of School Children*, Family Service Association of America, 1948, 134 pp.; P. M. Symonds, *The Dynamics of Human Adjustment*, Appleton-Century-Crofts, Inc., 1946, Chaps. 8–20; Schacter, *How Personalities Grow*, Chaps. 12–15; and L. P. Thorpe, *The Psychology of Mental Health*, The Ronald Press, 1950, pp. 133 ff.

honorable man who finds himself in love with his brother's wife. The difficulties in its use are twofold: emotions are hard to suppress, and after they have presumably been submerged they are likely to pop up somewhere else in more or less disguised form. In theory nothing should ever be suppressed, but in practice it is sometimes necessary, when, for instance, one must choose between two conflicting objectives. It is, of course, much healthier to divert the undesired drives rather than to suppress them, and in many instances this can be done.

2. The first escape on the list of distortions is rationalization. An individual is rationalizing when he gives a minor or faked reason for conduct that is actually motivated by some other reason that would be painful to admit. Thus, a dull freshman girl in high school may want to go to college but at the same time may be aware at least dimly that she has too little ability to do so. To admit openly that she is stupid would be most uncomfortable, so she rationalizes her conflict of desires by saying that she prefers the commercial to the college preparatory course because all her friends are taking it, because it leads to quicker financial returns, or because she had rather take "modern" subjects like shorthand than a stuffy dead language like Latin. She has distorted reality because she has not given a true picture of it—but the distortion is more palatable than the truth. Since these mechanisms are usually unconscious, the user is not aware of the distortion.

Projection is a less desirable mechanism than rationalization because it involves other people, upon whom the blame for a conflict is projected. Since, however, the human animal has great difficulty in saying the three simple words "I was wrong," this mechanism is popular. Suppose, for instance, that a pupil has tried very hard to pass a course in English composition. but finds he is failing. Failure is most uncomfortable, so he is likely to resort to a convenient "projection" of the blame. He may say that his father is a foreigner and speaks little English at home, that his mother was always a poor speller and never liked to write compositions when she was in school, and that his older sister also had trouble with English. In this way he can explain his own failure in terms of heredity and home environment, thus projecting the blame onto somebody else and relieving himself of the emotional discomfort that comes when one feels oneself a failure. He has absolved himself of guilt, and has escaped from the emotional situation altogether. The distortion of reality is here obvious.

Segregation is a name given to the practice of keeping different sets of motives and practices from interfering with each other and precipitating crises. The classic example of this mechanism is the factory owner who underpays and overworks his laborers, overcharges his customers, and generally makes money out of other people's misery, but who on Sundays is a devout worshiper and supporter of religion. The common interpretation of his conduct consists in dubbing him as a hypocrite, but this appellation is often erroneous. The man is actually sincere in accepting two contradictory sets of beliefs. His defense against emotional strain rests upon his ability to keep each set of principles in its own mental compartment. He honestly believes in Christianity, but his life would be thrown into confusion if he allowed such a precept as "Do unto others as you would have them do unto you" to get mixed up with his business. He distorts reality because he accepts as true in one situation what he rejects as false in another.

A fourth type of mechanism is called sour grapes, the name being derived from the fable about the fox who could not reach the grapes he wanted and so comforted himself with the conviction that they were too sour anyway. The adolescent who states loudly that all fraternities and other secret organizations are worthless is probably displaying exactly the same mechanism. At an earlier time he has very likely wanted badly to be elected to such a society but has failed to be among those chosen. Being rejected creates a most unpleasant situation. In fact, if the emotion generated by the rejection were continued long enough, the adolescent would become permanently crushed and defeated. Usually, however, the convenient sour-grapes rationalization develops, and the entire emotional problem disappears. It should be noted, however, that the lad has distorted reality.

The last of the escapes by distortion is called displacement. It is a mechanism by which an unpleasant and destructive emotion that is generated by one person or set of circumstances may be transferred to another. Suppose, for instance, that a pupil has been punished unfairly by his school principal and that he feels intense resentment. His first impulse may be to injure the principal, but he is restrained by a fear of consequences. As long as his hostility continues to boil inside him, he is intensely uncomfortable. On the way home from school he happens to meet a small, shy, inoffensive Negro boy, against whom he has no complaint, but he nevertheless attacks him and inflicts upon him at least some of the damage he would like to have done to the principal. His emotion was displaced from the real but untouchable object of his wrath to an object that he could assault with far less danger of punishment and no likelihood of damage to himself. This transfer of emotion is not conscious; the matter would be a lot less serious if the boy were consciously "working off" his anger. Unfortunately, he transfers his emotion so completely that he hates the Negro boy instead of the principal, and may presently begin to hate all Negroes. This mechanism is at the base of much race and intergroup prejudice. The distortion of reality is extreme.

3. The escapes in the next group are brought about by ignoring reality and erecting a neurotic bulwark against it. The commonest type is escape by regression or surrender. Thus, the shy daughter of a domineering mother finds her first efforts at life on an adult level quite impossible because she comes into frequent, sharp, painful conflict with her mother, by whom she is always defeated. If the daughter is kept by her conscience at her mother's side, her most probable escape is by surrender and regression to a childish level, at which her mother's domination seems natural, and her own chief urge is to please her mother. This mother—little girl relationship has at least the merit of being peaceful—but it is peace bought at the price of surrender.

Undoubtedly the commonest of all mechanisms is the substitution of daydreaming for action as a means of draining off painful emotions. Fantasy is fairly common at all ages and practically universal in adolescence. For the most part it is beneficial and does no apparent harm, as long as the daydreamer is perfectly sure which is the dream and which is the reality. For instance, the girl who is not popular or has to stay home from a dance because she owns no appropriate clothes can assuage her hurts to some extent by imagining herself the belle of the ball. It is only when the isolated daydreamer begins to think she *is* the belle of the ball that the mechanism becomes dangerous. When and if the substitution of fantasy for reality becomes habitual, the dreamer is mentally ill.

Finally, in this third group there is escape from harsh reality into illness or physical handicap that permits the individual to avoid adjustment altogether. This method of avoidance always looks spurious to the outsider, who has difficulty in believing that the illness or seizures of whatever type are real and not mere alibis. For instance, the writer once had a secondary school student who was under doctor's orders to cut all of her examinations because of the serious arm cramps that she developed. These were not mere imagination. The muscles in her arm stood out from the tissue and contracted so violently that on one occasion they dislocated a bone in her wrist and on another they pulled a tendon loose; her hand was drawn backward until it was almost against her forearm. The pain was excruciating. To imagine that anyone would undergo such agony on purpose is ridiculous. It is true that this student had a pronounced fear of examinations, which she began to dread by the end of her first year in school. On the day of an examination, she was in a state of profound misery, in which many conversion symptoms, such as diarrhea and dizziness, were already observable. She never succeeded in writing more than a few words before the cramps developed. Although it introduced a new kind of suffering, it removed her from her emotional conflict by making the writing of a test impossible and at the same time absolved her from any feeling of guilt.

It may already have been noted that these escapes by surrender and retreat, if they become fixed methods of resolving conflicts, will lead to neurotic or even psychotic behavior. In other words, neurotic reactions may be thought of as constituting a defense thrown up by the ego either against conditions that are intolerable or against drives that seem to be undesirable. Thus, a girl with a domineering mother may at first find herself wishing that her mother were dead, or even beset by an impulse to kill her mother; she cannot accept these urges, which seem to her so shameful and so degrading that they must be locked forever in the secrecy of her own heart and suppressed ruthlessly at the earliest possible moment. To deceive herself she waits on her mother more than ever, for it is only by immolating her natural urges that she can escape from them. Her regression to childishness is therefore a defense against the intolerable reality of her own instinctive impulses.

4. Some individuals are too vigorous to retreat or compromise and too clearheaded to deceive themselves by distorting reality, on major issues at least. They therefore attack the situations that are inhibiting the full expression of their desires and try to demolish the reality that is hemming them in. For instance, a vigorous boy from a poor family is likely to wish he had more money. He does not, however, sit down and daydream about the money he would like to have, nor does he tell people that all great men were once poor boys or that wealth is all delusion anyway and not worth

fighting for. He simply goes out and steals some money, or an object that he can turn into money. He may also let off some of his emotional steam by putting chalk marks on handsome new cars, by shouting scurrilous comments at well-dressed children, or by throwing a rock at a shiny top hat as its wearer is making his way to church on Easter Sunday. The less important modes of defiance are usually classed as rowdyism; if the reactions are serious, they are delinquencies. The delinquent is thus a person who is escaping from reality by attacking and changing it temporarily. The attack may be either physical or verbal. In the latter case, it takes such forms as excessive criticism, scurrilous remarks, rumors, cruel jokes, unpleasant nicknames, catcalling, and the like.

5. The last group of possible escapes contains those that are probably best for mental health. The individual does not distort reality to escape from his own guilt or inadequacies; he does not pretend that reality is not there, and he does not try to demolish it. He does, however, divert its impact and work out a compromise which, while not giving perfect satisfaction, at least gives enough to provide relief from tension and to divert instinctual urges into harmless and sometimes even useful modes of expression. The first of these mechanisms is called compensation. This term means simply that an individual compensates for a poor showing in one phase of existence by a good showing in another. A common example of this mechanism is seen in the pupil who is too small for athletic competition and too shy to be a social success, and who therefore compensates by getting the best grades in class and receiving mild admiration as an academic prodigy. Actually, success in his studies may be only his third choice, but it is better than obscurity. His concentration upon academic work may unfortunately serve to alienate him still further from the social intercourse and physical exercise that he badly needs. His compensation, however, makes him feel comfortable most of the time because he is no longer competing along lines in which he is sure to be a failure.

If one must pick out one mechanism as the best of the lot, most people would choose sublimation. One sees this process at work when the school bully is appointed as the school policeman. His urge to dominate has been diverted from twisting the arms of little children to seeing them safely across the street. His urge to inflict pain is being controlled by his urge to be admired. His exhibitionistic tendencies are satisfied by his uniform or armband, which sets him off from the others. His behavior now leads to satisfaction, whereas before it was not only undesirable in itself, but led to further punishment, further ostracism, further tension, and further discomfort. The boy's fundamental drives have not changed, however, only their mode of expression.

At the end of this long list of mechanisms comes a most convenient mode of adjustment known as identification. It is particularly useful to those who for some reason are inferior. For instance, a girl of average ability with brilliant parents and one or two older and equally brilliant siblings is in no position to reach the family standard of academic superiority. Although she might be admired as bright in some families, she is headed for strain, despair, failure, and tension in her own. Through hero-worshiping identification she can escape some of her troubles because one is not expected to compete with one's heroes. If she worships her mother, adores her father, and regards her older brothers and sisters as geniuses, she escapes strain, and nobody really notices that her own achievements are minor. Her attitude is real and sincere; it is no form of deliberate flattery. She gives admiration so thoroughly that the successes of others become hers just as truly as if she had had a hand in them. In this manner she avoids failure and tension and escapes even comparison with others, while she finds happiness and freedom from what could easily have become a chronic sense of her own inadequacy or inferiority. One sees the same mechanism in the humble bookkeeper who says with pride, "My firm did a half-million dollars' worth of business last year." He has escaped from his own insignificance by his identification with something bigger and more important.

The last three forms of escape are especially useful because they best meet the criteria set up at the beginning of this discussion: they are relatively healthy for the individual, they often lead to a better relationship with others, and they do not interfere with the usual goals of life.

All the mechanisms discussed above have their value because they permit an individual to get rid of his emotional tension toward situations about which he can do nothing. When they are used occasionally, their effect is beneficial rather than otherwise. Their extreme use, however, indicates the existence of some unsolved conflict that the individual cannot face and is consequently running away from. All these mechanisms permit him to escape reality, but it is not advisable that people do so too frequently. Persistent projection, rationalization, compensation, daydreaming, regression, conversion, hostility—these are all danger signals. They indicate the existence of chronic frustration and tension. Early recognition is essential if school pupils are to be prevented from developing warped personalities.

V. Summary

An emotion is an experience that affects an individual's vital processes, stimulating him to greater activity than is normal. The central changes that accompany emotions may be mild or intense, but their nature does not alter as one grows older. There is, however, an observable evolution in the types of stimulus that arouse emotional states and the types of response that are made. A child's causes of anger are relatively simple and personal; his reactions are direct and explosive. An adolescent reacts primarily to fear situations that are social in character, in which he feels his status to be involved; his reactions show some degree of subtlety, but he is quickly broken down to childish levels if he is exposed to pressure. A child's affection is usually centered first upon his mother, and then upon his father or other adults; in the case of a girl, fixation upon the mother is often supplanted at an early age by a possessive love for the father. During childhood, members of both sexes are deeply attached to other children of the same sex and age. In adolescence an interest in heterosexual love-objects arises; at first the interest is transitory and somewhat promiscuous, but soon it becomes centered on only two or three companions of the opposite sex, and eventually upon only one. Interests and attitudes change as a result of these developments. It is therefore possible to measure the level a given individual has reached by obtaining from him a statement of his interests, attitudes, hopes, fears, and identifications. From such measurement one derives an emotional age which should be used—along with mental, physical, social, and educational ages—in the handling of children and especially in their placement in the school grades. Emotional life furnishes the basic drives that impel an individual to action. These drives vary in strength not only from person to person but from age to age. When they cannot be satisfied, they lead to frustration and conflict, which may be resolved in a number of ways, some of which are more healthy than others. Emotions inevitably find some outlet; if one is blocked, another is substituted. ١٤

REFERENCES FOR FURTHER READING

BOOKS

1. Alexander, F. G., *Fundamentals of Psychoanalysis*, W. W. Norton & Company, 1948, 312 pp. (Chaps. 5, 6.)
2. Anderson, J. E., *The Psychology of Development and Personal Adjustment*, University of Minnesota Press, 1949, 720 pp. (Chaps. 10, 11, 17, 18.)
3. Barker, R. G., D. Tamara, and K. Lewin, "Frustration and Regression," in R. G. Barker, *et al.*, *Child Behavior and Development: A Course of Representative Studies*, McGraw-Hill Book Company, 1943, 652 pp. (Pp. 441–458.)
4. Blos, P., *The Adolescent Personality: A Study of Individual Behavior*, Appleton-Century-Crofts, Inc., 1941, 517 pp. (Pt. III, Chaps. 1, 2.)
5. Breckenridge and Vincent, *Child Development*, Chaps. 3, 13.
6. Cameron, N., *The Psychology of Behavior Disorders*, Houghton Mifflin Company, 1947, 622 pp. (Chaps. 3, 5, 6.)[20]
7. Cobb, S., *Foundations of Neuropsychiatry*, Williams & Wilkins Co., 1948, 1948, 260 pp. (Chaps. 1, 2.)
8. Cole, L., *Attaining Maturity*, Rinehart & Company, 1944, 218 pp. (Chaps. 7–13.)
9. Donahue, W. T., *The Measurement of Student Adjustment and Achievement*, University of Michigan Press, 1949, 256 pp. (Pp. 23–50.)
10. English, O. S., and G. H. J. Pearson, *Emotional Problems of Living*, W. W. Norton & Company, 1945, 438 pp. (Chaps. 5, 6, 10, 11.)
11. Fleming, *Adolescence: Its Social Psychology*, Chap. 5.
12. Freud, A., *The Ego and Mechanisms of Defense*, International Universities Press, 1950, 196 pp. (Chaps. 11, 12.)
13. Garrison, *Growth and Development*, Chaps. 7–15.
14. Garrison, *Psychology of Adolescence*, Chaps. 5, 15.
15. Garrison, *The Psychology of Exceptional Children*, Chaps. 19–21.
16. Hurlock, *Adolescent Development*, Chap. 4.
17. Jersild, A. T., and R. J. Tasch, *Children's Interests and What They Suggest for Education*, Columbia University Press, 1949, 173 pp. (Chaps. 2, 5, 7, 11.)
18. Josselyn, J. M., *Psychosocial Development of Children*, Family Service Association of America, 1948, 134 pp. (Chaps. 8–9.)
19. Kuhlen, *The Psychology of Adolescent Development*, Chap. 6.

---

[20] Or M. Cameron and M. Margaret, *Behavior Pathology*, Houghton Mifflin Company, 1951, 645 pp. (Chap. 2.)

20. Landis, *Adolescence and Youth,* Chaps. 13, 14.
21. Malm and Jamison, *Adolescence,* Chaps. 6, 7, 9.
22. Merry and Merry, *The First Two Decades of Life,* Chap. 9.
23. Pearson, G. H. J., *Emotional Disorders of Children,* W. W. Norton & Company, 1949, 368 pp. (Chap. 4.)
24. Richards, T. W., *Modern Clinical Psychology,* McGraw-Hill Book Company, 1946, 303 pp. (Chaps. 8, 9.)
25. Sadler, *Adolescence Problems,* Chaps. 5, 24.
26. Saul, L. J., *Emotional Maturity,* J. B. Lippincott Company, 1947, 339 pp. (Chaps. 2–9, 11, 13, 21.)
27. Saul, L. J., "Physiological Effects of Emotional Tension," in Vol. I of J. McV. Hunt, *Personality and the Behavior Disorders,* The Ronald Press, 1942, 1242 pp. (Pp. 269–305.)
28. Schacter, H., *How Personalities Grow,* McKnight & McKnight, 1949, 256 pp. (Chaps. 3–9, 11–15.)
29. Seguin, C. A., *Introduction to Psychosomatic Medicine,* International Universities Press, 1950, 320 pp. (Chap. 3.)
30. Sokoloff, B., *Jealousy: A Psychiatric Study,* Howell, Soskin, Publishers, Inc., 1947, 262 pp. (Chaps. 1, 6, and any one of Chaps. 2–5.)
31. Steckle, L. A., *Problems of Human Adjustment,* Harper & Brothers, 1949, 351 pp. (Chaps. 3, 13.)
32. Strain, F. B., *The Normal Sex Interests of Children,* Appleton-Century-Crofts, Inc., 1948, 210 pp. (Chaps. 3, 5, 8–13.)
33. Symonds, P. M., *The Dynamics of Human Adjustment,* Appleton-Century-Crofts, Inc., 1946, 666 pp. (Chaps. 1–3, 7, 10, 11, 13, 14, 17, 19, 20.)
34. Symonds, P. M., *The Ego and the Self,* Appleton-Century-Crofts, Inc., 1951, 229 pp. (Chaps. 2–4, 8–11.)
35. Thorpe, L. P., *The Psychology of Mental Health,* The Ronald Press, 1950, 747 pp. (Chaps. 2, 4, 5.)
36. Tiegs, E. W., and B. Katz, *Mental Hygiene in Education,* The Ronald Press, 1941, 418 pp. (Chaps. 1, 3.)
37. Travis, L. E., and B. Baruch, *Personal Problems of Everyday Life,* Appleton-Century-Crofts, Inc., 1941, 421 pp. (Chaps. 2–5, 8.)
38. Wallin, J. E. W., *Minor Mental Maladjustments in Normal People,* Duke University Press, 1939, 298 pp. (Chaps. 2–5, 10, 11.)
39. Warters, *Achieving Maturity,* Chaps. 5, 7, 8.
40. Weiss, E., *Principles of Psychodynamics,* Grune & Stratton, Inc., 1950, 268 pp. (Chaps. 3, 5, 6, 8, 11, 12, 15, 20.)
41. Wheatley and Hallock, *Health Observations of School Children,* pp. 141–149.

MONOGRAPHS, BULLETINS, PROCEEDINGS, YEARBOOKS, ARTICLES

A. *Needs, Tensions, Frustrations, Conflicts, Solutions*

1. Bender, L., "Aggression in Childhood," *American Journal of Orthopsychiatry,* 13:392–399, 1949.
2. Blum, G. S., "A Study of the Psychoanalytic Theory of Psychosexual Development," *Genetic Psychology Monographs,* 39:3–99, 1949.
3. Dettleheim, "The Social Studies Teacher and the Emotional Needs of Adolescents," *School Review,* 56:585–592, 1948.
4. Hewitt, L. E., and R. L. Jenkins, "Fundamental Patterns of Maladjustment," *Illinois State Department of Public Welfare Bulletin,* 1946.
5. Meyers, C. E., F. J. Estran, and R. C. Perry, "Characteristics and Needs of Individuals," *Review of Educational Research,* 21:75–85, 1951.

6. Seagoe, M. V., "Characteristics of the Needs of Individuals," *Review of Educational Research*, 18:126–137, 1948.
7. Zander, A. F., "A Study of Experimental Frustration," *Psychological Monographs*, Vol. LVI, No. 3, 1944, 38 pp.

B. *Studies of Emotions*

1. Anastasi, A., N. Cohen, and D. Spatz, "A Study of Fear and Anger in College Students through the Controlled Diary Method," *Journal of Genetic Psychology*, 73:243–249, 1948.
2. England, A. O., "Non-Structured Approaches to the Study of Children's Fears," *Journal of Clinical Psychology*, 2:364–368, 1946.
3. Marsh, C. J., "Worries of College Women," *Journal of Social Psychology*, 15:335–339, 1942.
4. Martin, A. H., "A Worry Inventory," *Journal of Applied Psychology*, 29:68–74, 1945.
5. Meltzer, H., "Anger Adjustments in Relation to Intelligence and Achievement," *Journal of Genetic Psychology*, 50:63–82, 1937.
6. Pratt, K. C., "A Study of the 'Fears' of Rural Children," *Journal of Genetic Psychology*, 67:179–194, 1945.
7. Vollmer, H., "Jealousy in Children," *American Journal of Orthopsychiatry*, 16:660–671, 1946.
8. Winker, J. B., "Age Trends and Sex Differences in the Wishes, Identifications, Activities, and Fears of Children," *Child Development*, 20:191–200, 1949.

C. *Measurement of Emotional Maturity*

1. Furfey, P. H., "A Revised Scale for Measuring Developmental Age in Boys," *Child Development Monographs*, Vol. II, No. 2, 1931.
2. Pressey, S. L., "Changes from 1923 to 1943 in the Attitudes of Public School Children," *Journal of Psychology*, 21:173–188, 1946.
3. Pressey, S. L., and L. C. Pressey, "Development of the Interest-Attitude Tests," *Journal of Applied Psychology*, 17:1–16, 1933.
4. Raths, L., and L. Metcalf, "An Instrument for Identifying Some Needs of Children," *Educational Research Bulletin*, 24:169–185, 1945.
5. Sullivan, Sister C., "A Scale for Measuring Developmental Age in Girls," *Studies in Psychology and Psychiatry*, Catholic University Press, Vol. III, No. 4, 1934, 65 pp.
6. Van der Merwe, A. B., and P. A. Theron, "A New Method of Measuring Emotional Stability," *Journal of General Psychology*, 37:109–123, 1947.

CHAPTER SIX

Personality:
Measurement and Types

According to the dictionary "personality" is the "totality of an individual's characteristics, especially as they concern his relations to other people"; it is also defined as an "integrated group of emotional trends, interests, behavior tendencies, etc." There are almost as many definitions among psychologists as there are investigators of the subject. In this book personality will be regarded as a fairly stable configuration of tendencies that determine one's customary behavior, by means of which an individual tries to satisfy his fundamental needs. One's personality is not fixed by heredity; it grows, sheds some traits, acquires others, is sometimes supported by environmental pressures and sometimes warped by them, and is quickly affected by illness, disease, or unusual emotional strain. The central core, however, is more likely than not to remain constant and merely to express itself in different ways as environmental conditions discourage one manifestation and encourage another. It should be noted in passing that personality is always measured by the manner in which a person behaves; it is always an inference, not a direct observation, although the inference is based upon numerous direct observations of behavior.

Thus one observes that a given man wears old and rather dirty clothes, that he lives alone in a hovel, that he is undernourished, that he owns no car, radio, or other modern convenience; one notes that he haggles over prices in the local stores, that he lugs his groceries home on foot, that he is never seen in a restaurant or theater—although he frequents the bank and the public library—that he refuses to contribute to churches or charities; yet, one is told that this man earns and for many years has earned a good salary, that he has no one dependent upon him and no direct heirs, and that he has never, so far as is known, invested any money. One describes such a man as stingy, insecure, selfish, obsessed by a fear of poverty and so on, summing up the total complex of traits by calling him a miser. Presumably, his need for personal safety is so strong that he has sacrificed his social needs to gain greater security. The existence and extent of his miserliness are an inference, however, based upon repeated observations of his behavior in a number of circumstances.

When one investigates personality, it is only the behavior or an individual's report of his behavior that is measured. Hence, one of the basic difficulties of tests in this field. The reactions can often be measured and recorded with great accuracy, but there may be sharp differences of opinion as to what the scores mean, though no one doubts that they mean *something*. The question lies in the interpretation. A copy of test results may be sent to five "experts" and five more or less divergent opinions assembled. This statement does not mean that tests of personality are useless. Even the least valid are probably better than unsupported personal observation. It should always be remembered, however, that one cannot measure personality directly, as a doctor determines blood pressure or bodily temperature, but indirectly, as a doctor observes symptoms and diagnoses disease. Any two doctors will agree, within the narrow limits of error in making the measurement, on what a patient's blood pressure is on a given day because the measurement is direct and objective, but they may not agree in the least upon what disease he has, because a diagnosis is a subjective inference. So also is a diagnosis of personality.

I. Tests of Personality[1]

Objective measurement of specific traits began some three decades ago, just as soon as tests of intelligence had proven their worth in dealing with practical situations. These tests are of numerous types, each of which has its merits and its shortcomings. The earliest forms consisted of questionnaires, inventories, and life histories. In all three of these the individual gives evidence about himself, usually in answer to specific questions. The most obvious shortcoming of this approach is that it rests upon the test taker's unsupported, subjective report.

For instance, a young man says—either orally or in answer to a written question—that he has never had a girl friend. There is no easy way of checking this statement. He may have different standards from other people's as to when a feminine acquaintance should be classified as a girl friend, he may have forgotten some experiences, or he may be lying, intentionally or unintentionally. Moreover, he obviously cannot tell what he does not know. In many instances his own explanations of his motives may not be correct because his true motives are unconscious. If he has a mother complex, for example, he probably does not know it. In short, any form of direct verbal or written inquiry has all the disadvantages of any subjective mode of inquiry. It does, nevertheless, often contribute to an understanding of personality as the taker of the test sees himself.

A second type of personality test consists of measures that are somewhat more objective than the inventory or questionnaire. The earliest form, the rating scale, supplements an individual's opinion of himself by the ratings other people make about him. The rating scale is, however, a somewhat unreliable instrument, even under the best of circumstances, perhaps be-

---

[1] For a good, short discussion of the various types of test, see S. Rosenzweig, "Available Methods for Studying Personality," *Journal of Psychology,* 28:345–368, 1949. For longer expositions, see: J. E. Bell, *Projective Techniques,* Longmans, Green & Co., 1948, 533 pp., and L. K. Frank, *Projective Methods,* Charles C Thomas, Publisher, 1948, 86 pp.

cause one person's opinion of another is not notably accurate. In one modified form, called the "Guess-Who" Test, the estimate is fairly reliable and very useful. More will be said about this type of test presently. Another kind of objective test consists in presenting a pupil with a life situation in which he does not know he is being tested or observed, and to record what he does. Thus, in an investigation of a single trait, such as honesty, one can give a pupil a chance to steal money and see if he does so. This technique is limited in its application, but has a convincing reality where it can be used at all.

The most recent tests are of the so-called "projective" type. They merit this name because the individual taking the test unconsciously reads into the materials his own life experiences and attitudes. That is, he projects himself. The theory underlying such tests is that the ego habitually thrusts onto the external world its own unconscious wishes; if these were ever to become conscious, they might be most painful, so they are disowned and attached to something or someone outside the self. If, then, a pupil is presented with a set of materials that give him a chance to project his attitudes, he will follow his customary pattern of response and do so. For instance, if the examiner shows a child a picture of a woman crying (but with no clue in the scene as to why she is crying) and asks what the picture is about, the child has to project into his narrative his own reasons for crying or his own idea of other people's reasons. Whatever he says, he is going to reveal something about himself. Or, he may be presented with a series of puppets and asked to select a family from them. His selections and his rejections, the reasons he gives for either, and his arrangement of his puppets are all significant because he is almost certain to project into his selection his feelings toward his own family. The materials used are of many types, but the underlying idea is the same—that the taker of the test will reveal himself by his reactions. The difficulty in the use of such materials lies in the interpretation. If, for example, a child selects a family of puppets without any mother, especially if he has one himself, this rejection of the mother-like puppets indubitably means something. It probably indicates an unconscious conflict of so disturbing a nature that even the idea of a mother has been repressed. Further play may give some clue as to the underlying attitudes.

It will be noted that each kind of test contributes some element that the others do not. A comprehensive series of questions honestly answered will tell what the test taker thinks of himself; any form of rating scale will add pertinent information as to what other people think of him; a projective technique will give him a chance to reveal the things that are disturbing him and to some extent the structure of his personality. All three kinds thus have their uses.

One warning about certain personality tests should perhaps be given. Some of them were devised for the express purpose of revealing which individuals have at least the beginnings of an abnormal personality. The items were therefore selected as covering the common symptoms of those who are neurotic or psychotic. As a result, one cannot make a "normal" score because there are no items based upon acceptable personalities. By no means all tests are of this type, but the user should be forewarned that some are.

1. Questionnaires and Inventories: There is no room in a book about adolescence for more than a sampling of each type of measuring instrument. No effort will be made to present a survey of the field. Two tests of this type are especially well known: the California Test of Personality[2] and the Minnesota Multiphasic Personality Inventory. The former yields two scores, one for self-adjustment and one for social adjustment. A few sample items will serve as illustration:

2. Is it hard for you to be calm when things go wrong?
22. Are people often unfair to you?
34. Do you feel that you are punished for too many little things?
54. Are you usually invited to school and neighborhood parties?
67. Have you often felt that older people had it in for you?
88. Do you usually find it hard to go to sleep?
116. Do you find it easy to make new friends?
141. Do your folks seem to feel that you are interested in the wrong things?
156. Are some of your teachers so strict that it makes schoolwork too hard?
179. Do you like most of the boys and girls in your neighborhood?

As may be seen, the test covers a wide range of topics. The Minnesota Test is so arranged that its scores fall into patterns which reflect basic groupings of personal traits. It is used primarily to indicate those students who deviate from the normal. The patterns are therefore patterns of abnormal personalities—the paranoid, the schizophrenic, the depressed, or the hysteric. In common with all inventories it is intended for use in surveying and sifting entire groups. That it has some diagnostic quality as well is an added attraction.[3]

Questionnaires and inventories are not substitutes for personal interviews but should be used as preparatory steps toward interviews. They serve also to call attention to those pupils who are most in need of help.

2. Rating Scales: A good and quite recent example of this type of test is the Guilford-Zimmerman Temperament Survey.[4] It consists of ratings upon ten traits of personality, as listed on the following page.

---

[2] Published by the California Test Bureau and used here with its permission. For a description, see E. W. Tiegs, W. W. Clark, and L. P. Thorpe, "The California Test of Personality," *Journal of Educational Research*, 35:102–108, 1941. For another inventory test, see S. R. Hathaway and J. C. McKinley, *Manual for the Minnesota Multiphasic Personality Inventory*, University of Minnesota Press, 1943, and R. J. Hampton, "The MMPI as a Psychometric Tool for Diagnosis of Personality Disorders among College Students," *Journal of Social Psychology*, 26:99–108, 1947.

[3] See, for instance, R. J. Hampton, "The MMPI as a Psychometric Tool for Diagnosis of Personality Disorders among College Students," *Journal of Social Psychology*, 26:99–108, 1947; S. R. Hathaway and J. C. McKinley, *Manual for the Minnesota Multiphasic Personality Inventory*, University of Minnesota Press, 1943.

[4] J. P. Guilford and W. S. Zimmerman, *The Guilford-Zimmerman Temperament Survey*, Sheridan Supply Company, 1949.

1. General activity, energy, drive
2. Restraint, self-control
3. Ascendency through persuasiveness and power of conversation
4. Sociability, making of friends, social contacts
5. Emotional stability: lack of moodiness, optimism, composure
6. Objectivity: lack of hostility or suspiciousness
7. Friendliness: acceptance of domination, responsibility for others, tolerance of hostility
8. Thoughtfulness: reflectiveness, interest in thinking
9. Tolerance of others, freedom from self-pity
10. Masculinity: interest in masculine activities, not easily frightened or disgusted

Results for four girls who have been very close friends for many years appear in Figure 58 below. L is a child of tremendous activity and great objectivity; she has a passion for ideas and is highly masculine in her attitudes. She was rated above average on all traits except self-control. E is

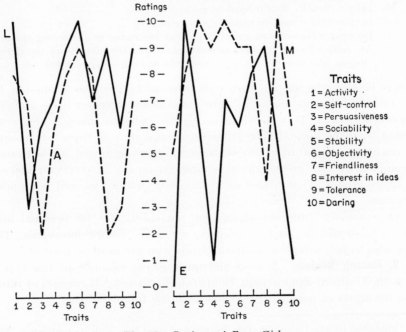

Fig. 58. *Ratings of Four Girls*

in many respects the exact opposite. She is abnormally inactive, she has no ability to influence others, she is extremely feminine, and her self-control is phenomenal, but she gets as high a rating in intellectual activity as L, whose mind and body are both hyperactive. M is strong on all characteristics that relate to social skills; she is highly persuasive, sociable, objective, friendly, and tolerant, but her mental activity is relatively low and her physical drive only average. A is active, stable emotionally, quite sociable, and somewhat masculine in her interests and attitudes, but she lacks self-control and persuasiveness, and she has little interest in ideas. She is of the same general type as L but lacks L's intellectual interests and abilities. From the ratings one can not only see four highly individual children but can also sense some of the interrelationships that hold them together. L and E furnish the ideas, L and A have the drive to carry them out, M provides the social control, and A participates a little in everything except the furnishing of ideas. L is a doer and dynamic thinker, E is a passive thinker and follower, M is a leader, and A is definitely a follower. All four received high ratings in friendliness and tolerance.

The "Guess-Who" test is an indirect sort of rating scale. It has many forms, of which the items below are examples:

1. In this class there is a pupil who does good work, is very bright, and recites a lot in class, but isn't popular, and sometimes tells on the other children. Who is it? ....

2. In this class there is someone the other pupils think is a "screwball." Who is it? ....

3. There is another pupil who stays alone a good deal, seems to be half-asleep much of the time, and often doesn't hear what the teacher says. Who is it? ....

4. Two pupils, one a girl and one a boy, are very popular. All the other children like them and often crowd around them on the playground. When partners are being chosen everyone wants these two as partners. Who are they? ....

5. Suppose your class was giving a play and you needed the following characters, which child would you choose for each?

a. a sissy	d. a sneak ....
b. a tough guy	e. a leader ....
c. a show-off	f. a bully ....

The pupils who take such a test are rating their comrades, sometimes on only a single trait, sometimes on their total personality.

3. Projective Techniques: There are so many of these that only a few of the most widely used can be discussed. Those selected are the Sentence Completion Test, the Picture-Frustration Test, the Thematic Apperception Test, the Mosaic Test, and the Rorschach. Brief mention will later be made of several others that are either not too well validated as yet or are not as widely used as those just enumerated.

The sentence-completion form of projective test is by far the simplest to understand. It consists merely of such sentences as these:

1. I feel hurt when ....
2. I object strenuously to ....
3. I often make believe that ....
4. My father used to ....
5. I liked one teacher in high school because she ....
6. The people I dislike most are those who ....[5]

Each introductory clause presents the student with a situation for which he must supply a conclusion, presumably by telling what he would do, or

---

[5] A. D. Tendler, "A Preliminary Report on a Test for Emotional Insight," *Journal of Applied Psychology,* 14:123–136, 1930, and J. Shor, "Report on a Verbal Projection Technique," *Journal of Clinical Psychology,* 2:279–282, 1946.

customarily does, in similar circumstances. No two people are likely to complete the sentences in the same way. Incomplete sentences of the types listed above require an individual to project his own personality into the finishing of the sentence.

The Picture-Frustration Test[6] is another one that presents the taker with a situation and asks what he would do about it. The test items are in the form of cartoons, each depicting a scene in which two people are involved. The scenes are of a more or less provocative nature. One of the two people has already made a remark, which is recorded as coming from his or her mouth, after the fashion of the comic strips. There is a similar but empty space in which the test taker is to write in what answer the second person might make to the entire situation.

One of the cartoons, for instance, shows a most exemplary taxicab driver leaning out of his cab window and apologizing for splashing mud on a pedestrian's clothes. The possible answers by the pedestrian may be grouped into three types: those that put the blame on the taximan, those that put the blame on himself, and those that put it on what Sir Henry Merrivale calls "the awful, terrible cussedness of things in general." Of the first type are such answers as: "Why don't you watch what you're doing?" or "People like you ought to be locked up." Of the second type: "Oh! that's OK! The suit's dirty anyway," or "I shouldn't have been standing so close to the curb." Of the third type: "Well, I suppose accidents will happen," or "On wet days you can't keep water from splashing." The first kind of answer is called extrapunitive; that is, the blame is assigned to someone or something outside the speaker, whose aggression is directed into the environment. The second type is called intrapunitive; that is, the speaker accepts the blame, thus turning his aggression in upon himself. The third is called impunitive and represents an effort to mask the frustration, to de-emotionalize the situation, and to evade any aggression at all. These different reactions to the same series of situations seem to be related in varying degrees to such traits of personality as dominance, neuroticism, scholastic aptitude, or religious interest.

Of all the projective techniques, the Thematic Apperception Test[7] and

---

[6] S. Rosenzweig, *Psychodiagnosis: An Introduction to Tests in the Clinical Practice of Psychodiagnosis,* Grune & Stratton, Inc., 1949, 380 pp.; R. P. Falls and R. R. Blake, "A Quantitative Analysis of the Picture Frustration Study," *Journal of Personality,* 16:320–325, 1948; J. Bernard, "The Rosenzweig Picture-Frustration Study, I and II," *Journal of Psychology,* 28:326–332, 333–344, 1949.

[7] For a description of this test and the methods of scoring it, see the following articles: B. Aron, *A Manual for the Analysis of the TAT: A Method and Technique for Personality Research,* Willis E. Berg, Berkeley, Calif., 1949, 163 pp.; R. M. Clark, "A Method of Administering and Evaluating the TAT in Group Situations," *General Psychology Monographs,* 30:3–55, 1944; C. D. Morgan and H. A. Murray, "A Method for Investigating Phantasies," *Archives of Neurology and Psychiatry,* 34:288–306, 1935; Z. A. Piotrowski, "A New Evaluation of the TAT," *Psychoanalytic Review,* 37:101–127, 1950; M. I. Stein, *The Thematic Apperception Test,* Addison-Wesley Press, 1948, 95 pp.; S. Tomkins, *The Thematic Apperception Test: The Theory and Technique of Interpretation,* Grune & Stratton, Inc., 1947, 297 pp.; R. Wittenborn, "Some Thematic Apperception Norms and a Note on the Use of the Test Cards in the Guidance of

the Rorschach are the best known and most widely used. In 1950, the former—usually known as the TAT—had already been the subject of 377 articles in professional journals,[8] and as many more have probably appeared since. The test consists of a series of pictures, each of which shows a dramatic or emotional scene that might have a number of explanations. The individual who takes the test is asked to explain the picture and to give an imaginary reconstruction of what went before and what followed. While a good deal of emotion is portrayed in each picture, it is not clear just what the excitement is all about. Thus, a man may be shown pointing excitedly toward something but there is no clue as to what he is pointing at. The subject must therefore read into the pictures some fantasies or interpretations of his own. In giving meaning to the picture, a person is certain to reveal something about himself. The raw material for a pupil's story comes from his own experiences and is colored by his own personality needs. His stories are scored for evidence of basic, unsatisfied urges and for environmental pressures. The nature of the outcome is also examined, since it is a product of the needs and the pressures, and is rated as a successful or an unsuccessful solution.

One of the most interesting and valuable studies using the TAT consists of the administration of 42 cards to 20 adolescent boys and 20 adolescent girls.[9] Four of the pictures are reproduced in Figures 59–62 on pages 164 to 167. These children told a total of 1,680 stories. The investigator collected a complete life history of each pupil, also an autobiography written by the pupil himself, ratings from teachers, results from questionnaires concerning such matters as likes and dislikes, or relations to family and age-mates, a record of each pupil's dreams, and several observational samples of behavior. The investigator thus had a great deal of information about each adolescent, to which he could relate the stories stimulated by the pictures.

The first point about the results has to do with the themes of the stories. These are of two types, environmental and psychological. Both types exist for every story; that is, a story can be about school life and show aggression, or about family relationships and show ambition, or about punishment and show repentance. Usually, a story had more than one theme; the 1,680 stories produced a grand total of 4,804 environmental and 5,499 psychological themes. Both numbers include repetitions. The themes that made up 88 and 87 per cent, respectively, of the two types are listed in Table 6. The first three environmental themes equaled 59 per cent of the total. By far the commonest psychological theme was aggression. There was no adolescent among the 40 studied who did not have some aggressive themes

College Students," *Journal of Clinical Psychology*, 24:319–330, 1947. See also L. E. Travis and J. J. Johnston, *The Travis-Johnston Projection Tests*, Griffin-Patterson Company, 1949.

[8] R. R. Holt and C. Thompson, "Bibliography for the Thematic Apperception Test," *Journal of Projective Techniques*, 14:82–100, 1950.

[9] P. M. Symonds, *Adolescent Fantasy: An Investigation of the Picture-Study Method of Personality Study*, Columbia University Press, 1949, 397 pp.

Fig. 59. *TAT Picture (1)*

Figures 59 to 62 are from P. M. Symonds, *Adolescent Fantasy*, Columbia University Press, 1949, Nos. 17, 22, 28, and 1, and are used by permission of the publisher.

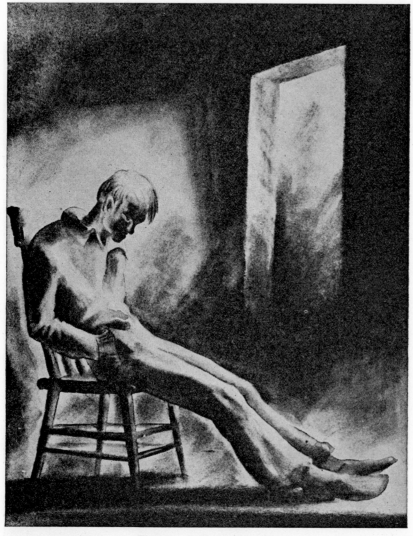

Fig. 60. *TAT Picture (2)*

Fig. 61. *TAT Picture (3)*

Fig. 62. *TAT Picture (4)*

in his or her stories. The chief differences between the rank order of environmental themes for boys and girls was that the former told relatively more stories about punishment, accidents, and strangeness, while the latter told relatively more about separation or rejection, school, and appearance. In

Table 6

THEMES

Environmental					Psychological				
	Number	*Per cent*	*Rank Order*			*Number*	*Per cent*	*Rank Order*	
			Boys	Girls				Boys	Girls
Family relationships	1,595	33	1	1	Aggression	1,562	28	1	1
Economic conditions	632	13	3	2	Eroticism	459	8	2	4
					Altruism	401	7	5	2
Punishment	614	13	2	5	Depression	349	6	6	5
Separation or rejection	397	8	5	3	Excitement	312	6	3	10
Accident or illness	297	6	4	6	Anxiety	310	6	8	3
					Repentance	305	6	4	9
School	251	5	6	4	Ambition	268	5	7	8
Peer social life	130	3	8	7	Thinking, decision	248	5	9	6
Strangeness	125	3	7	10	Joy, happiness	193	4	11	7
Place of residence	98	2	9	9	Escape	136	2	10	. . .
Appearance	75	2	. . .	8	Concealment	119	2	13	11
					Goodness	112	2	12	12
Total	4,214	88	. . .	. . .	Total	4,774	87	. . .	. . .
All Others	590	12	. . .	. . .	All Others	725	13	. . .	. . .
Grand Total	4,804	100	. . .	. . .	Grand Total	5,499	100	. . .	. . .

From P. M. Symonds, *Adolescent Fantasy*, Columbia University Press, 1949, pp. 80–81. Used by permission of the publisher.

psychological themes, the boys show more motifs reflecting eroticism, excitement, repentance, ambition, and escape than the girls, but fewer motifs concerning altruism, depression, anxiety, thinking, joy, and concealment. The escape theme occurs so rarely among girls that it is not among the first thirteen; its place is taken by the theme of guilt or conscience.

The individual stories told by the boys and girls are interesting and revealing. The few quoted below illustrate a number of themes and show what the raw material as produced by adolescents looks like. The last two were told about the same picture by two different boys.

Story A (Aggression)

This boy's father had died twenty years ago, when he was one. The boy is now 21. Father left insurance. Boy got a car. Decided to show it to mother. Drove it 80 miles per hour. Sped along. Saw old woman coming out on street. Hit her. Drove home. Screamed "Mother, Mother." Realized it was his own mother. Rushed back to street of accident. She was dying and said she hoped he wouldn't be so mean after this. She died. He went to jail and got life imprisonment.[10] (Harold, age 13; Story 22)

[10] This and the following excerpts are from Symonds, *op. cit.*, pp. 85, 84, 85–86, 85, and 86, respectively. Used by permission of Columbia University Press.

Story B (Depression)

Appears as if woman receiving letter is expecting bad news. Look in face doesn't seem to indicate any enthusiasm in receiving letter. Seems as if she's in a different world, the look in her eyes. Seems her taking letter was just a mechanical motion. Woman is very ordinary looking and looks more like secretary than housewife. Perhaps her boy friend has written her that due to financial conditions and the tie-up in work they cannot be married for at least a year. She had an inkling this would happen because of his actions in recent weeks. She feels, perhaps, he doesn't love her any more and is merely using that as an excuse to break off. I don't feel they ever will get married (I am awfully pessimistic). Girl will never forget him. (Albert, age 17; Story 1)

Story C (Altruism)

Teachers planning annual festival at school. In one class two girls were being considered for a large part. Girls were different. Sue was gentle—wanted part, but would give it up gladly. Mary—just the opposite—very bitter about it. Didn't know what to do. Teacher chose Sue. Sue very glad. Mary bitter over it. Resolved she would make it difficult for Sue. Sue noticed this. Gave part to Mary. Knew she wanted it. When Sue went to see festival felt good because she knew through her sacrifice she had made someone else happier. Had a pang of envy. But felt in the end that she had done a better thing. (Viola, age 14; Story 41)

Story D (Guilt)

Boy's name is John. Mother a widow. He got in trouble in school. Mother had to go up to school. Teacher told her he was fooling around too much in school. He said he was sorry. Here she's describing how her husband died. Boy never knew this. He was small. Telling how big brother ran away because he didn't have enough money from mother. Mother telling how much she'll have to depend on him when he's old enough to work. He'll have to support her. He's thinking over situation. Promised not to get into trouble. From then on, a good boy in school. (Jack, age 15; Story 17)

Story E (Ambition: success; realization)

Young Johnny lived in New York City. Pretty bad. Bad reports. Father dead. Mother had to support him. Wash woman. One ambition that her one son would go to college. Took him aside and talked to him. He was smart, but never tried. Now he did. Great raise in marks. Realized he could get scholarship. Studied hard. Mother helped. Physics exam, psychology exam which they taught—an unusual subject; mother helped. He also studied chemistry. At first he thought it a lot of stuff. Now realized there was something to it. Gets scholarship. Years later this young fellow is one of the greatest scientists ever and president of experimental scientific concern. (Sam, age 14; Story 17)

It will probably have been noted that these stories indicate the existence of conflicts, almost inevitably conflicts that are unsolved. In general, if an individual works out a conflict in reality its nature is revealed by his behavior. Thus a delinquent boy often acts out his conflicts, and the observer can deduce a good deal about them from the boy's symptoms. If, however, an individual inhibits the outward expression of his conflicts, he works them out in fantasy, either openly or in disguised forms. If the underlying drives are acceptable to both the child and society, the expression is usually open;

but if they are unacceptable, they will be expressed through symbols and through displacement.

The Mosaic Test[11] is a projective technique of quite another type. The materials consist of 456 small pieces of flat, colored, geometrically shaped bits of wood or plastic. The person who takes the test may arrange

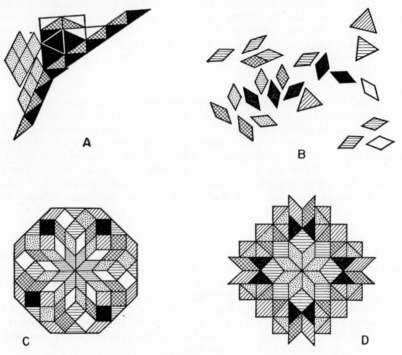

Fig. 63. *Results from the Mosaic Test (1)*

From M. Lowenfeld, "The Mosaic Test," *American Journal of Orthopsychiatry,* 19:537–550, 1949. Used by permission of the publisher. The items for this figure and for the next were selected from Figures 2–6.

the pieces into any kind of pattern he likes. A few sample results appear in Figure 63, and in Figure 64 on page 171. The patterns are scored for their coherency, their completeness, their use of color, their symmetry, their conceptual basis, and the arrangement of the spacing.

In Figure 63, A is an incoherent, compact result; B is also incoherent, but spaced. Design C is an unspaced, not quite symmetrical design, while D is a successful pattern of the same type. In Figure 64, E shows a simple but symmetrical, spaced pattern. Pattern F is incomplete and shows little coherence, with a poor use of space. Pattern G has some artistic merit, although this does not enter into the scoring; it is complete, symmetrical, well spaced, and well planned. Pattern H shows a relatively ambitious but unfinished plan. The "normal" patterns are D, E, and G, but the introduction of wide spacing into E and the balanced compactness of D suggest different personalities. The individuals who made Patterns A and B were either mentally defective or in a state of profound emotional disturbance. Patterns C, F, and H are characteristic types produced by neurotics. There seems to be some significance also in the extent to which the colors are disregarded or worked into the plans. In general, neurotics attempt to make the same kinds of patterns that normal people do, but they fail to

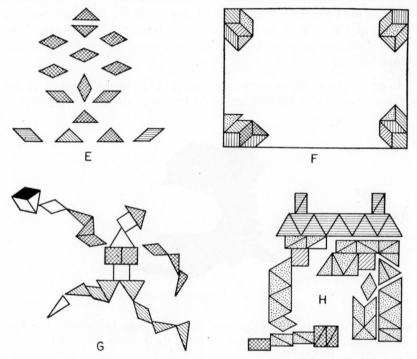

Fig. 64. *Results from the Mosaic Test (2)*

From Lowenfeld, "The Mosaic Test," *loc. cit.*

complete them in a satisfactory way. The degree of failure, which varies from a jumbled incoherence to a slight asymmetry, gives a clue to the severity of the condition.

No other projective technique is as old, as well known, or as widely used as the Rorschach.[12] A mere list of the existing references dealing with

[12] For good and not too technical discussions, see S. J. Beck, *Rorschach's Test*, Vol. I, *Basic Processes*, 2d ed., rev., 1949, 227 pp., and Vol. II, *A Variety of Personality Pictures*, 1945, Grune & Stratton, Inc., 402 pp.; M. R. Harrower-Erickson and M. E. Steiner, *Large Scale Rorschach Technique*, Charles C Thomas, Publisher, 2d ed., 1951, 353 pp.; M. R. Hertz, "Evaluation of the Rorschach Method in Its Application to Normal Childhood and Adolescence," *Character and Personality*, 10:151–162, 1941; B. Klopfer and D. M. Kelley, *The Rorschach Technique*, World Book Company, 1942, 436 pp.; and M. G. Siegel, "Description of the Rorschach Method," *Family*, 27:51–58, 1946.

it would fill an entire book. It consists of a series of cards on each of which there is an irregularly shaped blotch of ink. The person taking the test is merely asked, "What might this be?" He then reads his own interpretation into the blot by telling what he thinks it is. The scorer notes not only the total responses, but also the number of associations given, their quality, type, and originality, the lack or the profusion of detail, and so on. The person taking the test perceives in the meaningless ink blots only what his experiences to date have conditioned him to see, just as he bases the story he invents for each picture in the TAT test upon his personal experiences, emotions, and reactions. In the latter case, however, he has some hint of meaning from the picture, whereas in the former he must supply all the meaning himself.

In order to provide a simple illustration of the basic technique involved, the writer showed the ink blot in Figure 65—not taken from any test—to a

Fig. 65. *A Sample Ink Blot*

thirty-year-old veteran who had just returned from the war in the Pacific, to his twenty-eight-year-old wife, and to their seven-year-old son. Their replies were as follows:

> Boy: a bird, a dog, an old man with a long nose, a rat with a curly tail, a bat, a crooked finger, the edge of a saw.
> Man: a coral atoll, the guns on a battleship, a ragged sail.
> Woman: a lace collar, a map, a grass hula skirt, a flower dish.

The child did not see the blot as a whole at all, but picked out bits here and there, in which he could see a likeness to something he had known. Both adults interpreted it as a whole, each being influenced, however, by his or her experiences; the man gave one detail, the guns, but the woman made no effort to interpret the separate parts of the blot. All variations in the nature of what is seen give clues to personality and to problems of adjustment. The complete scoring of the Rorschach is too complicated to explain here, and the interpretation still remains more an art than a science. In the hands of a skillful tester, however, the Rorschach gives consistent and valuable information as to the structure of personality, especially in its unconscious elements.

Several other techniques may be mentioned briefly. The Szondi Test[13] presents the taker with forty-eight photographs of mental patients—six each of eight types—from which the subject chooses the ones in each set that he likes best and likes least. Szondi's own theory concerning the test is highly elaborate and does not seem related to the facts, but the test does appear to have value. The users believe the choices reflect both the taker's basic tensions and the manner in which he is handling them.

Another approach to the measurement of personality has been made through the analysis of handwriting[14] or simple drawing[15] and finger painting.[16] The drawing of a man or a house has been used for many years as a measure of intelligence, but its use in the investigation of personality is quite recent. Study of handwriting is a perennial method for "reading" character but has been so frequently coupled with palmistry and other pseudo sciences as to be regarded with suspicion. However, since everything people do reveals something about them, there seems no reason to think that handwriting cannot yield to scientific analysis. The handwriting and the drawing of normal individuals, mental defectives, delinquents, neurotics, and psychotics do show differences which are being studied and evaluated. An effort is also being made to use music and other sounds as the basis for a projective technique.[17]

II. Types of Personality

There have been many efforts to classify people into types. The trouble has always been that after one has selected from the population those who, upon any basis, may properly be grouped together, one still has a great many individuals left over who do not fit into any category. These "mixed" types are, indeed, so numerous as to arouse some doubts as to the practical value of "typing." However, it seems desirable to illustrate some of the current efforts at classification. There appear to be three modes of approach. One is statistical. Many single traits are measured in a given group of individuals, and the results are correlated to find out which traits are funda-

[13] S. R. Deri, "The Szondi Test," *American Journal of Orthopsychiatry,* 19:447–454, 1949; and S. R. Deri, *Introduction to the Szondi Test: Theory and Practice,* Grune & Stratton, Inc., 1949, 354 pp.

[14] P. Castelnuovo-Tedesco, "A Study of the Relationship between Handwriting and Personality Variables," *Genetic Psychology Monographs,* 37:167–220, 1948; and T. S. Lewinson and J. Zubin, *Handwriting Analysis,* King's Crown Press, 1942, 147 pp.

[15] P. Elkisch, "Children's Drawings as a Projective Technique," *Psychological Monographs,* Vol. LVIII, No. 1, 1945, 31 pp.; A. O. England, "Psychological Study of Children's Drawings," *American Journal of Orthopsychiatry,* 13:525–530, 1943; and K. Machover, *Personality Projection in the Drawings of the Human Figure,* Charles C Thomas, Publisher, 1949, 181 pp.

[16] E. Phillips and E. Stromberg, "A Comparative Study of Finger-Painting Performance in Detention Home and High School Pupils," *Journal of Psychology,* 26:507–515, 1948; T. Schmidel-Waehner, "Interpretations of Spontaneous Drawings and Paintings," *Genetic Psychology Monographs,* 33:3–70, 1946.

[17] D. R. Stone, "Recorded Auditory Apperception Tests: A New Projective Technique," *Journal of Psychology,* 29:349–353, 1950.

mental and independent of each other and which tend to occur together. A second approach is through the measurement of body build. In this case one makes the assumption that certain traits of character are associated with each type of build. A third method is to approach the matter through needs, drives, urges, problems, conflicts, escapes, and adaptations, observing how these tend to reinforce or offset each other to produce different types of personality. No one method seems adequate by itself but all three come out with certain similar groupings of traits that are recognizable as the same type of person. The agreement is naturally not perfect, but it is sufficient to suggest that all three methods have value.

As soon as one begins to interrelate measurements of separate traits it becomes evident that certain constellations or clusters appear often. Each cluster presumably represents a group of characteristics that coalesce to form a type of personality. One type may share some traits with others, to be sure, but each constellation appears as a unit often enough to justify its being regarded as distinct. The number of such clusters, as well as the particular selection of characteristics, varies with the nature and extent of the data used by an investigator, and with his method of handling them. One investigator[18] has found twelve primary trait clusters which suggest definite and recognizable types of people. Four samples appear below:

Unit 1: arrogant, exhibitionistic, talkative, boastful, argumentative, conceited, stubborn, pugnacious, tactless, rigid, hostile, ruthless, egotistical, acquisitive; blames others, is unkind to inferiors, flatters superiors

Unit 2: thoughtful, wise, original, constructive, intelligent, independent, persevering, reliable, mature, planful, analytical, versatile, orderly, cultured

Unit 3: naïve, modest, submissive, grateful, tolerant, peaceable, childlike, gentle, self-effacing, self-distrustful, self-dissatisfied, quiet, dependent

Unit 4: impulsive, changeable, thoughtless, playful, careless, wasteful, frivolous, humorous, lively, vivacious, foolish, unenquiring, amusing, entertaining

In common speech, persons having these groups of traits are dubbed the braggart, the scholar, the wallflower, and the playboy.

Investigations of body type have resulted in three basic types of personality, which are often referred to as psychotypes.[19] They are related to the three physical types described on pages 26–29. The ectomorph tends to be a restrained, self-conscious, inhibited, quiet, apprehensive, and somewhat secretive person. He likes privacy, and, when in trouble, he turns to solitude as a solution. Social contacts are hard for him, partly because he is usually afraid of people and partly because he becomes so horribly embarrassed if he makes a social blunder that he is not willing to run the risk of doing so. Analysis of the personality shown by fifty-one young men

---

[18] R. B. Cattell, "The Principal Trait Clusters for Describing Personality," *Psychological Bulletin*, 42:129–161, 1945, and *Description and Measurement of Personality*, World Book Company, 1946, 602 pp.

[19] W. H. Sheldon and S. S. Stevens, *The Varieties of Human Temperament*, Harper & Brothers, 1942, 520 pp.

whose body build was strongly ectomorphic seemed to show a significant degree of relationship between body structure and the type of personality indicated above. The endomorph has a personality in sharp contrast. He loves comfort, good food, good conversation, and plenty of companionship. He is a relaxed, slow-moving, amiable, sociable, tolerant, talkative individual who wants desperately to be loved and to give love to others. When he is troubled he turns at once to his friends; nothing disturbs him more than solitude. The mesomorph is reported as being characterized by great energy, a constant need for exercise, a great deal of physical courage, a love of both adventure and competition, and a Spartan indifference to discomfort. He is bold, reckless, aggressive, assertive of his position in a group, likely to dominate others, and often ruthless. His manner is direct, his voice is loud, and he makes a horrendous clatter as he rushes through life. When troubled, he takes a long walk, plays a vigorous game, or goes swimming, and finds relief in mere action. Since most people are not extreme types but mixtures, they usually show a less consistent picture than those just sketched. It is probable that personalities, as well as body build, form a continuous, unbroken series from the extreme introvert to the extreme extrovert.

One sometimes finds personalities indicated by descriptive phrases such as the "unsocialized-aggressive" or the "overinhibited" individual. These catch phrases may be translated rather easily into terms of basic drives. Thus, the first type has too much desire to dominate, to attract attention, to attack others, or to resist coercion, and too little desire to seek the approval of others, to surrender himself, or to seek protection. The second child wants overwhelmingly to seek protection, to surrender himself, and to avoid blame. In general, the earliest types of personality that were isolated and studied were abnormal types, since the practical need for their recognition was so great in order that children might be saved whenever possible from becoming criminal, neurotic, or insane. More recently, studies of personality have included many types, in which normal people constituted the majority of cases. Eventually, it is to be hoped that all personalities can be classified in a comprehensive and helpful manner.

One rather recent study[20] consisted of an intensive analysis of all the sixteen-year-old boys and girls in a single small town. These adolescents were studied by numerous questionnaires, tests of aptitude and personality, check lists, ratings, self-estimates, questions on beliefs and attitudes, measures of popularity and social status, tests of honesty, loyalty, and other traits, personal interviews, and so on. Five definite personality types emerged. The outstanding traits of each type appear in Table 7 on pages 176–177. These types included 66 (58 per cent) of the 114 adolescents who were sixteen years old during the year of the survey. The remaining 48 showed presumably mixtures of traits from at least two types. This proportion of "mixed" personalities is rather low—only 42 per cent.

---

[20] R. J. Havighurst and H. Taba, *Adolescent Character and Personality*, John Wiley & Sons, Inc., 1949, 315 pp.

Table 7

TYPES OF PERSONALITY

	Self-directive personality	Adaptive personality	Submissive personality	Defiant personality	Unadjusted personality
I.a. Personal traits (positive)	ambitious, responsible, orderly, persistent, introspective	outgoing, confident, sensitive to environment, good adjustments, no observable fears or anxieties			
I.b. Personal traits (negative)	self-doubt, self-criticism, some anxiety, some aggressiveness, low in warmth	submissive	timid, lacks initiative, stubborn, self-doubting, self-critical, lacking in aggression		dissatisfied, complaining, feelings of insecurity, occasional aggressiveness
II.a. Social traits (positive)	leadership, activity in school affairs	very popular, active in student affairs, social skills well developed, popular with opposite sex, self-assured, no family conflicts, permissive home training, high ratings in friendliness, tends to move toward others	no conflict with family, slight tendency to move toward others		
II.b. Social traits (negative)	some conflict with family, strict home training, awkwardness in social skills, tends to move away from others		always a follower, a nonentity, awkward in social skills, very strict home training	unpopular, hostile to school activities, moves against people, family training inconsistent, neglect, much conflict with family	any level from low to high

III.a. Intellectual traits (positive)	average to high intelligence, better schoolwork than IQ would indicate	average to high intelligence	any level from low to high	schoolwork lower than level indicated by IQ
III.b. Intellectual traits (negative)	schoolwork sometimes lower than expected	low to average intelligence, schoolwork corresponds to IQ	schoolwork lower than level indicated by IQ	
IV.a. Moral traits (positive) high ratings in character (especially in honor and responsibility), concern about morals, moral attitudes not rigid, high standards	good ratings in honor and responsibility	average to good ratings in honor and responsibility		
IV.b. Moral traits (negative)	adopts current standards without thinking, moral standards uncertain	uncertain of moral standards and attitudes	low character ratings except on courage, moral standards and attitudes low	low to average ratings in character, low to average moral standards and attitudes
V. Methods of gaining security	gains security through relations with others	gains security through submission to authority	gains security through personal hostility to authority	does not gain security
	gains security through achievements			

Reprinted with permission from R. J. Havighurst and H. Taba, *Adolescent Character and Personality*, pp. 118–119, copyright 1949, John Wiley & Sons, Inc.

The fundamental trouble with the classification of personalities has always been that the human animal is a highly complex and sensitive organism that continues to modify itself as long as it exists. Even if an individual starts with a basic type of personality, life soon pokes in a dent here and puffs up a bulge there. Moreover, any human being has many contradictory drives, such as the desire to be dominating and the desire to be submissive, but these competing tendencies are stimulated by different circumstances. For instance, the writer has a lifelong friend who is, as a general thing, argumentative, intolerant, aggressive, and outspoken, but in the presence of her crippled sister she is a model of charm, politeness, consideration, thoughtfulness, tact, and submissiveness. Both personalities are real, coexistent, and spontaneously natural. Such contradictions make the path of the classifier hard.

III. Summary

The last two decades have seen a great development of tests and other measures designed to investigate personality, or at least some of the traits that make up the complex of personality. Almost anything a person does and almost any attitude he expresses show his personality to a greater or lesser extent. The inventories of traits and attitudes were the first type of measurement to appear. More important at present are the various types of projective techniques, among which the Rorschach and Thematic Apperception Test are of outstanding importance. The grouping of traits into clusters has not progressed quite as far as the measurement of personality, but some constellations of traits are now fairly recognizable.

REFERENCES FOR FURTHER READING

BOOKS

1. Abt, L. E., and L. Bellak, *Projective Psychology*, Alfred A. Knopf, Inc., 1950, 485 pp. (Pp. 7–68, 75–145, 185–229, 230–256, 298–321, 357–402.)
2. Anderson, *The Psychology of Development and Personal Adjustment*, Chap. 16.
3. Beck, S. J., *Rorschach's Test*, Vol. I, *Basic Processes*, Grune & Stratton, Inc., 2d ed. rev., 1949, 227 pp. (Chaps. 1–4, 7–9), and Vol. II, *A Variety of Personality Pictures*, Grune & Stratton, Inc., 1946, 402 pp. (Chaps. 2–3.)
4. Bell, J. E., *Projective Techniques*, Longmans, Green & Co., 1948, 533 pp. (Chaps. 1, 3, 6, 8, 11, 12.)
5. Breckenridge and Vincent, *Child Psychology*, Chap. 12.
6. Cattell, R. B., *Description and Measurement of Personality*, World Book Company, 1946, 602 pp. (Chaps. 4, 8–12.)
7. Donahue, *et al.*, *The Measurement of Student Adjustment and Achievement*, pp. 23–50, 59–70.
8. English and Pearson, *Emotional Problems of Living*, Chaps. 10, 11.
9. Erickson, M. R., and M. E. Steiner, *Large Scale Rorschach Techniques*, Charles C Thomas, Publisher, 2d ed., 1951, 353 pp. (Pt. I, Sec. 1, and Pt. III, Secs. 1 and 2.)
10. Eysenck, G., *Dimensions of Personality*, The Macmillan Company, 1949, 308 pp. (Chap. 2.)

11. Fleege, U. H., *Self-Revelation of the Adolescent Boy,* Bruce Publishing Company, 1944, 384 pp. (Chaps. 11, 12.)
12. Garrison, *Growth and Development,* Chap. 14.
13. Garrison, *Psychology of Adolescence,* Chap. 14.
14. Frank, L. K., *Projective Methods,* Charles C Thomas, Publisher, 1948, 86 pp.
15. Goodenough, F. L., *Mental Testing,* Rinehart & Company, 1949, 609 pp. (Chaps. 26–27.)
16. Harsh, C. M., and H. G. Schrickel, *Personality Development and Assessment,* The Ronald Press, 1950, 518 pp. (Chaps. 8–11, 17.)
17. Havighurst, R. J., and H. Taba, *Adolescent Character and Personality,* John Wiley & Sons, Inc., 1949, 315 pp. (Chaps. 3, 10–16.)
18. Hurlock, *Adolescent Development,* Chap. 14.
19. Landis, *Adolescence and Youth,* Chaps. 5, 6.
20. MacKinnon, D. W., "Structure of Personality," in Hunt, *Personality and the Behavior Disorders,* I, 3–48.
21. Maller, J. B., "Personality Tests," in Hunt, *Personality and the Behavior Disorders,* I, 170–213.
22. Merry and Merry, *The First Two Decades of Life,* Chap. 11.
23. Murphy, G., *Personality: A Bio-Social Approach to Origins and Structure,* Harper & Brothers, 1947, 999 pp. (Chaps. 20–25.)
24. Rosenzweig, S., "An Outline of Frustration Theory," in Hunt, *Personality and the Behavior Disorders,* I, 379–388.
25. Rosenzweig, S., *Psychodiagnosis: An Introduction to Tests in the Clinical Practice of Psychodiagnosis,* Grune & Stratton, Inc., 1949, 380 pp. (Chaps. 3, 4, 6, 7.)
26. Sadler, *Adolescence Problems,* Chap. 6.
27. Sutherland, J. D., "The Types of Personality," in J. R. Rees, *Modern Practice in Psychological Medicine,* Paul B. Hoeber, Inc., 1949, 475 pp. (Pp. 86–102.)
28. Symonds, P. M., *Adolescent Fantasy,* Columbia University Press, 1949, 397 pp. (Chaps. 2–5, 11, 13–15.)
29. Thorpe, L. P., *Psychological Foundations of Personality,* McGraw-Hill Book Company, 1938, 602 pp. (Chaps. 1–4.)
30. Tomkins, S., *The TAT: The Theory and Technique of Interpretation,* Grune & Stratton, Inc., 1947, 297 pp. (Chaps. 1, 2, 3, 6, 7, 8.)

MONOGRAPHS, BULLETINS, PROCEEDINGS, YEARBOOKS, ARTICLES

A. *Surveys*

1. Frank, L. K., "Understanding the Individual through Projective Techniques," *American Council on Education Studies,* No. 14 (Ser. 1, No. 40), 1950, pp. 52–62.
2. Goldhamer, H., "Recent Developments in Personality Studies," *American Sociological Review,* 13:555–565, 1948.
3. Kutash, F. V., "Recent Developments in the Field of Projective Techniques," *Rorschach Research Exchange,* 13:74–86, 1949.
4. Raths, L. E., "Understanding the Individual through Anecdotal Records, Sociometric Devices, and the Like," *American Council on Education Studies,* No. 14 (Ser. 1, No. 40), 1950, pp. 63–73.
5. Rosenzweig, S., "Available Methods for Studying Personality," *Journal of Psychology,* 28:345–368, 1949.
6. Symonds, P. M., and M. G. Hessel, "Development and Educational Significance of Projective Techniques in Personality Measurement," *Review of Educational Research,* 20:51–62, 1950.

B. *The Rorschach Test*

1. Carr, A., "An Evaluation of Nine Nondirective Psychotherapy Cases by Means of the Rorschach," *Journal of Consulting Psychology*, 13:196–205, 1948.
2. Hertz, M. R., "Evaluation of the Rorschach Method and Its Application to Normal Childhood and Adolescence," *Character and Personality*, 10:151–162, 1941.
3. Hertz, M. R., "Some Personality Changes in Adolescents as Revealed by the Rorschach Method," *Psychological Bulletin*, 37:515–516, 1940.
4. McCandless, B. R., "The Rorschach as a Predictor of Academic Success," *Journal of Applied Psychology*, 33:43–50, 1949.
5. Northway, M. L., and B. T. Wigdor, "Rorschach Patterns as Related to the Sociometric Status of School Children," *Sociometry*, 10:186–189, 1947.
6. Siegel, M. G., "Description of the Rorschach Method," *Family*, 27:51–58, 1946.

C. *The TAT (Thematic Apperception Test)*

1. Bellak, L. E., R. Eckstein, and S. Braverman, "A Preliminary Study of Norms for the Thematic Apperception Test," *American Psychologist*, 2:271, 1947.
2. Clark, R. M., "Methods of Administering and Evaluating the TAT in Group Situations," *Genetic Psychology Monographs*, 30:3–55, 1944.
3. Combs, A. W., "A Comparative Study of Motivations as Revealed in Thematic Apperception Test Studies and Autobiography," *Journal of Clinical Psychology*, 3:65–75, 1947.
4. Combs, A. W., "The Use of Personal Experience in Thematic Apperception Test Story Plots," *Journal of Clinical Psychology*, 2:357–363, 1946.
5. Lasaga, J. I., and C. Martinez-Arango, "Four Detailed Examples of How Mental Conflicts of Psychoneurotic and Psychotic Patients May Be Discovered by Means of the TAT," *Journal of Psychology*, 26:299–345, 1948.
6. Morgan, C. D., and H. A. Murray, "A Method for Investigating Phantasies," *Archives of Neurology and Psychiatry*, 34:288–306, 1935.
7. Murray, H. A., *Thematic Apperception Test Manual*, Harvard University Press, 1943.
8. Piotrowski, Z. A., "A New Evaluation of the TAT," *Psychoanalytic Review*, 37:101–127, 1950.
9. Rosenzweig, S., and A. C. Ishan, "Complementary TAT Patterns in Close Kin," *American Journal of Orthopsychiatry*, 17:129–142, 1947.
10. Wyatt, F., "The Scoring and Analysis of the Thematic Apperception Test," *Journal of Psychology*, 24:319–330, 1947.

D. *The Picture Frustration Test*

1. Bernard, J., "The Rosenzweig Picture-Frustration Study: I and II," *Journal of Psychology*, 28:326–332, 333–344, 1949.
2. Falls, R. P., and R. R. Blake, "A Quantitative Analysis of the Picture Frustration Study," *Journal of Personality*, 16:320–325, 1948.
3. Rosenzweig, S., "The Picture Association Method and Its Application in a Study of Reactions to Frustration," *Journal of Personality*, 14:3–23, 1945.
4. Rosenzweig, S., E. F. Fleming, and H. J. Clarke, "Revised Scoring Manual for the Rosenzweig Picture-Frustration Study," *Journal of Psychology*, 24:165–208, 1947.

E. *Other Tests*

1. Deri, S. R., "The Szondi Test," *American Journal of Orthopsychiatry*, 19:447–454, 1949.

1. Costin, F., and P. E. Eiserer, "Students' Attitudes toward School Life as Revealed by a Sentence Completion Test," *American Psychologist*, 4:289, 1949.
2. Shor, J., "Report on a Verbal Projection Technique," *Journal of Clinical Psychology*, 2:279–282, 1946.

1. Diamond, B. L., and H. T. Schmale, "The Mosaic Test: I. An Evaluation of Its Clinical Application," *American Journal of Orthopsychiatry*, 14:237–250, 1944.
2. Lowenfeld, M., "The Mosaic Test," *American Journal of Orthopsychiatry*, 19:537–550, 1949.

1. Guilford, J. P., and W. S. Zimmerman, *The Guilford-Zimmerman Temperament Survey*, Sheridan Supply Company, 1949.
2. Hampton, R. J., "The MMPI as a Psychometric Tool for Diagnosis of Personality Disorders among College Students," *Journal of Social Psychology*, 26:99–108, 1947.
3. Hathaway, S. R., and J. C. McKinley, "Manual for the Minnesota Multiphasic Personality Inventory," University of Minnesota Press, 1943.
4. Rogers, C. R., "Tests of Personality Adjustment in Children 9 to 13 Years of Age," *Teachers College Contributions to Education*, No. 458, 1931, 107 pp.
5. Sheriffs, S. A., "The 'Intuition' Questionnaire: A New Projective Technique," *Journal of Abnormal and Social Psychology*, 43:326–327, 1948.
6. Symonds, P. M., "The Sentence Completion Test as a Projective Technique," *Journal of Abnormal and Social Psychology*, 42:320–329, 1947.
7. Teigs, E. W., W. W. Clark, and L. P. Thorpe, "The California Test of Personality," *Journal of Educational Research*, 35:102–108, 1941.

1. Elkisch, P., "Children's Drawings as a Projective Technique," *Psychological Monographs*, Vol. LVIII, No. 1, 1945, 31 pp.
2. Napoli, P. J., "Interpreting Aspects of Finger Painting," *Journal of Psychology*, 23:93–132, 1947.
3. Naumberg, M., "Studies of the 'Free' Art Expression of Behavior Problem Children and Adolescents as a Means of Diagnosis and Therapy," *Nervous and Mental Disease Monographs*, No. 71, 1947, 225 pp.

1. Castelnuevo-Tedesco, P., "A Study of the Relationship between Handwriting and Personality Variables," *Genetic Psychology Monographs*, 37:167–220, 1948.
2. Secord, P. F., "Studies of the Relationship of Handwriting to Personality," *Journal of Personality*, 17:430-448, 1949.

1. Stone, D. R., "Recorded Auditory Apperception Tests: A New Projective Technique," *Journal of Psychology*, 29:349–353, 1950.

F. *Factors of Personality*

1. Banks, C., "Primary Personality Factors in Women: A Re-analysis," *British Journal of Psychology, Statistical Section*, I, Pt. III, 1948, 204–218.
2. Cattell, R. B., "Primary Personality Factors in the Realm of Objective Tests," *Journal of Personality*, 16:459–487, 1948.
3. Cattell, R. B., "The Principal Trait Clusters for Describing Personality," *Psychological Bulletin*, 42:129–161, 1945.

CHAPTER SEVEN

Emotional
Deviates

Adolescence is one of the periods in life during which there is an extraordinary amount of strain, both physical and emotional. It is not surprising therefore that even normal boys and girls show rather intense emotional reactions and that a few are unable to cope with the new demands made upon them.[1] Some adolescents break down under the strain of their maladjustments, sometimes with short periods of panic or acute anxiety, sometimes with the development of specific neuroses, and less often with regression into dementia praecox, a term which means early dementia. If this mental disease is going to develop at all it usually makes its appearance during adolescence.

Different investigators have estimated the number of emotional deviates in the adolescent population at widely varying proportions. Such figures obviously depend upon where one draws the line between what is normal and what is abnormal, and upon the adequacy of the survey from which each investigator made his estimate. The studies to date deal with the occurrence of abnormality either in colleges or in the general population, rather than with its frequency in secondary schools. However, one can use these studies as a base from which the probable percentage of abnormality at any age level may be deduced. For instance, the rate of first admissions in New York to mental hospitals for those between the ages of fifteen and nineteen years in 1943 was 59 in 100,000.[2] This figure included only those so markedly abnormal that they had to be removed altogether from society. At this time, 68,000 in every 100,000 adolescents between the ages of fifteen and nineteen were in high school. The above rates would produce, in a single school enrolling 500 students, about 1 psychotic pupil every three years. If the current rate continues, approximately 7 in every 10,000 babies born in 1942 will some day enter a mental hospital, 5 of them before they are twenty-one.

Two mental health surveys of the public school children in entire

---

[1] H. C. Schumacher, "Mental and Emotional Disturbance in Adolescence," *Journal of Child Psychiatry*, 1:113–120, 1948, and H. Wilson, "Mental Disorders in Adolescence," *Practitioner*, 162:305–312, 1949.

[2] T. Tietze, "A Note on the Incidence of Mental Disease in the State of New York," *American Journal of Psychiatry*, 100:402–505, 1943.

counties give some indication of the number of maladjustments that exist in average school groups.

In one instance the survey was limited to those in grades 3 to 6, with a second survey being made of the same children a year later.[3] Of the 1,499 children, 287 or 29 per cent were seriously maladjusted. The percentage increased with each school grade. There were two maladjusted boys for each maladjusted girl. Almost half the retarded children were on the list. It is encouraging to note that in the retest during the following year, after the teachers had had a little time to help the maladjusted, the pupils who made the greatest improvement were those who had originally scored the lowest.

The second county survey included all children from the first grade through the senior year of the small local college, a total of 2,947 individuals.[4] From 5 to 10 per cent made very low scores. Two thirds of these cases were boys. There was a decrease of extreme maladjustment with age, the college students making the best scores of all. The results from these two surveys do not always agree, partly because the investigators did not use identical tests and methods and also because they did not regard exactly the same degrees of deviation as indicating severe maladjustment. The larger number of boys is, in the writer's opinion, due to the overwhelmingly feminine atmosphere of maternal supervision at home and female supervision at school. The majority of women, whether mothers or not, have little comprehension of a small boy's needs, even though they may love him dearly. If the situation were reversed, and little girls were supervised at home mainly by their fathers, and in school by adult men, their maladjustment would probably exceed that of the boys, although it might take other forms. It is also interesting that in one survey the frequency of maladjustment increases with age, while in the other it decreases.

For two or three decades colleges and universities have been maintaining mental clinics to which many students might come of their own free will for advice, and to which a few were sent each year by members of the administrative or instructional staffs. One report[5] that covers twelve years of work in a university gives the following figures: in a yearly student population of over 13,000 there was an average of 55 cases a year of serious mental disorder, or a rate of 4 in each 1,000. The number with acute conditions was less than 1 in 1,000, however. Each year, 8 per cent of the students consulted members of the clinic about something that was troubling them. In another university,[6] 3 per cent of the students came for consultation. The most common complaint, as reported in this study

[3] A. R. Mangus and J. R. Seeley, "Mental Health Problems among School Children in an Ohio County," *Understanding the Child,* 18:74–78, 1949.

[4] E. C. Hunter, "The Summary of a Mental Health Survey of Spartanburg County, South Carolina," *Journal of Experimental Education,* 17:294–308, 1948.

[5] T. Raphael and L. E. Himler, "Schizophrenic and Paranoid Psychoses among College Students," *American Journal of Psychiatry,* 100:443–451, 1944.

[6] H. A. Carroll and H. M. Jones, "Adjustment Problems of College Students," *School and Society,* 59:270–272, 1944.

and in others of similar nature, was poor schoolwork, which was often merely a result of inadequate preparation without emotional involvements. Minor social and emotional maladjustments brought about a third of the students who came to the clinics. The remaining third was composed mainly of neurotics, but included a few cases of more serious nature. Mental abnormality is, then, a real problem among those adolescents still in school—just as it is in all age groups, in school or out.

Further information concerning the prevalence of mental and emotional abnormality comes from reports by Army and Navy medical staffs during World War II. These figures were profoundly shocking to civilians, most of whom were not aware of how common maladjustment is in everyday life. A total of 1,850,000 men were rejected on grounds of mental or emotional abnormality.[7] Of this number 37 per cent were mental defectives, 42 per cent neurotic, and 1 per cent psychotic; the remaining 20 per cent suffered from nervous, not mental, diseases.

The original screening eliminated those with obvious mental and emotional peculiarities. It did not and could not tell in advance which men were going to break down under training. As the war progressed and the pace and strain increased, the number of men who had to be given a neuropsychiatric discharge became greater. In 1944, 48 per cent of all discharges for disabilities of any kind were for neuropsychiatric disorders.[8] Actual psychoses made up only 10 per cent of this total. The most frequent conditions were anxiety neuroses, psychosomatic disorders, and psychopathic personalities.

The types of symptom and underlying condition seen among soldiers differ only in details from those seen in civilian life, except as the shock of actual wounds and extreme physical fatigue may complicate the picture. The thumbnail sketches quoted below are included to illustrate the wide variety of abnormal personalities that came to the attention of a Navy psychiatrist. One can easily see why the Navy could do little with them and why they were given neuropsychiatric discharges.

No. 1: Two years of high school, involved in domestic friction at home, left school because of grief over parents' quarrels. Shy, easily fatigued, complained of his stomach. In brig for going to sleep on duty, which he persistently did.

No. 2: Left in third year of high school to enter Navy, very homesick, seasick, could not stay on duty on tanker as member of gun crew. Cried, very unhappy, and talked of suicide.

No. 3: A somewhat dull man, completed ninth grade at 17 years of age. During any excitement went into hysterical attacks. On one occasion was mute for several days. On another, frenzied excitement; particularly upset by gunfire.

No. 4: An adopted child who graduated from high school, worked with foster father in beauty parlor. On stage in the evenings, impersonating a female. Picked

---

[7] From figures furnished by the Office of the Surgeon General of the Department of the Army.

[8] W. C. Menninger, "The Mentally or Emotionally Handicapped Veteran," *Annals of the American Academy of Political and Social Science,* 239:20–28, 1945.

up spare money by prostitution to male homosexuals. Admitted in an acute anxiety state, afraid he would transgress in Navy and be sent to prison.

No. 5: Began stealing in early childhood. During high school forged checks, ran away, and enlisted in the Marines. Ran away and was sent to hospital where he again escaped. Attempted suicide by gas. Following a medical discharge he enlisted in Navy, immediately ran away, and again attempted suicide.

No. 6: Several arrests as young man, one term in prison. In 1937, when out of work and in domestic trouble, had period of amnesia lasting 12 days. Brought to hospital by shore patrol in cataleptic state, did not speak for several days. Had recently served a sentence in brig for AWOL, and a fine of $150.

No. 7: A good boy, devoted to his mother, became discouraged over failure to get type of transfer he wanted. Given leave, went home, somewhat sad, hated to go back. Brother took him to train, later found him in an alleyway with both wrists cut and having drunk a bottle of Mercurochrome.

No. 8: Sent in because of tendency to seek a weapon when he lost his temper. Much trouble in Navy through violent attempts upon others, with weapons. A haughty, belligerent, egotistic individual, thoroughly unreliable, a bully, and a petty thief.[9]

During the years of adolescence, boys and girls are under a good deal of strain, and most of them show at least occasional bits of peculiar behavior. The great majority manage to "muddle through" the period, with or without a few permanent emotional scars. Others make one or more of the overt, aggressive types of response—exhibitionism, outbursts of temper, or delinquencies of various kinds. The remaining pupils make withdrawal reactions, as will later be described. Students with inadequate intelligence or psychopathic personalities are practically certain to get worse. Fears and anxieties in regard to sexual matters are common, as also are feelings of inferiority and of guilt.

In this single chapter it is obviously impossible to present more than a few salient facts about each of the most common types of abnormal individual. Since the teacher may be the only person so situated as to make early diagnosis possible, she should have some idea of the behavior that characterizes emotionally and mentally unstable pupils. The writer has therefore attempted some brief sketches of the more common types of emotional deviates. These descriptions are necessarily somewhat dogmatic and oversimplified, but from them a teacher may gain a few clues as to what reactions are "peculiar." Since a teacher should not attempt treatment of emotional abnormality any more than she should try to cure physical disease, the present discussion is limited to descriptions of behavior. When a teacher recognizes reactions as peculiar, she should send the pupil showing them to an expert for diagnosis and treatment.

The reader will notice that the underlying conflicts are much the same from one type of emotional disturbance to another, but that the stimuli which produce in one person one kind of behavior may produce in another

[9] A. W. Stearns, "Unfit Personalities in the Military Services," in J. McV. Hunt (ed.), *Personality and the Behavior Disorders,* The Ronald Press, 1944, II, 828–830. Used by permission of the publisher.

a totally different kind. The inclinations to one mode of release rather than another lie within the individual, not in the situations. The ten types described below differ from each other in the reactions shown, rather than in the situations to which the responses are made.

I. Phobias and Compulsive States

Obsession and phobias do not look alike to the casual observer, but they have their origin in the same motivation. Two possible explanations will be given, one that is psychoanalytical and one that is not.[10]

The former presupposes that both difficulties begin with the pressure exerted by strong instinctual drives that the ego cannot accept. The first reaction, accompanied by a good deal of anxiety, is a direct repression of the drives. The pressure, however, continues with the generation of further anxiety lest the drives break through. The resulting tension is highly uncomfortable. An ego that is too weak to reconcile the drives with the restrictions of conscience may make either of two reactions in attempting to reject that part of its total make-up that is inacceptable to the rest. It can project the feeling of anxiety onto a particular object, person, or situation, or it can concentrate upon erecting a defense through which the offending drives cannot pass. In the first case, the individual develops a phobia. Instead of fearing himself, he fears cats, or thunderstorms, or sharp knives. Part of himself has thus been rejected and part retained. His projection helps him in two ways: he has apparently rid himself of the blame for having started the whole thing, and he has freed himself of tension during the absences of the feared object. If, however, his ego has enough strength to put up a fight, he tries to prevent the fear from ever arising, instead of projecting it after it has arisen. To this end he tries various rituals in the belief that if he goes through a certain set of avoidance reactions the drive will not break through. When the defensive reaction first appears the individual usually fights against it, but his conscious opposition is to no avail, because the reaction *does* bring relief from the underlying fear by preventing it from arising. The only safety for the ego now lies in following out the ritual exactly, and the individual soon feels compulsion to repeat a given act or to carry out a series of acts in a given order. That is, he has an obsession.

Another and less psychoanalytic explanation of phobias and obsessions should perhaps be presented. This theory presupposes the existence of a severe, long since forgotten, traumatic, emotional episode, to which the reactions of fear and anxiety were quite natural but were accompanied by equally strong feelings of guilt or shame and were therefore repressed. At some subsequent date an object, situation, or person reminiscent of the original experience appears and precipitates a reaction that was once sensible but now seems ridiculous. The sufferer from this condition cannot give

---

[10] See G. H. J. Pearson, *Emotional Disorders of Children: A Casebook of Child Psychiatry*, W. W. Norton & Company, 1949, Chap. 9; B. Crider, "Phobias: Their Nature and Treatment," *Journal of Psychology*, 27:217–229, 1949; and N. Cameron, *The Psychology of Behavior Disorders*, Houghton Mifflin Company, 1947, Chap. 10.

an explanation because he has forgotten the missing links in his story, either through passage of time or through repression. A similar type of explanation may be offered for obsessions. Presumably, while the traumatic experience was only partly repressed, it kept popping back into consciousness. Since sheer repression was not burying the objectionable memory fast enough, the individual tried prevention. At the first hint of returning recollection he diverted his attention by such distractions as walking three steps backward and blinking the eyes twice with each step. As a result of his distracted attention, the painful memory never became fully conscious. It should be noted that in all probability the defensive behavior really did work the first few times it was tried. The now-unconscious memories keep on trying to thrust themselves up and succeed sufficiently to make the individual feel tense and apprehensive. When the pressure gets high enough he performs his ritual and gets relief for a while, although he has long since forgotten what he is defending himself from. He has lost the connecting link between stimulus and response, but he has not forgotten that his mannerism, whatever its nature, has in the past brought him relief. There is no sense in trying to "educate" such a person out of his obsession, because he will succeed only in adding to his other troubles a new feeling of guilt and distress at his lack of self-control.

Phobias: Although a person may develop a phobia about anything, certain types of stimuli are more common than others: fear of small, closed spaces—claustrophobia; fear of open spaces; fear of looking down from a high place; fear of being alone, of falling down, of death, of knives, tunnels, storms, wind, or lightning. Generally, the stimuli are such as might normally cause a feeling of disquiet. Most people do not like to be shut in a closet or to look down from the top of a tower, but such experiences are only unpleasant, not terrifying. Similarly, most persons have more or less fear of the water, but they can inhibit it long enough to learn how to swim; a person with a phobia about water cannot be persuaded even to take a bath. The abnormal thing about most phobias is, therefore, their terrifying intensity rather than their nature. The writer knows a woman who lives in California, far from all her relatives and friends, doing work considerably below the level of which she is capable, and suffering much from loneliness and unhappiness because she has a phobia about thunderstorms. She has twisted her entire life out of shape in order to escape them. A similar warping of normal human relationships by a central fear is shown in the case study below:

Edna S. was a sophomore in college. She was twenty years old and had an IQ of 122. Her chief complaint was that she had a pronounced fear of being alone with any man; it made no difference if the man were a professor, a student, a relative, a casual acquaintance, young or old. She never accepted invitations that would involve her being alone with a male acquaintance. This settled policy on her part resulted in absence from practically all social affairs. During high school she had never attended a dance or evening party of any kind, even at the school, unless she was sure she could go and come with a group of girls. Edna could give no explanation for her phobia of men and believed that nothing could be done to help her. On the rare occasions when circumstances left her and a man together, she began at once to tremble, to perspire, and to become faint.

Edna had been the only child during her early years. She was a great favorite of her father, who adored her. He died when she was only five years old. In spite of her extreme youth, she cried and asked continually for her father for over a week after his death. Two years later her mother remarried. The mother was a highly emotional woman with little control over herself. She had infantile temper tantrums and hysterical attacks, which contributed to the emotional tension of the home. Edna never liked her stepfather, and he did not care much for her. Moreover, he attempted to provide the home discipline she probably needed, with the result that she came to hate him.

At school Edna always did good work and got along well with her age-mates, as long as she was in the elementary grades. In high school she made the school honor society, partly because of her good native ability, partly because she used for study the extra time she saved from parties, and partly because she had displaced her emotional drives from heterosexual interests to academic pursuits.

Investigation disclosed that when Edna was about eight years old—shortly after her mother's remarriage, while she was still in an upset condition from efforts to adjust to a new regime—she suffered a severe emotional shock. One evening she was left at home in the care of a male boarder, who attempted to molest her. Although he did not actually rape her, he frightened her badly, and then terrified her with threats of bodily harm if she should ever report his actions to her parents. Since he remained thereafter for some time within the family circle, Edna was constantly reminded of her experience, which she repressed completely for many years and until recently could not speak of without signs of emotional strain.

Treatment of this girl consisted primarily in leading her to talk freely of the repressed episode. When she first revealed it, she wept copiously. Seeing that this experience was a focal point in her difficulties of adjustment, the therapist encouraged her to relate the story over and over until it had lost its emotional content. Gradually she became objective about the whole episode and no longer showed fear, guilt, or shame. She read a little about the genesis of phobias in general and applied what she had read, under the therapist's supervision, to her own case. She began to show improvement almost at once. Within about four months she had her first date with a young man, with whom she walked to and from a theater without feeling anything more than a mild pleasure in his company. From this time on she improved rapidly and was able to make an almost normal adjustment. For the present at least she has lost her phobia, although no one can say that it will not return, in case she marries—especially if she marries a man who is thoughtless and callous in his advances to her.[11]

A person who is obsessed feels an inner compulsion so strong that he cannot resist it. He may, for instance, feel that he must use his left foot whenever he steps over a crack in the pavement; if by mistake he steps over one with his right foot, he feels compelled to go back and do it over again with his left. A failure to remedy his error makes him uncomfortable and may give him a sense of oncoming disaster. Some high school pupils have distinct obsessional tendencies. Thus one boy may want always to sit in the same seat, another to use the same space at the blackboard day after day, a third to settle down to study by performing a routine series of preparatory acts. Interference with these habits causes distress and some-

---

[11] Adapted from Thorpe, *op. cit.*, p. 373.

times guilt. The two histories given below describe the nature of compulsions and to some extent suggest the basis for the reactions.

Bryon is a young man of twenty-two, a sophomore in college. In his childhood he carefully avoided stepping on cracks in the pavement; he also felt compelled to pick up every smooth stone he saw. A little later he began to do everything by threes: he counted by threes, tore paper into three pieces, touched each shoe three times after putting it on, arranged objects in groups of three, and so on. Later, he changed to sevens, and felt compelled always to count exactly to seven whenever he urinated. At present he has changed to doing everything by fours. The fundamental compulsion has, of course, not altered. He also feels that he must pick up bits of paper, peelings, scraps, nails, pins, and all manner of small objects.

Bryon's home has been reasonably pleasant, although his mother is a highly emotional woman who broods, worries, takes things too seriously, and is rather uneven in her discipline. The father is a quiet, retiring sort of person, a professional man, whose chief interests are in his home and children. He is much more permissive that the mother. There are two brothers, one older and one younger, with whom Bryon has the usual number of brotherly arguments, but the relationship does not seem abnormal.

Bryon was always fearful, timid, sensitive, and physically weak. He often had terrifying nightmares. He thought other boys at school and in the neighborhood picked on him. By the time he was ten years old he had become quite fat, and he consequently became the butt of childish ridicule, which hurt his feelings. He was too clumsy to fight with other boys, and this inability gave him a sense of helplessness. Like many fat boys he had unusually small genitals and some deposit of fat under the nipples, which gave him a feminine appearance and caused comment. In recent summers he has refrained from going swimming, a sport that he enjoys, because he is sensitive about his appearance. At present he is not seriously overweight, but the attitudes he built up while he was fat have continued to influence him. During his adolescence he learned to masturbate and for a while indulged often in the habit, but has abandoned it of late. He has had some dates with girls, but denies that he has ever attempted any intimacies with them.

In school Bryon has always done good work. He graduated from high school at seventeen in the upper third of his class and entered the university, where he has made normal progress. After spending two years in the Army he has returned to school to major in agriculture.

Since early childhood this boy has experienced feelings of insecurity and inadequacy, although it is not altogether clear why he should have done so in the years before his obesity began to interfere with normal boyish pursuits. His compulsive and phobic patterns were apparently developed as protective mechanisms in order to preserve his ego from further assaults. He has always had a strong sense of magic in the carrying out of his rituals and has evidently believed that if he picked up every smooth stone all would go smoothly with him, or if he counted everything in whatever number grouping appealed to him at the moment he would ward off danger. Whenever he failed to take the precaution he thought essential—that is, if he inadvertently stepped on a crack in the pavement—he had a strong feeling of guilt and a conviction that something dreadful would soon happen. Like the primitive witch doctor, he developed so many taboos that he was almost certain to violate one or more of them every day, and he thus kept himself in an upset state of mind.[12]

Obsessions have played a rather prominent part in the mental make-up of the subject. The earliest recollection he has, going back to the time he was yet in his

---

[12] Based upon L. P. Thorpe, *The Psychology of Abnormal Behavior*, The Ronald Press, 1948, pp. 373–374.

high chair, is of an intense discomfiture at the table unless his chair was placed in such a position that both arms were exactly the same distance from the edge of the table. It is all very clear in his memory. . . . His father remarked one day that he should have a ruler with which to measure the distance, whereupon he was completely out of sorts until the ruler was obtained. . . . Always in school he was very careful to see that his pencils were sharpened to a perfectly symmetrical point. Even in eating an apple he was very careful to eat around the apple so as always to leave a circular shape. This preciseness has continued in the adult in the form of an intense desire to have everything with which he works arranged in the most acceptable manner, pictures always precisely straight on the wall, pencils adjusted to a minute degree, and, above all, his automobile always in as near perfect cond:tion as possible. Those who know him call him "an old maid.". . .

Another obsession is his desire to glance at the toe of first one shoe and then the other as he walks along, often at the cost of considerable discomfort. The more dangerous the terrain, the more likely is he to become obsessed with the desire. Frequently he stops, looks at the toe, and then walks on. He has even stopped running to look at the shoe toe. He has overcome this to a large degree, but he feels that bringing it vividly to mind as he is now doing is going to make the obsession more prominent for several days, until he can get it off his mind again. . . .

Another of these compulsive acts is the driving urge always to return, after locking a door, to see that the door is really locked. This is being gradually overcome through exertion of will power, of which it takes plenty.

While a child driving cows to and from the pasture it was practically impossible for the writer to pass a picket fence without touching every picket. Frequently he would return to touch one that he had missed. This tendency seldom appears now and is promptly put down when it does come. . . . He is also constantly running his hand over the buttons of his clothes to see that they are properly buttoned. This he has tried to overcome, but with little success.

He could probably enumerate several more of these phobias, obsessions, and compulsive acts were he to devote the time necessary, but suffice it to say that they have played, and still play, a rather important part in his everyday life.[13]

Both the phobia and the obsession are survivals of an actual adjustment to an actual emotional trauma, and they persist because the emergency still exists. The original shock has never been discharged, only hidden, and it is still trying to force its way into consciousness. Against this intrusion the obsessions and phobias stand guard, either to prevent the emergence or to convert the inner panic into fear of some external object. The usual method of treatment has been, therefore, to try to discover of what the trauma consisted, to drag the hidden episode out into the light of day, to solve the conflict, and to discharge the fear once and for all.

II. Anxiety Neuroses

The symptoms of an anxiety neurosis are numerous, and depend in some measure upon whether or not the state is openly expressed. If so, it is not hard to recognize. As the name of the condition indicates, the main symptom is a deep anxiety. The sufferer complains of difficulties in concentration, feelings of tension and strain, a sense of unreality, and feelings

[13] Condensed from J. E. W. Wallin, *Minor Mental Maladjustments in Normal People,* Duke University Press, 1939, pp. 132–133. Used by permission of the publisher.

of mental exhaustion.[14] He is irritable, apprehensive, and restless. He cannot sleep, and he has little appetite. His pupils are dilated, his hands tremble, his heart beats too fast, he feels faint and breathless, he sometimes thinks he is suffocating, he perspires easily, he is alternately flushed and pale, and he sometimes has digestive disturbances, especially diarrhea. The fundamental cause of the anxiety may be real or imagined; and if real, it may be either serious or trivial.

The anxiety itself may best be thought of as an escape mechanism[15] which, while unpleasant, is by no means as devastating to the ego as facing the underlying conflict would be. It is, of course, not a good form of escape because it promptly produces so much maladjustment that the sufferer has to use further forms in order to escape from the escape! The person with an anxiety neurosis originally develops the condition in response to some situation that threatened his security, but either the threat never materialized or it is a chronic threat that never disappears. Usually, this type of response to conflict makes its appearance in childhood if it is going to appear at all, and has become a habitual condition by the time adolescence is reached.

The state of anxiety may not be expressed openly. The individual may deny it, project it, convert it, repress it, or sublimate it, in case the open expression makes him feel too uncomfortable or brings upon him the scorn of others, especially of his age-mates. If he tries to rid himself of his anxiety through the usual escape mechanisms, he is most likely to convert it into some physical symptom, about which he can be anxious without feeling ashamed. Or he may take refuge behind an overconfident manner and forced cheerfulness. Thus, if a student is profoundly anxious over his schoolwork, he may brag about his good marks, real or fictitious, not only to conceal his anxiety but to reassure himself. Or he may sublimate his personal anxiety by joining in civilian defense work and openly worrying about atomic bombs—an expression of insecurity that has social approval. Or, if the real fear is a loss of his mother's love, a possibility he cannot face, he may project his anxiety by constant and intensive concern for her, by helping her, waiting on her, admiring her, or praising her in an exaggerated way. All these types of reaction are useful because they give relief from tension.

The commonest anxiety neuroses are of the simple types described below, in which the pressure, the anxiety, and the compulsive reactions to it stand out clearly.

Mildred M. is a high school girl with an anxiety neurosis that centers around the marks she receives on assignments, reports, and examinations. She becomes

---

[14] K. Hazell, "The Anxiety Syndrome," *Medical Progress,* 216:153–155, 1946; D. W. MacKennon, "Topological Analysis of Anxiety," *Character and Personality,* 12:163–176, 1944; and H. C. Kramer, "Orthogenesis of Anxiety," *Nervous Child,* 5:25–36, 1946.

[15] T. A. C. Rennie, "Anxiety States: Their Recognition and Management," *Medical Clinics of North America,* 32:597–610, 1948.

apprehensive as soon as she is notified of an examination or given an assignment. She bores her age-mates by her constant chatter about marks—what per cent she received, her general up-or-down trend in each course, her apprehensions about examinations, and so on. Twice, when she knew that a teacher was correcting papers, she has sneaked into the teacher's homeroom at recess and been discovered as she searched through the papers to see if hers had been scored. She has been caught also changing the marks on her papers before she took them home. She has saved every returned paper since her entry into high school (except a few that she threw away during the first month, an action she now greatly regrets), and every Sunday afternoon she spends two or three hours leafing through them and pondering her progress or lack of it. She is often greatly upset by the weekly review. As the day of an examination approaches, she becomes more and more apprehensive. After it is over, she usually vacillates between a gloomy conviction of absolute failure and a faint hope that she did not do *too* badly. She gives her family and friends a play-by-play account of what she wrote and why. Unlike pupils who become hysterical about examinations and are unable to take them because their hands are paralyzed, or because their heads ache violently, or because they are suffering from nausea, Mildred remains apprehensive without discharging her emotional load by means of any projective technique. What little relief she gets comes through the normal channel of answering questions correctly or from preparing assignments well. Unfortunately, however, Mildred's successes do not occur often enough to discharge more than a fraction of the pressure.

The reasons for this girl's condition are not far to seek. She is the one person of average ability in a family of superior verbal intelligence. Both parents and two older siblings made Phi Beta Kappa, and an older sister, now in college, almost certainly will do so. The parents became acquainted with each other when they were members of a high school honor society. After they graduated from college, the father went into business, and the mother concentrated on raising a family. Neither has had contact with professional people—who might have influenced them to evaluate marks more temperately—and both have sought refuge from their present boredom by reliving their own academic success in their children. Ever since she can remember, Mildred has heard high marks praised and admired as the *ne plus ultra* of life. She would be blissfully happy if she could even approach her older brother's four-year high school average of 98.9 per cent. Her parents want Mildred to be happy, but they cannot seem to envisage any success that is not measured in terms of marks. Thus Mildred continues to be afraid of examinations, anxious about assignments, fearful of an unsuccessful college career, and apprehensive of eventual failure in a life that is rigidly evaluated in tenths of a per cent!

N. T., aged twenty-two years, complained of nervousness, faintness, dizzy spells, heavy breathing, a pain up and down the breastbone, pounding of the heart at the least excitement, difficulty in breathing, and difficulty in swallowing. These symptoms had been present for six months, and continued unabated. "On December 26th, the night before leaving for a vacation, I was driving the car home. Suddenly I was seized by a terrible pounding of the heart, and I couldn't catch my breath. I felt I was going to die. These other symptoms have come on me since. I have taken all sorts of pills and some 'red medicine' but it made me dopey for a while and didn't stop my trouble." After several interviews, I learned that the boy, before leaving for his vacation, had been gambling and owed some money which he was to pay by borrowing from a loan company, the matter to be taken care of by a friend of his in whom he did not have much confidence. Although this chain of events seemed to be the cause of his troubles it was difficult to believe that a full-grown young man could develop such a lasting neurosis from one difficulty of this kind. Closer analysis, together with interviewing the parents, brought to light the following. The father told of the boy's being a "mama's boy" and of his never having been allowed by the mother to "be on his own." In addition, the father told of always insisting that the "boy make something of himself" instead of going to school and playing football, which the father insisted was too dangerous a sport. The father was short-tempered and irritable. He wanted his son, who worked in his store, to display more initiative and energy. The mother vehemently denied keeping the boy "tied to her apron strings" and insisted that he could go where he wished and do what he wished. "Of course, he is the kind of boy who always tells me just where he goes and what he does. He always wants me to buy his clothes for him, and he asks my advice whenever anything comes up that he's worried about." The boy's version (he was 6 feet tall and weighed 190 pounds of solid muscle and bone) was somewhat different. "I guess I was always babied and spoiled. My father is high-strung, and my mother always gets her own way. They always were afraid I'd make mistakes, and they'd tell me what to do and even what to say. They were afraid to let me play football because I'd be hurt, and I didn't want to be called a 'sissy.' If I go to buy a suit of clothes, Mother comes with me and she selects the color and the style, and talks about the price. At the store, Father watches me like a hawk. I guess he wants me to take his place eventually; but he's so anxious about everything I do that I'm afraid to do anything. When I come into the store now, it is as if a cloud settles over me and I can't breathe. I want to do my own thinking for a change. That's why I started to 'play the ponies'; I got a thrill out of it at first; but now every time I think of it and what my parents would do to me if they found out, I shudder and my heart begins to pound. I guess it's because I've always been a worrier. I can't stand to owe anyone money and I worry until it's paid. Every small thing which wasn't just right annoyed me and I worried about it. If a customer wasn't quite pleased, if I promised to do something and failed, if I had to hand in a theme in college and had little time to prepare it, if anything occurred in which I might not do the *right* thing, I worried."[16]

III. Psychosomatic Conditions

With every decade what was once regarded as a sharp line of demarcation between physical and mental health becomes thinner and hazier. Purely physical treatments, by drugs or surgery, are used to relieve mental symptoms, and emotional pressures are accepted as causes for physical illness. For instance, a prolonged emotion is accompanied by an engorgement of the blood vessels in the lining of the stomach. For a while this does no harm, but eventually the vessels begin to erode, and bare, unprotected spots appear. The gastric juice, being highly acid, burns these already eroded surfaces, and in the end ulcers appear. The emotion produced a hyperactivity of the stomach, which in turn produced the ulcers.

Certain types of people are more subject to psychosomatic diseases than others. For instance, soldiers who suffered from duodenal ulcers showed as a group an unusual degree of anxiety, instability, infantilism, and hunger for affection.[17] Most of them were married, but they had not found satisfaction in the relationship, and the divorce rate had been high.

---

[16] Samuel H. Kraines, *The Therapy of the Neuroses and Psychoses,* Lea and Febiger, 2d ed., 1943, pp. 200–201. Used by permission of the publisher.

[17] J. Ruesch, *et al., Duodenal Ulcer: A Socio-Psychological Study of Naval Enlisted Personnel and Civilians,* University of California Press, 1948, 118 pp.

Another study of 110 consecutive cases of dyspepsia showed a "normal" personality in only 2 of the 110.[18] The majority tended to be either very passive or very aggressive, and a good many were compulsive as well. The emotions that act as causes are all of the depressing or aggressive types: anxiety, fear, worry, feelings of inferiority, guilt, hostility, jealousy, and hatred.[19] Apparently no one ever developed a psychosomatic disease by being continually happy. Good-natured, jolly, happy-go-lucky people do not have stomach ulcers, even though they overload and abuse their digestive systems; but the chronic worrier and misanthrope can develop them on a diet of poached eggs and milk toast.

Prominent among the situations that are likely to cause maladjustment, which in turn may be converted into physical disease, is that complex of stresses and strains that are lumped together under the term "maternal rejection." Since the need to be loved is extremely strong, the rejection has a profound effect, although it may take some other form of expression. One physician who studied sixty-three children that showed clinical symptoms of asthma, hay fever, or eczema, and compared them with thirty-seven nonallergic children, found maternal rejection to be of overwhelming importance.[20] Of the sixty-three allergic children, 98 per cent were rejected; of the thirty-seven nonallergic, who were also patients but with other complaints, the figure was 24 per cent. In a more or less comparable group of unselected school children, it has been reported to be 13 per cent. A quotation from the report is, however, more convincing than any figures:

Some of the mothers stated that the children were "accidents" and that they had not wanted them. Said one, "He was an accident. I hated having him. I didn't want him and I wouldn't look at him for at least three days.". . . Said another, who had never cuddled or played with her six-year-old child, "When she was a baby I could at least put her in bed and out of sight and forget I had her. . . ." Still another said of her eight-year-old, "I didn't really want her. I was scared to have her. I've just existed since she was born. If anybody mentions having a baby I think they're crazy." Incidentally, this mother had from the child's birth turned over her entire care to a relative.

Resentment in a good many women was unmasked. The mother of a small, blonde three-year-old gritted her teeth and muttered, "I actually felt I could kill her. I wanted to throw her against the wall and bash her brains out.". . . The mother of a boy almost seven exploded, "I've no other children, thank God! He almost killed me when he was born. I should never have had him. I'm a nervous wreck. He makes me ill. Physically ill. I spank him till he gets nervous and I get nervous. I threaten to send him away. He's driven me to distraction. Just mad.". . .

Sometimes a mother revealed the fact that she had gone to extremes in showering care and attention on the child to hide from herself the feelings of

---

[18] S. R. Rosen, H. Weinberg, H. Keeosian, I. R. Schwartz, and J. A. Halstead, "Personality Types in Soldiers with Chronic Non-Ulcerating Dyspepsia," *Psychosomatic Medicine,* 10:156–164, 1948.

[19] O. S. English, "The Nature of the Emotional States That Disturb Bodily Functions," *Pennsylvania Medical Journal,* 52:689–691, 1949.

[20] H. Miller and D. W. Baruch, "Psychosomatic Studies of Children with Allergic Manifestations: I, Maternal Rejection: A Study of Sixty-Three Cases," *Psychosomatic Medicine,* 10:275–278, 1948.

rejection, using an overprotective, oversolicitous attitude as a cover-up. Such was the mother of a six-year-old boy who claimed her "every breath was for her child" and that she would do anything in the world to make him well. In an interview she admitted that he had been unplanned and that "it was terrible having a baby and knowing nothing about them." Later, when it became clear to her that her own sexual maladjustment might be causing tension enough to upset the child, she suddenly lost control of herself and burst out, "It's one thing if he were sensitive to eggs, I would do something about that. But if it's my sex life that's affecting him, he can just go on coughing the rest of his life."[21]

It does not take much imagination to realize that a child who is exposed for years to such maternal attitudes is likely to develop abnormalities and distortions of personality.

Every teacher has some pupils who show symptoms of physical disease. One may have stomach upsets, another may have skin eruptions, while a third complains of violent headaches, and a fourth has periods of asthmatic breathing. If the symptoms appear only when there is need for Johnny to perform some task that he dislikes or dreads, for instance, only when he should begin to prepare his geometry assignment, one is tempted to assume that he has simply invented the pain in his eyes as a deliberate excuse to get out of work. Such is not the case. The pain is real. What is not "real" is the cause. That is, he has a true somatic condition, the pain, from a psychic cause, his dislike of geometry.

The two stories which follow should give substance to the general discussion:

Mrs. C. is now a woman of thirty-three, who has had a hard and unsatisfactory life. She was the youngest of a large family and during her childhood was regarded as timid and bashful but very obedient. Moreover, at an early age, she began to show an extreme fussiness about her appearance and her belongings. She wanted everything done just so, and since she was the youngest in the family, she was constantly being frustrated. When she was eleven years old a sister died and Mrs. C. was given the care of her sister's babies. She was by then the only girl left at home, where she lived with a harsh and domineering father. Eventually she managed to attend business school and to take piano lessons. She wanted to become a pianist, but she never learned to play well enough to support herself in this way. She tried giving music lessons but had no success. Her music was thus one more frustration. During her entire childhood and adolescence she had to wear "hand-me-downs" which ill fitted her and made her acutely unhappy. Mrs. C. did not fall in love with her husband; she merely seized upon the first offer of marriage as a chance to escape from her home.

The marriage went badly from the first, largely because Mrs. C. merely submitted to her husband's sexual advances, as a sort of payment due him for taking her away from a situation that was still less bearable. The husband was never able to provide adequately for Mrs. C. and her children. For the last four years he has been unemployed, and the family has lived on relief. Mrs. C. has augmented the allowance by peddling stockings from door to door. She is still meticulous about her house-keeping and makes herself endless work by being overfussy. She also irritates her

[21] From H. Miller and D. W. Baruch, "Psychosomatic Studies of Children with Allergic Manifestations," *Psychosomatic Medicine*, 10:276–279, 1948. Used by permission of the publisher, Paul B. Hoeber, Inc.

children by excessive demands upon them to conform to her standards. With her oldest daughter she has gotten into quarrels so violent as to lead to hysterical attacks and complete exhaustion.

Mrs. C. is by nature a tense, anxious, ambitious, determined, driving woman. Given an average environment and even a small but regular income, she could have been a great success in life. As it is, she has managed to provide for her children many cultural advantages that are rare among families of such limited income as hers. However, in spite of her constant efforts to better herself and to drag her reluctant family along with her, she is more often frustrated than not.

About a year ago her husband's sister came to live with the family. The sister is a maladjusted person who quarrels continually with both her brother and her sister-in-law. She is also disorderly in the house—a trait that is probably worse than anything else in Mrs. C.'s eyes. This final pressure upon her seems to have been the last straw. Since about a month after the sister's arrival, Mrs. C. has suffered from terrific migraine headaches which come once or twice a week and are so severe as to incapacitate her. It is not difficult to understand why some such phenomenon should appear. Mrs. C. is much too sane to indulge in neuroses for relief, she is too practical and sensible to flee into fantasy, she is too inhibited to indulge in destructive overt behavior, she is so meticulous that nothing satisfies her, she is thoroughly unhappy, and she sees no solution to her difficulties. The only surprising thing is that she did not develop psychosomatic symptoms earlier.[22]

Polly is a fifteen-year-old girl who had to leave high school during her sophomore year because she became so thin and ill. Her chief symptoms are loss of weight and impulsive vomiting, which prevents her from eating more than a few mouthfuls at a time. Polly has a long history of illness and is regarded by her mother as a most difficult child.

The family consists of Polly, her older sister, and her mother. The father deserted his family when Polly was about two years old; his present whereabouts are unknown. The older sister has always been successful in everything she undertook. Her schoolwork is excellent, and her adjustment good. She is something of a leader in school activities. Polly is just as intelligent as her sister, but she has a much more retiring personality. The mother has had to work to support her family. She is a tense, hyperactive, alert woman who makes a good first impression, but upon better acquaintance she turns out to be overambitious for her children, stubborn, painfully conscientious, perfectionistic, and emotionally cold. The mother's marriage was most unsatisfactory. She has always been frigid, and after the birth of the second child she refused to have further intercourse with her husband. She also admits that she probably nagged him a good deal. He seems to have been a sunny, happy-go-lucky sort of man, whose good nature appealed to her, while her dependability appealed to him. When they began to live together, however, each grated upon the other, and the marriage was troubled and unhappy. Aside from the absence of financial support, the mother is glad to be rid of him. Such affection as she has to give she centers upon her older daughter mainly because the child has never been a problem and is fulfilling her own ambitions.

In her earliest years Polly was very pretty. Her parents both spoiled her and made no attempt to encourage her in developing regular eating habits. After the father's departure, the mother instituted a strict regime of feeding and training. Polly did not react at all well to it. She was accustomed to being treated like a baby, and she wanted the situation to continue. In the course of the usual childhood illnesses she discovered that by being ill she could get a greater amount of attention

[22] Adapted from H. G. Wolff, "Personality Features and Reactions of Subjects with Migraine," *Archives of Neurology and Psychology*, 37:895–921, 1937.

than usual from her mother, who became oversolicitous perhaps because she felt guilty of a certain neglect arising from her preference for her older daughter.

With the onset of adolescence Polly found herself faced with more problems than her infantile personality could handle. She fears association with boys, she fears low marks in school, and she definitely does not want to grow up. Her reaction to her anxieties has been to revert to her earlier dislike of eating, which she evidently regards as more acceptable than any other form of fear. Moreover, it permits her to remain a child, waited on by her mother whom she adores, and it removes her entirely from the problems that face her in her daily life when she is well. The reaction is now so deeply entrenched that the girl is slowly starving to death.

IV. Feelings of Inferiority

The term "inferiority complex" has come into some disrepute through being applied in daily conversation to individuals for whom it is not appropriate. There is, however, such a thing as a true feeling of inferiority which appears among persons who for some reason, real or imagined, do not feel sure of themselves. Its basis may be almost anything. It arises in adolescence generally from social situations in which the boy or girl feels at a disadvantage. The youngster need not be really inferior, although he often is in some particular respect. Thus the crippled, defective, or ugly adolescent may feel himself inadequate and actually is; however, a considerable number of these truly handicapped individuals make a satisfactory adjustment to society and escape serious strain. In many cases the inferiority is either imaginary or entirely avoidable.

Feelings of inferiority manifest themselves at all ages but are perhaps more common in adolescence than at other times. It is during these years that the boy or girl first begins seriously to evaluate himself. He studies himself in the mirror and gets upset because his face is out of proportion. He examines his clothes and is distressed if they are not up to the standard he observes around him. He evaluates his friends and often makes efforts to get into social groups that he feels to be more successful than his own. He begins to consider his ability and personality. He wants to understand his place in the world, and he all too often fixes upon a vocational or social ideal that is almost impossible of attainment by a person of his personality and intelligence. For the first time differences in wealth and material possession become important. Social relationships between boys and girls precipitate adolescents into situations in which they feel awkward and incapable. It is not surprising, then, to find feelings of inferiority especially common in early adolescence, because boys and girls are facing many new situations and have not yet had time to evaluate adequately either themselves or the new needs in their lives.

There are two quite different forms of behavior that may be shown by adolescents who are suffering from serious and chronic feelings of inferiority. The first type is simple and obvious because the inner frustration shows on the surface. The pupil is unwilling to attempt any activity in which his real or imagined inability might become evident. He therefore withdraws from all competitive activities, even from those in which he could succeed. He is generally diffident, self-conscious, and unsure of himself. He complains of anxiety, fear of failure, inability to get his work done—perhaps of such physical conditions as insomnia, excessive sweating, and palpitations. If the situation continues long enough, the galling sense of inferiority spreads to other fields and the character of the boy or girl becomes permeated with a sense of futility.

Some pupils, however, are not content to stay in the background and admit their insufficiencies. Instead, they make every effort to cover them up so that others will not suspect the existence of an inferiority. Usually an individual with this type of reaction tries so hard to conceal his handicap that he overdoes the matter; his resulting "overcompensation" displays his true feelings quite as blatantly as a withdrawal, but less obviously to the uninitiated. Thus the pupil who is afraid of physical combat and ashamed of his fear boasts loudly of his prowess, secretly hoping no one will call his bluff. The pupil who knows he is stupid persists in volunteering several times a day. The pupil who has no social graces makes repeated attempts to be the life of the party. The student who has had an uneventful life invents thrilling experiences. All such behavior, directed toward the covering up of inferiority, even from the pupil himself, is of a compensatory nature. The teacher should learn to see through the ordinary forms of overcompensation and to recognize them for what they are—the drives of an ego that is frustrated but will not be suppressed.

Three examples of rationalizing and overcompensating for failure to get along with people appear below, expressed in the students' own words. The first student had in the past overcompensated by being rude for her failure to be popular. The second had flaunted her erudition in an effort to achieve popularity with boys but had been unsuccessful. The third seems to have been a social climber, who did not succeed in climbing far. All three are now on the defensive and are rationalizing their frustrations by blaming others:

I am too blunt and unpleasant to people. I usually insult them by telling them just what I think. They are usually offended to hear, for the first time, what has been obvious but concealed truth to others.

They (men) take it for a personal affront if a girl has a few ideas to rub together. I have not been able to contact male friends who are interested in music and literature as I am. They think a well-developed vocabulary a heinous crime against society.

I have no political pull to aid me in getting a job. My appearance isn't any too pleasing. I live at a level which does not throw me among influential people who might aid me in my schooling. I must depend on superior skill to outweigh my other defects. I am unable to command respect in any other way.[23]

---

[23] These three paragraphs are from A. F. Fenlason and H. R. Hertz, "The College Student and Feelings of Inferiority," *Mental Hygiene,* 22:389–399, 1938. Used by permission of *Mental Hygiene.*

These statements are illuminating and should give the prospective teacher an idea of how pupils talk when they are trying to compensate for an inferiority.

The following three studies describe, in turn, a young man who suffered from feelings of inferiority but had largely overcome them, a girl with a true mental inferiority, and a boy who showed marked overcompensatory behavior.

My difficulties apparently began at birth, for, I am told, my mother wanted a girl baby. When a boy arrived, she was bitterly disappointed. While she decided to make the best of it, she was resolved to rear me along her predetermined lines. Father, who was concerned with difficulties between mother and himself, had little to say about the matter. Before I was very old, their differences had grown so large that they had separated and a divorce soon followed. This left me without the guiding hand of a father, as I went with my mother, who continued to rear me along her chosen pattern. She treated me more like a little girl than a boy. I was pampered, overprotected, and dressed in beautiful clothes until I had become an exceedingly spoiled and dependent individual. As I grew older, I was given piano lessons which kept me so busy that I had little time to play with the boys of the neighborhood. This pleased mother immensely as she thought young boys too rowdy. She kept impressing upon me the importance of learning to play the piano and the good it could bring me later in life. She dilated on the unimportance of the neighborhood boys, emphasizing that their continual playing would never benefit any of them. My playmates were my cousins, whom I really enjoyed being with, but the trouble was that all nine of them were girls. . . . This pleased my mother and at first did not bother me. But trouble was brewing. My pretty clothes, my girl friends, and my easy ways won for me a hated nickname, one I cannot hear now without a feeling of revulsion. To boys I was a girl, and it wasn't long before they called me "Sissy," a name that was to stick and torment me until I finished high school. I often declined to go out with the few friends I had for fear they might hear that awful name yelled at me. Although the few who did not indulge in tormenting me became my friends, I did not rely on them too much or press our friendship for fear of losing their friendship by some foolish action on my part. I didn't want them to know me too well either, for by this time I had become convinced that I was a wholly undesirable individual.

Following my graduation from high school, I went to college in my home town. I contacted students as little as possible. As in my high school days, I still hated to make friends for fear they might find some idiosyncrasy in me that would make them laugh. I realized that I had nothing to offer anyone in return for his friendship and his positive personality. From lack of contact with other than relatives, I took little interest in others' affairs. Hence when I did get in a group, I was at a loss to know what to talk about. Afraid to meet people and not knowing what to talk about after I did meet them, I decided I would make no more attempts to secure close friends, since it brought me only misery.

After I graduated from college I received a position as teacher of music in a small coal-mining town and I thought that in my new surroundings I might perhaps be able to "fool" the people. But I was wrong. The children there had never had a male music teacher before. From the first moment when I opened my mouth and sang in a high-pitched, falsetto voice, necessary in teaching elementary music, I was lost. The first year in this position made me more miserable than I had been during previous years. I had a position demanding respect, yet my pupils made fun of me. Here a nickname even more deadly than the former "Sissy" was attached to me. I became "Percy Pitchpipe" which finally boiled down to "Percy." It was at the end of my first year here that I decided to fight my complex and to effect a change. I realized I couldn't keep on running away from myself and that I would have to undergo a change.

The following summer I came to the Duke Summer School and forced myself to meet strangers, although I still did not relish doing so. But I found that no one seemed to act as if I were a "sissy" and many people really seemed to like me. I talked to people, went places with them, and decided I wasn't so inferior. Here I met superior people. I found that I could dance better than most of them could, I could hold my own on the tennis courts, swim and dive with the best of them, and I noticed that my personal appearance was equal to that of most of the students. I asked myself the question, "Why should I feel inferior to everyone?" At home I had a job. In fact, I am one of the few of my early childhood days who have progressed in education and who are holding positions. All this made me feel that I must go home and make good in my teaching position.

The following year I continued to teach in the same mining community, but instead of being mean and revengeful to the children who had tormented me, I became friendly. Although taunts continued to come from them for a while, I talked with them, came down to their level, and tried to understand them. Little by little a friendly attitude arose between my pupils and me. I also began taking an active part in community work, giving musicals and plays and performing at the church, all of which I had refused to do the previous year. I had now come to realize that my plan of life must change if I were to gain the respect of my community, the thing I desire more than anything else in the world. And my efforts did bring success. People who had not liked me before began to take an interest in me, for they could at least see that I was anxious to please. I received more invitations, and I accepted them. At the end of my second year I really liked my teaching position.

Last year, my third of teaching, was my most enjoyable one. Toward the end of the year, freed from worries incident to my personality handicaps, I was able to spend more time with the children. They in turn began to realize that I was doing all in my power to make school enjoyable for them. If an entertainment was to be given, I was in charge; if a field trip was planned, I was the pilot. Thus a genuinely friendly attitude has arisen between my pupils and me, and I now look forward to my best year with them next year.[24]

Miss J. is a young woman of twenty-five. She is a typist in a large law office, where her work is said to be satisfactory. She is living with an older sister, who is dependent upon her for support.

This woman has been dominated by members of her family ever since she can remember. She has been constantly repressed and made to feel inferior. Her father prided himself upon being a good disciplinarian and, although she tried hard to please him, he often scolded and berated her. She early developed an attitude of fear toward life, of fear toward members of her family, of fear about what others might think of her, of intense insecurity. As an adolescent girl she was not allowed to go out in the evenings because her father "would not have a child of his running loose in the streets." She attended no movies because her father told her they were lewd and sinful. She had few acquaintances among girls and none among boys. The father seems, in his own way, to have been attached to her and to have been motivated by a wish to guide her, and he felt very virtuous that he allowed her to finish high school when he might have kept her at home to wait on him. The girl was inhibited in every way, at first by her family and later by her constant

[24] Adapted from Wallin, *Minor Mental Maladjustments in Normal People*, pp. 208–212. Used by permission of Duke University Press.

undercurrent of fear and her conviction of her own worthlessness. She tortured herself with doubts and self-reproach. She was unhappy, felt inferior, and was sure she did not do her work as well as the other girls in the office—a fact that does not seem to be true. She is convinced that she will never amount to anything.

Miss J. has never been permitted to make up her own mind, and she is now almost incapable of doing so. At present, her older sister is carrying on the oppression begun by her father. The sister nags, belittles Miss J.'s efforts to make her comfortable, and in general makes life miserable for the girl. It is probable that the sister—a real failure herself—is under a compulsion to build up her own self-respect by forcing Miss J. into bondage to her. There is, therefore, little hope of a change as long as the two live together.

Miss J. shows in simple form the conviction of worthlessness that is brought about by years of domination, insecurity, and oppression. Her feelings of inferiority are on the surface where anyone can see them, and she makes no effort to fight back against them. In fact, they are getting worse all the time and have recently culminated in such fear and distrust of those in her office that she precipitantly left her job.[25]

Tony was an Italian lad of seventeen who would have been handsome if it were not for his petulant expression. When someone began to talk with him his face underwent a change and a flashing smile appeared, but the radiance vanished the moment the other person's attention moved away from Tony to someone else. In a "Guess Who" test given by his English teacher Tony was selected as the "show-off" by 19 classmates, as the "tough guy" by 11, as the "screwball" by 9, and as the "lonely guy" by 2 pupils with unusual perspicacity for their age. Tony's teacher characterized him as being insolent, hyperactive, vain, peculiar, unpredictable, and uncontrollable. He frequently caused disturbances in class, chiefly because he could not bear to be out of the limelight and would draw down punishment upon himself by making a scene rather than remain ignored. His insolence often took the form of "wisecracks" at which the class would laugh.

Upon examination this boy turned out to have an IQ of only 94, a level that is a little low for success in high school unless a pupil is willing to compensate for his mental inadequacy by extra effort. Tony was doing either failing or barely passing work in every class. His worst subject was algebra, and he had a record of difficulty with arithmetic in elementary school, although he was unusually clever in trading and swapping actual objects with other boys. Tony believed that his teachers discriminated against him and gave his work poorer grades than it should receive. He showed the examiner one of his notebooks which was quite neat and legibly written, but upon closer examination it appeared that Tony had merely copied what his teachers had put upon the blackboard without any evidence of comprehension and without organization. He had no notes on reading because, as he freely admitted, he never read his assignments on the ground that "the stuff is all too silly to waste time on." On a reading test he scored at the sixth-grade level. It is probable that his abstinence from reading had resulted from his slow rate of progress, from his failure to comprehend what he read, and from his dislike of any occupation that required physical inactivity and offered no chance for showing off. On the playground Tony's behavior was objectionable in two ways: he liked to break into a game that was proceeding nicely—especially if the boys were younger and smaller than he—by grabbing the ball and refusing to give it back, and he liked to sit on the side lines making loud and generally abusive comments upon the progress of the game and the activities of the players. He was fairly

[25] Based upon S. H. Kraines, *The Therapy of the Neuroses and Psychoses*, Lea and Febiger, 3d ed., 1948, p. 212. Used by permission of the publisher.

adept at a number of games but no one wanted him on his team because Tony wished to do all the playing, even when his team was losing on account of his efforts to play all positions himself. His natural talents in athletics were good enough, had he been willing to put in hours of practice, to have won him prominence on school teams, but he would not submit to the grind of practice work and therefore missed the opportunity to shine as an athlete.

Tony lived with his mother and stepfather. His two older sisters were already married. Two brothers who had been born between the girls and Tony had both died in infancy. He was therefore the only boy in the family, and there was a gap of nearly ten years between his sisters and himself. During his childhood he received much attention from his mother and even more from his sisters, who greatly enjoyed having a live doll to play house with. Tony's father was an Italian immigrant. During his lifetime the family lived in a poor section of the city among other Italian immigrants, but after Tony's mother's remarriage they moved to a better part of town, where they still do not feel entirely comfortable. The mother's second marriage was a severe shock to Tony, and he was clearly jealous of his stepfather. Gradually, however, he accepted the situation with fairly good grace, probably because his stepfather, who is a traveling salesman, was away from home during the week and sometimes for longer periods. Tony was thus able to retain his position as the chief attraction in the family most of the time. Tony's mother has overprotected him, especially in making excuses for his misdeeds, in finding justification for him, and in protecting him from criticism. The mother has the same rather empty good looks as her son, and one suspects that she has the same rather empty mind. She has many explanations for her son's failure to be popular. Mostly she bases her excuses upon the supposed envy of other boys because Tony is so handsome and because they supposedly feel that he will supplant them if he has half a chance. His stepfather is aware that the mother is too indulgent with Tony, but he does not feel he can interfere because of his own rather precarious position as an outsider who has recently joined the family.

It seems probable that Tony is overcompensating for both an intellectual and a social inferiority. In his franker moments he admits that he is not a success, either in school or out. At home he has always been the center of admiration and affection, and he does not know how to get along with others in any other kind of relationship. If he is disregarded for a few hours his basic feelings of inferiority overtake him and so threaten his ego that he is stimulated into any kind of action that will center attention upon him again. It is possible that if Tony drops out of school, where the competition is too severe for him, and goes into some kind of work within his capacities that he could learn to relax. When Tony is older he would make an excellent maître d'hôtel, a position in which his natural charm and good looks would be an advantage, in which he would feel himself important, and for which his ability is sufficient. In the meantime he might find satisfaction in any occupation for which he can wear a uniform and have people looking at him. With careful handling he may yet be a success, but without it he is likely to become more and more of a problem because he cannot let down his defenses without damage to his ego.

V. Moodiness

Most normal adolescents change their moods somewhat from day to day. Moods of depression are especially common among them, perhaps because they want adventure, romance, and excitement but have to put up with the somewhat dull routine of life. They are not yet resigned to a reality that they are powerless to change. Moreover, they are sensitive to social and emotional stimuli and are consequently easily discouraged about their social ineptitude. Moods of exaltation also occur. A chorus of voices raised in alma mater, a hectic junior prom, a closely fought football game, an infatuation, a story of human courage, an hour of scenic beauty, or the completion of creative work may precipitate an intoxicating, exhilarated mood. Such experiences are common and normal at any age, but they are especially marked during adolescence, when the individual is easily stimulated and thrilled.

A moderate degree of moodiness is a normal concomitant of growing up. Some individuals, however, show an abnormal range of mood and often a sudden change from one extreme to the other. When they are excited they talk continually and loudly to anyone who will listen, they are in almost constant motion, and they flare up into worse disorder at the least restraint.[26] They are overactive, noisy, and inclined to exhibitionistic clowning. They seem highly elated, vivacious, optimistic, socially confident, and extremely friendly. They unconcernedly engage perfect strangers in the most intimate conversations. They are without inhibitions in either speech or action, and react with irritability and rudeness to any restrictions applied to them from without. Perhaps their most characteristic symptom is their speech. They not only talk constantly, but they seem to be under a terrific pressure to go on talking. The speech has also a highly characteristic loose-jointedness, with one statement leading to another, not by logical connection but by chance association of sounds or other superficial connections. There is often a good deal of rhyming and punning. If the reader will recall the most scatterbrained, fastest-talking, gossipy woman he ever knew and will concentrate upon the pressure behind her speech, her inability to keep on the point, her lack of coherence, and the difficulty of stopping her long enough to escape from the torrent of words, he will get some notion of the typical speech of a person driven by euphoria. Such people are, however, sometimes equally possessed by a diametrically opposite mood. Their behavior is slow, inhibited, restrained, quiet, reserved, and subdued. They seem dejected, melancholy, pessimistic, hopeless, tired to exhaustion, brooding, anxious. They remain alone, if allowed to do so. If they talk at all, they complain of sundry aches and pains, of certainty that they have an incurable disease, of guilt for some heinous crime (often the "unforgivable sin," the exact identity of which has never been discovered), or of concern over some other personal problem. Their speech is slow, and their thinking seems to be not only retarded but extremely difficult. Any given person is likely to vary more frequently in one direction than in the other, and some people vary from their normal well-being in only one direction; most, however, go both up and down at different times.

High school teachers soon become familiar with the normal moodiness of adolescence. It differs from abnormality in three quite recognizable ways. First, it has a discernible and sensible cause, although at times the reason

---

[26] See, for instance, P. H. Hoch, "Manic-Depressive Psychoses," *Medical Clinics of North America,* 32:641–646, 1948.

seems inadequate. Thus a boy may become deeply despondent because he did not make the second track team or a girl may be all agog because she received a good mark on her weekly theme. In contrast, the moods of abnormal persons do not seem related to environmental stimuli. Second, the moodiness is too extreme and too intense to be mistaken for an ordinary variation of attitude. Third, the abnormally moody adolescent is driven by his moods. He does not possess them; they possess him. A teacher should be able to recognize the difference between the ordinary ups and downs of adolescent emotion and the apparently causeless, extreme, driving moodiness that is not normal. The two studies below describe typical states of moodiness:

J. R. was described as a quiet, shy young man of 21 who three years ago had gone through a four-week period of depression, following a recovery from influenza. He is said to have done fairly well at school, but had to study particularly hard. His father and one uncle were successful physicians and he had his heart set on finishing medicine. At the time of his second breakdown he was in the third year of college and was experiencing great difficulty in the science courses. He returned home from the physics laboratory one evening and went immediately to his room and drank a large quantity of iodine. He was rushed to a general hospital for treatment, but was so morose and dejected that he was transferred to the mental hospital. When he was admitted he was in a dull, depressed state, feeling hopeless and much concerned that he had not been learning as he should. It was difficult to get him to talk or answer questions and if he responded at all it was usually in monosyllables. He stated that he was melancholy, that his mind was occupied with morbid things, and that he would be better off dead. His general physical condition was good and his intellectual faculties were not impaired. There was very little response to things about him and he refused to participate in any activity. For the most part he sat in the ward rubbing his head and eyes, beating his fist on the chair and occasionally moaning, "My God, please let me die." He said that he was not as efficient as others, that he could not hold his own and would never be successful. There was much talk about being a burden on others and there was one attempt at suicide within the hospital.

After about three weeks in the hospital the patient gradually began to discuss his problems more easily. It was learned that he never wanted to study medicine, always had found science difficult, but was attempting to satisfy his father, who wanted him to be a physician. He had never done well in science and had begun to believe himself inferior and doomed to failure. An attempt had been made to secure approval in athletics, but he had recently been dropped from the school basketball team. A thorough study of the patient's intellectual and personal traits was attempted, and it was discovered that he was of above average intelligence, had an unusual facility in language, was a fair tennis player, and was greatly interested in finance. Through careful supervision of his activities and discussion of his problems he gradually became more interested in his environment. After four months' stay in the hospital he was discharged with good insight into his problems and definite plans for the future.

He has since graduated in law with honors, won the third place on the tennis team of the school, and appears to be very well adjusted. A good bit of his leisure time is spent in modeling, an activity begun at the hospital.[27]

---

[27] R. M. Dorcus and G. W. Shaffer, *Textbook of Abnormal Psychology,* Williams & Wilkins, Co., 1939, p. 352. Used by permission of the publisher.

Pauline is at present nearly eighteen years old. She has always done fairly good work in school, but she is by no means a brilliant student. Her IQ is not much over 100, and she is unable to use what ability she has to the best advantage because of her "nervousness," as her parents have always termed her sudden changes of mood. She sometimes goes along for a month or two on an even emotional keel, but then she becomes either wildly excited—usually about nothing—or unduly depressed. The most remarkable thing about these changes is the absence of adequate cause, or often of any cause at all. These alternations of mood become more extreme as she grows older. When she is excited she talks continually, tells jokes, laughs at everything, will not go to bed or if forced to do so does not go to sleep. Her parents have tried leaving her alone, but she talks rapidly to herself and does not relax. Her mother regards Pauline as being extremely sensitive and attributes each attack to some outside stimulus, but the explanations are not convincing to others. Her father is greatly worried, especially as his means are limited and he fears that Pauline will become a financial burden at just about the time when she should support herself. Ever since Pauline entered high school she has had to be absent from time to time because she was too excited to keep quiet in class. The visiting teacher has urged the parents to take their daughter to a psychiatrist, but thus far they have not done so. Pauline is anxious to finish high school, but it is probable that she will undergo more strain than she can bear in her efforts to do so. There is no observable situation in her home or school or social contacts that could be thought of as furnishing a serious conflict. Pauline does not complain of any difficulty, and in between attacks of excitement or depression she seems entirely normal, well-adjusted, and happy. Of late, Pauline has begun to take measures of her own against her difficulties. At the advice of the school doctor, she now remains at home when she feels herself beginning to get excited, takes a very hot, long bath every two hours, uses a sedative that has been given her, and stays in bed, dozing and reading. This treatment has not cured the attacks, but it has diminished their length and severity. The depressions are rare, occur not oftener than once in two years, and are of short duration. Pauline's routine of school life holds her together until they are over. It is the excitement that most needs to be controlled. Pauline is a typical manic-depressive in that she is entirely normal in between attacks, does not show the slightest sign of deterioration, reacts normally to good or bad news if she happens to be feeling herself, and develops periods of great excitement in response to inner stimuli rather than to environmental pressures.

VI. Neurasthenia

Typical neurasthenic behavior is of the withdrawal type. Neurasthenics impress the observer as being already defeated by their environment. They are negative, quiet, frustrated, repressed individuals. In general, three definite characteristics are outstanding. (1) Neurasthenics are in an exhausted physical condition because of the prolonged tension and frustration to which they have been subjected. Their vitality is too low for much exertion. They are tired, but usually without obvious reason for being so. (2) The neurasthenic has an intense preoccupation with his emotional problems. He may not attend to objective stimuli, such as the directions given by the teacher in class, because he is too preoccupied with his own troubles and too indifferent to what is going on around him.

(3) The neurasthenic is usually a socially isolated person. If he were not, he would be more likely to find a solution to his drives for ego satisfaction, many of which cannot be gratified in isolation. Thus an isolated girl with a domineering mother who will not allow her daughter a reason-

able independence may develop into a neurasthenic because she has sacrificed her own ego and no longer has the drives that characterize a normal girl. If, however, such a girl had had a number of intimate friends she might have escaped this development, because her friends could have helped her in her earlier efforts at satisfaction. Part of her collapse is doubtless due to social isolation and the failure of her social contacts to support her in moments of acute distress. A characteristic type of behavior shown by the neurasthenic adolescent is a failure to make friends, a preference for staying alone, and a tendency to eliminate tension by eliminating desire.

The neurasthenic is thus a person who is tired, preoccupied, and isolated. Obviously, such a condition soon gives rise to new problems to which the same type of response is made, and the vicious circle may continue until the ego is annihilated. In the early stages an outsider is sometimes able to arrest further unfortunate developments. At all events, teachers can be trained to recognize those individuals who are socially isolated and of negative personality. These are the pupils who may, under strain, develop into neurasthenics. The teacher can learn also to recognize emotional preoccupation when she sees it and to observe a discrepancy between work done and fatigue shown. Those pupils who are developing a neurasthenic condition rarely make trouble in the classroom; in fact, they are in the process of losing their own personalities to such an extent that one hardly notices their existence. A neurasthenic adolescent is rarely a disciplinary problem; his trouble is that he has too little overt behavior rather than too much.

The neurasthenics as a group come from a family background that is significantly different from that of normal people. The differences give some suggestion as to probable causation of the neurotic conditions. In one study[28] the homes of 138 young neurotics were compared with those of 370 normal college students. Several bases of comparison were used, as shown in Figure 66 on page 207. The first three items dealt with physical inheritance and indicated that there was some hereditary basis even for the neuroses, which do not arise from physical causes. Other items showed that the parents did not get along together, and that the neurotic was rejected by or was in conflict with his family. The least difference between the two groups was 13 per cent; in five items it was 30 or more; in 3, it was 40 or more, and in one it was over 50.

The following story is illustrative of the personality and history of a neurasthenic individual.

Mrs. X is a forty-year-old woman who had a "nervous breakdown" when she was about twenty-five and was in bed for a year, after which she remained an invalid for a decade. Recently she has made a good recovery, and the nature of the "cure" proves beyond doubt the emotional basis of her illness.

Mrs. X was the middle one of five children. Her childhood was not remarkable in any way, except that she had a great many colds and was somewhat less active

---

[28] H. V. Ingham, "A Statistical Study of Family Relationships in the Psychoneuroses," *American Journal of Psychiatry*, 106:91–98, 1949.

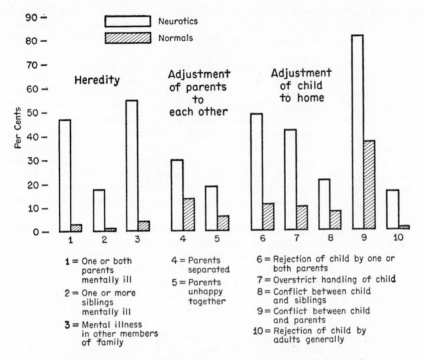

Fig. 66. *Family Backgrounds of Neurotic and Normal Individuals*

Based on figures in H. V. Ingham, "A Statistical Study of Family Relationships in the Psychoneuroses," *American Journal of Psychiatry*, 106:91–98, 1949.

than other children. Her school record was good but not distinguished. Her teachers found her amiable and docile but a little inclined to be finicky and fussy. After leaving high school she got a job as typist with a firm in a near-by large city. At first, she lived at home and commuted, but presently she moved to the city, telling her parents that she was going to live with two other girls. Actually she lived alone. A degree of estrangement from her family developed at about this time, although there was no quarrel of any kind. Mrs. X continued to write to her mother once every two weeks and to go home for holidays, but there was no close bond. On her visits home she talked a good deal about her roommates, her friends, and her dates. No one ever bothered to check any of the stories, so no one discovered that they were pure fantasy, invented to cover a social isolation that was constantly becoming more marked. After five years of work with the same firm, Mrs. X was transferred to another branch in a city some 500 miles away from her family. There she was unable to make any social life at all for herself. From Friday night till Monday morning she stayed in bed, getting up only to prepare inadequate meals for herself. She often had colds and other minor illnesses. Because of her frequent absence from work she was sent to the company's doctor, who found no physical abnormality except a mild anemia, but he gave it as his opinion that she was neurotic and would soon be unemployable. Mrs. X's chief symptom was fatigue. Her work gradually became slower and less and less satisfactory, and her superiors were glad when she notified them that she had decided to quit her job. The precipitating cause for this decision was a small inheritance from an aunt, for whom she had been named. The amount was so small that the income paid only for her room, about half a normal amount of food, the rent on a few books from a loan library, and simple toilet necessities. Mrs. X apparently just went to bed and was too tired to get up for a year and too tired to live a normal life for another nine years.

During this period Mrs. X acquired her married title, although she had never been married. She wrote long letters to her mother and sisters about her suitor, her engagement, her marriage, and her subsequent divorce. She sent them pictures of the "husband." She even developed enough energy to move her few belongings to another address, where she became known as Mrs. X. There is no evidence that she showed any signs of deterioration during the decade of her illness. She was clean, she had no mannerisms, and she was rational. The persons who saw her most frequently were her landlady and the owner of a loan library, who brought her books three times a week. Both these witnesses regarded Mrs. X as being ill, but not as being queer, although they did think it odd that no relatives or friends came to see her. "Mr. X" was supposed to be dead and therefore understandably absent.

Mrs. X continued to live this shadowy existence for a decade. During this time her major effort consisted of one short trip home, made in order to stall off a visit from her parents. During her week at home she stayed in bed till noon, on the grounds that she was on a vacation, and she refused to meet people because she wanted to "rest from a crowded social calendar." There was no suspicion of the true state of affairs, but her mother remarked to a friend that her daughter seemed altogether *too* unchanged. She felt that several years of work, marriage, the responsibility of a home, and a divorce[29] should have produced at least a few alterations of personality as well as a few facial wrinkles.

The ten years of voluntary retirement and invalidism were brought to an end by events outside Mrs. X's control. Her sister, brother-in-law, and their oldest child were killed in an accident, leaving two younger children to be cared for. Mrs. X seemed the logical person to take over the responsibility, since she was supposed to have a good job and alimony, plus her inheritance. Upon receiving the news that the children would soon be sent to her, a remarkable change came over Mrs. X. She rented an apartment, got herself a half-time job doing typing for an agency, and made a home for the orphans, who had inherited a large life insurance. Six years have now elapsed since this change. Mrs. X lives a perfectly normal life and has never shown any tendency to return to her former state.

Presumably Mrs. X is a person who has a strong need to give and receive affection. She never got enough from her family, not because they did not give her an average amount but because her need was excessive. She found no one who especially appealed to her—perhaps no one who was sufficiently helpless to want the amount of love she had to give—and no one fell in love with her. There is a hint from one man who took her out a few times that she was too demanding. Upon the two orphans she can pour out the affection and devotion that have been bottled up inside her. The repression of her main desires was apparently the cause of her illness and of the fantasies, which she developed apparently as protection to her ego. She never had any doubt as to their imaginary character, but they prevented people from seeing the true nature of her maladjustment. Mrs. X's neuroticism may have been cured by the turning of her attention from herself to someone else, but it is likely that as the children grow up and away from her it will return, perhaps in another form. She is "normal" temporarily because she is emotionally satisfied.

---

[29] Presumably to account for the missing husband.

VII. Hysteria

Hysteria is another kind of response made to an insoluble emotional difficulty. The difference between the neurasthenic and the hysteric lies in the individual, rather than in the external conditions. The neurasthenic is a person of relatively low vitality, excellent powers of inhibition, and negative personality who will sacrifice himself rather than put up a fight. The hysteric is a person of high vitality, slight powers of inhibition, and extroverted personality who will not sacrifice himself no matter into what maladjustments his drives may lead him.

When such an individual is blocked he does something vigorous and often explosive. Sometimes the reactions consist chiefly in crying, screaming, or swearing. In severe attacks a girl may throw herself upon the floor and become perfectly rigid. The most common symptoms are, however, physical, and consist in the alteration in the functions of some system of the body.[30] Thus a hysteric may act as if she were choking to death; she may become temporarily blind or paralyzed; she may vomit; she may develop a violent headache; or her attacks may mimic the symptoms of almost any physical disease. The pronoun "she" has been used because hysteria is found more frequently among girls and women than among boys and men. In fact, the name of the disease comes from the Greek word for uterus. The appearance of physical symptoms as expressions of emotional difficulties occurs through a mechanism called conversion, which means merely that other possible reactions are "converted" into physical symptoms. Thus, the girl who dreads social contacts becomes mute, or another who feels guilty because of a drive—probably unconscious—to kill her mother develops a paralysis in her arm. The immediate value of the symptom is obvious, since it prevents the girl from undergoing a strain that she cannot endure; but in the long run, it is undesirable, because it is an avoidance reaction that allows the fundamental conflict to continue as before. It does not solve but merely postpones.

As in the case of the neurasthenic, the only cure consists in a careful analysis of each individual case and a determination of what emotional problems are producing the inner tension. This work, however, is not the teacher's business. Her task is to recognize the behavior as abnormal and to send the pupil to someone else for expert diagnosis and remedial treatment. Two typical histories appear below:

Miss S., an attractive but very thin woman of thirty-five, is at present paralyzed in her legs and has been in this condition for the past six months. There have been three previous periods of paralysis, at the ages of fifteen, twenty-one, and twenty-seven.

From her earliest childhood, Miss S. had been the only child of a widowed

[30] E. A. Bennett, "Hysteria," *Postgraduate Medical Journal,* 22:323–325, 1946.

mother, who was both adoring and oversolicitous. One cannot perhaps blame the mother too much for her attitude, since her two sons, older than Miss S., and her husband had all died. She therefore clung to her one remaining child, babied her, watched her solicitously, and gave in to every whim. As a child Miss S. usually got her own way without much effort, but when she did not she had tantrums, during which she became rigid and seemed to be almost unconscious. This technique for reducing her mother and her teachers to submission continued until the girl was about twelve years old and tried to use it on her age-mates, who merely laughed at her and advised her to grow up. The first attack of paralysis came on during her first year in high school. She was barely passing most of her courses, she had not been encouraged to participate in the activities of the school, she had no boy friends, and she was quite isolated and unpopular. Instead of dominating her surroundings as she did at home and in her small elementary school, she found her surroundings threatening to overwhelm her. Her response to this situation was to become paralyzed and thus to withdraw from a situation that seriously threatened her ego. Doctors could find no cause for her condition. After some weeks of comfortable invalidism and of being the center of her mother's attention, the girl recovered the use of her legs—but she did not return to school.

Since the mother and daughter had only a very small income, Miss S. was encouraged to find at least a part-time job. She tried a half-dozen positions, as cash girl, bundle wrapper, waitress, and clerk, but she was unable to hold any job for more than two or three weeks. After each failure there was a good deal of weeping and complaining, until the girl had succeeded in displacing all blame from herself to her employer. The daughter's earnings were so erratic and inadequate that the mother took on a regular job from ten to two making sandwiches at a soda fountain in the neighborhood.

By her eighteenth year Miss S. had persuaded herself that she was not strong enough to work under usual conditions, but since she had a good deal of spare time she began to do volunteer work in various church organizations. The other workers soon discovered that she volunteered only for what she wanted to do and was completely irresponsible if given any other type of work. She was tolerated but not liked. At this point a young curate fell in love with her. To everyone's surprise the engagement went on and on for three years. Always Miss S. had some excuse for not setting a date for the wedding. Finally the young man became tired of waiting and insisted upon a definite date within the immediate future being chosen. The next day Miss S. was again paralyzed and remained so until after she had persuaded her fiancé that she could never be a proper wife and mother. After being released from her engagement she recovered the use of her legs. When she was twenty-seven, the same episode was repeated. In this case, she had become engaged to a young dentist in whose office she had worked afternoons as receptionist. Miss S. enjoyed the attention she received during her engagements, but she feared marriage, loathed housework, dreaded possible motherhood, and regarded sexual activity as dirty and indecent. Both engagements were terminated by a retreat into hysteria.

This woman has shown certain traits almost from birth: (1) she is remarkably self-centered, (2) she craves constant attention, (3) she cannot bear competition, (4) she is determined to have her own way, (5) she explodes when she is blocked, and (6) she is of dull-normal intelligence. She desperately wants more attention than her mediocre talents are likely to obtain for her, she is not bright enough to be scheming or to think out satisfactory rationalizations, and she cannot retreat into fantasy because she is dependent upon real people for her satisfaction. Her early habit of domination through tantrums has therefore become a fixed type of response, growing more extensive as her problems became more serious.

I have suffered more or less from writer's cramp ever since I was about eleven years old. I cannot recall that I was ever very much worried over answering questions orally in class, but I have always dreaded the first few minutes of a written test, and have had a more or less severe cramp in my hand. Very seldom have I gone into a classroom unprepared, and therefore the cause of the writer's cramp lies elsewhere. Just as soon as the questions are written or dictated, I am in the grip of a paroxysm of fear. During the first few minutes of the examination I am almost numb, even though I know I have no cause for alarm. Sometimes I have fully recovered before I had written many sentences, but on other occasions the cramp has persisted, and I was unable to write anything at all. A short written test always bothered me the most. Sharp limitation of time on one or two questions causes me to become "fussed," although I could answer the same questions orally with ease. During my undergraduate days I remember very distinctly being given a short test for which we were allowed about twenty minutes. We had to write our paper on a small arm of a desk, and I suffered from writer's cramp on that occasion more than on any preceding or subsequent occasion. I knew the work but had difficulty in writing the answers. The professor thought my standing in this test deviated too much from his grading of my class work and casually asked me what was the trouble. I have experienced a little of the same trouble in this class (in which a written quiz on one question was given daily). The strange thing is that I should experience this writing difficulty in connection with a question or questions with which I am very familiar. Usually the cramp is not so severe as to interfere with the quality of the answers, unless the examiner walks up and down the aisle and frequently announces "just —— minutes left," or unless I have to write in an uncomfortable place.[31]

VIII. Fanaticism

For this type of emotional deviate there is no technical name; the condition described is similar to paranoia, although it is less serious. The type may, however, be recognized rather easily. The individual is unreasonable, dogmatic, opinionated, hostile, and prejudiced, sometimes about almost any topic and sometimes about only one or two. He shows a tendency to develop a permanent mental rigidity and to systematize his erroneous ideas —twisting and distorting them until he has achieved an explanation that is satisfying to his ego. He protects himself by being either overtly aggressive or passively resentful whenever one tries to argue with him. Like other abnormal manifestations, the condition arises from a deep emotional insecurity and unadmitted fears of inferiority, both of which the fanatic hides even from himself by his unshakable belief in the correctness of his own convictions.[32]

The outstanding symptoms of a fanatic personality are three in number. In the first place, adolescents of this type have a chronic attitude of suspicion and mistrust. They expect unfair treatment, and they read into other people's behavior the worst possible interpretations. They feel the

---

[31] Wallin, *Minor Mental Maladjustments in Normal People*, pp. 117–119. Used by permission of Duke University Press.

[32] I. H. Rosen and H. E. Kane, "Paranoia and Paranoid Reaction Types," *Journal of Diseases of the Nervous System*, 7:330–337, 1946.

world is distinctly against them, and they will trust no one. In the total experience of such individuals the attitude observed may at one time have been a reasonable reaction to particular circumstances, but it has persisted in the face of all kinds of situations until it has become a settled frame of mind and now warps even the kindliest of approaches.

The second symptom is their tendency to be dominated by ideas which are markedly fixed and systematized. Fanatics are so driven by their ideas that they cannot change their minds, once they have decided upon something, no matter how many or how cogent reasons may be advanced. Furthermore, they usually build up a whole system of interrelated ideas, some of which at least are demonstrably untrue to anyone but the person involved. Pupils with this paranoid tendency complain, for instance, that a teacher is unfair to them—although other students insist she is perfectly just—and they support this contention with a systematically organized series of ideas in which the true and the false are inextricably interwoven. Presumably, they feel safe only so long as they have their basic principles to sustain them.

The third characteristic is their hostility, whether passive or active.[33] By means of it, they protect themselves from influences that might arouse doubts in their minds. Therefore they resist the efforts of anyone who would help them. On the whole, the passively resentful are harder to deal with than the overtly aggressive.

Fanaticism is a mode of response to tension and frustration. It is an unsatisfactory mode for it does not lead to a better adjustment but to a worse one because it estranges the fanatic still further from normal social life. It is an abnormal response which is made to situations that for some reason are not endurable to the ego. The building up of a system of beliefs is a means of escape from the chronic burden of emotional tension and maladjustment, but the escape is not toward sanity.

The case history below covers an entire lifetime. It is only by following development for many years that one can see the working out of fanaticism. This woman has been selected for description because her fanaticism has a long and instructive history, reaching from childish manifestations to adult paranoia.

As a child Mrs. K. was lively, alert, and full of driving energy. At home she was rejected from an early age by her mother, a singularly domineering woman who greatly preferred two older, quieter, and easily controlled daughters. The father liked his youngest child because of her vivacity, but he was a rather pale and negative creature, too much under his wife's domination to give more than an occasional furtive smile to his littlest daughter. Her mother's chief attitude was one of simple neglect and indifference. As a child Mrs. K. screamed when she was happy, groaned and wept when she was disappointed or hurt, struck other children when she was angry or jealous. Only by such outbursts could she get her mother's attention. It was never difficult to follow her moods, because she talked about them continually and revealingly. Her most conspicuous characteristic, however, was her

---

[33] See B. Crider, "The Hostility Pattern," *Journal of Clinical Psychology*, 2:267–273, 1946.

tendency to develop and to be dominated by unique, bizarre ideas, each of which in turn dominated her until another took its place. On one occasion she was seized with the rather common childish notion that she was an adopted daughter, probably as a result of maternal rejection. She accused her parents of concealing her real origin from her, told her friends that she did not expect them to play with her any more, refused to believe either the family doctor or a neighbor who was present at her birth, insisted upon staying in the schoolroom at recess time and on sitting in a corner like a pariah. She even walked—or rather ran—a round trip of six miles to a convent, where she demanded to be admitted at once so that she might escape from the world and the ignominy of her adoption. This obsessive behavior continued for about two weeks and then ceased as abruptly as it had begun.

In her secondary school years, Mrs. K.'s fundamental fanaticism became more marked. She took the molecular theory as a personal insult and argued against it so loudly and persistently that her chemistry teacher had her removed from his class. He could have saved himself the trouble, because she soon took sides vehemently and garrulously in the Bacon-Shakespeare controversy and forgot all about molecules. Other pupils were amused by Mrs. K. because she was never dull, but they did not trust her. Throughout her college days her teachers were delighted by her wit and liveliness, her talent for either oral or written expression, her industry, and her originality, but sooner or later they came up against the intransigent, truculent, stubborn, hostile, fanatic streak in her make-up. Even the teachers whom she most admired could not talk her out of a blatantly preposterous idea. The most they could do was to persuade her not to project her notions into class discussions.

After graduating from college, Mrs. K. taught ancient history in high school for about ten years. Her pupils were fascinated by the nimbleness of her wit, by her strong though highly individual sense of humor, by her vivid imagination, by her fluent speech, and by her general air of friendly camaraderie. But sooner or later, most pupils managed to tread innocently upon one of her many prejudices; in return, they received a completely unexpected and unnerving blast of criticism. She soon got the reputation of being "cranky" in class. Her colleagues found her delightful to talk to and practically impossible to work with. Usually, her outbursts were on purely intellectual grounds. The personal habits or emotional maladjustment of others seemed merely to interest her, when she noticed them at all. It was only a difference of opinion on some quite impersonal matter, such as whether or not a given biographer had drawn an unjustly ignominious picture of Alcibiades, that she flared into vehement protest and would not let the matter rest for days or even weeks.

It was at the close of her teaching career that she was seized by one of her major delusions. A boy in her freshman history class had committed suicide, for reasons that had no relation to his schoolwork, but she was convinced, the instant she heard the news, that he had taken his life in a moment of despondency after getting a failing mark on a history test. Although it turned out that he was already dead before Mrs. K. returned the papers, nothing could shake her conviction that she killed him. An inspection of the examination paper soon gave a clue as to the mental mechanism behind this self-accusation. The boy had answered five of six questions well enough but had unknowingly made a statement in his last answer that touched off one of her weird convictions. She had scrawled a violent and biting criticism across his last answer and she had marked the whole paper as failing. When she heard of his death, she was at once swamped by feelings of guilt, since she knew that she had been unfair. Once this conviction had seized upon her, it would not let her go. She could talk of nothing else. She did not meet her classes, but walked the floor of her room, and wept and beat the walls in the anguish of her remorse until her landlady sent for the police to take her to the nearest mental hospital. There she remained for six weeks, during which time she gradually relinquished her certainty of guilt and seemed to accept the proof that the boy had never seen his returned paper. As she recovered her normal gaiety of spirit, her incisive drive, and her charm of wit, she attracted the affections of a young interne, whom she subsequently married, at the age of thirty-five.

Mrs. K.'s married life was extremely happy. She acted as if she had finally found a safe harbor where she could relax, and for twenty years she stayed "right-side-up" emotionally most of the time. She did not cease to be stubborn and opinionated, but her husband could always restrain her. He loved her dearly, but he did not let his affections blind his judgment as a psychiatrist. He probably knew that her continued sanity rested mainly upon him, and he was certainly aware that his wife's bizarre ideas were merely shoved into the background, not abandoned.

After some twenty years of married life, Mr. K. died very suddenly. His wife weathered the immediate shock quite well, but it was not long before her earlier delusions again took hold of her, and she became convinced that she was responsible for his death. Other notions also crept back into the foreground of her consciousness. She realized more or less what was happening and went into a sort of panic, during which she packed a few belongings and fled from the house, leaving no indication behind as to her intentions. Her friends made efforts to find her, but no one was close enough to her to feel justified in authorizing a police search. For over a year nothing more was heard of her. Subsequently it was learned that she spent this time in a large city, living alone and brooding. She ate irregularly, slept badly if at all, had nightmares, and became quite ill from mere neglect. During this year of seclusion she did what she had never done before—she systematized her delusions. Eventually she had another outbreak of remorse during which she believed she had killed her husband. She was again sent to a mental hospital. By then, however, her delusions had become so rationalized and woven together that she was inaccessible to argument. Moreover, there was no one left in whom she had confidence. Her manner was bellicose and truculent, and she would brook no interference with her system of ideas. She has been in the hospital for over a decade, and it is unlikely that she can ever maintain herself without close supervision. She is still a remarkably vital and interesting person and can be as charming as ever, as long as a visitor keeps to neutral topics. Ten years of professional care have thus far failed to make a dent in her delusional system.

This woman showed the fanatic disposition of a future paranoic by the time she was of school age. She was suspicious, emotional, unable to tell a true from a false idea, closed to argument, and dominated by successive notions that popped into her head. Because she valued friendships she learned to push out of sight the weirdest of her ideas, but even her husband could not break her life-long habit of letting ideas dominate her. As soon as he was gone, her old delusions plus a few new ones seized upon her, and they will not let her go.

IX. Psychopathic Personality

The term "psychopathic personality" has been used in psychological literature to cover a multitude of slightly abnormal but highly divergent characteristics. It has been a sort of mental wastebasket into which one put those cases that were not neurasthenic, not hysteric, not fanatic, not inferior, not obsessed, and not moody, but were still too odd to be normal. Of late years, however, a good deal of research and observation have been devoted to clearing up the concept and to characterizing the psychopathic personality as a recognizable entity.[34]

Perhaps the first thing to do in describing this type of personality is to state what it is not. It is not a neurosis or a psychosis. There is a complete absence of delusions or other signs of irrational thinking. There is usually no indication of nervousness. There is no immediately obvious distortion of personality and no defect in theoretical reasoning. The individual shows no depression and no anxiety. His intelligence is usually normal and is sometimes superior.

The possessor of a psychopathic personality may have great superficial charm. To the casual observer he gives an appearance of complete sanity, and he shows in everyday situations an outer layer of acceptable functioning. This mask of sound mental health is, however, only a façade. Upon further acquaintance the psychopath shows his true personality. His condition reveals itself in five main types of reaction.

First, psychopaths are basically unreliable, irresponsible, untruthful, and deceitful, even when they have nothing to gain thereby. They can lie without the slightest indication of discomfort. It is generally not difficult to convince them that some particular thing they have done is wrong. They admit their guilt cheerfully and often promise to do better, but then they continue to do exactly as they please.

A second characteristic is their extreme emotional shallowness. They may, for instance, go through the motions of making a fluent apology for some misdeed, but the apology is fluent because there is no feeling behind it. They have little affection to offer, and they often remain throughout life unattached to other people. They show neither remorse nor shame for even their most glaring misdeeds. Because they are barren emotionally, they are conspicuously callous and unfeeling in their treatment of others, not appreciating at all the emotional impact of their acts upon other people.

Third, psychopaths are essentially solitary people, unresponsive to interpersonal relationships. Their behavior is in general asocial rather than antisocial, although under slight stress they become antisocial as well. They are extraordinarily unresponsive to human kindness from other people. While they have affairs with members of the opposite sex, these affairs do not seem to have any real emotional significance for them. Their sexual relationships are casual, trivial, and quite unimportant to them. They seem to have no capacity to see themselves as others see them, or to realize how other people feel about them.

Fourth, they are highly egocentric. Their reactions are made to gain pleasure and to avoid pain, without the intervention of such inconveniences as a conscience or an awareness of social pressure. They do what seems amusing to them at the moment.

---

[34] H. Cleckley, *The Mask of Sanity: An Attempt to Clarify Some Issues about the So-called Psychopathic Personality*, C. V. Mosby Co., 1950, 569 pp.; and B. Karpman, "The Myth of the Psychopathic Personality," *American Journal of Psychiatry*, 104:523–534, 1948.

Finally, psychopaths live a disordered and purposeless life. Even a consistent revolt is beyond their powers of organization. To be sure, they are sometimes defiant and explosive, but these manifestations are reactions to incidental blocking of some momentary desire. These people do not commit major offenses, although they are likely to be constantly in difficulty for minor infractions of the law, their most frequent clashes occurring because they are drunk and disorderly. They do not live lives of crime because crime requires planning, and psychopaths are thoroughly purposeless.

Presumably the psychopath's asocial, purposeless, and often self-defeating behavior is an expression of drives, disturbances, and conflicts that lie deep in his unconscious and urge him to self-destruction. For he does destroy himself as far as deriving either pleasure or value from life is concerned. The satisfactions of emotional life are denied him because he has essentially no emotions. The satisfactions that come from personal interrelationships elude him because what other people do, think, and feel are matters of no interest to him. He does not even seem to get pleasure or relief out of his sins and misdeeds. He does not, for instance, drink to escape an intolerable strain or insoluble emotional conflict; he does not drink to be sociable; he drinks without obvious pleasure and in the same casual, purposeless way in which he does everything else. Alcohol promptly disorganizes him still further and urges him on into even greater uselessness. What a normal person cannot usually grasp is that the psychopathic enjoys being disorganized and has no interest in improving himself. He is not ashamed of his life; it is his normal relatives who feel the shame for him. The psychopath does not act in a normal human way basically because he does not have normal human impulses.

The two studies below describe the development of boys who are typical of this group of abnormal children and adolescents:

Ronald is a boy of sixteen who recently entered high school where, in two weeks' time, he antagonized practically everyone he met. Ronald is an only child. His mother has been a semi-invalid ever since his birth. The father, a paint salesman, is away from home two or three weeks at a time during most of the year. Ronald's mother has always idolized the boy and has steadily refused to believe—in the face of evidence—any of the complaints made against him. In his preschool days Ronald was already so self-centered, so determined to have his own way, and so abusive at the first hint of restraint that other children would not play with him. When he was four years old he went up to a little girl who was peacefully walking along the sidewalk and pushing a doll carriage with her best and newest doll in it, snatched her toys away from her, pushed her carriage in front of a passing truck—which promptly demolished it—and smashed the doll into a hundred pieces on the curbstone. There were no adult witnesses of the scene, and Ronald's mother did not accept the little girl's version, as relayed to her by the child's mother. A day or two later, Ronald managed to clamber up on top of an ornamental gate at the entrance to the subdivision where he lived, lugging a fairly large stone up with him. He crouched there hidden for some time, until the little girl's mother came through the gate from the near-by market; he then rolled the stone off on top of her. His aim and his timing were bad and he did not injure her, but there was no doubt as to his intention. The following year, Ronald burst unasked into a kitchen, where two elderly maiden ladies were baking cookies for a church bazaar. He had smelled the cookies as he passed the house, so he just walked in and took a handful, although the women were complete strangers to him. When the ladies tried to stop him, he threw the whole tray of cookies on the floor and stamped on them. The ladies called on Ronald's mother that evening, but he flatly denied ever having seen them before, and she believed him. Episodes of similar nature continued. The summer when Ronald was six, he methodically trampled a neighbor's vegetable garden every week, stamping down every sprout he could find. The police finally caught Ronald in the act, but his mother would not believe the police, although she finally paid a fine, as she said, "to stop the talk" against her son. The next fall, Ronald went to school for just two days before he was expelled and brought into juvenile court for destruction of school property. Here he was given a Binet test and earned an IQ of 140—but he tore up half of the examiner's materials, spat on her when she tried to rescue them, and nonchalantly heaved a book end through a windowpane, in full sight of the police matron who had come to escort him back to the courtroom.

For the next year, Ronald was taught at home, at first by teachers who came after school hours, and then by his mother, since the boy sooner or later made a vicious attack upon each of the teachers. By this time Ronald's father had become greatly concerned about his son and made a real effort to control him, but his wife offset every bit of discipline by coddling Ronald, accusing her husband of cruelty, and refusing to accept any blame for the boy's misconduct. The tension between the parents mounted, until one evening when Ronald attacked his father with a kitchen knife. In spite of hysterical resistance from the mother, Ronald was arrested and taken into juvenile court. The court sent the boy successively to a detention home, to two foster homes, and eventually to a reform school. Kindness and firmness proved equally ineffectual. Ronald remained completely selfish, determined to do as he pleased, and vindictive when crossed. He was in reform school for eight years. His mother visited him as often as she was allowed to do so and was suspected of having once helped him to escape for a few days, although this was never proved.

The reform school did not offer work above the eighth grade, but the teachers felt that Ronald should go on to high school. The boy's conduct under the supervision and restraint of the reformatory had been passable during the previous year or two, and there had been no serious outbreak of viciousness for several years. The school therefore recently gave him a semester's parole, during which time he was to live at home and attend high school. From the first day at school Ronald began his campaign of deviling everyone. What he has learned during his reform school years is to be more cautious, subtle, secretive, and cunning. The other students give in to him, although they detest him; they are frankly afraid to resist him because his methods of fighting are highly unorthodox and very painful. Since school began, Ronald's English teacher has fallen downstairs and broken her arm, and his science teacher has nearly died from fumes that gathered where no fumes should have been. There were marks of a cord having been stretched across the stairs where the English teacher tripped, and in the small cloak closet where the chemist was overcome were found fragments of a stink bomb. Nothing definitely connects Ronald with either episode, nor with any of the following minor depredations: buttons have been slashed from coats as they hung in the dressing rooms, pages have been torn from books, notebooks have been defaced, and two wastebaskets have mysteriously caught fire during recess periods. Ronald jeers at those who question him, including the police, and he tells so many different stories that no one believes any of them. His mother still adores him, and she is certain that he is being wrongly accused, just as he was wrongly incarcerated in reform school. There is no doubt in anyone else's mind that Ronald is guilty.[35]

This boy has been through a series of experiences that should have altered his behavior, but he seems to have changed none at all, except to become more dangerous, more determined to have his own way, more resistive to discipline, more tortuous in his thinking, and more boastful. He does not even have enough normal feelings of affection to appreciate his mother's blind devotion, but callously capitalizes on it. Ronald displays in an unusually clear way the great vitality, the ceaseless drive, the egocentricity, the resistance to modification, and the callous insensitivity that characterize the psychopathic personality.

Philip is an eight-year-old boy. Ever since his earliest efforts to play with toys or to crawl around the house, he has been an abnormally destructive child. His chief pleasure with toys has been to smash them as quickly and as noisily as possible. He has tremendous outbursts of temper whenever he does not get what he wants. There is a younger sister, two years younger than himself, against whom his behavior is so aggressive that the mother is afraid to leave the two children together. He has frequently struck her, pushed her, and otherwise mistreated her.

For the past two years Philip has been in a special class for problem children. On his first test of intelligence he earned an IQ of 122. This figure was so much higher than expected that the test was given again some six months later by another examiner, who apparently did not appeal to Philip and was unable to win much co-operation from him. The resulting IQ was 91. Since that time he has had three more Binet tests with IQ's running from 87 to 140. The deciding factor appears to be the ability of the examiner to get Philip's attention and cooperation and to keep him sufficiently interested to prevent aggressive outbursts.

Upon first contact Philip talks quite intelligently and rather well on a somewhat superior level for his age, but he does not actually converse. It is more like a lecture than a conversation. Once started upon a topic, he goes right on talking about it even though the person to whom he is talking tries to introduce some other topic by means of questions.

Philip's mother is a rather young, good-looking, and extremely social individual. She has no real interest in her two children and has not disciplined them any more than is necessary to prevent injury to the younger child. Most of the time the children do precisely as they please. Her chief feeling toward Philip seems to be resentment that she has to be home after school because she does not dare to leave him in the house alone with the sister. If it were not for this anxiety she would apparently not bother to be home when the children come back from school in the afternoon. She is usually not there for lunch and has the children fed at the school cafeteria, paying the school a sum in return for this service. Since the family lives within two blocks of the school there is no reason why the children should not come home, except that it interferes too much with her own activities. Her husband is a small, neat, fiercely ambitious man of middle age. He was over fifty when the younger of the two children was born. He too is highly conscious of social status and extremely ambitious to move into what he regards as a higher social group than the one in which he was born. He is quite unsympathetic toward both children and punishes Philip regularly and severely. The mother's treatment varies from a rather lazy indifference toward most of Philip's misdemeanors to an occasional outburst of quite harsh punishment when she herself happens to be annoyed or

[35] This boy was eventually caught and returned to reform school. The episodes ceased after his departure.

inconvenienced. Neither parent seems to be aware of the needs of children, and each in his or her own way rejects and disregards them.

At the present time Philip is only eight years old, but he is already a terror in the neighborhood. The parents of other children send him home whenever he comes to their houses; they simply do not dare to have him play with the children, because he is rough at all times and extremely aggressive if things do not go exactly to suit him. Two or three times during the past year he has been reported to the police for acts of vandalism which were instigated by his desire to get even with someone who had sent him home or had otherwise criticized his behavior. This vindictiveness is a new manifestation which has appeared only during the last six months.

The above is a quite typical picture of the young psychopathic. He shows almost from birth a history of aggression, violence, destructiveness, brutality, indifference to social pressure, and vindictiveness. There is nothing in his home environment to counteract these tendencies, although his home would not be classed from its outward appearance as poor, but the emotional currents are such as to encourage the development of abnormality.

X. Schizophrenia

There is perhaps no other mental disease that casts before itself as long a shadow as does schizophrenia. Yet the illness usually takes both parents and teachers by surprise, perhaps because the patient was always a "good" child. He was quiet, obedient, and orderly. He had good manners, liked his school, and was a model pupil. He accepted discipline well and was never a behavior problem. It is not surprising that a teacher who has to persuade forty active children to control themselves enough to get their work done is likely to be thankful that she has one child in the room who sits quietly and is never rowdy. What usually is not noticed is that such a child has achieved his model deportment by a process of self-immolation.

When one examines the history of a schizophrenic one finds a record such as the following. The child discovered at an early age that he had been rejected by his parents. His only chance of avoiding punishment and of getting any parental affection at all was to concentrate upon perfection, inhibit his normal childish impulses, remain very quiet indeed, and stay away from other children who would stimulate him to get into mischief. He has therefore become a lonely, isolated, serious, inhibited, seclusive child. He does not express his feelings directly, he is beset by a chronic conviction that he is somehow inferior, he is shy and hesitant in his dealings with his age-mates, partly because he has little experience in getting along with them, partly because he is afraid of them, and partly because they are likely to subject him to a degree of competition that he cannot meet. Because he has few real pleasures he soon begins to substitute imaginary ones, and he often loses himself in daydreams. His ideas are likely to be rather peculiar, because he does not check them against either physical reality or the reactions of other people. Since he is too repressed to talk much, his odd notions may not be discovered for years. By the later years of childhood he has developed a typically "shut-in" personality; that is, he has become isolated, asocial, apathetic, introverted, and queer. In this precarious condition he is totally unable to meet the problems of adolescence. Since he has spent his life retreating from reality, he retreats still further and usually still faster until he is living in a private and distorted world of his own from which he may never emerge.

Recognition of the "shut-in" personality is essential for the prevention of mental abnormality. Symptoms appear by the time a child enters school, and the configuration is clearly discernible before the end of childhood. In one state hospital an investigator found that he had sixty-six young adult schizophrenic patients who had been sent to a school clinic when they were in the third, fourth, or fifth grade.[36] Their average age was only ten years at the time, but 48 per cent of them were already apathetic, inattentive, and indifferent; 20 per cent had odd attitudes or mannerisms, 17 per cent were markedly shy and fearful, and over 66 per cent were asocial and seclusive. The psychologists who examined them foresaw trouble, but a school clinic can only recommend changes to teachers or parents; it cannot enforce them. Since "shut-in" children have altogether too little overt behavior and since none of it is of the destructive, delinquent type, they do not come under court jurisdiction and cannot, therefore, be forcibly removed from their home environments. Nor do these children revolt against their homes and families and thus sever the bonds of their own accord. Presumably the parents of these sixty-six children did not succeed in changing their children's attitudes, assuming that they tried, and the seclusiveness increased until, during adolescence, it had separated them from normal life.

As schizophrenia develops under the strain of adolescence, the predisposing forces produce recognizable symptoms.[37] The prospective teacher would do well to memorize the following symptoms, picturing to herself the kind of person that would have this combination of traits. If, in subsequent years, she sees a student in her classes who shows any considerable number of these symptoms she should lose no time in getting him in touch with an expert.

1. *Appearance:* Usually untidy and sometimes dirty. Body build usually slender. Movements awkward. Body held in stiff and rigid poses. Frequent and meaningless grimaces. Repeats mannerisms or postures.

2. *Behavior:* Does not play games or take part in sports. Shuns exercise. Stays away from social affairs. Avoids contacts with members of opposite sex. Shows artificial mannerisms and silly, unappropriate laughter.

3. *Personal traits:* Seclusive, prudish, scrupulous in details, religious, sometimes suspicious, apathetic, sensitive to criticism, shy, lacking in ambition or interests, preoccupied.

---

[36] P. Whittman, "Diagnostic and Prognostic Significance of the Shut-in Personality Type as a Prodromal Factor in Schizophrenia," *Journal of Clinical Psychology,* 4:211–214, 1948.

[37] See, for instance, P. Polatin, "Schizophrenia," *Medical Clinics of North America,* 32:623–629, 1948, and G. C. G. Thomas and D. C. Wilson, "The Recognition of Pre-Schizophrenic States," *Virginia Medical Monographs,* 76:405–410, 1949.

4. *Mechanisms of adjustment:* Projects blame for difficulties on others, lives in a world of fantasies.

5. *Mental traits:* Incoherence, confusion, childishness, delusions, especially of persecution, possession, or grandeur.[38]

In spite of some success during recent decades with drugs or surgery, the greatest hope for controlling this mental disease still lies in an early recognition. Teachers are not only the best-placed adults for recognizing deviations in behavior on the part of young people, but in these cases they are likely to be the only ones, since the parents have probably become so indifferent or even antagonistic toward their child that they either do not notice the aberrant behavior or do not care. While an adolescent remains sufficiently in touch with reality to be in school at all, he is still accessible—that is, he hears when he is spoken to, understands what is said, and may be argued with—but without help he will soon become inaccessible, and then the damage is done.

In recent years there has been a good deal of research into the home background of those young people who have become schizophrenic. There seems to be almost complete agreement among investigators as to the character of parents and the nature of parent-child relationships in the homes that produce this type of mentally ill individual. To put the matter in a nutshell, the father is a nonentity, the mother is either overtly or covertly rejective, and the child is not wanted. Most of the research has concerned the mothers, partly because they were the dominant parent in the homes studied and partly because mothers are the central figures in a child's environment during the early years of his life, when his basic traits are developing. Upon adequate study, the mothers divide themselves into three distinct types which have in common a basic rejection of the child, although the forms of rejection are different.

The first is the openly hostile, domineering, aggressive mother who does not want to be bothered with her child and simply neglects him. These women are severe in their discipline, they constantly emphasize their child's shortcomings, they compare him unfavorably with others, they are emotionally cold, and by nagging, threatening, and ridiculing him they openly express their attitude by showing scorn or disgust at behavior that is entirely normal for their child's age. Quite often behind this attitude there is a burning resentment because the child's birth thwarted some ambition of the mother's, or a profound disgust on her part toward sexual relationships, or a fierce resentment toward the pains of childbirth. In short, the child has, in his mother's view, wrecked her life or caused her unnecessary shock and pain, and she never forgives him for it. The second type shows quite different reactions. These mothers are overanxious, overprotective,

---

[38] Typical delusions of persecution: that others laugh at and make fun of one behind one's back, that somebody is trying to poison one, that one is being followed. Of possession: that another person is controlling one's mind or putting ideas into one's head, that the devil has entered one's body. Of grandeur: that one has quantities of money, that one is irresistibly fascinating to any man (or woman), that one has magic power over others.

and oversolicitous. They baby their child, fuss over him, protect him from the ordinary hazards of childhood, keep him away from age-mates, prevent him from growing up emotionally, and generally surround him with what is often referred to as "smother love." This behavior looks like the exact opposite of rejection, but there is reason to believe that it often arises from the same sources as openly rejective behavior and is, indeed, mainly a guilt reaction. Such a mother can never do enough for her child because she can never escape the feelings of guilt that come from an unconscious hostility and rejection. Her maternal overprotection is therefore a defense against herself, and she cannot relax it lest her shameful guilt of not wanting the child overcome her. Other overprotective mothers have different motivation, although their treatment of their children shows no significant differences from that just described. They are not compensating for an underlying hostility. They have identified their children with themselves, concentrated their whole lives upon them, and they protect them as they would protect themselves. An overprotective mother smothers her child just as completely, whether her behavior is "pure" or "compensatory." A third type of mother, whose behavior may push a child along the path toward schizophrenia, is the perfectionistic type. She is very ambitious for her child, she demands perfection from him, and her standards of behavior are higher than any small child can reach. She puts her faith in a rigid schedule and rigid training. She loads her child with cultural "extras"— music lessons, dancing lessons, singing lessons, riding lessons—she insists fanatically upon good manners, and she pushes her child into superior social groups if she can. She is prim, proper, and prissy. She regards sexual interests as disgusting and sinful. She is oppressively righteous. She is concerned with the externals of life and with fitting her child to take his place in her social world, but she is stingy with expressions of affection. Thus she wants her child to achieve the impossible, she constantly urges him on to greater efforts, criticizes even his best performances, and she denies him any real reward by denying him love. These three types—the hostile, the overprotective, and the perfectionistic—may exist either separately or in several combinations. Perhaps the worst complex of traits is shown by the mother who is both rejective and perfectionistic. She is cold, hard, critical, severe, domineering, restrictive, rigid, righteous, and ambitious. In her defense, it should be said that she is usually the product of a childhood quite as unhappy as that of her children.

Many investigators have studied groups of mothers, each of whom has had at least one child that grew up to be an adult schizophrenic. Three sample studies from the much larger possible number will serve to bring out the main conclusions. In one instance[39] the investigator of 79 such mothers found 60 of them to be the dominant parent in the home and 50 to be covertly and 10 of them overtly rejective of their children. Another investigator[40] studied twenty-five mothers of schizophrenic patients. He found all of them tense, anxious, nervous, and defensive. All were righteous, re-

---

[39] S. Reichard and C. Tilliman, "Patterns of Parent-Child Relationships in Schizophrenia," *Psychiatry*, 13:247–258, 1950.

[40] T. Tietze, "A Study of Mothers of Schizophrenic Patients," *Psychiatry*, 12:55–65, 1949.

pressed, perfectionistic, and insecure unless they could be in control. Five of them were so domineering that they even tried quite openly to control the investigator! Seventeen were friendly on the surface but hostile underneath. They went through the motions of well-mannered affection toward others, but there was no warmth.

The third investigator[41] compared the behavior shown toward children by parents of schizophrenic, neurotic, and normal children. The groups were small, not over twenty-six in any of them, but the homes studied were carefully selected. In all cases both parents were alive and living together, the father's job was such as to demand no long absences from home, there were no outsiders living with the family, there were from two to four children (but no delinquents or defectives), the family did not belong to a minority race or low social group, and there were available informants who were well acquainted with the family but not related and were entirely objective in their attitudes. These rigid standards were imposed to eliminate incidental influences as much as possible. The parental treatment of the children was classified as being demanding and antagonistic, superficial and casual, encouraging and affectionate, or protective and anxious. The summary appears in Table 8. Demanding and protective parents have already

Table 8

RELATION OF PARENTS TO SCHIZOPHRENIC, NEUROTIC, AND NORMAL CHILDREN

Parents of same sex				Characteristic	Parents of opposite sex			
Demanding (%)	Casual (%)	Encouraging (%)	Protective (%)		Demanding (%)	Casual (%)	Encouraging (%)	Protective (%)
50	17	12	20	Schizophrenic	25	17	23	35
49	16	5	30	Neurotic	53	70	3	37
22	32	44	2	Normal	17	17	58	8

From J. E. McKeown, "The Behavior of Parents of Schizophrenic, Neurotic, and Normal Children," *American Journal of Sociology*, 56:175–179, 1950. Used by permission of the publisher.

been described. Superficial, casual parents are merely indifferent toward their children and do not want to be bothered by them, although they are kindly and affectionate when they happen to think of it. The parents described as encouraging were those who gave their children love and security, and helped them to grow up. They understood their children's limitations. They were patient, and, within reasonable limits, permissive. The results from this study are given separately for the parent of the same sex as the child and for the parent of the opposite sex. The parents of normal children tend to be either of the casual or the encouraging type, while those of neurotics or schizophrenics tend to be either overdemanding or overprotective. Actually the neurotic children seem to have had fewer encouraging, affectionate parents than the psychotics.

---

[41] J. E. McKeown, "The Behavior of Parents of Schizophrenic, Neurotic, and Normal Children," *American Journal of Sociology*, 56:175–179, 1950.

The two studies that follow describe, first, a girl in the beginning stages of withdrawal from life and, second, a young man who has already developed the characteristic traits of dementia praecox.

Helen Masterson is fourteen and in the eighth grade where, with a Binet IQ of just a shade above 100, she is scraping along with D's that come dangerously close to failures. She is a quiet soul who never misses a day of school, never requires correction. You might call her "colorless," though it is more likely that your comment would be: "I'm sure that she'd be interesting if I could get to know her." She is never impolite—answers any question you ask, quietly goes through with any task that is assigned. She comes to school on the bus, withdrawn and shy, having practically no contact with the others. If you watch her there, or in the schoolroom, you *guess* that she is dreaming through a quite satisfactory world of her own; if you speak to her, there is just that little hesitancy before the reply, as though at the moment she had been thinking of something else.

And it is the same at home. The oldest of three, Helen is very different from her two younger brothers, who carry on a constant running noisy fight. She is helpful about the house; her mother says, "She's always willing to do what I ask, even if her nose is always in a book." In spite of her lack of companionship and her constant struggle to keep from failing in school, one could not really call this youngster unhappy. There is an expression of placid acceptance on her face that means that her world is one of satisfaction.

One cannot help wondering why. We do not know just what part the father plays in the whole situation. A persistent drinker, he has always kept the family fearful and on the verge of poverty. With a drink or two he is mean, bristling, argumentative; while he does not manhandle his family, his homecoming means a noisy fight. The mother is a nervous, tense, energetic follower of prescriptions. When Helen sucked her thumb, Mrs. Masterson "tried everything" she'd ever even heard of. For several months she sent the child to school with a milk bottle and nipple securely tied about her neck. A social worker visiting the home always had to listen to a long tirade about the child's bed-wetting or her long, quiet playing with dolls—with Helen in the room, learning what the world thought of her.

One scarcely dares to forecast the future—no one even knows what the present is. This quiet conformist has certainly long since retreated to a daydream life that is quite adequate for her needs. Admittedly, it is of this stuff that schizophrenia is made; such people go completely into a life of unreality if the problems which they have to meet seem to offer no real chance for success and growth. But we cannot predict this sort of insanity with assurance because so many of our friends or co-workers are trudging along as Helen is, ritualistically meeting the demands of a job, sometimes even of family life, always living in a dream of how things might have been or of how things some day will be. People such as Helen never make trouble. If they go to a mental hospital (and several hundred thousand do take that road each year), they show up on our tax bill; if they quietly conform to society's demands, they are perhaps equally expensive in what they do not contribute to the country's growth; if they marry, they fail to bring to spouse or children any richness of experience.[42]

A is next to the youngest of five living children. The mother had fifteen pregnancies, seven of which resulted in miscarriages. Three of the eight children born alive died during the first few months of infancy. A's oldest brother, who is about ten years his senior, was hospitalized in a state hospital at the age of twenty-one

[42] J. F. Plant, "Who Is the Delinquent?" *Forty-seventh Yearbook of the National Society for the Study of Education,* 1948, Pt. I, pp. 20–21. Quoted by permission of the Society.

with a diagnosis of schizophrenia, catatonic type. The second brother, who is nine years his senior, enlisted in the Army in 1941. . . . After some months in the Army he became mentally ill, was hospitalized at the station hospital, and was diagnosed as schizophrenia, hebephrenic type. He was later transferred to a veterans' hospital. Next in line is a sister who is about four years older than A. She exhibited some delinquent behavior, ran away from home frequently, and tended to be sexually promiscuous. She finally graduated from high school, and is reported to be steadily employed in an office doing secretarial work. The youngest brother, who is one year younger than the patient, quit school at sixteen and is engaged in unskilled work. He had not been reported to show any abnormalities of behavior. The family was always poor. After the father's death, the mother lived mainly on state and municipal aid.

A has always been extremely shy, especially with strangers. Even as a small child, when visitors came to the house, he would run away and hide in a nearby barn. He had some boy friends, but was particularly shy with girls. He never associated with them and consequently did not enjoy school parties or similar functions. The older members of the family teased him frequently about it. He was mildly interested in baseball and football but never played much. In later childhood he became more interested in magazines, comics, and "little big books." He also started a stamp collection. He was particularly friendly with two boys who were his school friends.

Shortly before leaving school at the age of sixteen, the patient's shyness increased considerably. He began to express fears that he was "changing" and that he was different from other boys. He had a feeling that he did not look as well as formerly and that his features had been transformed. According to his complaints the children at school called him "Nasty." He did become rather untidy, refusing to wash or to wear clean clothes. . . .

His behavior became more seclusive, and gradually he withdrew from community life. When people visited the house he would run out of the room and hide under the bed. He would sit with his head bowed most of the time. Sometimes he would refuse to dine with the rest of the family. He also neglected his personal appearance, refusing to bathe or get a haircut. It was also noticed that he frequently covered his face with his hands, because he felt that he looked "funny." On some occasions he made rather strange remarks to his mother; e.g., "I am automatic."

A visiting social worker finally persuaded the mother to bring A to the local mental hygiene clinic for an examination. It took some time to get him out of the worker's car and persuade him to enter the clinic building. He seated himself under the stairs near the waiting room, facing the wall. Finally, after some additional coaxing, he entered the examination room. The interview is described briefly by the psychiatrist as follows:

He was pale and malnourished and definitely depressed. For about 15 minutes . . . he sat with his head bowed and face turned away; finally he was persuaded to turn around. . . . He grimaced quite often, squinting his eyes and wrinkling his forehead and smiling in a silly and inappropriate way. Occasionally he would giggle. He was correctly oriented and answered all questions slowly in a flat tone of voice. His conversation was relevant and coherent. He stated, "I am afraid to look at people; there's nobody like me, nobody like me. I should have gone to church; I did not go. I used to be better in grammar school. I don't look like I used to. I don't want to hang around the house all day." And then he voiced a wish to get some help, so that he would be able to go to work. He was inclined to repeat his sentences. He also complained of having the same thoughts coming to him over and over again. It is quite evident that he has some guilt feelings around sex activities. He was quite reticent about talking on this subject; when it was brought up he grimaced a great deal, and finally said that he did worry about masturbation, but appeared blocked when the subject was pursued. . . . He also said "I used to be independent and now I am dependent."

Whenever anyone talked to him, A answered in a rather jerky fashion. He had to be coaxed to speak. His speech was somewhat disconnected, but in the main, the questions were answered relevantly. His emotional reactions appeared rather immature; he smiled and laughed frequently, foolishly, and sometimes inappropriately. At times, amid embarrassment, he expressed a great deal of worry and feelings of inadequacy.[43]

Several factors contributed to A's inability to face the world. In the first place, he came of an inadequate family, only one member of which had managed to live a reasonably normal life. His mother was a spineless creature, who had no warmth or affection toward her children. His father neglected his home and had endless affairs with women. Two older brothers had already set a pattern of escape into futility. In his early childhood A got no emotional support from his parents. When faced with a stranger he literally ran away, thus setting a pattern for himself. He does not seem to have received help from his teachers in solving his problems during his school years. With the onset of adolescence his difficulties increased, because he could make no satisfactory response to girls or to social pressure. With normal expressions largely denied him, he escaped more and more completely into the already-familiar, isolated world of fantasy. The only hopeful feature is that he is not content with himself, but whether his desire to be like others is strong enough to build upon remains to be seen. In the meantime, he shows the typical symptoms of dementia praecox—withdrawal, mannerisms, dirtiness, anxiety, preoccupation with sex, feelings of guilt, and a general sense of futility.

XI. Summary

When adolescents are confronted with a situation to which they cannot adjust, when they suffer from tension and frustration, they show emotional reactions, some of which may be outside the bounds of normality. Various types of individual have been described, much too briefly; however, the sketches may be adequate to make teachers think about the problems of aberrant personality. Sometimes there is little a teacher can actually do for a pupil with an abnormal adjustment to the world, but she can at least get him in touch with an expert. A teacher can hardly help observing deviations from the normal among her pupils; if she can be trained to recognize the significance of aberrant behavior she can contribute much to the mental health of her classes by dealing understandingly with minor problems and by sending seriously maladjusted pupils to the school psychologist or other expert at an earlier stage in the development of emotional deviation than is usually the case.

---

[43] Condensed from A. Burton and R. E. Harris (eds.), *Case Histories in Clinical and Abnormal Psychology,* Harper & Brothers, new ed., 1947, pp. 23 ff. Used by permission of Harper & Brothers.

REFERENCES FOR FURTHER READING

BOOKS

1. Alexander, *Fundamentals of Psychoanalysis*, Chaps. 4, 9.
2. Alexander, F. G., and T. M. French (eds.), *Studies in Psychosomatic Medicine: An Approach to the Cause and Treatment of Vegetative Disturbances*, The Ronald Press, 1948, 568 pp. (Pp. 3–13, 173–191, 266–288, 401–421, 501–513.)
3. Alexander, F. G., and H. Ross (eds.), *Dynamic Psychiatry*, The University of Chicago Press, 1952, 578 pp. (Chaps. 5, 6, 12.)
4. Blos, *Adolescent Personality*, Pt. III, Chaps. 2, 3.
5. Breuer, J., and S. Freud, "Studies in Hysteria" (translated by A. A. Brill), *Nervous and Mental Disease Monograph*, 1947, 241 pp. (Chap. 1 and any one study from Chap. 2.)
6. Bromberg, W., *Crime and the Mind*, J. B. Lippincott Company, 1948, 214 pp. (Chap. 4).
7. Burton, A., and R. E. Harris (eds.), *Case Histories in Clinical and Abnormal Psychology*, Harper & Brothers, 1947, 680 pp. (Chaps. 10–13, 31, 42.)
8. Cameron, N., "The Functional Psychoses," in Hunt, *Personality and the Behavior Disorders*, II, 861–921.
9. Cameron, *The Psychology of Behavior Disorders*, Chaps. 9–12.
10. Cleckley, H., *The Mask of Sanity: An Attempt to Clarify Some Issues about the So-called Psychopathic Personality*, C. V. Mosby Co., 1950, 569 pp. (Any two studies in Sec. 1; Sec. 3, entire; Chap. 53.)
11. Dunbar, F., *Synopsis of Psychosomatic Medicine*, C. V. Mosby Co., 1948, 501 pp. (Chaps. 4, 10, 15.)
12. Eidelberg, L., *Take Off Your Mask*, International Universities Press, 1948, 230 pp. (Any one chapter.)
13. English and Pearson, *Emotional Problems of Living*, Chap. 13.
14. Garrison, *Psychology of Adolescence*, Chap. 12.
15. Kraines, S. H., *The Therapy of the Neuroses and Psychoses*, Lea and Febiger, 3d ed., 1948, 642 pp. (Chaps. 2, 3, 7, 14, 17.)
16. Landis, C., and M. M. Bolles, *Textbook in Abnormal Psychology*, The Macmillan Company 1947, 576 pp. (Chaps. 4–7.)
17. Malmud, W., "The Neuroses," in Hunt, *Personality and the Behavior Disorders*, II, 833–860.
18. Masserman, J. H., *et al.*, "The Neuroses," in E. A. Spiegel, *Progress in Neurology and Psychiatry*, Grune & Stratton, Inc., 1942, IV, 455–466.
19. Oberndorf, C. P., *Which Way Out? Studies Based on the Experiences of a Psychiatrist*, International Universities Press, 1948, 236 pp. (Any two studies.)
20. Pearson, *Emotional Disorders of Children*, Chaps. 3–7, 8, 9, 13, 14.
21. Preu, P. W., "The Concept of the Psychopathic Personality," in Hunt, *Personality and the Behavior Disorders*, II, 922–937.
22. Richards, *Modern Clinical Psychology*, Chaps. 1–3, 10–14.
23. Ruesch, J., *et al.*, *Duodenal Ulcer: A Socio-Psychological Study of Naval Enlisted Personnel and Civilians*, University of California Press, 1948, 118 pp.
24. Saul, *Emotional Maturity*, Chaps. 10, 11, 14.
25. Seguin, G. A., *Introduction to Psychosomatic Medicine*, International Universities Press, 1950, 320 pp. (Chaps. 1, 4, 6.)
26. Stearns, A. W., "Unfit Personalities in the Military Services," in Hunt, *Personality and the Behavior Disorders*, II, 822–832.
27. Steckle, *Problems of Human Adjustment*, Chap. 6.

28. Stevenson, G. S., "The Prevention of Personality Disorders," in Hunt, *Personality and the Behavior Disorders*, II, 1164–1192.
29. Stone, C. P., *Case Studies in Abnormal Psychology*, Stanford University Press, 1943, 98 pp. (Any five cases.)
30. Symonds, *Dynamics of Human Adjustment*, Chap. 22.
31. Thorpe, *Psychological Foundations of Personality*, Chaps. 8, 9.
32. Thorpe, *The Psychology of Mental Health*, Chaps. 9–11, 13, 14.
33. Tiegs and Katz, *Mental Hygiene in Education*, Chaps. 17, 18.
34. Wallin, *Minor Mental Maladjustments in Normal People*, Chaps. 2, 3, 5, 6, 8, 9, 16, 17, 20.
35. Weiss, *Principles of Psychodynamics*, Chaps. 21, 24, 25.
36. Weiss, E., and O. S. English, *Psychosomatic Medicine*, W. B. Saunders Company, 1949, 801 pp. (Any three chapters from Chap. 8 to Chap. 23.)
37. Weiss, E., and L. J. Saul, "Psychosomatic Medicine," in Spiegel, *Progress in Neurology and Psychiatry*, IV, 467–472.
38. Zachry and Lighty, *Emotion and Conduct in Adolescence*, Chap. 11.

MONOGRAPHS, BULLETINS, PROCEEDINGS, YEARBOOKS, ARTICLES

A. *General Summaries and Surveys*

1. Bradley, C., "Early Evidences of Psychosis in Children," *Journal of Pediatrics*, 30:529–540, 1947.
2. Cameron, N., "Abnormalities of Behavior," *Annual Review of Psychology*, 1:189–206, 1950.
3. Jensen, R. A., "Relationships between Physical and Mental Health," *Review of Educational Research*, 19:371–378, 1949.
4. Pacella, B. L., "Behavior Problems of Children," *Medical Clinics of North America*, 32:655–667, 1948.
5. Rose, H., and M. Johnson, "Psychiatric Interpretations of the Growth Process: Part II. Latency and Adolescence," *Journal of Social Case Work*, 30:148–154, 1949.
6. Schumacher, H. C., "Mental and Emotional Disturbance in Adolescence," *Journal of Child Psychiatry*, 1:113–120, 1948.
7. Wilson, H., "Mental Disorders in Adolescence," *Practitioner*, 162:305–312, 1949.

B. *Mental Health Surveys*

1. Hunter, E. C., "The Summary of a Mental Health Survey of Spartanburg County, South Carolina," *Journal of Experimental Education*, 17:294–308, 1948.
2. Mangus, A. R., and J. R. Seeley, "Mental Health Problems among School Children in an Ohio County," *Understanding the Child*, 18:74–78, 1949.

C. *Anxieties, Obsessions, Phobias*

1. Crider, B., "Phobias: Their Nature and Treatment," *Journal of Psychology*, 27:217–229, 1949.
2. Hazell, K., "The Anxiety Syndrome," *Medical Progress*, 216:153–155, 1946.
3. Ivimey, M., "Basic Anxiety," *American Journal of Psychoanalysis*, 6:3–11, 1946.
4. Kramer, H. C., "Orthogenesis of Anxiety," *Nervous Child*, 5:25–36, 1946.
5. Rennie, T. A. C., "Anxiety States: Their Recognition and Management," *Medical Clinics of North America*, 32:597–610, 1948.

D. *Psychosomatic Disorders*

1. English, O. S., "The Nature of the Emotional States That Disturb Bodily Functions," *Pennsylvania Medical Journal,* 52:689–691, 1949.
2. Martin, A. R., "The Body's Participation in Dilemma and Anxiety Phenomena," *American Journal of Psychoanalysis,* 5:28–48, 1945.
3. Miller, H., and D. W. Baruch, "Psychosomatic Studies of Children with Allergic Manifestations: I. Maternal Rejection: A Study of Sixty-Three Cases," *Psychosomatic Medicine,* 10:275–278, 1948.
4. Rosen, J. R., *et al.,* "Personality Types in Soldiers with Chronic Non-Ulcerating Dyspepsia," *Psychosomatic Medicine,* 10:156–164, 1948.
5. Weiss, F. A., "Neurotic Conflict and Physical Symptoms," *American Journal of Psychoanalysis,* 6:35–43, 1946.

E. *Psychopathic Personalities*

1. Karpman, B., "The Myth of the Psychopathic Personality," *American Journal of Psychiatry,* 104:523–534, 1948.
2. Lipton, H. R., "The Psychopath," *Journal of Criminal Law and Criminology,* 40:584–596, 1950.

F. *The Neuroses*

1. Bennett, E. A., "Hysteria," *Postgraduate Medical Journal,* 22:323–325, 1946.
2. Ingham, H. V., "A Statistical Study of Family Relationships in the Psychoneuroses," *American Journal of Psychiatry,* 106:91–98, 1949.
3. Madow, L., and S. E. Hardy, "Incidence of Broken Families in the Background of Neurosis," *American Journal of Orthopsychiatry,* 17:521–528, 1947.

G. *The Functional Psychoses*

1. Ewalt, J. R., and E. I. Bruce, "Newer Concepts of Schizophrenia," *Texas Reports of Biological Medicine,* 6:97–107, 1948.
2. Gerard, D. L., and J. Siegel, "The Family Background of Schizophrenia," *Psychiatric Quarterly,* 24:47–73, 1950.
3. Hoch, P. H., "Manic-Depressive Psychoses," *Medical Clinics of North America,* 32:641–646, 1948.
4. McKeown, J. E., "The Behavior of Parents of Schizophrenic, Neurotic, and Normal Children," *American Journal of Sociology,* 56:175–179, 1950.
5. Polatin, P., "Schizophrenia," *Medical Clinics of North America,* 32:623–629, 1948.
6. Raphael, T., and L. E. Himler, "Schizophrenic and Paranoid Psychoses among College Students," *American Journal of Psychiatry,* 100:443–451, 1944.
7. Reichard, S., and C. Tilliman, "Patterns of Parent-Child Relationships in Schizophrenia," *Psychiatry,* 13:247–257, 1950.
8. Rosen, I. H., and H. E. Kane, "Paranoia and Paranoid Reaction Types," *Journal of Diseases of the Nervous System,* 7:330–337, 1946.
9. Thomas, G. C. G., and D. C. Wilson, "The Recognition of Pre-schizophrenic States," *Virginia Medical Monographs,* 76:405–410, 1949.
10. Tietze, T., "A Study of Mothers of Schizophrenic Patients," *Psychiatry,* 12:55–65, 1949.
11. Whittman, P., "Diagnostic and Prognostic Significance of the Shut-in Personality Type as a Prodromal Factor in Schizophrenia," *Journal of Clinical Psychology,* 4:211–214, 1948.

CHAPTER EIGHT

Emotions
and the School

The work of a teacher has altered greatly during the past thirty years. She is now responsible not only for mastery of subject matter but also for the development of each child socially and emotionally. These new concepts of a teacher's work involve new kinds of emotional strain for both teacher and pupil, they call for character traits in teachers that are different from those admired in previous generations, and they demand a permissive, relaxed atmosphere in the classroom. Because of the enlarged concept of the teacher's functions, it becomes imperative for her to understand and to use in her daily instruction such facts as have been presented in the last three chapters on emotional growth, abnormality, and measurement.

The material of the present chapter is divided into two sections. The first deals with the interrelationships between a teacher and her class and includes such topics as the teacher's personality, bases of class control, and discipline. The second section discusses mental hygiene in the schoolroom. It includes presentation of common difficulties among pupils, the recognition of maladjustment, the provision of outlets for the emotions, and instruction in mental hygiene for the pupils.

I. The Teacher

Next to a child's parents, his teachers are likely to be the most formative influence in his life. He is with them five to six hours a day, five days a week, nine months a year, for eight to twelve years—a total between seven thousand and eleven thousand hours. In all those hours of contact there are sure to be many changes and modifications in the child's reactions, whether for better or for worse depending upon what his teachers were like. The teacher is thus the key person in the educational world.[1] She is sure to influence the pupils by her personality, by the atmosphere she creates in her classroom, by the discipline she uses, by the keenness with which she observes the pupils, and by her instructional methods.

1. The Teacher's Personality: There are probably not enough people with superior personalities in the educational world to fill all the teaching

---

[1] E. B. Cason, H. V. Funk, R. Harris, R. Johnson, F. L. Newbold, and H. H. Willis, "School Practices in Promoting Mental Health," *American Council on Education Studies*, Series I, No. 40, XIV (1950), 121–136.

positions, but fortunately personalities are modifiable and will develop in desirable ways if properly stimulated. There are, however, some people with personalities that are too disagreeable for work involving close personal contacts or that contain elements which not only make teaching extremely hard for them but also exert a destructive influence upon the pupils. In order to emphasize the qualities that are needed and to compare them with those that are undesirable, the clearest contrast is provided by comparing the best with the worst teachers, although most individuals will rank somewhere between the two extremes.

In reading through the descriptions given in Table 9, a prospective teacher would do well to try a little soul searching to make sure that he or she is fitted for teaching, or can develop the essential traits. Many fine individuals of irreproachable character do not make good teachers because, fundamentally, they are not interested in people. They make excellent research chemists, cataloguers in libraries, or commercial artists. Other, and most admirable, people belong in social work or in some form of religious endeavor rather than in teaching. It is no disgrace to be a type of person who makes a poor teacher; what is disgraceful is to persist in teaching when one has no talent for it. The person who is sure to be a failure, even though she may keep her job for a lifetime, is the immature, maladjusted, egocentric, insecure, unhappy individual who basically detests children. It is, of course, probable that such teachers were once young and reasonably happy, and that part of their maladjustment is due to their having projected onto their pupils the blame for their adult unhappiness.

One might suppose that care in the selection of teachers and a moderate degree of supervision in service would either prevent abnormal people from entering the profession or would soon eliminate them once they are in. Several studies suggest that such is not the case. Thus, one investigator classified 278 teachers in service by assigning each into one of three groups: those who were satisfactory, those who were slightly maladjusted, and those who were so neurotic as to be inacceptable.[2] Of the entire group, 67 per cent were rated as having good mental health and as being stimulating to the growth of their pupils. The slightly maladjusted totaled 20 per cent; this figure included those rated as neurotic (17 of the 278, or 6 per cent). It was felt that the oddities of these teachers, while undesirable and cramping to their own development, were not such as would not yield to treatment. In some cases, the maladjustment was of a kind that did not interfere seriously with teaching. The remaining 13 per cent of the total group were seriously maladjusted and were having a destructive influence upon their pupils. Another study of one hundred women teachers enrolled in a summer school class classified 33 per cent as emotionally maladjusted and 12 per cent as so eccentric as to be in need of psychiatric advice.[3] Neither of these

[2] N. Fenton, *Mental Hygiene in School Practice*, Stanford University Press, 1943, p. 289.

[3] P. Leigh, "Study of the Adjustment Difficulties of a Group of Women Teachers," *Journal of Educational Psychology*, 27:401–416, 1936.

Table 9

CHARACTERISTICS OF GOOD AND POOR TEACHERS

The "Good" Teacher	*The "Bad" Teacher*
1. Has a genuine love of children and young people and enjoys being with them.	1. Dislikes children and young people and resents spending so much time with them.
2. Finds great emotional satisfaction in teaching.	2. Regards teaching as a form of drudgery.
3. Is an emotionally mature person.	3. Is an emotionally childish person.
4. Is an emotionally stable person.	4. Is an emotionally unstable person.
5. Has a life outside school of so satisfactory a nature that she does not need to work off her own emotions through the children.	5. Has so unsatisfactory a life outside of school that she uses the children either to pour out her love upon, or to work off her frustrations on.
6. Is a personally secure individual.	6. Is a personally insecure individual.
7. Is reasonably free from anxieties and fears.	7. Is ridden by anxieties and fears.
8. Is more interested in others than in herself.	8. Is more interested in herself than in others.
9. Gets along well with other teachers.	9. Has feuds and quarrels with other teachers.
10. Is well integrated.	10. Is disorganized.
11. Can accept pupils emotionally, even those who may be hostile to her.	11. Rejects children emotionally, whether directly or indirectly.
12. Identifies herself with children.	12. Cannot identify herself with children.
13. Sees and treats pupils as individuals.	13. Sees pupils as a group and rarely treats members as individuals.
14. Is able to understand children and adolescents.	14. Is unable to understand children and adolescents.
15. Adjusts to pupils by being friends with them.	15. Adjusts to pupils by domineering over them.
16. Prevents most disciplinary situations from arising.	16. Does not usually try to head off disciplinary crises, and may enjoy them.
17. Uses, when necessary, discipline that is constructive to the pupil's growth.	17. Uses discipline that is destructive to the pupil's growth or attitude toward school.

studies throws light on whether the unsatisfactory teachers were maladjusted before they began to teach or if they became so subsequently. What is needed is a long-time study in which the personal adjustment of several classes of graduates from teachers colleges is measured while they are still in school and the results allowed to sleep for twenty years, until time has had a chance to give the investigator the answers.

Among the commonest symptoms of maladjustment among teachers may be listed the following: (1) the presence in the class of favorite pupils and "goats"; (2) the use of status or size to overawe or menace pupils; (3) an abnormal classroom quietness that comes from repression, alternating with outbursts of noise, quickly repressed and punished; (4) general physical inactivity of the children, plus much minor, unofficial, secretive activity; (5) punishment or criticism of pupils for things they cannot help— such as scolding a nearsighted child for getting out of his seat to see what is on the blackboard, or punishing a hysterical child for vomiting, or ridiculing a fast-growing adolescent for being lazy; (6) use of many dogmatic statements and absence of discussion; (7) frequent displays of emotion, whether appeals to the pupils to perform certain tasks out of loyalty to the teacher or threatening attitudes toward childish wrongdoers, or habits of caressing the pupils, or frequent outbursts of rage against the whole class; (8) reluctance of the pupils to talk in class; (9) use of frequent punishments or constant nagging; (10) use of sarcasm or ridicule or any attempt to shame a given pupil, especially in public. To these observable symptoms may be added the less objective characteristics of an inability to get on with one's colleagues and supervisors and a bad reputation among one's students.

Teachers have their own problems just as other human beings do. These are unavoidable, but certain mental and emotional hazards that affect their work are not inherent in the task of instruction but in various restrictions and situations that do not need to exist. If a teacher could be sure of progressing upon the basis of her merit, if she could participate in the determination of the policies under which she must live and in the development of the curriculum that she must teach, if she could be paid a salary commensurate with her social usefulness, if she could enjoy a secure status of respect, and if she could be asked to handle only a third to a half as many children as are generally assigned to her, many of her worst difficulties would never arise.[4]

Communities do not seem to learn very rapidly that good teaching has to be paid for just as much as good dentistry, or good carpentry, or good plumbing. As long as teachers are underpaid and overworked many of them are going to develop warped personalities unnecessarily. There are, to be sure, some elements of tension that are more or less inherent in the teaching situation. Teachers as a group suffer from an inability to relax, from overstrain, from a sense of futility—especially when their best efforts do not seem to be producing a reasonable amount of learning in their pupils—from fatigue, from too-restricted social contacts, from boredom with routine, from too much verbalism, from too much administrative and supervisory pressure, and—unless married—from sex starvation.[5] Like other human

---

[4] G. M. Meredith, "Administrative Procedures That Improve the Morale and Mental Health of Teachers," *Education*, 63:627–630, 1943.

[5] R. C. Bryan, "Pupil Ratings of Secondary School Teachers," *School Review*, 46:357–367, 1938; M. L. Hayes, "A Study of Classroom Disturbances of Eighth Grade Boys and Girls," *Teachers College Contributions to Education*, No. 871, 1943, 139 pp.;

beings, when they have personal maladjustments, they are likely to project their troubles upon those nearest, in this case their pupils, and to use their teaching as an outlet for their own frustrations. The stories below are illustrative of different types of teachers, all of whom were unsatisfactory:

Miss Banks teaches the eighth grade. She is a large, tall woman in her middle thirties, good looking in an icy way. In her class there is no foolishness, for she rules with an iron hand. To some of her pupils she is a cool, even-tempered, and benevolent despot; to others, especially some of the boys, she is a cold and rigid drill-mistress. These boys do not like her. In fact, they hate her.

Miss Banks was strictly reared by ultrarespectable parents. Her attachment to them has remained strong, especially to her father, who is a dominating man and who demands faithful service and respect from his employees and from all others with whom he deals. To her invalid mother she is a dutiful daughter, often sacrificing good times to stay home and care for her. A younger sister and a brother, brought up partially under Miss Banks' supervision, have long since left home to make their own lives. For them and for her parents Miss Banks has indeed sacrificed much, including the chance to marry. Twice she has declined offers of marriage, both times after careful consideration.

She was a superior student in a near-by teachers college and a success in her very first school job. She has had none of the discipline problems that plague so many young teachers. If she did not have to stay with her parents she could get better jobs in other towns. In her home town she will probably become a principal—unless the small group of "anti-Banks" parents gets to work and heads her off before long. These are parents whose children have feared and hated her. . . .

Miss Banks feels the hostility of some of her pupils and a few of the parents, but she shrugs it off. She knows she is in the right. If she could speak her unspoken mind, she would say, "The world owes me something. I've been perfect all my life, but other people don't seem to appreciate it. They don't seem to understand how much I have sacrificed; not even my own father and mother understand it. All my pupils should treat me as a perfect person. . . ."

She should never have become a teacher. She is entirely out of sympathy with teaching. She has no sympathy with children and their problems and simply cannot work in the kind of relationship that must exist between good teachers and pupils.[6]

Mr. Frame teaches general science and biology in high school. In appearance he is just about average—not tall, not short, not anything in particular. One could hardly say whether he is thirty or forty. The only unusual thing about him is his liking for neckties of bright color and loud pattern. These are noticed by a few of the girls in his classes, but most pupils go through his courses and forget both him and the stuff he teaches in less than the usual time.

A. T. Jersild and F. B. Holmes, "Characteristics of Teachers Who Are Liked Best and Disliked Most," *Journal of Experimental Education,* 9:139–151, 1940; J. E. Moore, "Annoying Habits of High School Teachers," *Peabody Journal of Education,* 18:161–165, 1940; A. S. Neill, *The Problem Teacher,* International Universities Press, 1944, 160 pp.; H. N. Rivlin, "The Personal Problems of Teachers," *Mental Hygiene,* 23:12–25, 1939; D. L. Simpson, "Personal Reasons for the Dismissal of Teachers in Smaller Schools," *Journal of Educational Research,* 30:585–588, 1936; P. M. Symonds, "How Teachers Solve Personal Problems," *Journal of Educational Research,* 38:641–652, 1945; P. M. Symonds, "Problems Faced by Teachers," *Journal of Educational Research,* 35:1–15, 1941.

[6] R. J. Havighurst, "Preparing Teachers to Meet the Problem of Delinquency," *Forty-seventh Yearbook of the National Society for the Study of Education,* pp. 230–231. Quoted by permission of the Society.

With his two children and his wife, whom he met as a fellow teacher in his first school, he lives in a small house on the "wrong" side of town. The house and yard get a good deal of his attention. When he is not puttering about the place, he can usually be found lying on a daybed in the parlor, reading mystery stories. Mr. Frame complains of his health but is never ill enough to miss school.

Perhaps he lacks self-confidence. That is what his college teachers used to say of him. (He was just an average student in a small college.) They thought that he drifted into teaching because there was no other white-collar job he could get without competing for it. . . .

Frame's own childhood was uneventful—perhaps too little marked by attention from his father and mother, who gave their affection more fully to his older brother, a brighter and more outgoing person. His father, who was a mail carrier, kept the boys in school and sent them to college but let them grow up in their own way while he spent his own spare time at the Odd Fellows clubroom.

As a teacher, Frame uses the "take it or leave it" technique. He knows that some pupils will do well no matter what he does as their teacher, while "the dumb ones couldn't learn anything, anyway." Why bother with them? In other words, Mr. Frame is not convinced of the importance of education or of the teacher's place in the educational scheme . . . It is as if he said to himself, "Nobody cares about me and I don't care about anybody else. I could have a good time out of life if I didn't have to work so hard. Anything I can do to make life easier for myself is the right thing to do."

Consequently, Frame avoids or overlooks opportunities to make his teaching meaningful to boys and girls in terms of their own developmental tasks. In biology it never occurs to him that he could help some youngsters understand and accept the disquieting physical changes which adolescence is bringing too early to some, too late to others. Biology, to him, is 568 pages in a textbook, plus exercises and tests to correct and record.[7]

Mr. L. was a teacher of German in a private boys' school, the graduates of which usually entered one of five colleges. Mr. L.'s students always were well prepared and did excellent work if they continued with the subject. Mr. L. knew that he was a success from the school's point of view, and he evidently felt strong enough in his position to do as he liked in his classroom.

Mr. L. was harsh, demanding, sarcastic, and critical. In his early years of teaching he had used corporal punishment, but the principal had made it clear that such treatment of the boys would not be permitted. Since then, Mr. L. has taken out his resentment verbally, but it is a question if the corporal punishment were not the easier for the boys to bear. Mr. L.'s main virtues were his clearness and his skill in pounding grammar into adolescent minds. It was also true that boys who had left his classes and gone on with German in college often told the principal that they were grateful to Mr. L. for his training, even if at the time it might have seemed severe. Other graduates also mentioned Mr. L. as a good teacher because he was the first one in their lives who had really made them work. These voluntary testimonials caused the principal to be more tolerant of Mr. L.'s highhanded methods than he would otherwise have been.

The source of Mr. L.'s maladjustment is not far to seek. Many years ago he married a beautiful American girl, with whom he is still deeply in love. She has borne him four sons, all of whom he hates and of whom he is profoundly jealous. He wants his wife all to himself, and he is so savage with his sons that she keeps them away from him as much as she can. He has never permitted the boys to

---

[7] Havighurst, "Preparing Teachers to Meet the Problem of Delinquency," *loc. cit.*, pp. 231–233. Quoted by permission of the Society.

learn German because he says that he and wife must have some language in which they can talk privately without interference from the children. Mrs. L. is still a very good-looking woman. In the earlier years of their marriage she attended a few social gatherings at the school, but Mr. L. was infuriated because other male teachers and most of the boys so openly admired her. She has not been near the school for years. Her sons all attend public school. Mr. L.'s extreme possessiveness about his wife and his hatred of his sons, which becomes greater as they approach manhood, are the dominant passions of his life. His dislike and abuse of the boys in his classes is presumably a form of displacement. He hates all boys because his own four have taken a share of their mother's attention and love away from him.

One point that had never been brought out clearly until recently was the abnormally high elimination rate from Mr. L.'s classes. The students called them "sudden death" classes, and with good reason. Out of each ten pupils who had been assigned to Mr. L. during the twenty years he was at the school, six had dropped out or flunked out at the end of the first semester, and eight by the end of the first year. The two who remained were boys who could take the rough treatment without being disturbed and were bright enough to profit by clear instruction. These were the graduates who went on to college and made good records. Almost any teacher who could dispense with eight out of every ten pupils could have a good record as far as mastery was concerned. It is quite possible that Mr. L.'s "good" record as a teacher depended upon nothing more than his willingness to frighten the weaker pupils out of his classes.

2. The Rating of Teachers: It is not at all difficult to find out what takes place within the four walls of a classroom, even without being there. One need only watch the behavior of the pupils; if evidence is desired one can ask the pupils to reply to a series of objective questions. Adolescents can give excellent testimony concerning what goes on from day to day in class. For the rating of teachers this method of approach is better than supervision from above, because supervisors see only the teachers' best efforts, while the pupils see their teachers on good days and bad ones. A systematic, objective, routine report by every student in every class at the end of every semester is greatly preferable to the usual method of waiting for enough individual pupils to come with complaints to the principal's office. For one thing, the routine report *is* routine and is therefore made with relative lack of emotion, whereas an investigation of complaints is an upsetting affair for everyone. It is quite true that some pupils give superficial judgments; so do some parents and some supervisors. But if all students are asked for opinions, the superficial guesswork of a few is not important. If a principal really wants to find out what his teachers are like from day to day, he has to ask the only people who know—the teachers' students. He can do so most easily by introducing a routine procedure by which every teacher in school is rated anonymously by every student every semester. The plan is relatively simple and has been carried out with success in several places. At the end of each semester all the students in the school are provided with a sufficient number of questionnaires to rate each teacher with whom they have just studied. The questionnaires consist of such inquiries as those listed on the opposite page.

1. How regularly do you feel afraid of this teacher?
   Answer: very often, often, sometimes, occasionally, never.
2. How often did this teacher have to punish students?
   Answer: very often, often, sometimes, occasionally, never.
3. How regularly did this teacher "pick on" a single student?
   Answer: very often, often, sometimes, occasionally, never.
4. How often did this teacher lose her temper and scold students?
   Answer: very often, often, sometimes, occasionally, never.
5. How often was this teacher sentimental about or toward students?
   Answer: very often, often, sometimes, occasionally, never.
6. How often was this teacher sarcastic?
   Answer: very often, often, sometimes, occasionally, never.

Since the ratings are anonymous, pupils may express themselves without fear of personal involvements. There will usually be, for each teacher, two or three unfavorable ratings, handed in by pupils who dislike her and have taken this opportunity to express their feelings. If such results appear only rarely they can be disregarded, but if a hundred students report a teacher as losing her temper very often, fifty more as losing her temper sometimes, and another fifty as losing it occasionally, while only ten or a dozen report that she never loses her temper, the administrator can be sure that the teacher under consideration is too poorly inhibited a person to be trusted with teaching.

3. **Control of the Class:**   Class control should be constructive. That is, it should lead the pupils to control themselves. Its objective is not quietness but the creation of an environment in which pupils can grow in both achievement and personality. The modern theories of control condemn the use of fear or intimidation in any form, and not only on humanitarian grounds. Fear leads to rigidity, not relaxation, it introduces a destructive emotion into what ought to be a constructive relationship, it prevents learning, it does not lead to a healthy attitude of mind, it favors the growth of all manner of escape mechanisms. In short, except for producing quiet, it is useless. Instead of fear, today's teacher is supposed to base her control upon the interests of the pupils and upon their friendly feelings toward her and toward each other. She is supposed to develop such good group morale that the pupils will control each other for the most part. The latest way of describing the best form of control is to call it "permissive," "accepting," and "nondirective." A teacher is "permissive" if she has few rules and if she does not demand routinized schoolroom manners from her pupils. She is "accepting" if she lets the pupils act naturally and if she remains unruffled in the face of whatever conduct the "natural" behavior may consist of. She is "nondirective" if she does not tell her pupils what to do but sets before them a problem and then lets them tell her. The good modern classroom is not especially quiet, but it is a hive of industry in which most of the pupils are engaged in doing something useful and in minding their own business.

Investigations of classroom atmospheres have taken as their criterion of good teaching either the behavior of the pupils or the rating of the teacher by experts. Either criterion is open to criticism. The pupil's behavior is obviously the end product of many forces, of which the teacher's methods form only one element. Since emotions are easily displaced, a pupil may show toward his teacher the aggression and hostility that he really feels toward his mother, merely because this expression is less damaging to his need for security. It is only when the same types of behavior appear in one class after another under the same teacher that one can prove a case either for or against her. The use of the pupils' behavior as a criterion has the great advantage of being fairly objective. Ratings, on the other hand, depend upon highly subjective concepts in the mind of the rater. They have their value, but one must remember their nature in evaluating studies in which they form the only or the main criterion.

One important investigation[8] concerned pairs of teachers in elementary school, but the conclusions are equally applicable on the secondary level. The basic method of studying these teachers consisted of observations made by expert observers, who watched what went on in the classroom on several occasions. They classified each contact between a teacher and either an individual or the class as being integrative or dominative. Correlations of reliability among different pairs of observers varied from 0.74 to 0.81 for the former type of behavior and from 0.85 to 0.93 for the latter. The reactions of the children were also studied. Teacher A of each pair made several times as many integrative contacts both with pupils and with the entire class as Teacher B and rarely made a dominative contact, while Teacher B showed the exact reverse. The children in the rooms of the A teachers showed an excess of such behavior as making voluntary suggestions, expressing voluntary appreciation, making voluntary social contributions, telling experiences or making contributions in response to the teacher's open invitation, and conducting themselves without conflict either with the teacher or with each other. The children in the classes of the B teachers showed an excess of such behavior as looking up from their work, playing with sundry small objects that had no relation to the subject under discussion, and blind conformity to domination or open revolt against it. They also showed a tendency to dominate each other in a manner that seemed modeled on the teacher's attitude toward them, they had an excess of nervous habits, and they showed more openly rebellious behavior. In one series of comparisons, the A teacher made eight times as many integrative contacts with evidence of working with the pupils as the B teacher; moreover, she worked with the pupils twice as often as she worked against them. By contrast, the B teacher worked against her class three times as often as she worked with it. The number of integrative, co-operative contacts between each teacher and her pupils was compared to the number of dominative contacts with resulting conflict, a ratio being based on these figures. The two teachers at the extremes of those studied had ratios of 100:12 and 42:100. These ratios mean that the best A teacher made 100 integrative

---

[8] H. H. Anderson and J. E. Brewer, "Studies of Teachers' Classroom Personalities: II," *Applied Psychology Monographs*, No. 8, 1946, 128 pp.

contacts to every 12 dominative, while the poorest of the B teachers made 42 integrative for every 100 dominative.

There seems no question that the dominating, authoritarian teacher of each pair pressed the children into molds that fitted the pattern of her own personality, or that these molds were unfavorable to healthy emotional growth. The second teacher, whose contacts with pupils were constructive, whose own personality was healthy, and whose classroom atmosphere was permissive produced quite different and far more desirable behavior in her pupils. The typical reaction patterns shown by the first class of children studied in both rooms were repeated by subsequent classes.[9] Moreover, the pupils who entered other rooms and worked with other teachers altered the reactions that had been recorded to suit the personality and demands of their next teacher. It has also been noted that a teacher who starts the year in conflict with her pupils and proceeds to control them by domination is more in conflict with them at the end of the year than she was at the beginning. As usual, maladjustment breeds more maladjustment.

The nondirective teacher controls her class by many methods: absence of rules, great flexibility of her plans, adjustment of work to the individual capacities of her pupils, absence of any considerable amount of tension plus the discharge of what little there is, transfer of the responsibility for discipline for any acts of aggression from herself to the pupils, her own efforts to give each child the stimuli he needs for healthy growth, encouragement to participation for the already-withdrawn, affection for the neglected, self-confidence for the insecure, diversion of expression for the attention seeker, and so on. As will be noted, such a teacher's efforts are directed toward avoiding situations that demand discipline. By so doing she prevents the arousal of the destructive emotions that ruin the relation between her and her pupils and make learning difficult. The strict, authoritarian, domineering teacher piles up emotional problems for herself and for her students. They become hostile toward her and perhaps, by displacement, toward all teachers and all schools.

4. Discipline and Punishment: The best teachers of all ages have been unalterably opposed to cruelty, corporal punishment, severity, or harshness, and overwhelmingly in favor of kindness and friendliness toward pupils, but the ordinary, untrained teacher of former times did not know how to interest pupils, and the curriculum he taught was too difficult for most children. He therefore resorted to whipping the children, probably because he did not know what else to do. With the entrance of women into the teaching profession, severe punishments of any kind soon became less frequent, and with better training, revision of the curriculum, and wider knowledge of child nature, teachers gained enough skill to avoid most situations that precipitate difficulties and to deal constructively with such as cannot be avoided. The number of occasions for discipline become less with

---

[9] H. H. Anderson, J. E. Brewer, and M. F. Reed, "Studies of Teachers' Classroom Personalities: III," *Applied Psychology Monographs*, No. 11, 1946, 156 pp.

each decade, partly because there are fewer rules and the atmosphere of the schoolroom is more permissive.

In theory, discipline should never be necessary. The need for punishment is evidence of someone's failure—not necessarily the teacher's. However, even after a teacher has prevented all the friction she can, has made her classwork as interesting as she knows how to make it, has created a relaxed and permissive atmosphere in her room, has reduced the rules and formalities to the smallest possible number, and has led her pupils to a reasonably high level of self-control, she still finds herself faced with an occasional situation that requires punishment. For the discouragement of mere restlessness or unintentional lack of manners, nothing more than a word of restraint or reproof is generally needed when the relationship between the class and the teacher is good, but as all teachers know, in any class there are a few who are at times recalcitrant and a few who are so impertinently aggressive that their bad manners cannot be overlooked. Teachers are therefore forced into using punitive measures from time to time.

Good discipline for adolescents has certain outstanding characteristics.[10] It is, first, the natural result of the misbehavior. For instance, if a boy loses his temper and throws an ink bottle at the wall, the natural punishment is to make him clean up the mess, not to require him to solve six extra problems in algebra after school. Second, punishment must be certain; if a Latin teacher sometimes laughs at smart-aleck exhibitionism and sometimes punishes it, the offender is actually encouraged to continue his antics because the possible satisfaction derived from making the teacher laugh more than offsets the possibility of disapproval. Third, punishment should be just; the English teacher who gives a failing mark to a boy because, on the final examination, he split one infinitive is being so unjust as to defeat her own ends. Fourth, punishment must be impersonal; the history teacher who gets annoyed at a pupil's general inattention and assigns a penalty that springs primarily from her own exasperation will never succeed with adolescents. They know that the penalty is only an outlet for the teacher's emotions and they blame her rather than themselves. Fifth, punishment should always be constructive and conducive to better self-control. Letting pupils suggest and carry out their own punishment is more likely to develop self-control than penalties assigned from above. Sixth, punishment should be withheld until the teacher is sure that she understands the student's motives and that she is seeing through the symptoms to the causes. Perhaps when her grasp of the situation is adequate, she will find little or nothing to punish. Seventh, punishment must avoid the arousal of fear, partly because fear is disorganizing and partly because it is useless. A frightened pupil will agree to anything, but after he has recovered, his behavior may be worse instead of better. Finally, punishment should never involve the assignment of extra schoolwork. Adolescents should have only pleasant associations with study

---

[10] G. V. Sheviakov and F. Redl, "Discipline," *Yearbook of the Department of Supervision and Curriculum Development,* National Education Association, 1944, pp. 7–8.

and learning. In spite of one's best efforts they will acquire some unpleasant associations with certain elements of their schooling, but the teacher who requires a boy to translate twenty-five extra lines of French because he threw a spitball in class is doing her best to kill any interest he may ever have had in the subject. One cannot use schoolwork as a big stick on Monday and expect pupils to find it interesting and stimulating on Tuesday.

Teachers may well follow the advice given to parents: to realize that most aggressive behavior stems basically from a need to be loved and to feel secure, and is preceded by a period during which the aggressor feels hurt, angry, or scared. The constructive approach is to give the offending pupil a normal amount of affection and security and to determine what hurt, angered, or frightened him. If possible, he should take an active part in the study of his motives. In the end, some punishment may yet seem desirable, but it can then be given on the basis of understanding and with the offender's cooperation.

In one especially important study of teachers' reactions to the misconduct of their pupils, the frequency of each scholastic sin was first determined for **874** pupils, and teachers were asked to grade the offense in terms of their seriousness.[11] A total of 51 different offenses or personal traits that interfered with good order was found, ranging from whispering and inattention to the stealing of money and the use of obscene language. Those offenses committed or traits shown by **20** per cent or more of the pupils are listed in Table 10. Of the entire 51 reactions, the average boy showed 10; the

Table 10

MISDEMEANORS IN SCHOOL

	Per cent		Per cent
Whispering	75	Daydreaming	35
Inattention	50	Lack of interest	32
Careless work	44	Overactivity	31
Tattling	42	Cheating	29
Disorder in class	39	Oversensitiveness	26
Interrupting	39	Neglect of work	25
Taking little or no part in		Laziness	21
activities	35	Rudeness, impertinence, etc.	20

Based on E. K. Wickman, *Children's Behavior and Teachers' Attitudes*, The Commonwealth Fund, 1929, pp. 30–32.

average girl, 6. The 60 children who were most maladjusted averaged 17 offenses, the 28 chronic liars and 39 chronic thieves each averaged 19, and the 32 aggressive delinquents, 21.

The investigator asked several teachers and also a group of mental hygienists to rate the seriousness of the traits and offenses. The two sets of results appear in Table 11. As will be seen, the two sets are in almost exact contradiction. What the mental hygienist regards as a serious menace to

---

[11] E. K. Wickman, *Children's Behavior and Teachers' Attitudes*, The Commonwealth Fund, 1929, 247 pp.

Table 11

OPINIONS OF TEACHERS AND MENTAL HYGIENISTS

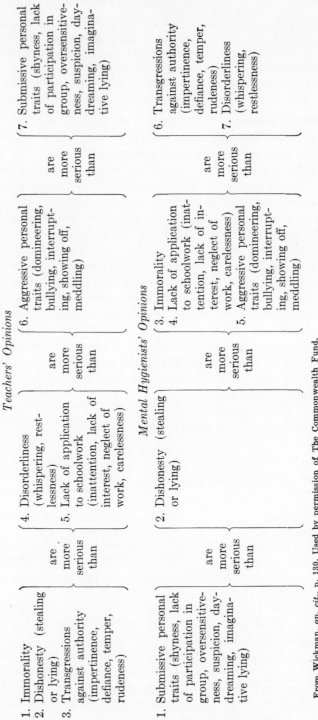

Teachers' Opinions

1. Immorality
2. Dishonesty (stealing or lying)
3. Transgressions against authority (impertinence, defiance, temper, rudeness)

} are more serious than {

4. Disorderliness (whispering, restlessness)
5. Lack of application to schoolwork (inattention, lack of interest, neglect of work, carelessness)

} are more serious than {

6. Aggressive personal traits (domineering, bullying, interrupting, showing off, meddling)

} are more serious than {

7. Submissive personal traits (shyness, lack of participation in group, oversensitiveness, suspicion, daydreaming, imaginative lying)

Mental Hygienists' Opinions

1. Submissive personal traits (shyness, lack of participation in group, oversensitiveness, suspicion, daydreaming, imaginative lying)

} are more serious than {

2. Dishonesty (stealing or lying)
3. Immorality
4. Lack of application to schoolwork (inattention, lack of interest, neglect of work, carelessness)
5. Aggressive personal traits (domineering, bullying, interrupting, showing off, meddling)

} are more serious than {

6. Transgressions against authority (impertinence, defiance, temper, rudeness)
7. Disorderliness (whispering, restlessness)

From Wickman, *op. cit.*, p. 130. Used by permission of The Commonwealth Fund.

mental health, the teacher rates as of little significance, and vice versa. The reason is not far to seek. These teachers were clearly interested in maintaining order and were inclined to overlook those traits that did not interfere with the daily conduct of the classroom. The mental hygienists were concerned with the prevention of abnormal personalities.

5. Emotional Involvements: Another source of disturbance in school is the emotional attachment that sometimes develops between a student and a teacher. Since the teachers are mostly women and since they are too old to appeal to the average boy as love-objects, the most frequent and distressing manifestation is the "crush" of a girl in the early years of adolescence. The handling of a crush demands from the teacher tact, sympathy, objectivity, and friendliness. Teachers are sometimes so harsh in trying to suppress a crush that they cause a complete disorganization of personality in an already overexcited girl.

The exact details of a desirable treatment will vary, of course, with the temperament of the individual teacher and the girl, but three general principles may be laid down. First, the teacher should remain friendly but objective, and should never betray any emotional interest in the girl, even though she may feel it. If she is herself a well-adjusted person, she will have no particular desire to fasten upon the emotional offerings of a half-developed adolescent. The idea is to redirect the girl's emotional interests, at the same time keeping her friendship and respect. Second, the teacher should not allow herself to be caught alone with the girl. Most of the embarrassing and difficult situations into which an adolescent girl with a crush may precipitate both herself and the teacher are prevented if other people are present. Since the girl's devotion is only a temporary affair, any unpleasant situations are soon looked back upon with embarrassment by both the persons concerned. A teacher should therefore make certain that the girl will not have an opportunity to see her alone. The third general rule is that the teacher should provide the girl with a great many helpful things to do. If she is an intelligent girl, she may be allowed to become of real assistance in the classroom; in any case, she can be used to run errands, wash blackboards, and do other routine jobs. While the crush is in an intense stage the girl is burning up with energy and devotion and is only too pleased to have tasks assigned to her. If they are not assigned, she will probably think up more emotional ways to demonstrate her feelings. Two or three weeks of washing blackboards, cleaning erasers, counting out books, and so on, are usually quite sufficient to calm down the emotional fires of the most intense crush. In this way a girl may succeed in working off her emotional energies through accepted channels. At the end of the intense stage, the teacher and the girl are still friends, and there are no unpleasant episodes for either to look back upon.

From time to time a teacher has as a pupil some boy who has never outgrown his infantile devotion to his mother. Such a boy may accept the teacher as a substitute and may fall quite completely and sincerely in love with her. If it happens that she returns the feeling, an extremely awkward situation arises. The two individuals not only belong to different generations but have met as teacher and student; no matter what their subsequent relations may be, she will always remain the teacher and he the pupil. This relation, while entirely satisfactory during childhood and adolescence, is a poor basis for adult happiness. Usually, however, the teacher does not return the boy's devotion. In this case the same advice just given for the handling of crushes is applicable.

The teacher should remain objective and unemotional, but at the same time friendly and sympathetic. She should not allow herself to be alone with the boy. Aside from the considerations already presented in the case of the girl with a crush, there is the wholly practical difficulty that if the teacher is caught in an emotional scene with a boy student she may lose her job. Finally, she should not attempt simply to crush the boy's feelings toward her, but should present him with a number of objective, normal ways in which he can work them off. In all probability the emotion will last for some period of time. During this period the boy is likely to write love letters, waylay the teacher on her way to and from class, and precipitate emotional scenes unless something is done to divert his modes of expression into more practical and less emotional channels. The writer recalls one high school boy who developed a tremendous devotion to a Latin teacher. It happened that the class was reading the fourth book of Caesar and had about reached the famous description of the bridge across the Rhine. The teacher seized upon this situation and asked the boy to build for her a really adequate model. He built a model about three feet long and completely correct in every detail. This work required the better part of his leisure time for nearly a month. By the time it was done he had recovered completely from his devotion, and nothing had happened to interfere with the establishment of normal relationships between the teacher and the boy.

Teachers influence children and adolescents for good or ill through their personalities, their procedures, and their punishments, all of which arouse some kind of emotional response in the pupils. Mildly stimulating, pleasant emotions are among the best of aids to learning, whereas violent or disruptive emotions prevent it. A teacher must, therefore, watch for the emotional reactions of her students.

II. Mental Hygiene in the High School

The secondary school teacher of today is responsible for teaching subject matter, just as teachers have always been, but in addition she is responsible for improving her pupils' mental health. Consequently she needs to understand the principles of mental hygiene, to be familiar with the nature of adolescent problems, and to become skilled in recognizing the symptoms of maladjustment. A high school needs also to provide the students with outlets for their emotions and to give them instruction in emotional control. These are various phases of the mental hygiene problem at the secondary school level.

1. Fears Caused by Schoolwork: Three fears are so common that they sometimes seem a natural and unavoidable accompaniment of schoolwork: fear of teachers, fear of examinations, and fear of reciting. None of these is necessary, all are destructive to either progress in school or normal personal development, and all are learned from experiences in school.

Teachers of whom pupils are afraid may have any of several unpleasant characteristics, but perhaps sarcasm and ridicule are the most common traits. Sarcasm is an unfair weapon that the sophisticated adult in a position of authority uses against pupils whose respect she cannot obtain. It usually precipitates even worse manners on the part of the student involved, and it is always emotionally disrupting. The shy students are hurt, the verbally quick students "talk back," and the ill-mannered and the hostile make scenes. In the resulting emotional storm no one in the room gets much learning done.

Fear of examinations arises when teachers stress the police functions of examinations instead of their educational functions. It may also come from too great a pressure for marks by either parents or teachers. This fear is quite real; indeed, its physical effects can be measured.[12] Most pupils, however, recover from their apprehension as soon as they start working on a test. If the fear of examinations in the future is sufficiently intense, it prevents the learning of the subject matter, although the student conscientiously makes what should have been an adequate preparation, and it sometimes produces an actual distortion of the material.[13] Perhaps some degree of anxiety is unavoidable, but at least teachers should do what they can to alter this attitude on the part of those pupils who show it.

Fear of reciting in class is common among adolescents, especially among boys, perhaps because their voices are changing. If pupils are required to stand when reciting, they may be embarrassed by their own awkwardness. Except for the occasional student who is pathologically shy, a good teacher should be able to eliminate this fear by making classwork informal and by giving special help to those who are apprehensive.

2. Discrimination: Throughout the average school one finds discriminations, intentional or unintentional. Such attitudes are fatal to the emotional equilibrium of those against whom the attitude is expressed. The writer has heard several teachers say they would never give a Negro more than a passing grade, no matter how good his work was. Similar attitudes are found toward Chinese, Japanese, Mexicans, foreigners generally, Jews, or children coming from some particular section of a city. It is the writer's opinion that teachers with such attitudes have no business in a public high school. Many emotional problems can be avoided if a school insists upon real equality. A high school should, for instance, not agree to sponsor any extracurricular activity, whether an athletic team, social club, or other organization, that on principle excludes any pupil in the high school from admission. Naturally, social relationships that are purely personal would not be affected. That is, children would still choose their friends as they wished, eat their lunch in whatever company they preferred, ask those they liked to their own homes, and so on. Such activities are not backed by school authority and require no stamp of approval except from the pupils' own families. The point is that the officially sponsored activities of a school

---

[12] C. H. Brown and D. von Gelder, "Emotional Reactions before Examinations: I. Physiological Changes," "II. Results of a Questionnaire," and "III. Interrelations," *Journal of Psychology,* 5:1–9, 11–26, 27–31, 1938.

[13] E. Liss, "Examination Anxiety," *American Journal of Orthopsychiatry,* 14:345–349, 1944.

should be open to anyone—and equally open to all. Clubs based on common interest—such as the nature study club, the radio club, the literature club, and so on—should require as the basis for admission nothing but a real interest in the matter under consideration. Athletic teams, debating teams, or honorary clubs should ask no more competency for admission from a foreigner, Jew, Negro, or Oriental than from an American white child. The official school dances should be open to everyone who wants to come; the school swimming pool should exclude only those who have infections that might be communicated to others and should never base exclusion upon the silly notion that a black or yellow skin may pollute the water. In classes in which work is sometimes done by small groups of children, the units should be made up either by putting together those of equal standing in the subject or by sheer chance—as when one groups children according to the alphabetical arrangement of their names or by the row in which they happen to sit. Such groups should not be made on the basis of race or social class. In short, school routine should be of a type which leaves no possibility for discrimination in its official procedures.

The results of unnecessary discrimination may be shown by the following case of a Negro boy who had been arrested for attacking a white high school girl. He had, to be sure, merely put his arms around her and tried to kiss her, but his attack might have gone further. The boy, who was sent to the writer for examination, told the following tale. He had never, in his ten years of school, had a teacher who would call on him as often as she called on the white children. He had never been allowed to collect papers, erase blackboards, run errands, or do any of the other things that so delight the soul of the school child. He had always been made to work by himself whenever there were group projects, unless there happened to be another Negro in the room. He had been forced to work repeatedly with one very stupid Negro girl during the preceding year because she was in many of his classes. He had never heard one of his own compositions read and commented on in class, though he wrote well. In high school he had been excluded from the swimming tank. The football coach would not even allow him to try out for the team. When he tried to take his girl to a supposedly public school dance he was refused admittance. He was not allowed to eat in the school lunchroom. His teachers often passed him on the street without speaking to him. On the day before the attack he had stumbled over a girl's foot in the aisle as he went toward the blackboard; she had slapped his face, and the teacher had scolded him for being careless, but had not made the girl apologize. Finally, this discrimination had worn him down until he had to assert himself or be crushed for the rest of his life. His manner of self-assertion might well have cost him more than an arrest. This boy's problems and attitudes were in the main created by the school itself; the blame is with the teachers and administrators who permitted a child's spirit to be broken with the load of countless small insults.

Any school that permits open intolerance is letting itself in for trouble because it is developing warped personalities both among those who discriminate and among those who are discriminated against. A spirit of tolerance can be built up in a school and often has been.

A school should not be content with merely discouraging discrimination; it should take positive steps toward equality for all, not only by admitting all children to activities for which they can qualify by either interest or ability, but by regulating the clothes which the children wear to school—a relatively simple practice. One high school in which the writer has worked required that the boys wear either cords or jeans, any colored shirt they liked, and sweaters; neckties were permitted but by no means regarded as essential. The girls were allowed cotton blouses of any color and either cotton or woolen skirts, or any plain cotton or woolen dress; if they arrived in a silk dress or blouse they were sent home to change. Such regulations make a positive contribution to equality, because discrimination on the basis of wealth is not possible. A child cannot acquire prominence through being better dressed than other children; he or she must stand out because of ability, not merely appearance.

3. The Problems of Boys and Girls: Some of the problems of adolescents are those of everyone else, but others are closely associated with their stage of development. Their problems are no more serious than those of the child or of the adult, but they certainly are more numerous. The list to be presented shortly is based upon a large number of studies that reported findings for many groups of students—some large, others small—from high school or the first two years of college. Some reports are based upon questionnaires, others upon personal interviews, and a few upon autobiographical materials. Well over ten thousand individual students contributed to the total.

The list of problems presented on pages 248–252 is detailed. It has been made so purposely in order that one may see the problems in as concrete a form as possible. The main divisions and the subgroupings are intended to give the list some degree of organization and to make it easier to grasp. The figures in Table 12 are percentages and are taken from several different sources. Some items were mentioned in only one study, in which case the per cent comes from that one. Other items appeared in two or more reports; in such instances, the percentages from all of them have been averaged. These figures are only approximations of frequency and are included because they provide a rough estimate of how common a difficulty is among adolescents. An average student in high school will have at least a dozen of these problems; many will have thirty or forty, of which, however, only two or three are basic, the rest being pyramided on top of the fundamental ones. There is nothing abnormal in having a large number, provided the pupil is taking sensible steps toward solving some of them. Adolescence is an age of doubts and conflicts, and no teacher can hope to do more than eliminate those that are unnecessary or superficial, but she can show a lively sympathy, a quick recognition, a hopeful assurance that age and experience will solve most difficulties, and a determination to help in the solution of as many as possible, not merely when she is consulted by students, but consistently in her day-to-day presentation of subject matter and in her day-to-day procedures in class.

It is necessary that the insecurity which comes from anxieties and fears be reduced as soon and as completely as possible, even if a teacher has as

Table 12

PROBLEMS OF HIGH SCHOOL STUDENTS

I. *The Problems of Health*

	%			%
1. Not getting enough sleep	42		Eating the wrong foods	24
2. { Getting tired too easily	19		Having poor appetite	8
Feeling tired all the time	11	5. { Being overweight or under-	
3. { Not getting enough exercise	8		weight	52
Not having time for relaxa-			Suffering from nausea	64
tion	27			
Having bad posture	39		Having headaches	12
Having poor figure	25	6. { Having stomach trouble	10
Having bad complexion	31		Having too many colds	12
Having bad breath	10		Having toothaches	9
4. { Having body odor	12		Being nervous and tense	30
Being ugly	11	7. { Biting nails	26
Blushing very easily	12		Feeling always below par	8
Having poor motor co-ordina-		8. { Feeling faint or dizzy	8
tion	22		Worrying about health	11

II. *The Problems of Personality*

	%			%
Feeling inferior	41		Worrying over little things	31
Feeling bashful	19		Being blue frequently	18
Disliking responsibility	22		Getting discouraged easily	24
Lacking self-confidence	30		Having thoughts of suicide	5
Feeling self-conscious	28	3. { Taking things too seriously	37
Feeling pushed around by others	25		Being underactive	12
1. { Feeling of not being wanted	21		Wondering if life is worth	
Feeling unsure of oneself	24		while	12
Fearing criticism	20		Seeing no future for oneself	10
Fearing failure or humilia-			Daydreaming too much	32
tion	26		Feeling guilty about things one	
Feeling one is not as smart as			has done	26
others	33	4. { Feeling lonesome	20
Having outbursts of temper	33		Feeling not wanted by others	17
Being too restless (over-			Feeling different from	
active)	24		others	11
Being too excitable	23		Being unhappy	16
2. { Being too careless	26		Wanting a pleasanter personality	35
Losing head in emergencies	23	5. { Being too easily hurt	31
Getting into too many argu-			Feeling that others do not	
ments	12		understand one	19
Being too impulsive	14		Being too intolerant	18
		6. { Being tactless	19
			Hurting the feelings of others	21

III. *The Problems of Home and Family*

%

1.
- Interference of parents in:
  - buying one's own clothes — 9
  - selecting one's own friends — 13
  - spending of money one has earned — 11
  - making one's own decisions — 11
  - making one's own dates — 14

2.
- Having no place to study — 31
- Having no room to oneself — 18
- Having no privacy — 26

3.
- Feeling too distant from parents in interests — 19
- Being unable to discuss personal things with parents — 20
- Being unable to discuss sex problems with parents — 30
- Being afraid to tell parents when one has done wrong — 19
- Being unable to think of parents as friends — 28

%

4.
- Quarreling with parents — 13
- Quarreling with siblings — 18
- Feeling discriminated against — 10
- Talking back to parents — 26
- Hearing constant bickering about money at home — 15
- Having parents who quarrel with each other — 16

5.
- Being treated as a child — 34
- Being denied use of family car — 29
- Not being trusted — 11
- Not being allowed to go out on school nights — 39
- Being made to get home by a certain hour — 31
- Being constantly criticized — 14
- Being expected to tell parents everything — 10
- Being regarded as irresponsible — 21
- Having too little freedom — 29

6.
- Feeling that parents expect too much of one — 14
- Being constantly nagged to study harder

IV. *The Problems of Social Status*

%

1.
- Feeling awkward at social affairs — 27
- Fear of making social errors — 43
- Fear of meeting people — 28
- Feeling that people dislike one — 11
- Feeling unable to maintain a conversation — 35
- Feeling of being insignificant in one's own group — 21
- Feeling awkward among one's age-mates — 17
- Wanting to be included in a "crowd" — 18

2.
- Worrying over what to wear — 16
- Worrying over correct manners — 34
- Wanting to learn how to dance — 34
- Not knowing how to act at parties or other formal affairs — 28
- Not knowing how to introduce people

%

2.
- Not knowing how to get rid of someone one does not like — 20
- Wanting to know how to plan a party — 16
- Not knowing how to select right clothes for figure — 15
- Not knowing how to order in a restaurant — 11
- Not knowing good table manners — 17

3.
- Having too few friends — 38
- Wanting to be more popular — 54
- Being left out of things — 26
- Wanting to join more clubs — 15
- Having too few activities — 18
- Having no one for a pal — 38
- Having no one to discuss personal problems with — 26
- Wanting to make new friends and not knowing how — 42
- Being unpopular — 20

4. Wanting to be more of a leader — 25

Table 12—*Continued*

V. *The Problems of Heterosexual Relationships*

	%			%
1. { Not having a boy (girl) friend	35		3. { Worrying over selecting the right mate	19
Wanting more dates	45		Wondering how to prepare for marriage and family life	21
Falling in and out of love	23		Wanting to marry now	27
Having brief, intense love affairs	17			

1.
- Not having a boy (girl) friend — 35
- Wanting more dates — 45
- Falling in and out of love — 23
- Having brief, intense love affairs — 17

2.
- Not knowing how to ask a girl for a date — 19
- Wondering how much initiative to take in getting a boy to ask for a date — 15
- Not knowing what to do on a date — 24
- Not knowing what are good manners on a date — 17
- Not knowing how to refuse a date politely — 26
- Not knowing if one should go on a "blind" date — 22
- Not knowing how to break off dating with someone — 19
- Not knowing if one should "go steady" — 26

3.
- Worrying over selecting the right mate — 19
- Wondering how to prepare for marriage and family life — 21
- Wanting to marry now — 27

4.
- Wanting to be more attractive to boys (girls) — 38
- Wanting to be more interesting to boys (girls) — 30

5.
- Being embarrassed by tales of sex — 11
- Being embarrassed by dirty stories or jokes — 21
- Not knowing if necking is right or necessary for popularity — 21
- Not having any vocabulary for discussing sex — 9
- Thinking too much about sex — 18
- Needing correct information about sex — 35
- Wondering if one is normal sexually — 13
- Worrying about masturbation — 29

VI. *The Problems of Religion and Morals*

1.
- Feeling the need for advice on religious matters — 28
- Wondering if there is a life after death — 24
- Fear of death — 34
- Being confused in religious beliefs — 17
- Worrying over differences between teachings of Bible and of science courses — 13
- Searching for something to believe in — 5
- Worrying over losing one's faith in religion — 9
- Knowing one is not living up to one's own ideals — 19

2.
- Not knowing what is right or wrong — 28
- Not knowing how one sets up standards for right and wrong — 19

3.
- Having a guilty conscience — 11
- Yielding to temptation — 9
- Trying to break a bad habit — 21
- Being tempted to cheat — 12

4.
- Wondering what life is all about — 18
- Wondering about one's place in the world — 11
- Wondering what is really important in life — 12

5.
- Worrying over world problems — 14
- Worrying over the next war — 31
- Worrying over racial prejudice — 25
- Worrying over social inequalities — 16
- Worrying over problems of government — 15
- Worrying over problems of intolerance — 18
- Worrying over problems of reform — 29

VII. *The Problems of School and Study*

	%
Being unable to concentrate	47
Having inadequate methods of study	36
Being unable to plan time	34
Being unable to use library	21
1. Being unable to pay attention in class	39
Not having enough time to study	27
Spending too much time in activities that interfere with study	31

	%
Having difficulty in taking notes	27
Having difficulty in outlining	17
Being unable to express oneself in writing	37
2. Having too small a vocabulary	26
Being unable to spell	11
Being slow in mathematics	17
Being unable to read well enough or fast enough	28

	%
Having teachers who are unfair	15
Having teachers who are sarcastic	17
Having teachers who give no encouragement	15
Having teachers who are not interested in one	12
3. Having teachers who have favorites	22
Having teachers who do not like one	6
Having teachers who are too strict	13
Having teachers of whom one is afraid	9
Having teachers who are dull	11

	%
Doubting the value of what is taught	21
4. Taking courses too far removed from life	10

	%
Worrying over examinations	51
Worrying about marks	28
Not knowing how to prepare for tests	26
5. Wanting to know more definitely just how well one is doing	40
Getting low marks	29

	%
Disliking courses	14
Disliking school	22
6. Wanting to quit school	9
Being restless in class	14

	%
Being afraid to recite	36
7. Being unable to speak before a group	53
Being unable to express oneself in words	35

	%
Wondering how much ability one really has	59
Doubting ability to do school-work	40
8. Doubting ability to go to college	42
Fearing failure in college	27
Having unstable interests	12

	%
Needing help in selecting courses	26
9. Needing help in selecting college	38

Table 12—*Continued*

VIII. *The Problems of Choosing a Vocation*

	%
1. { Needing help in selecting vocation	43
Needing help in selecting courses to reach objective	42
Needing practical experience in different types of work	49
Needing help in discovering one's abilities	43
Needing help in finding out about opportunities and requirements in different fields	28
Having no interest in any vocation	14
Not knowing where to look for a job	35
Not knowing what work is suitable for one's abilities	56

	%
2. { Needing to earn more money now	27
Needing to earn more money for college	21
Needing to budget money	28
3. { Not knowing how to write a letter of application	18
Not knowing how to act during an interview	24

This list is based mainly upon the following references: H. J. Baker, "Mental Hygiene Problems of Adolescent Boys," *Nervous Child*, 4:151–158, 1945; N. A. Congdon, "Perplexities of College Freshmen," *Educational and Psychological Measurement*, 3:367–375, 1943; C. W. Heath and L. W. Gregory, "Problems of Normal College Students," *School and Society*, 63:355–358, 1946; R. A. Hunter and D. H. Morgan, "Problems of College Students," *Journal of Educational Psychology*, 40:79–92, 1949; M. C. Klohr, "Personal Problems of College Students," *Journal of Home Economics*, 40:447–448, 1948; H. C. Koch, "Shifting Emphasis in the Problems of Pupils in Certain Michigan High Schools," *School Review*, 51:79–84, 1943; R. G. Kuhlen and H. S. Bretsch, "Sociometric Status and Personal Problems of Adolescents," *Sociometry*, 10:122–132, 1947; R. L. Mooney, "Personal Problems of Freshmen Girls," *Journal of Higher Education*, 14:84–90, 1943; C. Pope, "Personal Problems of High School Pupils," *School and Society*, 57:443–448, 1943; H. H. Remmers, A. J. Drucker, and B. Shimberg, *Examiner's Manual for the SRA Youth Inventory*, Science Research Associates, 1950, 12 pp.; G. L. Stone, "Student Problems in a Teachers College," *Journal of Educational Psychology*, 39:404–416, 1948; H. Taba and D. Elkins, *With Focus on Human Relations*, American Council on Education, 1950, 227 pp.; C. W. Valentine, "Adolescence and Some Problems of Youth Training," *British Journal of Psychology*, 13:57–68, 1943.

her objective only the mastery of subject matter, because insecurity is a basic cause of failure to learn among pupils of normal intelligence.[14] Only mental defect is as pervasive and important a factor in the etiology of school failure. The reduction of anxiety and the furnishing of emotional security are therefore essential to the work of the teacher.

4. Provisions for Emotional Outlets: Another important contribution of the school to emotional stability is the provision of adequate outlets for the easily aroused emotions of adolescents. It is better for all concerned if the school allows emotions to be expressed as they are generated by providing frequent outlets, so that a feeling, which must in the interest of others be temporarily suppressed, will soon be worked off. Such outlets are of various types.

Fortunately for mental hygiene, man is a talkative creature and finds

---

[14] D. McCarthy, "Personality and Learning," *American Council on Education Studies*, Series I, No. 35, 1948.

it possible to work off much of his tension by merely talking. Modern school methods provide adolescents with abundant opportunities for conversation. Much work is done by committees of students, who plan their assignment, talk over what each has to contribute, and work out a joint report. These informal groupings produce relatively little tension and provide an excellent means for the draining off of destructive emotion and the expression of integrative feelings.

Since emotions generate nervous and muscular tension, anything that requires exertion acts as a relief. Games of all sorts give excellent opportunity to work off pent-up feelings generated either in or out of class. If every pupil in a high school has some agreeable form of exercise during his last period in school, or after school, he is automatically provided with an outlet of a socially accepted sort. Kicking a football is just as good as kicking a chair and much better than kicking the cat. Sheer physical exertion uses up the extra supply of blood sugar with which the muscles are already well provided and allows them to relax again. Games may also act as compensatory activities for those pupils whose academic work is poor but whose athletic skills are superior.

Any kind of extracurricular activity may also function in the same way, even though little or no physical exertion is involved. Such developments distract the pupil's mind from his worries, provided the activities are interesting to him and he does not find them too competitive or too difficult. Then, too, they offer such opportunities for emotional expression as singing, acting, or pursuing an emotionally satisfying hobby. If a boy has a lively interest in radio, for instance, he may be able to work off, during the time he spends with the radio club, the feelings of inferiority and discouragement he has developed earlier in the day because his English composition was unsatisfactory. Or a girl may be able to express her drives for domination and prestige by making a stunning poster to support an appeal for funds on behalf of some charity. Extracurricular activities do not always function automatically as outlets for emotional stress, but they may be made to do so if they are correctly guided.

Finally, the school should provide plenty of opportunity for social intercourse in the form of purely social meetings, dances, picnics, chances for groups to lunch together, and so on. One has to remember, however, that school dances and parties can sometimes precipitate more emotional stress than they relieve if discrimination becomes involved. The high school needs no new techniques or equipment in order to provide for the working off of tensions. It needs merely to use what it has and use it wisely.

5. Instruction in Mental Hygiene: The list of problems presented in a previous section might well serve as the basis for a course in mental hygiene. Many adolescents are greatly helped by the relatively impersonal and intellectual approach inherent in the study of any subject. High school students are old enough to understand the basic concepts of mental hygiene and, with help, to apply these concepts to their own lives. They have so many problems, great and small, that it is hard to imagine a more immediately useful course than one in mental hygiene. Moreover, each teacher should apply the tenets of mental hygiene to her own instruction and should use her assignments, when possible, to aid in the normal development of her pupils.

The teacher of English is in a particularly good position to provide emotional outlets and emotional stimulation through her assignments, both in writing and in reading. Creative writing gives great satisfaction to its author and often serves as an outlet for emotional problems. The form is a minor consideration, and a teacher who fusses unduly about spelling and punctuation is almost sure to diminish the therapeutic values of writing. Naturally, one has to correct errors, but the time for correction is after a pupil has expressed his interests and drives and feels that his manner of writing could be improved. One might consider the following excerpts, which are quoted as originally composed:

1. Last truthday a friend of min were have a ras. We were still ras antilt we come to a car and my frend ran me of road and hit the car the biskly trind a somer saw and I flow through the air.

2. I think I'm coming out this summer only I'm not staying on the desert. Wiht rattle snakes crawling around my neck, and cactuses in my pants, with a black widow crawling up my leg and a teranchla biting my tow and a scorpion stinging my back. A hawk pecking my head. I hope to go to the mountain.

3. I am in the fourth grade now. I sit in the fourth row in the sixth seat from the front. On my report card I got three A and three B four S. I weigh 61 pounds. I am 52 inches tall.

4. We made a poster about dogs. We has all kinds of dogs. And they were pretty dogs. I like they all. We had a bule dog and he was looking in a mirer. And there were huting dog and some puppy too.

5. Yesterday my dad and I went riding on our horses. We went down to the field to hunt for fish in the ponds the river had left when it flooded. Once my dad looked around and I was in a mud puddle and the poney was on its side. My dad thought I was mud turtle with a cowboy hat and boots.[15]

These compositions leave much to be desired in the matter of form, but they are spontaneous and vivid. The writers of No. 1 and No. 5 had experiences that, if suppressed, might have become traumas; No. 3 is showing something of an obsession about his schoolwork; No. 2 is expressing his overdeveloped anxiety about things that crawl and bite; and No. 4 is demonstrating his interest in dogs. Such creative writing is good for children because it provides both a satisfaction of and an outlet for emotional drives.[16]

It is the school's duty to give its students scientific information in regard to emotional life. Adolescents need it so badly they will try to get it somehow, but too often they have to depend upon quacks and pseudo psychologists for help. As matters now stand in the ordinary high school,

[15] E. J. Swenson and C. G. Caldwell, "The Content of Children's Letters," *Elementary School Journal,* 49:149–159, 1948. Used by permission of the Journal.
[16] L. H. Buckingham, "Creative Writing Based on Experience: Some Psychological Values," *English Journal,* 30:553–557, 1941.

most references to emotional problems come incidentally into class discussions or in private interviews with teachers. Neither of these arrangements is satisfactory. Instruction concerning such important matters as emotional development and control should not be left to chance.

6. Recognition of Maladjustment: In general people seem to be somewhat inattentive to the signs of emotional disturbance, but most normal people can learn to recognize the major symptoms of maladjustment once they know what to look for. A list of those deviations which have appeared with the greatest frequency in the extensive research done in recent decades will guide teachers in the recognition of abnormal behavior, the first step in the prevention of abnormal personalities. Children showing regularly more than one or two such behavior traits as those given below are showing clear symptoms of emotional or nervous difficulty. These are the danger signals. The teacher's task is to make sure that they are not flown in vain.

Physical symptoms: Frequent headaches, attacks of nausea, dizziness, loss of weight, loss of appetite, habitual twitching of muscles, grimacing, nail biting, stammering, lack of co-ordination, sudden blushing or paling, frequent complaints of aches and pains, obesity, mannerisms, rigidity, constant restlessness, chronic fatigue, nervousness, affectations or posturings, jumping at sudden noises, inability to stop talking.

Symptoms of emotional immaturity: Dependence on teacher, frequent requests for help, efforts to attract teacher's attention, crushes on teachers, efforts to curry favor with teacher, staying voluntarily after class to talk with teacher, behavior too young for age, irresponsible behavior, impulsive behavior, mischievousness, frequent interruptions in class, inability to work alone, frequent requests for special attentions and favors, unwillingness to state an opinion, preoccupation with marks.

Symptoms of social inadequacy: Excessive shyness, lack of self-confidence, preference for remaining alone, overt rejection by other pupils, lack of friends of either sex, avoidance of members of opposite sex, absence from school parties or other events, homesickness, chronic attitude of insecurity or anxiety, unwillingness to recite, refusal to take part in games, tendency to stay alone at recess or to go home alone from school, refusal of recognitions or rewards, expectation of special privilege as a right, snobbishness, efforts to join groups where one is not wanted.

Symptoms of abnormal emotionalism: Frequent absorption in daydreaming, irrelevant answers to questions, failure to hear when spoken to, tendency to worry unduly, lack of voluntary participation in class, absent-mindedness, withdrawal from work that looks new or difficult, chronic attitude of apprehension, moodiness, overexcitability, melancholy or apathy, indifference to stimuli that excite other pupils, unusual sensitivity to annoyances, frequent laughing at nothing or failing to laugh when others do, uncontrolled laughing or giggling, high distractibility, tendency to get feelings hurt, marked fears or anxieties or obsessions, shrieking when excited, sudden attachments to people (usually older), extravagant expression of any emotion, undue and prolonged anxiety over mistakes, marked distress over failures, meticulous interest in details, frequent bad dreams, hangdog attitude of guilt or hopeless acceptance of frustration or rejection.

Symptoms of exhibitionism: Teasing other pupils, pushing or shoving them (especially in corridors between classes), trying to act tough, trying to be funny, wanting to be conspicuous on public occasions, effusiveness, exaggerated courtesy, marked agreement with everything the teacher says, constant bragging about exploits or places seen or people met, frequent attempts to dominate younger or small children, inability to accept criticism, constant efforts to justify self, frequent blaming of failures on accidents, on false causes, or on other individuals, refusal to admit any personal lack of knowledge or inability, frequent bluffing, attempting either far too little or far too much work, showing off.

Symptoms of intellectual involvement: Marked pressure of ideas that crowd forward so fast that one sentence is left unfinished as another is begun, marked slowness of answers to questions, frequent breaking off of speech in the middle of a sentence, apparent blocking of ideas, fixity of ideas, explosive tone in argument, unwillingness to change opinions in the face of evidence, seeming inability to grasp the basic ideas of a course, tendency to repeat gestures or words several times, false interpretations of other people's behavior, false accusations of others, complaints that teachers or parents "pick on" or "have it in for" one or that other pupils are antagonistic, constant negative criticism of others, frequent complaints of unfair treatment, rationalization and projection of failures, "chip-on-the-shoulder" attitude, marked suspiciousness of other people's motives, interest in schoolwork to the exclusion of everything else.

Symptoms of antisocial tendencies: General attitude of aggressiveness in all relations, insolence, frequent loss of temper when corrected, destructiveness of school property, defacing of books, bullying, abusive or obscene language, undue interest in sex, telling of dirty stories, writing obscenities on walls, showing pornographic pictures, fierce resentment of authority, unwillingness to conform to regulations, bad reaction to discipline, "hoodlum" behavior whenever unsupervised, irresponsibility, frequent minor delinquencies—lying, cheating, swiping things—profound dislike for schoolwork, inability to profit from experience, truancy, delight in nonintellectual competition.

III. Summary

Teachers inevitably influence their students through their own personalities. The maladjusted teacher has a class full of maladjusted pupils, many of whose difficulties are directly attributable to her own attitudes and behavior. The first duty of teachers in promoting mental health among their pupils is therefore to promote their own. Teachers can also learn as much as they can about emotional life and its expressions, about reactions and their meanings, and they can try to avoid the arousal of unpleasant emotions as much as possible, at the same time providing adequate outlets for the expression of normal drives. They should also be aware of the many problems that beset adolescents and should learn to recognize the common symptoms of maladjustment. In their disciplinary measures, when these cannot be avoided, they should utilize all they know about the nature of adolescent boys and girls. Most adolescents are in school several hours a day. The experiences they have there are numerous and sufficiently important to have an influence upon their emotional development. A school can, and should, be as concerned about the emotional growth of its pupils as it is about their educational achievements.

REFERENCES FOR FURTHER READING

BOOKS

1. Blos, *The Adolescent Personality,* Chap. 5.
2. Bullis, H. E., E. O'Malley, and J. Jastak, *Human Relations in the Classroom,* Delaware State Society for Mental Hygiene, 1944, 155 pp. (Part II and any five lessons in Part IV.)
3. Fenton, N., *Mental Hygiene in School Practice,* Stanford University Press, 1943, 455 pp. (Chaps. 6, 8, 10–12, 16–18.)
4. Fleege, *Self-Revelation of the Adolescent Boy,* Chap. 8.
5. Fleming, *Adolescence: Its Social Psychology,* Chap. 13.
6. *Helping Teachers Understand Children,* American Council on Education, 1945, 468 pp. (Chaps. 5–10.)
7. Landis, *Adolescence and Youth,* Chap. 18.
8. Louttit, *Clinical Psychology of Children's Behavior,* Chaps. 10, 13.
9. Neill, A. S., *The Problem Teacher,* International Universities Press, 1944, 160 pp. (Pp. 32–39, 54–80, 107–114.)
10. Preston, G. H., *The Substance of Mental Health,* Rinehart & Company, 1943, 147 pp. (Chap. 7.)
11. Sadler, *Adolescence Problems,* Chaps. 13, 15.
12. Thorpe, *The Psychology of Mental Health,* Chaps. 16, 17.
13. Tiegs and Katz, *Mental Hygiene in Education,* Chap. 10.
14. Travis and Baruch, *Personal Problems of Everyday Living,* Chaps. 2, 8.
15. Turner, *School Health and Health Education,* Chap. 13.
16. Wallin, *Minor Mental Maladjustments in Normal People,* Chaps. 10, 14.
17. Wickman, E. K., *Children's Behavior and Teachers' Attitudes,* Commonwealth Fund, 1929, 247 pp. (Chaps. 2, 3, 6–8.)
18. Zachry and Lighty, *Emotion and Conduct in Adolescence,* Chap. 11.

MONOGRAPHS, BULLETINS, PROCEEDINGS, YEARBOOKS, ARTICLES

A. *Teachers: Personality and Methods*

1. Anderson, H. H., and J. E. Brewer, "Studies of Teachers' Classroom Personalities: I," *Applied Psychology Monographs,* No. 6, 1945, 157 pp.
2. Anderson, H. H., and J. E. Brewer, "Studies of Teachers' Classroom Personalities: II," *Applied Psychology Monographs,* No. 8, 1946, 128 pp.
3. Anderson, H. H., J. E. Brewer, and M. F. Reed, "Studies of Teachers' Classroom Personalities: III," *Applied Psychology Monographs,* No. 11, 1946, 156 pp.
4. Arbuckle, D. S., "The Teacher as a Source of Maladjustment," *American Psychologist,* 4:294, 1949.
5. Dodge, A. F., "A Study of Personality Traits of Successful Teachers," *Occupations,* 27:107–112, 1948.
6. Jersild, A. T., and F. B. Holmes, "Characteristics of Teachers Who Are Liked Best and Disliked Most," *Journal of Experimental Education,* 9:139–151, 1940.
7. Leigh, P., "Study of the Adjustment Difficulties of a Group of Women Teachers," *Journal of Educational Psychology,* 27:401–416, 1936.
8. Meredith, G. M., "Administrative Procedures That Improve the Morale and Mental Health of Teachers," *Education,* 63:627–630, 1943.
9. Moore, J. E., "Annoying Habits of High School Teachers," *Peabody Journal of Education,* 18:161–165, 1940.
10. Symonds, P. M., "Problems Faced by Teachers," *Journal of Educational Research,* 35:1–15, 1941.

B. *Mental Hygiene*

1. Baron, D., Mental Health Characteristics and Classroom Status," *Education*, 69:306–310, 1949.
2. Cason, E. B., *et al.*, "School Practices in Promoting Mental Health," *American Council on Education Studies*, Ser. I, No. 40, XIV (1950), 121–136.
3. Chase, W. W., "Mental Hygiene and In-Service Training of Teachers," *Education*, 69:288–292, 1949.
4. "Fostering Mental Health in Our Schools," *Yearbook of the Association of Supervision and Curriculum Development*, National Education Association, 1950, 320 pp. (Chaps. 11, 17.)
5. McClusky, B. Y., "Mental Health in Schools and Colleges," *Review of Educational Research*, 15:405–412, 1949.

C. *Attitudes Caused by Schoolwork*

1. Brown, C. H., and D. von Gelder, "Emotional Reactions before Examinations: I. Physiological Changes," *Journal of Psychology*, 5:1–9, 1938.
2. Liss, E., "Examination Anxiety," *American Journal of Orthopsychiatry*, 14:345–349, 1944.

D. *Discipline*

1. Hayes, M. L., "A Study of Classroom Disturbances of Eighth Grade Boys and Girls," *Teachers College Contributions to Education*, No. 871, 1943, 139 pp.
2. Sheviakov, G. V., and F. Redl, "Discipline," *Yearbook of the Association of Supervision and Curriculum Development*, National Education Association, 1944, pp. 7–8.
3. Symonds, P. M., "Classroom Discipline," *Teachers College Record*, 51:147–158, 1949.

E. *Difficulties of Adjustment*

1. Baker, H. J., "Mental Hygiene Problems of Adolescent Boys," *Nervous Child*, 4:151–158, 1945.
2. Graham, A. W., "Personal and Social Adjustment of High School Students," *School Review*, 55:468–473, 1947.
3. Heath, C. W., and L. W. Gregory, "Problems of Normal College Students," *School and Society*, 63:355–358, 1946.
4. Hunter, R. A., and D. G. Morgan, "Problems of College Students," *Journal of Educational Psychology*, 40:79–92, 1949.
5. Klohr, M. C., "Personal Problems of College Students," *Journal of Home Economics*, 40:447–448, 1948.
6. Kuhlen, R. G., and H. S. Bretsch, "Sociometric Status and Personal Problems of Adolescents," *Sociometry*, 10:122–132, 1947.
7. Pope, C., "Personal Problems of High School Pupils," *School and Society*, 57:443–448, 1943.
8. Remmers, H. H., A. J. Drucker, and B. Shimberg, "Examiner's Manual for the SRA Youth Inventory," Science Research Associates, 1950, 12 pp.
9. Schrader, W. B., and N. Fredriksen, "Worries of Veteran and Non-Veteran Students as Related to Disparities between Prediction and Actual College Grades," *American Psychologist*, 5:344–345, 1950.
10. Stone, G. L., "Student Problems in a Teachers College," *Journal of Educational Psychology*, 39:404–416, 1948.

PART THREE

Social
Development

CHAPTER NINE

Social
Growth

The adolescent years are, pre-eminently, a period of social development and adjustment. During the preceding years of childhood there has been, to be sure, a beginning of socialization, through the acquisition of fundamental social skills. The elementary school child can learn how to get along with others of his own age and sex in such social situations as arise during his schoolwork or his play outside school. He can also develop a workable relationship between himself and his parents or teachers. It is quite necessary that these childish adjustments take place, since they serve as a basis for the more complete development of the adolescent years. The social development of children is, however, limited both by their immature mentality and by their inattention to many social stimuli.

With the oncoming of adolescence, the boy or girl becomes acutely aware of social pressures and relationships. It is this sensitivity that leads the adolescent into the conformity characteristic of the period. The boy or girl wants to have exactly the same kind of clothes, to use the same slang expressions, to do the same things in the same way, to study the same subjects in school, and to enjoy the same forms of amusement as his or her friends. Deviations in dress or manner from the mode of the group are painful. As the adolescent grows older, he learns to react to some situations but not to others, and he develops greater self-confidence, so that he does not feel the need for dependence upon his friends. He tends, however, to remain very sensitive to the reaction of his group to his behavior. It is therefore essential that the teacher should realize the strength of these social drives, and should always try to work with rather than against them.

The normal course of development from the onset of puberty—when social situations first become critically important—through the adolescent years is outlined in Table 13. In general, the change is from an excessive, emotionalized interest in social relationships to a stable, more objective adult level.

1. Spontaneous Social Life among Adolescents

When the mother of an adolescent boy or girl asks her child where he or she is going, the answer is likely to be "just out with the crowd." A few years earlier the reply is "just out with the gang." From the adult point of

Table 13

SOCIAL GROWTH

Growth from	*Toward*
1. Variety and instability of interests	1. Fewer and deeper interests
2. Talkative, noisy, daring with a great amount of any kind of activity	2. More dignified controlled masculine and feminine adult behavior
3. Seeking peer status with a high respect for peer standards	3. The reflecting of adult cultural patterns
4. A desire for identification with the herd, the crowd of boys and girls	4. Identification with small select group
5. Family status a relatively unimportant factor in influencing relations among peers	5. Family socioeconomic status an increasingly important factor in affecting with whom boys or girls associate
6. Informal social activities such as parties	6. Social activities becoming more formal, such as dances
7. Dating rare	7. Dates and "steadies" the usual thing
8. Emphasis on building relations with boys and girls	8. Increasing concern with preparation for own family life
9. Friendships more temporary	9. Friendships more lasting
10. Many friends	10. Fewer and deeper friendships
11. Willingness to accept activities providing opportunities for social relations	11. Individual satisfying activities in line with talent development, proposed vocation, academic interest or hobby
12. Little insight into own behavior or behavior of others	12. Increasing insight into human relations
13. The provision of reasonable rules important and stabilizing	13. Growing independence from adult and dependence on self for decisions and behavior
14. Ambivalence in accepting adult authority	14. Seeking relations with adults on an equality basis

L. H. Meek, *The Personal-Social Development of Boys and Girls*, Committee on Workshops, Progressive Education Association, 1938, p. 121. Used by permission of the Association.

view the "gang" and the "crowd" may be more or less synonymous, but the adolescent uses the terms to denote somewhat different groups. The gang is typically a spontaneous social unit of late childhood. Its members are generally of the same sex, and it is relatively small. The activities of a gang are, of course, influenced by the outlets provided in a given neighborhood, but its general objective is to seek adventure and excitement. The crowd, on the other hand, is typically composed of both boys and girls, preferably an equal number of each. It contains from six to a dozen members, who usually live within two or three blocks of each other, attend the same school, and have much the same socioeconomic background. Its chief activities consist of talking, listening to the radio, watching television, eating, and dancing at home to radio or phonograph.

In the summer the crowd sits around on someone's porch, with occasional excursions to the neighborhood drugstore. In the winter it sits around in someone's house, plays the radio, and makes raids on the icebox. None of this comes under the heading of adventure as seen through the eyes of late childhood, but it is apparently exciting to the adolescent. It is adventure, not into the world of things but into the world of social relationships. An adult listening to the conversation of such a crowd for an evening can hardly see that the chatter has been worth while. It does not seem to start anywhere, to go anywhere, or to be about anything. It is, however, satis- factory to the participants. It obviously gives them an opportunity to de- velop their conversational powers on other people whose abilities are no better than their own. Other values obtained from such a crowd include experiences in getting along with other people, practice in social skills, de- velopment of loyalty to a group, practice in judging people, assistance in the emancipation-from-home procedure, and experience in love-making un- der circumstances in which the participants are protected from serious con- sequences. Moreover, the group gives its members a feeling of social security, of "belonging."

On the debit side, it is probable that the crowd encourages some degree of snobbery and that it has an undesirable effect upon those who belong to no crowd at all. Sometimes an intense rivalry springs up between two crowds and leads to extremely silly behavior, but such situations do not usually last long. If some observant and tactful older person can bring about an attachment to an existing crowd for the isolates or can influence the growth of a new crowd among those who belong to none, and can manage to curb the occasional excesses of loyalty, this spontaneous social group could be- come even more valuable than it is naturally. Even as it is, the crowd probably does more to bring about normal social growth than teachers and parents combined.

The "peer culture," the sum total of spontaneous social manifestations among age-mates, is most clearly defined and most influential during the middle years of adolescence.[1] At this time adult values have less power to produce behavior than peer values. That is, if "everyone" is wearing berets, it is almost impossible to persuade an adolescent to wear any other sort of headgear, no matter how formal the occasion or how inappropriate the beret; if "no one" is wearing berets, then an adolescent will not wear one even to keep the hair out of his eyes while he is sailing a boat. Apparently, one of the deepest of adolescent needs is the need to be supported and approved by his peers. The actual values of the peer group change and mature as the boys and girls grow older, and gradually they lose some of their power, partly because the youngsters have learned more about thinking for them- selves, partly because they have already achieved a secure place in their own group, and partly because peer values are becoming merged with adult values instead of being in opposition to them.

The clique, the fraternity, and the sorority are less healthy manifesta-

---

[1] C. M. Tryon, "The Adolescent Peer Culture," *Forty-third Yearbook of the National Society for the Study of Education*, 1944, Pt. I, pp. 217–239.

tions at the secondary school level. Adolescents go to enough extremes in social adulation and social ostracism even at best, without the encouragement of group support. The clique, of whatever character, is too tight an organization for a member's own good, it is by nature intolerant, it is usually based upon either wealth or social class, and it demands a loyalty from its members that prevents many possible social contacts from taking place and reduces the effectiveness of those that do occur. A clique is really a caricature of a crowd, an out-of-proportion drawing with the least desirable traits overemphasized. Cliques are unhealthy both emotionally and socially, and they precipitate unhealthy reactions among the outsiders as well as among the members. Two excerpts below are illustrations of this point:

I want to tell you something about that school [the high school]. All the kids in it are broken up into little groups. Those gangs start in the seventh and eighth grade, and they carry them on into high school. If you're in the gang you're all right, and if you aren't you're left out of things. When I started to high school, I was lost. I did not know anyone but Harry Swenson. We graduated from the Dickerson School together. I tried to get in with some of the girls, but I never did. They made me feel like I wasn't wanted. About the fourth week, I heard Anne Hogate [Class III] call me "that hick." I wanted to quit after that, but Mom made me go on for a few weeks. Pop said if I didn't want to go I didn't have to; so I quit.

Frankly, for a lot of us there is nothing here, but just going to classes, listening to the teacher, reciting, studying, and going home again. We are pushed out of things. There is a group of girls here who think they are higher than us. They look down on us. I won't mention any names, but they are a group of girls from the higher families. They have a club that is supposed to be outside of school, but it's really in the school. They just go from one club to the other and hog all the offices. They're in all the activities. They talk about what they're doing, what they're going to do, and they won't pay any attention to us. They snub us and they won't talk to us. Some of them will speak sometimes, but most of the time they just ignore us. I'd like to be in the school activities and the school plays, go to the dances, and things like that, but they make us feel like we're not wanted. I went to some of the activities when I first started high school. Last year, I was in the Home Makers' and the Cheer Club, but they ignored me. Now I'm not in anything. If we go to the high school dances, nobody will dance with us. They dance among themselves and have a good time and we're nobody. If we go to the football games, it's the same way. Those Cheer Club girls are supposed to sit together at a game and root, but they don't. They break up into little groups and, if you're not in one of the groups, you're left out of things.[2]

To an adult, the social behavior of boys and girls when they are left to themselves often seems silly, awkward, or merely wasteful of time that might well be used otherwise. It is true that adolescent social skills are undeveloped and awkward, but for that very reason boys and girls need precisely the kind of experiences they crave, in order that they may acquire poise and adjust themselves to the demands of society. One investigator explored the matter of social competence, as measured by knowledge of such

[2] Reprinted with permission from August B. Hollingshead, *Elmtown's Youth*, pp. 202–203, 343, copyright 1949, John Wiley & Sons, Inc.

relatively superficial skills as knowing how to invite, introduce, and meet people, how to write acceptances and thank-you notes, how to make dates, and so on. As noted on page 249, adolescents worry a great deal over their ineptitude in such simple social techniques. As would be expected, the girls scored far above the boys. Senior boys had less knowledge of accepted social usages than freshman girls. Both sexes showed gains in these skills during the high school years.[3]

The spontaneous speech of adolescents also reflects their social immaturity and their emotional instability. It is idiomatic, slangy, and colorful but overloaded with the catchwords and clichés of the moment. It is highly charged with emotion, although ostentatiously careless. Most of the content, between the ages of thirteen and sixteen, has to do with personal relationships, gossip, clothes, and social affairs. For girls, the order of frequency was clothes, dates, boys, parties, jokes, books, teachers, movies, movie stars, sports, money. For boys it was sports, jokes, girls, dates, clothes, machinery, money, drink, jobs, teachers, politics, movies. In the later years of adolescence a somewhat larger proportion of the spontaneous conversation is concerned with academic matters, vocational plans, attitudes toward life, and world events, and there is a decrease in the earlier concentration upon clothes.[4] A large group of adolescent boys reported concentration of conversation upon sports and girls, with a small admixture of remarks about school, social affairs, sex, jokes, and movies.[5]

Perhaps the best way to get a picture of adolescent social life is to read a few accurate and detailed descriptions of typical episodes and developments. As one reads one should try to see that the somewhat diffuse and disorganized behavior is an expression of underlying social drives and that the clumsy experimentation is a first step toward adult social behavior.

The following descriptions give an account of spontaneous adolescent reactions in the clubrooms that have been opened as a part of certain research programs in a few high schools:

It became more and more evident, as the clubhouse attracted more students, that its *raison d'être,* as far as the majority were concerned, was to offer a place for social contact and consequently a place in which to work out one's social relationship to the group. For some the chief concern was to work out relationships with the same sex. Boys who did not feel equal to the competition afforded by the organized sports on the school grounds came over and learned how to play with other boys in the informal small group games in the back yard. Five or six who found themselves together in the yard would get the football and have a makeshift game and enjoy it. Two or three who would not dare enter a real football game would play with one or two who were recognized athletes without any feelings of inferiority. They were necessary in order that there be a game and the physical

[3] J. R. Leevy, "Social Competence of High School Youth," *School Review,* 51:342–347, 1943.

[4] M. C. Jones, "A Functional Analysis of Colloquial Speech among Adolescents," *American Psychologist,* 1:252–253, 1946.

[5] U. H. Fleege, *Self-Revelation of the Adolescent Boy,* Bruce Publishing Company, 1944, p. 234.

set-up was such that it could not be a "high-powered" game. Those who, for some reason, had missed the rough-and-tumble of neighborhood street games, made up for lost time. The standards of achievement were so much lowered that girls were even admitted to boys' games. Standards of sportsmanship were not lowered, however, and it was interesting to see how those who started out criticizing others or blaming the other fellow for their own mistakes soon learned not to do so. Bean bag wars were fun and taught some the needed lesson in how to "take it." When basketball was in season, at almost any time from one to five could be seen practicing throwing baskets. The less skillful came over during their study periods to get in an extra practice when there was no competition and practically no audience. This same thing happened especially during the pole vaulting season. At noon it was a spectacular affair, gathering an admiring audience, and only the skillful cared to compete. During study periods and after school, however, nearly everyone took a try at it and several worked daily at mastering this sport.

The girls learned to get along with one another, not so much through activities although they did take part in some of them, but rather through a trial and error method of handling social situations. Some learned through watching what sort of conduct seemed to bring popularity. Some tried loud attention-getting behavior until they found it wasn't welcome or they tried bossing others around until someone "told them off." The "Scandal" sheet kept them posted as to public opinion. Anyone could write this sheet who felt inspired. Usually he or she had several assistants as soon as he started to compile the news items. It was rather an honor to "make" this sheet, as it usually indicated that one's latest boy or girl friend had been recognized as such by the group. Sometimes, however, the item was a group reprimand for behavior of which it did not approve. As such it was far more effective than anything an adult could say.

The girls danced a great deal together but always with an audience of boys. The audience might be playing checkers, cards, Ping-pong and table games, or reading, doing puzzles, listening to the radio, or just "horsing," but it was a satisfactory audience just the same. Any of its activities, except listening to the radio, might better have taken place in one of the other rooms, but that was something that almost never happened, no matter how crowded the living room and dining room became. Three of the boys knew how to dance when the clubhouse started. They declared it a silly activity—then proceeded to ask the young lady in charge of the clubhouse to teach them privately. In public they practiced on adults and on each other and finally had the courage to ask dances of the more boyish sort of girls (the ones with whom they were accustomed to playing games). Dancing was never a favorite nor consistent activity among the boys although there were a few who could be counted upon to dance at least once during the day. The girls engaged in some activities other than dancing. Usually these were games such as Ping-pong or cards which involved members of the opposite sex. The only activities which the girls engaged in together were tap dancing and cooking. Even the cooking groups became mixed finally.

The boys engaged in many activities which did not include girls nor have girl audiences. Some boys never took part in activities except with girls or in the vicinity of girls. These were older boys. This included a group of boys who were very much interested in the girls, although they had no techniques for getting along with them and limited themselves to watching and teasing them. Those who had developed their social techniques and were successful with the girls, alternated between spending their time in mixed groups and in groups of boys. Conversations among these boys touched frequently on parties, girls, clothes, as well as on sports, radio, etc. There was also a group of boys who were only interested in the activities of boys. They came into the house just long enough to get their equipment and showed no interest in the mixed group activities. They were for the most part younger boys. Sometimes they made comments about the boys whose interests lay within the house. Members of the "outside group" graduated to the "inside" as they became interested in the opposite sex. Some never did come to the club-house until they were interested enough in girls to at least watch the group inside. Another group of boys were not mature enough to be interested in the social activi-ties and were so busy at school and with special interests outside school that they had neither time nor interest in the activities at the clubhouse.[6]

A few boys and quite a number of girls who came to the clubhouse regularly from the start made effective gains in social experience. Through their persistent attendance at noon and after school, as well as at parties on Friday nights, they became the staunch supporters of a variety of clubhouse activities. Their popu-larity was established, and they possessed an attractive aspect of maturity in the eyes of their classmates.

Leaning on these central figures as heroes and heroines on their social horizons were larger groups of boys and girls, often lacking in adequate social techniques and self-assurance, but eager for all the firsthand experience they could get by just being present and hanging around with the crowd. Their rising social interests were reflected in their anticipation of approval by their more popular and grown-up classmates. For some months it was essential that they share such visible means of support as games of checkers, throwing darts or bean bags, playing Ping-pong, or merely having a book open in their hands. But as courage mounted and con-versation between these boys and girls became easier, they dispensed with such props and mingled with each other more freely and informally.

Still further removed from these levels of mixed social activities were many other groups, usually made up of one sex only, exhibiting a diversity of interests, and often moving about almost independently of each other as well as of the more sophisticated groups. For several months, two or three smaller girls met quietly and contentedly for lunch in the kitchen by themselves; or, when this space was invaded by a vigorous game of tag, they would retire to an upstairs room. In the garage at a carpenter's bench some more mechanically inclined boys carried over interests they were enjoying in the school shops. In the back yard, groups of smaller boys tirelessly worked on the improvement of their skills at basketball or football, with a view toward increasing the effectiveness of their competition with larger groups on the school grounds. A few less popular boys and girls preferred the company of the secretary to the hazards of ridicule from their classmates, and these would remain at her side busily trumping up means of capturing her attention.[7]

The activities described above are anything but aimless. Most of the boys and girls had little social facility, but in their inept way they were ex-pressing the fundamental drives that hold society together.

The last sentence of the above quotation brings up the question of the role of the adult, whether teacher or parent, in relation to the spontaneous social life of adolescence. The main thing is that the adult should be on hand and available when wanted but should not interfere when not wanted or make attempts at guidance that can be detected for what they are. Attempts to mingle with the group as if one were of the same generation

---

[6] L. H. Meek, *The Personal-Social Development of Boys and Girls*, Committee on Workshops, Progressive Education Association, 1938, pp. 220–222. Used by permission of the Association.

[7] W. J. Cameron, "A Study of Early Adolescent Personality," *Progressive Education*, 15:556–557, 1938. Used by permission of the publishers.

are not only futile and ridiculous but are practically certain to alienate the adolescents. Any obvious effort at control has the same effect. It is one of the minor mysteries of life that some fine, educated, well-intentioned men and women are quite incapable of providing acceptable supervision, while certain quite ordinary, uneducated, only moderately interested adults do so admirably. The writer remembers one family from her own adolescent days in which the mother was unable to make any but the most distant contacts with the cronies of her adolescent daughter, whereas the Irish cook was perfect in the role of "teacher, philosopher, and friend." The mother greeted her daughter's guests courteously and pleasantly, but then retired to the second floor. The cook stayed in her kitchen, except when she was bringing food to the guests, but almost every boy and girl in the group went to her once or twice every evening with problems, great or small, and was given hardheaded advice. She never intruded, but she was available when wanted, and her mere presence not only prevented misbehavior, but spread a feeling of complete security.

II. Selection of Friends

Adolescent boys and girls are most eager to have friends of both sexes and are inclined to measure their social status in terms of their ability to establish friendships with their peers. The paramount importance of friends is well expressed in the words of an adolescent boy, who wrote the following paragraph in his diary:

It is evening. My watch is ticking softly. Everyone is asleep. I closed a just-finished book and wiped the tears from my eyes. Whether this was weakness or nothing to be ashamed of, I don't know. The book tells the story of a boy who at the side of a friend struggles and obtains work and faith. This friend dies, and the boy ceases to develop. I always feel that I lack a friend, one who can completely enter into my personality, to whom I could utter all my thoughts, and who would be fond of me. . . . I also know that few people love me, but I shouldn't care about that if I had one who was willing to be my friend. Then I could say I am of value to one person, and could ignore others with indifference, but, as it is, knowing that I have not completely won over anyone, knowing that there is no one who likes me better than all the rest of his comrades, it seems to me as though I were worth very little. I should not, like Socrates, like to look for men, but for one man. *I think it is a disgrace to be without a friend.*[8]

1. Bases for Friendship: Many studies have been made to determine which adolescents in a school are likely to become friends with each other. Several factors seem to contribute to the choices made by boys and girls.

The greatest single reason for selecting an individual as a friend is neither dramatic nor psychologically revealing; it is mere propinquity. Obviously the environment limits the number of possible associates, but it does not force boys and girls to choose as best friends those who live in the

---

[8] Translated from C. Bühler, *Das Seelenleben der Jugendlichen,* G. Fischer, Vienna, 1927, p. 51. Used by permission of G. Fischer.

same block or the same dormitory or are in the same classes in school. Yet in all studies, the factor of mere propinquity emerges as of utmost importance.[9] Thus, college girls who were asked to name what three girls they would most want to keep in touch with after college chose over 50 per cent from their own dormitories.[10] The next most important basis was membership in the same college class; the 103 freshmen cast 74 per cent of their votes for other freshmen; the sophomores, 60 per cent for other sophomores; the juniors and seniors, 50 per cent for their own classmates. A third and much less important basis was concentration in the same major subject, but one does not know how much of this result was again due to propinquity, since majors meet each other more often than they meet other classmates and with increasing frequency as they advance through college. In another study, made of members of college fraternities, a similar basis for selecting classmates appeared.[11] In addition, members tended to give most of their remaining votes to seniors, probably a reflection of hero worship for campus leaders.

Another factor, obvious yet usually overlooked, is the sex of the chooser and the chosen. High school friends were found to be of the same sex in 86 per cent of pairs of friends.[12] In this same study, 68 per cent lived within a block or two of each other. Social class, economic level, occupational status of the father, and religious affiliation are also known to have some relationship to friendship choices.

One excellent study concerned both choices and rejections among school children in the fifth and sixth elementary school grades and in the tenth and eleventh grades of high school in a small midwestern city that had five rather clearly defined social groups: (A) the "Old Families," (B) the professional men and business officials, (C) the average man—clerk, small storekeeper, skilled laborer, (D) the lower-income group—semiskilled, unskilled, and casual labor, and (E) the "Nonrespectables"—keepers or inmates of brothels, gamblers, known criminals, and other shady characters.[13] Results from Group A were not presented, presumably because there were too few children. The sixth-grade children selected their friends from their own social level more frequently than from any other; when they went outside it they tended to select a friend from a higher social class rather than from a lower. The highest degree of rejection—and it was mutual—occurred between the "highest" group of children and the "lowest." The results from high school, as shown in Figure 67 on page 270, are of a similar nature but less marked. One explanation for the difference is the absence

[9] G. A. Lundberg, V. B. Hertzler, and L. Dickson, "Attraction Patterns in a University," *Sociometry*, 12:158–169, 1949.

[10] G. A. Lundberg and V. Beazley, "Consciousness of Kind in a College Population," *Sociometry*, 11:59–73, 1948.

[11] F. M. Vreeland, "Social Relations of a College Fraternity," *Sociometry*, 5:151–162, 1942.

[12] M. Smith, "Some Factors in Friendship Selections of High School Students," *Sociometry*, 7:303–310, 1944.

[13] B. L. Neugarten, "Social Class and Friendship among School Children," *American Journal of Sociology*, 51:305–313, 1946.

from the high school group of those who had left school or had been retarded or sent to a special class. The small proportions from social groups
D and E who still remained included only those who were bright, had a
real interest in books, and had imitated best the clothes and manners of the
two upper groups. The resulting protective coloring led to somewhat less
rejection. However, the pupils of the B and E groups still selected most of
their friends from their own social level and rejected those from the opposite extreme.

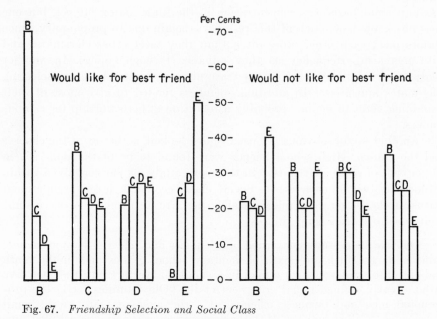

Fig. 67. *Friendship Selection and Social Class*

From B. L. Neugarten, "Social Class and Friendship among School Children,"
American Journal of Sociology, 4:311, 1946. Used by permission of the
publisher.

Religion is a relatively unimportant basis of friendship among college
students, but it does have a slight influence, perhaps because freshmen
may first become acquainted with each other through attending meetings
in churches near or on the campus. The number of actual choices of friends
who have the same religion is slightly in excess of the number that would
be selected if church affiliation had no influence at all.[14] Similarities between
friends in academic achievement, vocational interests, and traits of personality are all low.[15]

In general, then, a boy or girl tends to choose friends from among those

[14] M. E. Bonney, "A Study of Friendship Choices in College in Relation to Church
Affiliation, Church Preference, Family Size, and Length of Enrollment in College,"
Journal of Social Psychology, 29:153–166, 1949.

[15] M. E. Bonney, "A Sociometric Study of the Relationship of Some Factors to
Mutual Friendships in Elementary, Secondary, and College Levels," *Sociometry*, 9:21–
47, 1946.

of the same age and sex, from the same social background, from the immediate neighborhood, and of about the same intelligence. In addition, an adolescent tends to select others who have reached the same level of physical maturity.[16] Such facts as these are too general to be of much use in individual cases, although they sketch in the background. There may be, for instance, fifty adolescents who are potential chums of any given boy, insofar as the above criteria are concerned; yet he develops friendships with no more than a few of the total number who seem, from an external point of view, equally appropriate. Much more study of individual friendships is needed before one can state with any certainty who will like whom—and why.

2. Heterosexual Friendships: Normally, boys and girls develop friendships with each other during the period of adolescence. Sometimes the transfer from preadolescent friendships with members of one's own sex to the heterosexual interests of adolescence takes place gradually and easily and sometimes it is sudden and bewildering. The wise parent not only refrains from comment or opposition, but is thankful that the transfer has occurred. Whether sudden or gradual, the boy-and-girl friendships of adolescence are essential to normal adjustment. Nothing that results from them could possibly be as serious as their failure to develop.

The reports of adolescents concerning their early heterosexual interests are most illustrative. A few samples appear below:

Girl, age 16: In the very earliest part of this (adolescent) period I had a queer feeling toward boys. I did not care for their company; in fact they rather bored me, yet I rather liked to be noticed by them. I considered it the proper thing to disagree with boys continually and rather prided myself upon my continual wrangling. A favorite scheme of my chums and myself was to pretend that we did not see the boys but put ourselves where they would surely see us. But on the whole we considered them a silly lot. Some of the girls of our age went to dances, and we considered this the most stupid and silly thing possible. Often, while I was sitting on the porch in the evenings with Mother, many boys would pass and naturally speak. Mother would answer, but I coolly cut them and considered it very smart and especially when, afterward, people remarked what a stubborn person I was. Until I was fifteen I loudly asserted that I would be an "old maid," and then in my sophomore year I suddenly changed my mind.[17]

Boy, age 18: I still recall that once our whole family was taking a walk. Going home we met a father with his daughter. I could not turn my eyes from her beautiful figure, her attractive dress. I still recall that I was amazed and saw nothing but her. Then I heard Mother saying to Father, "Just look at our Fritz." Thus, I was dragged back into grim reality, only furtively so that no one noticed it, I had to glance back again and again toward the heavenly child.

O when I kissed the first girl! In the evening I wanted to go to Röders'. On the way, I met my longed-for Anna. She wanted to go to a gardener in order to bring a little flower pot to a friend. I said, "Oh, Anna, this suits me swell. I can go along." I still hear her expectantly consenting voice, so bashful, chaste, and yet

---

[16] M. C. Jones, "Adolescent Friendships," *American Psychologist*, 3:352, 1948.
[17] E. L. Mudge, *Varieties of Adolescent Experience*, Appleton-Century-Crofts, Inc., 1926, pp. 53–54. Used by permission of Appleton-Century-Crofts, Inc.

yielding. When we were halfway, I said, "Come, Anna, let us go out there." And I laid my arms around her childlike form. Thus we walked along happily. She also liked to hold me in her clasp. In the meadow in front of the wide street— I still remember quite distinctly—I stood still. Her head rested on my cheek, but I could not muster up courage to kiss her. I recall the sensation of this first uncertain groping toward an experience. Oh, and when on the way home, I pressed, clasped, and kissed her, there was no such intoxicating bliss as I had expected. I was overwhelmed by embarrassment because I seemed now to be responsible for this girl.[18]

The "boy-crazy" and "girl-crazy" periods, which occur at the ages of thirteen to fourteen and sixteen to seventeen, respectively, are extremely trying to adults, but this stage and the many brief, intense episodes during it serve a practical purpose. They give experience in courtship and provide the basis for the subsequent selection of a mate. If a girl is "protected" from such youthful love affairs she is likely in later years to think herself in love with the first man who courts her. If a boy has already had a few attacks of puppy love he knows how to discount mere excitement. Far from being dangerous, the somewhat sentimental boy-and-girl attachments of adolescence are highly educative at the time and are essential for self-protection in the years after home supervision has been left behind.

There was, for instance, a young man of twenty-seven who had been "protected" from girls, partly by an oversolicitous mother, partly by an absorbing interest in schoolwork, and partly by being accelerated so far in school that he was thrown with people socially too old for him. At twenty-seven John had never had a girl friend. He had begun to feel himself abnormal in this respect and had made a few tentative efforts to remedy the matter. He had taken two or three clerks or stenographers to the movies, treating them with exaggerated courtesy. Evidently he did not feel confident enough to make a date with girls from his own social class. After a few months of these tentative social contacts he met and fell in love with a young woman of about his own age—a thoroughly sophisticated girl who had had a number of "affairs," more or less serious. She liked John, enjoyed his somewhat erudite conversation, and found him most useful in running errands for her. Because she generally kissed him good night John assumed they were engaged. In the course of time the inevitable happened. John found out about her affairs, some of which were continuing, and was both hurt and horrified. Suddenly he realized that she was not the good and beautiful maiden he had imagined, but a rather ordinary person of far from conventional morality. This sort of episode should have taken place when John was sixteen or seventeen, living at home with his family. Falling in love with a girl who is not good enough for him is part of every intelligent boy's education, but not after he becomes a man. John's affair took place too late. Instead of getting over it and charging it up to experience, he has developed a hatred for all women and now he has nothing more than purely business contacts with them. At the age of sixteen he might have made a similar response, but it would hardly have lasted long. At present it bids fair to become permanent. There is a time when puppy love is educative, but after the period has gone by it is only destructive.

Investigators have of late years been turning the light of scientific inquiry upon the path of true love. Most high school boys and girls report as

---

[18] Bühler, *op, cit.*, p. 68. Used by permission of G. Fischer.

normal a series of boy-and-girl affairs, courtships, engagements, quarrels, friendships, crushes, and broken engagements. Numerous difficulties are encountered, especially at first in meeting a sufficient variety of the opposite sex. If the advertisements in the "personal" columns of newspapers and the number of "clubs" of the matchmaking type are any criterion, this problem does not stop with the end of adolescence.

There have been a number of articles that listed the stages of courtship. One of the best of these classifications appears below:

1. No dating
2. Occasional dating
3. Frequent dating
4. "Going steady"
5. Having a definite understanding to be married at some future time
6. Having a definite understanding to be married on a specified date in the near future
7. Being formally engaged
8. Married[19]

The fourth stage is generally reached at least once by the end of high school, and is almost sure to be reached by the end of college unless conditions are most unfavorable. "Going steady" has certain advantages that lure youngsters before they sense its disadvantages. It gives security because one always has someone with whom to go to a social function, it makes both members feel popular and grown-up, it gives time for friendship and understanding to develop, and it costs less. It is, however, a relationship that is easier to start than to stop, it may become too serious too soon, it is likely to arouse family opposition, it prevents the development of other friendships, and it often ends in a good deal of strain, after which there is likely to be a period of isolation until others discover that the erstwhile "steadies" are back in circulation again.

Dating behavior and success in courtship are related to family background and interrelationships. Whenever any circumstance had intervened to affect normal relationships between parents and children, the latter were less successful in having dates during high school and in progressing through the normal stages of courtship.[20] The most obvious of such background conditions were the absence of one parent from the family group, the foreign nativity of the parents, open revolt of the children against parental authority, and serious tension of any kind. Senior high school students who did not date at all were found to have an appreciably less wholesome family background than other seniors. Boys who had no fathers and girls who had no mothers tended to be low in their ability both to make social contacts

---

[19] R. F. Winch, "The Relation between the Loss of Parents and Progress in Courtship," *Journal of Social Psychology,* 29:51–56, 1949.

[20] R. F. Winch, "Interrelationship between Certain Social Background and Parent-Son Factors in the Study of Courtship among College Men," *American Sociological Review,* 11:333–343, 1946, and "The Relation between the Loss of Parents and Progress in Courtship," *loc. cit.*

and to progress through the usual stages of courtship, as shown in Table 14.

Table 14

EFFECT OF BROKEN HOMES UPON DATING

Courtship Status	Boys (Father missing) %	Boys and Girls (Both parents missing) %	Girls (Mother missing) %
High	18	35	43
Low	82	65	57

Based on R. F. Winch, "The Relation between the Loss of Parents and Progress in Courtship," *Journal of Social Psychology*, 29:51–56, 1949.

Orphans were equally ineffective. The figures are clearer for the boys than for the girls. In another study, high school seniors who did not date at all presented a picture of inadequate family relationships, unwholesome attitudes toward themselves, negative attitudes toward others, and poor adjustments in even the most casual of heterosexual contacts.[21]

Most early adolescent love affairs come to an end. Thus, one investigator found that only 15 per cent resulted in marriage. The commonest reasons for the end of romance were geographical separation, dissatisfaction of one or both members, and interference of adults.[22] In the same study, college students of both sexes were asked a number of questions concerning their previous and current attachments. The results appear in Figure 68 on page 275. The students admitted frequent affairs, conflicts over becoming too involved, over jealousy, friction, or tension, and over the feeling that they had become trapped. The chief cause for termination of an affair was a loss of interest on the part of one or both of the partners. The resulting feelings of relief, satisfaction, happiness, and indifference far outweighed those of bitterness, sorrow, or remorse. Over half of the students reported no shock at all, although in a few instances the trauma was severe. Readjustment was immediate for half the boys and girls, but for a few, the aftereffects lingered on for a year or more. When an adolescent does not recover from a broken affair within six weeks or so, there is probably some weakness in the structure of his personality.

3. Popular and Unpopular Individuals: It is obvious to the most casual observer that pupils differ markedly in both their ability to react to others and their ability to arouse in others reactions to themselves. The investigations to be reported in this section measure and objectify this well-known phenomenon.

The first study was based upon results from 665 college girls who named

[21] O. P. Walford, "How Early Background Affects Dating Behavior," *Journal of Home Economics*, 40:505–506, 1948.

[22] C. Kirkpatrick and I. Caplow, "Courtship in a Group of Minnesota Students," *American Journal of Sociology*, 51:114–125, 1945.

which girls of the group they regarded as best friends and which they disliked.[23] The total number of positive choices was 1,860, or 2.8 per girl; for

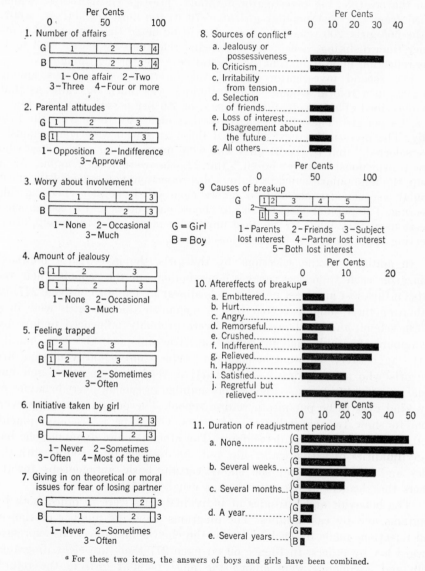

^a For these two items, the answers of boys and girls have been combined.

Fig. 68. *Love Affairs*

Based on figures in C. Kirkpatrick and I. Caplow, "Courtship in a Group of Minnesota Students," *American Journal of Sociology*, 51:114–125, 1945.

negative choices, or rejections, the total was 682, or 1.02 per student. By assigning positive numerical values to first, second, or third position of

[23] C. Smucker, "Management of Group Tension through the Use of Negative Sociometric Data," *Sociometry*, 10:376–385, 1947.

choice on another girl's blank and negative values for first, second, or third position of rejection on another's blank, and then subtracting the negative from the positive, the investigator obtained "prestige status scores" which varied from the least popular girl at -76 to the most popular at $+607$. Of the 665 girls, 200 rejected no one. It will be noted that liking was commoner than disliking; acceptances exceeded rejections by a rate of 3 to 1. This reflection upon human nature should be a comforting thought.

The second investigator studied the interpersonal relations among 400 girls in a reform school.[24] The technique was much the same as that just described. There were 1,045 choices, or 2.6 per person, and 587 rejections, 1.4 per girl. These figures agree well enough with those from the first study. The investigator next identified those girls who were conspicuously "overselected," that is, the 21 girls who were most popular; also, those who were conspicuously "underchosen," the 22 who were least popular. As a group, the unpopular tended to claim a disproportionate number of the most popular as their friends and to ignore each other, neither choosing nor rejecting. The popular girls tended to choose each other and to assign such rejections as they made to the most unpopular members of the group, often rejecting the very girls who had chosen them.

In addition to the selections by the girls, the investigator obtained ratings on each from the various housemothers in the school. Their reports on the most and least popular girls appear in Table 15 on page 277. In evaluating these judgments, one has to remember that the girls were in a reform school, and the housemothers were probably influenced unduly by the amount of trouble each girl caused her. The unpopular girls were mainly of the aggressive, "chip-on-the-shoulder" type. Conspicuously missing are the girls who are withdrawn, shy, inactive, repressed, negative, and unsocial, presumably because they do not indulge in enough overt behavior of any kind ever to be put into a reform school. The popular girls, however, seem to show two constellations of traits. One type is friendly, placid, motherly, and reasonably dependable. The other is more dynamic; she has many qualities of active leadership, but she does get into trouble with the rules and regulations and she shows certain basic antagonisms toward others that leaders of her type do not usually show.

The behavior and attitudes of individual girls were recorded both by diagrams and by case studies. The diagrams show the number of choices and rejections made by each girl, plus the choices and rejections expressed toward her by others. In Figure 69 on page 277 there are eight diagrams. Jean and Jacqueline were among the most popular girls in the reform school; Beatrice and Sarah were also popular, but less so. Vera, Alice, Eva, and Amelia were all extremely unpopular. Vera was a complete isolate; she received no votes at all. The other three were near isolates, each being chosen once. The diagrams are constructed in the following manner: in the smallest circle is the girl's name; in the next larger is a record of her choices

---

[24] H. H. Jennings, *Leadership and Isolation: A Study of Personality in Interpersonal Relationships*, Longmans, Green & Co., 2d ed., 1950, 349 pp.

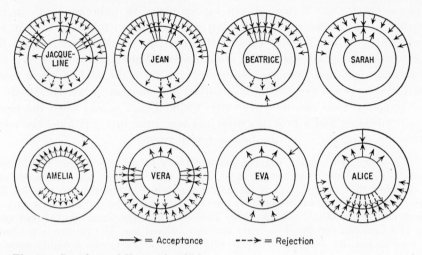

→ = Acceptance   --→ = Rejection

Fig. 69. *Popular and Unpopular Girls*

From H. H. Jennings, *Leadership and Isolation,* Longmans, Green & Co., 1950, pp. 105–111. Used by permission of the publisher.

Table 15

RATINGS OF POPULAR AND UNPOPULAR GIRLS

Characteristic	Unpopular (22 girls) %	Popular (21 girls) %
1. Quarrelsome and irritable	15	1
2. Aggressive, domineering	12	2
3. Interfering actively with others	11	1
4. Interfering passively with others	13	1
5. Resistive to criticism	16	8
6. Attention seeking	11	1
7. Praise seeking	10	2
8. Suspicious, believes she is not treated fairly	19	0
9. Is cooperative	7	40
10. Is even-tempered	6	27
11. Shows ingenuity in handling "problem" girls	0	37
12. Is solicitous toward new girls	2	39
13. Requires no attention from housemother	0	30
14. Does own share of work voluntarily	0	26
15. Willingly accepts background roles	3	26
16. Plans and organizes well	0	26
17. Has initiative	2	28
18. Believes in her own ability	1	17
19. Is sometimes retaliatory	2	14
20. Makes minor changes without permission	2	13
21. Is impatient with slower girls	0	13
22. Is sometimes rebellious	4	11

From H. H. Jennings, *Leadership and Isolation,* Longmans, Green & Co., 2d ed., 1950, pp. 145–150. Used by permission of the publisher.

and rejections—the former shown by arrows with unbroken lines in the upper half of the diagram and the latter by arrows with broken lines in the lower half; the outside ring records the reactions of other girls toward the one whose name appears in the middle area. When the heads of two unbroken arrows, one from the outer and one from the middle circle meet, the liking between the two girls involved was mutual; when the heads of two broken arrows just meet, the girls disliked each other; when the heads of an unbroken and a broken arrow just meet, the first girl liked the other while the second rejected the first—or vice versa.

Jacqueline is the most outgoing and sociable of the leaders. She made relatively many choices—ten. Of the ten she chose, all but one chose her. She was chosen also by another thirteen girls whom she had not selected as friends. She rejected five girls, but was not herself rejected by anyone. Jean made fewer choices (seven), of which five were mutual; nineteen other girls also chose her. Jean rejected four girls, one of whom rejected her. One other girl also disliked her. The picture is not quite as good as that for Jacqueline, but nevertheless shows a girl who is highly popular, even if she does arouse occasional friction. Beatrice's diagram shows five mutual choices, one unreciprocated choice on her part, and eleven additional choices directed toward her. She rejected three girls and was rejected by one. Sarah is near the lower limit of the twenty-one overchosen girls. She made one mutual choice, and three additional ones; eleven other girls liked her. She neither has nor arouses dislikes. Her own selections are remarkably few. Her acceptance seems to consist largely in being unobjectionable rather than in being truly popular. Eva has little emotional reaction toward others. She has established no mutual contacts either positive or negative with anyone. Two girls disliked her and one liked her, but perhaps without her knowing it. Amelia, equally isolated, although less actively disliked, does not share Eva's resignation to the indifference of others. She made fifteen positive choices and nine rejections, but got only one vote in return. She is emotionally active but seems unable to establish even enough contact with others to be disliked. Alice and Vera are of a different type altogether. Alice expressed a liking for five girls, one of whom liked her. She thus does have *one* friend. On the debit side, she was involved in seven mutual antagonisms and was disliked by an additional nine girls, toward whom she is neutral. Alice gives evidence of being a fighter who meets hate with hate. Vera shows a pathetic attempt to make contacts, which lead her into rejection. Of her nine choices, six disliked her. She rejected four girls, and was rejected by two of them, plus ten others, not counting the six already mentioned. No one voted for her. Unlike Alice, she has no friend to fall back on, and she has a positive genius for persuading people to dislike her.

More light is thrown upon these popular and unpopular girls by the case histories, of which portions from those of Jacqueline, Jean, Amelia, and Vera will be presented. While reading these histories, the student should keep in mind the diagram for each girl—perhaps making a rough copy so that the diagram can be conveniently matched with each history.

JACQUELINE (Leader: chosen by twenty-two; rejected by none)
1Q 114; age 17 years 2 months.

Appearance. A supple, lithe physique excellently proportioned; pretty features; expression winsome and contemplative; large, luminous brown eyes, tan complexion, wavy dark brown hair. Fine, colorful speaking voice. Well-poised. Manner gracious.

Personality-Behavior Picture. Very self-aware and equally aware of others. Feels others' moods practically as if they were her own; emphatic in her reactions to people; seems to understand "the whole person" of the individual; rapidly gets into rapport with a wide range of individual's troubles, problems, or special gifts. . . . Exceptionally articulate verbally as well as mimically. Particular facility in "tuning" her words to the person with whom she is talking. "Gets away with" the suggestions and criticisms she gives to others. Is herself very conscious of the impression she is making upon others whom she cares to impress favorably; will go out of her way and undergo great sacrifices to make the adult or other girl realize her worth. Tenacious. Will undergo more than necessary rather than ask to be relieved, whether it is work assigned to her or a situation causing her acute emotional distress. Aspiration level high and ability likewise high. Wants a lot of recognition and succeeds in getting it in a bona fide, well-earned way. Cares nothing about the kind of recognition anybody can earn; it must convince her that she has accomplished more than another could accomplish. When she has excelled so very much beyond others that the few whose good opinion is important to her know her quality, then a simple word or look is all she wants from them. . . . Never asks privileges and favors not given without the asking although she knows they would be granted. Unusually appreciative of any "nice thing" another person may do for her and shows her appreciation in unusual ways. Shows exceptional esthetic appreciation of nature, literature, and painting, but not of music. . . . Hides any disappointment she may have; displays an evenness of disposition covering a variety of moods, well controlled. Takes in the nuances of a situation, astutely sizes up the participants, and then remakes it without a dissenting voice protesting; shows such tact and subtlety in dealing with others that they hardly realize she has "managed" them and they appear to think they changed their minds themselves. . . . Cares nothing about clothes. . . . Not self-conscious about appearance.[25]

JEAN (Leader: chosen by twenty-four; rejected by two)
1Q 112; age 17 years 2 months.

Appearance. Athletic, well-proportioned physique, square shoulders, bounding walk; alert, bright blue eyes; confident, merry, look-you-through expression; a poised-to-go posture; bright gold hair very curly and tangled; complexion covered with freckles to appear quite dark. Gives immediate impression of adequacy, tenseness, and jovial outlook. Attractive, resonant voice. Manner somewhat arrogant. Speech and gesture have a decisive quality.

Personality-Behavior Picture. A dynamic, strong personality, very self-aware and apparently little aware of others as individuals; camaraderie manner, loud, cheery, and friendly towards others, chiefly as a group. Skips the verbal efforts of person-to-person rapport that other leaders make or seek to make with others. Calls out to a roomful of girls as she enters, "How's everybody?" in a manner that makes them all feel equally "near" to her. Seems to get a "group-response" rather than a person-to-person response for the most part. Pitches into things without hesitation; epitomizes "freshness," vivacity, gayety, and urge for endless activity. The group often appears to be interpreted in her conduct; others would like to have the "nerve" to do as she does. . . . Her satisfactions appear to lie in what she does, the outlets she gets, doing what she wants to do (and there is always something she wants to do), rather than showing dependence on whether or not other girls or staff members think her accomplishments worthy of comment. . . . Lives actively, participates fully, with never a thought as to whether she has captured the front seat and most desirable role or not. But no one takes these from her very often. Everybody

---

[25] Jennings, *Leadership and Isolation,* pp. 199–200. This and the following excerpts are used by permission of Longmans, Green & Co.

appears to enjoy her performance in play and in work. Is sincerely dismayed if her "usurping" is brought to her attention. . . . In speech is dramatic, quick, seldom at a loss for words, spontaneous, and witty in repartee; never offended at jokes directed at her; immediately enlarges upon them, making herself twice as ridiculous as the joker did; a person who is very easy to caricature who wins others' esteem by her lack of touchiness when she is the object of such attempts. Highly entertaining member of any group. Large-minded in her talk about others; will not tolerate "fussiness" and "putting down" girls who are obviously not very cooperative or in other ways have the disfavor of the group; says, "Live and let live; you're not so perfect yourself if you want my opinion." Her presence in any group seems to bolster the members' confidence and enthusiasm.[26]

VERA (Isolate: chosen by none; rejected by eighteen)
IQ 118; age 14 years 9 months.

Appearance. Petite figure; pale complexion; dreamy, thoughtful, rather sad expression; slate-blue eyes; nose small and retroussé, seeming out of proportion with rest of face. Gives a first impression of being self-absorbed, timid, somewhat withdrawn; in speech, however, shows herself highly articulate. Voice confident and well modulated but increases in tempo the longer she talks.

Personality-Behavior Picture. Diffident and hesitant in approach to peers but readily enters into conversation with an adult if she feels the adult responds adequately. . . . Shy and retiring in manner when observed in a group, wears an expression suggesting she is entertaining private thoughts and is "not among those present" except when the main focus of attention, as when others are listening to her; then becomes very animated in expression and seems to be swept away by desire to make listeners grasp the importance of what she is saying; a curious increase in tempo of speech accompanies increase in general emotionality the longer she talks; when listeners indicate they understand, animation sharply subsides and she becomes quiet and apparently again absorbed with private thought trends; when listeners indicate misunderstanding, lack of interest, or difference of opinion an expression as of anguish or physical pain passes over her face, lingers a while, and then her expression takes on again a look of private occupation. She does not give in at once except to a reaction of lack of interest; towards persons who argue back, she vehemently argues in return, becoming so excited that discussion is rudely ended by one or another participant.

Always requires overt demonstration of warmth of reception when talking to others; otherwise apparently feels others are disinterested. Never known to talk to peers about self or others; discourses with them only about ideas and expresses herself in a vocabulary that lacks humor and is described by peers as "dictionary stuff." In tone of talk with peers, in contrast to that with adults, there is a marked absence of a casual touch or of a spirit of fun. Is characterized by other girls as "an intellectual," "ethereal," "doesn't know how to be herself." Is avoided by others apparently because of their feeling uncomfortable in her presence. . . .

While showing pronounced lack of social facility to make other members of the group appreciate her potential contribution, gives repeated evidence of exceptional insight both into herself and peers. Very appreciative of other individuals and gives no evidence of entertaining feelings of self-pity when similar appreciation does not greet her. Never complains of other individuals' treatment of her. Sensitive, discriminating, but emotionally overintense in her reactions. Ambitious, patient, studiously inclined.[27]

---

[26] *Ibid.,* pp. 196–197.
[27] *Ibid.,* pp. 179–182.

AMELIA (Near isolate; chosen by one; rejected by none)
IQ 96; age 17 years 8 months

Appearance. Small in stature and features; straight black hair; blue eyes; expression practically devoid of animation, almost apathetic; voice low and monotonous, very slow speech tempo; gentle, shy manner; overly polite and unassuming.

Personality-Behavior Picture. Extremely passive and unassertive in reactions; says very little about herself or others; rarely volunteers information; makes no requests of others yet invites their imposing requests upon her; has to be deterred from doing work of others; is indiscriminate in offering her services to others; appears to crave affection and to seek outlets for her affectionate feelings towards others by doing "kindnesses" (in the form of tasks which are mainly menial or uninteresting) for anyone who happens to be near her; makes herself promiscuously available for duties so that whoever cares to may impose upon her invariable good nature. Shows no initiative in exerting pressure on others to obtain what is her due in return for her labors. Is almost painfully unassuming. Very impressionable and suggestible. Shows practically no insight into herself or the motives of others in respect to their conduct towards her. Conforms to school rules without questioning. Uncritical to the point of being gullible. Appears not to be able to endure anyone's not thinking well of her; excuses her waiting upon others by saying, "I did it because I thought she would be mad at me if I didn't." Apparent difficulty in marshalling herself to take a stand on conflicting issues; consequently is considered "wishy-washy" by other girls. Actually her behavior is consistent (a "yes" to everything) but it is interpreted by peers as vacillation—sometimes standing for this and sometimes for that; this produces a feeling she cannot be counted upon to act as a situation calls for one to act. Frank, naïve, and uncircumspect in general behavior. . . . Timid, unexpressive, "uncrystallized" personality; calm and restful but gives impression of being sad because of lack of animation.[28]

The two studies mentioned above both deal with the interrelationships among age-mates and under situations that were not average, i.e., life in a woman's college and in a girl's reform school. It seems worth while to add one more set of charts that depict in some detail the social contacts made during a sample week by one popular and one unpopular adolescent, both of whom were living at home, attending school, and otherwise carrying on a normal life. The social contacts of these two high school students reflect a profound difference in the entire mode of life followed by those who are popular and by those who are not.

The diagrams in Figures 70 and 71 on pages 282 and 283 consist of seven concentric zones, each of which represents a different degree of intimacy, the innermost one indicating the closest relationship and the outermost the most remote. The degrees may be described as follows:

    I. The confidant—an almost inseparable friend
    II. The intimate—a close friend
    III. The familiar—a friend who is seen often, but for whom one feels little emotional warmth
    IV. The acquaintance—a person barely known.
    V. The active group acquaintance—a person with whom one works in a group, but does not know otherwise

[28] *Ibid.,* pp. 166–168.

    VI. The passive group acquaintance—a person who attends the same group meetings but takes no part

    VII. The spectator—a person known by name, with whom one has never spoken[29]

The frequency of contact between two people and the amount of emotional warmth determine the varying degrees of intimacy, which may also be called differences in "social distance."

Several segments are marked off within each diagram to indicate the main sources of social contact. Members of one's family form one group, those whom one has met through family friends form another, and friends made at school or through church affiliation furnish two more. There are also some friends and acquaintances that one picks up through being on the same team with them, playing on the same playground or in the same street, skating on the same pond, and so on. The diagrams also show the attitude of each friend or acquaintance toward the central character: an arrow pointing toward the center indicates liking, an arrow pointing toward the periphery indicates dislike, a lack of arrow means indifference, and an arrow with heads in both directions shows ambivalence—that is, sometimes liking and sometimes antagonism. The boys on each chart are represented by small black circles, the girls by small white ones, and the adults by large white circles. The relationship of the adults to the central individual is also given. Finally, the heavy lines around a few of the circles point out those who are idealized by the central character. There is a mark of some kind for each person whom the central character met, talked to, played with, or worked with over a period of a week,[30] plus a few people voluntarily mentioned as among his "acquaintances" although he did not know anything about them beyond their names.

Figure 70 on page 283 records the social contacts of Tess, a popular girl in high school. Her family consists of a father, mother, two brothers, a grandmother, and an aunt. She is on terms of intimacy with her father, whom she idealizes, and with her younger brother. Her relations with her mother are less close, and her mother is ambivalent in her feelings toward Tess, alternating between loving her intensely and being jealous of her closeness to the father. The older brother has been away at school, college, and university ever since Tess can remember, and she sees him only occasionally, but she idealizes him. She and her aunt are on extremely casual terms. Her grandmother rarely leaves her room on the third floor of the house, and Tess does not see her often, although there is no enmity between them. Some of Tess's many friends have been met through her home and family—seven boys and five girls, who range from confidants to acquaintances. Of these twelve individuals, six have chosen Tess as a friend whom they like, as indicated by the arrows. The school has furnished Tess with social contacts that seem of varying importance to her. These range from an intimate girl friend to people whom she does not even know to speak to but likes the looks of. Eleven schoolmates—six boys and five girls— are close enough to Tess to be called friends; then come five students and four teachers with whom Tess worked on committees or under whom she studied in class. In Zone VI are one hundred and nine more classmates, plus one teacher; these

---

[29] These categories are quoted from J. R. Runner, "Social Distance in Adolescent Relationships," *American Journal of Sociology,* 43:428–429, 1937. The figures are of the same type as those in this article.

[30] Minus clerks in stores, motormen on buses, and so on, with whom contact was too unimportant or impersonal to record.

students took no active part in the class or committee, and the teacher was a substitute who kept the pupils writing during most of every hour and had the barest contacts with them. The eighteen girls and thirteen boys among the classmates who expressed an emotional attitude toward Tess appear as individual circles, but those who were indifferent—thirty-nine boys and thirty-nine girls—are represented only

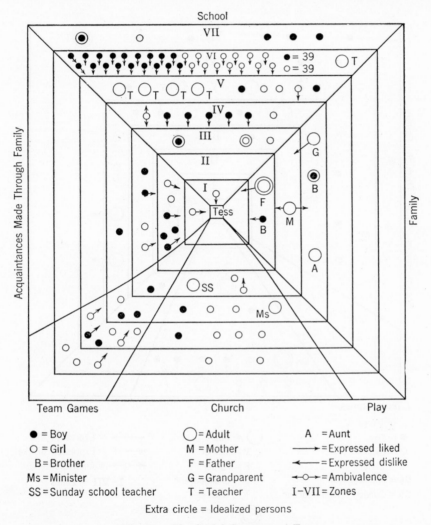

Fig. 70. *The Social Contacts of Tess*

by a numeral. In the outermost area of the diagram there are four boys and one girl, all known to Tess only by name. One of the boys is a football hero whom she worships from afar but has never spoken to. With the one hundred and nine classmates recorded in Zone VI Tess had only the most casual of contact, if any, beyond merely sitting with them in class. Of the fifty-seven boys in this group, eighteen expressed a liking for Tess, as did thirteen of the fifty-two girls.

In organized games Tess made contact with thirteen other adolescents who were not in her classes: three girls on the basketball squad, two on the swimming team, four boys and three girls with whom she played softball on an intramural team, and a boy who was her doubles partner in tennis—with whom, curiously enough, she is on rather distant terms. He is a foreign-born lad who adores Tess, but she has no contact with him except on the tennis court. Four of the thirteen expressed a liking for her. The remaining area of contact was the church. Tess knows the minister only

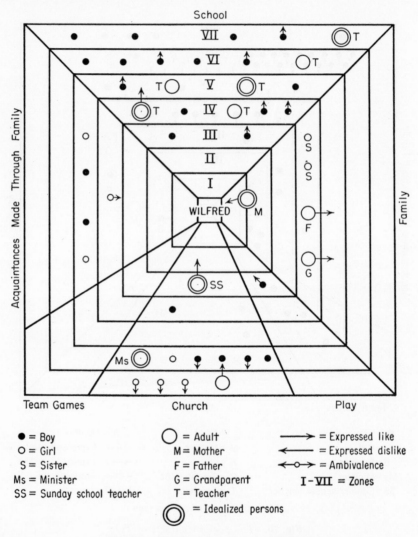

Fig. 71. *The Social Contacts of Wilfred*

to speak to, but she knows her Sunday school teacher rather better. Her roster of friends and acquaintances of her own age received eleven additions. These boys and girls are not in her classes at school nor among her neighborhood friends. None of her "church" friends are close to her, and all but one seem indifferent to her.

In all, Tess had contact of some sort with one hundred and seventy-nine people during the sample week. Of this total, eighty-five were boys, eighty-three were girls, and eleven were adults. Of the eighty-five boys, twenty-eight expressed a liking for her; of the eighty-three girls, twenty-two expressed a liking, and of the adults, two. One girl and one adult were ambivalent toward her, and no one expressed a dislike. It is a curious thing that the relation between Tess and all four of her regular teachers is one of indifference on both sides. Admittedly, Tess is no academic genius, but one would suppose that she would be of some interest to her teachers and they to her. Aside from her identification with her father, her own admirations are for three boys, two her own age and one somewhat older. With the exception of her relationship with her mother—and the problem there is more the mother's than the daughter's—Tess is an unusually well-adjusted, popular, sociable, happy young girl.

Wilfred presents a contrast, as shown in Figure 71 on page 284. The only person who can be rated as a confidante or intimate is his mother. His Sunday school teacher and three boys of his own age are casual friends, while eleven other people rate as acquaintances. This level of intimacy includes four members of Wilfred's family, one boy in his Sunday school class, three boys in school, one girl who is the child of family friends, and two teachers. In Zone V appear four age-mates met through family connections, two schoolmates, and two teachers. In Zone VI there are ten age-mates and two adults, met either at church or in school. The remaining nine individuals—known only by sight to Wilfred—appear in the outermost area. The only game Wilfred plays is chess. Mostly he plays with his mother but he has one familiar friend whom he met through his chess playing. The bulk of his contacts are with those whom he barely knows. Wilfred attends a small private school where he is taking college preparatory work. There are not more than four other pupils in any class; and there are so many duplicates from one class to another that he has contacts with only sixteen boys and six teachers at school.

Wilfred's family relationships are abnormal. His mother adores him, his two sisters are completely indifferent to him, his father and his paternal grandmother have rejected him. Indeed, since birth he has been a pawn in a game between his mother and her mother-in-law, who has always lived within the family circle. Wilfred's admirations and idealizations are all fixed on adults—his mother, the minister, his Sunday school teacher, and three teachers at school, one of whom he has never spoken to. His total contacts number forty-five. Of these people, five expressed a liking for Wilfred—his mother, his Sunday school teacher, an isolated girl who is the daughter of a family friend, a widow with three marriageable daughters, and the chess opponent, who is as isolated as Wilfred. Fifteen persons expressed a positive dislike, including one of the teachers he idealizes, two members of his family, and all the daughters of the scheming widow; the remaining twenty-five are indifferent. Since the only age-mates who accept him are themselves isolates, it is not likely that he will extend his acquaintanceship much. Wilfred's social contacts reveal a person who is maladjusted, rejected, neglected, and unpopular.

III. Social Acceptance and Rejection

Study of the traits which make an adolescent popular or unpopular has indicated that both acceptance and rejection of an individual by a group are complex phenomena. The commonest method of investigation has been to have each student in a class select from his schoolmates the one or two whom he most admires, most prefers to work with, likes best to play with, would choose as an intimate friend, would want for a class or club president, and the like. The students also list the names of anyone they dislike. In addition, the teachers may submit what evidence they have as to who

is accepted and who is not. The popular students are those who are mentioned by the largest number of classmates as first or second choice in the
largest number of situations, are not listed as being disliked, are considered
by their teachers as being easy to find partners for in any group undertaking, are noticed by their teachers as being continually with others and
often in the center of a group, and have a record of having been actually
elected by their classmates to sundry positions of honor. The unpopular
students are those who are never or almost never mentioned as admired or
liked in any situation but are often listed as disliked, are avoided by others
and rejected if they make advances, are difficult to find partners for in group
undertakings, and are regularly the last ones to be chosen for team games
on the playground.

Analysis by means of tests, questionnaires, ratings, and interviews has
revealed two trait syndromes that characterize the popular pupil[31] and
three that characterize the unpopular.[32] Some greatly admired individuals
have (a) a high degree of social aggressiveness; that is, they are expansive,
talkative, daring, energetic, and enthusiastic. Others who are equally popular
have no dash or verve whatever and have achieved their acceptance through
being (b) friendly, kind, sympathetic, good-natured, and happy. They are
also more emotionally and socially mature than their friends. Individuals
of this second type are not so much admired as loved. The first group of
"outsiders" includes those maladjusted youngsters who are (a) aggressive,
noisy, rebellious, boastful, overtalkative, and selfish. These children are actively disliked by their age-mates. The second type includes those who are
(b) not interested in social life and are therefore immature in social skills,
shy, easily embarrassed, passive, and quiet when in a group. The boy or
girl who loves to study belongs in this last category; so also does the radio
enthusiast or the eager young philatelist who pores over his stamp collection
instead of going to football games and cheering for the team. This second
type of unpopular pupil is the isolate whom no one mentions at all. He does
not repel people; he merely fails to get their attention. The third type includes those pupils who are (c) introverted, listless, under par physically,
and withdrawn emotionally. The normal youngsters disregard such human
oddities, label them as "queer," relegate them to social limbo, and forget
them.

Among young girls, at least, the commonest response to rejection is
to withdraw from social situations altogether. Such girls tend to become
self-conscious, to refuse to recite in class, to avoid meeting new people, to
stand in the back of an audience rather than take a vacant front seat, and
to avoid drawing attention, even of a favorable nature, to themselves.[33]
Boys often make overcompensatory reactions, push themselves forward into

---

[31] M. E. Bonney, "Personality Traits of Socially Successful and Socially Unsuccessful Children," *Journal of Educational Psychology*, 34:449–472, 1943.

[32] M. L. Northway, "Outsiders," *Sociometry*, 7:10–25, 1944.

[33] A. A. Rose, "Insecurity Feelings in Adolescent Girls," *Nervous Child*, 4:46–59,
1944.

groups where they are not wanted, recite too often, indulge in noisy speech and general rowdyism. Of the two responses, the second is the more healthy, but it certainly presents problems to the teacher.

Traits Admired or Disliked: The list of traits to be presented shortly was derived from a number of sources. In some cases a trait that contributed to unpopularity is merely the reverse of one that is admired, but this contrast does not always appear. The combined list is given in Table 16.

According to this list, appearance and manner are often of great importance in determining social acceptance. An attractive face, a trim figure, a pleasant manner, a fluency in small talk, a stylish hair-do, and clothes prescribed by the fad of the moment are elements of attractiveness. Homeliness, dirtiness, excessive fatness or thinness, excessive perspiration, out-of-date or shabby clothes, hesitancy in speech, crudeness in manner or any real variation from the group norm are sources of unpopularity. Those girls who rate lowest in appearance are found to be negative, withdrawn, self-effacing, and not interested in people or events.[34] Rejected by their age-mates, they have evidently stopped trying to maintain social contacts. An unpopular girl could presumably improve her status by remedying her defects of appearance; indeed, this is precisely the path that unpopular girls of financially adequate families follow, often with success.

There are some changes from early to late adolescence in the traits that are admired, although the chief difference lies in emphasis rather than in the selection of characteristics. In one group of adolescents, cheerfulness, enthusiasm, and friendliness were rated high at all ages; being good-looking was less important at eighteen than at thirteen, but ability to initiate activities was more important.[35] At both thirteen and eighteen, pupils disliked those who wanted to fight, who sought attention, who were bossy, restless, or talkative, or who tried to act older than they were. There was little difference between boys and girls in the traits selected for approval or disapproval.

IV. The Influence of Social Class

In general, popularity has a definite relationship with social class. In practically all studies in which the influence of class has been considered, the children from the upper classes have been overchosen, those from the middle class slightly underchosen, and lower-class children even more underchosen. For example, in a small Ohio city, pupils from these three social levels received, respectively, an average of 4, 3.5, and 2.5 choices as desired friends or work partners.[36] There is some evidence that the inability of children from the lower socioeconomic levels to establish themselves in the

[34] S. S. Silverman, "Clothing and Appearance: Their Psychological Implications for Teen-Age Girls," *Teachers College Contributions to Education,* No. 912, 1945, 140 pp.

[35] R. G. Kuhlen and B. J. Lee, "Personality Characteristics and Social Acceptability in Adolescence," *loc. cit.*

[36] L. A. Cook, "An Experimental Sociographic Study of a Stratified Tenth-Grade Class," *American Sociological Review,* 10:250–261, 1945.

Table 16

Liked

A. *Appearance and manner*

1. Has good looks
2. Is neat and clean
3. Wears appropriate clothes
4. Is natural
5. Is well-mannered

B. *Leadership type of popularity*

6. Makes many contacts
7. Is active, energetic
8. Is enthusiastic
9. Is a good talker
10. Pursues many activities
11. Shows initiative
12. Is usually good in athletics

C. *Social type of popularity*

13. Is kind
14. Is co-operative
15. Is unselfish
16. Is usually cheerful
17. Is even-tempered
18. Is friendly
19. Is sympathetic
20. Is responsible
21. Is loyal
22. Is truthful
23. Has high ideals
24. Has good sense of humor
25. Has maturity
26. Is a good listener
27. Has adequate social skills

D. *Miscellaneous*

28. Is intelligent
29. Gets good marks
30. Has good reputation
31. Is a good sport
32. Has a good home

Disliked

A. *Appearance and manner*

1. Is unattractive
2. Has physical handicap
3. Dresses inappropriately
4. Is dirty
5. Uses too much lipstick (girls)
6. Uses hair grease (boys)

B. *Withdrawal behavior*

7. Is listless
8. Is too much absorbed in self
9. Is too bookish
10. Is too prissy, too "good"
11. Is timid, shy, embarrassed
12. Is overdependent on others
13. Is poor in athletics
14. Has no interest in activities
15. Is "queer"
16. Has inadequate social skills

C. *Retaliatory, attention-seeking, or paranoid behavior*

17. Is resentful, carries a grudge
18. Is quarrelsome
19. Is a bully
20. Is rude and bad-mannered
21. Shows off, brags
22. Is stuck-up, snobbish
23. Interferes with others
24. Is domineering
25. Thinks he is picked on
26. Is constantly alibi-ing
27. Is stubborn
28. Is untruthful
29. Is disloyal
30. Is moody

D. *Miscellaneous*

31. Is stupid
32. Is immature
33. Is nervous
34. Is a poor sport
35. Is lazy

Based upon traits reported on one or more of the following references: A. Anastasi and S. Miller, "Adolescent Prestige Factors in Relation to Scholastic and Socioeconomic Variables," *Journal of Social Psychology,* 29:43–50, 1949; M. C. Austin and G. G. Thompson, "Children's Friendships: A Study of the Bases upon Which Children Select and Reject Their Best Friends," *Journal of Educational Psychology,* 39:101–116, 1948; Bonney, "A Sociometric Study of the Relationship of Some Factors to Mutual Friendships on the Elementary, Secondary, and College Levels," *loc. cit.;* Jones, "Adolescent Friendships," *loc. cit.;* R. G. Kuhlen and B. J. Lee, "Personality Characteristics and Social Acceptability in Adolescence," *Journal of Educational Psychology,* 34:321–340, 1943; M. Lucina, "Sex Differences in Adolescent Attitudes toward Best Friends," *School Review,* 48:512–516, 1940; Northway, "Outsiders," *loc. cit.;* R. Potashin, "A Sociometric Study of Children's Friendships," *Sociometry,* 9:48–70, 1946; Smith, "Some Factors in Friendship Selections of High School Students," *loc. cit.;* G. G. Thompson, "Age Trends in Social Values during the Adolescent Years," *American Psychologist,* 4:250, 1949; E. V. van Dyne, "Personal Traits and Friendship Formation in Adolescent Girls," *Journal of Social Psychology,* 12:291–303, 1940; F. M. Vreeland and S. M. Corey, "A Study of College Friendships," *Journal of Abnormal and Social Psychology,* 30:227–236, 1935.

school community is a source of considerable frustration and tension among them.[37]

Teachers have known for many years that pupils from the same socio-economic level tended to form more or less exclusive groups, which sometimes have a disruptive influence upon the social life of the school. One quite recent study of all the sixteen-year-old adolescents in a small city makes clear the pervasiveness of social class in the activities and attitudes of the pupils.[38] As a first step, all the families that had sixteen-year-old children were grouped into five socioeconomic classes, upon the basis of several types of evidence. The investigators then administered tests of various kinds, interviewed the adolescents, collected their opinions, and studied their social interrelations. The relation of the data on social class to the activities and attitudes of the pupils in the high school is of special interest because it demonstrates how social stratification, even in a democracy, can produce marked inequalities of many types. A few outstanding examples are shown in Figure 72 on page 290. Since there were relatively few pupils in the two upper classes, they have been put together.

As one might expect, intelligence showed a rough relation to class. No pupil in Classes I and II had an IQ below 90. The bulk of the lowest IQ's was found in Class V. It should be noted, however, that there were also some high IQ's in the lowest class. Marks showed an even higher relationship with social class than intelligence did. Half the pupils in Classes I and II were doing good work, and no one was failing; in Class V, nearly a third were failing and less than a tenth were doing good work. Every pupil in Classes I and II wanted to continue in school, and everyone took some part in extracurricular activities. Almost 90 per cent of the Class V pupils wanted to leave school at once, and only 25 per cent of them participated in activities. Those from Classes II and III occupied a position between the two extremes in almost every trait or measurement. The data on attendance at football games are particularly revealing. Ninety per cent from Classes I and II and 65 per cent from Class III attended all or almost all the games. Evidently they felt the team was "their" team and the school was "their" school. Pupils from Class V and over half of those in Class IV attended few if any games, thus giving indisputable evidence that they did not feel themselves bound to the school by emotional ties. The data on vocational plans followed the lines one might expect, in view of the home backgrounds from which the pupils came. Both boys and girls had from a half to two thirds of their dates with members of their own social class, although it is improbable that they made their selections with social standing in mind. In no instance was there any dating between the members of the highest and the lowest classes. In the particular high school under consideration the students attached "labels" to each other, thus expressing their spontaneous attitudes. The three labels in current usage were the "elite," the "good kids," and the "grubbies." The members of the first two groups were socially accepted, the difference being that the elite set the tone and furnished the

---

[37] A. Davis and R. J. Havighurst, "Social Class and Color Differences in Child Rearing," *American Sociological Review,* 11:698–710, 1946.

[38] Hollingshead, *op. cit.*

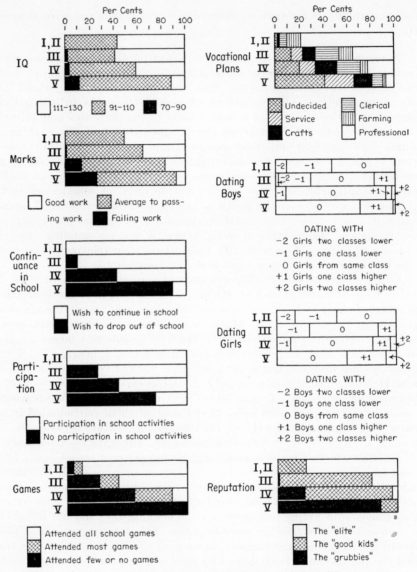

Fig. 72. *Influence of Social Class upon Attitudes and Activities*

Based on figures in A. B. Hollingshead, *Elmtown's Youth,* John Wiley & Sons, 1949, pp. 172–216.

leadership. The grubbies were rejected. No one in Class I or II was charac-terized as a grubby, and only 1 per cent of those in Class III were so labeled. The per cent increased to 20 in Class IV and burgeoned to 85 for the lowest social group, from which there was no contribution to the ranks of the elite.

In the above sample, the boys and girls who had dates with adolescents one or two classes above their own, those from the lower groups who did well in school and participated in its activities, and those who were planning to enter the professions were all trying, by various routes, to improve their status. Some of them will succeed, and their children will start upon a higher rung of the social ladder than that originally occupied by their parents. At the other end, the small number of births in Class I and II families leads to a constant shrinking of their proportional representation. Some of these families die out, some deteriorate, and some meet financial reverses; their places are then taken by families from Classes III and IV who have prospered financially and have made adequate social contacts for acceptance. These processes go on all the time, and their effects are reflected in the attitudes of high school pupils toward each other. Probably the high school involved in this study should initiate measures to make school more attractive to boys and girls from Classes IV and V and to help them make themselves more attractive to other students. The degree of exclusion and rejection as reported seems somewhat higher than it needs to be. One has to remember, however, that differences in ability and achievement will continue to exist and will inevitably lead to differences in the attitudes of pupils toward each other.

V. Leadership

Because of the social prominence of the leader and because of his strategic position, psychologists have been trying for years to find out what qualities result in leadership. Although the number of leaders is small, their influence is always large because of their position in their own society. The high school that can influence its student leaders to exercise their power along desirable lines is not likely to have serious difficulties with the student body as a whole. An understanding of leaders thus seems highly desirable.

Within the last decade there has been a revival of interest in leadership, possibly as a reflection of how badly the world needs wise leaders in most of its activities. Individuals and committees have made out lists of problems to be answered before the phenomena of leadership can be adequately understood. Some of the more important questions appear below:

Who are the leaders?
Of what does their leadership behavior consist?
What traits are associated with leadership behavior?
What situational factors produce leadership behavior?
What are the results on the participants of leadership behavior?
What motivates the leader and what satisfaction does he receive?
How permanent is leadership?
Can leadership be developed?
How can leaders best be identified?
Why is the relation between leadership and either high intelligence or high academic achievement usually so low?[39]

---

[39] R. T. Morris and M. Seaman, "The Problems of Leadership: An Interdisciplinary Approach," *Journal of Sociology*, 56:149–155, 1950.

To date, a beginning has been made on some of these problems. Within another fifteen or twenty years most of them will have received at least a partial answer.

It already seems quite clear that leadership rests not only on the traits of the leader, but also on the needs of the followers at the moment. That is, a given group situation calls for, and gets, a leader; the leader does not go hunting for a group. Hence, presumably, the many "types" of leaders, since different individuals are required to meet the varying needs of the same or different groups at different times and in different situations. Leadership is therefore both a function of group structure and a result of personality. Thus, an Augustus, a Savonarola, a Metternich, a Robespierre, a Garibaldi, or a Hitler is called forth by the needs of the people, but these men became leaders because they possessed the particular cluster of traits that fitted them to meet the needs. If American students of 1953 cannot understand why Hitler *could* have become a leader, it is mainly because they are not German students of 1930. Leadership is therefore a spontaneous sort of social interaction between individuals and groups. If the needs continue or if the behavior and personality of the leader arouse emotional reactions of an enjoyable sort, the leader maintains his position, but if the needs are satisfied or if the leader arouses antagonistic emotions, his position becomes precarious and he is able to continue only if in the period of his real leadership he has built up enough control and power to maintain himself, even though he has become unpopular. As time passes, both the members of a group and its leaders change, and yesterday's idol becomes today's forgotten man.

Groups have many characteristics, and no two are exactly alike. Some of the determining factors are quite obvious, but others are considerably less so. The most important determinants are listed below, with a pair of contrasting examples, taken from college life, after each:

GROUPS VARY FROM ONE ANOTHER IN:

1. *Size*

    Lecture class in elementary chemistry (large)
    Seminar in metallurgy (small)

2. *Homogeneity*

    College preparatory Latin class in an expensive, exclusive, private girls' school (homogeneous)
    Freshman English class in an average American high school (heterogeneous)

3. *Flexibility*

    College glee club (established, persisting mode of behavior)
    Departmental clubs (no established model, clubs come and go)

4. *Permeability*

    Small, self-contained, highly "social," snobbish fraternity, whose members mix little with others
    Good-fellowship club, to which anyone can belong and whose members mix with everyone

5. *Polarization*

    Campaign committee for electing the campus queen (a group with a single, clear goal)

    Executive committee of the student government (a group that deals with whatever needs to be done)

6. *Stability*

    Basketball team, honors society (these exist year after year)

    Chess club, fencing team (these depend on whether or not anyone is interested)

7. *Intimacy*

    Sorority (everyone knows everyone else)

    Political club (members are only acquaintances)

8. *Control*

    Training table (diet is controlled)

    Eating club (for pleasure and sociability; no control over diet)

9. *Potency*

    Phi Beta Kappa, fraternities, varsity teams (strong drives satisfied by membership)

    Debating teams, dance committees, newcomers' club (relatively weaker drives satisfied by membership)

10. *Affective tone*

    Special sections for best students (agreeable feelings associated with membership)

    Special sections for students on probation (unpleasant feeling tone)

11. *Participation of members*

    Discussion class ⎫
    Lecture class   ⎬ of same size

12. *Dependence*

    Cast of a play (dependent on stage manager, without whom rehearsals usually do not even start)

    Staff of college newspaper (not dependent upon the physical presence of the editor to get started)[40]

As the groups that need leaders vary in their composition, so does the nature of the leader who best meets the requirements.

Personality is, however, also of importance, partly in preventing many people from ever becoming leaders and partly in making a relatively small number in each generation more likely to be chosen than anyone else. Those who are shy, timid, easily flustered, weak of voice, slow of thought, and hesitant of manner are not going to be leaders because others do not pay enough attention to them, no matter how good their ideas may be. Other clusters of traits, possessed naturally by not over a tenth of the population,

---

[40] Based on R. M. Stogdill, "Personal Factors Associated with Leadership; A Survey of the Literature," *Journal of Psychology*, 25:35–71, 1948; and J. K. Hemphill, "Situational Factors in Leadership," *Bureau of Educational Research Monographs*, Ohio State University, No. 32, 1949, 136 pp.

make leadership possible but they do not guarantee it. Thus, a young girl in the year 1800 might have had every desirable trait and still have spent her life on remote prairie farms, helping wrest a living from the soil, having children under exhausting conditions, seeing few people, and leading no one. When an opportunity to lead arises, it does not knock at every door—only at the doors of those who possess, by nature or by training, certain basic traits, plus any other specifically called for by the situation—and these few do not become leaders unless external conditions are favorable.

Most studies of student leaders have consisted in locating, either through observation or by the adolescents' own ratings of each other, the leaders in a school and then comparing the standing of these leaders in a number of traits with the standing in the same traits of the other students of the same age in the school. In some cases, rating scales have been used to measure various traits; in others many tests have been administered, individual interviews given, and personal histories obtained. A typical study of leaders is summarized in the next few paragraphs.

An investigator asked all the 223 students in a private junior college, between the ages of sixteen and twenty, to state their choices (a) for the chairman of a certain project and (b) for a roommate. They were also asked to give the names of those they thought least likely to succeed as chairman or least acceptable as a roommate.[41] The entire student body was then divided into four sections, as shown in Table 17. More students were rejected as leaders than as roommates, presumably because many amiable

Table 17

GROUPINGS ON THE BASIS OF POPULARITY

	Chairman of Committee (%)	Roommate (%)
1. Those who received more choices than rejections	17	40
2. Those who received more rejections than choices	50	23
3. Those who received the same number of each	18	34
4. Those who received neither rejection nor choice	15	3

Based on M. A. Price, "A Study of Motivational and Perceptual Factors Associated with Leadership Behavior of Young Women in a Private School," *Ohio State University Abstracts of Dissertations*, No. 58, 1950, pp. 59–64.

people who are nice to live with have no ability to lead. Study of the first and second groups showed three main differences between them. The leaders expressed the positive emotions—joy, pleasure, satisfaction, humor, happiness—while the rejected specialized in negative reactions—gloom, anxiety, and hurt feelings. The leaders had definite goals in their activities, while the rejected did not seem to be going anywhere in particular. The leaders gave others a sense of security, but the rejected merely made others feel uncom-

---

[41] M. A. Price, "A Study of Motivational and Perceptual Factors Associated with Leadership Behavior of Young Women in a Private School," *Ohio State University Abstracts of Dissertations*, No. 58, 1950, pp. 59–64.

fortable. The neglected ones, who were simply forgotten, proved upon investigation to show little emotional reaction of any kind, to be formal and correct in their demeanor, to be easily distracted from any goal they might have, to be quite banal in their thinking, and to have few friends or even acquaintances. They were not noticed even enough to be rejected.

A psychologist cannot yet definitely say which child will become a leader, but the many specific investigations at least set the limits of personality within which to look for the leaders of the next generation. The necessary traits may be listed and classified as indicated in the following list:

1. *Capacities* (inborn or acquired early in life): Average or better intelligence, mental alertness, verbal facility, good health, efficiency, animal courage, cheerfulness, humor
2. *Attainments to date:* Average or better schoolwork, athletic accomplishments, former experience as leader, special knowledge needed by situation
3. *Appearance and manner:* Average or better attractiveness, well and appropriately dressed (by standards of group to be led), good voice, features, body build, and clothes typical of group
4. *Motility:* Unusual degree of participation in whatever is going on, greater than average activity, enthusiasm for undertakings
5. *Contacts with others:* (1) Aggressiveness, self-confidence, ambition, initiative, persistence, (2) dependability, integrity, (3) sociableness, kindliness, approachability, co-operativeness, adaptability, capacity to mix with subordinates without making them feel subordinate, willingness to stay within conventional limits
6. *Special intellectual qualities:* Judgment, originality, insight into people and situations, impartiality (ability to see both sides)
7. *Background factors:* Better than average social status, better than average income, membership in family that already has leaders in it.[42]

It should be noted especially that under the fifth heading there is a subdivision of traits, some of which not only seem contradictory but are. They are all needed, however, in order to maintain balance. A leader is aggressive, but his aggressiveness is controlled by his sociability and his willingness to conform to social standards. If these other traits were lacking, he might become a braggart or a delinquent, both of whom are also aggressive. A leader gets along well with others, but without his ambition and persistence he would be just another good mixer and pleasant companion. And even

[42] Based on Stogdill, "Personal Factors Associated with Leadership," *loc. cit.;* C. W. Burnett, "A Study of College Campus Leaders," *Abstracts of Dissertations,* Ohio State University, No. 58, 1948–1949, pp. 59–64; R. M. Drake, "A Study of Leadership," *Character and Personality,* 12:285–289, 1944; E. G. Fleming, "Factor Analysis of the Personality of High School Leaders," *Journal of Applied Psychology,* 19:596–605, 1935; O. O. Hunter and A. M. Jordan, "An Analysis of Qualities Associated with Leadership among College Students," *School Review,* 46:523–531, 1938; Price, *op. cit.;* F. Redl, "Group Emotion and Leadership," *Psychiatry,* 5:573–596, 1942; M. K. Remmlein, "Analysis of Leadership among High School Pupils," *Journal of Experimental Education,* 46:413–432, 1938; M. Roff, "A Study of Combat Leadership in the Air Force by Means of a Rating Scale," *Journal of Psychology,* 30:229–239, 1950; M. Smith and W. C. Nystrom, "A Study of Social Participation and of Leisure Time of Leaders and Nonleaders," *Journal of Applied Psychology,* 21:251–259, 1937; R. E. Wakeley, "Selecting Leaders for Agricultural Programs," *Sociometry,* 10:384–395, 1947; L. D. Zeleny, "Characteristics of Group Leaders," *Sociology and Social Research,* 24:140–149, 1940.

though an individual has great initiative and much social ability, he still will not lead for long unless he can be trusted. As one thinks of the various types of would-be leaders, one can see what they lack. Thus, the fanatic has great enthusiasm, self-confidence, and drive, but lacks judgment and can see only one side of a question at once. And the foreign agitator comes a cropper because his appearance, features, build, voice, clothes, and manners are not those of the people he wants to lead.

In general, leaders are superior individuals who come from a superior background[43] in which they have found the elements needed for adequate self-development. One of the better ways to become a leader is to be born into the right family! This idea is thoroughly undemocratic, but it is true. It is especially true in a high school because the pupils are at an age when they put great stress upon appearance, dress, manners, and social competence—exactly the traits that an adolescent from a good home acquires without effort. Those from inferior social backgrounds may and do sometimes become leaders, but not easily.

It may be noticed that the capacity to learn out of a book does not contribute much to leadership, perhaps because the student who reads many books learns about books instead of about people. Also, he has less time to be with people than he would otherwise have. He can therefore hunt down an elusive reference in a catalogue but not an elusive antagonism in a group. It is not surprising that the student who impresses his age-mates as undisguisedly intelligent or as having superior academic standing does not often become a leader. This is not the same thing, however, as saying that intelligence has no relation to leadership. Certain phases clearly have—judgment, versatility, organizing ability, originality, alertness, and insight, for instance. Even tests of "intelligence," which admittedly measure only one or two phases of mental ability and measure academic skills at the same time, show a medium amount of correlation with leadership, probably because they indubitably measure the alertness and quickness of one's mental machinery. If they tapped other mental abilities also, the correlation would probably be much higher.

The two students described below belong to quite common types of high school leaders. An experienced teacher can probably identify both among the boys and girls she has known.

Dot and Fritz are both leaders in a small high school. Both are seniors. In a recent sociometric study they were the two main "stars" of their class.

Dot is a rather small but extremely lively girl. She radiates good health and normalcy. She is not pretty, but she is attractive in both face and figure. Her intelligence is in the highest 25 per cent of the class, but not in the highest 5 per cent. She comes of a good family, and she is always well and appropriately dressed. Her classwork is above average but not so good as to arouse either envy or scorn among her peers. She does a reasonable amount of studying, but not too much.

---

[43] F. J. Reynolds, "Factors of Leadership among Seniors of the Central High School of Tulsa, Oklahoma," *Journal of Educational Research*, 37:356–361, 1944; and Cook, "An Experimental Sociographic Study of a Stratified Tenth-Grade Class," *loc. cit.*

Her mind is nimble and of an inquiring nature, but she is satisfied with small bits of knowledge about many things and shows no desire for real mastery in any field. She is an excellent conversationalist. Dot has many interests; she is the drum major for the school's band, a cheerleader, a member of the school glee club, secretary of the senior class, president of two school clubs, and a member of the editorial board for the school yearbook. She never lacks invitations to dances and parties. Both boys and girls like Dot, and she has become an arbiter in social matters. She has a fair amount of tact and a moderate understanding of people, but she depends upon appearance, family background, and manner for her popularity rather than upon any remarkable ability to understand others. When one examines Dot's record and watches her behavior, one learns something more about her. She has never been in any disciplinary difficulty, she observes the conventions, and her behavior, while lively, is never indiscreet or indecorous. This strain of propriety in her make-up is of value to her because it commands respect from both boys and girls and prevents her name from being linked with scandals, unfavorable gossip, or revolts. Dot has abounding vitality, manifold interests, a quick mind, a pleasant appearance, a good background, irreproachable manners, a moderate degree of extroversion, and a fair understanding of people. Presumably, like everyone else, Dot has some small problems, but there are no serious conflicts or tensions in her life. Dot's chief charm lies in her normalcy.

Fritz is high-strung, handsome, intelligent, and very successful as an athlete. He is a member of all the school's major teams, but has been especially satisfactory as a quarterback. Fritz is a good student and would be an excellent one if he had more time for study. As it is, he will be on the school's honor list. His IQ has varied on different tests from 130 to 150. He intends to be a doctor, and will probably become a serious student as soon as he passes beyond the age for school and college athletics. Fritz tends to burn himself out by the intensity of his application to whatever catches his interest, and to be rather moody; his periods of exertion and excitement are often followed by periods of sloth and irritability. He is nervous, but he has remarkable control; and the greater the pressure, the cooler he gets. Fritz's good looks make him popular with the girls, and his athletic success makes him the idol of the boys. Fortunately, Fritz's real interests are in intellectual pur-suits—although he keeps this fact carefully hidden—and his prowess at running and throwing and jumping strikes him as incidental, childish, and amusing. Athletic success has its values for him, and he uses it for all it is worth, but he has no illusions about it, and his ideals lie elsewhere. This boy's greatest defects of per-sonality are the shortness of his temper, his impatience, and his sensitiveness. Leadership was made easy for him by his size and strength; at entrance to high school he was already postpubescent, he was taller and heavier than his classmates, and he had already passed through the period of poor muscular co-ordination. His social abilities are only average, but they are good enough to maintain his status. Fritz's interests are rather narrow. He belongs to only one club, in addition to athletic teams, and is the president of the school's athletic association. During his junior year he was one of the student judges, and was re-elected this year but resigned because the sessions conflicted with his chemistry laboratory.

As may be seen, these two leaders are successful for different reasons. Fritz depends upon maturity, physical size, good looks, intelligence, athletic success, a controlled quickness, a high degree of concentration, and general good judgment. He was not a leader in childhood and is one of those who had to conquer himself before he could lead others. He has proceeded along the usual path to male adoles-cent leadership, via size and athletic prominence. Although Fritz is still quick-tempered and although he has moods and is a sensitive boy, he has no strain of the prima donna in him. He is modest about his success as a quarterback largely because he does not enjoy the furor and because he does not think football really important. Dot is of quite a different type. She shares Fritz's pleasant appearance, but she depends chiefly upon her healthiness, her vivacity, her drive, her quick interests, her alertness, her skill at repartee, her social prominence, her conformity, and her musical talents for her success. Moreover, she enjoys being a leader. She has been one ever since she can remember. She probably has more understanding of people on a rather superficial level than Fritz, but his grasp is deeper. She is also less mature, except in her willingness to conform to approved custom. In both cases, family status is an important background factor.

Some investigations have classified leaders into types. In one case they were characterized as the entertaining, the brilliant, the athlete, the good fellow, the talented, the just, the good neighbor, and the diplomat.[44] In another as the patriarchal sovereign, the tyrant, the organizer, the hero, the love-object, and the recipient of aggressive drives.[45] In a third study, leaders are described as "charismatic"—a word coined to mean the ability to make others aware of a common end—organizational, intellectual, and informal.[46] The first type tends to excel in dramatizing an issue but to become rigid in thinking and procedures; the second, to excel in efficiency but to drive others too hard and often to lose sight of the goal; the third, to excel in producing ideas but to be deficient in the ability to attract people or to precipitate action; and the fourth, to have great warmth and insight into the feelings of others but to lose these traits after he has become a leader. Although such classifications and labels are suggestive and interesting, an adequate typing of leaders, assuming it can be done, is yet to be made.

Leaders are more active than nonleaders in the social life of the school, but one does not know if they are leaders because they are active or are active because they are leaders. For instance, one group of 40 leaders[47] had a total of 272 participations in extracurricular activities as compared with only 70 for 40 nonleaders. They averaged nearly 7 activities each to 2 each for the latter group. The leaders received 80 special recognitions of one kind or another and spent a total of 255 hours a week in sports as compared with 1 special recognition and 47 hours spent in sports for nonleaders. They drove cars more, danced more, went to three times as many parties, listened twice as much to the radio, went twice as often to movies, and read more. In short, they were leaders!

The leader is a fundamental source of social control because of his strategic position in his community. The effect a leader may have upon his followers is well illustrated by the example in Figure 73. This chart depicts the emotional bonds between a group of students in a boys' school and their history teacher. The positive bonds or attractions are shown by straight lines; the negative bonds, or repulsions, by broken ones. In this class of

[44] Redl, "Group Emotion and Leadership," *loc. cit.*

[45] Fleming, "Factor Analysis of the Personality of High School Leaders," *loc. cit.*

[46] F. Levine, "Approach to Constructve Leadership," *Journal of Social Issues,* 5:46–53, 1949.

[47] Smith and Nystrom, "A Study of Social Participation and of Leisure Time of Leaders and Nonleaders," *loc. cit.*

eleven boys, nine disliked the teacher and two admired him intensely. The explanation of the entire configuration lies in Boy A. He has an active dislike for the teacher, but he stands high in the affection of his age-mates. Boys B, C, D, E, F, G, H, and I are so positively attracted to him as to be his disciples. Between him and Boy M, however, there is a bitter feud. Boy M's chum, Boy N, is his only ally. Through the emotional bonds between Boy A and his followers, everyone in the clique has come to dislike

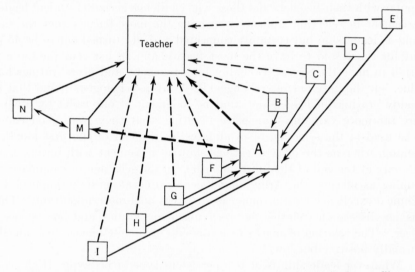

Fig. 73. *Effect of a Popular Student's Attitudes upon the Attitudes of Class Members toward Their Teacher*

the history teacher. A single pupil of great popularity may thus influence his admirers into antagonism toward a teacher against whom they often have no personal objection. Boy M, who returns Boy A's dislike but cannot compete with his popularity, has found his place in the sun by becoming friendly with the teacher and has carried Boy N along with him. The teacher was so unwise as to have made "pets" of these two, thus further increasing the gulf between himself and Boy A and his satellites. Such emotional crosscurrents as those shown here wreck the serenity of the classroom. In this example, Boy A is the key to the situation. If the teacher can somehow win this one boy's respect, he will obtain similar attitudes from Boy A's followers. Here, on a small scale, is demonstrated the need for expert education and guidance of those who are natural leaders.

Selection of Leaders and Prediction of Leadership: If one wants to find out who are the current leaders one had best ask the students. An observant teacher can contribute something, but she is not among those being led. Moreover, a single teacher knows only a portion of the pupils in her school; in actual fact, nearly half the students in a large school may not be sufficiently known to any teacher to receive even one rating from the entire faculty. Perhaps ratings by both age-mates and teachers should be collected in any selection of leaders, since the two generations use different criteria. Teachers tend to overrate those who are courteous and responsive in class and those who work well as long as they are controlled from above.[48] They tend to underestimate any student who annoys or challenges them or does poor work. Since teachers see students primarily in class, it is natural that they should make these errors. Students rate each other mostly on what happens outside class. They tend to underrate those who are popular with their teachers and those who challenge accepted student leaders. Agreement in selecting students who have the most friends (not the same thing as leadership but certainly connected with it) turned out to be 45 per cent for those said to have the most friends and 28 per cent for those reported to have the fewest. Probably both teachers' and peers' ratings have value, but they are not interchangeable. Army psychologists found that the "buddy" ratings of leadership—that is, judgment of one cadet by others— were far more valuable than officers' rating, that they were good enough to be used in the selection of candidates by the end of the first month of training, whereas the officers' ratings showed agreement with ultimate success only at the end of the fourth month.[49] In the selection of candidates for training as officers, the Army found personality at least as important as technical excellence and in some cases a great deal more important.[50] There was no discernible relation between academic grades and success as an officer.[51] The relation of marks to leadership or of intelligence to leadership is usually positive but low.[52]

Whatever leadership is, it is a persistent type of behavior. High school leaders who go to college are four times as likely to be leaders in their college years as are those who were not prominent in high school; their chances for community leadership, subsequent to leaving school, are also four times as good.[53] Ability to influence others is therefore a fairly permanent coalescence of traits that appears in one social setting after another.

The task of following up a group of students after the members leave school requires an enormous amount of work and a staff of fieldworkers who have a dash of both the bulldog and the bloodhound in them. The American family's well-known habit of constantly changing its abode and of losing contact with its younger members makes the tracing of experience subsequent to school days extremely difficult. There are, therefore, relatively few studies on this point. One, however, may well be quoted.[54] A follow-up of

---

[48] M. E. Bonney, "Sociometric Study of Agreement between Teachers' Judgments and Students' Choices," *Sociometry,* 10:135–146, 1947.

[49] R. J. Wherry and D. H. Fryer, "Buddy Ratings: Popularity Contests for Leadership Criteria," *Personnel Psychology,* 2:147–159, 1949.

[50] Roff, "A Study of Combat Leadership in the Air Force by Means of a Rating Scale," *loc. cit.*

[51] H. E. Page, "Detecting Potential Leaders," *Journal of Aviation Medicine,* 19:435–441, 1940.

[52] C. E. Howell, "Measurement of Leadership," *Sociometry,* 5:163–168, 1942.

[53] M. E. Courtney, "Persistence of Leadership," *School Review,* 46:97–107, 1938.

[54] J. J. Crowley, "High School Backgrounds of Successful Men and Women Graduates," *School Review,* 48:205–209, 1940.

all the 485 living graduates of ten consecutive classes, 1927–1936, of a small high school to determine their degree of leadership in their community gave interesting results, which are summarized in Table 18. Adult success in leadership was judged on the basis of general reputation, positions of trust (school superintendents, bank managers, judges, superior officials), or superior positions in business or industry, ownership of business, and election to chairmanship of community undertakings. In their high school days the 186 male graduates had shown the four levels or kinds of leadership in school life: 64 were prominent athletes, 22 played dominant roles in nonathletic

Table 18

LEADERSHIP IN COLLEGE AND COMMUNITY

	Number of Men	Number and Per Cent Who Became Leaders
1. Leadership in athletics	64	10 (15%)
2. Leadership in student affairs	22	14 (65%)
3. Leadership in both	23	14 (60%)
4. Leadership in neither	77	11 (15%)
Total	186	

Based on J. J. Crowley, "High School Backgrounds of Successful Men and Women Graduates," *School Review*, 48:205–209, 1940.

student affairs, 23 were outstanding in both the above classifications, and 77 had no record of any leadership. Nearly two thirds of the second and third groups became leaders in adult life. The student who was prominent in athletics but nothing else did not fare so well in later years. Only a few nonleaders in high school became leaders as adults. Among the 299 women graduates, only 59 had occupied positions of leadership in school. Of these, 37 per cent held such positions as adults. Only 2 per cent of the 240 other women graduates, all nonleaders in high school, had had success as leaders in their communities.

Studies, however efficient, of current leaders are not likely to give certain of the facts that are most necessary for understanding the phenomenon of leadership. Longitudinal studies that began when a child entered Grade 1 and went on when he left school (or college, if he attended one) would add much that cannot otherwise be discovered. It is the writer's conviction that a research fund could hardly be spent more wisely than on a study of leadership as comprehensive as the long-time study of genius now well into its fourth decade of work at Stanford University. With such a program it might be possible to determine what makes a leader and why he or she can influence others. This knowledge would naturally result in an effort to educate adequately the leaders of the next generation. Through the training of leaders the situation offers unparalleled possibilities for influencing public opinion, both during the school years and in adult life.

VI. Ratings of Social Behavior

There have been numerous attempts to formulate rating scales for measuring socialization. Those that are based upon the impressions of the raters as to some pupil's personal characteristics are relatively unsatisfactory, partly because the impressions are too general and partly because the opinions are too subjective. Ratings that are based upon descriptions of actual behavior are much better, probably because they are less subjective. Samples from one such scale appear below. The numbers from 1 to 7 are values to be assigned by the rater. The verbal descriptions tell what traits are being considered. A rating of 1 is the highest; 4 is average, and 7 is the lowest. Values of 2, 3, 5, or 6 are used to rate those who come between the extremes and the average.

1. ATTRACTIVENESS OF APPEARANCE

1 2	3 4	5 6 7
Extremely attractive and pleasing appearance, including clothing, features, proportions of body, carriage, cleanliness, facial expression, becoming clothes, proper distribution of fat.	Pleasing and attractive in some of the factors listed in "I."	Very unattractive; unattractive coloring and features; poor carriage, asymmetrical proportions; unpleasing expression; unkempt; ill-fitting, inappropriate clothes, excessively fat or thin.

3. ACTIVITY

1 2	3 4	5 6 7
Overtly active practically all the time, including gross movements and aggressive contacts with physical environment; eager, animated, bodily movements.	Not conspicuous either because of activity or inactivity.	Very little overt movement; stationary; indifferent attitude; idle; stolid, listless bodily movements.

4c. INTEREST IN OPPOSITE SEX (*Without Participation*)

1 2	3 4	5 6 7
Keenly alive to and curious about social-sex environment. Lacking the necessary techniques, persistently hangs around opposite sex and tries to initiate contacts.	Hangs around members of opposite sex as an onlooker. Self-conscious and embarrassed in their presence or by their advances.	Not only lacks techniques for mingling with, but has no interest in, members of opposite sex.

12. COMPLIANCE WITH AUTHORITY

1	2	3	4	5	6	7

Eager to comply with adults' wishes. Anticipates what adults might want. Asks adult assistance in enforcing regulations. Extremely suggestible with adults.

Takes rules and adult requests as a matter of course. Resistance or compliance dependent upon the situation or the person in charge.

Deliberately breaks rules. Refuses to comply with requests of person in charge. Subtly resists authority; evasive, sly, two-faced, smooth.

13 & 14. SOCIAL SELF-CONFIDENCE (*With Same and Opposite Sex*)

1	2	3	4	5	6	7

Very assured social behavior with both adults and children. Takes failure in matter-of-fact way. Invites new situations requiring poise and confidence.

Is assured with friends and in accustomed situations. Capable of adjusting to new situations requiring poise and confidence.

Panicky in social situations. Makes excuses for self. Shrinks from making new adjustments.

27 & 28. SENSITIVITY; DEPENDENCE ON APPROVAL (*With Same and Opposite Sex*)

1	2	3	4	5	6	7

Explosively concerned about the sort of impression he makes on his associates. Very sensitive and easily "hurt." Reacts strongly to praise or blame. Constantly leaning on others for approval of his actions, or help in his decisions.

Moderately concerned about the impression he makes on his associates. Fairly stable and self-reliant in his relationships with others. Emotional give-and-take. Not oversolicitous for approval in most situations.

Unconcerned about the impression he makes on his associates. Insensitive and indifferent to the opinions of him held by others. Arrives at and acts upon his own decisions. Does not depend upon social approval.

30. GROUP (VS. SELF) INTEREST

1	2	3	4	5	6	7

Quickly adapts himself and buoyantly carries the load or enthusiasms for group interest and activities, or quickly adapts and devotes himself unreservedly to the interests of the group. Enthusiastically encourages activities in which most of the group are interested.

Assumes the attitude of the majority of the group and does what they seem to expect.

Persists in putting personal preferences before the group interests. Makes an issue of little things. Tries to force others into his pattern of interests. May even blow up with an emotional reaction whenever he can't have his way.[55]

[55] F. B. Newman, "The Adolescent in Social Groups; Studies in the Observation of Personality," *Applied Psychology Monographs*, No. 9, 1946, 94 pp. Quoted by permission of the Institute of Child Welfare.

In order to demonstrate the use of such scales, the writer has rated a young acquaintance whom she has known for several years and has had adequate chances to observe. The ratings appear in Figure 74 on this page. The entire scale has been used.

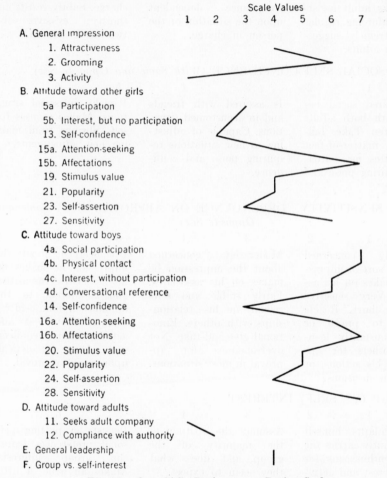

Fig. 74. *One Girl's Ratings on a Rating Scale*

This girl has certain social peculiarities that are brought into sharp focus by the ratings. She is a vigorous and overactive girl who has little thought for her appearance and spends little time in caring for herself. Her adjustment to other girls is fair; she gets along well with them, but her many mannerisms and her lack of sensitivity decrease the popularity engendered by her ready participation and interest in other girls' activities. Toward boys, she has a definitely odd sort of attitude. She shows no fear of them, is self-confident when she meets them, is interesting to them in spite of her indifference—but has not one jot of interest in them and is unwilling to go out of her way to attract them. She does not, however, have such a good adjustment to members of her own sex that an overconcentration upon them would seem the explanation of her lack of interest in boys.

It is the ratings of her relationships with adults that tell the story. She likes them, seeks them out, is with them whenever possible, and is greatly stimulated by them. Her outstanding traits in the social field are, then, her great activity, her self-confidence in all situations, and her marked preference for adult society. The ratings tell nothing more about her, but they do point out an adjustment to society that is not average. Further details about her explain the ratings. She is a girl of unusual mental maturity; ideas interest her so much that she likes nothing better than to discuss them. From her age-mates she gets little stimulation because she is far in advance of them in her intellectual development. Her conversation bores them, and theirs bores her. She has grown up in a family of men and boys. As a result, her adjustment to the opposite sex is good but casual, because she has been with boys and played with them all her life. At her present age—seventeen—the boys in her classes are even younger in their interests than the girls. She is therefore dependent upon adults for both social and intellectual stimulation. Her emotional fixations are also in the main upon adults, although she likes individual boys and girls well enough. Because of her unusual maturity she is stimulating to her age-mates of both sexes, and is even something of a leader among them. Her social adjustment is not desirable as a permanent thing, but as the adolescents of her own age become more mature, it is likely that she will develop more interest in them. In any case, the situation is understandable in terms of her personal history.

Perhaps a word should be said about the concept of social age, a measurement parallel to that of mental or emotional age, which could be derived from the use of such scales as that presented above. Pupils show an infantile social age if they are noisy, if they get their materials into a mess and then walk off and leave them, if they grab what they want, if they are destructive, if their humor runs to slapstick, if they have little perception of their own relation to their peers, or if they resent adult guidance.[56] Abject conformity and clique or gang loyalty represent a somewhat higher social age. A socially mature person is characterized by his awareness of his own role in his group, by his desire to keep the peace, by his sense of fair play, by his honest, considerate treatment of others, by his use of general principles in guiding his conduct, and by his customary conformity to the mores, which is, however, linked with a willingness to be a nonconformist if necessary when the mores run counter to his convictions. In the course of time it is probable that measurements of social age will be in as common use as those of mental maturity.[57]

VII. Summary

Adolescents are tremendously sensitive to social stimuli; no other problem seems to them as important as the establishment of themselves in their own society. They react faster and more deeply to the influence of their age-mates than to that of adults. High school boys and girls tend to form

[56] E. H. Penchef, "The Concept of Social Age," *Sociology and Social Research,* 34:177–183, 1950.

[57] See, for instance, the Vineland Scale of Social Maturity, by E. A. Doll in *Your Child Grows Up,* John Hancock Insurance Company.

small, shut-in cliques, the members of which are intensely loyal to each other and highly critical toward outsiders. Degrees of popularity among students vary from those who are desired as "best friend" by a large proportion of their classmates to those who are rejected or ignored. The traits that are admired by adolescents are known, and the combinations most likely to lead to either acceptance or rejection can be recognized. Recent intensive studies of leadership have made clearer what traits are necessary, but it is not yet known whether or not individuals can be trained to be leaders; perhaps the best that can be done is to select those adolescents who already have the necessary traits and to train them in the social responsibilities of leadership. It is possible to measure with some accuracy the social adjustment of a student and to see in which phases of his life his adjustment is adequate or inadequate. In the course of time it is probable that social age, as a definite measurement, will take its place with intellectual and emotional age as an indication of maturity.

REFERENCES FOR FURTHER READING

BOOKS

1. Anderson, *Psychology of Development and Personal Adjustment*, Chap. 14.
2. Breckenridge and Vincent, *Child Development*, Chap. 12.
3. Davis, K., H. C. Bredemeier, and M. J. Levy, *Modern American Society*, Rinehart & Company, 1948, Vol. I, 399 pp.; Vol. II, 379 pp. (Vol. I, Chaps. 9, 10, 22, 23, 25.)
4. Dimock, *Rediscovering the Adolescent*, Chaps. 4–6, 9, 10.
5. Fields, M. R., T. A. Goldberg, and H. S. Kilander, *Youth Grows into Adulthood*, Chartwell House, 1950, 246 pp. (Chaps. 4, 6.)
6. Fleege, *Self-Revelation of the Adolescent Boy*, Chaps. 11, 12.
7. Fleming, *Adolescence: Its Social Psychology*, Chaps. 11, 12.
8. Garrison, *Growth and Development*, Chap. 12.
9. Garrison, *Psychology of Adolescence*, Chaps. 8, 10.
10. Havighurst and Taba, *Adolescent Character and Personality*, Chap. 5.
11. Hollingshead, A. B., *Elmtown's Youth: The Impact of Social Class on Adolescents*, John Wiley & Sons, Inc., 1949, 480 pp. (Chaps. 3–7, 9–12.)
12. Hurlock, *Adolescent Development*, Chaps. 5–7.
13. Jennings, H. H., *Leadership and Isolation*, Longmans, Green & Co., 1950, 349 pp. (Chaps. 2–6, 8.)
14. Jennings, H. H., and H. Taba, *Sociometry in Group Relations*, American Council on Education, 1948, 55 pp. (Chaps. 2, 3.)
15. Jones, *Development in Adolescence*, Chap. 4.
16. Kuhlen, *Psychology of Adolescent Development*, Chap. 7.
17. Landis, *Adolescence and Youth*, Chaps. 7, 13, 14.
18. Malm and Jamison, *Adolescence*, Chap. 3.
19. Meek, L. H., *The Personal-Social Development of Boys and Girls*, Progressive Education Association, 1940, 243 pp. (Pt. I.)
20. Merry and Merry, *The First Two Decades of Life*, Chap. 10.
21. Roberts, D. M., *Leadership of Teen-Age Groups*, Association Press, 1950, 195 pp. (Chaps. 8–12 and any one chapter in Pt. IV.)
22. Rockwood, L. D., and M. E. N. Ford, *Youth, Marriage, and Parenthood: The Attitudes of 364 University Juniors and Seniors toward Courtship, Marriage, and Parenthood*, John Wiley & Sons, Inc., 1945, 298 pp. (Chaps. 5–7.)

23. Sadler, *Adolescence Problems*, Chaps. 17, 18.
24. Steckle, *Problems of Human Adjustment*, Chap. 9.
25. Stendler, C. B., *Children of Brasstown*, University of Illinois, Bureau of Research and Service, 1949, 103 pp. (Chaps. 4, 5, 7, 9.)
26. Taba, H., and D. Elkins, *With Focus on Human Relations*, American Council on Education, 1950, 227 pp. (Chap. 4.)
27. Wile, *The Challenge of Adolescence*, Chap. 11.
28. Zachry and Lighty, *Emotion and Conduct in Adolescence*, Chaps. 7, 8.

MONOGRAPHS, BULLETINS, PROCEEDINGS, YEARBOOKS, ARTICLES

A. *Personal Traits*

1. Anastasi, A., and S. Miller, "Adolescent Prestige Factors in Relation to Scholastic and Socioeconomic Variables," *Journal of Social Psychology*, 29:43–50, 1949.
2. Bonney, M. E., "Personality Traits of Socially Successful and Socially Unsuccessful Children," *Journal of Educational Psychology*, 34:449–472, 1943.
3. Bonney, M. E., "Popular and Unpopular Children: A Sociometric Study," *Sociometry Monographs*, No. 9, 1947, 81 pp.
4. Kuhlen, R. G., and B. J. Lee, "Personality Characteristics and Social Acceptability in Adolescence," *Journal of Educational Psychology*, 34:321–340, 1943.
5. Northway, M. L., "Outsiders: A Study of the Personality Patterns of Children Least Acceptable to Their Age-Mates," *Sociometry*, 7:10–25, 1944.

B. *Friendships*

1. Austin, M. C., and G. G. Thompson, "Children's Friendships: A Study of the Bases upon Which Children Select and Reject Their Best Friends," *Journal of Educational Psychology*, 39:101–116, 1948.
2. Bonney, M. E., "A Sociometric Study of the Relationship of Some Factors to Mutual Friendships on the Elementary, Secondary, and College Levels," *Sociometry*, 9:21–47, 1946.
3. Hoult, T. F., and R. S. Bolin, "Some Factors Involved in High School Friendship Choices," *Sociology and Social Research*, 34:273–279, 1950.
4. Lundberg, G. A., and V. Beasley, "Consciousness of Kind in a College Population," *Sociometry*, 11:59–73, 1948.
5. Lundberg, G. A., V. B. Hertzler, and L. Dickson, "Attraction Patterns in a University," *Sociometry*, 12:158–169, 1949.
6. Neugarten, B. L., "Social Class and Friendship among School Children," *American Journal of Sociology*, 4:305–313, 1946.
7. Potashin, R., "A Sociometric Study of Children's Friendships," *Sociometry*, 7:303–310, 1944; 9:48–70, 1946.
8. Smith, M., "Some Factors in Friendship Selections of High School Students," *Sociometry*, 7:303–310, 1944.
9. Thompson, G. G., and J. E. Horrocks, "A Study of the Friendship Fluctuations of Urban Boys and Girls," *Journal of Genetic Psychology*, 70:53–63, 1947.
10. van Dyne, E. V., "Personal Traits and Friendship Formation in Adolescent Girls," *Journal of Social Psychology*, 12:291–303, 1940.
11. Vreeland, F. M., "Social Relations of a College Fraternity," *Sociometry*, 5:151–162, 1942.

C. *Leadership*

1. Carter, L. F., and M. Nixon, "Investigation of the Relationship between Four Criteria of Leadership Ability for Four Different Tasks," *Journal of Psychology*, 27:245–261, 1949.

2. Crowley, J. J., "High School Backgrounds of Successful Men and Women Graduates," *School Review*, 48:205–209, 1940.
3. Drake, R. M., "A Study of Leadership," *Character and Personality*, 12:285–289, 1944.
4. Gibb, C. A., "The Principal Traits of Leadership," *Journal of Abnormal and Social Psychology*, 42:265–284, 1947.
5. Hemphill, J. K., "Situational Factors in Leadership," *Bureau of Educational Research Monographs, Ohio State University*, No. 32, 1949, 136 pp.
6. Morris, R. T., and M. Seaman, "The Problems of Leadership: An Interdisciplinary Approach," *American Journal of Sociology*, 56:149–155, 1947.
7. Page, H. E., "Detecting Potential Leaders," *Journal of Aviation Medicine*, 18:435–441, 1948.
8. Preston, M. G., and R. K. Heintz, "Effects of Participatory *versus* Supervisory Leadership on Group Judgment," *Journal of Abnormal and Social Psychology*, 44:345–355, 1949.
9. Reynolds, F. J., "Factors of Leadership among Seniors of the Central High School of Tulsa, Oklahoma," *Journal of Educational Research*, 37:356–361, 1944.
10. Roff, M., "A Study of Combat Leadership in the Air Force by Means of a Rating Scale," *Journal of Psychology*, 30:229–239, 1950.
11. Stogdill, R. M., "Personal Factors Associated with Leadership: A Survey of the Literature," *Journal of Psychology*, 25:35–71, 1948.
12. Stogdill, R. M., and B. L. Shartle, "Methods for Determining Patterns of Leadership Behavior in Relation to Organic Structure and Objectives," *Journal of Applied Psychology*, 32:286–291, 1948.
13. Wherry, R. J., and D. H. Fryer, "Buddy Ratings: Popularity Contests for Leadership Criteria," *Personnel Psychology*, 2:147–159, 1949.

D. *Measures of Social Relationships*

1. Bogardus, E. S., "Measurement of Personal and Group Relations," *Sociometry*, 10:306–311, 1947.
2. Bonney, M. E., "Sociometric Study of Agreement between Teachers' Judgments and Students' Choices," *Sociometry*, 10:133–146, 1947.
3. Cook, L. A., "An Experimental Sociographic Study of a Stratified Tenth-Grade Class," *American Sociological Review*, 10:250–261, 1945.
4. Inkeless, A., "Development of Sociometry: The War Years, 1941–1945," *Sociometry*, 9:379–385, 1946.
5. Northway, M. L., "Social Acceptability Tests," *Sociometry*, 5:180–184, 1942.
6. Raths, L. E., "Understanding the Individual through Anecdotal Records, Sociometric Devices, and the Like," *American Council on Education Studies*, Ser. I, No. 40, XIV (1950), 63–73.
7. Runner, J. R., "Social Distance in Adolescent Relationships," *American Journal of Sociology*, 43:418–439, 1937.

E. *Spontaneous Adolescent Society*

1. Davis, A., "Socialization and Adolescent Personality," *Forty-third Yearbook of the National Society for the Study of Education*, 1944, Pt. II, pp. 198–216.
2. Hartley, R. E., "The Sociality of Pre-adolescent Boys," *Teachers College Contributions to Education*, No. 918, 1946, 117 pp. (Chaps. 3, 4.)
3. Jones, M. C., "A Functional Analysis of Colloquial Speech among Adolescents," *American Psychologist*, 1:252–253, 1946.
4. Leevy, J. R., "Social Competence of High School Youth," *School Review*, 51:342–347, 1943.

5. McGuire, C., and R. J. Havighurst, "Social Development," *Review of Educational Research,* 17:345–355, 1947.
6. Newman, F. B., "The Adolescent in Social Groups: Studies in the Observation of Personality," *Applied Psychology Monographs,* No. 9, 1946, 94 pp.
7. Skubic, E., "A Study in Acquaintanceship and Social Status in Physical Education Classes," *Research Quarterly of the American Association for Health, Physical Education, and Recreation,* 20:80–87, 1949.
8. Tryon, C. M., "The Adolescent Peer Culture," *Forty-third Yearbook of the National Society for the Study of Education,* 1944, Pt. II, pp. 217–239.

F. *Courtship*

1. Christenson, H. T., "Courtship Conduct as Viewed by Youth," *Journal of Home Economics,* 40:187–188, 1948.
2. Christenson, H. T., "Students' Views on Mate Selection," *Marriage and Family Living,* 9:85–88, 1947.
3. Cuber, J. F., "Changing Courtship and Marriage Customs," *Annals of the American Academy of Political and Social Science,* 229:30–38, 1943.
4. Cupps, R. D., and M. S. Hayner, "Dating at the University of Washington," *Marriage and Family Living,* 9:30–31, 1947.
5. Hill, R., "Campus Values in Mate Selection," *Journal of Home Economics,* 37:554–558, 1945.
6. Himes, J. F., "Mate Selection among Negro College Students," *Sociology and Social Research,* 33:204–211, 1949.
7. Vail, J. P., and V. M. Standt, "Attitudes of College Students toward Marriage and Related Problems: I. Dating and Mate Selection," *Journal of Psychology,* 30:171–182, 1950.
8. Walford, O. P., "How Early Background Affects Dating Behavior," *Journal of Home Economics,* 40:505–506, 1948.
9. Winch, R. F., "Interrelationship between Certain Social Background and Parent-Son Factors in the Study of Courtship among College Men," *American Sociological Review,* 11:333–343, 1946.
10. Winch, R. F., "The Relation between the Loss of Parents and Progress in Courtship," *Journal of Social Psychology,* 29:51–56, 1949.

CHAPTER TEN

The Adolescent
and His Home

Teachers have at least two good reasons for wanting to understand homes. The first is that homes have a profound effect upon the behavior and attitudes of pupils. Without some knowledge of their home conditions, a teacher cannot understand her students and cannot, therefore, adjust her work to their needs or help them in their personal development. The second reason is that her classroom is a kind of home, and she should know what the characteristics of a good home are so that she can introduce these into her classroom, thus making it a good environment for her students. This chapter will therefore present certain basic data about the trends in the modern development of the family, the structure of families, the patterns of parental behavior, the effects of the home upon its children, the special sources of difficulties during adolescence, the desirable characteristics of a home for adolescent boys or girls, and some of the undesirable outcomes if normal developments do not occur.

I. The Modern Family

The American family has changed greatly during the last fifty or sixty years, especially in regard to the basis of mate selection, the number of children, the relative authority of father and mother, the relation of the parents to each other, the nature of home discipline, and the stability of the union. All of these changes have affected the position of children and their relations to their parents.[1]

Modern marriage is based upon a mutual sexual attraction, romantic interest, and glamour, with little consideration of suitability, financial arrangements, social contacts between the two families involved, future care of any children, or more thought of stability than the perennial conviction that love will last forever. The present theory seems to be that these practical problems will be worked out after the marriage, not before. Most young men are looking for a glamorous, exciting mistress with a pretty face rather than for a good housekeeper or a satisfactory mother for their children. A young woman is trying to attract a handsome, exciting, romantic lover, although she does have some thought of improving both her social

---

[1] O. R. Rice, "Ethical Elements in the Etiology of the Unstable Family," *Journal of Clinical Pastoral Work*, 2:53–60, 1949.

and financial standing, if possible. To be sure, in a choice between a poor but romantic suitor and a rich but stodgy one, she will usually choose the former, but up until the time of actual emotional involvement, even a modern girl considers it advisable to fall in love, if she can, with a man whose wealth and social status are above her own. At the beginning, marriage is chiefly a man's diversion, but to a woman it is always a career, even if she has a profession or a job outside her home. As the marriage continues, the woman's role becomes more difficult, especially if there are children. She must remain glamorous, she must be motherly, she must be domestic, she must be an intelligent companion, she must maintain the family's social prestige, she must be the chief emotional prop of the household, and quite possibly she may want to pursue some line of work outside her home. The father's role, while onerous, is simpler: he has to earn money. He almost always spends the major part of the day away from his home and family. He is likely to find satisfaction and stability in his occupation, if it is at all suitable, but he often becomes a secondary figure in his home because his children see so little of him. The patriarchal father whose word is law has practically disappeared from the American scene, largely because social conditions have caused the foundations on which he stood to crumble. He no longer has any actual power over either his wife or his children. Thus, his wife *can* support herself if necessary, his children are encouraged from the cradle to "be themselves" without much reference to his desires, any earnings of his wife or children belong to them rather than to him, his wife has a legal existence separate from his—that is, she can vote, she can own property, she can enter practically any occupation that he can, and as far as the law is concerned she is his equal. The modern father usually tries to be a friend to his children and is sometimes so successful that they look to him for their main emotional satisfactions.

The mother's relation to the children is complex. She is almost the only influence in a baby's life until the age of about two and is the main figure until the child enters school. Her position is so commanding that American families are more in danger of matriarchal than patriarchal domination.[2] The mother's position as the most immediate love-object is, however, more or less offset by her position as the source of control. She does most of the reproving and punishing because she is on the scene, and in the case of her daughters she does practically all of it. The American mother serves, also, for her daughters as a figure with whom they can identify themselves— that is, she can be, and usually is, a model that her daughters imitate. As long as her sons are little boys, they too are likely to worship their mother, but as they grow older, they cannot identify themselves with her. They must leave her and prepare to enter the masculine world. The boy's typical revolt against the dominating feminism of both home and elementary school is to become tough, to excel in games, to be irresponsible, to pummel his companions and be pummeled by them, to play hookey, to be unpunctual, to neglect home chores, to admire "badness," to protest against going to church or Sunday school (unless his father also goes), and in general to react in a negative way to whatever seems to him to be feminine. This reaction is

[2] E. A. Strecker, *Their Mothers' Sons: A Psychologist Examines an American Problem,* J. B. Lippincott Company, 1946, 220 pp.

normal and healthy, and it parallels that of girls three generations ago against a predominately masculine world. Perhaps the members of those primitive groups who separated boys of nine or ten from their mothers and educated them together under exclusively masculine guidance were not such poor psychologists. In the modern family, the father should step in to become the guide, friend, and model of his son.

The modern marriage is seriously lacking in permanence. The causes of its dissolution are many, but important among them is the basis upon which the marriage rests. Both husband and wife founded their marriage on romance, sex, and glamour. The romance may survive, but the glamour will not. If the partners become good friends, wholly aside from their sexual attraction for each other, the marriage has at least a chance. Since, however, the man was originally attracted by his wife's appearance, he is likely to find her first pregnancy a trial. Gone is the slender, alluring, eager, energetic girl he fell in love with, and in her place is an awkward, lethargic, unaesthetic young woman. If a man marries because he wants children, he may be as interested and excited about the pregnancy as his wife; but if what he wanted was a mistress, he is likely to react negatively and perhaps vehemently to her condition. He also finds the next year or two after the child's birth very difficult. Even if his wife regains her previous appearance, which is by no means certain, he has to share her attention with her child. Moreover, he and she cannot go out together any longer, unless the child can go with them or a baby sitter can be found. A marriage founded upon romance, good times together, and glamour is ill-equipped to survive such strains.

A second source of difficulty arises from the modern theory that marriage is a relation between two people and not between two families. When any two people fall in love, there is no guarantee that their backgrounds are such that they can live together in harmony, no matter how much attraction they may feel toward each other. As long as families did the choosing, certain problems of adjustment did not arise. For instance, Catholic families did not choose Jewish ones, a native family did not choose a foreign one, and wealthy or high-status families did not choose their opposites. Consequently, the young people had much in common, and they were not likely to have trouble with their in-laws, since each had been approved by the other's relatives. The modern engagement is usually contracted between two young people who are unknown to each other's families. They may be of different creed, race, nationality, or social status. The marriage may or may not receive family approval. The older method of using marriage for furthering family alliances had its great disadvantages, but it avoided most of the clash that comes from antagonisms based upon divergent backgrounds.

Finally, a word should perhaps be said concerning the modern social forces that operate to pull a family apart. The different members find many competitors for their attention and affection outside the home: their sports, their friends, their interests, their diversions, to mention the most obvious. Thus, on a given afternoon the father of a family is at work, the mother is at a PTA meeting, one daughter at a music lesson, one son at football practice, another son in the YMCA swimming tank, and the younger daughter watching animated cartoons in a movie theater. No one is home, and no two are carrying on a joint enterprise. It is not surprising that family life has a tendency to disintegrate. The family automobile ride, the family picnic, the family vacation, and now the family television are forces that still bind members together, but there are not as many integrative as disintegrative forces operating upon the average family group.

Modern psychologists and sociologists have been studying homes in great detail in recent years. The main results of their researches have been to demonstrate the extreme importance of a child's home upon his personality, attitudes, reactions, and behavior. The balance of this chapter will deal with the results of outstanding investigations into such topics as the classification of homes into types, the emotional interrelationships among the members, the discipline in the home, the special problems of maintaining a good home for adolescents, and the effect upon all concerned by such factors as size of family, absence of one parent, socioeconomic status, and so on.

II. Classification and Characteristics of Homes

As a stranger visits a home, he inevitably notices its characteristics more or less, depending upon his powers of observation, and, on the basis of what he has observed, draws his own conclusions as to familial affections and tensions. Use of a rating scale for homes requires primarily a series of such observations as any visitor might make, except that the trained adults who study homes are more systematic, careful, and thorough than a casual visitor is likely to be.

Within the past few years two especially important contributions to the understanding of family interrelationships have appeared. One contains a rating scale of thirty items, by means of which one may classify homes. The other gives a classification of the patterns of authority and control within the home. The present section will be concerned primarily with the presentation of results from these two studies.

1. Patterns of Parental Behavior: Although each pair of parents has its own individuality, the behavior of parents in general toward their offspring may be classified roughly into eight types,[3] based upon different combinations of three main variables. The first of these is the degree to which the parents accept the child. They may reject him, accept him, or be casual or indifferent toward him. The second variable concerns the extent of their indulgence and varies from subservience to his every whim to a nonchalant indifference to his needs. The third is the pattern of authority within the family, which may vary from an autocratic issuing of commands by the parents to a family democracy in which everyone's vote is of equal value. In theory there could be many possible combinations of these three

---

[3] A. L. Baldwin, J. Kalhorn, and F. H. Breeze, "Patterns of Parental Behavior," *Psychological Monographs*, Vol. LVIII, No. 3, 1945, 75 pp.

variables, but actually there are only eight frequent configurations. These will be described briefly.

1. *Actively rejectant* parents are consistently hostile, unaffectionate, disapproving, critical, and distant. They seek actively to dominate the child by means of autocratic commands. Warm, social, trusting relations are missing. The home is full of tension and conflict, and there is a feeling of resentment on both sides. These parents dislike children, have no understanding of them, and rule them in a dictatorial manner. They are not intentionally cruel and they do not physically mistreat their offspring. They are cold, unsympathetic, and irritable toward those who are to them mainly a nuisance.

2. *Nonchalant, rejectant* parents have the same basic dislike for and indifference toward the child, but instead of continually nagging at him, they are merely indifferent to what he does, as long as he does not bother them. They ignore him as completely as possible and maintain only the slightest contact with him. When, however, the child does get in their way, they become autocratic and hostile, so as to get the point at issue settled quickly and with as little inconvenience to themselves as possible.

3. *Casually autocratic* parents neither accept the children with understanding nor reject them with resentment. Some are more consistently autocratic than others. All of them believe that a parent's authority is definitely above the desires of a child, but some of them are autocratic on principle, all day and every day, on matters large or small; whereas others try to maintain a friendly atmosphere, but resort to commands on important matters, merely from expediency. These autocratic-by-expedience parents have no theories about child training, so they react to each situation as it arises. They are likely to have no fixed policy about anything, and their home is usually on the chaotic side, with the children having a good deal of freedom and a moderate degree of affection, but meeting an autocratic handling if an issue is important enough.

4. *Casually indulgent* parents are mildly indulgent and in general tolerant, but rather haphazard. They maintain a fairly pleasant atmosphere in the home, and they often let the child do as he pleases, provided he does not bother them too much. They do not go out of their way to be indulgent, but they find that giving in is easier than resisting. They take their children easily, have no rigid standards for them, have no fixed policy about handling them, are often diverted from punishing them, and are inclined to baby them at times, although not consistently.

5. *Acceptant-indulgent* parents show a deep emotional attachment to the child, they are unduly anxious about him, they protect and baby him, they identify themselves so completely with him that they try to live their own lives over in his. They almost smother him with demonstrations of affection, and they put themselves to endless inconvenience in order to keep him happy. They do not, however, admit him as an equal who helps them make decisions. Their attachment to him is definitely neurotic and is so close that they cannot be objective about him or his problems. These parents have, however, definite standards for their child's behavior, although their method of procedure consists in leading him gently through their love for him rather than in coercing him.

6. *Acceptant-casual-indulgent* parents are sometimes just as indulgent as those in the above groups—although usually they are less extreme—but their indulgence is based on impulse, and they do not identify themselves with their child. They let junior have almost unrestrained freedom, and they submit to a good deal of disobedience and bad manners on his part. They admit their child's shortcomings, but they think freedom is the best way to let him develop his capacities, even though it may be trying at times. Because they are basically casual in their relationship, they do not smother their child with affection, or seek to overprotect him, or try to make

him conform to an ideal. They just let him run wild most of the time and give in to him when conflict arises, because it seems to them easier than opposition.

7. *Acceptance-indulgent-democratic* parents are basically indulgent and believe in treating children as their own equals in a family democracy. The children are

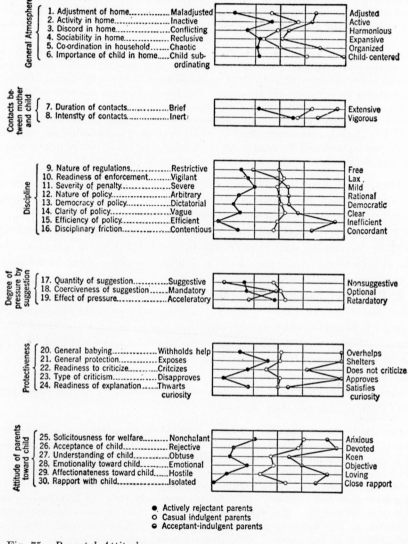

Fig. 75. *Parental Attitudes*

Based on A. L. Baldwin, J. Kalhorn, and F. H. Breeze, "Patterns of Parental Behavior," *Psychological Monographs,* 58:19, 26, 43, 1945.

allowed to criticize their parents, to express their own views, and to make decisions on most minor and some major issues. They are treated on the surface as if they were adults, but they are also subject to a good deal of parental pressure that is applied indirectly via the close bond between parent and child. The parents use democracy as a means of making their child into the ideal companion they want him to be. The home is child-centered and rests upon a neurotic degree of contact between parent and child, and a neurotic identification of the former with the latter.

8. *Acceptant-democratic* parents are emotionally mature people who believe in the participation of children in family decisions and the independence of the child as an indivdual. Some parents of this type purposely repress expressions of affection and try to be objectively scientific in their treatment of their children. They are so afraid of influencing him too much that they often do not help him, even when he needs their aid to resolve a conflict. They make little or no effort to protect him from dangers of any kind. The more "scientific" parents do not act impulsively, but think matters over in view of basic educational principles and try to be rational. The child is respected as an individual, is encouraged to voice his opinions, is often consulted, and his decisions are allowed to stand without adult coercion. Children in such families often call their parents by their first names, an outward evidence of complete democracy. Parents and children meet on a companionable intellectual ground, but there is little overt affection between them. The child has his own place in the family council, and his desires are given whatever weight seems just in relation to the needs and wishes of the remaining members of the group.[4]

The chart in Figure 75 has been constructed to show the contrasts among these various home atmospheres. Since the figure would be more confusing than helpful if all types of parents were included, it has been limited to only three: the actively rejectant, the casually indulgent, and the acceptant-indulgent. As may be seen at once, the first and third types of parent score at the two extremes, while the casually indulgent scores nearly in the middle of the figure on most traits.

2. Effects of Parental Attitudes upon Children: A careful and experienced observer can make a shrewd guess about a child's parents from noticing his behavior when he is away from them, because the child reflects to some extent at least the environment in which he has lived and the treatment he has received. It should be understood, however, that there are individual variations in the reaction of children and adolescents to their homes and that the following remarks apply only in general when one summarizes results from a large number of cases.

Thus the child who has been actively rejected by his parents is passive toward authority, docile, outwardly decorous—since only by such behavior can he escape their nagging and punishment—but he is also hostile, withdrawn, fearful, frustrated, insecure, stubborn, and passively resistant.[5] He is hostile in response to his parents' hostility, withdrawn because his contacts have been reduced to a minimum, fearful with good reason, but stubborn and resistive, since only thus can he achieve a small assertion of his ego, a slight retaliation of hostility, and an inactive expression of resentment. In one interesting study of twenty-six children who had dominating parents, fifteen of the children were passive, submissive, and dependent, six were rebellious and resentful, and five were passively resistant.[6]

---

[4] Condensed from Baldwin, Kalhorn, and Breeze, *op. cit.* Used by permission of the publishers.

[5] L. R. Wolberg, "The Character Structure of the Rejected Child," *Nervous Child,* 3:74–88, 1944; and D. D. Mueller, "Paternal Domination: Its Influence on Child Guidance Results," *Smith College Studies in Social Work,* 15:184–215, 1945.

[6] Mueller, "Paternal Domination: Its Influence on Child Guidance Results," *loc. cit.*

The child of nonchalant, rejectant parents shows a different picture. He does not have to fight against hostility but against indifference. He is a type of neglected child. There is so little interaction between him and his parents that he can get their attention only by misbehaving. He has a moderate degree of independence, thrust upon him by parental refusal to help him. He makes desperate attempts to get attention, to arouse affection, and to achieve status. He soon discovers that he can obtain from age-mates the satisfactions that his parents deny him, and from then on he is likely to be in open conflict with his home.

Children whose parents maintain a neutral attitude but are at the same time autocratic in discipline are likely either to be nervous, timid, and compliant in their efforts to win recognition, or else to be aggressive and rebellious, in order to assert their independence and individuality. If, in addition, the autocratic handling alternates with indifference—as is the case if treatment is based upon expediency and impulse—the children learn to be sly, to wriggle out of difficulties, to test the limits to which they can go, to bend temporarily before the storm, to delay requests until mother is in an amiable mood, and generally to circumvent a discipline that is of an uncertain and varying nature. If the casual parent is indulgent rather than autocratic, the less assertive child reacts by feeling insecure and anxious, by showing a tendency to be withdrawn when among other children, and by clinging silently to the fringe of groups without trying to take an active role. The aggressive child reacts to the same situation by running wild, by being destructive, and by thrusting himself into groups. Children of indifferent parents thus tend either to resign themselves to receiving little attention or else to become determined attention getters.

The children of indulgent parents are likely to feel secure, protected, and comfortable. They soon learn to give an outer conformance to parental desires, at the same time getting their own way by being loving, cute, wheedling, disappointed, hurt, or amusing, as the occasion demands. Behind the façade of compliance and close attachment, however, they are domineering, self-centered, selfish, and determined to do as they please. Because they feel absolutely secure, they become smug, self-confident, somewhat self-righteous, and certain of their power over others. When they go to school, however, they discover that their age-mates are not so easily handled, and these overprotected children are usually unpopular. If they are smug enough to resist the shock, they become more aloof from others than before and more firmly entrenched in their own superiority. Success in meeting parental pressure intensifies the complacency of the accepted child into a precocity of mind, a maturity of outlook, a cocksureness of attitude, and an absolute belief in his own powers that makes him thoroughly obnoxious to everyone but his parents. Since, however, "democratic" parents tend to withhold open demonstrations of affection toward a child—lest they overprotect him—he is inevitably caught in a conflict: those who approve of him give him little warmth, and those from whom he might get affection either dislike or despise him. A vigorous child makes violent attempts to break out of his isolation. Since his democratic home treatment has taught him that he need fear no one, he is uninhibited, aggressive, and confident. As he grows older and develops understanding, his desire to be popular may lead him to try a more friendly means of approach. An extreme of democratic treatment may thus set up undesirable reactions.

Parents who are acceptant, moderately indulgent, democratic, and warmly affectionate have a home that is as near to satisfaction as can be expected, and their children are generally well balanced, secure, and happy. They may, however, be a little too comfortable within the family circle and reluctant to leave it, either actually or emotionally. They are sometimes too much exposed to pressure from siblings because their parents will not step in and protect them from aggression. Those who can come up to expectations, protect themselves, and adjust their desires to those of other people emerge as successes from this type of home.

2% Teachers in general tend to prefer as pupils those youngsters who come from homes in which the parents are dominant to those who come from homes in which the parents are submissive to their children's demands. Since teachers have twenty-five to forty children in a class, one can see the reason for this preference. The child with dominating parents is usually courteous, obedient, interested in school, modest, generous, responsible, docile, attentive, loyal, and careful. He accepts authority, keeps his desk in order, is careful of his clothes, has good manners, does not talk back when reproved, puts things back where he found them.[7] Children from homes with submissive parents are rated by their teachers as being disobedient, irresponsible, disorderly, lazy, selfish, stubborn, sulky, aggressive, self-confident, talkative, independent, and antagonistic. They defy authority, are fussy about their food, lack interest in school, have bad manners, are often tardy, express themselves well and fluently, get on with their age-mates, and are general classroom nuisances. It should be noted that the two groups of children show both virtues and faults. One child is pleasant for a teacher to have around, but lacks initiative; he depends upon authority, he is hesitant in speech, and he has a better adjustment to older people than to his age-mates. The other child has the faults of irresponsibility, selfishness, and disobedience, but the virtues of independence, initiative, and fluent self-expression.

3. Patterns of Authority in the Family:[8]   Since there are two parents, there can be only three general patterns, although subdivisions within each are possible. Authority may be in the hands of the father or of the mother, or it may be equally divided between them. In the investigation here reported, based upon an intensive analysis of thirty-seven homes, five main types were recognized: the mother-controlled, the mother-led, the father-controlled, the father-led, and the equal-controlled, of which there were four subtypes. These groupings are listed in Table 19. Brief descriptions are given below.

The mother-controlled family contains the *passive* husband so frequently referred to in discussions of the (supposedly) increasing number of matriarchal families in America. Characteristically, this husband is indifferent to his wife; he looks upon child rearing as a woman's responsibility; and he prefers men's companionship and masculine activities to the company of his wife and children. His wife controls the home and family, first, because he apparently delegates that responsibility to her while he earns the living or not, as the case may be; and second, because she apparently feels some compulsion or need to assume the dominant role in family control.[9]

In the mother-led family the decisions regarding family policy are jointly made, but with the wife assuming the lead. She is apparently recognized as the stronger, more capable person of the partnership, and her leadership appears to be accepted without resentment on the husband's part. There is warmth and affection in this

---

[7] P. M. Symonds, *The Psychology of Parent-Child Relationships,* Appleton-Century-Crofts, Inc., 1939, 228 pp.

[8] Based upon H. L. Ingersoll, "A Study of Transmission of Authority Patterns in the Family," *Genetic Psychology Monographs,* 38:225–302, 1948.

[9] The quotations are condensed from pp. 287–293 of Ingersoll, *op. cit.* They are used by permission of the publisher.

Table 19

TYPES OF PARENTAL CONTROL

A. Mother-controlled, autocratic   4 ⎫
B. Mother-led, democratic   5 ⎬ 9

C. Balanced
  1. Equalitarian, democratic   7 ⎫
  2. Equalitarian, indulgent   2 ⎬ 13
  3. Equalitarian, neglectful   2 ⎪
  4. Equalitarian, inconsistent   2 ⎭

D. Father-led
  1. Autocratic   2 ⎫
  2. Democratic   7 ⎬ 15
E. Father-controlled, autocratic   3 ⎪
  1. Pseudo father-controlled   3 ⎭

From H. L. Ingersoll, "A Study of Transmission of Authority Patterns in the Family," *Genetic Psychology Monographs*, 38:239, 1949. Used by permission of the publishers.

family. The husband tends to be less secure emotionally, and thus to need more affection than his wife.

The partners in a democratic marriage have worked out a complex but unified system of authority based on a common philosophy of family life. This philosophy becomes so much a part of their thinking about the family that one partner often knows without asking what the other's reaction will be to a proposal. Therefore, authority over the various spheres of home and family life in the equalitarian family, for the most part, becomes a joint activity except in areas where one partner is felt more capable of judgment than the other. The husband and wife of the equalitarian marriage express their flexibility in adjustment in a variety of ways. Both have developed successful techniques of resolving conflicts, although the techniques used vary from sharp quarrels that are soon over to various means of avoiding a conflict when one partner is irritable, or withdrawing a point when it seems not worth the cost. The use of humor and "kidding the other out" of his peevishness are more common in this authority pattern than in the others.

In the father-led family the father is definitely the head of the family. Although family policy is apparently unified and arrived at through agreement of both husband and wife, the husband's leadership is more often followed in family planning and decision making than is his wife's, although she manages the home and family, including the rearing of the children, to conform with joint family policy and with his expectations. His authority supports her discipline consistently and firmly. Occasionally he may "lay down the law" or become autocratic in his control but for the most part he is the respected and loved democratic husband and father.

In the father-controlled family the husband expects to be absolute master of the home. He sets the family policy and makes the major plans and decisions. His unpredictable temper is his keenest and most feared weapon in maintaining control over his wife and children. He is likely to set standards of behavior for his children that are beyond their abilities to achieve. He expects his wife to see that his children are brought up to suit him. He criticizes her when they are not a credit to him. He takes the attitude that he is a superior being and his wife is inferior. He goes about in some mixed crowds but prefers men's company and masculine sports and activities. Wife and children are almost compelled to share his interests. Conflicts between him and his wife are often unresolved. He insists on having his way. If his wife tries to gain some concession, she is only ignored, berated sarcastically, or overrun. She is forced to make all the adjustments in order to keep the marriage intact. There is little or no affection expressed toward each other by either of the partners.

The reaction of the children could be prophesied from the family situation. In the mother-controlled homes they are erratic in maturing, some showing parental "fixations," some rebelling against or withdrawing from parental authority, and others escaping from the family group as rapidly as possible. Generally speaking, these children show symptoms of disturbance in personality adjustment.

When the mother is a leader but not a despot the children appear to be more attached to her than to their father. They respect, admire, and love her, but like their father also. The children confide in their parents. The general family atmosphere is warm and acceptant. The husband and wife who are equalitarian in their relationship to each other tend to guide their children from early dependency to a place of responsibility and individuality in the family group. These children learn how to co-operate, how to share in family crises, how to contribute to family planning, and how to use so-called democratic techniques in group living. They are encouraged to become self-reliant and independent of parents as they approach adulthood. Children in a father-led home often feel that their punishment is unfair and unnecessarily strict. The authoritarian father loses the confidence of his children, especially during adolescence. They may rebel, withdraw, or become overdependent. He may tie them to himself by his overprotection or force them to premature independence in order to escape his domination.

Since the father in the father-controlled home is autocratic, erratic, and unpredictable, he is not loved. He sets up adult standards for his children that suit his ends and represses them into docile submission. He discourages adolescent independence, and is disapproving of his children's association with the opposite sex. He apparently hopes to run their lives as long as he can.

The two extreme types and a typical equalitarian pattern are described below in the words of students who wrote statements concerning their own families.

My mother is the one who tells us what to do and the one we go to for the answers. . . . My mother is the recognized head of the family. . . . The house we live in belongs to my grandfather, but my mother drew up the designs for it and planned the furniture. Dad has had very little to say about any of it. It is Mother's money that we spend. Now that Dad is home he pays her for his room and board, and she is the one who keeps the accounts, figures the income tax, and hands out the money.

We all have such a good time together! Arguments and disagreements occur, but are easily patched up. . . . Everyone helps with jobs, and there seems to be a unity in which everyone is pulling together for a common goal. We are all very honest with each other, and everyone can take criticism.

Our family has always been subordinated to my father's needs and desires. He would do anything for us if it didn't interfere with *his* plans. He is still a little boy. He has to have everything his own way. Mother does the adjusting. She sometimes tries to reason with him, but it doesn't do any good. . . . He decided where we were to live, selected the house furnishings, planned our vacations, decided when and whom we should entertain, and to some extent decided upon our vocations. . . . He always expects too much of my mother, and she almost had a nervous breakdown trying to live up to his expectations.[10]

---

[10] These paragraphs are quoted from Ingersoll, "A Study of Transmission of Authority Patterns in the Family," *loc. cit.,* pp. 246, 254, and 274, by permission of the publisher.

4. Factors Affecting the Impact of the Home upon the Child and Adolescent: The "normal" home contains two parents, their children, and no one else. If the home is broken by the absence of a parent, whether through death, divorce, or desertion, the home has a different character. If the number of children is unusually large or small, the family customs and relationships show differences. If there is conflict and tension in the group, such as arises when one child is jealous of another or when the parents quarrel frequently, the children are affected. The nature of the discipline in the home is of importance in a child's development. So also is the economic level of his home and its social status. The effects of variation from "normal" in these matters are of considerable importance in conditioning the behavior of adolescents, especially in influencing the nature and course of their emancipation from home control.

The broken home exists everywhere even without divorce, because one parent dies, or deserts his family, or is in an institution. In America the high divorce rate increases the number of such homes. At the time of World War II, one child in every nine, or 11 per cent, was growing up in a broken home.[11] At present, owing to the death of men during the war and the dissolution of many hastily contracted "war" marriages, the proportion is not far from 15 per cent. Broken homes leave their traces upon both personality and achievement. High school students from such homes do poorer schoolwork and rate lower on personality scales than do those who come from complete families. Even when one equates pairs of boys for intelligence, in each pair the adolescent from the broken home has more social and emotional problems than the other boy.[12] He is quicker to anger, more self-centered, less sensitive to social approval, less able to control himself, and more easily discouraged when things go wrong. Many of the boys studied in this investigation entered the Army, and some of them were discharged as being maladjusted to Army life and requirements; all the dismissals were boys from broken homes. Investigation of 211 hospitalized neurotic soldiers showed that 36 per cent came from broken homes. Since this number is over three times the corresponding percentage in the general population, it is clear that these homes are producing a disproportionate number of those with personalities that break down under strain.[13]

The size of a family affects the development of those who grow up in it, especially at the extremes.[14] Members of relatively large families, six or more children, tend to be more popular among their classmates and to be rejected less frequently than children from smaller families. Their supe-

[11] Anon., "One Child in Nine in a Broken Home," *Statistical Bulletin of the Metropolitan Life Insurance Company,* 25:3–6, 1944.

[12] R. Torrance, "The Influence of Broken Homes on Adolescent Adjustment," *Journal of Educational Sociology,* 18:359–364, 1945.

[13] L. Madow and S. E. Hardy, "Incidents and Analysis of Broken Families in the Background of Neurosis," *American Journal of Orthopsychiatry,* 17:521–528, 1947.

[14] C. P. Loomis, W. B. Baker, and C. Proctor, "The Size of the Family as Related to Social Success of Children," *Sociometry,* 12:313–320, 1949.

riority persists, though somewhat reduced, into the years of adolescence. One can understand that members of large families acquire social skills, sensitiveness to others, responsibility, and the habit of co-operation because they live in a highly social milieu. Their superiority might be more marked and more consistently shown if large families did not occur mostly at the lower end of the social scale and were not therefore subject to privations that offset some of the home's social values. The large family is conspicuously the one in which the rituals of family living persist, such as the religious ritual of saying grace before meals, or the social rituals of hanging up a Christmas stocking, or of having baked beans on Saturday evening, or of walking in a park on Sunday, or of measuring the children's heights against a wall and leaving the successive marks on the wallpaper, or of wishing on a wishbone, and so on. Such rituals are indicative of integration, and, in turn, they help to preserve the *status quo*.[15] When a family starts to disintegrate it soon loses its little customs, which, while of no importance in themselves, often furnish a cement that helps to hold the family together and to perpetuate its characteristics into the homes of the next generation.

At the other end of the distribution in respect to size of family is the only child. He is automatically deprived of constant contact with other children and he is continually subjected to adult presence, adult ways of life, and adult conversation. It is not necessary for an only child to be maladjusted, but it is easy for him to become so. For one thing, his mother has enough time to baby and spoil him, if she wants to. For another, he is not forced to overcome jealousy of his siblings and to content himself with his fair share of his mother's attention, and, if he is a boy, he comes into sharp and direct rivalry with his father for his mother's affection. If his parents quarrel, the only child has little if any protection from the resulting emotional atmosphere, even when the quarrel has nothing to do with him. On the other hand, an only child usually matures faster in social, emotional, and intellectual reactions than a member of a large family.

There is certainly a tendency for only children to be overprotected; that is, they receive too much maternal attention and companionship, they are abnormally protected from the ordinary hazards of childhood, they receive constant indulgence of their desires and such an outpouring of maternal love as to isolate them from other influences. The mother in these instances is usually not an abnormal person and shows no abnormal drives; she merely displays too much ordinary maternal behavior, too intensively and over too long a period. The danger of this development is greater if the child is a boy, if the father is ineffectual as a person, if the child is sick a great deal in infancy, if he is not merely the only child but the only possible one, or if he was born or adopted toward the end of the mother's years of possible childbearing.[16] The "only" child who is overprotected is sure to have difficulties in school, since neither his teacher nor his age-mates are going to give him the treatment he receives at home. If he rejects his peers

[15] J. H. S. Bossard and E. S. Boll, "Ritual in Family Living," *American Sociological Review,* 14:463–469, 1949.

[16] Harry Bakwin, "Pure Maternal Overprotection," *Journal of Pediatrics,* 33:788–795, 1949.

and they reject him, he becomes more tightly tied than ever to his mother; if he tries to win status among them, he is soon in conflict with her. One of the relatively late evidences of overdependency is the chronic homesickness of a few college freshmen each year.[17] Some cannot survive the separation, and others do so only with difficulty. One hears more about homesick girls at the college level, probably because boys regard the attitude as unmanly and therefore repress the symptoms if they can or assign some other explanation to them, but in boarding schools both boys and girls are homesick and show it.

The two mothers described below show in the genesis of maternal overprotection the difference between the "pure" and the "compulsive" types:

Nancy is at the present time the curse of a young kindergartener, who came to the writer for assistance in dealing with the child. Nancy, aged six, wants all the teacher's attention, all the teacher's time, all the teacher's affection—and she raises merry Cain when she cannot get them. The basis for the behavior was not hard to find. Nancy is the only child of a very young, pretty, rather stupid, socially isolated widow, who has no interest in anything but her small home and her small daughter. The mother's behavior bears out her assertion that she does not miss her husband and rarely even thinks of him. She has an independent income, and her husband's absence seems to mean to her only that the child is entirely hers. The home is meticulously neat. Everything in it is arranged for Nancy's comfort. Mother and daughter have never been separated for more than an hour or two since Nancy's birth. When Mrs. M. gets a permanent, Nancy goes along and gets one also; when Mrs. M. goes to the market, Nancy accompanies her and makes most of the selections. The child has rarely played with other children, partly because the mother had no friends and partly because the two were completely absorbed in each other. So far as could be determined, Mrs. M. is not overcompensating for any underlying guilt and is not an abnormal person. She merely prefers her daughter's company to anyone else's. No compulsion or phobia could be detected. The relationship is normal, but there is too much of it. Mrs. M. is willing to co-operate with the school in helping Nancy learn how to get along with her age-mates. She sees that she has unwittingly spoiled the child and wants to repair the damage. It is probable that she and the teacher can gradually accustom Nancy to being part of the chorus instead of constantly playing the leading role. The writer urged Mrs. M. to join some women's groups—Red Cross, Women's Volunteers, Grey Ladies, or whatever interested her—and to find work that would fill her empty days and would help prevent too great a centering of attention upon Nancy. It would appear that Mrs. M. was showing pure maternal overprotection, largely as a result of having nothing on her mind but her child and nothing to do except to be with her and amuse her.

In contrast to Mrs. M. was another widowed mother of an only child, in this case a boy of seven who had several times wandered away or run away from home—no one was quite sure which. Mrs. B. was emphatic that little Teddy had wandered off because, while he was a darling child, he was not very bright. After

---

[17] A. A. Rose, "The Homes of Homesick Girls," *Journal of Child Psychiatry*, 1:181–189, 1948; "Insecurity Feelings in Adolescent Girls," *Nervous Child*, 4:46–59, 1944; "A Study of Homesickness in College Freshmen," *Journal of Social Psychology*, 26:185–203, 1945; W. H. McCann, "Nostalgia: A Descriptive and Comparative Study," *Journal of Genetic Psychology*, 62:97–104, 1942; S. H. Jameson, "Adjustment Problems of University Girls Because of Parental Patterns," *Sociology and Social Research*, 24:262–271, 1940.

the police had found and returned him for the fifth time, a social worker was sent to the home to make inquiries. She took the precaution of visiting Teddy's school first and there discovered that he had never been absent from school and that he had earned an IQ of 142 on a Binet test that had been given him because his teacher thought he seemed too mature for first-grade work but too insecure for advancement.

The mother seemed on the surface to be quite co-operative, but she soon began to complain about how the child tied her down and prevented her from enjoying life. On the other hand, she was very anxious that he should be a credit to her. Sympathetic questioning brought out the fact that she had not wanted to have children, that she had always been frigid, and that she resented the child's failure to be a girl. After her husband's death, she had had a series of gentlemen friends, one or more of whom would have married her had she not been burdened by a child. She still often had to turn down invitations because there was no one to leave him with.

Warring with her desire to enjoy herself while she was still young was a stern sense of her duty toward Teddy. She had been carefully brought up by a meticulous but emotionally cold mother to believe that any natural mother loved her children, and she could not face the fact that she disliked hers. As a result, she was in conflict with herself and was unable to give the boy any security.

Her attitude toward him swung from one extreme to the other. At times she simply dumped him on a neighbor and went off for an evening with one of her friends, but she was so conscience-stricken by her neglect that for days she smothered Teddy with affection. In general, she overprotected him in a compulsive way as a means of protecting herself against the inner voice of conscience. The results upon the child were much the same, except that he had to face occasional short periods of neglect and open rejection in favor of someone else. He ran away, not during his mother's absence but just after her return. The response seemed composed of a desire to punish his mother for her neglect and of a true revulsion to the gushing affection with which she felt compelled to assuage her own feelings of guilt.

There is less prospect of an early modification of behavior by Mrs. B. than by Mrs. M. of the previous study, because this overprotection of the child is a form of obsession which serves as a buffer between the mother and a conflict of desires. After she has spent a few days in smothering her son with an outpouring of mother love, *she* feels better. Her chief concern is to protect her own ego, whereas Mrs. M. had no such need to protect hers. To judge from the running away to date, Teddy will eventually solve his problems by rejecting his home and leaning upon his friends for security, but in the meantime there are sure to be many periods of difficulty. Incidentally, with each experience of rejection, Mrs. B. is making it harder for Teddy to accept a stepfather, if he should ever have one.

The emotional interrelations within the family are of the utmost importance in affecting a child's development. A series of questions answered by five hundred college girls gives a view of the variation that one can normally expect. The girls testified to the following relationships within their homes:

I. Attitudes of parents to each other: deep love, 29 per cent; strong love, 26; moderate love, 19; little love between them, 12; no love or active dislike, 11; no answer to question, 3

II. Attitudes of parents toward daughters:
A. Mother: loved her dearly, 64 per cent; loved her a good deal, 25; loved her some, 7; loved her little or none, 3; no answer, 1

  B. Father: loved her dearly, 54 per cent; a great deal, 28; some, 8; little or none, 8; no answer, 2

III. Attitudes of daughters toward parents:

  A. Toward mother: loved her greatly, 75 per cent; loved her some, 24; no answer, 1; hated her sometimes, 48 per cent

  B. Toward father: loved him dearly, 59 per cent; loved him more or less, 35; loved him none, 3; no answer, 3; hated him sometimes, 45 per cent

IV. Conflicts between daughters and parents:

  A. With mother: no conflicts, 25 per cent; few conflicts, 41; some, 17; many, 16; no answer, 1

  B. With father: no conflicts, 39 per cent; few, 33; some, 13; many, 13; no answer, 2[18]

This summary may be taken as the normal variation in interpersonal relationships within homes of the upper social and economic levels. The degree of friction and rejection is not excessive.

The relationship between adolescents and their parents is more likely to be good than poor, although the overwhelming amount of literature on maladjustment easily leads to the opposite opinion. Happy, normal, contented families have little news value and are not often investigated, except as "control" groups. Thus, among nearly two thousand high school pupils who were queried about home conditions, nearly two thirds had no criticisms.[19] Possibly they were too immature, too cowed, or too stupid to give any, but it seems more probable that they were happy and well adjusted in their home life. Those who had criticisms—32 per cent of the boys and 39 per cent of the girls—complained that their parents gave them too many instructions, criticized them, nagged them, asked them too many questions, interrupted them, quarreled with them, required them to get home from parties at too early an hour, were stingy with money, embarrassed them by bad manners, or showed such traits as partiality, sarcasm, or worry over nothing. The parents, on the other hand, complained mainly that their adolescent children were disobedient, impertinent, lazy, and untidy.

These 1,878 high school boys and girls were also asked what home discipline they had been given during the week just before they were questioned. About two thirds of them were not punished at all. Of the 313 disciplined boys, 172 (55 per cent) were punished by their mothers and 141 (45 per cent) by their fathers. For the 307 disciplined girls, the corresponding percentages were 80 and 20. The commonest punishment was scolding, but occasionally parents deprived adolescents of some desired liberty. The boys and girls felt that perhaps half the punishments were deserved.

The three basically dangerous disciplinary attitudes on the part of the parents are control by domination, a lack of any discipline beyond that based upon temporary annoyance, and an unpredictable variation between

---

[18] A. Ellis, "Love and Family Relationships of American College Girls," *American Journal of Sociology,* 55:550–558, 1950.

[19] L. H. Stott, "Adolescent Dislikes Regarding Parental Behavior and Their Significance," *Journal of Genetic Psychology,* 57:393–414, 1940, and "Home Punishment of Adolescents," *Journal of Genetic Psychology,* 57:415–428, 1940.

extreme severity and extreme leniency. The first type produces either shy, insecure children or overbold, insecure ones—depending upon how much vitality they have to fight back with—and is certain to precipitate severe storms during adolescence. The second type produces either a child who can manage himself or one that can manage his parents. In the former case, he has acquired independence at the cost of considerable strain. Adolescence in a permissive home is likely to be relatively free of disciplinary difficulties (although there may be other kinds), but in a child-dominated home the emancipation is far from simple, because the adolescent who has dominated his parents practically ever since his birth has never learned much about self-control. The third case, that of alternating control and neglect, combines the disadvantages of both and has the advantages of neither. The adolescent has not been able to develop either security or self-confidence, and his childhood uncertainties pursue him into adolescence, if not longer.

In the "good old days" it was tacitly assumed that in cases of conflict between parents and children, the former were always right. In recent psychological literature it sometimes seems as if they were always wrong! Parent-child—or teacher-pupil—relationships are complex, interdependent, ever-changing social phenomena. Considering the vast differences in objectives, interest, outlooks, and basic needs between adults and children, it is surprising that they get along as well as they do. When there is difficulty, especially between adolescents and their parents or their teachers, both sides would do well to administer to themselves a series of questions concerning their own basic attitudes and customary behavior. A few sample questions appear below:

A. FOR PARENTS (OR TEACHERS):

   3. Is your child exposed to parental bickerings and arguments?
   5. Is your child expected to perform duties around the home suitable to his age?
   7. Does your child receive a weekly allowance and training from you in the wise spending of money?
  10. Do you expect your child to report to you all his activities outside the home?
  14. Is the room in which your child studies reasonably free from distraction?
  22. Do you listen to your child's opinions and try to understand them?

B. FOR ADOLESCENTS:

   1. Do you believe that your parents' advice to you is usually sound and reasonable?
   4. Do you think that you are misunderstood by your parents?
   8. Do you expect your parents to treat you as if you were an experienced adult?
  12. Do you make excessive demands upon your parents for money or attention?
  19. Does your mother constantly have to pick up your belongings and put them away?
  21. Are you as polite to members of your family as you are to outsiders?
  25. Do you honestly try to meet your parents' wishes concerning the time of your return from parties or dates?
  28. If you have a party at home are you and your friends careless of the furniture and inconsiderate of the comfort of other members of your family?[20]

---

[20] From L. D. Crow and A. Crow, *Adjustment Problems from Eighteen to Eighty,* Christopher Publishing House, 1949, 192 pp., pp. 89–90. Used by permission of the Christopher Publishing House.

These questions suggest that adjustments should not be all on one side, but that both parents and adolescents need to respect each other and to consider seriously each other's desires and attitudes.

The social status and prestige of the family has an effect, mostly indirect, upon the children and never more so than during adolescence. In a democracy there is no automatic inheritance of caste, but a democratic society is by no means a classless one. It merely uses bases that are different from those of other societies. The social level of a family determines in large measure the type of friends the children will have, the neighborhood they will live in, the schools they will attend, and the material advantages they will command. Since adolescents are extremely sensitive to social pressures, the well-dressed, poised, sophisticated pupil from a socially prominent family has some advantage over one from a good, solid, middle-class family, and an enormous advantage over the poorly dressed, insecure, uncultured, but intelligent and ambitious pupil from the slums. High school students react to the social system about them by consistently overrating members from the upper classes and consistently underrating those from the lower strata. Since they are only reflecting the culture they see about them, they can hardly be blamed. They do not consider the family background of a candidate for the president of student government as being any more important than adults assume the family background of a candidate for the state legislature to be.

III. Homes for Adolescents and Adolescent Attitudes toward Homes[21]

1. Emancipation from Home Control: One major objective to be reached by the end of the adolescent period is the emancipation of the boy or girl from home control and from intense parental attachment. The first need, then, in a home for those of adolescent age is a wise surrender of the supervision necessary for children and a wise development of adequate self-control in the adolescents themselves.[22] This process presents a difficult task for parents. During the twelve or thirteen years of childhood, successful parents have consistently, if indirectly, controlled the behavior of their children. After adolescence begins, they must learn *not* to control them. Naturally, the shift from complete supervision to complete independence cannot be made overnight, but it must be finished by the time the boy or girl is an adult. Attempts to continue childish dependence result in the production either of adults who act like children or of adults who continue an adolescent revolt against parental pressures into their adult years. Adoles-

---

[21] See also P. M. Symonds, "Essentials of Good Parent-Child Relations," *Teachers College Record,* 50:528–538, 1949.

[22] C. E. Meyers, "Emancipation of Adolescents from Home Control," *Nervous Child,* 5:251–262, 1946; F. McKinney, "Personal Adjustment of College Students as Related to Factors in Their Personal History," *Journal of Applied Psychology,* 23:660–668, 1939.

cents make many mistakes in their efforts to escape continued parental domination, but the only way in which they can learn to manage themselves is to try to manage themselves. During the process, there will be difficulties.

There are numerous ways in which an adolescent may gradually achieve the necessary freedom from parental attachments. For instance, there is the matter of handling money. As children approach adolescence it is highly desirable that their allowance be increased so that they may buy independently a large proportion of what they need. Naturally they will buy some things inappropriate for their age, they will use up their allowance before the week is over, and they will buy things they do not really want. However, they will never learn to spend money wisely and appropriately by any other method than by actually spending it. If parents do not make some such arrangement as that suggested above, they encourage their adolescent sons and daughters to ask or tease for money, exactly as if these near adults were children. Such a situation not only prolongs childishness but may eventually bring on real revolt.

Dan, a young man of twenty-seven, is the despair of his parents because he seems unable to realize the value of money. Dan's family is quite wealthy. His mother has been a semi-invalid ever since his birth—he is the youngest of four children—and she has left his care to nursemaids, governesses, teachers in day schools, counselors in summer camps, and to housemasters and teachers in boarding school and college. During his childhood and early adolescence, whatever he wanted was procured for him. He constantly saw his parents charging things, and as he grew older he simply used their accounts in various stores. At the boarding school he attended the boys were supposed to be given only two dollars a week for spending money, but Dan's parents usually sent him five dollars or ten dollars, although the headmaster asked them several times to observe the limit more conscientiously. When Dan was sixteen, his father opened a cash account for him. There followed four or five years of constant difficulty because Dan overdrew his account almost every month. He did not intend to write bad checks, but he was unwilling to keep track of what he spent. When Dan was nineteen, he went into the Army, where he remained for two years as a private. He was constantly in monetary difficulties of one sort or another, and on a few occasions spent time in the guardhouse because he had failed to pay the bills he owed to the local merchants. Dan was kept in the United States as a clerk because he seemed too irresponsible for active service. When he developed fallen arches the Army was quite willing to let him go back into civilian life. At twenty-five he came into an inheritance from his grandfather. Dan's habits are not in the least wicked but they are expensive, and he has each year spent a good deal more than his income. His capital is therefore decreasing at an alarming rate. The endowment is enough to last, with moderate care, for his entire lifetime, but at the present rate it will be used up by the time he is forty. His parents worry constantly, partly because they do not like to see Dan remain so childish and partly because they feel some concern over leaving him a fourth of their own wealth. The older brother and the two sisters have shown no tendency to irresponsibility. The parents have about decided to put Dan's portion into a trust fund, of which he will be allowed to spend only the income.

In contrast, the writer is reminded of her own training in the proper handling of money. One of her earliest memories is of the Sunday morning ceremony of being given three new, shiny pennies for each week's allowance. One she put at once into the bank, one she put upon the collection plate in church, and the third was hers to spend as she liked. In the course of time, the amount was raised to five cents, then ten, twenty-five, and fifty cents, and eventually to one dollar and two dollars. With each advance, however, the contributions to bank and church were raised correspondingly. Also, as the amount of the allowance increased so did the number of things it was supposed to cover. There were three rigid rules about this allowance: first, no more money was forthcoming when it was gone; on many a cold winter's morning the writer tramped two miles to school through the snow because she had spent her allowance and had nothing left for carfare. The only way of adding to the amount was to earn small sums by doing whatever errands or other work could be found in the neighborhood. Second, there was no adult interference in the spending of the "free" portion of the allowance, nor were the more silly and childish uses of it belittled or commented upon. Third, items that were supposed to come out of the allowance were not forthcoming from any other source. If the writer did not buy toilet soap for herself, she did not borrow someone else's or raid the family supply; she washed with Fels-Naphtha from the kitchen. Such systematic and eminently fair training results in the establishment of habits that last a lifetime.

An adolescent's friends should not be chosen for him by his parents. If he allows such childish treatment of himself, he will never grow up. If he does not allow it, he is soon in open conflict with his parents and may be driven into many unwise friendships by his desire to show them that they cannot dominate him. Naturally, adolescents will choose some undesirable acquaintances. Instead of getting into a panic and attempting to terminate such friendships by sheer authority, the parents should use these incidents as so much education in the judgment of character. No serious harm is likely to come unless the parents, by an uncompromising attitude, drive the adolescent out of his home and force him to meet these undesirable individuals secretly in places where there is little or no protection. As in the case of spending money, a shifting of control from parent to child cannot take place overnight; but take place it must, sooner or later.

Fifteen-year-old Priscilla has recently been the center of a family storm. One evening she had supposedly gone to the neighborhood movie with two other girls. About an hour after she left home her father had an errand at the drugstore, where he was surprised to find his daughter and her friends sitting in a booth with a half-dozen boys of about eighteen. She did not see him, and he had enough sense to leave at once. He then parked his car so that he could watch the door to the drugstore. The three girls eventually came out, hung around outside for awhile, and then went home together, minus their escorts—and unknown to them trailed by Priscilla's father. The next day, after he had had time to discuss matters with his wife and to calm himself somewhat, he talked to his daughter alone. He did not scold her, either for her interest in boys or for her deceit. In fact, he assured her that an interest in boys was normal at her age and that he should be profoundly disturbed if she did not have it. On the other hand, he was sorry that she had so poor a view of her parents that she felt deceit necessary, and he wanted to know why she had not asked the boys home. Priscilla knew she was in the wrong on several counts, and she was completely surprised at her parents' willingness to understand her point of view, and most grateful to her father for not lowering her prestige by ordering her home in front of her friends. She was not at all certain that the boys she had met the night before would want to come to her house, since she admitted they were not really "nice" boys, but she promised in the future not to have clandestine, even though harmless, dates. She was assured that her parents would welcome anyone she brought home—even the drugstore wolves, if they would come. She and her friends might use the front rooms for dancing, but in common courtesy she should always introduce her parents to her friends. After her long talk with her father Priscilla went to see her two girl friends and talked over developments with them. Gradually she persuaded them to try bringing their boy friends openly to her house. Both girls and boys came hesitantly at first, but it was not long before Priscilla's house was a center for normal adolescent social life. In the course of her development Priscilla brought home some curious specimens—both male and female—but her parents never relaxed their graciousness, although they did sometimes point out later certain gaucheries or other failings on the part of the guests. By the time she was eighteen Priscilla was bringing home boys whom her parents liked. The most difficult part of the girl's experimentation in heterosexual-social relationships was over, and she had never been in an unprotected situation.

Insofar as it is possible, parents should allow an adolescent boy or girl to get himself out of his own difficulties. Thus if a boy gets into a row with one of his teachers, he should not be allowed to run away from the situation while his parents see the teacher and patch up the trouble. If a girl buys a dress and then suddenly decides it is not suitable, she should return the dress to the store and do the necessary explaining herself; if the store will not take the dress back, then she should not be given money to buy another. If a girl has offended some acquaintance she may, of course, be given advice about what to do, but she should certainly carry out the advice independently. If a boy insists upon taking an extra course in school, he should not be allowed to drop out of it as soon as he thinks himself overworked. If a boy wants to ask a girl to a dance he should ask her himself—not get some member of the family to do it for him. The first impulse of an adolescent who gets into difficulty is to follow a childish pattern of behavior and run at once to a sympathetic adult who, he hopes, will straighten out matters for him. This behavior cannot, however, be allowed to continue. Most adolescents are not resourceful and therefore need advice, but they should never be allowed to dodge the outcome of their own bad judgment. The sooner they learn that the tail goes with the hide, the better. Parents and teachers both need to learn how to stand aside and let adolescents make mistakes, and then see to it that the youngsters profit by their errors. Protection from experience does not educate; it only prolongs childishness. Life will usually pound in the lesson, if parents will only let it.

Finally, the youngster in the late years of adolescence must be left free to choose his own mate. If since the age of twelve or thirteen there has been reasonable opportunity for social relations with members of the opposite sex, the adolescent has probably already gone through a series of temporary attachments and has educated himself sufficiently to know what he wants. Even though the final attachment leading to marriage may not find favor with the parents the latter are likely to produce only revolt and estrangement by opposition. Parents can prevent many tragedies if, in their children's early years of adolescence, they arrange for an abundance of social contacts for their children. When permanent attachments are made, the time for parental control has already gone by.

2. Parental Adjustment to Society: An adolescent needs a home in which the parents do not pass on to him their own maladjustments. Antagonism between the parents is too obvious a source of difficulty to need special comment. What is not so obvious is the frequent maladjustment of parents to modern social life and ideals. Conflict may be seen in its simplest form in the immigrant home, in which the parents are attempting to maintain their native customs or religion in the face of American social forces. Thus foreign parents who will not accept American standards of behavior, pass on their own maladjustment to the next generation. Parents who insist upon a fundamentalist view of religion force their children into conflict between schoolwork and home beliefs. Parents who will not tolerate smoking, use of cosmetics, or social dancing are almost sure to have maladjusted adolescent children. If boys and girls from such homes insist upon maintaining their parents' standards, they will become ostracized by their own social group; if they secretly abandon parental ideas, they develop a chronic habit of deceit; if they show the proscribed behavior openly, they are forced into revolt against their homes. Many parents who have not formulated a consistent point of view on modern life force their adolescent children to make decisions on exactly the same problems for which they themselves can find no comfortable solution.

These statements do not mean that parents must approve of every passing fad or custom. If, however, they wish to prevent serious difficulties for their children, they must find for themselves some reasonable adjustment to modern life. Otherwise they are certain to pass on their own difficulties in an intensified form. The examples below illustrate parental solutions, good or bad, to their own problems.

One of the writer's friends has a boy who passed his sixteenth birthday last year. Young Edwin has three sisters younger than himself, but he is the only boy in the family. For eight consecutive generations the oldest son has had the same name as his father, and the family has come to have a regard for descent in the male line that is beyond the ordinary degree of concern. As a result, Edwin has been carefully guarded, perhaps more carefully than is good for him. For some months before he became sixteen he was increasingly vocal in his demands that he be allowed to take out a license and drive the family car, just as soon as he was legally able to do so. His parents did not want him to drive until he was twenty-one, but Edwin was most resistive to the postponement. During the week after his sixteenth birthday he took his driving test and secured a license, but his father refused him permission to drive the family car. His mother soon realized that Edwin's prestige among his friends was slipping and that he was developing feelings of inferiority. Gradually she came to feel that the dangers inherent in *not* driving were more important than those that might come from doing so. She therefore prevailed upon her husband to allow Edwin a reasonable use of the car. She still feels faint with apprehension every time she sees Edwin step into the car and buzz off down the street, but she grits her teeth and does not let him know how she worries. This woman is putting herself through a stiff course of self-discipline so that she will not let her own prejudices interfere with her son's normal development. Aside from her concern about Edwin's carrying on the family name, she has no real liking for a car, although she has driven one for years. She grew up in the horse-and-buggy days and has never felt comfortable in an automobile. Edwin grew up in a large city and knows nothing of life without a car. This mother has refused to hand on her own attitudes—based on a rural childhood—to her cosmopolitan and more sophisticated children. As a result of her wisdom Edwin his matured in his entire adjustment to life, has lost the galling sense of inferiority he was developing, and has regained his prestige among his friends.

Mrs. M. and her three children came to America in about the year 1900. She had been carefully brought up in the old country and had absorbed her native customs and manners so thoroughly that they seemed to her the only acceptable mode of life. Mrs. M. liked the material comforts of America, but she never made head or tail of American social life. She guarded her children as if she expected them to be kidnaped at any moment. The two oldest ones, both boys, were eager to become "real Americans" as soon as possible. Gradually they rejected their home and parents and escaped from maternal control.

Helene, the daughter, however, lived at home and docilely absorbed what her mother told her. Since she heard no English in her home and since she spent more time there than elsewhere, her English is still hesitant and accented, although she was only two years old when she arrived in America. Little Helene was not exactly unpopular in school, but she was rejected on account of her queerness—broken speech, foreign clothes, foreign manners, and so on. Her mother had managed so to imbue Helene with her own love of the old country that Helene gladly wore clothes markedly different from those of other people and willingly submitted herself to the regime considered proper by her mother. There was never any revolt of consequence, even when her high school classmates laughed at her gaucheness. In her youth Helen might have attracted masculine attention, since she was a rather good-looking girl, but her appearance was foreign and her ideas about the conduct of escorts were rigid. American boys would not be squeezed into the desired mold, American girls liked the process no better, and most second-generation foreigners were trying to escape similar parental molds and had no intention of handicapping themselves with an un-American wife or friends. Helene lived at home, worked in a nearby library, and never questioned her mother's judgment. Three years ago the mother died suddenly. Helene now finds herself in a difficult position. She has tried living with several different acquaintances, but her ways of doing things and her modes of thought are so alien that no one can be comfortable with her. A year ago she became desperately unhappy because of her extreme isolation and loneliness, and she finally initiated attempts to become Americanized. She now finds that her mother has passed on to her the same problems of Americanization that she herself found insoluble in 1900.

3. Pride in the Home: If an adolescent is not proud of his home, or if he does not find it an attractive place, he will rarely ask his friends to it, no matter how devoted he may be to his parents. Since adolescents set such great store by externals, the needed alterations in the home are usually only on the surface. Often nothing more is required for keeping an adolescent girl at home evenings than to let her remove one or two shabby pieces of furniture from the living room, rearrange the remaining pieces, and buy a new set of curtains. These superficial changes may suffice to make her willing to entertain her friends at home. Naturally, a family unit—composed, for instance, of two parents, one sixteen-year-old, and one child—cannot reorganize itself entirely around adolescent prejudices, but it can take them into account in its thinking, especially since the issues are often relatively insignificant. If they can afford it, wise parents have new wallpaper hung in the dining room and engage a maid to wait on table when the daughter of the family has guests. They make such concessions not to baby her but because they prefer to reserve their authority and influence for more important matters and because they want her to go on loving her home.

Being ashamed of one's home leads to serious maladjustment. The adolescent is upset over what he thinks is unique and unjustifiable treason to those he loves; he also feels he must not accept invitations from his friends because he is not willing to return them. Many a girl who would not ask friends to her home because her father sat around in shirt sleeves has gradually become isolated and friendless. If she is too vigorous to be crushed, she will resort to meeting her friends—especially boys—in drugstores, theaters, restaurants, amusement parks, or other public places that give her no protection. Such a girl may realize the situation perfectly, but she prefers to take a chance of getting into trouble rather than let her friends think her home unrefined.

Pauline is the only daughter of doting and indulgent parents who have devoted their lives to making her a lady and a beauty. In the process they have neglected themselves. They scrimped to buy her pretty clothes, went without adequate food to keep her supplied with luxuries, and borrowed money to send her to a select boarding school. In a way, Pauline still loves them, but she refuses to live at home and has invented a "past" for herself in which shabbily genteel parents play no part. She is determined to marry a wealthy man—and soon, partly in order that she may pay off the parental indebtedness and partly to escape from her home completely. Pauline is not heartless, but she feels she cannot at this stage handicap herself with parents who are commonplace, old before their time, uncouth by her friends' standards, dowdy, and quite unpresentable in her social group. The mother and father are bewildered, worried about their debts, half-sick, tired, and badly hurt. They cannot understand that in educating their daughter far above her normal station in life they have given her desires and ambitions which cut her off from them permanently. It is probable that Pauline will manage somehow to relieve them of their financial difficulties, and in times of crisis she will probably help them, but in their daily life she and they move in orbits that have no point of intersection. Pauline has hours of remorse over her rejection of her father and mother, whose sacrifices on her behalf she appreciates, and she intends to do what she can for them, but she wants to dissociate her present and future from her past. If she marries an understanding man with whom she can be honest, all may yet be well; but if she cannot confide in her husband, Pauline will be forced into a life of deception.

4. Security in the Home: A fourth characteristic of a desirable home for an adolescent is the existence of physical and emotional security in his home, especially during periods of distress. He often goes along for days or even weeks at a time without need of assistance, but when he gets into difficulties he needs a secure and sympathetic home quite as much as a small child does. As his independence increases, he falls back upon his home less and less frequently, but until he has set up a home of his own—and sometimes even later—there are sure to be occasions when he needs emotional security above everything else.

A week or two ago a local newspaper carried an item about a nearly fatal accident to a sixteen-year-old boy. The lad had come home from high school about two in the afternoon and had begun to do some work on his car in the garage. When his younger brother and sister arrived home at three thirty they found the house open but empty. Then they heard the motor running in the garage and ran into it, hoping to persuade their older brother to take them out for a ride. They found him lying unconscious on the floor. The younger boy, aged ten, shut off the motor and ran out of the garage, pulling his sister with him. He told her to take two or three deep breaths of air and to hold them while they went into the garage and pulled their brother's body toward the door, but not to breathe while she was inside. By alternately running in for a minute and then out for air, the children got the boy out. The younger brother then told his sister to telephone the police while he tried to revive his brother by artificial respiration that he had learned in camp, the summer before. The little girl, who was barely eight, then fetched blankets and put a hot water bottle at her big brother's feet, carefully removing his shoes first. The police brought an inhalator and completed the resuscitation that the children had begun. Then they tried to find a responsible adult in the family but none of the children knew where either parent might be. In the meantime a still smaller child, aged six and one half, wandered in, with no very clear account of where she had been since two thirty when she left school. Finally, the police officer sent the adolescent boy to the nearest hospital and ordered a policewoman to come and stay in the house until the parents came home. The mother telephoned about six thirty to tell the children to eat their dinner—not that any had been prepared—because she would not be home until later, and was told by the policewoman to return at once. Evidently she got in touch with her husband, since they presently came in together. Each parent was asked to tell where he or she had been. The mother had left the house about ten in the morning, had gone shopping, had had lunch with a friend, had had her hair waved, had gone to a bridge club, and subsequently had gone home with one of the women there. The father had taken a "prospect" out to lunch and then played a round of golf with him; by that time it seemed hardly worth while to go back to the office, so he sat around the club, wrote a couple of letters, had some cocktails, and was just ordering dinner when his wife called him. In the meantime the three younger children had come in by themselves for lunch, which had been left for them, had gone back to school, and had come home again. Neither parent regarded the arrangement of the day as at all unusual. The adolescent son of this family did not even have physical security in his own home. He lived because a ten-year-old boy kept his head and knew what to do. It presently developed that the older boy did not have other kinds of protection, either. He was tuning up his car before taking a notoriously "bad" girl out to a roadhouse, where he had already twice spent most of a night with her without even being missed at home. These facts came to the surface when he wanted the hospital authorities to notify the girl that he could not keep his appointment with her.

This family had failed in its first function of providing safety for its offspring. The youngest child had taken three hours to get home from a school two blocks away—no one ever discovered where she had been—and the oldest child was over-come by carbon monoxide while preparing for an assignation. Neither parent had more than casual daily contact with the children and did not know them well enough to inspire their confidences.

5. Harmony in the Home: The desirability of harmonious interrela-tionships among members of a family group is too obvious to require dis-cussion. Two other points are, however, not so clear: the frequency of such dissensions as occur, and their nature.

Responses from several thousand high school boys and girls indicate that in approximately one third of the homes there is some degree of con-flict between children and parents.[23] In a group of 259 college sophomores, all men, who were selected as being normal in health, academic progress, and social adjustment, the majority admitted some degree of friction with their parents.[24] For 17 per cent of these students, the conflict was acute. The majority of the quarrels and arguments for both groups centered around (1) economic matters—size of allowances, part-time jobs in order to earn more money, support of students while in school; (2) social mat-ters—attendance at dances or movies, selection of friends, selection of clothes, accounting for how time has been spent, discipline, determination of how late the adolescents may stay out, or proper chaperonage; and (3) purely personal matters—the refusal of the father to wear his coat when there is company, the mother's irritability and bad temper, parental insistence that the children speak some other language than English at home, and so on through an infinitude of conflicts over personal traits, habits, and reactions ranging all the way from chronic alcoholism on the part of a parent to the dirt under Johnny's fingernails. Some conflicts are sure to arise whenever people live together, and the number of chances for friction increases if the individuals are of varying ages. No home is without problems and conflicts, but some homes are far more successful than others in reaching a sensible basis for daily living.

Jack is a frightened rabbit of a lad, who goes in constant fear of his father. The latter is strongly opposed to Jack's attendance in college and is not hesitant to say so. Jack is next to the youngest in a family of fourteen, of whom only the three youngest remain at home. The father has a job at the moment as a clerk in a neighborhood grocery, but he would like to "retire" on the wages Jack could earn if he were not in school. As each child in the family has reached sixteen, he or she has taken out working papers, gotten a job, and turned in most of the earn-ings for family use. As each child married, the next in order took up the burden. One older sister finished high school, but Jack is the first of the children to attempt a college education. He lives at home, partly to save money and partly because of the housing shortage. In addition to doing his college work, he has to earn every cent he spends. It is therefore necessary for him to plan on at least five years in college, perhaps six. His father is antagonistic, sarcastic, and domineering. He is unfortunately possessed of a low form of wit, by means of which he can overwhelm Jack with self-consciousness and embarrassment. Jack avoids the family meals by

[23] H. H. Punke, "High School Youth and Family Quarrels," *School and Society,* 58:507–511, 1943.
[24] C. W. Heath and L. W. Gregory, "Problems of Normal College Students and Their Families," *School and Society,* 63:355–358, 1946.

eating at odd moments, preferably when his father is out, and he tries to stay away from home as much as he can. Thus far, Jack has managed to hold out against pressure, but at a cost to both health and personality. He is badly underweight, his digestion is not good, he is highly nervous, anxious, and apprehensive, he hates his father, and he seems constantly on the point of tears. Somewhere behind the frightened exterior there lies a gallant soul, but one wonders if it can take much more of the savage pressure to which the boy is constantly subjected.

6. Identification in the Home: As youngsters grow into adolescence the parents should voluntarily change the nature of the relationship between themselves and their children. Parents can become friends of their adolescent children, a friend being defined as a person who is around when needed and not underfoot when not wanted. An adult cannot have such a relationship with a small child; one can be friendly, but not a friend. The adolescent, however, should emerge from the childhood pattern and should gradually enter the relationship of older and younger friends. This change will not often be made unless the parents take the initiative.

Whether they intend to or not, parents serve as models, good or bad. From them and their attitudes toward each other an adolescent gets many of his notions about home life and marriage. Adolescents are already beginning to think about a home of their own. They can have no greater help in developing desirable attitudes than a good model of happy marriage on the part of their parents.

Duncan Smith is a high school sophomore. He has a sister who is just through college and a foster brother in the eighth grade. His mother is dead. The three adults in his home are his father, his father's younger sister—who has lived with the family since Duncan's birth—and a faithful Negro servant of more than middle age. This somewhat heterogeneous group has been welded into a real family by the efforts of the aunt, nicknamed "Dodo" by the children. She is still a young-looking woman of whose appearance Duncan is very proud. The father is a lawyer by profession and an educated gentleman by preference.

Duncan's sister, Marie, graduated from college last year and is now at home. She has a boy friend whom she hopes some day to marry; in the meantime she is learning how to run a house, cook, plan meals, and make simple repairs. She and Dodo have a session every morning while they divide the day's work between them. Marie admires her aunt's gay disposition, her good looks, and her efficiency. The girl's ambition at the moment is to become as capable as her aunt, to have her fiancé develop into as nice a man as her father, and to have a home in which her children can have as much fun as she has always had in hers. She threatens to take white-haired Nannie, the maid, with her. In short, she wants her home of the future to duplicate her home of the past.

Duncan studies at home most evenings, going to his father whenever he needs help. During the past summer he and his father visited about a dozen colleges, staying at each two or three days, so that he might be better able to decide which he prefers to attend. He and his father play tennis together in the father-and-son doubles in the summer and bowl together in the winter. He goes out with various girls, but says he won't fall in love till he finds a girl who is as pretty as Dodo and can cook as well.

The family have many joint enterprises and amusements. On a stormy evening Mr. Smith reads aloud, Dodo darns socks, Marie hems dish towels for her hope chest, Duncan whittles wooden buttons and brooches that he will later use for

Christmas presents, and Nannie goes to sleep in a corner. On Sunday mornings there is a great stir all over the house; Nannie makes popovers for breakfast, Marie and Duncan pull the linen off the beds and make them up fresh, and at ten thirty the family is ready to set out en masse for church, where Duncan and Mr. Smith both sing in the choir.

One day last summer, when Marie had had an argument with her boy friend, Dodo told her about her own most serious love affair that had gone on the rocks after a quarrel. The two talked more as if they were older and younger sister than niece and aunt. With similar frankness and companionship Mr. Smith has recently talked over some of his cases with Duncan.

At the beginning of every month the family makes a joint budget. Mr. Smith announces what funds are available, Dodo presents the house accounts of the previous month, everyone puts in bids for the things he or she needs or wants, there is much discussion, and eventually a budget emerges. One small sum is always set aside for joint expenditures, such as a family visit to the movies. The money is given in turn to each child, who keeps an account on what Dodo calls the "swindle sheet" and reports his expenditures at the beginning of the next month.

As a result of all these activities, Duncan and Marie are reaching maturity with a deep love for all three of the adults in their home and a sincere admiration for each. To be sure, Duncan refers to his father merely as a "good egg." Marie says her aunt is "crazy but O.K.," and all the children call Nannie "Gold Dust" when she is not around, but the careless speech does not fool anyone but themselves. All three are modeling themselves upon the adults they know best, with whom their relation is now more nearly that of one friend to another than that of a child toward a parent.

7. Interest in the Home: A home should be as interesting, exciting, and stimulating as possible so that adolescents will feel a desire to stay there during a portion of their leisure time. If hours spent at home mean only an endless round of chores and the ever-present likelihood of being scolded or criticized, adolescent boys and girls will remain there only long enough to eat, bathe, dress, and sleep. Of course, as a place of entertainment, homes cannot compete with such commercialized offerings as the movies or the amusement parks, but they can furnish the adolescent with interesting things to do or think about, and with a background for an abundant social life. A radio or record player, a clearable space for dancing, simple equipment such as a ping-pong table, access to the larder, privacy, and a relaxed atmosphere will do much to make home an interesting and exciting place in which adolescents want to stay because they enjoy themselves. Parents may have to help their sons and daughters with suggestions, but they should rarely try to take part in the activities.

The Jones family lives in a large, one-story, rambling house. There are four children—two boys, ages 16 and 15, one daughter, aged 13, and an adopted daughter, aged 14. All four children are just entering adolescence. Up until a year ago each child had his or her own room, but as they approached adolescence and began to go out to movies and parties, the parents suggested that the two girls should share a bedroom and the two boys another, while each pair fitted up one room for social purposes. A small fund was made available to them, and while the parents made some suggestions, the expenditure was determined mainly by the children. The boys first bought a secondhand pool table, the girls a ping-pong table and a small radio. Later on, the boys bought a number of small items—cards, an ancient slot machine, a basketball, and a hoop which they affixed to the wall. The girls took out sub-scriptions to two magazines, acquired a number of puzzles, and got some paints. Both boys and girls made some of the furniture for their rooms. They are also responsible for keeping the rooms in order. All four of them are permitted to play anything that is quiet even on weekday evenings, if they feel they do not need the time for study. The rooms are usually occupied by a number of youngsters Friday evenings, Saturday, and Sunday afternoons. There is a fireplace in the girls' room, where they cook wieners and toast marshmallows. The ping-pong table folds up when not in use, and the youngsters have a space for dancing. In the course of the past two years they have accumulated quite a number of books and magazines, and it often happens that they and their friends spend hours together reading, sometimes aloud. They make Christmas presents, May baskets, Easter gifts, and so on, in these rooms, and they have a number of collections—stamps, rocks, miniature animals, and the like. They have recently acquired a Victrola and some records, to which they listen avidly. Since these two rooms have been available for their use, the children have made their home the center of their social activities, simply because they can have more fun there than they are likely to have in any other place. They still go to the movies sometimes, to school dances, or to parties at their friends' houses, but home is the most interesting place they know.

A desirable home for adolescent boys and girls has thus seven main characteristics: first, it allows its children to grow up; second, it does not pass on its own maladjustments; third, it is willing to modify externals; fourth, it provides a haven of security at all times of stress; fifth, it keeps a harmonious balance among its members; sixth, it serves as a model; and seventh, it is a stimulating and interesting place.

8. Application of Principles to the Classroom: A teacher who wishes to maintain a classroom in which adolescents will feel comfortable can do no better than to imitate the characteristics of a good home. She can encourage her pupils to be just as independent of her as possible. She can keep her own troubles and problems to herself. She can let her students decorate the class-room from time to time according to their own taste. She can keep on good terms with her pupils and be available for help in times of stress. She can develop her own maturity so that she will appear to adolescent boys and girls as a model to be admired. And she can make her work so interesting and ex-citing that the pupils want to stay in her classes as long as they can. The good home and the good classroom are thus similar in their fundamental psychological characteristics.

Another writer on adolescence has expressed similar convictions about homes and schools, characterizing those best adapted to the needs of youth in the following way:

Homes in which interesting things happen and in which the co-operation of the children is welcomed. Parents who have attained some measure of emotional maturity and some awareness of their own philosophy of living. A corner for some treasured possessions and a certain measure of responsibility for some part of the common welfare. An atmosphere of courtesy and consideration. The security which follows upon the consciousness of family affection. These are the requirements of youth in the home.

Schools in which meaningful activities occur and in which the willing participa-tion of the pupils is encouraged. Teachers who are themselves emotionally and socially mature. A measure of acceptance and recognition by an admired group. Opportunities for adventures in learning and a chance to contribute deliberately to the corporate life of the whole. These are the needs of youth in the school.[25]

9. Typical Behavior of Unemancipated Adolescents: The adolescent who is overdependent upon his home may show his childishness in either of two ways. He may constantly seek the advice and help of others because he has had no practice in meeting situations alone. In the schoolroom he is frequently in need of extra help, not because he does not understand what he is to do, but because he has no independence in doing it. He often cannot follow printed directions because he is so dependent upon personal relationships. If he is given a choice of several assignments, he cannot make up his mind which he prefers. If a decision must be made at once, he asks for a special dispensation until the next day so that he can consult his parents. He usually cannot study without supervision; at home his parents help him with his work as if he were a child, and he finds independent work too lonely. He attaches himself emotionally to almost any sympathetic adult. He cannot submerge himself in a group because he is dependent for his emotional satisfaction upon being the center of attention. He constantly makes ridiculous judgments if he is forced into thinking for himself. He frequently asks privately for some special arrangement: he wants some other partner in the laboratory, he prefers some other work to that assigned, he asks permission to hand in work a day late, he wants to have his seat moved nearer to the window, he keeps library books out when others need them, he wants to be excused from class early, he wants a special arrangement of classes; if he gets into trouble, he begs his teachers to excuse him from punishment. In brief, he expects exactly the indulgent treatment one can expect from older people to whom one is emotionally attached. Every high school teacher has a few such pupils in her classes. They are emotional and social children who are so dependent upon their parents that they transfer this same attitude to their teachers. This simple type of childish adolescent is not difficult to recognize. A description of one appears below:

Foster is a very bright boy of sixteen and a Grade A pest in the classroom. Often he is mischievous and talkative, and much of the time he is unable to guide his own activities. After the other pupils have opened their history books to page 98 and have started to read their assignment, Foster is out of his seat asking an acquaintance where he is supposed to begin. Three minutes later he finds an unfamiliar word and asks another friend what it means; if sent to the dictionary, he is again in trouble because he either cannot find the word or will not read the definition carefully enough to understand it. He wants someone to tell him the meaning. At the end of a fifty-minute period he has perhaps read three pages, has interrupted other pupils several times, has been to the teacher with two or three questions, has been out of the room once or twice, and has chatted with friends en route during each pilgrimage. In contrast to his inefficient work during a study

---

[25] C. M. Fleming, *Adolescence: Its Social Psychology,* International Universities Press, 1948, p. 243. Used by permission of the publisher.

period in school, his homework is always well prepared. Every evening his parents go over his lessons with him; they explain obscure passages—often incorrectly; they read an entire textbook through before they let him begin it, in order to decide whether or not it is suitable for him. If they think it is not, they call upon the teacher who has assigned it and complain. They—and Foster—then pester the teacher until she either substitutes a book the parents like better or precipitates an open break with them. Two or three such breaks have occurred, and the parents have called upon and written letters to the school principal, the supervisors of the teacher concerned, and the superintendent of schools. A few teachers have solved their own problem by giving Foster the special attention he craves; if he is placed in a front seat and allowed to interrupt the teacher twenty times a day he does good work and is well behaved. This treatment does not in the least solve Foster's problems, however, because the teacher is, in self-defense, strengthening the very reactions that are already too strong. The situation is a difficult one. If a teacher insists upon trying to push Foster into greater independence, she upsets the development of other members of the class and decreases the efficiency of her instruction; if she pampers him, she not only prevents him from growing up but uses time and energy that should be given to others in the group. Some teachers have tried talking with Foster and explaining to him how childish he is. This method of approach is successful for a few hours, but Foster soon relapses into his earlier attitudes. If one had only the boy to deal with, more progress could probably be made, because he is intelligent and would sooner or later grasp the situation well enough to make efforts of his own to behave in a more mature way, but each step in the right direction during school hours is offset by the smothering attention given to him at home. Until Foster gets old enough to resent parental control, he is likely to remain childish and troublesome.

The second type is more complicated. Although an adolescent is deeply attached to his home and dependent upon it, he may at the same time desire profoundly to be independent, but he does not know how to free himself from home domination by ordinary methods. To cover up his social and emotional attachment to his home and parents, he makes numerous and dramatic overcompensations. This type of unemancipated adolescent is seen in the boy who gets drunk, uses profanity, or has illicit sexual relations as a means of demonstrating his independence to the world. When an over-attached adolescent sets out to break the bonds between himself or herself and the family by unwise and violent methods, it is generally because all ordinary methods have failed. A boy or girl rarely succeeds in growing up by such violent means; all he does is to build up a habit of childish resentment. The adolescent who is free to buy his own clothes (provided he keeps within his allowance), free to bring anyone he will to his own home, free—within reasonable degrees of guidance—to choose his own work, and free to plan his own time, has adequate opportunity for self-assertion without going to undesirable extremes. The boy who gets into serious difficulties to prove he is grown up is no more independent of his home than the boy who cannot make up his mind which book to read until he has asked his mother for her advice. One is positively conditioned, the other negatively; neither is mature, and neither can regard his home objectively.

One type of overcompensation on the part of an immature boy with deep emotional reactions to his home situation is described below:

Roy is now nearly eighteen years old and a senior in high school. He matured rather late and has been interested in girls only during the past year and a half. His record shows no clashes with school authorities and no need for discipline until recently.

Roy is the youngest of a family of three boys. His two older brothers attended the same schools and made satisfactory records. One of them was a class officer and a member of several school teams. Both of the older boys had fallen in love when they were eighteen or nineteen with girls whom their parents did not like. There had been a good deal of parental interference, and in the end one son had left home for good, although he did not marry the girl in whom he was at the time interested, and the other had eloped after a bitter quarrel with his parents. There is thus evidence that the children of this family were not encouraged to become mature but had to assert themselves against parental authority and make a break with the family if they were to grow up. The father and mother had evidently not learned much from their experiences with their two older sons. They had merely tightened the control over the youngest one, lest he too should leave them. They did everything they could to keep him a little boy for as long as possible. His delayed maturity aided them in their efforts, so that the dreaded interest in girls, dancing, and parties did not arise until Roy's last year of high school, after most of his friends had already established themselves as more or less independent individuals in their family groups.

At present Roy is going through a girl-crazy stage that should have taken place about two years earlier, when his friends were suffering from a similar afflic-tion. At sixteen he would have been more easily controlled than now. This phase is presumably only temporary, but his parents are frightened by it. It does not interfere greatly with his schoolwork, although his marks are somewhat lower than they were during the first three years of high school. The boy's worst symptoms of maladjustment are shown in his relation to his age-mates and his parents. The former, who have themselves recently emerged from the same silly stage, find him endlessly amusing. They are never tired of poking fun at him, telling him dirty stories, and giving him false advice about how to act with a girl. The rough initiation has produced a good deal of confusion in Roy's mind and has made him uncertain about his social status. He is, however, overcoming this difficulty and will probably re-establish himself among his peers. The situation with his parents is more serious.

As soon as Roy began to have appointments in the evening—before his interest in girls developed—he was most carefully watched. He had to tell in advance just where and with whom he was going, and he was required to be home at a given hour, the time being set so that he would not have any moments of leisure after completing whatever business took him out of the house after dark. The restric-tions became even stricter after he started to go out with girls. Usually the dead-line for his return was earlier than the hour at which the girl he was with had to get home. Wholly aside from his desire to be with a girl as long as possible, he could hardly be expected to ditch her and leave her to go home alone merely because his parents were stricter than hers. Roy remembers how his mother suf-fered when his older brothers were going through the period of emancipation from home, and he does not want to cause her further grief. On the other hand, he cannot keep his self-respect or the respect of his age-mates unless he insists upon having greater independence than his parents wish to give him.

Up until about a month ago Roy had tried to be reasonable, but finally he ran out of patience and began to be resistive and assertive. He hardly speaks to his parents, goes out every night, stays out as late as he wants to, and refuses to listen to their remonstrances. Recently he has told them that he will leave home if they do not stop their constant criticisms. To be sure, Roy is reacting on a childish level, but this is to be expected since he has never had a chance to be anything else.

His parents are not willing that he should grow up and become a man. They realize that growing up is a dangerous business, but they do not see that failure to do so is even more dangerous. In the meantime they are forcing their son to react violently against them because they cannot bring themselves to release him from supervision in a normal manner. At present Roy is overcompensating for his earlier submission and for his earlier lack of experience with girls. He actually feels insecure, inferior, and unhappy, but he talks loudly, boasts of his independence from home control, uses a good deal of profanity, and tries desperately to convince everyone that he is now a grown man.

These two types of adolescent appear occasionally in any teacher's class. The conditions cannot be remedied quickly. A "cure" requires both time and a reasonable degree of co-operation from the home. The chief thing a teacher can do for such an adolescent is to explain to him the nature of his difficulties. Once he understands what the matter is, he is often able to work out his own adjustment, either by obtaining greater freedom from his parents or by conforming superficially to their demands until he is old enough to leave home. An individual teacher can do little toward modifying a home situation, but much can be done through a vigorous parent-teacher association by the open discussion of adolescent problems of adjustment. Such an organization permits an impersonal approach and does not imply the criticism which is always inherent in dealing with a single family. The teacher's chief individual efforts, however, are generally centered upon showing an adolescent how he can adjust himself to things as they are.

IV. Summary

A student's home is extremely important in molding his attitudes toward life. In the best type of home, an adolescent is allowed to grow up and take responsibility for himself as soon as he is able to do so. His parents do not pass on to him their own unsolved problems. The boy or girl is proud of his home and feels secure in its harmony. By the end of adolescence the parents in a good home have become friends with, rather than the controllers of, their children. If homes are inadequate in these respects, an adolescent either fails to grow out of his emotional and social childhood, or else he is driven into open revolt. Neither situation is desirable, but the latter is healthier than the former.

REFERENCES FOR FURTHER READING

BOOKS
1. Anderson, *The Psychology of Development and Personal Adjustment*, Chaps. 13, 22, 25.
2. Anshen, R. N., *The Family: Its Function and Destiny*, Harper & Brothers, 1949, 443 pp. (Chaps. 1, 9–12, 18.)
3. Blos, *The Adolescent Personality*, Pt. II, Chap. 6.
4. Bossard, J. H. S., and E. S. Boll, *Family Situations: An Introduction to the*

Study of Child Behavior, University of Pennsylvania Press, 1943, 265 pp. (Chaps. 3, 4, 6, 7.)

5. Bossard, J. H. S., and E. S. Boll, *Ritual in Family Living,* University of Pennsylvania Press, 1950, 228 pp. (Chaps. 2–5, 8–9.)
6. Breckenridge and Vincent, *Child Psychology,* Chap. 5.
7. Burgess, E. W., and H. J. Locke, *The Family,* American Book Company, 1945, 800 pp. (Chaps. 16–22.)
8. Dimock, *Rediscovering the Adolescent,* Chap. 7.
9. Fields, Goldberg, and Kilander, *Youth Grows into Adulthood,* Chap. 7.
10. Fleege, *Self-Revelation of the Adolescent Boy,* Chaps. 3–6.
11. Fleming, *Adolescence: Its Social Psychology,* Chaps. 6–8.
12. Garrison, *Psychology of Adolescence,* Chap. 11.
13. Groves, E. R., E. L. Skinner, and S. J. Swenson, *The Family and Its Relationships,* J. B. Lippincott Company, 1948, 582 pp. (Chaps. 4, 5, 10–12.)
14. Kuhlen, *Psychology of Adolescent Development,* Chap. 12.
15. Landis, *Adolescence and Youth,* Chap. 12.
16. Levy, D. M., *Maternal Overprotection,* Columbia University Press, 1943, 417 pp. (Chaps. 3–6, 8, and any three cases from the appendix.)
17. Malm and Jamison, *Adolescence,* Chap. 12.
18. Sadler, *Adolescence Problems,* Chaps. 8–12.
19. Strecker, E. A., *Their Mothers' Sons: A Psychologist Examines an American Problem,* J. B. Lippincott Company, 1946, 220 pp. (Chaps. 2–6, 12, 16, 17.)
20. Symonds, P. M., *The Psychology of Parent-Child Relationships,* Appleton-Century-Crofts, Inc., 1939, 228 pp. (Chaps. 2, 3.)
21. Taba and Elkins, *With Focus on Human Relations,* Chap. 3.
22. Taylor, K. W., *Do Adolescents Need Parents?* Appleton-Century-Crofts, Inc., 1939, 380 pp. (Chaps. 2, 3, 5.)
23. Thorpe, *The Psychology of Mental Health,* Chap. 15.
24. Tiegs and Katz, *Mental Hygiene in Education,* Chap. 11.
25. Wallin, *Minor Mental Maladjustments in Normal People,* Chap. 13.
26. Wile, *The Challenge of Adolescence,* Chap. 10.
27. Zachry and Lighty, *Emotion and Conduct in Adolescence,* Chaps. 8, 9.

MONOGRAPHS, BULLETINS, PROCEEDINGS, YEARBOOKS, ARTICLES

A. *Various Elements of Family Life and Interrelationships*

1. Anderson, J. P., "A Study of the Relationships between Certain Aspects of Parental Behavior and the Attitudes and Behavior of Junior High School Pupils," *Teachers College Contributions to Education,* No. 809, 1940, 196 pp.
2. Baldwin, A. L., J. Kalhorn, F. H. Breeze, "Patterns of Parental Behavior," *Psychological Monographs,* Vol. LVIII, No. 3, 1945, 75 pp.
3. Bossard, J. H. S., and E. S. Boll, "Ritual in Family Living," *American Sociological Review,* 14:463–469, 1949.
4. Ellis, A., "Love and Family Relationships of American College Girls," *American Journal of Sociology,* 55:550–558, 1950.
5. Ellis, A., "Some Significant Correlates of Love and Family Attitudes and Behavior," *Journal of Social Psychology,* 30:3–16, 1949.
6. Gardner, L. P., "An Analysis of Children's Attitudes toward Fathers," *Journal of Genetic Psychology,* 70:3–28, 1947.
7. Gordon, L. P., "A Survey of the Attitudes and Activities of Fathers," *Journal of Genetic Psychology,* 63:15–53, 1943.
8. Ingersoll, H. L., "A Study of Transmission of Authority Patterns in the Family," *Genetic Psychology Monographs,* XXXVIII, No. 5 (1948), 225–302.
9. Radke, M. J., "The Relation of Parental Authority to Children's Behavior

and Attitudes," *University of Minnesota Institute of Child Welfare Monographs,* No. 22, 1946, 123 pp.

10. Rice, O. R., "Ethical Elements in the Etiology of the Unstable Family," *Journal of Clinical Pastoral Work,* 2:53–60, 1949.

11. Symonds, P. M., "Essentials of Good Parent-Child Relations," *Teachers College Record,* 50:528–538, 1949.

B. *Conflicts and Difficulties in the Home*

1. Bakwin, H., "Pure Maternal Overprotection," *Journal of Pediatrics,* 33:788–795, 1948.

2. Block, V. L., "Conflicts of Adolescents with Their Mothers," *Journal of Abnormal and Social Psychology,* 32:193–206.

3. Field, N., "Maternal Attitudes Found in 25 Cases of Children with Primary Behavior Disorders," *American Journal of Orthopsychiatry,* 10:295–312, 1940.

4. Lewis, W. D., "Influence of Parental Attitudes on Children's Personal Inventory Scores," *Journal of Genetic Psychology,* 67:195–201, 1945.

5. Mueller, D. D., "Paternal Domination: Its Influence on Child Guidance Results," *Smith College Studies in Social Work,* 15:184–215, 1945.

6. Punke, H. H., "High School Youth and Family Quarrels," *School and Society,* 58:507–511, 1943.

7. Symonds, P. M., "A Study of Parental Acceptance and Rejection," *American Journal of Orthopsychiatry,* 8:679–688, 1938.

8. Torrance, P., "The Influence of Broken Homes on Adolescent Adjustment," *Journal of Educational Sociology,* 18:359–364, 1945.

9. Wolberg, L. R., "The Character Structure of the Rejected Child," *Nervous Child,* 3:74–88, 1944.

C. *Emancipation from Home*

1. Frank, L. K., "The Adolescent and the Family," *Forty-third Yearbook of the National Society for the Study of Education,* 1944, Pt. II, pp. 240–254.

2. Hacker, E. J., and E. R. Geleerd, "Freedom and Authority in Adolescence," *American Journal of Orthopsychiatry,* 15:621–630, 1945.

3. Meyers, C. E., "Emancipation of Adolescents from Home Control," *Nervous Child,* 5:251–262, 1946.

4. Sherman, A. W., "Emancipation Status of College Students," *Journal of Genetic Psychology,* 68:151–180, 1946.

D. *Discipline*

1. Baruch, D. W., "How to Discipline Your Child," *Public Affairs Pamphlets,* No. 154, 1949, 31 pp.

2. Hymes, J. L., *Discipline,* Bureau of Publications of Teachers College, Columbia University, 1949, 46 pp.

3. Stott, L. H., "Home Punishment of Adolescents," *Journal of Genetic Psychology,* 57:415–428, 1940.

E. *Homesickness*

1. Heath, C. W., and L. W. Gregory, "Problems of Normal College Students and Their Families," *School and Society,* 63:355–358, 1946.

2. Jameson, S. H., "Adjustment Problems of University Girls Because of Parental Patterns," *Sociology and Social Research,* 24:262–271, 1940.

3. McCann, W. H., "Nostalgia: A Descriptive and Comparative Study," *Journal of Genetic Psychology,* 62:97–104, 1942.

4. McKinney, F., "Personal Adjustment of College Students as Related to Fac-

tors in Their Personal History," *Journal of Applied Psychology*, 23:660–668, 1939.
5. Rose, A. A., "The Homes of Homesick Girls," *Journal of Child Psychiatry*, 1:181–189, 1948.
6. Rose, A. A., "A Study of Homesickness in College Freshmen," *Journal of Social Psychology*, 26:185–203, 1945.

CHAPTER ELEVEN

Delinquency

Attitudes toward the cause of delinquency and crime have shown an interesting development. When efforts were first made to understand the criminal, the assumption was that his abnormality was basically physical. /1/ That is, he was a "type." Measurements of hundreds of criminals soon exploded this idea, as far as the scientist was concerned—although the general public is still wedded to the notion that a criminal looks like Neanderthal man—since they show a normal human variation, and nothing more. The next assumption was that delinquents and criminals were mental de- /2/ fectives. This idea did not hold up under scientific investigation. Use of mental tests has proved that low intelligence is at most only a contributing cause in perhaps a quarter of the cases. Attention was then turned from the man to his surroundings, on the assumption that a child became first a delinquent and later a criminal because of his environment. This idea /3/ seemed the more likely since it had long been known that some areas of any city produced more delinquents than others. Under the sway of the environmental theory, investigators analyzed the families, homes, friends, schools, neighborhoods, and districts from which delinquents came. They found a great deal that was amiss, and for two or three decades social scientists thought they had the answer to the age-old problem of wickedness: if there were no congested, filthy slums, there would be no crime. However, the environmental theory alone could never explain why one of two brothers who grew up in the same family, in the same tenement, in the same dirty street became a criminal while the other did not. Nor did it account for the delinquent who emerged from an excellent home situated in a good neighborhood. The fact that delinquents come in larger numbers from some areas than from others suggests that the environmental theory contains some elements of truth. The latest assumption is that the delinquent has a person- /4/ ality with a different structure from that of his brothers and sisters and that he derives his characteristic attitudes from the "different" treatment he receives, first in his home and later in his school and neighborhood. This theory is probably not adequate alone to explain all cases, but it is strong precisely where the environmental theory is weak. If one accepts either or both the current theories, one has to agree that delinquents are made, not born.

It is the writer's guess that emotional insecurity, emotional retardation, emotional distortion, and social inadequacies are of utmost importance

346

in the making of a criminal, but that social deprivations, bad examples, cultural conflict, and an insufficient number of normal outlets for fundamental drives also play a vital part. It is probable that in some cases one element is the more significant and in some cases, the other. Certainly, the slum child has one strike already called on him—but one strike does no harm provided there are no more.

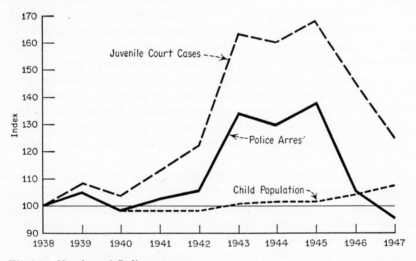

Fig. 76. *Number of Delinquents*

Sources: Police arrest data from section on fingerprint records in Uniform Crime Reports (annual bulletins) issued by Federal Bureau of Investigation.
  Juvenile court cases from data reported by the U. S. Children's Bureau on delinquency cases disposed of by 76 large urban juvenile courts participating in the federal-state juvenile court reporting system from 1938 to 1947 inclusive.
  Child population under 18 years of age for 1940–1944 estimated by Bureau of the Census. Data for 1945–1947 estimated by the U. S. Children's Bureau.

From E. E. Schwartz, "Statistics of Juvenile Delinquency in the United States," *Annals of the American Academy of Political and Social Science,* 261:11, 1949. Used by permission of the publisher.

I. The Number of Delinquents

It is difficult to find out just how many children are delinquents, partly because records are not uniform from place to place and partly because only those children who are arrested are included in the counts. The small boy who steals food out of other children's lunch boxes, is caught, and subsequently punished by his father is not included in any set of figures, and it is anyone's guess how many such cases there are. The official situation is, however, bad enough, as is shown in Figure 76 on this page. The lowest curve gives the increase in the entire population of children and adolescents under eighteen years of age. The number in 1938 was taken as a basis. In 1947 the child population was 107 per cent of that of 1938. Figures from juvenile court cases in seventy-six large, urban, juvenile courts are plotted in the uppermost curve, which was also constructed by using the number of delinquents in 1938 as a base. During and immediately after the war, the number of delinquents increased until it was 160 to 170 per cent of what it had been five to eight years earlier. This phenomenon would seem to support the environmental theory. The median age of these juvenile offenders was fifteen. On the basis of adequate returns from seventy-six districts, it was estimated that there were in the United States at least 275,000 delinquent children and adolescents. This number works out to 6 in every 1,000 under eighteen years of age. Another study[1] of delinquency is confined to results within a single state. In 1946, there were 9,434 juvenile court cases, or 2 children in every 100. In the years since the war the number of delinquents has decreased, but it is not yet as low as it was in 1938. In 1952, according to the Federal Bureau of Investigation, there was an increase in juvenile delinquency over 1951, thus reversing the previous downward trend. In 1950, 14.4 per cent of all arrests were of persons under twenty-one years of age.[2]

In all studies boys greatly outnumbered girls. Of all the children and adolescents included in the first study above, 74 per cent were boys, and in the second, 85 per cent. The proportion of delinquent boys to delinquent girls has, however, changed appreciably during the years since 1935, as shown for the entire country in Figure 77 on page 349. Figures from New York City alone give an even greater change. From 1900 to 1935, 93 per cent of the juvenile court cases in New York City were boys.[3] After 1935 the cases among girls became more numerous. The increase for girls of 1942 over 1941 was 30 per cent and that of 1943 over 1942, 70 per cent. Apparently girls were becoming the equal of boys in some ways that were not altogether desirable!

II. Characteristics of the Delinquent Adolescent

Many people have studied large or small groups of delinquents in an effort to determine what traits the delinquent shows and how important each may be in contributing to his delinquency.

A recent and excellent study[4] gives a detailed comparison of five hundred delinquent and five hundred nondelinquent boys who were carefully paired for age, residence in the same area of the same city, intelligence, and racial origin. The delinquents were first selected, and then public school

---

[1] M. Van Waters, "Special Community Program to Prevent Delinquency," *Forty-seventh Yearbook of the National Society for the Study of Education*, 1948, Pt. I, pp. 214–229.

[2] Figures are quoted from the *San Francisco Chronicle* for April 21, 1952, p. 1.

[3] J. B. Maller, "Juvenile Delinquency in New York," *Journal of Psychology*, 3:1–25, 1937.

[4] S. S. Glueck and E. T. Glueck, *Unraveling Juvenile Delinquency*, published by Harvard University Press for The Commonwealth Fund, 1950, 399 pp.

boys were located who matched the delinquents. The five hundred boys of
the control group had no record of delinquency. Searching inquiry failed to
reveal more than an occasional, ordinary, childish misdeed, such as swiping
a neighbor's fruit from his tree or jumping onto the backs of trucks or trolley
cars, and 75 per cent of the nondelinquents did not show even such minor
misbehavior. The five hundred delinquents were all chronic offenders. Over
80 per cent of both groups lived in tenement or business areas. Their
ages were between eleven and seventeen, two thirds of them being over

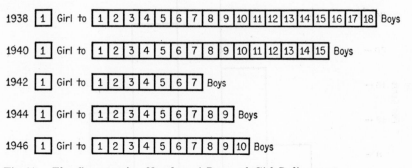

Fig. 77. *The Comparative Number of Boy and Girl Delinquents*

Based on data in Schwartz, "Statistics of Juvenile Delinquency in the United
States," *loc. cit.*, p. 14.

fourteen. The entire thousand, minus two to nine cases who moved away or
became otherwise inaccessible, were given a medical examination, a test of
intelligence, achievement tests in reading and arithmetic, a Rorschach test,
and a psychiatric interview. This study will be referred to at various points
in this chapter as the Glueck study.

One important question about delinquents concerns their mental level.
The IQ's for several delinquent groups have been found to distribute themselves in a normal scatter, but with the center at some point between 80
and 90 instead of at the normal 100. The extremes usually vary from below
50 to above 150. In one study of 1,731 delinquents with an average chronological age of fourteen, an average mental age of eleven years eight months,
and a median IQ of 84, the range was from 45 to 130.[5] Seventy-one per cent
of these delinquents would be classed as normal or low-normal, 4 per cent
as bright, 2 per cent as brilliant, 8 per cent as borderline, and 15 per cent
as definitely defective.

The distribution of IQ's from the Glueck study appears in Figure 78
on page 350. The range is from below 60 to above 120, with a median at 82.
Fifty-three per cent would be classed as normal, 5 per cent as bright,
32 per cent as low normal, and 10 per cent as defective. On the basis of such
results, one can hardly regard low intelligence as the only cause of delin-

---

[5] W. W. Wattenberg, "Boy Repeaters, 1946–1947," Crime Prevention Bureau,
Detroit Police Department, 1949, 58 pp., mimeographed.

quency. Moreover, for every delinquent adolescent with a low IQ there are many socially normal adolescents of no higher intellectual level.

There is little evidence to suggest that delinquents are in poorer physical condition than others from the same economic levels. One careful investigator[6] gave physical examinations to 282 delinquent boys and 282 nondelinquent boys of the same age, grade, and intelligence. The excess of

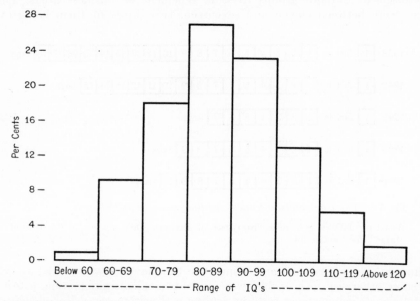

Fig. 78.   *Distribution of IQ's for a Delinquent Group*

Based on S. S. Glueck and E. T. Glueck, *Unraveling Juvenile Delinquency,* The Commonwealth Fund, 1950, p. 356.

the former over the latter group for each type of physical abnormality varied from 45.8 per cent for dental caries to 0.3 per cent for deafness, but only three items—dental caries, poor dental hygiene, and defective tonsils —showed differences of more than 8 per cent between the two groups.

The 1,000 boys of the Glueck study were given a thorough medical examination, and pictures were taken for purposes of studying their body type. The results of the examination were entirely negative, in the sense that both groups showed the same defects in approximately the same proportions. The delinquents grew a little more slowly up to the age of fourteen, when they overtook and surpassed the other group. In body build, the delinquents tended to the mesomorphic type;[7] almost none of them were conspicuously ectomorphic. They usually had clearly masculine proportions and relatively heavy muscles.[8] It does not, therefore, seem that physical defects are outstanding causes of delinquency.

---

[6] A. Christie, "Physical Defects in Adolescent Boys," *Journal of Juvenile Research,* 18:13–22, 1934.

[7] See pp. 26–29.

[8] W. H. Sheldon, *Varieties of Delinquent Youth,* Harper & Brothers, 1949, 899 pp.

One outstanding characteristic of delinquents is their educational retardation, which is usually more than can be explained by their slight intellectual inferiority. They generally average about a year's retardation mentally, but nearly three years educationally.[9] In one study, the educational
retardation of 152 delinquent boys ranged from 2.8 to 5.5 years; their
average chronological age was 14.5 years and their average mental age
was nearly 13 years, but they showed an average educational age of only
11.5 years. Another group of 345 sixteen-year-old delinquent boys of normal intelligence averaged in their schoolwork at only the low sixth-grade
level.[10] Of 977 juvenile offenders, 85 per cent were retarded from one to five
years, 12 per cent were at age for their grade, and only 2 per cent were
accelerated.[11]

The Glueck study showed similar results. All but 16 per cent of the delinquent boys had repeated grades in school; 69 per cent were retarded from
two to five years. Twice as many of the nondelinquents as delinquents had
always been promoted. The reading and arithmetic quotients of the control
groups averaged five or six points higher than those of the delinquents,
although both groups had the same range and both made relatively poor
showings. The delinquents disliked school, wanted to leave it at once, and
were persistent truants. The normal boys liked school, wanted to complete
high school and rarely misbehaved. Only a few of them played truant, and
they were not persistent in this behavior. Even when matched with boys of
similar mentality, the delinquents make heavy work of their schooling.
Comparison of the delinquents with the nondelinquents in regard to their
attitudes toward school and their behavior when there appears in Figure 79
on page 352. They disliked school intensely (62 per cent), wanted to leave
school (43 per cent), were chronic truants (63 per cent), misbehaved persistently (96 per cent) and from an early age (73 per cent). Delinquents
generally show an especial incapacity where verbal symbols are involved.
Reading is difficult for them, and many of them never read well enough
to get enjoyment from books. As they pass through the grades, they find
the work less and less suited to their needs because of the ever-increasing
need to read easily. The nonverbal type of delinquent outweighs the verbal
type by six to one.[12]

Delinquents do not like the traditional school, as indicated by three

---

[9] The facts in this paragraph are taken from C. J. Eckenrode, "Their Achievement
Is Delinquency," *Journal of Educational Research*, 43:554–560, 1950; A. K. Eccles, "An
Inquiry into the Verbal Facility of Delinquent Boys," *Training School Bulletin*, 43:157–
160, 1946; J. Jastak and E. Allen, "Psychological Traits of Juvenile Delinquents,"
Delaware State Medical Journal, 16:100–104, 1944; H. A. Lehman and P. A. Witty, "The
Educational Attainments of Delinquent Boys," *Journal of Educational Psychology*,
25:695–702, 1934; J. E. Moore, "Comparative Study of the Intelligence of Delinquent
and Dependent Boys," *Journal of Educational Psychology*, 28:355–366, 1937.
   [10] Lehman and Witty, "The Educational Attainments of Delinquent Boys," *loc. cit.*
   [11] S. S. Glueck and E. T. Glueck, *One Thousand Juvenile Delinquents*, Harvard
University Press for The Commonwealth Fund, 1934, p. 137.
   [12] Eccles, "An Inquiry into the Verbal Facility of Delinquent Boys," *loc. cit.*

reports. In one case, 67 per cent of the boys disliked school;[13] in a second, 90 per cent;[14] and in a third, 83 per cent.[15] Since they are uninhibited, they react to their dislike by becoming chronic truants. Indeed, truancy is often the first "delinquent" act by which a pupil calls attention to himself. In all groups of delinquents studied, some percentage between 50 and 60 had been truants from school.

There seems to be little if anything the matter with the native social capacities of delinquents. They are unpopular enough with their teachers

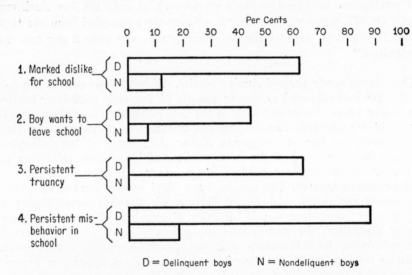

Per Cents

0 10 20 30 40 50 60 70 80 90 100

1. Marked dislike for school { D / N }

2. Boy wants to leave school { D / N }

3. Persistent truancy { D / N }

4. Persistent misbehavior in school { D / N }

D = Delinquent boys   N = Nondeliquent boys

Fig. 79. *School Attitudes of Delinquent and Nondelinquent Boys*

Based on Glueck and Glueck, *Unraveling Juvenile Delinquency,* pp. 145–148.

and other school officials, but once they are on the playground or in the gymnasium they participate freely and naturally in whatever is going on. They usually show a capacity to get on with their age-mates that others would do well to imitate. Some delinquents even show distinct qualities of leadership. Although the forms of expression are usually inacceptable, the underlying social competency of delinquents seems at least average. One investigator, however, has found the typical delinquent boy to be less social than normal boys, as well as less intelligent, less well adjusted, less academic, and less healthy.[16] In another study, the social activities of one hundred delinquent and one hundred nondelinquent boys of the same age and intelligence were observed.[17] The former showed greater increase in participa-

---

[13] Wattenberg, *op. cit.*

[14] Eckenrode, "Their Achievement Is Delinquency," *loc. cit.*

[15] F. C. Zakolski, "Studies in Delinquency: I. Personality Structure of Delinquent Boys," *Journal of Genetic Psychology,* 74:109–117, 1949.

[16] *Ibid.*

[17] B. S. Atwood, "Social Participation and Juvenile Delinquency," *Indiana Bulletin of Character and Correction,* No. 210, 1933, pp. 208–211.

tion from the lower to the higher ages than the latter and a consistently
higher average participation at all ages.

It is in the field of emotional development that one finds the important
differences between delinquents and normally behaved children or adolescents. Many investigators have found the delinquent to be emotionally immature. His emotional age is below both his mental and his chronological

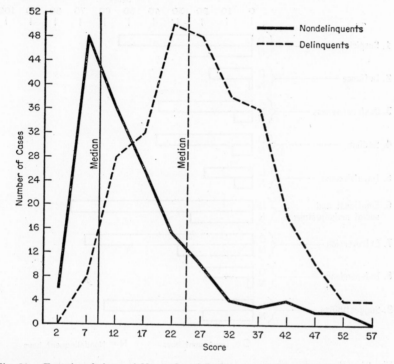

Fig. 80. *Emotional Ages of Normal and Delinquent Adolescent Girls*

Based on figures in M. A. Durea and A. L. Assum, "The Relation of Personality
Traits as Differentiating Delinquent and Non-Delinquent Girls," *Journal of
Genetic Psychology,* 72:307–311, 1948.

ages. One study of 276 delinquent and 151 nondelinquent adolescent girls
between the ages of thirteen and seventeen gave especially interesting
results, which are shown in Figure 80. As the test used was scored
for this study, the possible scores ran from 0 to 58, the higher scores indicating the lower degree of maturity. The median score of the normal adolescents was 10 points. Ninety-one per cent of the delinquents scored
higher. Over a third of them scored above the ninetieth percentile for the
normals.

Delinquents are emotionally unstable individuals, and they are abnormally sensitive to emotional tensions in their families or neighborhoods.
One study reports the following facts about members of a delinquent

group.[18] They are unhappy and emotionally disturbed (91 per cent), irresponsible (36 per cent), without purpose (40 per cent), indifferent toward others (44 per cent), unimaginative (48 per cent), and emotionally unstable (48 per cent). They feel themselves to be insecure, rejected, unloved, inferior, guilty, and frustrated.[19] Unlike the neurasthenic, who may experience similar feelings, they do not allow themselves to be beaten by the

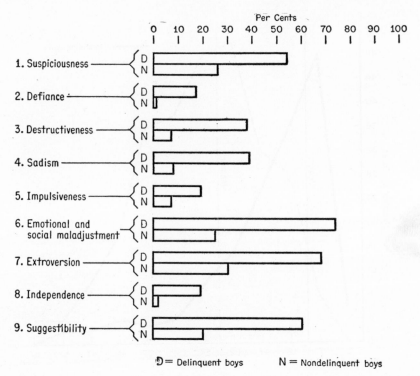

D = Delinquent boys   N = Nondelinquent boys

Fig. 81. *Personality Traits of Delinquent and Nondelinquent Boys*

Based on figures in Glueck and Glueck, *Unraveling Juvenile Delinquency*, pp. 219–236.

world. They fight back. As a result, they become aggressive, hostile, suspicious, jealous, and quarrelsome. They blame others for their own shortcomings. This tendency for projection appeared in results obtained from 250 delinquents, ten to thirteen years of age.[20] Of the entire group, 189, or 76 per cent, gave responses that projected blame onto others, as compared with only 36 per cent among normal children.

The Glueck study reveals the personality traits of delinquents to be as indicated in Figure 81 on this page. They are resentful, hostile, suspicious,

---

[18] V. Birkness and H. C. Johnson, "A Comparative Study of Delinquent and Nondelinquent Adolescents," *Journal of Educational Research*, 42:561–572, 1949.

[19] W. Healy and A. F. Bronner, "What Makes a Child Delinquent?" *Forty-seventh Yearbook of the National Society for the Study of Education*, 1948, Pt. I, pp. 30–47.

[20] F. T. Gatling, "Frustration Reactions of Delinquents, Using Rosenzweig's Classification System," *Journal of Abnormal and Social Psychology*, 45:749–752, 1950.

unconventional, self-centered, emotionally unstable, suggestible, extroverted, and destructive. The nondelinquents give a quite contrasting picture as a group, although some of them show each separate trait. They are outstandingly submissive and stable, and they lack the destructive trends, the impulsiveness, and the defiance that characterize the delinquents with whom they were paired.

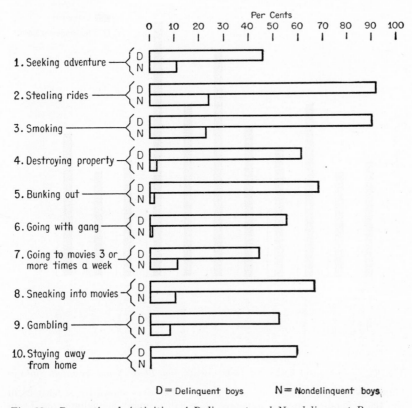

Fig. 82.   *Recreational Activities of Delinquent and Nondelinquent Boys*

Based on figures in Glueck and Glueck, *Unraveling Juvenile Delinquency*, pp. 160–163.

The recreational life of the two groups in the Glueck study also shows marked differences and is revealing of personality. The results appear in Figure 82. The delinquents favored adventurous activities and shunned competition; they were heavy patrons of the movies; their idea of fun consisted in stealing rides on streetcars or trucks, in staying away from home, in destroying property, in smoking, and in gambling. They played in the streets, and they roamed afar. Their companions were more often than not members of a gang. The nondelinquents show contrasts in almost all respects, although they also attended movies frequently and played on street corners, presumably for lack of any better place. However, they used playgrounds wherever these were available. What the delinquent does when he is just amusing himself shows clearly what kind of person he is. One can easily understand that he would be in constant conflict with others and in constant disciplinary difficulties.

However, delinquents are not psychotic. The percentages of abnormality among them are about the same as those for the general population.

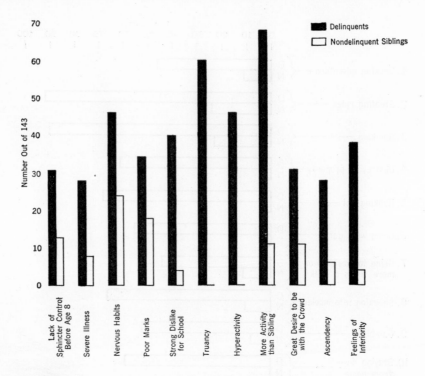

Fig. 83. *Differential Traits of Delinquents and Their Nondelinquent Siblings*

Those traits were considered "outstanding" that were shown by at least 28 of the 105 delinquents and by not more than half as many nondelinquents. From W. Healy and A. F. Bronner, *New Light on Delinquency and Its Treatment,* Yale University Press, 1936, pp. 73–77. Used by permission of the Yale University Press.

Of 9,958 criminals, 2.4 per cent were found to be mentally defective, 1.5 per cent were mentally ill, and 14 per cent were neurotic, leaving 82 per cent who were considered normal.[21] Even the neurotic individuals among the delinquents differ, however, from the neurotic nondelinquents in the forms their neuroticism takes. They may be hysterics, paranoiacs, or psychopaths, they may have compulsions or driving fears, they may show overcompensatory behavior, but they definitely do not belong to the submissive, solitary,

---

[21] W. Bromberg and C. B. Thompson, "The Relation of Psychosis, Mental Defect, and Personality Types to Crime," *Journal of Criminal Law and Criminology,* 28:70–89, 1937.

introverted type of neurotic. Their behavior is not typically withdrawn but typically explosive.[22]

The instability of delinquents is well brought out by a study that reports findings for 105 delinquents, each of whom was paired with a non-delinquent sibling.[23] The two children in each pair therefore had the same home and neighborhood influences—although the treatment of the two by their parents was sometimes dissimilar. Both members of each pair were carefully studied. The outstanding differences between them appear in Figure 83, page 356. The delinquents were more nervous and neurotic, they were hyperactive and dominating, they felt thwarted and inferior, they were more sociable, and they had a greater interest in sports, reading, and movies. Perhaps the most outstanding point in these results is the underlying aggressiveness and vitality of these delinquents. They were children with strong drives and desires who would not succumb quickly to strain. When one avenue of expression was blocked they tried another.

The vital differences between the normal and the delinquent child are to be found, then, not in intelligence, health, or basic social competency, but in the emotional immaturity, instability, and frustration that produce in them a maladjustment to home, school, and society.

III. Characteristics of a "Delinquent" Environment

Three elements in the total social situation seem to be of utmost importance in influencing the behavior of delinquents—the home, the neighborhood, and the school. Because of their outstanding importance they will be dealt with in some detail.

1. The Delinquent Home: The most obvious characteristic of a home is its physical condition. Out of one thousand delinquent children studied by one investigator, 62 per cent lived in dilapidated, poorly furnished houses or tenements; 25 per cent came from homes of fair condition, and only 13 per cent from homes that were sanitary, well equipped, and reasonably prosperous.[24] In the Glueck study, the homes of the delinquent and non-delinquent boys were of much the same external type—overcrowded tenements with poor sanitation and poor furnishings—but the homes of non-delinquents were cleaner, and fewer of the families were on relief.

The family stock, the physical condition of the parents, their educational level, and their moral attitudes are all below average. In one study 52 per cent of the families from which delinquents came contained at least one person who was insane, feebleminded, epileptic, or syphilitic; and

---

[22] M. Stern, "Some Differences between Neurotic Delinquents and Other Neurotic Children," *Smith College Studies in Social Work,* No. 16, 1945, pp. 62–81.

[23] W. Healy and A. F. Bronner, *New Light on Delinquency and Its Treatment,* Yale University Press, 1936, 226 pp.

[24] Glueck and Glueck, *One Thousand Juvenile Delinquents.*

in 84 per cent of these same families there was at least one delinquent.[25] Results from a second investigation appear in Table 20. In this study the

Table 20

HOME CONDITIONS OF DELINQUENT CHILDREN

	Number of Homes
Both parents uneducated	36
Both parents subnormal	10
One parent with criminal record	20
One parent heavily alcoholic	26
One parent vicious	13
One or both parents of low ethical standards	36
One or both parents of poor emotional control	58
One or both parents neurotic or psychotic	21

From W. Healy and A. F. Bronner, *New Light on Delinquency and Its Treatment*, Yale University Press, 1936, 226 pp.

total number of homes was 133. The total number of parental handicaps, as listed in Table 20, was 220, or 1.6 per home.

The family stock of the two groups in the Glueck study is poorer for the delinquents. Among both the immediate ancestors and the living relatives there are appreciably more defectives, emotionally disturbed people, drunkards, and criminals. The parents and siblings of the delinquents also show

Table 21

FAMILIES OF DELINQUENT AND NONDELINQUENT BOYS

Characteristic of Home	Mothers		Fathers		Siblings	
	Delinquent (%)	Nondelinquent (%)	Delinquent (%)	Nondelinquent (%)	Delinquent (%)	Nondelinquent (%)
Serious physical ailment	49	33	40	29	41	23
Mental retardation	33	9	18	6	50	25
Emotional disturbances	40	18	44	26	37	26
Drunkenness	23	7	63	24	21	15
Criminality	45	15	66	34	65	39

From Sheldon Glueck and Eleanor T. Glueck, *Unraveling Juvenile Delinquency*, Cambridge, Mass., Harvard University Press, 1950, p. 98. Reprinted with permission of the publishers and The Commonwealth Fund, 1950.

an excess of these same traits, as indicated in Table 21. The differences run from 6 to 39 per cent and are all larger among the delinquents.

In present-day society 1 child in 9—or 11 per cent—grows up in a

---

[25] *Ibid.*

home that lacks either father or mother.[26] If the proportion were the same for delinquents, only 11 in each 100 would come from such homes, but actually over 50 out of each 100 of them do. Thus, in 300 consecutive cases of delinquents, 51 per cent came from broken homes, whereas only 27 per cent of matched nondelinquents did.[27] The breaking of the normal family constellation therefore appears to be influential in producing delinquents.

Of late, the emotional currents and tensions within the homes of delinquents have been analyzed and studied. Many investigators feel the fundamental causes of delinquency are to be found in the treatment accorded a child by his parents, especially during his preschool years. The basic theme is one of rejection, for various reasons, on the part of the parents.[28] For instance, in a group of 116 delinquent boys, 55 (47 per cent) had been rejected by their mothers and 40 (34 per cent) by their fathers. Maternal rejection began before birth in 20 cases, before the age of two in 6 more, and during early childhood in the remaining 29.[29] In addition, the parents showed a profound maladjustment to each other. There were 11 divorces, 22 separations, and 50 cases of severe quarreling with intermittent desertion. Thirty-one mothers and 36 fathers showed severe emotional instability in their own personalities. A total of 99 out of the 116 boys, or 85 per cent, suffered from at least one of these family situations: maternal rejection, paternal rejection, parental incompatibility, "disturbed" mothers, or "disturbed" fathers, while 62—or 53 per cent—suffered from more than one—three of the boys suffering from all five. In a second group consisting of 143 delinquents,[30] 131—or 92 per cent—showed major emotional disturbances in their home relationships. Fifty-three of them felt rejected and unloved; 45 had deep feelings of frustration; 62 felt inferior and inadequate; 43 were disturbed over family disharmonies; 43 were markedly jealous of their brothers or sisters; 20 had deep-seated conflicts of other types centering in the home.

The emotional interrelationships of the families in the Glueck study are summarized in Figure 84 on page 360. The parents of the normal boys expressed warm affection for them and received affection from them. The boys felt that their parents were really interested in them. The discipline was usually firm and kindly and included other types of punishment than merely physical. Between the delinquent boys and their mothers, affectional relationships were fairly good, but between the boys and their fathers there was too little warmth and too much hostility. Discipline by both parents was lax, erratic, or overstrict, and both depended mainly upon physical punishment as a means of control. Although the two groups of boys came from the

[26] Anon., "One Child in Nine in a Broken Home," *Statistical Bulletin of the Metropolitan Life Insurance Company,* 25:3–6, 1944.

[27] M. A. Merrill, *Problems of Child Delinquency,* Houghton Mifflin Company, 1947, p. 66.

[28] H. M. Shulman, "The Family and Juvenile Delinquency," *Annals of the American Academy of Political and Social Science,* 261:21–31, 1949.

[29] J. Lander, "Traumatic Factors in the Background of 116 Delinquent Boys," *American Journal of Orthopsychiatry,* 11:150–156, 1941.

[30] Healy and Bronner, *New Light on Delinquency and Its Treatment.*

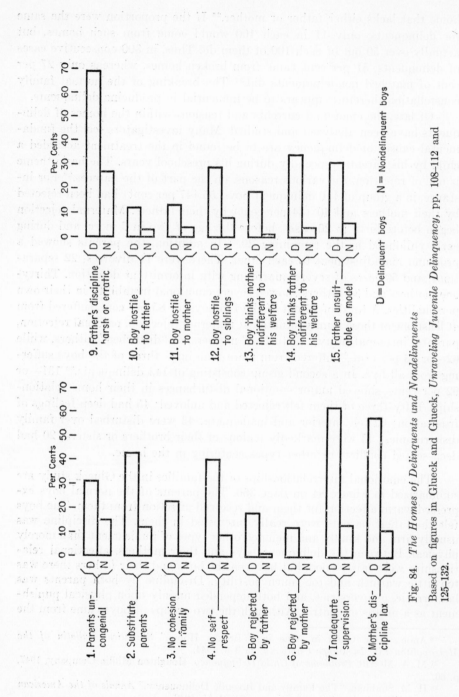

Fig. 84. *The Homes of Delinquents and Nondelinquents*

Based on figures in Glueck and Glueck, *Unraveling Juvenile Delinquency*, pp. 108–112 and 125–132.

D = Delinquent boys   N = Nondelinquent boys

9. Father's discipline harsh or erratic
10. Boy hostile to father
11. Boy hostile to mother
12. Boy hostile to siblings
13. Boy thinks mother indifferent to his welfare
14. Boy thinks father indifferent to his welfare
15. Father unsuitable as model

1. Parents uncongenial
2. Substitute parents
3. No cohesion in family
4. No self-respect
5. Boy rejected by father
6. Boy rejected by mother
7. Inadequate supervision
8. Mother's discipline lax

Per Cents

same social milieu and although the external features of their homes were similar, the affectional interrelationships show marked differences. The non-delinquent has the affection, interest, and support of his parents; the delinquent does not. Furthermore, the families of the normal boys were characterized by careful planning, self-respect, good relations between the parents, adequate supervision of children, and marked cohesiveness of the group. The families of delinquents lived in a haphazard sort of way and had poor standards of conduct; the parents did not get along together, the children were not supervised, and joint family recreations were virtually absent. Nearly twice as many delinquents as nondelinquents came from broken homes, and nearly four times as many were living with people who were substituting for their parents.

When one talks with delinquents and with their parents one is struck with the lack of normal friendliness between them, with the attitude of each toward the other, and with the inability of the parents to establish control without arousing resentment. For instance, among the parents of 1,465 delinquent boys, only 8 per cent played with their children or went on excursions or picnics with them; an even smaller proportion was found among 672 boys who were "repeaters"; and the smallest proportion of all was found for parents of boys who were before the court on serious charges.[31] Such facts suggest an unusual degree of estrangement between the two generations. In general, parents of delinquent children are ashamed of their offspring and disown them publicly.[32] It usually happens that a child's early, minor, normal misdeeds meet with shocked surprise and temporary parental rejection, which in turn stimulate the child to resent his parents' attitude. Each undesirable act on his part calls forth more rejection, and each rejection produces more resentment and subsequently more misdeeds.[33] The discipline in the homes from which delinquents come is usually harsh or inconsistent, and often both. Renouncing of an instinctive desire always results in some degree of frustration, but the pleasure derived from parental approval in good homes is sufficient to offset the frustration. In poor homes, however, there is no such compensation, and the frustration soon turns into rebellion against the parents. The children become resentful, hostile, and unwilling to conform, and this attitude, originally directed toward the parents, soon carries over into rebellion against authority outside the home, against school, and against society.[34] Finally, there are some parents who use their child either to satisfy their own suppressed desires or to serve as a scapegoat for these desires. They derive satisfaction through their child's delinquencies. They maintain their own emotional equilibrium at the expense of the child's development. If the parents would like to be quarrelsome and get into fights

---

[31] W. W. Wattenberg, "Family Recreation and Delinquency," *Focus*, 29:6–9, 1950.

[32] M. Van Waters, *Parents on Probation*, New Republic, Inc., 1927, 333 pp.

[33] G. Foulds, "The Child-Family Relationship and the Frustration Types among Mental Defective Juvenile Delinquents," *British Journal of Psychology*, 20:255–260, 1945, and H. H. Zucker, "Affectional Identification and Crime," *Archives of Psychology*, No. 286, 1943, 60 pp.

[34] Healy and Bronner, "What Makes a Child Delinquent?" *loc. cit.*

but repress this desire, their child is likely to fight; if they have repressed impulses to steal, he is likely to steal. This process works just as efficiently when it is unconscious as when it is not. The child's response to the situation is usually a deep hostility toward the person who has so overburdened and misused him.[35]

An interesting comparison revealed differences between boys from juvenile court and college students who had, in their precollege days, committed the same offenses but without being brought into court.[36] The college boys showed a history of acceptance by their parents and support by both home and community at the time of their offenses. The juvenile delinquents were friendless and rejected by their parents, and confused in their moral standards. Almost all adolescents get into difficulties, but those who are supported by parents and friends manage to weather the storm.

2. The Delinquent Neighborhood: During the last thirty years many studies have been made in various places to show the occurrence of delinquency in different areas of a city. The approach has been entirely pragmatic. Investigators have first taken a detailed map of the city or area under investigation and have tabulated upon it the location of those homes from which delinquents came. In all cases these homes centered in a few districts, sometimes in not more than two or three. Having located the critical neighborhoods in this way, the investigators next made a careful survey of these localities to determine the characteristics which differentiated them from other districts. Most of this work was done under the influence of the environmental theory of delinquency. It remains valuable and contains contributions to an understanding of delinquency.

A map of New York City appears in Figure 85, page 363.[37] The number of juvenile court cases per thousand inhabitants is indicated by the different shadings. The blackest districts are the "delinquency areas," while the light districts are those in which the rate is lowest. Comparison of the districts having the highest and the lowest delinquency rates gives the facts shown in Table 22.

Study of these delinquency areas in the many surveys that have been made indicates that they are of three general types: (1) business districts, (2) manufacturing districts, and (3) districts in which the nature of the population is changing. In no investigation was there more than a scattering of delinquents from strictly residential parts of a city.

A business district is typically a place where adults are busy with work or amusement and have no time or attention for children. The adults there, except

---

[35] A. M. Johnson, "Sanctions for Superego Lacunae of Adolescents," in Eissler, *op. cit.*, pp. 225–245.

[36] A. L. Porterfield and C. F. Clifton, "Youth in Trouble: Studies in Delinquency and Despair, with Plans for Prevention," *Bulletin of The Leo Potishman Foundation*, Fort Worth, 1946, 132 pp.

[37] This material is twenty years old, admittedly, but in the last two decades attention has been turned away from such studies of the environment. There are therefore no better studies of this nature that are any more recent. The basic situation here revealed has changed little, if any, since this study was made.

possibly policemen, feel no responsibility for what children are doing. Consequently, the youngsters have none of the supervision that comes to all children who are living or playing in a residential district, where the mothers especially pay attention to anything any child is about. Manufacturing districts are not much more accept-

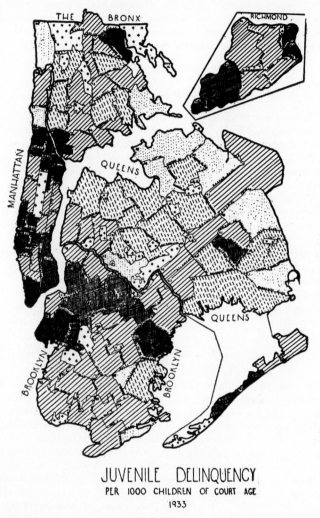

JUVENILE DELINQUENCY
PER 1000 CHILDREN OF COURT AGE
1933

Fig. 85. *Neighborhoods of New York City*

From J. B. Maller, "Juvenile Delinquency in New York City," *Journal of Psychology*, 39:314, 1936. Used by permission of the Journal.

able than business districts as places in which to bring up children. In the first place, the smells and sights are likely to be so unsavory that only those who cannot afford to live elsewhere will live there. Only cheap houses are built, and the inhabitants are those who work in the nearby factories—mostly families of unskilled or semiskilled laborers. Recreational facilities for children are usually missing because the land is too valuable to be used for playgrounds. A business district usually abounds in forms of amusement intended for adults, but a factory district is rather worse in this respect because the amusements are of a lower type—poolrooms, cheap theaters with burlesque shows, houses of prostitution, saloons, men's "clubs," hangouts of gangs, and so on. Neither factory nor business district offers the protection or the normal outlets for activity that children need.

The third type of district presents a somewhat different problem. Suppose the houses in a few blocks have been tenanted primarily by Hungarians, for instance; while this situation lasts, there is formed a little, closed-in colony, the members of which feel responsible for its children. Suppose, then, these people begin to drift

Table 22

COMPARISON OF GOOD AND BAD NEIGHBORHOODS

High delinquency areas are characterized by	Low delinquency areas are characterized by
1. Excessive retardation of children in school (35%)	Moderate retardation of children in school (26%)
2. Low intelligence	Average intelligence
3. High birth rate and high infant mortality rate (83 per 1,000)	Low birth rate and average infant mortality rate (50 per 1,000)
4. Low rents ($40)	Average rents ($50)
5. Few automobiles owned (15 per 100 families)	Many automobiles owned (156 per 100 families)
6. Great overcrowding (223 people per acre)	No overcrowding (36 people per acre)
7. High adult crime rate	Low adult crime rate
8. Few Boy Scout troops	Many Boy Scout troops
9. Few copies of the New York Times sold	Many copies of the New York Times sold
10. Many tabloids sold	Few tabloids sold

Based on J. B. Maller, "Juvenile Delinquency in New York City," *Journal of Psychology,* 3:20–22, 1936.

away—perhaps toward some new place where the men are employed. The cohesion begins to break up almost at once, and is further broken if, for example, Italians start moving into the vacated houses. If the process goes on and the neighborhood becomes entirely populated with Italians, there is again social cohesion. But during the period of the shift, the district is pulled apart by antagonistic social forces. The adults of the two groups do not get on with each other; the children inherit these antagonisms and develop competing gangs. The looseness of social control is furthered if the adults of both groups speak much less English than do their children. In any case, the neighborhood has lost one set of standards without acquiring another. While the change is in process it becomes an area in which the rate of delinquency is higher than the rate in nearby districts that are inhabited solidly by members of either nationality alone. "Mixed" districts—regardless of the elements entering into the mixture—are also unsettled districts in which delinquency is likely to flourish.

Perhaps the outstanding characteristic of all these "bad" districts is that they offer no social cohesion, little protection, little supervision, and only warped outlets for childish activities. The "good" district presents the opposite picture. It is one in which there are social traditions, excellent protection (in the form of observant adults), and adequate outlets for the restlessness and emotional drives of childhood and adolescence.

The neighborhood furnishes the setting in which a child is educated either for an acceptance of conventional attitudes or for an acceptance of rebellion toward such attitudes. It furnishes him with his models. It limits the forms in which he may express his instinctive drives. It provides him with standards—either the conventional ones or those of organized crime. Perhaps the most confusing neighborhoods are those in which both standards thrive alongside each other. Delinquency is learned behavior; it therefore requires association with and instruction by other delinquents, who are provided by the neighborhood—and sometimes by the immediate family. In such cases, the children learn their delinquency through the perfectly normal process of identification, either with their parents or with outstanding adults in their environment.[38] The neighborhood also makes its pressure felt after a child's first misdeeds. It may label him as a delinquent, deprive him of participation in normal childhood groups, and eventually banish him to those areas that will sanction his aggressiveness; or it may take him to its bosom—if it is already well populated with adult criminals—and give him the first real approval and acceptance he has ever known.

The greater world outside his immediate neighborhood also exerts an effect upon the young offender through the various means of communication—the newspapers, the comics, the radio, the movies, and television.[39] Newspapers that glorify crime in lurid pictures and morbid detail have their greatest sale in the most delinquent neighborhoods of a city. Such publicity not only focuses the attention of the children on crime but furnishes them with rationalizations for any later misconduct. From newspapers the children learn also of the inconsistent moral values of adults, of sexual misconduct, of business dishonesty, of fraudulent tax returns, of bribery, of abortions, of fee splitting, of bootlegging, of black markets, and of political corruption. From this type of reading children derive the ideas that any crime is all right if you can get away with it and that adult obedience to law is only selective at best, not at all the cast-iron system of right and wrong about which they have been told. Since the sensational press wastes no space on the ordinary citizen who behaves himself, it is not surprising that children get extremely warped ideas about adult morality from their newspaper reading. This conflict of attitudes is very unsettling, especially to adolescents.[40] The movies have improved a great deal in the last two decades through their own enforcement of better standards, but some of the cheaper shows are still objectionable. It cannot be mere accident that the delinquent goes to the movies oftener than the nondelinquent. Boys who take no part in the extracurricular activities of their schools or in other organized recreation and derive their chief social satisfaction from delinquent activities spend twice as much time at the movies as nondelinquents.[41]

---

[38] Healy and Bronner, "What Makes a Child Delinquent?" *loc. cit.*

[39] M. B. Clinard, "Secondary Community Influences and Juvenile Delinquency," *Annals of the American Academy of Political and Social Science*, 261:42–54, 1949.

[40] H. D. McKay, "The Neighborhood and Child Conduct," *Annals of the American Academy of Political and Social Science*, 261:32–41, 1949.

[41] E. Shanas, *Recreation and Delinquency*, Chicago Recreation Committee, 1942.

The radio and television have not done as well as the movies in de-empha-
sizing crime, while many of the popular comics approve and even glorify the
more vicious forms.[42] Because of the pressure exerted directly and indirectly
by his environment, it would seem rather futile to attempt an understanding of a human being apart from the society in which he lives.

3. The Delinquent School: The public school in general is a contrib-
utor to mental health rather than to delinquency, but there are still a few
characteristics of the average school that may produce abnormal behavior.
The chief adverse element is the nature of the curriculum. The delinquent
is typically a nonbookish, nonintellectual, nonacademic, nonverbal individual who does poorly in the traditional school subjects. For instance, in
a group of 761 delinquents, 44 per cent had repeated at least one term of
school, as compared with 17 per cent of all other children in the same
school.[43] About 60 per cent of these delinquent children expressed a definite dislike for school, and 34 per cent had been truants, as compared with
7 per cent among nondelinquents. It is probable that these young delinquent
experience a considerable degree of frustration in connection with their
school life. By now it is certainly evident that delinquent children soon revolt against the traditional school and leave it at the earliest possible age,
usually after periods of truancy and long records of aggressive misconduct.
When they leave school they usually abandon the one potentially constructive influence in their lives.

It is highly probable that some teachers also contribute to the creation
of the delinquent child. They influence him, as they do all other children,
through the emotional atmosphere of their classroom. If they are demanding, harsh, domineering, and authoritarian, they arouse the aggressive hostility of the already rejected child, who now finds himself rejected once more.
If, as sometimes happens, such a child has a different teacher every semester
in elementary school and another eight during junior high school, he may
have gone through the painful period of rejection as many as twenty times.
One can hardly blame him for hating school, for playing truant, or for
leaving as soon as possible. Perhaps the worst teacher for the delinquent-
in-the-making is the one who not only cannot accept him but also takes his
reactions to her rejection as a personal insult.[44] Such a teacher regards misbehavior as a reflection upon her competence, she becomes so involved personally that she loses her self-control—sometimes descending to the child's
own level of bad manners—and she is quite unable to make an objective
study of the pupil and his problems, largely because she is a good deal
sorrier for herself than she is for him. School discipline is sometimes so

---

[42] See F. Wertham, "The Comics—Very Funny," *Saturday Review of Literature*,
May 29, 1948; and G. L. McIntyre, "Not So Funny Funnies," *Progressive Education*,
22:28–30, 1945.

[43] W. C. Kvaraceus, "Delinquency—A By-product of the School?" *School and
Society*, 59:330–341, 1944.

[44] N. Fenton, "The Delinquent in the Classroom," *Forty-seventh Yearbook of the
National Society for the Study of Education*, 1948, Pt. I, pp. 48–65.

administered as to be thoroughly inacceptable even to well-balanced, normal children and adolescents. The effect upon delinquents is disastrous and stimulates them to even greater hostility toward their school. The following story is a case in point:

Michael, aged sixteen, had no record of delinquency until he was in his sophomore year of high school. He was quick-tempered and occasionally got into fights on the playground, but he had never been a problem in school. During his sixteenth year he grew very fast, showed a ravenous appetite, and had periods of indolence, during which he had hardly enough energy to get out of bed. He was also in the midst of his first attack of puppy love, and he was somewhat bewildered by the changes that had come into his life, all at once. He was doing rather poor work in school. At this point, his family moved to another part of town, and Michael had to change teachers, classmates, and girl friends in the middle of a semester. His new teachers had somewhat higher standards of scholarship than those of his former school, and their conduct of classes was more formal. Michael was in no mood for a change, he disliked almost everything about his new school, he was lonesome, and he was at the moment too indolent to study much. The very first day Michael was sent to the principal's office for "talking back" and for interrupting the teacher. Actually, he had said nothing that would not have been accepted in the more permissive atmosphere of his former school. One remark was intended for a companionable joke but was regarded by his English teacher as an insult and an impertinence. Michael took the first violent dislike of his life to this teacher. The students of the school were already grouped into cliques and had selected girl or boy friends before Michael appeared, and there seemed to be no place for him in the student life of the school. The second day he got into a fight on the playground and was again haled into the principal's office. The principal, who had not taken the time to examine Michael's record, decided he had an incorrigible boy on his hands; after scolding Michael, he went to a faculty meeting, where he warned the teachers to be firm with this new boy, who seemed to be a troublemaker. The unfamiliar, strict discipline became stricter where Michael was concerned. His schoolwork got steadily worse, partly because it was poor to start with, partly because the classes were more advanced than those in the former school, partly because Michael liked neither the methods nor the teachers, and partly because he was too exasperated and too tired to study. In a short time Michael became moody, despondent, and indifferent, with occasional outbursts of resentment and violence. He "talked back" in class, criticized the methods used, and compared his present with his past teachers. A group of predelinquents soon began to be friendly toward him, presumably because they thought him a kindred spirit. Michael did not especially like them, but at least they were aware of his existence, and he went about with them some, thus convincing the school authorities that he was a budding criminal.

One day when the boy was feeling especially unhappy, a teacher took exception to his manner and insisted that he apologize to her before the class. Michael does not seem to have known just what he was to apologize for, but he mumbled something and then bolted out of the room in an agony of embarrassment. He cut his next two classes. At noon he went to the school cafeteria but was still so upset that he dropped his tray. After clearing the floor he left without having lunch, and went to his home room, where he sprawled in his seat with his feet on the next desk, and tried to relax. A teacher whom he had never seen before came through the room, went out of her way to scold him for his posture, became annoyed when he neither answered nor moved, tried to pull him up by the collar, and then struck him across the knuckles with a ruler she happened to have in her hand. Michael rose to his feet and slapped her face. For this behavior he was sent first to the principal's office, then home, and then to juvenile court. The judge was a sympathetic man, who had already become suspicious of the school that Michael attended, because the principal had brought too many youngsters into his court for trivial offenses. He therefore talked at length with the boy and brought out the full story of the strict insistence upon routine, the repressive discipline, the petty persecutions, and the total failure to understand an adolescent boy's needs. He told the complaining teacher that if she wanted a boy to stand up in her presence, she should be the kind of person who made him *want* to be on his feet; and if she could not inspire him to do so, she had no business yanking him up by his collar. He reprimanded Michael for slapping her, but on the grounds that gentlemen do not slap women. He dismissed the case against Michael and ordered him to be transferred to his former school. Since most of the semester had already passed, Michael entered only two classes, made up his back work, passed both courses, and successfully took a full schedule during the remaining semesters. There was never any more trouble.

A "delinquent" environment consists, then, of three main elements: a home in which parents are unsuccessful economically, are of not more than average native ability, are of undesirable personal habits, and are of questionable morality, who are ineffective in discipline, unable to furnish emotional security, and inclined to reject their delinquent child both before and after his misdeeds; a neighborhood that is devised for adults, quite without safeguards for children, largely without safe outlets for emotional and social life, and full of unsatisfactory models and conflicting standards; and a school that tries to make scholars out of nonacademic material and sometimes furnishes teachers who are too rejective in their attitudes. When all three elements are affecting the same unstable child at the same time, a delinquent is likely to be produced.

IV. Factors Contributing to Delinquency and Theories about Them

It is not difficult to list the factors that have been shown by various investigators to be related to delinquency. Some of those in the list appearing in Table 23 on page 369 are doubtless of more importance than others.

Because of the somewhat conflicting ideas current at present as to the causes, development, and treatment of delinquents, it seems wise to review briefly the possible causes and to present two somewhat opposed, but not mutually exclusive, interpretations. Delinquency is a highly complex phenomenon, for it is a way of life that a child develops during his first ten or fifteen years of existence. If there are two explanations, each emphasizing different phases supplementing each other, it seems worth while to consider both, and then to attempt a synthesis.

According to one outstanding authority, delinquency is an impulsive reaction made in order to find direct or indirect satisfaction for instinctive urges. The young delinquent does not find in his home and neighborhood enough love or attention or admiration to satisfy his needs, nor does he find many suitable outlets for his drives toward activity or play. His social urges find their readiest expression in the gangs that already exist. Such groups are made up of others like himself. The members are rejected by their homes

Table 23

Heredity
1. Bad family stock—incidence of feeble-mindedness, insanity, epilepsy higher than in families of nondelinquents.
2. Defective mentality—average IQ of delinquent groups is 85 to 90 instead of 100. (However, about two thirds of all delinquents are of normal or above normal mentality.)
3. Specific inability to handle verbal symbols, resulting in slow progress in school.
4. Unusual vitality, drive, and energy, resulting in restlessness, over-activity, and aggressiveness.

Home
5. Poverty and crowding in home.
6. Delinquency and crime among parents or older siblings.
7. Home broken by death, separation, divorce, desertion, or prison term.
8. Lack of emotional security, high degree of tension in home; lack of emotional stability in parents.
9. Lack of proper or uniform discipline.
10. Rejection of child by parents, neglect of child, lack of interest in his activities.

School
11. Poor work in school; one or more retardations.
12. Dislike of school.
13. More or less truancy.
14. Rejection by some of the teachers.

Neighborhood
15. Existence of many criminal models in the neighborhood.
16. Lack of adequate supervision and protection.
17. Lack of adequate outlets.
18. Exposure to low or conflicting adult morals.
19. Exposure to minority conflicts.

Resulting Personality Traits
20. Feelings of inferiority, insecurity, and rejection.
21. Constant frustration and development of deep hostility.
22. Emotional immaturity.
23. Aggressive drives turned toward parents, school, and society.
24. Identification with criminal models.
25. Emotional satisfaction found in antisocial groups.
26. Strong impulses, uninhibited by conscience.

and are in acute conflict with the community. They rebel openly with direct acts of aggression. Such behavior is well calculated to awaken a desire to imitate in the bosom of the child who has a similarly acute, but as yet only indirectly expressed, conflict of his own. His hostile urges are of the same sort as theirs, and by joining forces with them he can not only express himself more directly, but can even obtain in return admiration and absolution from a lurking sense of guilt that might otherwise mar his content. One can see that from the delinquent's point of view there is not much to be gained by a reform in his behavior. Moreover, a delinquent act, such as stealing, often becomes an outlet for tension. The connection between the act and the release may be quite accidental in the beginning, but soon the child discovers this new outlet for his insecurity and unhappiness. When tensions pile up inside him, he can discharge them by stealing something, an act which makes him feel much more comfortable. It is also probable that the delinquent act gives him pleasure. Thus, the tearing up of a small grocery by pulling things off the shelves and spilling them on the floor may serve not only to "get even" with a grocer against whom he has a grudge but also to give him a feeling of omnipotence, with accompanying release from his usual fears and inferiorities. He may therefore indulge in periodic destruction, perpetrated against entirely unknown owners of property, because these episodes contribute to his sense of success and well-being more than any resulting detection or punishment is likely to offset. The outstanding point in the above explanation is the constant interchange between childish needs and environmental rewards and pressures.[45]

The psychoanalytic school has presented an explanation that rests primarily upon a faulty personality structure that has already developed before the child is old enough to leave his home. During the first two or three years all children are "delinquent"—that is, they take what they want immediately, directly, and without inhibition, and they derive pleasure from their unsocial reactions. By the time they are three years old, however, they should have learned to wait a little while for satisfaction and to accept substitutes for gratifications that are denied them. That is, they can derive enough pleasure from the approval of their mother that they can keep themselves from tossing books on the floor, for instance. They should be able to bear a little tension in order to reach a goal. When there is a conflict between immediate instinctual gratification and their affective relationship to their parents, they should be able to inhibit the former in order to improve the latter. If, however, the child has not advanced to this level, he cannot bear the tensions that an increasingly active life puts upon him, so he regresses to his earlier direct, uninhibited behavior of letting his drives have full and immediate expression and deriving great satisfaction and pleasure from their fulfillment. Since the youthful predelinquent is already a rejected child, his natural attachments to his mother have become weak. His failure to gain what he deeply wants turns his love into hostility, and he expresses his feelings by aggression toward her. If development has been normal, between the ages of three and six a child should have developed a superego, or conscience, and a strong enough ego to control many of his impulses and to meet some of the demands of the superego; at least, he knows what he should do, and in general he tries to do it, even though his control is not always strong enough. Because the delinquent has already begun his regression, he makes little progress in the development of a superego. He is probably more comfortable if he fails completely, since then there is no inner conflict; but often he does develop just enough conscience to stir up feelings of guilt in himself and yet not enough to be of much guidance to him. Once in a while one finds a delinquent with a very severe superego that is strong enough to make him indulge in antisocial acts in order to punish himself. More often, however, any urge to self-punishment is transmuted into blame against the environment, a far more comfortable attitude, espe-

---

[45] This theory finds expression in the writings of Healy and Bronner, *New Light on Delinquency*, and "What Makes a Delinquent?" *loc. cit.*

cially as the child can now discharge some of his hostile feelings against the straw man he has just set up.[46]

As life becomes more complex and makes more demands upon him, the child gets into more and more open revolt. He continues to carry out his primary desires and to ignore environmental pressures. His attachments to people are never strong enough to act as inhibitions upon his drives. His parents usually meet his behavior either by excessive severity or by excessive indulgence, and sometimes by an oscillation between the two extremes. While the neurotic is greatly constrained by the attitude of others toward him, the delinquent is not affected at all by them. He continues to act on the pleasure principle. The delinquent is, then, an individual in whom instinctive drives are strong, conscience is weak, and the ego is bent upon immediate pleasure without respect to the generally accepted norms of behavior. This combination of traits keeps him in conflict with everyone and leads him to attack reality before it gets a chance to overwhelm him. Delinquency gives him, therefore, his most satisfactory defense against a world that frightens and annoys him without giving him any adequate compensatory pleasure.

These two views are not in contradiction, although they emphasize different aspects of the total problem. The most important difference between them is the emphasis put by the Freudians upon the first two or three years of life and the tracing of delinquency to a faulty structure of personality, without much apparent regard for other possible elements. Both views have much to offer to the student of human behavior.

After the student has read through the three brief histories below, he or she might try to analyze the contributing factors in each and to interpret them in terms of the theories just presented.

George R. has a long record of antisocial reactions. His parents are normal people, his siblings are normal, and there is nothing in the family interrelationships or in his parents' treatment of him that can account for his behavior. Almost from the cradle George was a stubborn, self-centered, destructive, emotionally cold child, with a strong streak of cruelty in his make-up. He seemed to have no normal human feelings. He rode roughshod over others if he could, and when he could not he had tantrums during which he destroyed whatever he could get his hands on and inflicted as much damage on others as possible. His older brothers and sisters were big enough to take care of themselves, but his younger sister was constantly in danger of attack from him. It was never safe to leave the two children together. When George was five years old he made such a vicious attack upon her that his parents took him to a good psychiatrist, who was unable to do much to modify the boy's behavior. As soon as George was old enough to enter school there was further trouble. He destroyed property and assaulted other children, especially girls. During his second week in school he was sent to the school psychologist, who gave him a Binet examination. He was rather un-co-operative, and the psychologist felt that his IQ of 87 was too low. The public school could not keep him although several teachers tried to control him. At some cost to their budget his parents hired a male teacher for him at home, but George refused to learn anything, and no teacher would remain

[46] This theory is presented by Eissler, *op. cit.*

long with him. During his seventh year George attacked and almost killed his younger sister. His parents then felt that they could do nothing more with him, so they took him to juvenile court, where he was declared an incorrigible child and put into an institution. George is now thirty-four years old. He has spent all but six months of the twenty-seven years since he was first committed to reform school in one institution or another. At present he is in state prison for an attempted rape, and since he is a totally un-co-operative prisoner, it is probable that he will serve his full term of twenty years. There is nothing in George's home and family background, in the attitude of his parents toward him during his early years, or in their treatment of him as a small child to account for his behavior.

In the fall of 1951 a brief article appeared in a large city newspaper concerning an eleven-year-old boy who had won nearly $3,000 at a nearby race track. He had been at the track and placed bets many times. On one occasion, he met his mother there. She was greatly surprised to see him, and astounded that he had just won $1,200, but she made no effort to prevent future visits. In fact, the matter came to official attention only because she wanted to have custody of his winnings.

This boy is a well-mannered, well-spoken, good-looking son of divorced parents. He spends the school year with his mother and the summers with his father, who has a box at the race track. He and the boy have often been there together. During the summer of 1951 the boy formed the habit of going by himself on weekdays when his father was at work. The boy learned about race tracks and betting, not from his age-mates but from his father, by the simple process of observation.

This boy, in talking with the judge, showed a good intelligence and a sophistication far beyond his years. It does not seem probable that a series of successful gambling experiences, resulting in a pocketful of "easy money," is any preparation either for a life of rectitude or for a return to such normal boyish pleasures as scrub baseball, camping trips, or visits to the old swimming hole. The parents have demonstrated their unfitness to care for a child. One suspects that this neglected child has had no proper supervision since his infancy. It seems clear that neither parent knew or cared what he did with his time. Presumably, during the summer at least, he had his whole day to himself, without guidance or supervision. One fears that the moral damage to the boy has already been done.

It should be noted that this boy entered a dubious activity only through the help of indifferent adults—his parents, who did not know where he was; the men at the race track who accepted his bets, although they must have known he was below legal age; and various adult acquaintances before whom he boasted of his winnings. He had attended the races often enough to attract the attention of officials, who determined his age and had just barred him from further betting when his mother sued for control of his earnings. A boy is certainly without proper guidance when he has to depend upon race track stewards for supervision.

Elaine was a child with a normal personality and a normal degree of intelligence. She was somewhat precocious, to be sure, but there was no sign of conflict or abnormal emotional preoccupation in her early years. Her progress in school was normal, and she was popular with both her age-mates and her teachers. She had no record of trouble until her thirteenth year, when she began to have sexual relations with boys and men.

Elaine's father had died when she was about four years old, and her mother had supported herself and her daughter by being the receptionist in the dining room of a large hotel. She and Elaine lived in a back room of the hotel. She tried hard to provide a normal life for her daughter and to shield her from the seamier sides of hotel life. Elaine had her lunch at school, and since her mother was free during the last part of the afternoon, they usually went to a park or out on errands together after school hours. Elaine was put to bed about six-thirty, just before her mother went on duty in the dining room. The mother sometimes augmented her income by visiting the rooms of men guests after the dining room closed. Although she was very discreet, Elaine nevertheless learned about these episodes and assumed them to be normal. She does not seem to have been upset in the least, but she did develop a precocity and indifference to conventional morality as a result. During her twelfth year she began to have relations with the bellboys and some of the waiters. It does not appear that she sought them out or that she was impelled by any strong inner urge. She seemed to think such behavior was expected of her and submitted to advances without much interest. Her mother was genuinely horrified when she was told of this development and much more deeply distressed over Elaine's misdeeds than Elaine was. At the suggestion of the school psychologist, she gave up her hotel job and took a place as companion to an elderly woman out in the country. So far as could be determined, the mother lived a strictly moral life from that time on. Elaine went to a consolidated school, finished the twelfth grade, and soon afterward married a boy who lived on a neighboring farm. She is now a happily married farm woman, with three small children. There has never been the slightest sign of further delinquencies. Elaine would appear to have been a normal child who lived under abnormal circumstances and wandered into delinquency mainly because she had developed at the age of thirteen the precocity and hardness that are likely to characterize adults who live in hotels.

V. The Prevention of Delinquency

Delinquency is, for the delinquent, a reasonably satisfactory pattern of living, since it provides him with what he wants with the least delay possible, gives him great satisfaction, and permits him to punish those who have neglected him. He does not therefore want to help himself to be different. He merely wants not to be caught. Moreover, there is a theory of extremists that society does not really want criminals to reform. The reasoning behind this idea goes as follows: that human beings are in need of suitable outlets for the many feelings of aggression that are created by the complex demands of life. For them a delinquent is a good scapegoat for the projection of their own inacceptable drives and inner tensions. They do not therefore really want the delinquent to recover. The writer does not guarantee the correctness of this explanation, but it is a type that one not infrequently meets in modern literature on criminals. With the delinquents and the righteous both quite happy as things are, it is not surprising that recoveries are less numerous than one might wish.

The results of two follow-up studies indicate the extent to which reformation may be expected. In one case a thousand juvenile offenders were followed throughout a fifteen-year period. Their history may be shown by the number of arrests before the period began and the number in each successive five-year interval. Table 24 shows the facts. The total number of arrests first increased and then decreased, although the average remained high throughout the fifteen years. The number who ceased to be delinquent rose to nearly 40 per cent of those who were still alive, could be located, and were not in an institution.

The second investigation gives results for 143 cases who were followed for only two years. These delinquents were classified, at the time of their

Table 24

NUMBER OF ARRESTS

Degree	Before the First Period	First 5 Years	Second 5 Years	Third 5 Years
0	374	190	297	356
1	294	154	111	114
2	151	167	118	83
3	80	126	75	61
4	50	96	72	60
5	24	78	59	28
6	11	41	40	33
7	10	31	25	30
8	4	56	78	71
Not known	2	61	125	164
Total arrests	1,324	2,551	2,194	1,819
Arrests per person, whose record was known	1.3	2.7	2.5	2.1

The totals were found by adding together one times the number with one arrests, two times the number with two arrests, and so on. The average was found by dividing this total number of arrests by 1,000, minus the number of persons "not known." From S. S. Glueck and E. T. Glueck, *Juvenile Delinquents Grown Up*, published by Harvard University Press for The Commonwealth Fund, 1940, p. 309. The data for this table are used by permission of Harvard University Press. For a similar follow-up study of 500 ex-reform school inmates, see *Criminal Careers in Retrospect* by the same authors, 1943, published by Harvard University Press for The Commonwealth Fund, 380 pp.

first appearance, into three groups: 26 children who showed markedly abnormal personalities, 50 normal or nearly normal children who lived in homes that were antagonistic and apparently unmodifiable, and 67 children who were normal and came from homes that, while having some undesirable traits, were co-operative. The situation for these three groups two years after treatment appears in Table 25. The children in the first group and the

Table 25

EFFECT OF TREATMENT UPON DELINQUENTS

	Group I (%)	Group II (%)	Group III (%)
Nondelinquent	19	38	72
Much improvement, rare minor delinquency	12	14	8
Delinquent	58	46	19
Unknown, dead, or in institutions	11	2	1

Based on material in Healy and Bronner, *New Light on Delinquency and Its Treatment*, pp. 171–172.

homes in the second were abnormal and difficult to modify. The results for both groups are therefore poorer than those for the third, in which both child and home were basically normal and could therefore manage to find a better solution than delinquency to their problems. However, the chances for recovery are better for a normal child in an abnormal home than for a child with an already warped personality.

Since, however, the best efforts do not produce complete success, it is necessary to focus one's attention upon prevention. It is now possible, by means of questionnaires, tests, and observation of behavior, to tell in advance which children are likely to become delinquent.[47] Most predelinquent children could be identified long before their first serious offense. It is possible that the early treatment thus permitted might offset undesirable influences and re-educate warped personalities.

The investigators of the Glueck study went over their data to study the possibility of using scores on tests of personality or items from case histories as bases of prediction, and worked out three prediction tables based on different groups of items. The records of 424 boys (205 delinquent and 219 nondelinquent) were next examined to find out to what extent each table correctly classified the boys. The results are summarized in Table 26.

Table 26

VALUES OF PREDICTION

	Percent	
1. Boy correctly classified on all three prediction tables	49 ⎱	87 %
2. Boy correctly classified by two but wrongly by one	38 ⎰	successes
3. Boy incorrectly classified on two and correctly on one	11 ⎱	13 %
4. Boy wrongly classified on all three	2 ⎰	failures

From S. S. Glueck and E. T. Glueck, *Unraveling Juvenile Delinquency*, published by Harvard University Press for The Commonwealth Fund, 1950, p. 268. Used by permission of Harvard University Press.

If selection of the most clearly related items of a boy's history and the most striking of test results can produce a prediction of 87 per cent, it would seem that an early identification of the delinquent is already feasible.

Although adolescence is the period during which delinquency reaches its height, the first deviations of conduct and personality take place much earlier. One investigator found that in 47 per cent of his cases the first offense had occurred before the age of eight and that in another 31 per cent it was committed before the age of twelve.[48] The first recorded offense among 1,000 juvenile offenders occurred before the age of four for 3 per cent, before six for 12 per cent, before eight for 36 per cent, before ten for 62 per cent, and before twelve for 84 per cent.[49] Since the chief offenses of female juvenile delinquents are sex offenses, girls do not show quite as early—or perhaps only not as recognizably—delinquent behavior as do boys. The proportion of 500 delinquent women who showed a first offense at eight or

---

[47] H. A. Weeks, "Predicting Juvenile Delinquency," *American Sociological Review,* 8:40–46, 1943.

[48] Healy and Bronner, *New Light on Delinquency and Its Treatment.*

[49] Glueck and Glueck, *One Thousand Juvenile Delinquents.*

earlier was 5 per cent; between nine and ten another 5 per cent had committed an offense, and between ten and twelve another 10 per cent.[50] Such figures show clearly that the predelinquent child was already sufficiently maladjusted to be recognizable some years before his behavior landed him in court. During the last decade the age of first arrests has become lower even than formerly, and the first evidences of maladjustment have appeared correspondingly earlier.

Three lines of investigation could contribute much to the identification of the criminal-in-the-making: study of the home, observation of each pupil's behavior, and measurement of his personality.[51] It does not take long to find out which pupils come from homes located in a deteriorated area or in an area of cultural conflict, or which have parents who are so poor or so maladjusted as to be known to welfare agencies or to the police. The pupil can give information concerning the emotional tensions in his home. The pupil's behavior can be measured by the use of rating scales made out by his parents, if they are not too much on the defensive. The significant type of behavior is consistent aggression. A predelinquent's life is already a protest against authority. He is in conflict with his parents, his teachers, and his age-mates. His emotional outlets are direct and destructive. He blames everyone but himself. He early begins to play truant from school, to lie about where he has been and what he has been doing, and to indulge in petty pilfering, which is usually not punished by his parents. He makes slow progress in school. He has a history of being unmanageable from nursery school onward, and since infancy in his home. He has already made a typical positive adaptation to his inadequacies and failures, a solution which keeps him from knowing that he has failed and gives him a sense of power over others. Personality tests show him to be hostile, aggressive, egotistical, and infantile. There is relatively little difficulty in identifying the child who will become a criminal because—on a childish level—he already is one.

The possible adjustments that might prevent a further development of delinquency among those who have already shown tendencies in that direction divide themselves rather naturally into the necessarily limited possibilities of the school and the almost unlimited possibilities of society. A school can recognize its potential delinquents early.[52] Then it can abandon its traditional curriculum and build a new one on the nonacademic interests these children undoubtedly do have. The objectives of this new curriculum should be to train the children in acceptable behavior and in earning their living at the levels open to them. These children should be under the super-

---

[50] S. S. Glueck and E. T. Glueck, *Five Hundred Delinquent Women,* Alfred A. Knopf, Inc., 1934, p. 429.

[51] H. Y. McClusky, "How Community Agencies May Help with Problems of Delinquency," *Forty-seventh Yearbook of the National Society for the Study of Education,* 1948, Pt. I, pp. 191–231.

[52] D. B. Harris, "Suggestions for the School from Recent Literature on Juvenile Delinquency," *Forty-seventh Yearbook of the National Society for the Study of Education,* 1948, Pt. I, pp. 247–266.

vision of the school from early morning until bedtime;[53] they should be fed at least two meals each day at school; their play activities should be carried forward on the school playground, with excursions under school control. Their homes and neighborhoods offer chiefly deteriorating influences; the one chance of preventing delinquency lies, therefore, in allowing the school to substitute for both home and neighborhood. As the pupils grow older they should receive direct vocational training and subsequent placement. At all ages they need plenty of acceptable outlets for their emotional drives. True, such a procedure would not prevent all delinquencies, but it gives promise of reasonable effectiveness.

Society could do much more if it were willing to make sweeping changes. It could, for instance, abolish all dwellings now located in business or industrial districts. It could pass and enforce a law that people having children must live in residential areas, it could make sure that a sufficient number of decent houses with low rents were available, and it could, by zoning restrictions, keep these districts permanently residential. It could relieve the congestion and squalor that are so often preludes to delinquency. It could instruct its police to keep children away from business and industrial areas and to return them to their homes when they stray. It could provide adequate recreational grounds; the opening of parks, playgrounds, club-houses, and swimming pools has a prompt effect in lowering the delinquency rate. Society could provide also for some degree of supervision, and it could make it impossible for children to enter places of amusement unsuited to them, to obtain stimulants and drugs, or to undertake occupations that are harmful. Society could build enough schools to prevent overcrowding, and it could pay teachers so well that the most effective people in every genera-tion would enter teaching as a profession. It could prevent the hindrances to healthy living that have their basis in poverty by raising substandard wages, making more medical service available, and giving greater economic se-curity.[54] Society brings about its own human deterioration because it is too indifferent to pass and enforce the measures necessary for the elimination of unsuitable districts and for the adequate teaching and protection of children. Such changes would not prevent all delinquencies, but they would remove many of the causes that lead to discomfort, inadequacies, and frus-tration, which in turn produce delinquency.

Any agency, whether school, church, community center, or settlement house, that institutes work with the parents of predelinquents and with the children themselves can contribute a good deal to the prevention of future crime. The children should be brought into contact with such groups as the Boy Scouts, Campfire Girls, 4-H Clubs, YMCA, YWCA, Junior Farm Boys, Future Farmers of America, and any local church groups that may be avail-able. The church is often an effective agency in individual cases but does not always live up to its potentialities. Thus, among 2,137 delinquent boys, 44 per cent were regular attendants at church. Of the 2,137 boys, 672 were repeaters and 1,465 were not.[55] Forty-six per cent of the nonrepeaters had

[53] R. J. Havighurst, "The School and Juvenile Delinquency," *School Review*, 52:72–73, 1945.

[54] R. H. Felix, "The Responsibility of the Community for Juvenile Delinquency," *Proceedings of the National Conference of Social Work*, 1947, pp. 377–383.

[55] W. W. Wattenberg, "Church Attendance and Juvenile Delinquency," *Sociology and Social Research*, 34:195–202, 1950.

been attending church regularly, as had 38 per cent of those who continued their delinquencies. The church can do and has done much better than these figures indicate. Such membership may do little good, but sometimes a predelinquent begins, finally, to identify himself with desirable models and to derive enough pleasure from the good opinion of others to inhibit some of his worst forms of aggression. He may find a father-substitute in the leader.

It has been found useful to suggest that parents and children have one night together every week and that it be spent at home in pleasurable activities.[56] No listening to radio, watching television, or going to a movie or a hockey game was to be considered as a proper activity for "family night," because these, while all right for other evenings, did not involve group effort. Many simple amusements of former generations had to be gotten out and relearned: taffy pulls, making a birthday cake, charades, simple card games, pinning the tail on the donkey, bobbing for apples, putting on a family show, reading aloud, singing together, developing a family orchestra, designing and making Christmas cards or Easter baskets together, or joint construction of new furniture. The only rule was that everyone in the family should take an active part in reaching some group objective, however trivial either the part or the objective. At first these efforts at man-made enjoyment in a machine-made age were not too successful, but gradually parents and children learned to like and trust each other, and the basic hostility vanished. For the parents there should be several frank talks and discussions at first with leaders and later among the parents by themselves. They have a common problem, and they are more likely to solve it together than separately. Some parents resist outside interference, some project all the blame for their child and his misdeeds onto his playmates, some recognize their problem but are too secretive and ashamed to ask for help, while others beg for aid from any and all agencies.[57] The first meetings of parents with such different outlooks are likely to be stormy, but gradually a better understanding develops, and the children begin to receive a different treatment in their homes, usually with a marked reduction of tension.

Most of the recommended procedures for the prevention of delinquency—or for its treatment during its early stages—are aimed at providing activities in which the child or adolescent can be successful, experiences that make him feel accepted, and outlets that are socially approved for his emotional drives. The attack upon the problem is indirect and consists essentially in substituting acceptance for rejection by means of activities that are within the established social norm but are *more satisfying to the adolescent than his delinquency*. A series of suggestions to teachers by one writer on the subject are listed on the following page.

---

[56] McClusky, "How Community Agencies May Help with Problems of Delinquency," *loc. cit.*

[57] *Ibid.*

1. Provide children with a variety of experiences—crafts, art, music, athletics—covering a wide range of difficulty and interests, so that every child engages in some activity in which he can win outstanding success.

2. Understand each child's capacities and help him to recognize and develop his abilities—social, emotional, and artistic as well as intellectual—and accept his irremediable limitations.

3. Help him to gain skills and knowledge without unnecessary failure. Be on guard against occasions and incidents which might cause him to feel inadequate.

4. Guide the experiences of the class so that each pupil will gain satisfaction and moderate success in human relationships when he is acting along socially constructive lines.

5. Provide opportunities for normal emotional responses and accept minor instances of bad manners without comment.

6. When an outburst of delinquent behavior occurs in the classroom, do not be disturbed; handle it with objectivity and understanding; try to get into the delinquent's world and see things from his point of view.

7. Do what you can to change conditions in the home, school, or community that seem to be giving rise to types of behavior that are "expensive" to the individual and to society.[58]

None of these recommendations is either revolutionary or dramatic, but taken together they are likely to be effective. The writer would add one more precept to the list: Try to *like* the delinquent, even when he is being most objectionable. Children are exceedingly quick to sense rejection, no matter how well it is camouflaged, and will see through a pretense. Since the delinquent adolescent has probably not been loved since he was a baby, a small amount of genuine affection will often do more to help a boy rehabilitate himself than all other "treatments" combined.

The following brief account shows what can be done if the members of a community really want to reduce delinquency.

Grand Rapids, Michigan, was having an epidemic of juvenile delinquency in 1938. In one area of approximately 190 families, 156 youngsters had been arrested. The superintendent of police, Mr. Frank J. O'Malley, was suspicious of so much trouble concentrated in one spot. He and his colleagues concluded that the young folks in the area did not have the right kind of things to do in their free time. So they decided to take matters into their own hands.

With very little encouragement and even less financial assistance, they started by renting the basement of the Methodist Mission near the center of the troubled area. After much struggle, the police opened the Grand Rapids Youth Commonwealth, Inc., on Christmas Eve, 1938. From the beginning, the youngsters have liked the program and have learned to think of the police as friends. The center is open afternoons and evenings, six days a week. The membership ranges in age from eight to twenty-one and numbers about five hundred. It includes young folks from Mexican, Italian, Indian, Negro, and mixed, as well as from old stock, families. Racial and ethnic differences have never caused a problem.

The center provides a library of 1,450 donated books; classes in metal, leather, and wood crafts; lessons on string instruments and the piano; a cooking school for boys and girls conducted by the policewomen; table games; outdoor shower for

[58] Condensed from R. Strang, "First Steps to Progress in the Prevention of Delinquency," *Forty-seventh Yearbook of the National Society for the Study of Education,* 1948, Pt. I, pp. 267–269. Quoted by permission of the Society.

summer cooling-off; a skating rink in winter; boxing and basketball in the rear yard; equipment for competitive team sports played on the schoolground nearby; occasional entertainments; a Cub Den and a Boy Scout Troop; a plan whereby youngsters working on maintenance and improvements earn money payable in stamps which can be cashed in for schoolbooks, shoes, clothing, scouting equipment, athletic equipment, etc.; a self-government plan in which children hold positions of mayor, judge, police commissioner, librarian, etc.

In 1942, land was purchased a few miles from Grand Rapids for a camp site. The property was prepared and equipped for a diversified program, and by the season of 1943 more than a hundred young people had attended for successive periods of ten days each. Since then the camp has become an established feature of the over-all program of the center.

The Grand Rapids Youth Commonwealth, Inc., embodies a number of important principles. It has concentrated its program in an area known to have a high percentage of vulnerable youth. It has made effective use of the resources already existing in the neighborhood and the city. These resources include nearby school property, equipment, and books, the Methodist Mission, adjacent land for family gardens, personnel from various youth organizations, and other agencies and resources. It has placed great stress on the contribution of the young people themselves; their leadership, responsibility, and enthusiasm are immeasurable assets to the program. This enterprise has also thrown new light on the preventive job of police officials; in Grand Rapids, Captain Winslow, Sergeant Deming, Chief O'Malley, and their associates are more distinguished as leaders of youth than as apprehenders of youth who have gone astray. Finally, it has shown that a basic attack on delinquency requires a strong, positive program for all youth in the area served.[59]

VI. Delinquency and World War II

Wars are always accompanied by outbreaks of crime because wars interrupt the stable habits of peace, pull people up by the roots and drop them in strange places, break up many homes temporarily and some homes permanently, distract women's attention from their children, stir the emotions, generate tensions, produce new mental stresses, tempt older children to leave school either to work or to enter military service, and shake people out of their customary routines of existence.[60] The more the needs of war affect the daily lives of the people, the more profoundly does society become disorganized and disintegrated. The rise in juvenile delinquency during World War II was merely one concrete evidence of the widespread disorganization of individuals, homes, schools, and communities. The increases in the rates of delinquency correlated with the degree of breakdown in normal living. Thus, in London, the combination of broken homes—as a result of evacuation or of fathers in the service—of irregular life in shelters, of increased adult crime in the blackout, of terrific emotional tension, of

[59] McClusky, "How Community Agencies May Help with Problems of Delinquency," loc. cit., pp. 205–206. Quoted by permission of the National Society for the Study of Education.

[60] See, for instance, C. Towle, "The Effect of the War upon Children," Social Service Review, 17:144–158, 1943; and D. A. Thom, "The Psychological Response of Adults and Children to Influences Exerted by the War," Bulletin of the New England Medical Center, 5:174–179, 1943.

bombings, and of decreased school and recreational facilities produced during the first two years of war an increase of approximately 60 per cent in juvenile delinquency.[61] By contrast, in some rural districts and small towns in the United States there was no upward change in the delinquency rates, nor was daily life vitally affected. The increase for the entire United States is given at 17 per cent;[62] some areas, however, went as high as 60 per cent. The proportion of girl delinquents increased more than that of boys, although in actual numbers delinquent boys are three to four times as numerous. The age levels for first arrests were lower than ever before.

The media through which the disorganization of society impinged most directly upon the lives of children were the home and the school. In the case of adolescents one must add the job, and in the case of boys the exciting, if sometimes disconcerting, prospect of military service. Some of the emotional tension felt by adults communicated itself directly to children and adolescents, who were deeply affected also by propaganda in newspapers and motion pictures. Many homes were moved about during the war, as the fathers followed the best wages from place to place, or the family followed the father from one Army post to another. The group did not settle down in a house that it intended to make into a permanent home, but into a few crowded rooms in a boardinghouse, a war housing center, a trailer camp, or some other equally impermanent place. If the family moved for economic reasons, both mother and father usually went to work in the nearest war industry. Any children who were above compulsory school age soon joined them, leaving the younger ones to their own devices. The greatest emotional needs of children are to be wanted, to feel absolutely sure that they can depend on their parents, and to know definitely just what is right for them to do and what is wrong.[63] After a mother has put in eight hours a day at welding, she is too tired to care much about what the children want or need. Moreover, her long hours of absence mean that the home is uncared for and unguarded. Thus from all sides the familiar pattern of life was interrupted, and children lost their security.

The golden deluge of war wages put money into many pockets that were generally empty. If a man, his wife, his wife's sister, his nineteen-year-old daughter, his seventeen-year- and fifteen-year-old sons all worked, they might earn, with overtime and with one person working on the graveyard shift, a total of $600 a week, instead of the $60 on which the group had been living. In such sudden affluence many families disintegrated. Adults and children ate what they pleased, when and where they pleased; no one

---

[61] C. Burt, "Delinquency in Peace and War," *Health Education,* 1:165–172, 1943; A. H. Jones, "An Inquiry into Juvenile Delinquency in an English Town: A Comparison between the Effects of Peacetime and Wartime Conditions," *Social Service Review,* 19:525–531, 1945; and M. H. Neumeyer, "Delinquency Trends in Wartime," *Sociology and Social Research,* 29:262–275, 1945.

[62] C. L. Chute, "Juvenile Delinquency in Wartime," *Probation,* 21:129–134, 149, 153, 1943.

[63] H. D. Williams, "Behavior Problems of Children in Wartime," *Nervous Child,* 2:346–352, 1943.

bothered to inquire where other members of the family were or what they were doing; children came home from school to empty houses; adolescents threw off any remaining parental restraints and walked out of the house in the evening with their pockets full of money. In short, home life, with its automatic controls for the protection of children and adolescents, broke down for certain segments of the population.[64]

It should be noted that the elements which produce delinquents in wartime are the same as those that produce them in peacetime. Some families are perennially rootless, shiftless, and incompetent to control their children. During the war the number of such families increased because thousands of normal family units joined the floating population.

Wars produce tensions and stimulate aggressiveness. Parents and teachers have both noticed an increase in aggressive, vigorous play among children during the war years.[65] War fantasies and some degree of abnormal preoccupation with the problems of war have also been reported.[66] The net result is a general aggressiveness toward society, the selection of "toughness" as an ideal, and the development of hatreds toward various groups that acted as the recipients of aggression.

For the first year of the war the schools did a rather good job of compensating insofar as possible for home neglect and in helping to prevent delinquency,[67] but soon they were themselves too swamped by the emergencies of war to do more than struggle along as best they could. Men teachers were drafted, some women teachers volunteered for war service, some married and followed their husbands all over the country, and others went into war industries—partly for patriotic and partly for financial reasons. In the course of the war years, some 350,000 more teachers left the ranks of teaching than could be replaced. Many country schools closed altogether, and rooms in city schools had to be combined. High schools had to reduce the number of courses offered in order to make the teaching staff go around. Some teachers had seven classes of 50 to 60 pupils every day in the week—a total of seven preparations each day, seven sets of records to keep, and between 350 and 400 students. They did not know most of the pupils by name, and their instruction inevitably suffered from too little time for preparation, for individualization, for testing, or for guidance. After the

[64] See E. Burgess, "The Effects of War on the American Family," *American Journal of Sociology*, 48:343–352, 1942; H. von Hentig, "Juvenile Delinquency and Adult Disorganization," *Journal of Criminal Law and Criminology*, 35:87–92, 1944; H. F. Helmholtz, "Emotional Disturbances of Children in Wartime," *Minnesota Medical Journal*, 26:1044–1046, 1943; W. Overholser, "Who Are the Juvenile Delinquents?" *Journal of Social Hygiene*, 30:304–308, 1944; J. H. S. Bossard and E. S. Boll (eds.), "Adolescents in Wartime," *Annals of the American Academy of Political and Social Science*, 236:33–42, 43–50, 67–73, 74–82, 1944.

[65] M. E. Odoroff and D. B. Harris, "Midwestern Children's Responses to Questions about War," *Nervous Child*, 2:353–359, 1943.

[66] C. Harms, "The American Child on His Front of This War," *Nervous Child*, 2:338–345, 1943.

[67] Anon., "Juvenile Delinquency and the Schools in Wartime," United States Office of Education, *Schools, Children, War Series*, No. 8, 1943, 26 pp.

actual hostilities ceased and men started to come home, the schools were soon even more critically overcrowded. With the shortage of teachers and the increase in students, it was not possible for the schools to maintain the services that might best supplement the home and help in the prevention of delinquency.

VII. Summary

Delinquents differ from nondelinquents in a number of significant traits. As a group they have a somewhat lower intelligence, they are retarded still more in their educational development, they dislike the traditional school, they are markedly overactive, and they are not content with modes of emotional expression that other children find adequate. They show a high degree of hostility, aggressiveness, and suspicion. Their typical escape from their frustrations consists in making an attack upon their environment. Their homes are usually undesirable, not so much because of poverty as because of emotional tensions of various kinds. From the neighborhoods in which they live they derive standards of behavior that put a prestige value upon delinquency. They come from neighborhoods in which lawbreaking, among both adults and juveniles, is an accepted mode of behavior. The frustration that lies at the basis of much delinquency comes in large measure from restrictions and attitudes arising from these various background factors, although individual children naturally differ greatly in the nature of their reactions to environment. During the war, delinquency increased rapidly because the disruptive influences that usually affect only a few homes spread to a larger number and because children—like everyone else—felt the tensions and insecurities of wartime living. Because delinquency is an expression of a total adjustment to life, it is difficult to cure and hard even to prevent. The best modes of attack upon the problem seem to be an early identification of the predelinquent, an alteration in his school environment so that it is attractive to him and will hold him, a re-education (if possible) of his parents, and a provision on the part of the community for better emotional outlets.

REFERENCES FOR FURTHER READING

BOOKS

1. Bromberg, W., *Crime and the Mind: An Outline of Psychiatric Criminology,* J. B. Lippincott Company, 1945, 219 pp. (Chaps. 2, 5, 6.)
2. Burt, C., *The Young Delinquent,* University of London Press, 4th ed., 1944, 662 pp.
3. Crow, L. D., and A. Crow, *Our Teen-Age Boys and Girls: Suggestions for Parents, Teachers, and Other Youth Leaders,* McGraw-Hill Book Company, 1945, 366 pp. (Chap. 11.)
4. East, W. M., P. Stocks, and H. T. P. Young, *The Adolescent Criminal: A Medico-Sociological Study of 4000 Male Adolescents,* Churchill, London, 1942, 237 pp. (Chaps. 3–5, 7–9.)

5. Eissler, K. R. (ed.), *Searchlight on Delinquency*, International Universities Press, 1949, 456 pp. (Sec. 4.)

6. Ellingston, J. R., *Protecting Our Children from Criminal Careers*, Prentice-Hall, Inc., 1948, 374 pp. (Chaps. 2, 3, 20, 25–27.)

7. Garrison, *The Psychology of Adolescence*, Chaps. 16, 18.

8. Garrison, *The Psychology of Exceptional Children*, Chaps. 19, 20.

9. Glueck, S. S., and E. T. Glueck, *Criminal Careers in Retrospect*, published by Harvard University Press for The Commonwealth Fund, 1943, 380 pp. (Chaps. 2, 4, 7, 10, 13, 16.)

10. Glueck, S. S., and E. T. Glueck, *Juvenile Delinquents Grown Up*, published by Harvard University Press for The Commonwealth Fund, 1940, 330 pp. (Chaps. 2, 4–7, 9.)

11. Glueck, S. S., and E. T. Glueck, *Later Criminal Careers*, published by Harvard University Press for The Commonwealth Fund, 1937, 403 pp. (Chaps. 1–3, 13.)

12. Glueck, S. S., and E. T. Glueck, *Unraveling Juvenile Delinquency*, published by Harvard University Press for The Commonwealth Fund, 1950, 399 pp. (Chaps. 4, 10–12, 10, 18, 19.)

13. Healy, W., and A. F. Bronner, *New Light on Delinquency and Its Treatment*, Yale University Press, 1936, 226 pp. (Chaps. 2–9.)

14. Healy, W., and A. F. Bronner, *Treatment and What Happened Afterwards*, Judge Baker Guidance Center, 1939, 54 pp.

15. Kuhlen, *The Psychology of Adolescent Development*, Chap. 8.

16. Lindner, R. A., *Rebel without a Cause*, Grune & Stratton, Inc., 1944, 290 pp. (Pp. 15–30, 285–289, and any five "hours" from pp. 31 to 294.)

17. Louttit, C. M., *Clinical Psychology of Children's Behavior*, Harper & Brothers, rev. ed., 1947, 661 pp. (Chap. 11.)

18. Lowrey, L. G., "Delinquent and Criminal Personalities and Behavior Disorders," in Hunt, *Personality and the Behavior Disorders*, II, 794–821.

19. Malm and Jamison, *Adolescence*, Chap. 11.

20. Merrill, M. A., *Problems of Child Delinquency*, Houghton Mifflin Company, 1947, 403 pp. (Chaps. 2–3, 5–9.)

21. Neumeyer, M. H., *Juvenile Delinquency in Modern Society*, D. Van Nostrand Company, 1949, 335 pp. (Chaps. 1, 2, 4–7.)

22. Pierce, J. D. W., "Physical and Mental Features in the Juvenile Delinquent," in L. Radzinowicz and J. W. C. Turner, *Mental Abnormality and Crime*, The Macmillan Company, 1944, 316 pp. (Pp. 208–216.)

23. Reckless, W. C., *Etiology of Delinquent and Criminal Behavior*, Social Science Research Council, 1943, 169 pp. (Chaps. 2–4 and pp. 131–137, 144–147, 148–151 from appendix.)

24. Sadler, *Adolescence Problems*, Chap. 25.

25. Shaw, C. R., and H. D. McKay, *Juvenile Delinquency in Urban Areas*, The University of Chicago Press, 1942, 451 pp. (Pt. II.)

26. Tappan, T. W., *Juvenile Delinquency*, McGraw-Hill Book Company, 1949, 613 pp. (Chaps. 2, 4–7, 18, 19.)

27. Van Waters, M., *Parents on Probation*, New Republic, Inc., 1927, 333 pp.[68] (Chaps. 2–4, 10.)

28. Whyte, W. F., *Streetcorner Society: The Social Structure of an Italian Slum*, The University of Chicago Press, 1943, 284 pp. (Chaps. 2, 35.)

MONOGRAPHS, BULLETINS, PROCEEDINGS, YEARBOOKS, ARTICLES

A. *Characteristics of Delinquents*

1. Adelson, E. T., C. Sugar, and B. S. Wortis, "Socio-Psychiatric Study of 25 Young Offenders," *American Journal of Psychiatry*, 105:619–622, 1949.

---

[68] This reference is old but excellent.

2. Bach, G. R., and G. Bremer, "Projective Father Phantasies of Preadolescent Delinquent Children," *Journal of Psychology*, 24:3–17, 1947.
3. Banay, R. S., "Immaturity and Crime," *American Journal of Psychiatry*, 50:170–177, 1943.
4. Birkness, V., and H. C. Johnson, "A Comparative Study of Delinquent and Nondelinquent Adolescents," *Journal of Educational Research*, 42:561–572, 1949.
5. Durea, M. A., and A. L. Assum, "The Relation of Personality Traits as Differentiating Delinquent and Non-Delinquent Girls," *Journal of Genetic Psychology*, 72:307–311, 1948.
6. Durea, M. A., and G. J. Taylor, "The Mentality of Delinquent Boys Appraised by the Wechsler-Bellevue Intelligence Tests," *American Journal of Mental Deficiency*, 52:342–344, 1948.
7. Eccles, A. L., "An Inquiry into the Verbal Facility of Delinquent Boys," *Training School Bulletin*, 13:157–160, 1946.
8. Gardner, G. E., "The Community and the Aggressive Child: The Aggressive Destructive Impulses in the Sex Offender," *Mental Hygiene*, 34:44–63, 1950.
9. Gatling, F. P., "Frustration Reactions of Delinquents, Using Rosenzweig's Classification System," *Journal of Abnormal and Social Psychology*, 45:749–752, 1950.
10. Jenkins, R. L., and S. Glickman, "Patterns of Personality Organization among Delinquents," *Nervous Child*, 6:329–339, 1947.
11. Jones, H., "Group Sentiment and Delinquency," *Mental Health*, 8:41–44, 1948.
12. Monachesi, B. D., "Personal Characteristics and Socio-Economic Status of Delinquents and Non-Delinquents," *Journal of Criminal Law and Criminology*, 40:570–583, 1950.
13. Zakolski, F. C., "Studies in Delinquency: I. Personality Structure of Delinquent Boys," *Journal of Genetic Psychology*, 74:109–117, 1949.

B. *Delinquency as an Adjustment to Life*
1. Eckenrode, C. J., "Their Achievement Is Delinquency," *Journal of Educational Research*, 43:554–560, 1950.
2. Healy, W., and A. F. Bronner, "What Makes a Child Delinquent?" *Forty-seventh Yearbook of the National Society for the Study of Education*, 1948, Pt. I, pp. 30–47.
3. Lesser, E. K., "Understanding Juvenile Delinquency," *United States Children's Bureau Publications*, No. 300, 1943, 52 pp.
4. Seidler, R., "Escape into Delinquency: The Case of Robert E.," *Individual Psychology Bulletin*, 5:79–83, 1946.
5. Zucker, H. H., "Affectional Identification and Crime," *Archives of Psychology*, No. 286, 1943, 60 pp.

C. *The Homes of Delinquents*
1. Abramson, D., "Family Tension: Basic Cause of Criminal Behavior," *Journal of Criminal Law and Criminology*, 40:330–343, 1949.
2. Foulds, G., "The Child-Family Relationship and the Frustration Types among Mental Defective Juvenile Delinquents," *British Journal of Psychology*, 20:255–260, 1945.
3. Lander, J., "Traumatic Factors in the Background of 116 Delinquent Boys," *American Journal of Orthopsychiatry*, 11:150–156, 1941.
4. Shulman, H. M., "The Family and Juvenile Delinquency," *Annals of the American Academy for Political and Social Science*, 261:21–31, 1949.
5. Wattenberg, W. W., "Family Recreation and Delinquency," *Focus*, 29:6–9, 1950.

D. *Delinquents and the School*

1. Fenton, N., "The Delinquent in the Classroom," *Forty-seventh Yearbook of the National Society for the Study of Education*, 1948, Pt. I, pp. 48–65.
2. Harris, D. B., "Suggestions for the School from Recent Literature on Juvenile Delinquency," *Forty-seventh Yearbook of the National Society for the Study of Education*, 1948, Pt. I, pp. 247–266.
3. Havighurst, R. J., "Preparing Teachers to Meet the Problems of Delinquency," *Forty-seventh Yearbook of the National Society for the Study of Education*, 1948, Pt. I, pp. 230–246.
4. Kvaraceus, W. C., "Delinquency—A By-Product of the School?" *School and Society*, 59:330–341, 1944.
5. Louttit, C. M., "The School as a Mental Hygiene Factor," *Mental Hygiene*, 31:50–65, 1947.
6. Mullen, F. A., "Truancy and Classroom Disorder as Symptoms of Personality Problems," *American Psychologist*, 3:360, 1948.
7. Roser, M., "The Role of the School in Heading off Delinquency," *Yearbook of the National Probation and Parole Association*, 1951, pp. 149–167.
8. "Schools and Wartime Delinquency," *Journal of the National Education Association*, 31:151–152, 1942.
9. Smith, S. G., "The School and Delinquency," *Yearbook of the National Probation and Parole Association*, 1949, pp. 274–279.

E. *Delinquency and the Community*

1. Clinard, M. B., "Secondary Community Influences and Juvenile Delinquency," *Annals of the American Academy of Political and Social Science*, 261:42–54, 1949.
2. Felix, R. H., "The Responsibility of the Community for Juvenile Delinquency," *Proceedings of the National Conference on Social Work*, 1947, pp. 377–383.
3. McKay, H. D., "The Neighborhood and Child Conduct," *Annals of the American Academy of Political and Social Science*, 261:32–41, 1949.

F. *Prevention and Prediction of Delinquency*

1. Denny, V., and M. Johnson, "Predelinquency and Juvenile Guidance: A Story of the Way Which Minneapolis Teachers Aroused Their Community to Do Something about Juvenile Delinquency," *Journal of the National Education Association*, 35:386–387, 1946.
2. Goodykoontz, "How School Services Help in the Prevention of Delinquency," *Forty-seventh Yearbook of the National Society for the Study of Education*, 1948, Pt. I, pp. 100–125.
3. McClusky, H. Y., "How Community Agencies May Help with Problems of Delinquency," *Forty-seventh Yearbook of the National Society for the Study of Education*, 1948, Pt. I, pp. 191–213.
4. National Conference on Prevention and Control of Juvenile Delinquency, "Report on Juvenile Detention," 1946.
5. Oyemann, R. H., "How to Work with Parents in Preventing Delinquency," *Forty-seventh Yearbook of the National Society for the Study of Education*, 1948, Pt. I, pp. 171–190.
6. Porterfield, A. L., and C. F. Clifton, "Youth in Trouble: Studies in Delinquency and Despair, with Plans for Prevention," *Bulletin of the Leo Potishman Foundation*, Fort Worth, 1946, 132 pp.
7. Strang, R., "First Steps to Progress in the Prevention of Delinquency," *Forty-seventh Yearbook of the National Society for the Study of Education*, 1948, Pt. I, pp. 267–269.

8. Strang, R., "Prevention of Delinquency through Guiding Community Experience," *Forty-seventh Yearbook of the National Society for the Study of Education,* 1948, Pt. I, pp. 66–98.
9. Van Waters, M., "Special Community Program to Prevent Delinquency," *Forty-seventh Yearbook of the National Society for the Study of Education,* 1948, Pt. I, pp. 214–229.
10. Wampler, W. N., "An Experimental Program for Delinquent Boys in Los Angeles County," *Nation's Schools,* 36:22–23, 1945.

G. *Delinquency in Wartime*

1. Anon., "Juvenile Delinquency and the Schools in Wartime," United States Office of Education, *Schools, Children, War Series,* No. 8, 1943, 26 pp.
2. Bell, M. (ed.), "Delinquency and the Community in Wartime," *Yearbook of the National Probation and Parole Association,* Vol. XXXVII, 1943, 307 pp. (Pp. 86–117, 183–224.)
3. Bossard, J. H. S., and E. A. Boll (eds.), "Adolescents in Wartime," *Annals of the American Academy of Political and Social Science,* 236:26–50, 60–82, 1944.
4. Gerard, M. W., *et al.,* "Psychology of Pre-adolescent Children in War Time," *American Journal of Orthopsychiatry,* 13:493–517, 1943.
5. Hentig, H. von, "Juvenile Delinquency and Adult Disorganization," *Journal of Criminal Law and Criminology,* 35:87–92, 1944.
6. Jones, A. H., "An Inquiry into Juvenile Delinquency in an English Town: A Comparison between the Effects of Peacetime and Wartime Conditions," *Social Service Review,* 19:525–531, 1945.
7. Preston, R. C., "Children's Reactions to a Contemporary War Situation," *Child Development Monographs,* No. 28, 1942, 96 pp.
8. Williams, H. D., "Behavior Problems of Children in Wartime," *Nervous Child,* 2:346–352, 1943.

CHAPTER TWELVE

The Social Life
of the School

The social life of the school has three major manifestations—the voluntary groupings among the students, the relationships developed in the classroom, and the co-curricular activities of the school. The first of these manifestations has been discussed in an earlier chapter. The present chapter will, therefore, be devoted to two main topics: the social anatomy of the classroom and the co-curricular interests of high school pupils.

I. Social Life of the Class

1. Social Anatomy of the Classroom: A class is, or soon becomes, a social unit, not just a random assortment of isolated individuals. Even if the pupils are strangers at the beginning of the year, they will not remain that way for long. During the elementary school years the social life of the classroom is extremely important to a child because he spends about half his waking time in it and, perhaps, another quarter in playing with the children he works with there. In secondary school, students have several classes and several teachers. Each class has a structure of its own, since the individuals composing it are different. But no single class is likely to be as important in the adolescent's social development as the elementary school class is to the child's. However, it is desirable for a teacher in secondary school to know how to investigate social relationships by making a sociogram and to know how to use the results. This form of inquiry represents a fairly new approach to the study of the individual and his group, and although its potentialities are probably not yet fully realized, it has already proved its usefulness.

The first step consists in asking the students, after they have had time to get acquainted, to write down the names of the one, two, or three classmates with whom they would most like to work and those of the one, two, or three with whom they would least like to work. The request is usually made just before the teacher intends to divide the pupils into groups or committees for independent work; there is thus an immediate and practical motivation that impels the pupils to tell the truth and to take the matter seriously. One usually limits the number of votes to not more than three, because the diagram otherwise becomes too complicated for use. Both the choices and the rejections may be recorded upon a single chart, but often they are put into separate diagrams, in the interests of clarity. The arrangement of the children's names upon the chart rests upon convenience. The

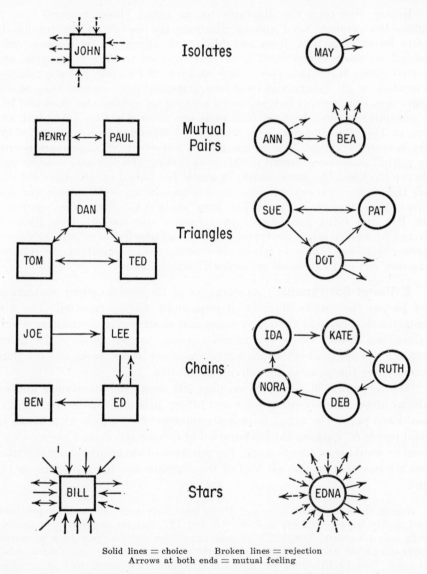

Solid lines = choice   Broken lines = rejection
Arrows at both ends = mutual feeling

Fig. 86. *Typical Results from Sociometric Studies*

only guiding principle is to prevent as many crossings of the lines as may be possible. Boys are usually represented by squares or triangles; girls by circles. Each child's name appears inside one of these symbols. The maker of the diagram next draws an unbroken line, terminating in an arrowhead, from the square or circle to that of each of the child's choices. For aversions, one uses a broken line. If either feeling is mutual, there is an arrowhead on both ends of the line. When the diagram is completed, one is almost certain to find certain arrangements and groupings.

Before discussing the diagrams for an entire class, it seems best to explain the symbols used and to illustrate the nature of the results. In Figure 86 on page 389, John and May both appear to be isolates. John received no choices, expressed none, was rejected by five classmates, and rejected three. May made two choices and rejected no one, but she received no mention at all. Henry and Paul form a mutual pair—in this case, an exclusive one, since neither boy expressed a liking for anyone else. Ann and Bea are not quite so close, because Ann made one other selection. Dan, Ted, and Tom, or Dot, Pat and Sue form triangles of attraction—in the case of the boys, a closed triangle. That of the girls is less exclusive since there is only one mutual attraction instead of three; moreover, Dot has attachments outside the triangle. The boys' chain, in which Joe likes Lee who likes Ed who likes Ben, is an open one, because there is no relation between Ben and Joe, while that of the girls is closed. The boys' chain is interrupted by one rejection. Bill and Edna are "stars," one positive and one negative. Bill was selected by twelve other boys, two of whom he selected in return. Edna was rejected by eleven others, of whom she rejected two; in addition, she rejected one other girl and expressed preference for three more.

2. Use of Sociograms: As examples of the uses to which sociograms may be put the results of three investigations will be reported. The first illustrates the practical value of a sociogram in arranging committees within a class, the second shows the interrelational changes in an entire group when the teacher used her sociogram to guide her in her work, and the third demonstrates the changes in individual children.

The sociogram in Figure 87 on page 391 shows the attractions and repulsions among the seventeen boys and fifteen girls in a high school English class. Each pupil was asked to indicate the two other pupils with whom he would prefer to work on the preparation of a joint report and the two with whom he would least like to work. For purposes of simplification, the attractions are recorded on the left half of the diagram and the rejections on the right.

Among these seventeen boys and fifteen girls there were one small clique, composed of five boys (Numbers 4, 6, 10, 11, and 12), and the suggestion of another among girls (Numbers 7, 8, 9, 10, 11, and 12). There are also four pairs of mutual friends among the boys, three pairs among the girls, and one pair composed of a boy and a girl. Pair 14–15 among the girls has no voluntary contacts with other members of the class. The pair composed of Boys 1–2 is nearly as isolated. The other pairs have some contacts beyond each other. There are also two chains (Boys 8, 9 and Girls 5, 1; Girls 1, 8, 9, 10, 12, 7, and 5). The stars are Girl 7 and Boy 10. There are five isolates (Boys 5, 7, 13, and Girls 2 and 13); they made choices, but no one chose them. Boy 1 chose only his chum, while Boy 10 unable to choose two from his three intimates and so selected all of them. There are eight choices of girls by boys and five of boys by girls. Boys 9 and 17 chose only girls. Boy 5, an isolate, is trying to attach himself to both a mutual pair and a chain. Boy 7 chose the most popular boy, and Girl 13 chose the most popular girl. This selection of central figures by rank outsiders is a common phenomenon.

One boy, Number 17, and two girls, Numbers 2 and 6, are the main centers of admitted hostility. In five instances a choice in one direction is met with repulsion in the other (Boys 1–5; Boys 8–5; Girls 8–9; Girls 8–6, and Boy 8–Girl 5). There

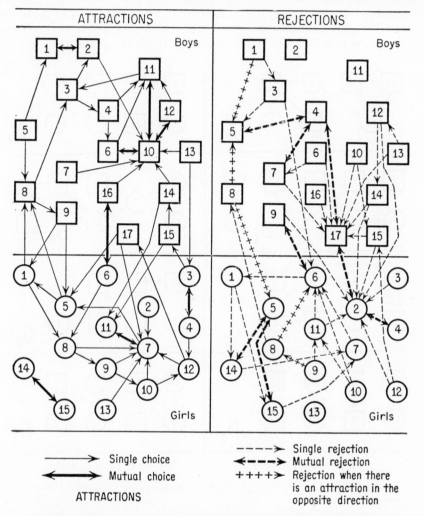

Fig. 87. *Attractions and Repulsions in a High School English Class*

were eight mutual rejections (Boys 4–5; Boys 4–7; Boys 4–17; Girls 2–4; Girls 5–14; Girls 5–15; Boy 17–Girl 2; Boy 9–Girl 6). The chums, Girls 14, 15, selected only each other, ignored boys, rejected the same two girls, were rejected jointly by two girls, and were jointly ignored by everyone else. Eight boys rejected girls, and four girls rejected boys. Boys 2 and 11 rejected no one; if they could not work with their chums or with the most popular boy they did not care with whom they worked. Girl 13 also rejected no one. Boys 5, 16, and Girls 3, 4, 7 made only one rejection each, while Boy 4 made 3. Boys 1, 2, 6, 10, 11, 13, and 16 and Girls 3, 9, 10, 12, and 13 received no rejections.

In order to try out the effect of these various interrelationships upon the work of small groups, the writer persuaded the teacher of the above class to divide it into (A) one good group, (B) one that was composed of small cliques, (C) one that contained many antagonisms, and (D) one in which the members had relatively few contacts with each other. The interrelationships are shown in the left half of Figure 88, below. The groups were given a list of a dozen topics, any one of which they might choose to work on, their first task being to select their subject. So far as the academic result

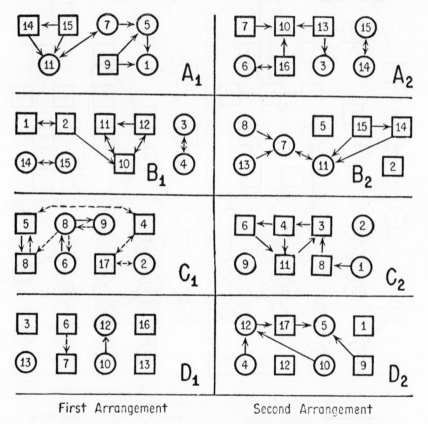

First Arrangement   Second Arrangement

Fig. 88. *Two Groupings of the Same Students for Committee Work*

was concerned Groups A and B turned in good reports; that from Group C was poor, while Group D never finished any joint report, although most of the members put in individual ones of varying merit. Girl 7 became the leader of Group A from the start. For a few days, Boy 10 tried through his general popularity to whip the cliques in Group B into line, but not without a good deal of resistance. Whenever he stopped prodding, the group fell to pieces. In the end, he broke the work up into units and assigned one unit to each clique—thus showing that his popularity rested upon the foundation of an insight into social behavior. Group C was full of discord and argument, as might have been expected, since there were three mutual rejections and three cases in which a liking in one direction was met by a dislike in the other. There was no leader, and twice the teacher had to intervene to keep the peace. If anything, the antagonisms among the members were deeper at the end of their joint effort than at the beginning. Group D discussed the selection of a topic in a listless and desultory way for nearly two weeks but never came to an agreement. In the end the group simply disintegrated; a few members wrote individual reports.

For the next assignment, the teacher rearranged the students to the best possible advantage, as shown in the right half of Figure 88. She put

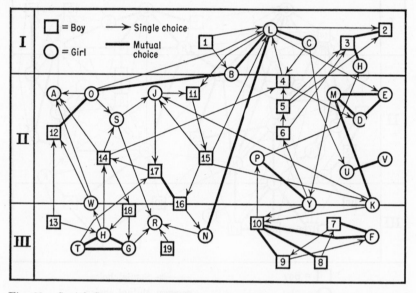

Fig. 89. *Social Structure in October, 1942*[a]

[a] There are two girls indicated by the letter H in this figure. In referring to them, Girl H in the upper right corner will be called H₁ and the other H₂. The same plan is used for Figure 90.

Adapted from L. A. Cook, "An Experimental Sociographic Study of a Stratified Tenth-Grade Class," *American Sociological Review,* 10:252, 1945. Used by permission of the publisher.

one student with some qualities of leadership into each group, broke up most of the cliques, and distributed the isolated and disliked pupils so that there were no more than two in each group. They were soon drawn into at least a slight degree of activity by their more socialized mates and by their leader. Aside from the isolates, positive bonds held the members of each committee together. All four groups worked through several projects in harmony and with excellent results academically.

The second investigation continued over a period of eighteen months. In the fall of 1942 a high school teacher made a sociogram of her class of forty-three pupils—twenty-two girls and twenty-one boys. The positive attractions are shown in Figure 89, above. On the basis of several types of evidence, the teacher divided the students into three "prestige" classes. These classes are indicated by Roman numerals at the left side of the figure.

Several boys and girls are on or very close to the borderline between two groups (Girls H, B, K, W, and Y and Boys 4, 16, and 18). One can see three small cliques (Girls M, E, D, Girls H_2, T, G, and Boys 7, 8, 9, 10 with Girl F). During the first year of work with this group the teacher relied mainly on individual guidance. A sociogram made in November, 1943 (not reproduced here), showed some minor changes in social structure; there were more attractions among the pupils, and two of the three former

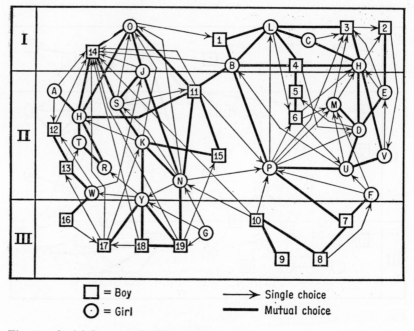

Fig. 90. *Social Structure in May, 1944*

Adapted from Cook, "An Experimental Sociographic Study of a Stratified Tenth-Grade Class," *loc. cit.*, p. 259. Used by permission of the *American Sociological Review*.

cliques had begun to break up. During the next semester the teacher tried a group approach, by means of sundry group undertakings, both in school and out. All of these were activity projects, in which the class as a whole did the planning and made the decisions, and in which all members participated. The last sociogram of the experiment, made in May, 1944, appears in Figure 90, above.

The first and most obvious change is in the number of positive relationships. The mutual likes, indicated by the heavy lines, have more than doubled. More single lines also appear. Each member of the class is thus bound to a larger number of classmates by positive ties at the end than at the beginning of the experiment. In 1942 the stars were Girl L, Boy 10, and to a lesser degree Girls A, H_2, J, and R and Boy 14. At the end there were eight girls (O, L, M, P, D, Y, N, and H_1) and four boys (14, 17, 19, and 11) who might be classed as stars. At the beginning Boys 1, 13, and 19 received no votes; at the end they received three, three, and four, respectively. A few pupils (Girls K, Y, N, H_2, T, O, and R, and Boys 14, 17, and 16) had changed their alliances so much that they had to be moved to another section of the diagram. Girl O and Boys 14 and 4 began in Prestige Class II and ended in Class I; Girls K, H_2, R, N, T, and F and Boy 13 emerged from Class III into Class II. Boy 17 moved from Class II to Class III. Whatever

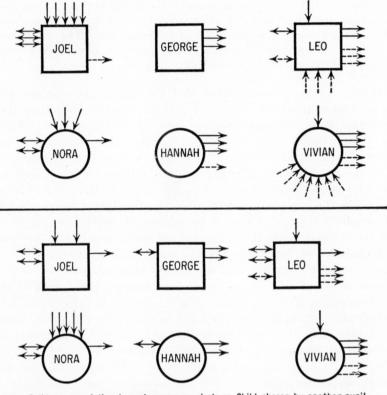

→ Solid arrow pointing toward square or circle = Child chosen by another pupil
--→ Broken arrow pointing toward square or circle = Child rejected by another pupil
← Solid arrow pointing away from square or circle = Child chooses another pupil
←-- Broken arrow pointing away from square or circle = Child rejects another pupil
←→ Solid arrow with points at both ends = Mutual choice
←--→ Broken arrow with points at both ends = Mutual rejection

Fig. 91. *Changes in the Contacts of Certain Children*

Based on H. Taba and D. Elkins, *With Focus on Human Relations,* American Council on Education, 1950, pp. 191–192.

else the pupils of this entire class may or may not have learned, they did learn to like each other. There is practically no sign of the small tight cliques, and the various mutual pairs have made many other contacts. The group has now three leaders (Girls L and O and Boy 14). Between the last two there is a mutual bond, and they furnish the leadership for one section of the class. The two factions are joined through several pupils who have friends in both halves (Boys 1, 11, 15, and 10 and Girls B, P, and N).

It remains to say a word as to the effect upon the structure of the class of procedures that take into account the already existing likes and dislikes of its members. The results are perhaps best seen by examining individual cases, taken from a third study. Figure 91 on page 395 shows the votes for and against two popular, two unpopular, and two neglected children in September, 1948, and again in April, 1949, after they had had a year of attention. The popular boy, Joel, lost votes, presumably because they were diverted to other children who needed them more; Nora, however, gained two additional votes. The unpopular boy, Leo, lost three rejections while gaining a chum. The unpopular girl, Vivian, lost all her rejections. The two isolates, George and Hannah, each gained a chum; they were still neglected, but at least they made some progress.

It is to everyone's advantage that the social interrelations within a class be used as much as possible, if only for purposes of getting the work done better, since harmony produces better results than strife.[1] Moreover, if the rejected pupils lose some of the antagonism directed against them, they have less need for hostile, aggressive defense reactions. The isolates and neglected ones begin to establish contact with the world. Even if they learned no more, and they often do, such results in character development would make the procedures worth while. The intelligent use of a sociogram thus permits a teacher to work with adolescent society instead of against it, as she is likely to do if she ignores the social behavior of her students.

3. Relation of Teacher to Class: Some of the relatively recent studies of the relation of teachers to their classes have consisted of obtaining a verbatim report of what went on in class during a given unit of time on several occasions, and of then analyzing this record. In many cases, however, the observation of experts was the main method of investigation. Sometimes the teachers knew they were being observed, and sometimes they did not. Naturally, no two records of a teacher's behavior, either by different observers on the same day or by analysis of verbatim records on different days, show perfect agreement. Wholly aside from any variability in the observers, the teacher does not proceed in exactly the same manner every day because of differences in subject matter, if for no other reason. Since she is influenced by human stresses and strains, she herself changes more or less. However, the reliability of samples taken over several days is high. In noting and classifying types of contacts, trained observers show correlations from 0.74 to 0.93.[2] The teachers also show remarkable consistency in the nature of their contacts with the children; if they are integrative on Monday they will probably be integrative on Friday. The children's reactions to the teacher show a good deal of consistency. That is, Sammy's hostility or helpfulness on a given day is likely to be followed by aggression (even though against another child or assuming a different

---

[1] N. E. Shoobs, "Sociometry in the Class Room," *Sociometry,* 10:154–164, 1947.

[2] H. H. Anderson and J. E. Brewer, "Studies of Teachers' Classroom Personalities: I," *Applied Psychology Monographs,* No. 6, 1945, 157 pp.

form) or thoughtfulness of others two weeks later, provided an opportunity arose for him to show his attitude. Examination of typical analyses of reliability leaves one with the conviction that good observers and good analysts of records really do agree with each other well enough to command respect for their findings.

Three studies seem to be of special interest to the prospective teacher. Two are concerned with the teacher's spoken comments and questions, and the third with the classification of a teacher's contacts, both group and individual, with her class, and with the effects of her contacts upon the behavior of the pupils.

The figures in Table **27** summarize results from the first study to be reported. The six teachers involved differed widely from each other in the intent behind their contributions to class guidance or discussion. One teacher (C) spent only **42** per cent of her time in making constructive suggestions. She used up **20** per cent of her time in making announcements, in giving directions, or in merely repeating what a pupil had said, presumably while she communed with herself as to what might next be done. She used the remaining **38** per cent of her time in dominative or destructive contacts with the pupils. Teacher F, on three separate occasions, used **85, 87,** and **86** per cent of her time constructively. Her need for neutral comments varied greatly, probably according to the subject matter and the practical needs of the moment. For example, such an occurrence as a special assembly, a bank day, a prospective fire drill, or an excursion will require more than the customary number of merely informative remarks. Her need to reprove members of the class was infrequent, and during two observation periods she neither gave orders nor spent time justifying herself.

A second study of teachers' remarks and questions is of a more restricted character and concerns the nature of verbal contacts between thirty student teachers and the pupils in their classes.[3] These "teachers" were naturally inexpert, but they were constantly under observation and could therefore be studied intensively. The comments were classified as "positive verbalism" (the direction of an individual pupil's attention to a desired act or attitude), "negative verbalism" (the direction of a pupil away from undesired behavior), and "blanket responses" (remarks directed at the entire class, such as, "Come now, let's all of us start working"). These verbal offerings were correlated with ratings of the teachers' general effectiveness. Two types of verbal comment showed relationship to the ratings. Positive verbalism correlated $+0.59$ with the ratings, while the issuing of "blanket" instructions correlated -0.62. The student teachers received marks in practice teaching at the end of the course. Four students received the highest and two the lowest grades given. These extreme cases show the trends better than the entire group does. The comparison appears in Table **28.** The contrast is clear. Good teaching consists of saying "do" and poor teaching of saying "don't" to particular children and of addressing the class as a whole too frequently.

---

[3] W. C. Olson and M. M. Wilkinson, "Teacher Personality as Revealed by the Amount and Kind of Verbal Direction Used in Behavior Control," *Educational Administration and Supervision,* 24:81–93, 1938.

Table 27

CLASSIFICATION OF THE SPOKEN COMMENTS OF TEACHERS[a]

	Teachers					*Three Ratings of Teacher F*		
	A	B	C	D	E	1	2	3
1. Statements reassuring or commending pupil	18	20	8	2	2	0	8	0
2. Statements conveying to the pupil the feeling that he was understood and to help him elucidate his ideas	5	8	3	0	5	69	58	64
3. Statements or questions proffering information or raising queries about the problem in an objective manner, with the intent of facilitating the solving of the problem	29	40	31	53	70	16	21	22
Constructive comments	*52*	*68*	*42*	*55*	*77*	*85*	*87*	*86*
4. Remarks consisting of polite forms, names of pupils, conveyance of brief administrative items, verbatim repetition of something already said								
Neutral comments	*10*	*22*	*20*	*21*	*9*	*15*	*11*	*0*[b]
5. Statements exhorting or directing the pupil to follow a recommended course of action	15	7	24	14	6	0	0	2
6. Statements reproving the pupil for undesirable action or deterring him from inacceptable future behavior	9	2	9	7	0	0	2	6
7. Statements justifying teacher's own position or course of action	14	1	5	3	8	0	0	6
Destructive comments	*38*	*10*	*38*	*24*	*14*	*0*	*2*	*14*

From J. Whithall, "The Development of a Technique for the Measurement of Social-Emotional Climate in the Classroom," *Journal of Experimental Education*, 17:347–361, 1949. Used by permission of the publisher.

[a] Figures express percentage of time spent by teachers in various types of contact with their pupils.

[b] This result seems most unlikely, though it is possible that a teacher might not call any pupil by name or say "Thank you" or "Would you please continue" during a period of observation. Since the figures are combined to the nearest whole number, a teacher may have used some per cent less than 0.5 per cent in neutral remarks.

Study of observations and records in the third investigation[4] suggested a fivefold classification of the contacts of a teacher with her pupils:

1. Dominative, with evidences of conflict
2. Dominative, with no evidences of conflict
3. Dominative, with evidence of working together

4. Integrative, with no evidence of working together
5. Integrative, with evidence of working together

[4] H. H. Anderson and J. E. Brewer, "Studies of Teachers' Classroom Personalities: II," *Applied Psychology Monographs*, No. 8, 1946, 128 pp.

The members of one pair of teachers were conspicuously different in their behavior. Teacher A was of the authoritarian type. She used domination of class and pupils as her main technique. Most of her contacts consisted either in giving directions or in making explanations. Her dominating procedures resulted in conflict, both with single pupils and with the class as a whole. When she did make integrative reactions, she worked against the children

Table 28

COMPARISON OF VERBAL COMMENTS

Student Teachers	Per Cent of Positive Verbalism	Per Cent of Negative Verbalism	Per Cent of "Blanket" Responses
Four Best	76	16	9
Two Poorest	27	41	32

Based on W. C. Olson and M. M. Wilkinson, "Teacher Personality as Revealed by the Amount and Kind of Verbal Direction Used in Behavior Control," *Educational Administration and Supervision*, 24:81–93, 1938.

three times as frequently as with them. Teacher B created a democratic atmosphere in her room. She had relatively little conflict with her pupils, and her contacts were usually integrative. She used eight times as many contacts classified under Number 5 above as Teacher A did. Teacher B's pupils showed a significant excess of the types of behavior classified by observers as being spontaneous, showing initiative, leading to problem solving or to co-operative efforts with other pupils, and a significant lack of behavior classified as attempts to domineer over other children or as nervous habits.

It is interesting to note that teachers in the same school tend to resemble each other, either because they were originally selected by the principal as embodiments of what he or she thought teachers should be, or because the yearly newcomers to the group gradually conformed to the norm. Thus all teachers in one school equaled or exceeded all teachers in another in the excess of their integrative over their dominative reactions.

The authoritarian type of teacher is no longer admired. Her domineering procedures break up or repress natural groupings among the students and result in frequent conflict between herself and them. It is reflected by the students toward each other, and it favors the dependence of a student upon authority. Since adolescents are going to work together anyway, they will form a resistive unit to the domineering teacher. Such a teacher may achieve good academic results but at the cost of injury, temporary or permanent, to the development of those in her charge and of no little injury to herself, because of the heavy strain under which she works. The acceptable teacher of the present makes every effort to enlist her pupils' natural social grouping in advancing her work, to study the interrelationships within her class, to use guidance and suggestion rather than coercion, and to maintain with the group and with its individual members an integrative attitude that permits her class to develop into a living social unit.

II. The Co-curricular Program

The social activities sponsored by the high school take the form of the "extracurricular" or, to use a more appropriate name, the "co-curricular" program. Although the activities should always be based upon the spontaneous interests of adolescent boys and girls, they are nevertheless to some extent organized and supervised by the school. Because of the intense social interests of most adolescents, these co-curricular activities constitute an important part of school life.

1. Nature and Types of Activity: Theoretically, the co-curricular program should include opportunities for students to develop their interest and skill along any line, whether or not it is already adequately provided for in the program of classes. Actually, however, the expansion of activities is always conditioned by the size and facilities of any particular school. Unless it owns a printing press, a school cannot, for instance, have a club in which pupils actually print their own stories. There is a limit also to the number of clubs a member of the faculty can supervise and the number a pupil can profitably belong to.

In order to demonstrate the wide variety of adolescent interests and enthusiasms, a summary is given below of the types of organization that are sponsored in junior and senior high schools, although not all of them appear in any one school.

I. Organizations concerned with school government
1. Student government, student council
2. Student court
3. Home room organization
4. Class organization
5. Assembly program committees

II. Organizations based on service to school or community
1. Know-your-city club
2. Improve-your-city club, neighborhood club
3. School newspapers, handbook, magazine
4. School police
5. Army, Navy, Marine, and Air Force clubs, women's corps
6. Patriotic clubs

III. Organizations growing out of academic classwork
1. Language clubs
2. Writing clubs
3. Debating clubs
4. Mathematics clubs, surveying clubs
5. Naturalist, Audubon, or Agassiz clubs
6. Astronomy, geology, geography, chemistry, physics clubs
7. History, current events, biography clubs
8. Civics, sociology clubs
9. Honor societies: Phi Beta Sigma, Cum Laude Society, Ephebian Society, National Honor Society, etc.

IV. Organizations based on commercial or home economics classwork
  1. Business correspondence clubs
  2. Stenographic and typing clubs
  3. Office practice clubs
  4. Market clubs
  5. Banking clubs
  6. Homemaking clubs: embroidery, knitting, crocheting, serving, millinery
  7. Fashion clubs
  8. Home nursing clubs
  9. Gardening clubs
  10. Cooking clubs: canning, freezing clubs
  11. Textile, basketry clubs

V. Organizations based on classwork in mechanical arts and applied science
  1. Mechanical drawing, blueprinting, printing clubs
  2. Carpentry, cabinetmaking, woodcarving clubs
  3. Forging, metalworking, jewelry-making clubs
  4. Model-making clubs: airplanes, sailboats, speed boats, automobiles
  5. Radio, television clubs; radio building or repair club
  6. Leatherwork club

VI. Organizations based on social needs and interests
  1. Dance clubs, school dances
  2. Bridge clubs
  3. Fraternities and sororities
  4. Etiquette clubs
  5. Leaders' clubs

VII. Organizations based on aesthetic needs and interests
  1. Music: orchestra, bands, glee clubs, school chorus, musical appreciation, radio, phonograph clubs
  2. Drawing and painting: sketching, camera, cartoons, posters, art collecting, art appreciation, designing
  3. Dancing: esthetic, folk, social

VIII. Organizations based on religious or moral needs and interests
  1. Girl Reserves, Hi-Y clubs, Junior YWCA or YMCA, 4-H Clubs, Boy and Girl Scouts, Camp Fire Girls, Junior Red Cross, hospital auxiliary
  2. Church clubs
  3. Chapel services, assemblies (if of religious nature)

IX. Organizations based on athletic needs and interests
  1. School teams: baseball, basketball, football, tennis, hockey, swimming, skating, track, gymnasium, etc.
  2. Class teams of same types
  3. Hiking or camping clubs
  4. Intramural clubs

The first type of activity to be discussed here is the organization for governmental purposes of the home room, the student council, and the assembly. Through these activities the pupils practice techniques of government and participate in the conduct of school affairs. They learn how voting is done, how laws are formulated and passed, how a court functions, how rules are enforced. These activities give practical training in citizenship. The more the students take part in their own government the better, but there are obvious limitations to their participation. In the first place, there are several matters that are not at all their business: for instance, the repair of buildings, the employment of teachers, and—in considerable measure— the curriculum. The main objective of student government is the education of pupils through the control of behavior in the school, the punishment of the violators of the students' own regulations, and the management of small units of government—such as the home room or any of the clubs developed by the school. These responsibilities usually appeal to adolescents because they feel themselves old enough to determine rules for their own behavior.

The range of topics included in the list on pages 400–401 suggests the catholicity of adolescent interest. Although some of these clubs are obviously related to the curricular work of various departments in the high school, they do not have the same objectives or values as the courses from which many undoubtedly developed. Students may use their activities for purposes of exploring various untried fields, for the development of avocations and of profitable and interesting uses of leisure time, as opportunities to develop normal social relationships with each other, for practice in self-direction and self-government, and as outlets for their emotional drives.

Athletic activities form a class by themselves. In the past they have shown a tendency to overshadow other elements in the nonacademic program of the high school. The social prestige and general publicity given the high school athlete have combined to produce abnormal personalities in many boys who were normal until their period of athletic prominence. Intense competition in high school athletics has led to the development of a few experts rather than to the rounded physical development of every pupil in the school. In recent years more and more people have realized that high school athletics might well have a damaging effect upon morale and might prevent rather than promote the development of good sportsmanship. To combat this tendency the intramural athletic program has been developed with great success in some schools.

As a means of physical development and as a preparation for leisure time, it seems desirable that every adolescent should learn to play reasonably well at least one game for which the equipment is not expensive and the demands on vitality are not excessive. This provision immediately rules out football, basketball, hockey, and baseball because the equipment is too expensive, the risk of injury too great, and the drain on energy too severe. Tennis, golf, softball, swimming, skating, or fencing, on the other hand, may be continued for many years after adolescence. So also may such minor games as badminton, handball, table tennis, or volleyball. As training for adult use of leisure, the less vigorous and less highly organized games and sports are to be recommended; but the time to learn them is during childhood and adolescence.

Most of the activities listed above are definitely wholesome and valuable, but the high school fraternity and sorority are generally condemned. They have all the faults of the college brand and practically none of the virtues.

Membership in them comes at just the time when boys and girls have the strongest drives to slavish imitation of each other, the least degree of social independence, the most sensitive feelings, and the highest degree of uncertainty about their general acceptability. Members are influenced to become more snobbish than is normal, and nonmembers develop increased feelings of rejection. The difference between the privileged few and the undervalued many is nowhere sharper than in a school divided into members of secret societies and everyone else.

2. Distribution of Co-curricular Activities: If adolescents are left to themselves, the activities will almost certainly be dominated by the best-adjusted students in the school. The pupil who tends to participate voluntarily and successfully is usually a little more intelligent and more mature than the nonparticipant, he comes more frequently from the upper socio-economic levels, his personality is better organized, and he has wider interests than the average. These statements are based upon a study of 115 adolescents who were mentioned in their school newspapers as compared with those whose names never appeared.[5] They are the "natural" leaders, and they tend to overparticipate, probably because they have the necessary traits and social position and because they derive satisfaction of their social drives by such activities. By contrast, the shy, self-conscious, or repressed pupils who most need co-curricular activities for their own best development are likely to have the least opportunity for the participation that would give them the experience they need in order to gain social poise and social skills.

It is not necessary for pupils who do not spontaneously participate in activities to remain aloof throughout their adolescent years. Those who are shy, easily embarrassed, and withdrawn can be helped to a better adjustment and eventually to some degree of participation in the social life of the school.[6] Counseling that is directed specifically toward helping students appreciate the value of co-curricular activities yields results.[7] It is not a matter of requiring participation but of readjusting isolated pupils so that they have a desire to join in the activities going on about them.

In many schools the administration has tried to regulate participation by a point system or other method. This technique, if used alone, has been rather ineffective for two reasons. In the first place, the number of points, indicating the number of positions a pupil may hold simultaneously, is generally too high. Second, those pupils who love to expand their egos by participation in nonacademic activities often resort to the following trick: they use up their own points and then get their friends elected to other

[5] M. C. Jones and H. E. Jones, "Factors Associated with Prominence in Extra-Curricular Activities at the High School Level," *American Psychologist*, 4:251, 1949.

[6] See J. C. Solomon and P. L. Axelrod, "Group Psychotherapy for Withdrawn Adolescents," *American Journal of the Diseases of Children*, 68:86–101, 1944; or P. L. Axelrod, M. S. Cameron, and J. C. Solomon, "An Experiment in Group Therapy with Shy Adolescent Girls," *American Journal of Orthopsychiatry*, 14:616–627, 1944.

[7] R. Hill, "An Experimental Study in Social Adjustment," *American Sociological Review*, 9:481–494, 1944.

positions that they covet, whereupon they shelve the obliging friends and do the work themselves. Some better method than those usually employed is needed for distributing participation in terms of needs as well as in terms of interest.

The study reported in Figure 92 on page 405 is admittedly old, and schools in which participation is as uneven as here represented are becoming infrequent, but the danger of such a distribution is always present merely because adolescents are adolescents. In this study, 313 pupils kept count of the amount of time spent during a single week in nonacademic activities; the same pupils also listed the number of organizations to which they belonged. The time spent shows, first, that 34 per cent participated in no co-curricular activities during the week of investigation. Another 49 per cent spent 1 to 10 hours. The remaining 17 per cent spent from 11 to 22 hours. To put the matter in another way, this group of 313 pupils devoted a total of 1,508 hours, of which 51 per cent were spent by only 14 per cent of the pupils. A similar situation is shown by the number of groups to which these students belonged. Thirteen pupils belonged to no club. On the other hand, there were two who belonged to eight different clubs. In this entire group of 313 pupils there was a total of 946 club memberships; of this number, more than half were held by less than a third of the pupils. From any point of view, the distribution of co-curricular activities was most uneven.

A report of a quite successful distribution of activities on the part of 1,584 students states that 88 per cent took some part, however small, leaving only 12 per cent without participation.[8] It is only a reflection of individual differences that the degree of participation among the 88 per cent (1,390 students) should vary a good deal. The students averaged a little less than 3 participations apiece, with a range from 1 to 7. Of the total 3,893 participations, 35 per cent consisted merely of membership and another 37 per cent of some minor contribution to a small committee; 17 per cent of the participations consisted in membership on a major committee, and 11 per cent of holding office. This showing gives evidence of guidance, since the participation, uneven though it is, is better than among unguided adolescents.

As an example of development in extracurricular activities within a single school, some statistics will be presented from a private school that has a complete set of yearbooks running back for nearly 100 years. The earlier ones sometimes mentioned the various clubs and sometimes gave the names of the officers—but not the names of the members of each club—and sometimes they reported nothing about extracurricular activities. The earliest yearbook to include all the facts needed for the present investigation was published in 1881. In this year there were 73 girls in the school and sixteen clubs, with a total membership of 189. The sixteen clubs were titled as follows: orchestra, choir, singing (for any girl who liked to sing without test of her ability to do so), drawing, painting, athletics, gymnasium, canoeing, literature, French, Latin, Greek, Christian Association, Bible, cooking, and drama. Each club had four officers, giving a total of sixteen presidencies and forty-

---

[8] E. H. Wilkins, "On the Distribution of Extra-Curricular Activities," *School and Society,* 51:651–656, 1940.

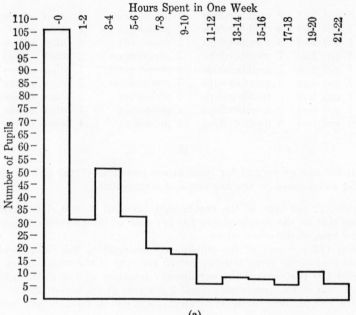

(a)

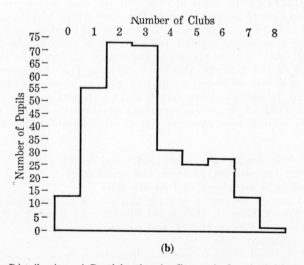

(b)

Fig. 92. *Distribution of Participation in Co-curricular Activities*

Based on W. J. Hayes, "Some Factors Influencing Participation in Voluntary
School Activities," *Teachers College Contributions to Education*, No. 419, 1930,
82 pp.

eight other offices. The record of the nine girls with the greatest degree of participation is listed below:

1 girl had	9 memberships	2 presidencies	3 other offices
1 girl had	8 memberships	3 presidencies	1 other office
1 girl had	8 memberships	1 presidency	6 other offices
1 girl had	7 memberships	2 presidencies	2 other offices
1 girl had	7 memberships	2 presidencies	4 other offices
1 girl had	6 memberships	3 presidencies	2 other offices
1 girl had	6 memberships	1 presidency	3 other offices
1 girl had	6 memberships	1 presidency	5 other offices
1 girl had	6 memberships	1 presidency	4 other offices
	63	16	30

The totals for this group and for three others including all the girls in the school are further summarized in another series of statements:

- 9 girls (12 per cent of the enrollment) belonged to 6–9 clubs, held 33 per cent of the memberships, 100 per cent of the presidencies, and 63 per cent of the other offices.
- 17 girls (23 per cent of the enrollment) belonged to 3–5 clubs, held 35 per cent of the memberships, and 35 per cent of the minor offices
- 36 girls (50 per cent of the enrollment) belonged to 1–2 clubs, held 32 per cent of the memberships, and 2 per cent of the minor offices
- 11 girls (15 per cent of the enrollment) belonged to no club, and held no offices

At this time the clubs were relatively unsupervised, and each girl joined as many as she wanted to. It will be noted at once that the most active girls carried the greatest load and that 15 per cent, even in this small school, had no part whatever in activities. Of the 73 girls in the school, 46 (63 per cent) had no office of any kind.

In 1951 the same school enrolled 164 girls. All of them belonged to Student Government, all but 4 to the Christian Association, all but 7 to the Dramatic Association, and all but 3 to the Athletic Association. The 14 nonmemberships in these four school groups represented only nine girls, of whom five abstained from two organizations. In addition, there were 42 clubs, a student court with five judges, a yearbook committee (with one chairman and seven members), and three dormitory committees, totaling three chairmen and six other members. The 42 clubs were as follows:

Orchestra, choir, singing, glee, opera, radio, and records clubs
sketching, art appreciation, painting, and architecture clubs
leather working, woodcarving, and jewelry clubs
gymnasium, games, swimming, skating, and rowing and canoeing clubs
literature, French, German, Italian and Spanish, and classical clubs
ancient history, European history, and current events clubs
Bible and philosophy clubs
biology, physics and chemistry, and mathematics clubs
child care, home economics, and family living clubs
drama production and puppet clubs
social dancing and folk dancing clubs
writing and newspaper clubs

There were 42 presidencies of clubs, 4 presidencies of the four large school organizations, 5 student judges, 4 chairmen of committees, and 4 presidencies of the school classes, making up a total of 59 major offices. The clubs each had one other officer (42 secretary-treasurers), the four large organizations had each 3 other officers (4 vice-presidents, 4 secretaries, and 4 treasurers), the committees had 13 members besides the chairmen, and each class had a secretary-treasurer, giving a total of 71 minor offices. The student government had passed rules several years earlier limiting membership to 4 clubs or committees in addition to the 4 large organizations to which practically everyone in the school belonged, and requiring membership by each student in at least 1 club. There was also a recognized principle that every student should hold at least one office every year, and the secretary of student government was charged with the responsibility of keeping a list of the students, rejecting the names for any proposed offices in excess of the number allowed and suggesting names of students who had held no office as substitutes for those who had reached their limit. Membership on the various school athletic teams was also counted on a student's record. There were therefore enough offices of some sort to go around for all, and the few girls who were inclined to be overactive were prevented from having more positions than they should.

The participation in 1951 is summarized below:

44 girls (27 per cent of the enrollment) belonged to 4 clubs, had 176 memberships, held 37 major offices, and 6 minor ones.

47 girls (28 per cent of the enrollment) belonged to 3 clubs, had 141 memberships, held 11 major offices and 28 minor ones.

60 girls (37 per cent of the enrollment) belonged to 2 clubs, had 120 memberships, held 9 major offices and 28 minor ones.

13 girls (8 per cent of the enrollment) belonged to 1 club, had 13 memberships, held 2 major offices and 9 minor ones.

In the first group, 43 of the 44 girls held some office; in the second group, 39 out of the 47; in the third, 37 of the 52; and even in the lowest, 11 of the 13 girls had some kind of responsibility. The others were all on so many athletic teams that they were not eligible for election to club offices. Counting the 4 large groups to which almost everyone belonged, no girl had less than 5 memberships. The important positions tended to be held by the more active girls, but this situation can hardly be avoided; students are not going to elect a shy isolate to a major office, and even if they could be persuaded to do so, the responsibility and the unwelcome attention might easily precipitate the isolate into a panic. However, there is a great gain over the figures from 1881. At present the most active 27 per cent of the girls hold 63 per cent of the major offices, whereas in 1881 the most active 12 per cent held 100 per cent of them. The minor offices are also much better distributed. One cannot hope for a completely even distribution because all students do not show the same degree of interest, ability, or social skill. All one can do is to persuade the students themselves to limit participation for several reasons: to prevent overfatigue and a too great distraction from classwork among their extremely active members, to give the isolates the experiences they need for developing greater security in their social milieu, and to provide training in leadership for the few who have the necessary qualifications.

The effect of participation in co-curricular activities upon scholarship is almost always favorable.[9] The pupil who has an integral part in the social life of the school does better academic work than the pupil of equal ability

---

[9] See, for instance, M. K. Remmlein, "Scholastic Accomplishment as Affected by Intelligence and Participation in Extra-Curricular Activities," *Journal of Applied Psychology,* 23:603–607, 1939.

who does not. Teachers who feel that co-curricular activities absorb too much time would do well to remember this point.

Most students have at one time or another belonged to clubs or other student groups from which they have, or have not, derived considerable value. It is suggested that each student might find it useful to write such a summary of his or her own secondary school experiences with activities as that given below:

In secondary school the writer belonged to a nature study club. During one year, by vote of the members, the club collected rocks. Every Saturday morning about twenty girls tramped over hill and dale looking for specimens. By the end of the year, several hundred had been gathered, classified—with considerable help from an instructor—and properly labeled. There was then an exhibit, with introductory remarks and explanations by the president of the club. During another year, the writer belonged to a Latin club whose members decided to translate into Latin and dramatize a story. For reasons long since forgotten, they selected *Bluebeard*. The Brothers Grimm were therefore consulted for a correct version of the tale, which was turned into execrable Latin by one of the girls; thereafter it was examined and rewritten, in even worse versions, by each successive member until all had had a chance at it. Not content with a classroom dramatization, the girls rehearsed their production and gave the play for the school. Since everyone knew the story no one was inconvenienced by the use of Latin words. The writer was Wife Number 2, who died a grueling death, probably from an overdose of bad syntax.

At a still later period there arose among the girls in the school a feeling that the faculty and students did not understand each other. For some obscure reason the means taken to bring about a *rapprochement* was the production by the students of a one-act play in which the teaching of a particularly stupid class was portrayed. Over this chef-d'oeuvre, a committee labored on and off for weeks; the members then assembled a cast of characters and trained them; they requisitioned the embryo artists of the school to create appropriate posters and invitations; eventually they gave their play—which was extremely funny, but not for any of the intended reasons. On another occasion several girls decided to publish a book of poems. They bullied something out of practically everyone in the school; next they persuaded two or three girls who could print nicely to write the poems on fancy paper; then they bound the sheets together and presented the volume to the principal of the school. Toward the end of the last year, about a dozen girls suddenly developed an interest in religion and formed the habit of meeting with one of the teachers every Sunday between breakfast and church. In the course of these meetings they discovered many beautiful passages in the Bible, reached numerous naïve conclusions on theological matters, and acquired the beginnings of a philosophy of life.

3. The Nonacademic Program: Co-curricular activities among high school students presumably date back to the first high school, since adolescence is a period of social interest. In most schools a variety of clubs and societies grew up in a decidedly hit-or-miss fashion. Thus, for a few years a literary society would be very attractive and then almost die out for a decade, only to be resuscitated by some strong personality or by popular interest. From the first there were school parties, school plays, and school ceremonies of various kinds. Within the past forty years these somewhat incidental activities have become more numerous and better organized. Many schools have supervisors who devote their full time to the routine necessary for keeping the entire program moving forward. While many of the societies and other forms of organization are old, an integrated program—functioning as a complement to the curriculum—is new. Consequently, one finds in only a few places a program of activities that approaches what it could become.

Some school officials and teachers do not understand the basic function of the program. They fail to see in the activities any values beyond enjoyment and relaxation. Some teachers regard the co-curricular program as a competitor with their own work—an unfair competitor with lower standards. The greatest values of these activities cannot be obtained if teachers have not learned to use them as supplementary methods for the education of adolescents.

Many clubs are outgrowths of the work in some department of the school; therefore the teachers in that department are the individuals best equipped to supervise these activities. Naturally, the boys and girls should exercise as much control as they can, but they are neither inventive enough nor mature enough to keep a club as interesting or as soundly managed as it will be if it has the assistance of a sympathetic teacher. It is not the idea at all that a teacher should dominate the activities of the students, but rather that she should help them to make the activities more interesting and valuable to themselves. Most teachers have fundamentally no objection to such participation in the nonacademic program of the school. Difficulty arises, however, when a teacher who has already taught six or seven classes in a day is asked to remain after school to assist with a club. Adequate supervision cannot be given casually because it imposes a real burden upon a teacher's time, vitality, and ingenuity. If a school wants its teachers to develop the co-curricular program as well as the course of study, it must make time in the teacher's schedule for work of this sort. The writer knows one school that requires its teachers to return one evening a week for club meetings; some of them are back at the school two or three evenings a week. No teacher can carry such a load of nonacademic work and still be able to give her pupils something worth while during class. The two school programs will have to find some way of co-operating, instead of competing, with each other. One method already tried is to lengthen the school day, two or three times a week at least, and to include the activities during the last hour or two as part of the school's regular program. If some such arrangement can be made, most teachers enjoy working with groups of adolescents who have come into a club because of spontaneous interest. Even so, a teacher's class load needs to be reduced before she is in a position to render her best service to the co-curricular program.

Perhaps the two basic difficulties are the lack of relationship between the academic and nonacademic activities of the school and the lack of clearly realized objectives. Adolescent social life tends to "just grow." It is often purposeless and inchoate. Pupils should, of course, enjoy their activities, but they should also grow into better poised and more mature individuals because of them. Merely having a good time is not enough. The academic and nonacademic work of a school should be so correlated that each reinforces the other and they become two related means by which pupils may best realize their possibilities, develop their talents, expand their horizons, and pursue their interests.

Several practical suggestions for carrying out the purposes of the co-curricular program appear below:

In some public schools a definite period is set aside once or twice a week for the meeting of school clubs. Every student in the school attends some meeting. Each pupil is entirely free to select the club he will attend and is also permitted to change from one group to another whenever he wishes. The only requirement is that he should attend some group meeting during the time set aside for club activities. This technique brings the "outside" activities inside the school where they belong. In some schools a similar arrangement has been made by extending the school days for an hour or more after the completion of classes, and by carrying on various activities during this additional period of time. Thus if the academic work closes at two thirty, the pupils do not leave school until four. Such arrangements are, of course, a step toward an educational use of nonacademic activities because all pupils in the school are automatically involved.

A second step consists in making arrangements whereby the responsibility for managing the various activities devolves upon many different students instead of upon a restricted few. In some schools the following arrangement has been found to work well: In each club there is a central committee of three pupils. Each week one pupil resigns and a new one is added. Each member thus serves for three consecutive weeks before he resigns. Continuity is provided for, since in any given week there are two members from previous weeks. A dispersion of control is also provided for because, in the course of the year, every member in the club will be on this central committee. This arrangement is greatly preferable to the election of three or four permanent officers. In the interests of continuity and student prestige there may be a permanent president for each club—in addition to the central committee—but no other officials are necessary.

For the really educational use of nonacademic activities, it is necessary that someone should be charged with the responsibility of bringing about participation on the part of those pupils who most need the training and socialization, and of giving the natural leaders the experience they need in leading. It takes a good deal of tact and quiet persistence to persuade an introverted adolescent to participate in anything; and it takes more tact and an occasional show of authority to prevent the exhibitionist from indulging in the tactics most harmful to his development.

On the other hand, one must not neglect the natural leader to whom adolescents turn spontaneously. These individuals are sure to lead others, and they need practice in the wise controlling of their followers. They are the pupils who have the natural authority to assume such positions as the head of the student government, the president of the senior class, the president of the athletic association, the chief editor of the yearbook, and so on. Such important posts are obviously no place for the inexperienced; it will not help the introverted pupil to be elected to an onerous position, even if school politics could be so managed as to elect him. The situation is best arranged if the natural leaders fill the outstanding posts in a school, where the authority they exercise will influence the largest number, while minor positions are used for the development of personality among those who need, for their own mental health, a little prominence and a little responsibility. Only by individualizing participation—exactly as the classroom teacher has learned to individualize instruction—can the co-curricular program grow constructively into a means for the development of healthy personalities, and for the expression of the social inclinations, emotional drives, and varied interests of normal adolescents.

III. Summary

A class is a social unit, the members of which are joined together by bonds of attraction or repulsion. These social pressures are very powerful, and in general a teacher should try to work with them, although small, tight cliques and closely bound mutual pairs are sometimes better off if the members do not work together. A sociogram is a most useful device in revealing to a teacher the forces that are operating in her schoolroom.

The position of the teacher in the group is steadily changing from the traditional authoritarianism to a constructive, nondirective, permissive type of leadership. A teacher is well advised if she develops a habit of checking her own classroom comments to determine what proportion of them could be classified as constructive.

The co-curricular life of the school can be of great value to the students and should therefore be encouraged by teachers. It is, however, necessary that all pupils should have some part in it and that no pupil should carry too heavy a load. The program should be as extensive as possible without trespassing upon the academic life of the school.

REFERENCES FOR FURTHER READING

BOOKS
1. Alexander, W. M., and J. G. Saylor, *Secondary Education*, Rinehart & Company, 1950, 536 pp. (Chap. 18.)
2. Crow and Crow, *Our Teen-Age Boys and Girls*, Chaps. 5–6, 9–10.
3. Dimock, *Rediscovering the Adolescent*, Chaps. 9, 10.
4. Fedder, R., *Guidance in Homeroom and Group Activities*. McGraw-Hill Book Company, 1949, 467 pp. (Chaps. 1, 4–7.)
5. Garrison, *Psychology of Adolescence*, Chap. 12.
6. Hollingshead, *Elmtown's Youth*, Chaps. 6, 8.
7. Jennings and Taba, *Sociometry in Group Relations*.
8. Meek, *The Personal-Social Development of Boys and Girls*, Pts. II and III.
9. Merrill, *Problems of Juvenile Delinquency*, Chap. 4.
10. Partridge, *Social Psychology of Adolescence*, Chap. 12.
11. Strang, R., *Group Activities in College and Secondary School*, Harper & Brothers, rev. ed., 1946, 361 pp. (Chaps. 1, 3, 9 and any one of Chaps. 4–8.)

MONOGRAPHS, BULLETINS, PROCEEDINGS, YEARBOOKS, ARTICLES
A. *Interrelationships in the Classroom*
1. Anderson, H. H., and J. E. Brewer, "Studies of Teachers' Classroom Personalities: II. Effects of Teachers' Dominative and Integrative Contacts on Children's Behavior," *Applied Psychology Monographs*, No. 8, 1946, 128 pp.
2. Deutsch, M., "The Effect of Co-operation and Competition upon the Group Process: An Experimental Study," *Human Relations*, 4:199–232, 1949.
3. Finley, M. H., "The Classroom as a Social Group," *American Journal of Orthopsychiatry*, 11:21–30, 1941.
4. Olson, W. C., and M. M. Wilkinson, "Teacher Personality as Revealed by the Amount and Kind of Verbal Direction Used in Behavior Control," *Educational Administration and Supervision*, 24:81–93, 1938.

5. Watson, G., "What Are the Effects of Democratic Atmosphere on Children?", *Progressive Education,* 17:336–342, 1940.
6. Withall, J., "The Development of a Technique for the Measurement of Social-Emotional Climate in the Classroom," *Journal of Experimental Education,* 17:347–361, 1949.

B. *Use of Sociograms*

1. Atkinson, G., "The Sociogram as an Instrument in Social Studies Teaching and Evaluation," *Elementary School Journal,* 50:74–85, 1949.
2. Cook, L. A., "An Experimental Sociographic Study of a Stratified Tenth Grade Class," *American Sociological Review,* 10:250–261, 1945.
3. Moreno, J. L., H. H. Jennings, and R. Stockton, "Sociometry in the Classroom," *Sociometry,* 6:425–428, 1943.
4. Shoobs, N., "Sociometry in the Class Room," *Sociometry,* 10:154–164, 1947.
5. Smucker, O., "Management of Group Tension through the Use of Negative Sociometric Data," *Sociometry,* 10:376–383, 1947.

C. *Extracurricular Activities*

1. Axelrod, P. L., M. S. Cameron, and J. C. Solomon, "An Experiment in Group Therapy with Shy Adolescent Girls," *American Journal of Orthopsychiatry,* 14:616–627, 1944.
2. Hand, H. C., "How to Conduct the Participation in Extra-Class Activities," *Illinois Circular,* Ser. A, No. 51, 1949, 66 pp.
3. Hayes, W. J., "Some Factors Influencing Participation in Voluntary School Activities," *Teachers College Contributions to Education,* No. 419, 1930, 82 pp.
4. Hill, R., "An Experimental Study in Social Adjustment," *American Sociological Review,* 9:481–494, 1944.
5. Jones, M. C., and H. E. Jones, "Factors Associated with Prominence in Extracurricular Activities at the High School Level," *American Psychologist,* 4:251, 1949.
6. McKown, H. C., "The Importance of Extra-Curricular Activities to the Adolescent," *Understanding the Child,* 8:14–20, 1939.
7. Remmlein, M. K., "Scholastic Accomplishment as Affected by Intelligence and Participation in Extra-Curricular Activities," *Journal of Applied Psychology,* 23:603–607, 1939.
8. Solomon, J. C., and P. L. Axelrod, "Group Psychotherapy for Withdrawn Adolescents," *American Journal of the Diseases of Children,* 68:86–101, 1944.
9. Wilkins, E. H., "On the Distribution of Extra-Curricular Activities," *School and Society,* 51:651–656, 1940.
10. Williamson, E. G., "The Extra Curriculum and General Education," *Fifty-first Yearbook of the National Society for the Study of Education,* 1952, Pt. I, pp. 230–249.

Moral
Development

CHAPTER THIRTEEN

Growth in Attitudes

The present chapter contains a number of sections, each of which contributes something to an understanding of growth in attitudes, habits, personal traits, and ideals that, taken together, constitute development in morality. Investigators have measured all kinds of attitudes with more or less success. The writer has limited the discussion to a relatively few topics upon which research has been especially fruitful and interesting, and has selected only two or three illustrative studies for inclusion in each section. The first section deals with attitudes toward racial or national sub-groups of the American population. The second section contains data on the religious growth of children and adolescents. In the third, the development of honesty is traced in some detail. The last two sections are devoted to the growth of ideals and of a philosophy of life—two matters that are of great importance to adolescents. The material on the various topics is somewhat difficult to put together into a picture of moral growth during adolescence. The raw data are presented with some interpretation, but the reader will need to think back to adolescent days and to recall his own early strivings for tolerance, his religious convictions, his idealism, his desire to understand the world, and his longing to make it a better place. Such memories should help in fusing the sundry lines of evidence included in this chapter into a coherent understanding of moral growth in adolescence.

I. Racial Prejudice: Its Nature, Causes, and Expression

In order that a teacher may see her role and that of the school in the prevention of intolerance, it seems best to begin the discussion by giving a brief explanation of its bases, its growth, its nature, and its causes.

1. Social Background of Intolerance: America is often and fondly referred to as the "melting pot." To it have come members of all races, nationalities, political faiths, and religious beliefs. Up to a point there has been the kind of assimilation that was expected, but it has now become obvious that some of the ingredients that went into the pot show little inclination to melt. If fusion is to take place there has to be a desire on the immigrant's side to become Americanized and on the American side to absorb the newcomer. Sometimes the immigrant wishes to remain apart. The orthodox

Jew, for instance, vehemently resists absorption and mourns as he sees his children, his grandchildren, and his great-grandchildren depart ever more and more from ancestral customs. Sometimes the aversion is mutual. Thus the small groups of Portuguese fishermen who settled nearly a century ago here and there along the coast of Maine wanted no truck with the native Yankees, who, in turn, regarded the Portuguese as a low order of humanity. Often, but not always, the prejudice is on the American side, as in the rejection in the West of the Japanese, who wanted desperately to be Americans. In the course of centuries, the problem of interracial adjustment is likely to solve itself through biological assimilation, and the discordant elements will disappear into the general population through intermarriage, just as the Indians of many former tribes have been absorbed, or as the Roman Empire absorbed the surrounding barbarians. This long view, however, does not offer much that is practical in the easing of present-day tensions.

The elements of the population that are proving most difficult to assimilate—in all parts of the country—are the Negroes, the Orientals, and the Jews. In limited areas, the Mexicans, French Canadians, Irish, Germans, Italians, Portuguese, and Poles are also proving resistive to absorption. Certain religious groups fight against assimilation—the Dunkards and the Mormons, for instance—as do a few political groups, of which the Communists may serve as an example. The Negroes, Japanese, Chinese, Filipinos, and Indians present racial variations that are of a fundamental nature. The biological differences remain even after the descendants of the original immigrants have become as Americanized as the Bostonian of purest Anglo-Saxon ancestry, and these differences mark off the individual and make him "feel different," a basic attitude that easily leads to submission in a timid soul and to violence in an aggressive one. Further differences between national groups are social, political, ethnological, religious, or economic, all of which are acquired by the respective groups through social tradition. They become almost as ineradicable as inborn differences between races, however, and are actually just as potent in causing prejudices as are inherited traits, although aversion may be centered upon the latter.

Intolerance of one group of people for another is as old as written history, but several recent developments have tended to create new tensions between groups and to reawaken old ones. World War II intensified antagonisms tremendously, because the need for millions of workers threw together people of all races and national extractions without providing instruction in how to get along together. Thus, in one manufacturing center, the Negro population increased, between 1941 and 1943, seventeen times as fast as it had been increasing from 1930 to 1940, whereas the white population grew much more slowly.[1] Consequently, there were more chances for

---

[1] D. W. Baruch, "Some Aspects of Discrimination in a War Area," *American Journal of Orthopsychiatry,* 14:714–721, 1944.

contact between the races, especially as the Negroes spilled out of their previous district and began to compete with whites for living quarters. Competition for high wages produced additional tension. Since the country needed, above all, able-bodied soldiers and workingmen—especially in the skilled trades— it became necessary to permit Negroes, the largest single unassimilated group, to enter many fields that had never been open to them before. In the Army they became fliers and officers; in industry, if they had the necessary abilities, they were advanced farther and faster than usual; as civilians, they occupied many voluntary positions of responsibility in the Red Cross, and the like. The war record of the Negroes is one to be proud of.[2] Their expanding activities brought them into more and more frequent clashes with white people. Like any other group, they need an acceptance of themselves by others, an equal opportunity for progress, a recognized and satisfactory social status, and a reasonable degree of security.

2. Development of Prejudice: A fanatic intolerance, being a form of projection, is one means of escape from emotional difficulties. The growth of a prejudice runs about as follows:[3] (1) An individual is frustrated in his efforts to satisfy his basic needs, is rejected and neglected; (2) he feels insecure and defenseless, he wants at least enough power to defend himself and, by preference, enough to compensate for his past and present low status; (3) he feels hostile toward almost everyone, but he cannot express his hostility toward those who are more powerful than he is, in any more active way than wishing them ill or grumbling about them. What he needs is a victim who is accessible and in no position to fight back. (4) The individual then displaces his hostility from its natural objects to his victim. If, at the same time, he is subjected to propaganda and furnished with ready-made attitudes, his prejudice develops faster than it otherwise would because it is reinforced from without. (5) The prejudiced person is now ready to commit an act of aggression, and will do so when outside stimuli prompt him. By this series of reactions the fanatic has rid himself of his emotional burden. He no longer feels helpless, because he has someone to attack; and he is no longer isolated, because he can ally himself with others of the same opinions and attitudes. (6) As a final stage, the fanatic adds reasons and justifications for his intolerance. This step is necessary in proportion to the fanatic's intelligence. If he has an otherwise logical and able mind, it soon tells him that he has no sensible reason for hating the people he does. Since this notion, if listened to, would reduce his prejudice and bring back his former state of insecurity, he makes haste to bolster his emotional attitude with "good" reasons. This step is always possible because no group is perfect; as long as one likes the members, or most of them, one overlooks the shortcomings, but as soon as one begins to hate the members, the faults are

---

[2] Symposium, "The American Negro in World War I and World War II," *Journal of Negro Education*, 12:263–585, 1943.

[3] M. F. A. Montagu, "Some Psychodynamic Factors in Race Prejudice," *Journal of Social Psychology*, 30:175–187, 1949.

not hard to find. When a fanatic is queried about his prejudice, he justifies it with his "reasons," which actually came at the end of the process, not at the beginning, as he probably thinks. He is usually not aware that the early steps were parts of the development. It should be noted that the basic causes of prejudice are emotional and have no necessarily integral connection with whatever group the prejudice is directed against. It is this lack of logic, plus the factitious logic of the superimposed justification, that makes intolerance so hard to "cure." Moreover, the prejudiced person's ego clings to his intolerance in sheer protection because it keeps him from sensing his own inferiorities.

The above account outlines the stages in the development of prejudice on the part of a person who received little or no help from others. Actually, most people short-circuit the process by imitating attitudes that they observe in people whom they admire or love. Thus, pupils' attitudes and those of their teachers agree more than they would by chance, and children's attitudes resemble closely those of their parents.[4] Adolescents, especially, imitate the opinions of their age-mates. An individual who is in the frustrated, insecure, hostile frame of mind that is the forerunner of prejudice can soon find in his environment people with already congealed attitudes and opinions. In addition to his family, teachers, and friends, the movies, the radio, books, and television are constantly presenting him with possible fixations. Society thus furnishes the models, which do not seriously affect those who have no need of them but are accepted uncritically by those who, for their own emotional comfort, need someone to project their frustrations upon.

3. Stereotypes and Scapegoats:[5]   Most people develop stereotypes for the nationalities or races with which they come into contact They generally assign to the groups they like the traits of which they approve and to the groups they dislike the traits of which they disapprove.[6] Also they tend to reject their own least acceptable traits when they think they recognize them in another.[7] A stereotype usually has or has had some slight basis in fact, but the fact may or may not have been relevant. For instance, the writer remembers one sentence from a childhood geography which gave the following stereotype: "The French are a gay people, addicted to light wines and dancing." This entire concept is presumably based upon the kind of entertainment furnished by enterprising Parisians to American tourists, upon the assumption that gaiety was a desideratum. At the time the geography was written the French were certainly "addicted to light wines" because their

---

[4] M. Weltman and H. H. Remmers, "Pupils', Parents', and Teachers' Attitudes: Similarities and Differences," Purdue University Division of Educational Reference, *Studies in Higher Education*, No. 50, 1946.

[5] See G. W. Allport, *ABC's of Scapegoating*, Anti-Defamation League of B'nai B'rith, rev. ed., 1948, 56 pp.

[6] Montague, "Some Psychodynamic Factors in Race Prejudice," *loc. cit.*

[7] I. I. Child and L. W. Doob, "Factors Determining National Stereotypes," *Journal of Social Psychology*, 17:203–219, 1943.

water was not potable. Certain facts thus served as a basis for the stereotype, but they were irrelevant.

The American stereotype of the Negro describes him on the negative side as being uneducated, lazy, stupid, ignorant, and dirty, and ascribes to him on the positive side a genuine interest in religion, a cheerful disposition, a pleasant singing voice, a superior sense of rhythm, and a good deal of dancing ability. This concept also has or has had some basis in fact. As long as Negroes were slaves, they were kept ignorant on purpose, and they were often lazy because slaves have little motive to be anything else. They were uneducated, and many southern Negroes still are, because the schools and teachers provided for them were inadequate; but wherever the same educational facilities are open to them, they have reached the same levels as white Americans. They appear to have the same range of intelligence as any other racial group. Surely a race that stepped out of slavery less than one hundred years ago and in that short period has reached its present level can hardly be regarded as being inherently stupid. It is, of course, true that individual Negroes may have one or more of these negative traits, but so also do individual white people. It is not surprising that Negroes are usually religious, for religion is the refuge of those who need it and serves the black man as an emotional outlet for his many frustrations. Another outlet is supremacy in athletics, one line of endeavor in which the Negro meets with much less discrimination than in other fields.

Stereotypes of similar nature but with emphasis upon different traits exist for the Jews, who have formed an "out-group" in almost all cultures, largely because they have resisted absorption on account of the religion. The feelings of inferiority aroused by intolerance are usually revealed only through the Jew's typical overcompensation. According to the stereotype, he pushes himself forward—lest he be overlooked—fawns upon those who can help him to be accepted socially, and puts his trust in money as a source of power. Since Jews are likely to be successful in material matters, they arouse envy and fear in a way that Negroes do not. The prejudice against them is thereby strengthened in proportion to their success.[8]

Members of a dominant group in a society feel safe and superior because they belong to the party in power at the moment. That is, they are members of the "in-group." In order to maintain their safety and security, those in the "in-group" have to do some things of which they cannot be proud, things that make them feel guilty, things that disturb them. Such feelings are uncomfortable bedfellows. Moreover, members of the in-group experience constant vague fears and anxieties that they will lose their position, even though no cloud is at present visible upon the horizon. These fears build up within the members of the in-group a degree of tension that gradually becomes unbearable. They therefore project their guilt, anxiety, uncertainty, or whatever strain needs to be reduced upon members of one or

---

[8] J. F. Brown, "Social and Psychological Factors in the Anti-Semitic Attitude," *Journal of Educational Sociology*, 16:351–354, 1943. See also G. Ichheiser, "Diagnosis of Anti-Semitism: Two Essays," *Sociometry Monographs*, No. 8, 1946, 27 pp.; and E. Simmel (ed.), *Anti-Semitism: A Social Disease*, International Universities Press, 1946, 141 pp.

more "out-groups," making them the scapegoats,[9] thus discharging their own tensions. Once a proper scapegoat is found, it can serve for the discharge of future anxiety, fear, guilt, or hostility, whether or not the situation causing the emotion has a logical connection with the chosen channel of release. After enough specific instances pile up, the basic attitudes harden into a prejudice, which is socially sanctioned by the majority of those belonging to the in-group, members of which are always conservative, since the last thing they want is a change in the *status quo*. They value conformity because it gives them greater security, and they organize themselves in whatever way seems most effective for keeping outsiders out. Once established and sanctioned, a stereotype is passed down from one generation to the next.[10] Stereotypes are especially pernicious because they are so crystallized that they are hard to modify, and they provide their holder with both a shield against the assault of new facts and a theory in the light of which he can interpret such facts as are too clamorous to be ignored.

It should be understood that scapegoating has inevitably an aggressive content. It is an extreme position at the lower end of a scale that represents the possible varieties of human intergroup attitudes. Such a scale appears in Figure 93, page 421. The phrasing suggests that the word "prejudice" should be used for the first level of negative feeling, but this word does not imply an emotion strong enough to lead to extreme overt behavior. It suggests, rather, a personal opinion. For the next lower level, the word "discrimination" has been used. This word implies action against a group. In everyday speech it refers to such actions as preventing Negroes from voting, closing certain apartment houses to Jews, requiring Negroes to attend separate schools, barring foreign-born men from being army officers, and so on. These actions are directed against certain groups, but they are not usually accompanied by violence. The word "scapegoating" appears at the bottom because it indicates not merely an extreme of prejudiced feeling, but an extreme of discriminatory behavior, an increase in hostility and violence, and a tendency to react toward individuals as well as toward groups.

The reaction of the out-group to its exclusion may take several forms. Its members may docilely comply with the restrictions set upon them and resign themselves to being unwanted. One sees this attitude among many of the Untouchables of India. Or they may seek protection from the worst

---

[9] The source of the term "scapegoat" and of the entire concept of "scapegoating" is to be found in the Bible. In the days of the Old Testament, the children of Israel had a ceremony once each year for the purpose of ridding themselves of their sins. The technique is described as follows: "And when he hath made an end of reconciling the holy place, and the tabernacle of the congregation, and the altar, he shall bring the live goat: And Aaron shall lay both his hands upon the head of the live goat and confess over him all the iniquities of the children of Israel, and all their transgressions in all their sins, putting them upon the head of the goat, and shall send him away by the hand of a fit man into the wilderness."—Leviticus 16:20, 21.

Students should note the spelling of this term—"scape-," not "scrape-." The animal is definitely not one that, to quote one of the writer's former students, is "called a scrapegoat because it gets you out of a scrape"!

[10] See C. I. Glickesberg, "Human Aspects of the Race Problem," *School Review*, 54:523–529, 1946.

of their wrongs by allying themselves with prominent individuals of the in-group. Thus, during the prewar and early war years in Germany, many Jews escaped persecution through individual alliance with powerful non-Jewish figures. A third and very common reaction is to close their ranks and

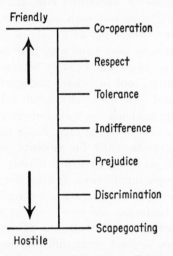

Fig. 93. *Range of Attitudes toward Racial or Ethnic Groups*

From G. W. Allport, *ABC's of Scapegoating,* Anti-Defamation League of B'nai B'rith, rev. ed., 1948, p. 11. Used by permission of the League.

live among themselves, ignoring others as they are ignored. One sees this in the Chinatowns, the Harlems, and the ghettos. Finally, they may fight back. The most conspicuous modern example of this reaction is furnished by the Jews of Palestine. After centuries of segregating themselves in ghettos and of trying to solve their problems by not attracting attention to themselves, they have finally decided to stand and fight.

4. The Intolerant Individual: The typically prejudiced person comes from a family in which the discipline was strict and arbitrary. The parents put great emphasis upon outward forms, conventional standards, and social status, but did not show much affection toward the child.[11] They were more concerned with mores than with morals and tended to be superior about whatever was "theirs"—their church, their home, their social set, their school, their clubs, and so on. The child identified himself early with his parents and eventually idealized them, taking over from them their glorification of whatever group they belonged to, their devotion to appearances, their rigidity of thought, their lack of emotion, and their absence of moral convictions. By the time such a child has reached adolescence, he has acquired a good enough adjustment on the surface. He is polite, self-confident, optimistic, conventionally moral, and kind, when kindness is no particular trouble. He

---

[11] E. Frenkel-Brunswik, "Family Patterns and Idealogy," *American Psychologist,* 3:350, 1948, and "A Study of Prejudice in Children," *Human Relations,* 1:295–306, 1948.

is markedly conservative, mentally rigid, and fanatically loyal to his own group.[12] He admires power, is a social or political climber, and believes in harsh punishment for misdeeds. He has an unusually deep need to feel superior to others. He solves his daily problems by projecting the blame for his difficulties onto someone or something else. He is markedly lacking in ability to love but is well equipped with suspicious, incipient hatreds and callousness toward those outside his own narrow group. He is usually a member of "the best church in town" and may give generously to its support —partly because it is "his" church and partly because he likes the increased status that follows the gifts—but he misses the spiritual values of religion. He shows prejudice toward practically any minor ethnic, racial, or religious group, without apparently noticing the wide individual differences that exist among members of even very small groups. Since the fanatic is rigid, self-righteous, and unfeeling, he is ready for violence, sadism, or hostility, the extreme to which he will go being governed mainly by his deep regard for his status. If he can become anonymous behind the sheets of the Ku Klux Klan, his aggressive cruelty may slip the leash completely. Since the typical fanatic has been slowly becoming one ever since he left the cradle, it is not surprising that he is hard to "cure." Like the delinquent, his disease is his way of life. Not only does he have great difficulty in changing his attitudes, he does not even want to change them.

It is unfortunately true that those adults who maintain their church affiliation and attend services regularly are more prejudiced than those who have no contacts with established religion.[13] It is not, however, clear which is cause and which is effect. To the writer it seems probable that people are not prejudiced because they go to church but that they go to church because they are motivated by a need for support that is also at the bottom of their prejudice. A true follower of Christian doctrine, whether allied to a church or not, cannot be brought to hate his fellow man. Many who become church members, however, need chiefly security; the projection of guilt upon others is another means of gaining the same end. It is therefore not surprising that the two traits are related. Incidentally, there is no difference between Catholics and Protestants in this respect.[14]

---

[12] N. W. Ackerman and M. Jahoda, *Anti-Semitism and Emotional Disorders,* Harper & Brothers, 1950, 135 pp.; W. Adorno, *et al., The Authoritarian Personality,* Harper & Brothers, 1950, 982 pp.; G. W. Allport and B. M. Kramer, "Some Roots of Prejudice," *Journal of Psychology,* 22:9–39, 1946; S. Crown, "Some Personality Correlates of War-Mindedness and Anti-Semitism," *Journal of Social Psychology,* 31:131–143, 1950; E. Frenkel-Brunswik and R. N. Sanford, *The Anti-Semitic Personality,* Harper & Brothers, 1950, pp. 26–124; N. C. Morse and F. H. Allport "Anti-Semitism; A Study of Its Causal Factors and Other Associated Variables," *American Psychologist,* 4:261, 1949; M. Rokeach, "General Rigidity as a Factor in Ethnocentrism," *Journal of Abnormal and Social Psychology,* 43:259–278, 1948.

[13] See Adorno, *op. cit.,* and R. N. Sanford and D. J. Levinson, "Ethnocentrism in Relation to Some Religious Attitudes and Practices," *American Psychologist,* 3:350–351, 1948.

[14] H. J. Parry, "Protestants, Catholics, and Prejudice," *International Journal of Opinion and Attitude Research,* 3:205–213, 1949.

The two brief studies below illustrate typical motivations for the development of intolerance:

Miss L. is a woman of fifty who is head clerk in a large business office. She is efficient in her work and has the reputation of being fair in her treatment of those whom she is willing to accept at all, but she shows a violent distaste for Negroes. There are usually two or three Negro girls working as typists in the large office she supervises, but they rarely stay long because she makes them uncomfortable by a number of petty persecutions and prevents them from being advanced, if she can. Miss L. makes no secret of her prejudice. She declares that Negroes are low class, dirty, and repulsive-looking and that Negro men are sexually aggressive toward white women. The firm for which she works employs many Negroes in their shipping rooms, and Miss L. expresses a real fear of an attack by one or more of them. She will not ride alone in an elevator operated by a male Negro of any age.

In disposition Miss L. is a rigid, repressed, precise, conventional woman. She was the only child of parents who were extremely unhappy together but did not believe in divorce and therefore continued to occupy the same house. The father usually paid little attention to his wife and daughter beyond eating breakfast and dinner with them and occasionally taking the child out for a walk on Sundays. At an early age Miss L. discovered that he visited prostitutes. About once every six weeks he came home drunk and quarreled loudly with his wife, sometimes insisting upon his "rights," and abusing her more or less. Miss L. grew up with the conviction that all men were brutal and that sex was dirty. At the same time she wanted a home of her own, and she was aware of an interest in sex herself. Her equation of sex with filth and her rejection of both in her father and in herself created a conflict which made her acutely uncomfortable during her adolescent years. She has escaped from this conflict by projecting these same qualities onto Negroes. She believes that she is quite without interest in sex, but she is a steady consumer of all types of erotic literature—presumably another form of escape. Miss L. has never had a disagreeable experience with Negroes, aside from such slight unpleasantnesses as she has precipitated by her own treatment of girls in her office. The projection is so useful to her that she will probably not relinquish it. Moreover, it satisfies her narrow, rigid, repressed personality because she feels that prejudice against a "lower" race and caste is a proper and conventionally acceptable point of view.

Mr. R. is a man of fifty-five who expresses a violent anti-Semitic attitude. He asserts that Jews are exploiters of others, Christ-killers, and fakers, that they are dishonest, that they sell second-rate goods at high prices, that they are too successful, too rich, and too powerful. Mr. R. will not work for a Jewish employer or for a firm that employs Jews, even though they may work at a distance from himself. He criticizes President Roosevelt for having been too friendly with Jews and he praises Hitler's anti-Semitism and regrets that a few European Jews escaped death.

Mr. R. is the son of a Presbyterian minister who ruled his numerous children with an iron hand. The atmosphere of the home was intensely and narrowly religious, permeated with the gloomiest of Calvinism. The father threatened his sons and daughters with hell-fire for minor transgressions and thrashed them for major deviations from what he considered proper conduct. The other three boys eventually escaped from their father by running away from home, and the girls all married at an early age, two of them eloping with suitors who had been sent away by the father in a dictatorial manner. Mr. R. was always terrified of his father, but at the same time he admired him for his strength and power. On the whole he conformed better to requirements than any other member of the family and never revolted openly against authority.

In the Jews Mr. R. has found a convenient target for the hatred he has for his father. They, like his father, are strong, successful, and powerful. Moreover, he can hate them without danger to himself, whereas he never dared to express openly his hostility toward his father. They are only substitutes, but they permit him to escape from the inferiority that he would otherwise feel because he lacks the courage to escape from parental domination. His hatred is great because his need is great.

These two individuals show different motives for their prejudice. What they and all other intolerant people have in common is an unresolved conflict, from which they can escape by projecting their feelings onto a group of people whom they dare to hate and toward whom they feel hatred to be socially acceptable. Just what form of prejudice each intolerant human being develops—whether against Jews, Negroes, Japanese, Irishmen, Mexicans, French Canadians, Catholics, Christian Scientists, Quakers, Mormons, capitalists, Communists, or any other group—depends upon the environment in which he lives, because it is essential that he should select a group that one can hate without becoming socially ostracized. The degree of prejudice is dependent chiefly upon the urgency of the intolerant individual's need to defend his ego and the amount of encouragement he receives from those of similar outlook.

5. Typical Degrees of Prejudice Shown by Children and Adolescents: What might be called the "normal" growth of attitudes toward two minority groups, the Negroes and the Jews, is shown by two studies that extended from the early grades through high school or college.

In one case, 1,065 children and adolescents were first asked to vote for one of three possible treatments of Negroes: the present segregation, more opportunity for them than at present, or equal opportunity with whites.[15] For the entire group, the percentages were 66, 14, and 18, respectively, for the three typical attitudes enumerated above, with 2 per cent not voting. In the elementary school, 71 per cent favored segregation; in the high school, 66 per cent; and in college, 55 per cent. Part of the decrease is certainly due to mere elimination of the less intelligent pupils, but one does not know how much. In the second study, pupils from Grades 5 through 12 wrote compositions on "What Is an American?" "What Is a Jew?" and "What Is a Negro?"[16] The topics were given as a routine assignment, without special preparation or reading. It is interesting, incidentally, that criticism of the United States made a spontaneous appearance in these productions, increasing from 6 per cent in Grade 5 to 21 per cent in Grade 12. More pupils actively opposed discrimination than actively supported it. Some per cent between 2 and 13 volunteered the information that they liked either Jews or Negroes and a similar range volunteered a dislike; in high school a few students (1 to 5 per cent) stated that they "hated" Negroes and from 3 to 6 per cent that they "hated" Jews. Those who read the compositions classified the characteristics imputed to each group as favorable, inferior, bad, or

15 R. Centers, "Attitudes and Beliefs in Relation to Occupational Stratification," *Journal of Social Psychology*, 27:159–185, 1948.

16 M. Radke and J. Sutherland, "Children's Concepts and Attitudes about Minority and Majority American Groups," *Journal of Educational Psychology*, 40:449–468, 1949.

unique. The percentages in each grade appear in Table 29. These particular pupils regarded Negroes mainly as inferior and different rather than bad, and Jews as bad but not inferior. The percentage of favorable comments decreased with age and that of unfavorable ones increased. Some children

Table 29

CHARACTERISTICS IMPUTED TO NEGROES AND JEWS
(The figures are percentages.)

Characteristics	Negroes Grades				Jews Grades			
	5–6	7–8	9–10	11–12	5–6	7–8	9–10	11–12
Favorable	34	36	27	21	20	13	13	16
Inferior	26	41	39	67	4	4	3	8
Bad	0	18	23	27	50	45	69	80
Unique	22	10	12	25	22	21	7	5

Based on M. Radke and J. Sutherland, "Children's Concepts and Attitudes about Minority and Majority American Groups," *Journal of Educational Psychology*, 40:449–468, 1949.

and adolescents expressed a favorable attitude toward both groups; others had a prejudice against only one, and some expressed intolerance toward both. The per cents appear in Table 30. It should be noted that prejudice

Table 30

CHANGES IN TOLERANCE TOWARD NEGROES AND JEWS

	Grades			
	5–6	7–8	9–10	11–12
	(%)	(%)	(%)	(%)
Favorable to both Negroes and Jews	54	47	32	32
Favorable to one group but not the other	29	20	20	8
Negative to both groups	17	33	48	60

Based on Radke and Sutherland, "Children's Concepts and Attitudes about Minority and Majority American Groups," *loc. cit.*

not only increases but that those who feel it toward one group tend to feel it toward the other also.

Prejudice against Negroes begins early and is sensed by young members of both races. A very interesting experiment consisted in letting kindergarten and first-grade children play with a Negro doll and a white doll, a new, brightly painted house that the dolls could be placed in, a shabby house of similar size, a set of "dress-up" clothes for each doll, and a set of ragged, dirty clothes.[17] Each child's play was watched. If he did not place the dolls in the houses or dress them voluntarily, the investigator asked him which doll lived in which house or which doll wore which clothes. Among the

[17] M. J. Radke and H. G. Trager, "Children's Perceptions of the Social Roles of Negroes and Whites," *Journal of Psychology*, 29:3–33, 1950.

152 white children, 77 per cent put the white doll into the new house; among the 90 Negroes 60 per cent also did so. When handed the Negro doll and asked which house it lived in, 73 per cent of the whites and 67 per cent of the Negroes assigned it to the ramshackle house. Sixty per cent of the white children dressed the white doll better than the Negro doll, while 63 per cent of the Negro children dressed the Negro doll better than the white doll. When they were asked why they assigned which house to which doll, 16 per cent of the whites and 5 of the Negroes expressed already formed prejudices and 34 per cent of the whites and 22 per cent of the Negroes implied a prejudice. That is, at the kindergarten level, half of the white children were already aware of racial discrimination. It will be noted that these small children expressed their attitudes not in words, but in deeds.

6. Reduction of Prejudice: Various people have attempted to reduce the amount of already measured prejudice in a given group. The logical assumption was that an intolerant person will lose his negative attitudes once he is given adequate information about, and adequate contact with, those whom he dislikes. The matter is, however, not so simple, because prejudice rests upon emotional rather than intellectual grounds. There seems to be practically no relationship between knowledge of and feeling toward a group,[18] and an already established prejudice is reduced only a little if at all by supplying facts to counterbalance it. In one study of the opinions and attitudes shown by 2,523 white people with varying degrees of formal education, the relationship between the last grade to be reached in school and information about Negroes was positive but that between educational level and attitude was zero.[19] In other words, increased education gave information about Negroes, their problems, and the conditions under which they lived but failed to dent basic attitudes. Specific teaching in a college course on race relations may modify prejudices slightly, although work in other courses in sociology seems to have no effect.[20] In some cases, both age and instruction seem to be related negatively to the degree of prejudice shown.[21]

Another favorite suggestion for the reduction of intolerance between races has been the establishment of personal contacts between individual members of two cultures. This idea is just a variation on the theme that prejudice is due to ignorance and will disappear if one becomes acquainted with members of a disliked group. Simple contact does not, however, prove effective, and it sometimes increases rather than decreases prejudice. In one actual experiment of having Negro and white boys in the same summer

---

[18] See, for instance, G. Nettler, "The Relationship between Attitude and Information concerning the Japanese in America," *American Sociological Review,* 11:177–191, 1946, and B. Shimberg, "Information and Attitudes toward World Affairs," *Journal of Educational Psychology,* 40:206–222, 1949.

[19] B. Samuelson, "Does Education Diminish Prejudice?" *Journal of Social Issues,* 2:11–13, 1945.

[20] M. Smith, "A Second Report on Changes in Attitudes toward the Negro," *School and Society,* 57:388–392, 1943.

[21] I. M. A. Myers, "A Study of Anti-Negro Prejudice," *Journal of Negro Education,* 12:709–714, 1943.

camp, the boys of both races who were already frustrated, inclined to aggression, and defiant of authority, became more intolerant than before.[22] There was, at the same time, a decrease in prejudice among those who already had many friends, were well adjusted, and showed few signs of aggressive needs. The contact in this instance acted selectively, having its greatest influence where it was least needed. Obviously, if contact alone were enough, some of the most deep-seated cases of intolerance would never have arisen. There is more daily contact between whites and Negroes in the South than in the North, but the intolerance is higher. What does seem to have some effect is acquaintanceship with *superior* members of another group.[23] Thus a concert by Marian Anderson or a commencement address by Ralph Bunche is more likely to modify anti-Negro prejudice than daily contact with the Negro men who collect the trash.

Two especially interesting experiments in the "contact" approach of reducing prejudice have been reported. One of these mixed contact with certain forms of instruction, while the other depended upon contact alone.[24] In the former instance, the investigator first selected a group of high school students who had strong anti-Negro feelings. These boys and girls became acquainted with a number of attractive, intelligent, interesting Negroes who talked vividly and pleasantly with them, both in lectures and in conversation. The students themselves expressed a desire for more information on racial matters. They were therefore given a "course" in which films, pictures, radio programs, maps, and charts were the main ingredients. In the other experiment, forty-six college students were exposed to intensive social and intellectual contacts with Negro leaders for four days. Prejudice was definitely lowered in both experiments. In the second, the greatest shift was in such matters as willingness to share dining-room accommodations with Negroes, or in having Negro guests, escorts, or friends. Greater respect for the abilities of Negroes was also evident. The attitudes that showed least change concerned intermarriage. If such alteration of attitude can be gained by a four-day conference, there would seem to be real hope of greater amity between groups by widespread and continued use of this approach.

7. Effect of Discrimination upon Individuals and upon Groups: A number of emotional reactions have been noted among individual members of minority groups, especially among Negroes and foreigners who have been subjected to discrimination by a white or native majority. Some Negroes are openly hostile and aggressive toward white people and are inordinately proud of their own race; others reject their own people and toady

[22] P. H. Mussen, "Some Personal and Social Factors Related to Changes in Children's Attitudes toward Negroes," *Journal of Abnormal and Social Psychology,* 45:423–441, 1950.

[23] B. K. MacKenzie, "The Importance of Contact in Determining Attitudes toward Negroes," *Journal of Abnormal and Social Psychology,* 43:417–441, 1948.

[24] S. Holbrook, "A Study of Some Relationships between Negro and White Students in the New York Public Schools," *High Points,* 26:5–17, 1944; and F. T. Smith, "An Experiment in Modifying Attitudes toward the Negro," *Teachers College Contributions to Education,* No. 887, 1943, 135 pp.

to the white race in an effort to be so useful as to escape the general dislike; still others merely accept things as they are and avoid contacts with whites when possible; most, however, are unhappy, discouraged, and frustrated but have not reached the point of aggression.[25]

In one study, a large number of Negroes were asked if they had felt racial discrimination.[26] A few reported that they had never experienced any humiliation based on racial discrimination, but most reported the appearance of prejudice at about the age of twelve; relatively little was felt during the childhood years. The situations in which discrimination appeared were social in character. The most frequent reaction on the part of the Negroes was a complete withdrawal from companionships, clubs, or other activities requiring social relationships with white children. The realization of prejudice against themselves was a severe blow to the Negroes' sense of security. Most of those involved in the study reported profound resentment against white pupils, with a consequent increase in the emotional attachments formed with adolescents of their own race. Nearly half the Negroes felt that their white teachers discriminated against them by seating them in the back of the room, ignoring them, grading their papers unfairly, refusing them opportunities for classroom leadership, and excluding them from extracurricular activities.

The kinds of difficulty reported by Negro children and the frequency with which these difficulties are encountered are shown in Table 31, which

Table 31

TYPES OF DISCRIMINATION REPORTED BY SCHOOL CHILDREN

Types	Per cent
Ridicule	71
Indirect disparagement	54
Aggression	40
Discrimination	31
Rude remarks	17
Physical abuse	10

From R. M. Goff, "Problems and Emotional Difficulties of Negro Children," *Teachers College Contributions to Education*, No. 960, 1949, 93 pp. Used by permission of the publisher.

rests upon the testimony of 150 elementary school pupils. Their reactions to the treatment they received consisted of resentment (69 per cent), inferiority, shame, hurt feelings, or embarrassment (47 per cent), and fear (6 per cent). Only 3 per cent remained indifferent. Their first impulse was either to accept the discrimination stoically or to fight, either actually or verbally. Their permanent solution was a voluntary and complete withdrawal from white

---

[25] O. Verin, "Racial Attitudes of Negro Clients," *Smith College Studies in Social Work*, 34:795–798, 1946.

[26] A. S. Beckham, "A Study of Attitudes of Negro Adolescents," *Journal of Abnormal and Social Psychology*, 29:18–29, 1934. See also J. H. Atwood, *This Be Their Destiny*, American Council on Education, 1941, 96 pp., for excellent individual accounts of emotional reactions to discrimination.

children, in order that future situations which might make them uncomfortable should not arise.

Jewish as well as Negro children also usually experience prejudice before the end of their elementary school days. The Gentile children strongly tend to select their best friends from among their own group—to the extent of 94 per cent—thus rejecting their Jewish age-mates except as casual acquaintances.[27] Jewish boys react to this situation by establishing friendships with other boys of the same faith, but Jewish girls often try to escape from prejudice by seeking social acceptance among Gentile boys and girls.

Foreign groups have similar experiences. A study of two thousand eleven- to-fifteen-year-old children of Italian-born parents shows that rejection by the majority group occurred and had definite effects upon personality. These children manifested feelings of inferiority, awareness of their rejection, poor social adjustment, and emotional instability.[28] If the feeling of frustration becomes sufficiently deep and permanent, serious maladjustment, delinquency, neuroses, and psychoses may result.

II. Religious Attitudes

Ideas on religious questions, interest in religion, degrees of conviction, and attitudes toward religious matters all vary with age and develop by a fairly orderly series of changes that continue into adult life.

Small children often show a free, unconventional, and vigorous imagination in their thinking about religion. For instance, one little boy drew three lines that swept across a page as if he were trying to represent a windstorm and said that he had drawn a picture of God. Another drew the back of a man's head and said that one could not draw God's face because it shone so brightly one never saw it. Many children show a tendency to deify their parents, as their first concept of God. One writer has postulated three stages of religious development among children:[29] the fairy-tale stage, during which children have all manner of fanciful beliefs; the realistic stage, during which they reject earlier imaginings and give explanations in terms of natural phenomena; and the individualistic stage, during which they begin to select from religion the elements that satisfy their own needs and drives. In general, children tend to accept such formal religious concepts as their elders choose to offer them, without doubt as to their correctness but not without many questions as to their nature. As children approach adolescence and begin to question authority of all kinds, they may revolt from church as well as from both home and school domination. A considerable number of

[27] A. Harris and G. Watson, "Are Jewish or Gentile Children More Clannish?" *Journal of Social Psychology*, 24:71–76, 1946.

[28] J. W. Tait, "Race Prejudice and Personality," *School*, 34:795–798, 1946; and R. L. Cooper, "The Frustrations of Being a Member of a Minority Group: What Does It Do to the Individual and to His Relationships with Other People?" *Mental Hygiene*, 29:189–195, 1945.

[29] E. Harms, "The Development of Religious Experience in Children," *American Journal of Sociology*, 50:112–122, 1944.

adolescents investigate religion anew as a possible source of both emotional and intellectual stimulation and satisfaction. At each age beyond fifteen, more and more boys and girls become critical of religion. After becoming adults, many of them settle down to a rather indifferent, though tolerant, attitude. Religion would seem to have some value to children, although prob-

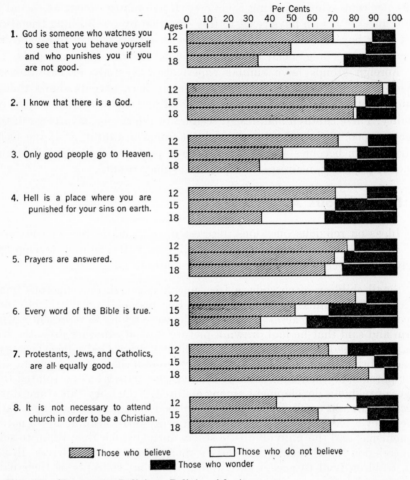

Fig. 94. *Changes in Religious Beliefs with Age*

Based on R. G. Kuhlen and M. Arnold, "Age Differences in Religious Beliefs and Problems during Adolescence," *Pedagogical Seminary and Journal of Genetic Psychology,* 65:291–300, 1944.

ably none of the usual adult values, since children do not have the mental ability to understand the basic ideas and ideals. Perhaps they derive a measure of security from their belief in a God who watches over them and a relief from their feelings of guilt if they have trust in God's forgiveness. Adolescents want to find something in religion, but most of them fail to do so, and their reactions to failure often take the form of intolerance, cynicism, and withdrawal from contact with church activities.[30] The hostility eventually dies out, however, and adults again find values, although not necessarily religious ones, in religion.

One author has traced the growth of attitudes on eighteen religious problems between the ages of twelve and eighteen. Results for a few typical items appear in Figure 94 on page 430. Eight sample propositions to which the pupils reacted are listed at the left. At the right are three shaded lines indicating the percentage of pupils at ages twelve, fifteen, and eighteen who believed, did not believe, or wondered about each proposition. In some cases the decrease in belief is due to an increase of pupils who rejected the proposition (No. 1); in some cases the decrease is due primarily to an increase in those who merely wondered about its correctness (No. 4).

Table 32

REASONS FOR PRAYER

Reasons	Per cent
1. To ask for personal benefits	22
2. To express thanks	19
3. To talk to God	15
4. To ask for guidance	11
5. To comply with habit	10
6. To seek comfort	8
7. To ask help for others	5
8. To ask for forgiveness	5

Based on E. Pixley and E. Beckman, "The Faith of Youth as Shown in the Public Schools of Los Angeles," *Religious Education*, 44:338, 1949.

In spite of more or less talk to the contrary, presumably by a highly vocal minority, there is still a good deal of interest in religion on the part of adolescents. One of the most impressive reports comes from an analysis of 3,676 essays written anonymously by high school seniors in Los Angeles.[31] Of this number, 36 per cent attended church regularly, 52 per cent irregularly, and 12 per cent never or almost never. Their urge for going came from a desire to honor or learn more about God (41 per cent), from pressure by their parents (28 per cent), from pressure by their own consciences (23 per cent), or from a desire for fellowship (8 per cent). Of the 436 who never went to church, only 18 (4 per cent) stayed away from lack of belief; almost 90 per cent of the nonattenders said they believed in religion, but were prevented from attendance by work or lack of transportation. A total of 3,317 seniors also wrote on prayer, but only 520 of the papers were sufficiently articulate to be worth analyzing. The reasons given for praying are listed in Table 32. The impression one gets from this study is that these adolescents, at least,

---

[30] F. E. Moreton, "Attitudes toward Religion among Adolescents and Adults," *British Journal of Educational Psychology*, 14:69–79, 1944.

[31] E. Pixley and E. Beekman, "The Faith of Youth as Shown in the Public Schools of Los Angeles," *Religious Education*, 44:336–342, 1949.

were far from godless. A few brief quotations from their papers on prayer are reproduced below:

Of course many people need prayer as a spiritual cleansing. Even as you sometimes feel you would like to talk to someone heart to heart, I can understand how others would get things off their chest and stabilize their perhaps tottering beliefs through prayer.

I, like many teen-agers, am very close to God in my feelings, yet often do not show this openly. Many young people have more faith than adults believe. I can talk to God when I can talk to nobody else. He is a friend who will always be with me in the darkness of my room. I often say prayers that are memorized but I get more satisfaction from making up my own—I feel that I am talking to God and that he is listening.

I feel rather guilty about my lack of prayer, but I cannot exactly believe, somehow, that rattling off a few memorized lines every night before jumping into bed does anyone any good. In serious times or times of stress, or at a time when success is wanted, I think most people of my age call upon prayer for help, and I think we all feel rather uneasy about not praying more, but maybe we have not lived long enough nor seen enough of the crises of life to feel the need of calling upon Him for help.

Like all humans, I only call upon God's help when everything else seems to fail. It is not right to do this; I think there should be time for prayer in every day. But to be truthful, I only give prayer when I need help, when a situation arises which is too large for me to untangle.

I, for one, do not pray often, and I know of few who do, except when they want something. Whether it was the same situation in past generations, I do not know, but I imagine it was different. Why the change is in our generation I do not know. But I do know that one who is brave enough to admit that he prays is laughed at by most high school students of today. This is not because of the training we have had, but the lack of it.

I don't believe in prayers. When I was ten years old I wanted a bicycle very much, so prayed in order to get it, I would pray every morning, and at night before I would go to bed; sometimes when I had time during the day I prayed too. I didn't get the bike, so I could never again see any sense in praying. Since that time on I never prayed again.[32]

This series of reactions represents a wide range of opinions and feelings, such as might probably be obtained from any other large group.

In the year 1930 an able investigator collected reactions to twenty-five religious propositions on the part of the 266 freshmen in the small college where he taught. In the fall of 1949, he repeated the same series with the 852 freshmen who had just entered.[33] In both instances, the students were asked to mark each statement according to the following plan:

A—If you believe implicitly
B—If you have an inclination to believe but cannot help doubting

[32] Pixley and Beekman, "The Faith of Youth as Shown in the Public Schools of Los Angeles," loc. cit., pp. 338–340. Used by permission of Religious Education.

[33] G. J. Dudycha, "The Religious Beliefs of College Freshmen in 1930 and 1949." Religious Education, 45:165–169, 1950.

C—If you do not know whether you believe or not
D—If you are inclined to disbelieve, but are not sure
E—If you absolutely do not believe

In general, the per cent in each classification on all twenty-five items put together changed relatively little over the nineteen-year period. Nine per

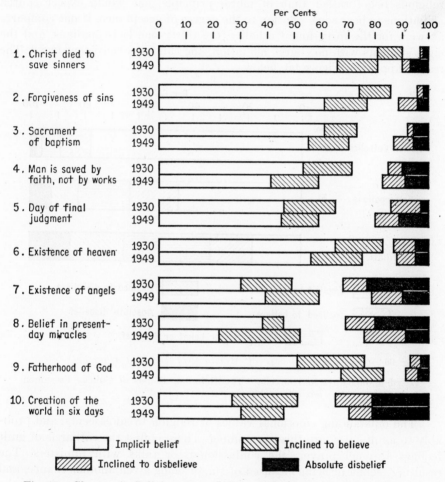

Fig. 95. *Changes in Beliefs among College Students from 1930 to 1949*

Based upon figures in G. J. Dudycha. "The Religious Beliefs of College Freshmen in 1930 and 1949," *Religious Education,* 45:166, 1950.

cent fewer students registered implicit belief, but 5 per cent more indicated an indication to believe, 4 per cent more were in doubt, 2 per cent more were inclined to disbelieve, and 1 per cent fewer were sure of their disbelief. The shift, though small, was rather consistently downward.

Ten sample items are shown in Figure 95, shown above, together with the results from the two groups of freshmen. In the interests of simplicity, the "C" answers have been omitted. Items 5, 3, and 10 registered little change. Items 1, 2, 4, 8, and 9 are those that showed the greatest shift in belief, Items 7, 9, and 10 showed an increase in implicit belief, but in the case of Item 7, an increase also in absolute disbelief.

Since the majority of the twenty-five propositions are statements of religious belief rather than of moral principle, one would expect church affiliations to bear some relation to the degree of acceptance. If one compares answers for the forty-four Catholics, the thirty-one Episcopalians, and the eight students with no church affiliation, one can see a consistent trend. The results appear in Figure 96, below.

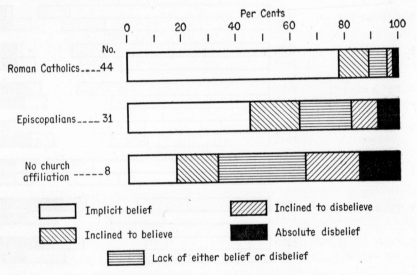

Fig. 96. *Comparative Beliefs of Members of Different Churches*

Based upon figures in Dudycha, "The Religious Beliefs of College Freshmen in 1930 and 1949," *loc. cit.,* p. 168.

The outstanding emotional values of religion to adolescents, and probably to adults also, are three in number. There is first the catharsis of guilt feelings through prayer, the confessional, or talks with ministers. The resulting feeling of being cleansed of sin, of being given another chance, and of reduced tension is of great value in adjustment. A second value is the increase of security, sometimes relatively superficial and sometimes profound, that may result from religious belief. A trust in God prevents the panic of despair, a belief in personal immortality with its promise of an everlasting perpetuation of the ego prevents the fear of death, the membership in a group gives a sense of belonging, and the chance to work with and help others leads to helpful identifications and attitudes. These values are not all of a religious nature, but they are of assistance in the search for happiness and adjustment. Finally, religion can become the basis for a sound philosophy of life, even though it does not always do so.

In contrast to its values, there are certain common disadvantages that sometimes result from religious belief. The most important of these are the narrow, intolerant, fanatic, prejudiced, rigid attitudes of mind that sometimes appear among those who call themselves religious. In some instances, the religious tenets in which these people have been educated are unmodified heritages from an earlier day and are far more rigid than is consonant with the mores of the present; the believers can therefore maintain their belief only by becoming blindly fanatical. Otherwise modern life would undermine the beliefs that give their egos the support they need. In other instances, people who are already intolerant in their attitudes seek religion because they can find in church doctrines an intellectual support for their prejudices, and can thereby rid themselves of guilt. It should be noted, however, that these disadvantages are not results of the religious spirit but of religious dogma. One should not condemn religion merely because its values can be misused.

III. Honesty

The studies to be reported are of three types. First comes a brief summary of an old but extremely good study into the behavior of school children and adolescents. The pupils were given chances to cheat without their knowing it, and a record was kept as to whether or not they availed themselves of the opportunity. Honesty was studied in both school and play activities. The second type of investigation deals with ideas of honesty, of one kind or another, as expressed by pupils in their early adolescent years. The third type of investigation deals wholly with honesty on examinations in school. Since the investigation of behavior covers the widest sampling of situations, it will be considered first.

In some schools the extent of dishonesty increased with age; in others it decreased;[34] in still others, dishonesty in schoolwork decreased, while other types of deceitful behavior increased with maturity. The nature of such changes is shown clearly in Figure 97 on page 436. In one school the degree of honesty increased from kindergarten through the twelfth grade; in the other, it decreased. School Y had a tradition of honesty, while School Z had a tradition of deceitfulness. When results of all tests of honesty from all schools are put together, there is a very slight increase from year to year. This result may be due to higher morality, greater maturity, or merely to elimination of the dullest and most delinquent members of the school population. The writer is inclined to believe the change in honesty represents little more than the normal elimination of dullards from grade to grade. The increase is relatively small, and the variability of performance from one group to another relatively great. Certainly there is no such increase as one hopes might result from education.

The extent of dishonest behavior correlates directly with a number of

[34] Most of the results in this and the next few paragraphs are from H. Hartshorne and M. May, *Studies in Character,* Vol. I, The Macmillan Company, 1928, 306 pp.

factors. The intelligent pupil cheats less on school tests than the unintelligent, but both the intelligent and the stupid cheat more in social situations than the child of average mental ability. There is only a slight relationship between knowledge of what constitutes honesty and actual behavior. Educational maladjustment leads to dishonesty, as shown by increased cheating on the part of neurotic children. Emotional instability and suggestibility both correlate positively with dishonest behavior. The level of honesty tends to

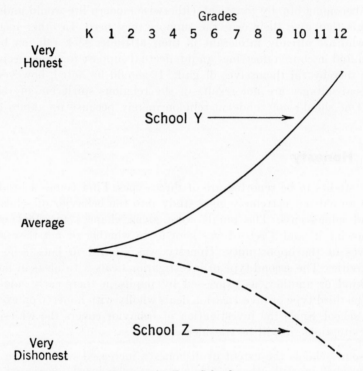

Fig. 97. *Comparative Honesty in Two Schools*

From H. Hartshorne, M. May, and F. K. Shuttleworth, *Studies in Character,*
The Macmillan Company, 1930, III, 331. Used by permission of the publishers.

be similar among friends, or among members of the same family. The correlation of scores between children and their parents is very high, and that between children and their friends quite high; but it is zero between pupils and either their schoolteachers or their Sunday school teachers. Finally, honesty correlates with the economic and cultural level of the home from which the children come.

Some of these relationships may be seen in Figure 98 on page 437. The first set of bars shows the percentage of cheating on school examinations by children at different levels of intelligence; the brighter the children were, the less they cheated. The second part of the figure gives the percentage of dishonesty shown by children from homes of different cultural and economic levels; the better the home, the less the dishonesty. The third set of bars illustrates the relation between suggestibility and dishonest behavior. The more suggestible children were, the more they cheated. The last section of the figure shows dishonesty to be related positively to retardation in school and negatively to acceleration. If a child is bright, accelerated, resistant to suggestion, and a member of a good family, there is little likelihood that he will be dishonest; if he is dull, retarded, suggestible, and a member of an uncultured family he is almost certain to be.

Two studies deal primarily with the opinions of children, in one case about stealing and in the other about different forms of dishonesty. Among 184 pupils in the eighth and ninth grades who answered a series of questions on various phases of stealing, only 12 per cent maintained an absolute

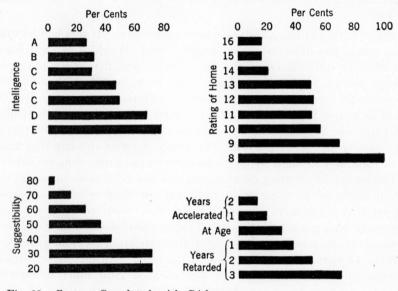

Fig. 98.   *Factors Correlated with Dishonesty*
(Bars Indicate Per Cent of Cheating.,

From H. Hartshorne and M. May, *Studies in Character,* The Macmillan Company, 1928, I, 183, 261, 215, and 279. Used by permission of the publishers.

standard of honesty in their answers and insisted that stealing was wrong, no matter what it was called, or what was stolen, or who had previously owned the stolen object, or what circumstances prevailed at the time.[35] Just two thirds of the pupils showed a sliding scale of morality by condoning stealing under at least one and often several such circumstances as these:

1. Stealing from a corporation, not an individual.
2. Stealing from either corporation or individual who would never notice the loss.
3. Stealing whatever careless people had left lying around.
4. Stealing from people who are strangers or members of a despised racial or social group.

[35] C. B. Stendler, "A Study of Some Socio-Moral Judgments of Junior High School Children," *Child Development,* 20:15–28, 1949.

    5. Stealing things of low intrinsic value.
    6. Stealing from members of the family.
    7. Stealing that is never detected.
    8. Stealing from a person whom you dislike or who has been disagreeable to you.

The remaining 22 per cent marked the statement that they would refrain from stealing only if they were fairly sure of being punished.

In the second study 328 normal boys of nine, twelve, and fifteen years of age were presented with a series of described situations, such as:

A boy got on to a bus. The crowd pushed him into the bus and got between him and the conductor, so that he could not drop his fare into the box. The boy thought that it was not his fault that he did not pay, so he got off the bus without doing so.[36]

The pupils answered two questions about each story: "If this had happened to you, would you have done what he did?" and "Would it be right for you to do what he did?" Between the ages of nine and fifteen the anticipated behavior became steadily less moral. That is, more fifteen-year-olds than nine-year-olds admitted they would indulge in minor dishonesties. But their opinion as to the "rightness" of such behavior increased markedly. Only 37 per cent at age 9 condemned the dishonesties, but by age 12, 84 per cent did so, and by age 15, 92 per cent. This study suggests strongly that knowledge of right and wrong is by no means sufficient to produce moral behavior.

The extent of cheating on examinations has been determined by three different methods. In some cases examinations were returned supposedly unscored, and pupils were allowed to mark their own; actually, the papers had already been graded. If students changed their answers, their dishonesty was apparent. In other cases advanced graduate students, who appeared to be taking an exam of their own, sat in the room with undergraduates and unostentatiously kept a record of who cheated. Still other investigators studied the problem by passing back objective examinations that had intentionally been graded incorrectly. In the course of a semester each student got back some papers scored too low and some scored too high; if he claimed the extra points in the former case and kept them in the latter, he was dishonest.

The results of the studies—whatever the technique of investigation—came out much the same.[37] At least a third of the students were dishonest, and on specific occasions the proportion ran as high as two thirds. The extent of dishonesty varied with intelligence, with the standing in the course to date, and with the presence of the teacher. The brighter the students were, the less they cheated. Those who were doing "A" work were the only group

---

[36] E. K. Beller, "Two Attitude Components in Younger Boys," *Journal of Social Psychology,* 29:137–151, 1949.

[37] See W. G. Campbell, "Student Honesty as Revealed by Reporting of Teachers' Errors in Grading," *School and Society,* 33:97–100, 1939; C. A. Drake, "Why Students Cheat," *Journal of Higher Education,* 12:418–420, 1941; T. H. Howells, "Factors Influencing Honesty," *Journal of Social Psychology,* 9:97–102, 1938; F. W. Parr, "The Problem of Student Honesty," *Journal of Higher Education,* 7:318–326, 1936.

with a clear record for honesty. These results do not, however, tell whether an A student is honest because he wants to be or because he can afford to be! The cheating was least when the teacher was constantly in the room, increased somewhat if he wandered in and out, and rose considerably if he went outside for a walk where he was in full view of the classroom windows.

A recent report concerning moral judgments gives data about the changes in various attitudes between the ages of five and fourteen among pupils in a private school.[38] There were a progressive shift from personal to co-operative bases of judgment, a growth in the "team" feeling, and a development of a better understanding of human motives. These changes led to a decrease in such antisocial and unpopular sins as tattling, but it led also to an increase in group cheating in the classroom.

The implications of such research for the teacher are clear. She can expect cheating in schoolwork from many pupils of average ability, from most dull pupils, and even from a few of the brightest children. She can expect greater dishonesty from retarded than from accelerated pupils and more from those who do poor work than from those whose work is satisfactory. If a given pupil's friends or siblings are known to be deceitful, she can anticipate dishonesty from him. Cheating in schoolwork does not appreciably decrease as the pupils grow older, perhaps because there is inevitably a group of pupils at the bottom of the class, no matter how much elimination has already taken place. By the high school period, childish motives for cheating have been reinforced by the emotional drives of adolescence. Failure in school is distressing enough to children, but it often means to the adolescent boy or girl a collapse of social as well as academic standing. Considering the strain put upon them by a too-difficult curriculum, it is surprising that so many adolescents learn to be honest.

IV. Ideals

One of the typical features of adolescence is the development of and interest in ideals. A child lacks ideals, and his behavior is based mainly upon the specific habits in which he has been trained. He regards as "right" those actions he has been allowed to do, or rewarded for doing; he regards as "wrong" both those actions of his own that have met with punishment and whatever other behavior he has heard condemned verbally by elders in whom he has confidence. Because a child lacks abstract ideas, such as an ideal of honesty, he is likely to be honest at some times and deceitful at others, according to whether or not he has received training in each particular situation. A good example of this point is given in Figure 99 on page 440. Two children who took twenty-one different tests of honesty had widely different degrees of consistency, although their average was about the same. Child A scored fairly high, and his performance was quite even. Child B, on the other

[38] B. Rosen, "The Development of Moral Judgment," *Clark University Abstracts of Dissertations,* 20:114–115, 1948.

hand, varied from a scrupulous honesty to arrant deceit. This second curve reflects the piecemeal concept of honesty that is so common among children.

The adolescent can identify the common element in his many previous experiences with honesty and can therefore obtain a generalized meaning of the term. He can also apply his concept to new situations. When this stage is reached, the adolescent has achieved an ideal, which becomes his "guide to conduct" in situations that are unfamiliar. Every normal adolescent has ideals, although they are not necessarily acceptable. The boy who sees in

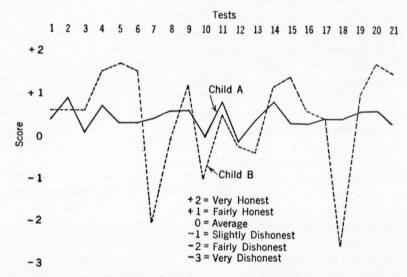

Fig. 99. *Honesty of Two Children as Measured by Twenty-one Tests*

From Hartshorne, May, and Shuttleworth, *op. cit.*, III, 291. Used by permission of The Macmillan Company.

many diverse situations the ability of the strong to coerce the weak may develop the ideal that "might makes right." He then uses it to guide his own conduct and as a basis for judging new situations. His generalization is just as truly an "ideal" as a conviction that the strong should protect the weak.

Since concepts grow out of experiences, the child with socially acceptable habits usually grows up into the adolescent with socially acceptable ideals. Hence the vital importance of training children in desirable habits. The small boy who "swipes" other pupils' erasers, buys candy with money given him to put on the collection plate, and cheats in games is laying the basis from which he will develop the ideal that dishonest conduct is wrong only when it is detected. No other general principle could reasonably be deduced from his earlier behavior. To be sure, the period of adolescence may bring new experiences, and these will, in turn, lead to modifications. However, the essential connection between childhood experiences and adolescent ideals should not be forgotten.

A few examples of how a guiding principle may grow out of specific experiences may be of interest. In some cases, the ideals were translated into vocational ambitions.

I happened to be living in a small mining town at about the age of eleven. Here I saw the horrors of the sickened miners. The pain they had to suffer because of the lack of a doctor. I was only about eleven or twelve years of age but I could understand the life of these mothers and fathers and children who lived at this great disadvantage and I determined at that time to do my best to help these conditions with my whole heart. I have never lost this ambition and I am sure I never shall.

One can see in every-day life the results of diseases. A wage earner may be afflicted and his family be forced to fall back on national support. When one sees a person in a hopeless condition, it awakes a desire to better this condition regardless of compensation or reward. There is no feeling so exhilarating as that which comes with the realization that you have helped some person to the extent of your ability, no matter how small this help may be.

The institution I would like to see exist some time would be a hospital which was supported by every individual in a city. Each family head would pay a small amount each year, regardless of whether anyone was sick in his family or not.[39]

When I was 15 years of age my daddy was out of work, as he is now. I liked to look through the catalogue of children's clothes and then tell mother how I would like to have a little girl and boy and buy them anything on that page that they wanted. I often said that I would like to have a big car piled full of packages and then go in some poor sections and give food, clothing, and toys to poor families. I joined the Girl Scouts when I was 10 and from them derived an ambition to become a leader. Then I have done a lot of welfare work in our community and I am greatly interested in it. My mother also had some influence over me in that matter because she said she always had the same desire.

My mother and I had been to the theatre and decided to follow Tremont Street and see where it led. It led to no pot of gold. I had never seen such absolute filth and laziness before, not even in New York (although I have never been to the poorest sections of New York). I never want to see it again.

It was not so much that these people are throwing their lives away but for the future generations that I care. No children should live like that. They should live in the country and bring up their children there. . . . I have seen the babies in the tenement houses with swollen heads because of lack of milk. The hot, sweaty odor that comes from unsanitary conditions. The mothers fainting, while trying to keep their young alive. The husbands drunk, beating their wives and children. The low, petty thief who never had a chance to better himself.

It sounds rather farfetched for me, a girl, to attempt to better these conditions, but in newspaper work, if you ever acquire much of a following, you can do most anything and I plan to make people see just what a little money and kindness can do for these people.

I became interested in this question when I learned what an appalling amount of unnecessary suffering comes from ignorance of the intricacies of sex, and how to treat them. I believe that modern people still hold quite a bit of false modesty along these lines, and are more willing to see insanity and suffering increase than to frankly discuss these problems and endeavor to do something about them. The book *Revolt of Modern Youth* by Judge Lindsey has given me some ideas, and

[39] H. H. Moore, "Autobiographical Sketches of High School Students Revealing Their Social Impulses," *Social Studies*, 26:436–439, 1935. These three excerpts are used by permission of *Social Studies*. The two following sketches are also from this reference.

though I don't agree with him in all of his beliefs, I do think that he has found the faults of the present time, and why they exist, if not a way to cure them.

My mother told me everything when I was nine and the older I get the more I appreciate it. My friend had been hushed all her life when she asked questions and she was befogged by questions she dared not ask. I tried to tell her but she could not understand me. She was mixed up with a rotter, I told her so, but she didn't believe me; she had faith in him and he owned her. When it was found out that she was pregnant she was sent to a home. Today she is handicapped by her child. Her mother will not speak to her and yet it is the mother's fault. There are more cases of the same; ignorance certainly is not bliss. I think frankness is a good characteristic. A lot of trouble would not be caused if people were frank. . . .

Since I have been old enough to be told the facts of life (eleven years old) and as I grew older and could understand more deeply I have wished somehow that the world could be rid of sporting houses. I have listened to lectures and read books about these things, not because I have a filthy mind, but because if I could do something I would want to have a thorough understanding of the matter.

Identifications: The world is full of heroes and hero worshipers of all ages and conditions. Identification of oneself with a hero and conscious imitation of him are presumably as old as humanity. The process is extremely useful at all ages and is especially so in adolescence, when ideals are in process of formation.[40]

Identification begins early, with the small child's intense love of his parents and his efforts to be like them. Most children develop a similar attitude toward at least one elementary school teacher or a Sunday school teacher, a boy scout or camp fire girls' leader, a movie hero, a camp counselor, or other adult who is the embodiment of perfection at the moment. That the hero has a great effect upon the young worshiper cannot be doubted. One has only to count the number of Hopalong Cassidy shirts worn by neighborhood small fry. Some children prefer a fictional character, or one taken from the more popular cartoons. During preadolescence and adolescence, most girls find the personification of their ideals in movie or television or stage actresses, or occasionally in men singers, and sometimes in their teachers. Adolescent boys tend to either purely athletic heroes or men who play glamorous but highly adventurous roles in the movies; they reject the "great lovers," who appeal mainly to girls in their late adolescence and to maladjusted women. As children grow older and learn about historical or present-day public figures, some of them substitute characters they read about for people they know.

Two investigations of ideals at different ages will be summarized briefly. The first concerns the identification of school pupils at three age levels— seven to eight, eleven to twelve, and fifteen to sixteen.[41] The main results appear in Table 33. There is a decrease in the proportion of school pupils who identify themselves with any member of their own family but especially in the identification with adult members. Hero worship of well-known

[40] O. E. Klapp, "Hero Worship in America," *American Sociological Review,* 14:53–62, 1949; and K. Lawrence and M. H. Frank, "One Way to Personality," *Childhood Education,* 25:389–393, 1948.

[41] J. B. Winker, "Age Trends and Sex Differences in the Wishes, Identifications, Activities, and Fears of Children," *Child Development,* 20:191–200, 1949.

characters increases. At later stages of adolescence the percentages would probably be even higher. Identification with age-mates begins to be impor-

Table 33

IDENTIFICATIONS AT DIFFERENT AGES

	Age Groups		
	7–8 (%)	11–12 (%)	15–16 (%)
With members of the family	52	20	13
With adults in family	38	17	10
With well-known persons	12	28	44
With movie or radio stars	8	30	31
With age-mates	7	5	21

Based on J. B. Winker, "Age Trends and Sex Differences in the Wishes, Identifications, Activities, and Fears of Children," *Child Development*, 20:191–200, 1949.

tant in the early adolescent years and continues to increase throughout the period.

The second study of personification[42] classifies the type of ideals expressed by children and adolescents as shown in Table 34, which gives the

Table 34

PERSONIFICATION OF IDEALS

	Ages									
	9	10	11	12	13	14	15	16	17	18–20
Characters	(%)	(%)	(%)	(%)	(%)	(%)	(%)	(%)	(%)	(%)
1. Characters from immediate environment	58	45	38	35	30	30	29	28	30	27
a. Parents	19	16	15	12	10	9	9	8	10	9
b. Teachers	10	10	7	8	8	7	8	9	8	9
c. Acquaintances	25	14	12	13	9	11	9	10	11	9
d. Others	4	5	4	2	3	3	3	1	1	0
2. Historical or public characters	32	45	53	55	61	61	65	64	61	61
3. Characters from fiction	2	4	4	4	2	3	1	3	3	3
4. Characters from religion	3	2	2	2	3	2	2	1	2	2
5. Miscellaneous	5	4	3	4	4	4	3	4	4	7

From D. S. Hill, "Personification of Ideals by Urban Children," *Journal of Social Psychology*, 1:379–392, 1930. Used by permission of the Journal.

percentages for each type at each age. The degree of personifications from the immediate environment is about half as large at age 18 as at age 9, while that for historical and public characters has almost doubled. In the early years of adolescence there is a tendency to stress physical beauty,

---

[42] D. S. Hill, "Personification of Ideals by Urban Children," *Journal of Social Psychology*, 1:379–392, 1930.

fame, wealth, or personality as the basis of admiration. In the latter years the emphasis shifts to those traits that are moral, intellectual, or altruistic.

To some extent ideals may be taught, largely by means of appropriate reading matter, movies, or concrete experiences. In one investigation,[43] the books and magazines read by two thousand high school pupils were classified as "good" or "bad" in their moral tone and the effect of such reading was studied by means of the imitative and identification tendencies shown by the pupils. About 75 per cent of the reading matter had a recognizable effect upon behavior or attitudes, and the effect was in the direction of the moral tone in the material read.

One effort to teach ideals gave some interesting results.[44] Nearly six hundred high school boys and girls took part in the experiment. At the beginning of the school year they wrote a paper telling who their ideal person was and why they had selected him or her. Late the next spring, after a considerable amount of study and discussion of ideals, these students again wrote out a statement parallel to the first. There was a slight increase in the proportion of religious and historical characters, and a slight decrease in acquaintances. A few pupils kept the same ideal for the same reason; some kept the same ideal but for different reasons; others chose a new ideal for reasons already given for the first; and still others changed both ideals and reasons. A few excerpts from the papers appear below:

Girl, age 12, IQ 105: In November: A classmate because she is prompt and gives a good example. In May: the same classmate because she is honest, intelligent, impartial, patient, and friendly.

Boy, age 14, IQ 115: In November: Jack Oakie because he is handsome, wealthy, pleasant, polite, and popular with the girls. In May: President Roosevelt because he is handsome, wealthy, polite, neat, upright, and broad-minded.

Girl, age 12, IQ 106: In November: Shirley Temple because she is pretty, and smart for her age. In May: St. Francis of Assisi because he was patient, kind, merciful, and a good Patron Saint.

Boy, age 13, IQ 74: In November: Thomas Edison because he was a great man, a great worker, and helped people. In May: S. F. B. Morse because he was industrious, helpful, and persevering.

Girl, age 13, IQ 70: In November: Her cousin because she is nice, polite, and has many clothes. In May: Florence Nightingale because she was a nurse, kind and helpful to the sick and poor.

Most of the boys—94 per cent—and 89 per cent of the girls felt that the study of ideals had been interesting and helpful in making them realize what an ideal was, in supplying them with information about possible ideal persons, and in assisting them to formulate an ideal for themselves.

Children build up their ideals slowly and somewhat erratically. The

---

[43] M. C. Lorang, "The Effect of Reading on Moral Conduct and Emotional Experience," *Studies in Psychology and Psychiatry of the Catholic University of America,* Vol. IV, No. 6, 1945, 122 pp.

[44] Sister Mary Inez Phelan, *An Empirical Study of the Ideals of Adolescent Boys and Girls,* Catholic University Press, 1936, 155 pp. The excerpts on this page are quoted by permission of the Catholic University.

process can be accelerated by teaching, but it takes place even without direct instruction. As soon as an adolescent has developed a few ideals, he is ready to integrate them into a consistent attitude, commonly referred to as a philosophy of life.

V. Philosophy of Life

The modern adolescent wants to find a meaning to life, a synthesis of its discordant values.[45] Certain elements in modern life make this effort of his especially difficult. First, he has from infancy been brought up on an objective, unemotional presentation of scientific facts. He usually knows just enough science to block his acceptance of traditional religion but not enough to make a synthesis of science with religious and moral beliefs. Second, he has moved about a good deal in a radius—large or small—around the center of his home and community; he is acquainted with many people, many customs, and many points of view; he often no longer has any roots in the place of his birth and early childhood. Consequently, he does not inherit a ready-made point of view from his surroundings. Third, he is met on all sides with the most divergent adult opinions. He sees no single, accepted mode of life, and he does not know what will satisfy his notions of right and wrong. Indeed, because of changes in adult opinions he does not know what *is* right and wrong—and probably the adults of his acquaintance do not, either. They have no clear-cut principles to hand down to him. Finally, he and his friends have extraordinary freedom from adult control. Many hours are his to do with as he pleases. It is not surprising that the world seems chaotic and meaningless. Some adolescents find consolation in organized religion, but more of them have to work out their own salvation.

Many adolescents have expressed themselves concerning the confusion they feel in trying to make sense out of life.

I am still wandering around in this maze of conflicting training, wondering what I will be like if I become molded to an acceptable pattern. My life has become without aim, without a goal to work forward to, a little without meaning. At present I have decided to step back into my shell, and out of the conflict of codes and desires and personalities that seem to make up society.[46]

My mother's tree spread with sturdy branches: Quaker, Puritan, Wesleyan, and Boone. If less conforming branches had grown there, they had been carefully pruned. This family, together with some half-dozen of their group, held rigid customs which they projected on each succeeding generation. They had three ambitions: to till the soil, to establish homes, to spend eternity in Heaven. My parents were the third generation of these upright pioneers.

Through me, a frail, nervous, little girl, they would project their way to life.

---

[45] See, for example, L. B. Murphy, "Background of Adolescent Religion," *Child Development*, 13:140–144, 1936; P. H. Landis, "Points of Strain in Adolescent Morality," *School and Society*, 51:612–616, 1940; H. S. Dimock, "Some New Light on Adolescent Religion," *Religious Education*, 31:273–279, 1936.

[46] Landis, "Points of Strain in Adolescent Morality," *loc. cit.*, p. 613. These three excerpts are used by permission of *School and Society*.

I would reach perfection; I would be devoutly religious, kind, gentle, soft of voice and manner, a little lower than the angels. I would keep a household running smoothly, be a perfect seamstress, a renowned cook. I would sing and play and drink deeply of the joy of music. I would have a deep and perfect understanding. "As a twig is bent, so is the tree," they reasoned.

Cut off from group contacts as a child, unhappy, living in the past in which my mother lived, I placed my faith in the future, and in my fantasy thinking built the foundation for a future different from the past. Left so often to my own thoughts, I began to question, to reason, to choose. The bonds which held me tightly to my primary group patterns still held firmly, but I felt that after graduation, when I went out "on my own," they would be severed and I would begin to live under new codes, to have new ideas, attitudes and habits which would make me a part of the society about me. Strange, illogical reasoning to believe that bonds so carefully tempered through the years would snap so easily!

I entered college mentally and physically exhausted. During the period of rest necessary to rebuild my body, I cut loose from the old inhibitions and began to give expression to long suppressed desires. Habits were difficult to break, but I found it could be done.

Here I must leave my analysis. With new stimuli, fewer taboos, more opportunity for borrowing new patterns, I will no doubt form new habits, but from the experience of recent years, it seems safe to conclude that I will never break entirely from the training of my childhood and of my youth.

From a study of my development, we may conclude that a personality may be shaped chiefly by the customs of a small group if that group is isolated by physical or taboo barriers, and that when this happens socialization in a larger group is difficult; that projection of the culture of an intimate "in-group" upon the child can be so effective as to practically eliminate the influence of "out-group" patterns and to make difficult the attainments of status in normal "out-group" life.[47]

Sometimes I wonder if it pays to behave one's self; there are naturally times when I do, and then again there are times when I don't.

I have my own code of morals, somewhat affected by my parents' views, but on the whole established by myself.

For instance, I don't smoke. I have been both complimented and embarrassed for that. Since most every girl I run around with smokes, and that excessively, they kid me, although for some reason, I feel that some of them at least admire me for refraining from it. Why do I? Well, first of all, it is too expensive, and it doesn't help one's health whatsoever; in fact, I hear it is most detrimental. Then, too, most every girl who so indulges is only doing it to show off and be smart. In my opinion, it lowers her to a great extent. And I feel well rewarded for my abstinence when the boys who are worth while appreciate the fact that I don't smoke. It is not only the boys, but middle-aged people who know and who have been around, who congratulate me for being so wise.

Once in a while when I'm out with a crowd of kids who are in the mood for drinking, I am rather puzzled as to what to do. If I refuse, they think I'm a prig and a wet blanket; if I do it, it hurts me because I hate the stuff and I know it isn't doing me any good. When I am tired and the evening is dull, a glass of wine does wonders, but to go to a café and spend a whole evening in such a wasteful manner is not my idea of a good time.

There is also the boys' side to it. They like to take out a girl who will be sociable and full of fun. If he wants some liquor, then she should be agreeable. But I try to accept dates where I won't be expected to be quite so agreeable.

---

[47] *Ibid.*, pp. 613–614.

That all goes for this business of necking and petting. I hate those words, so I'll use one commonly heard in my home town; namely, "checking."

A fellow will see just how far he can go with a girl, and the harder she is to get the more he likes her. He'll take out the one that is loose and will "check" with any one and every one where no one will see them. But the girl he is proud to show to his friends and the general public is the other girl, his real girl.[48]

These youngsters want an understandable set of morals, a meaning to life, some guiding principles to help them see the discordant details as a sensible whole. Adolescents have always needed such help, but never more than now. For most high school pupils the lack of traditional morality among their elders is a source of confusion. Because they cannot get consistent guidance from older people, they turn to the various youth groups, many of which are intentionally quite independent of and antagonistic to whatever they regard as characteristically adult opinion. These youth organizations tend to set up their own standards—some good, some bad, some radical, some conservative. Although they help boys and girls to become independent, they do not always add materially to the clarity with which their members view the world. However, one cannot blame the youth of today for trying in any way open to them to set up their own standards, since adults have few to pass on to them.

Young people want chiefly two things from their philosophy—a feeling of security that a rapidly changing society does not give them, and an emotional satisfaction that is not provided by the scientific world around them. Modern science can explain enough phenomena to divest the world of its awesome and highly exciting mystery, but it cannot yet—if ever—give an answer to the riddle of man's life and destiny. It feeds the mind but not the imagination or the emotions. In their efforts to interpret the world so that it has a meaning for them, adolescents want not only a sense of personal security but also a stimulus to imagination and an opportunity for emotional thrill. In the course of time modern youth may work out a new synthesis of values, a long-range concept that will almost certainly be independent of organized religion but probably will be an evaluation of human life in criteria that are social and ethical.

VI. Summary

Research into attitudes and beliefs shows that young people reflect faithfully the attitudes of their elders, but also that they tend to modify these points of view as they grow older and are influenced by various individuals and agencies outside the home. Their attitudes toward the members of various nationalities, races, and ethnic groups are compounded of those of their parents and teachers, plus those which grow out of current events. Certain traits of personality and certain background conditions tend to produce intolerance and prejudice, while contrasting influences tend to produce

---

[48] *Ibid.*, p. 614.

tolerance. Information, as usually given at least, does not seem to be an important factor in the development of attitude. Most prejudices are of emotional origin and may be merely projections by means of which an individual rids himself of emotional tension.

Honesty is not as high as one could wish, and cheating on examinations is quite extensive. Teachers should expect that children who are dull, maladjusted, or overburdened by their schoolwork will cheat. There is usually some advance in honesty with age, but one cannot tell how much of the gain is due to the elimination from school of those who are least able to pass the examinations. There is some evidence that pupils who are dishonest in school tend to be dishonest as adults.

All adolescents develop ideals, although some of these are of an antisocial nature. During adolescence, however, the normal boy or girl acquires some kind of generalized principles of conduct, the particular type depending upon his personality, his environment, and his experience to date.

Most young people want to find a satisfactory philosophy of life. In the course of their efforts they often subscribe to a number of more or less extreme points of view, most of which are transitory and experimental. Adolescence is the time par excellence of "isms." The desire to reform the work and to do some good during life is strong, partly because such ideas are new and partly because experience with the ways of the world has not yet had time to dent youthful idealism. The church and other religious forces do not contribute as much as they could to the formation of a philosophy of life.

REFERENCES FOR FURTHER READING

BOOKS

1. Ackerman, N. W., and M. Johoda, *Anti-Semitism and Emotional Disorders: A Psychoanalytic Interpretation,* Harper & Brothers, 1950, 135 pp. (Chaps. 3, 4.)
2. Adorno, T. W., E. Frenkel-Brunswik, D. G. Levinson, and R. N. Sanford, *The Authoritarian Personality,* Harper & Brothers, 1950, 982 pp. (Chaps. 1, 2, 16, 19 and either A and B of Chap. 4 or A and B of Chaps. 6 and 8.)
3. Allport, G. W., *ABC's of Scapegoating,* Anti-Defamation League, rev. ed., 1948, 56 pp.
4. Baruch, D. W., *Glass House of Prejudice,* William Morrow & Company, 1946, 205 pp. (Chaps. 1, 7–9, 10–12.)
5. Bettleheim, B., and M. Janowitz, *Dynamics of Prejudice,* Harper & Brothers, 1950, 224 pp. (Chaps. 2, 3, 6.)
6. Child, I. L., *Italian or American? The Second Generation Conflict,* Yale University Press, 1943, 208 pp. (Chaps. 3–6.)
7. Davis, Bredemeier, and Levy, *Modern American Society,* Chaps. 11–14, 17.
8. Dimock, *Rediscovering the Adolescent,* Chap. 8.
9. Frenkel-Brunswik, E., *et al.,* "The Anti-Democratic Personality," in T. M. Newcomb and E. L. Hartley (eds.), *Readings in Social Psychology,* Henry Holt and Company, 1947, pp. 531–541.
10. Garrison, *Psychology of Adolescence,* Chap. 9.

11. Havighurst and Taba, *Adolescent Character and Personality*, Chap. 8.
12. Hurlock, *Adolescent Development*, Chaps. 10, 11.
13. Klineberg, O., *Tensions Affecting International Understanding*, Social Science Research Council, 1950, 227 pp. (Chaps. 3–5.)
14. Kuhlen, *The Psychology of Adolescent Development*, Chap. 9.
15. Landis, *Adolescence and Youth*, Chaps. 8–11.
16. Lewin, K., *Resolving Social Conflict*, Harper & Brothers, 1948, 230 pp. (Pt. III.)
17. Locke, A., and B. J. Stern, *When Peoples Meet*, Progressive Education Association, 1942, 825 pp. (Chaps. 8, 10–12.)
18. Malm and Jamison, *Adolescence*, Chap. 8.
19. Merry and Merry, *The First Two Decades of Life*, Chap. 12.
20. Myrdal, G., *et al.*, *Democracy*, Harper & Brothers, 1944, 2 vols., 1483 pp. (Chaps. 36, 44, 45.)
21. Schermerhorn, R. A., *These Our People: Minorities in American Culture*, D. C. Heath & Company, 1949, 635 pp. (Chaps. 4–10, 16–19.)
22. Simmel, E. (ed.), *Anti-Semitism: A Social Disease*, International Universities Press, 1946, 141 pp. (Chaps. 2, 3, 6.)
23. Sperry, W. L. (ed.), *Religion in the Postwar World*, Vol. IV, Harvard University Press, 1945, 114 pp. (Any one of Chaps. 2, 3, or 4.)
24. Steckle, *Problems in Human Adjustment*, Chaps. 11, 13.
25. Tenenbaum, S., *Why Men Hate*, Beechhurst Press, 1947, 368 pp. (Chaps. 6, 9–11, 14–18, 36, 39.)
26. Williams, R. M., *The Reduction of Intergroup Tensions*, Social Service Research Council, 1947, 153 pp. (Chap. 3 in Sec. II and pp. 84–93.)

MONOGRAPHS, BULLETINS, PROCEEDINGS, YEARBOOKS, ARTICLES

A. *The Nature of Prejudice*

1. Allport, G. W., and B. M. Kramer, "Some Roots of Prejudice," *Journal of Psychology*, 22:9–39, 1946.
2. Frenkel-Brunswik, E., "Family Patterns and Ideology," *American Psychologist*, 3:350, 1948.
3. Frenkel-Brunswik, E., "A Study of Prejudice in Children," *Human Relations*, 1:295–306, 1948.
4. Lindzey, J., "An Experimental Examination of the Scapegoat Theory of Prejudice," *Journal of Abnormal and Social Psychology*, 45:295–309, 1950.
5. Miller, N. E., and R. Bugelski, "Minor Studies of Aggression: II. The Influence of Frustrations Imposed by the In-Group on Attitudes Expressed toward Out-Groups," *Journal of Psychology*, 25:437–442, 1948.
6. Montagu, M. F. A., "Some Psychodynamic Factors in Race Prejudice," *Journal of Social Psychology*, 30:175–187, 1949.
7. Morse, N. C., and F. H. Allport, "Anti-Semitism: A Study of Its Causal Factors and Other Associated Variables," *American Psychologist*, 4:261, 1949.
8. Preston, M. G., and L. A. Kahn, "Prejudices of Out-Groups," *International Journal of Opinion and Attitude Research*, 3:214–228, 1949.
9. Radke, M., and J. Sutherland, "Children's Concepts and Attitudes about Minority and Majority American Groups," *Journal of Educational Psychology*, 40:449–468, 1949.
10. Razran, G., "Ethnic Dislikes and Stereotypes: A Laboratory Study," *Journal of Abnormal and Social Psychology*, 45:7–27, 1950.
11. Sanger, G., and H. M. Schulman, "Some Factors Determining Intercultural Behavior and Attitudes of Members of Different Ethnic Groups in Mixed Neighborhoods," *Journal of Psychology*, 25:365–380, 1948.

12. Thistlethwaite, D., "Attitude and Structure as Factors in the Distortion of Reasoning," *Journal of Abnormal and Social Psychology,* 45:442–458, 1950.
13. Zeligs, R., "Reasons Given by Children for Their Intergroup Attitudes," *Journal of Genetic Psychology,* 76:145–161, 1950.

B. *Prejudice against Negroes*

1. Baruch, D. W., "Some Aspects of Discrimination in a War Area," *American Journal of Orthopsychiatry,* 14:714–721, 1944.
2. Bayton, J. A., and E. F. Byoune, "Racio-National Stereotypes Held by Negroes," *Journal of Negro Education,* 16:49–56, 1947.
3. Blake, R., and W. Dennis, "The Development of Stereotypes concerning the Negro," *Journal of Abnormal and Social Psychology,* 38:525–531, 1943.
4. Goff, A. M., "Problems and Emotional Difficulties of Negro Children," *Teachers College Contributions to Education,* No. 960, 1949, 93 pp.
5. MacKenzie, B. K., "The Importance of Contact in Determining Attitudes toward Negroes," *Journal of Abnormal and Social Psychology,* 43:417–441, 1948.
6. Mussen, P. H., "Some Personal and Social Factors Related to Changes in Children's Attitudes towards Negroes," *Journal of Abnormal and Social Psychology,* 45:423–441, 1950.
7. Radke, M. J., and H. G. Trager, "Children's Perceptions of the Social Roles of Negroes and Whites," *Journal of Psychology,* 29:3–33, 1950.
8. Smith, F. T., "An Experiment in Modifying Attitudes toward the Negro," *Teachers College Contributions to Education,* No. 887, 1943, 135 pp.

C. *Changing Attitudes*

1. Jones, H. E., "Attitude Changes of High School Youth," *American Psychologist,* 3:352, 1948.
2. Mayo, G. D., and J. R. Kinzer, "A Comparison of Racial Attitudes of White and Negro High School Students in 1940 and 1948," *Journal of Psychology,* 29:397–405, 1950.
3. Remmers, H. H., and N. Weltman, "Attitude Inter-Relationships of Youth, Their Parents, and Their Teachers," *Journal of Social Research,* 26:61–68, 1947.
4. Rose, A. M., "A Study in the Reduction of Prejudice," *American Council on Racial Interrelationships,* rev., 1948.
5. Watson, J., "Some Social and Psychological Situations Relative to Change in Attitude," *Human Relations,* 3:15–36, 1950.
6. Wirth, L., "Research in Racial and Cultural Relations," *Proceedings of the American Philosophical Society,* 92:381–386, 1948.

D. *Religious Attitudes and Practices*

1. Arbuckle, D. S., "Religious Services in Colleges," *Journal of Higher Education,* 20:317–320, 1949.
2. Beller, E. K., "Two Attitude Components in Younger Boys," *Journal of Social Psychology,* 29:137–151, 1949.
3. Dudycha, G. J., "The Religious Beliefs of College Freshmen in 1930 and 1949," *Religious Education,* 45:165–169, 1950.
4. Kirkpatrick, C., "Religion and Humanitarianism: A Study of Institutional Implications," *Psychological Monographs,* LXIII, No. 9, Whole No. 304 (1949), 1–23.
5. Kuhlen, R. G., and M. Arnold, "Age Differences in Religious Beliefs and Problems during Adolescence," *Journal of Genetic Psychology,* 65:291–300, 1944.

6. Moreton, F. E., "Attitudes toward Religion among Adolescents and Adults," *British Journal of Educational Psychology,* 14:69–79, 1944.
7. Mull, H. K., "A Comparison of Religious Thinking of Freshmen and Seniors in a Liberal Arts College," *Journal of Social Psychology,* 26:121–123, 1947.
8. Parry, H. J., "Protestants, Catholics, and Prejudice," *International Journal of Opinion and Attitude Research,* 3:205–213, 1949.
9. Pixley, E., and E. Beekman, "The Faith of Youth as Shown in the Public Schools of Los Angeles," *Religious Education,* 44:336–342, 1949.
10. Vinacke, W. E., J. Eindhoven, and J. Engle, "Religious Attitudes of Students at the University of Hawaii," *Journal of Psychology,* 28:161–179, 1949.
11. Weaver, T., "Youth and Religion," *Annals of the American Academy of Political and Social Science,* 236:152–160.

E. *Moral Attitudes and Behavior*

1. Dowd, M. A., "Changes in Moral Reasoning through the High School Years," *Studies in Psychology and Psychiatry,* Catholic University of America, Vol. VII, No. 2, 1948, 120 pp.
2. Jones, V., "A Comparison of Certain Measurements of Honesty in Early Adolescence with Honesty in Adulthood: A Follow-Up Study," *American Psychologist,* 1:261, 1946.
3. Landis, P. H., "Points of Strain in Adolescent Morality," *School and Society,* 51:612–616, 1940.
4. Lorang, M. C., "The Effect of Reading on Moral Conduct and Emotional Experience," *Studies in Psychology and Psychiatry of the Catholic University of America,* Vol. IV, No. 6, 1945, 122 pp.
5. Stendler, C. B., "A Study of Some Socio-Moral Judgments of Junior High School Children," *Child Development,* 20:15–28, 1949.

F. *Identifications and Hero Worship*

1. Hill, D. S., "Personification of Ideals by Urban Children," *Journal of Social Psychology,* 1:379–392, 1930.
2. Klapp, O. E., "Hero Worship in America," *American Sociological Review,* 14:53–62, 1949.
3. Lawrence, K., and M. H. Frank, "One Way to Personality," *Childhood Education,* 25:389–393.
4. Rudolph, M., "Identification through Finding a Hero," *Childhood Education,* 25:407–408.
5. Russell, D. H., "Identification through Literature," *Childhood Education,* 25:397–401.
6. Stoughton, M. L., and A. M. Ray, "A Study of Children's Heroes and Ideals," *Journal of Experimental Psychology,* 15:156–160, 1946.

CHAPTER FOURTEEN

Community
Influence

Individuals of any age above infancy are to some extent affected by the standards and customs of the community in which they live. As an adolescent approaches maturity, he becomes more and more aware of the cultural influences about him and begins to adjust himself to adult social pressure, as distinct from either home or school pressures. This matter is relatively difficult to investigate or to measure, and few studies have been made, although several have thrown light incidentally upon the ways in which customs and conventions influence adolescent life.

The present chapter will consist of three main topics: (1) the changes in the physical environment since 1900 and the influence of these changes upon the daily life of the adolescent, (2) the common defects in communities, and (3) the constructive influences that can and often do exist and might be developed further by communities that are willing to put time, energy, and money into the protection and guidance of youth.

I. Changes in the Physical Environment since 1900

It is common knowledge that the typical American community has changed markedly during the last fifty years, but only those who have either studied the period or lived through it can know how much change there has been.

For example, the author grew up in a small eastern city in which, until she was about twelve years old, there were no telephones and no electric lights, and until she was about eighteen, no automobiles, no movies, and no phonographs. Not more than half the houses had toilets, and about 10 per cent of them had no running water and no gas. Cooking was done, even in the wealthiest of families, on a coal stove, which required constant feeding, banking at night, shaking down in the morning about an hour before breakfast, and enough knowledge of drafts and fuel to qualify a cook as an engineer. To appreciate the differences between life not very long ago and life now, let the reader make a list of all his activities during the last twenty-four hours, then go through and cross off any activity that depended upon one or more of the modern inventions listed below, and finally note what proportion of his day's occupations remains untouched.

Means of communication: telephone, radio, typewriters, dictaphones, television, wire recorders

Means of travel: streamliners, automobiles, busses, trucks, airplanes

Electrical equipment: lights, toasters, percolators, ovens, vacuum cleaners, fans, irons, mixers, heaters, electric razors, refrigerators, freezers, washing machines, sewing machines

Use of leisure: movies, cameras, skating rinks, record players, swimming pools, public playgrounds, loan libraries

Modern conveniences: running hot water, toilets, bathtubs, gas or electric stoves, gas or oil-burning furnaces, power tools, gasoline motors, electric motors

As can be imagined, the population did not move about much, except on foot. The members of the family were constantly thrown together by necessity, since it took the combined and continuous labor of all members to keep the household economy functioning. In the evenings there was some visiting in the neighborhood among adolescents, but most evenings found the family together and amusing itself with singing, playing games, reading aloud, popping corn, dancing, drawing, painting, whittling, and so on, or continuing with quieter forms of work, such as darning stockings or casting up accounts. Thus, both work and play were shared, and parents could not help knowing where their children were and what they were doing; in fact, most adults in a neighborhood knew every child who lived in it. The family and neighborhood were of a custodial or trustee type;[1] that is, they guarded tradition and knowledge and handed them down, relatively unchanged.

In 1947, there were nearly thirty-eight million automobiles in the United States, and by the date of this book's publication there will be over fifty million.[2] Americans travel one hundred million miles by air each year, and no one knows how many billion miles by automobile. There are nearly one hundred million radio sets, and barely 10 per cent of American homes are without at least one. The number of television sets is small by comparison, only two or three million, but this seeming scarcity is due only to newness. Before many years are over they will be as common as radios. The number of telephones comes to more than half the total number in the world.[3] Because their means of transportation are both easily available and cheap, Americans are the world's most persistent travelers. In an ordinary year, something over two million people leave their own state and enter another; during the war years a third of the population changed states, at least temporarily. It is nothing unusual to meet ordinary working people of modest incomes who have lived in five or six different states and have

[1] J. H. S. Bossard and E. S. Boll, *Family Situations,* University of Pennsylvania Press, 1943, 265 pp.

[2] J. H. S. Bossard, "Social Changes in the United States," *Annals of the American Academy of Political and Social Science,* 265:69–79, 1949.

[3] Of the material leadership of the United States there would seem to be no question, although Switzerland is a close competitor. As summarized by C. E. Wilson, then President of General Motors, over CBS on December 5, 1951: "With 6 per cent of the world's area and 7 per cent of the world's population, we have 46 per cent of its electric power, 48 per cent of its radios, 54 per cent of its telephones, 59 per cent of its steel capacity, 60 per cent of its life insurance policies, 85 per cent of its automobiles, and 92 per cent of its modern bathtubs."

driven through thirty to forty of the others. This mobility of large segments of a population is new.

The extremely rapid changes in physical environment since about 1900 have so altered society as to destroy the old values without yet establishing new ones. The adolescent of today finds himself faced with an adult society in which habits are unsettled and ethics are heterogeneous and conflicting. His home is without roots and has been shorn of many of its former functions. His urban neighborhood has little if any community existence, and his daily life is overexciting, overdemanding, overdangerous, and overstimulating. One doubts that human beings were ever intended to live in such an environment of constant strain, constant noise, and constant stimulation as now exists, especially since the pressure of modern life has destroyed the familiar guideposts and left the coming generations to decide upon what new ones should be erected. There may come a time when society catches up with its own progress and again becomes stable, but that hour is not yet, nor in the foreseeable future. In the meantime adult chaos will continue to have its effects upon children and adolescents.

II. Common Community Defects

In most states children of sixteen may drive automobiles. As the adolescent social world is at present organized, the ability to drive a car and the permission to do so are integral factors in adolescent maturity and prestige. The boy or girl who cannot or will not drive is looked down upon. A sixteen-year-old is competent, physically and mentally, to drive a car, although one may question his judgment, but it is doubtful if any but the most unusual boy or girl of sixteen is sufficiently self-controlled to be permitted the widespread freedom which comes from the unchaperoned use of a car. The boy who owns or borrows an automobile can, in an hour's time, get so far away from home that no one is likely to know him. He thus escapes the supervision which comes from the mere presence of those who may recognize him. Most adolescents cannot safely dispense with this indirect form of protection. As matters now stand, parents and teachers have to protect their adolescents against temptation as well as they can by the development of self-control. It would seem a more sensible and simpler measure, if a community wishes to guard boys and girls from the dangers of unsupervised adventure in an automobile, to raise the legal age at which a license may be obtained.

In most states the legal age at which cigarettes or liquor may be bought is eighteen. It is, however, an unusual clerk in a drugstore who refuses to sell cigarettes to high school boys and girls. It is not a question here of whether adolescents should or should not smoke. It is rather a matter of cigarettes and liquor being generally available to those who are not yet old enough to exercise discretion in their use. In most high school groups there are some pupils who apparently have free access to whatever liquor they want, and not through their own families. In most cities there is an occasional outbreak of the use of drugs among high school pupils, and in some parts of the country drug addiction is a serious menace to normal development and health. If an adolescent can easily obtain tobacco, alcohol, or drugs, the fault lies in adult indifference.

When a large city high school disbands for the day, the boys have to run a more or less extensive gauntlet of prostitutes and pimps. When the situation comes to the attention of school authorities or parents—often through the venereal infection of some boy—there is an agitation, and the police drive temptation away from the school. In a few weeks, however, the panderers of vice are back again. High school boys do not, to be sure, have much money, but they furnish a small, steady income for prostitutes who could do no better in an adult market. Only doctors and juvenile courts are constantly aware of the perils that most high school boys manage to avoid or of the tragedies that overtake those who cannot resist temptation. Every year tobacco, liquor, drugs, and vice take their toll of adolescent vitality. And the blame lies fundamentally with the indifference of the community to its young.

A community may also regulate its places of amusement. Some effort in this direction is usually made, but the laws are by no means rigidly enforced. In fact, the owners of places of amusement depend primarily upon the young people for support. The usual amusement park is probably the least harmful type of entertainment furnished by adults and consumed mainly by adolescents and children. Naturally, the character of such places varies with the ownership, but many proprietors attempt to give reasonable protection to those who frequent their place of business. There are also public dance halls, night clubs, and roadhouses where reasonable standards are enforced, but no owner can be too scrupulous or his income will rapidly diminish. Most such places offer practically no protection to the adolescent using them, and some make a direct appeal to the baser motives of boys and girls. Dancing is a definitely exciting procedure, which readily deteriorates into the primitive rituals from which it sprang. By serving liquor and by allowing pimps, prostitutes, drug handlers, perverts, and other undesirables to linger about, the cheap dance hall lays a trap to catch the stimulated boy or girl. The low-class night club intends to get boys and girls intoxicated and is not above giving them knockout drops if there is any profit to be gained. Roadhouses and the poorest of the tourist cabins offer facilities for immoral conduct. Burlesque shows and vaudeville houses are also without protection for adolescents, who are, in theory, excluded. The programs deliberately seek to arouse sex interest; the acts are designed for the lowest levels of intelligence and moral attitude in the audience; the jokes need to be laundered. The age limit below which individuals are excluded is low and is often not enforced. In any case, the matter is usually left to the judgment of the ticket seller as to whether a given adolescent is to be admitted. The community that permits dance halls with low standards of morality, cheap shows, unsupervised night clubs and roadhouses, and salacious burlesque will reap a harvest of adolescent moral collapse that is its own fault.

Finally, there are the various places maintained by organized vice. Public houses, gambling rooms, poolrooms, and the like, damage thousands of adolescents every year. Adolescents lose money on gambling machines, horse racing, dog racing, roulette wheels, crap shooting, and card games. Gambling is often carried on openly if not legally, with the authorities looking the other way most of the time and contenting themselves with sporadic raids. The community in which the laws are "liberal" can expect some of its adolescents every year to be forced into stealing in order to meet debts incurred through gambling. Some of them commit suicide. Boys and girls of high school age do not have the judgment, the knowledge, or the financial resources to gamble with safety. The lure of the house of prostitution is too obvious to need comment. There is nothing inherently wicked in shooting pool or playing billiards; the trouble comes from the nature of the adults who hang around the ordinary poolroom. In its indifferent attitude toward organized vice the average community sows the wind—and reaps the whirlwind.

Cities are convenient places for certain types of adult work and activities, but they do not—without considerable modification—meet the needs of children and adolescents, partly because they do not furnish easy and safe outlets for social and emotional drives and partly because they do not provide for the natural and harmless kind of thrill demanded by youngsters. In a city, children are frankly in the way. Both children and adolescents are likely to develop a sophistication that comes from constant contact with too much adult thought. Some children and adolescents are overstimulated by it, some are bored, some are resentful, and some are stifled. Perhaps this ever-present grown-up world furnishes the greatest handicap of all to the healthy development of children and adolescents who live in the heart of a big city.

Bill F. was twelve years old when he first came to the attention of the juvenile court in a large city. The misdeed for which he was arrested proved to be more a comedy of errors than a crime, but the intention behind his activities was definitely criminal. Just before closing time one evening he had slipped unseen into a drugstore, crouched down behind a counter, tied a bandana over his face, tied a pair of wooden blocks on his feet (to make him seem taller), put on gloves, and seized a pair of dime-store cap pistols. Thus accoutered he waited a few moments till the store was empty and then rose, like Venus from the waves, nearly scaring the druggist into a fit. Subsequent events soon offset the magnificent entry, however. Bill had not realized that his voice was still a childish treble until his, "Hands up, or I'll shoot," sounded unconvincing even in his own ears. As he spoke, the bandana fell down, and in his embarrassment he fired off the caps in his pistols, making a noise that bore about the same relation to a real pistol shot as his voice did to a man's shout. The druggist, seeing now with what he had to deal, charged at Bill, who promptly tried to run away, but one of his wooden blocks fell off while the other hung on just long enough to trip him. The druggist grabbed him up by the seat of the pants and held him upside down while telephoning the police to come and collect the young marauder. Aside from possible strain to the druggist's heart, no harm was done, but everyone concerned felt that Bill's state of mind needed attention.

Upon investigation, it appeared that, in the main, Bill's home and environment were good, from an external viewpoint. Bill's parents were separated and he occupied a small apartment with his mother. His father lived in another apartment only a few blocks away. Bill had had a key to both apartments from the age of eight. He often spent Sunday with his father. His mother was head of a department in a large store. Six days a week she was up before Bill was, made a pot of coffee, ate a meager breakfast, and rushed off to work. She purposely did not waken Bill until she was on the point of leaving, because he was under foot. About half the time she picked up a meal from a delicatessen on her way home in the late afternoon, and the other evenings she and Bill went to a restaurant. The apartment was so small that there was really no room for Bill in it. He slept in a bed that let down from the wall in the living room, kept his clothes in one of his mother's bureau drawers and in a corner of her closet, had no space of his own, and owned almost no toys. There was neither any place to keep them nor any place to play with them.

Bill usually drank warmed-over coffee for breakfast, supplementing it with cookies, leftover cake, or crackers. His mother left fruit juice and milk for him, but he had for years poured them down the sink. After browsing through the paper, he pushed his bed back into the wall, rinsed off the dishes, and went to school, where he remained till three thirty. He loathed the nutritious school lunch and often patronized the corner drugstore instead, making a lunch from soft drinks, doughnuts, and cream puffs. Bill's schoolwork was satisfactory, though below his capacities, his manners were above reproach, his clothes were faultless, and he had never been a disciplinary problem. His teachers had, however, sensed in him a rather sneering attitude toward school, and his age-mates regarded him as stuck-up. He had no interest in games and thought the Boy Scouts were "kid stuff," but he had never made any real trouble during school hours, except that he had to be watched at lunchtime. If he could not slip away unseen, he bowed to necessity in a polite way and ate the school lunch. After school hours he went, usually alone, to the movies. During the previous year he had sometimes substituted watching television for the movies. Saturdays he remained in bed till noon reading detective fiction and westerns, and spent the entire afternoon in the movie. On his way home, he bought two or three tabloids and read them until his mother came home. Quite often she had visitors in the evening, mostly other women from the store and sometimes their husbands. There was no place but his mother's tiny bedroom or the bathroom or the minuscule kitchenette for Bill to go, and he could not retire because the guests were sitting right where his bed would descend, so he listened to adult conversation, drank a diluted cocktail, and leafed through magazines. Mostly, he was bored but sometimes he picked up nuggets of sophistication.

Ever since he could remember, Bill's only free play had taken place in the streets. It was rarely very active, partly because a downhill slope made running dangerous for small children, partly because the same slope made all games involving the use of a ball impossible, and partly because Bill learned early in life that the best way to win approval from his pretty young mother was to keep his clothes clean. The "play" consisted in a little mild roughhousing among the other boys, a good deal of storytelling and wisecracking, and an occasional hopping on a truck for the ride. Bicycles or wagons were utterly impossible, and the basements of apartment houses do not include space for children's workshops. The nearest park was quite a distance away, and the activities of the boys, once they got there, were so wild and unrestrained that Bill was not interested in going to the park. By the time he was eight years old, the movies had become Bill's chief form of "play," with the radio his second choice.

Bill's mother was a pleasant though superficial sort of person, his father was a good but sophisticated man, his neighborhood was better than average but without outlets for children's interests, and his school was excellent in caring for Bill's mind and body. But nowhere except at the movies and in the tabloids did Bill's soul get any nourishment. His environment was "good," but his life was wrong. He was as neglected as any tenement child. His normal emotional drives had no outlets. He could not identify himself with his father, because he knew that his father drank, gambled, had mistresses, and—while invariably kind to his son, in a casual sort of way—was not an admirable character. Bill's emotions were already stunted and blighted; although his callousness had no cruelty in it, only indifference, it was marked in one so young. His only comment after reading a nauseatingly detailed account of the murder of a prostitute was, "Well, I guess the bitch asked for it." What emotional life Bill had left was due to the movies, which gave him something to feel. They also presented him with the notion of holding up a drugstore, but this negative contribution is of minor importance. He could have obtained the same or similar ideas from other sources, but only the movies kept the tepid bath of adult indifference in which he lived from killing his emotions altogether.

Bill's essay into crime did not seem to have been motivated by desire for money, for revenge, or for prestige. He did not belong to a gang, and most of his acquaintances were unlikely to respect him for acting like a hoodlum. What he wanted was to "feel" like a desperado, to experience one episode of acute emotional pleasure, to escape just once from the dull life that he had to live, and to identify himself in a realistic way with the only "he-men" he had ever come in contact with. In short, Bill's motives were normal, and he was not a real delinquent, although he could readily have become one.

The city, with its comforts, its easy life, its sophistication, and its indifference provides a passable environment for adults, but it smothers children. There is literally no room for them. Schools, playgrounds, and settlement houses try to provide a little normal life, but their combined efforts are usually inadequate. The city teaches normal, intelligent children like Bill too much too soon on the one hand, and on the other, it gives them too little too late, since a small child cannot reach a park or other place where he can run and play without adult help because of the traffic.

Epilogue: The above account was written some years ago. At the present time, a postscript is possible. Bill's parents fortunately had plenty of money and could send him away to a school in Wyoming, where he probably made less academic progress than he would have made at home, but where horseback riding and marksmanship were part of the curriculum. For six years Bill remained in the Great Open Spaces, living what to him was an exciting life, until he was ready to return voluntarily to the city in order to go to college. There has never been another delinquent episode. Bill's fantasies were no longer necessary because reality was so exciting that he did not need them. He is now a normal young man who bears little resemblance to the pale, sophisticated, overrepressed little boy who tried to save his soul by holding up a drugstore.

At present, three fifths of the population of this country live in cities of one hundred thousand or over, and two thirds in cities of ten thousand or over.[4] One feature of urban life is the splitting up of the family, even though all members continue to reside under the same roof, largely because the many facilities offered by city life are commonly used by different age groups, even though there is no law about it.

[4] Bossard, "Social Changes in the United States," *loc. cit.*

A comparison of a typical Sunday in the author's childhood and a typical urban Sunday of today as spent by a neighborhood family composed of parents and four children ranging in age from nine to eighteen may serve to highlight the changes that have occurred. It will be seen in Table 35 that the modern example shows a group of individuals who live together and share such home activities as happen to be convenient. At no time during the day is everyone together. There is constant coming and going, as each member pursues his or her own life. There is little division of labor, and far more responsibility is put on the children, who essentially "run" themselves. Even on the day of leisure there is no group undertaking. This feature of a separate life for each person has led sociologists to call the modern family "atomistic." The present arrangement separates children and adolescents from the constant support of their main "primary" group—their family— even though the support may be easily available when needed. In general, the less the identification with other members of a primary group and the fewer the contacts with them, the smaller the degree of security and the less the pressure for conformity to the standards of the group. The second important primary group, the gang or crowd, providentially continues to exist, and it often outbalances the family because it has retained the close-knit dependence of the members upon each other, while many families have lost this feature.

Urban life greatly increases the number of "secondary" groups to which one is likely to belong: one's work group, school, union, recreational club (golf, tennis, swimming, and so on), social or business groups or clubs of all sorts, committees, associations, or professional societies, plus mere membership in a number of organizations. The secondary groups afford a great many contacts of different kinds with different people, but the contacts are superficial. The demands made upon a single individual by his various secondary groups are numerous and often conflicting. There is no unity of either goals or attitudes. For many people the contacts are too numerous and too fatiguing. Urban life is composed largely of many diversified, superficial contacts with many secondary groups. As a result, the individual who belongs to twenty such groups but is still isolated and confused is a common phenomenon.

Since the beginning of the machine age, with its prolongation of education and its postponement of gainful employment, adolescents have had more and more leisure. Even the adolescent who has begun to work still has many unassigned hours. This universality of leisure is so new that there has not been time to educate communities into supplying youth with adequate means of recreation. Surveys have made clear the inadequacies of the average community as a place in which young people with little or no money can find healthy diversion. Because of the demands made upon them by modern types of work and by modern life, all youngsters need opportunities for outdoor activities, for creative experiences, and for a full social life. The underprivileged boy or girl in either city or country is especially handicapped in his efforts to find recreation. Even adequate physical exercise—

Table 35

SUNDAY ACTIVITIES IN 1910 AND IN 1950

	Yesterday	*Today*
7:30 A.M.	Family prayers, led by father.[a]	Extra half hour of sleep.
8:00–8:30	All members of family ate breakfast.	Members of family ate breakfast by ones or twos, except son who was sleeping late after a dance on Saturday evening.
9:00–10:00	Women and girls washed dishes and made beds; men and boys filled wood boxes, fed the stock, and did other necessary chores.	Each person washed his own cup and plate. Just before dinner mother washed the coffeepot, and cleaned the toaster and orange juicer.
10:00–12:00	Entire family went to church, where father and both sons sang in choir.	Children read the comics, father washed car, older daughter shampooed her hair, mother went to church, younger children went to Sunday school. Each person made his own bed at some time during the day except the younger son, who didn't bother.
12:15 A.M.–1:00 P.M.	Children were in Sunday school; women prepared dinner; men read newspaper or talked. Sunday dinner; everyone present.	Older son just getting up; younger boy at friend's house; older girl talking on telephone to friends; older daughter missing from dinner to go with friends on a picnic; younger one bolted her meal and left early to go to the movies.
1:00–2:00		
2:00–6:00	Adults read or rested; children read or did something quiet in their own rooms by themselves.	Mother remained at home, father played golf, older son went out somewhere in car, one daughter was at picnic, another at the movies, a younger son was swimming in YMCA pool. Later, younger son went with his pals to a hotdog stand for a snack and went home with one of them (notifying his mother by telephone after he had arrived at friend's house).
6:00–6:30	Supper; everyone present.	Mother fixed plate of sandwiches and some fruit, and put Coca-Colas on ice. Parents ate supper about six. The others strayed in any time up to midnight. Paper plates and cups were used and thrown away, and the last man in washed the service plate.

[a] Not a minister, who might be expected to show unusual interest in religion.

Table 35—*Continued*

	Yesterday	*Today*
7:00–8:30	Father read. Sons sang in choir at church. Daughters read or wrote letters. After mixing dough for 6–8 loaves of bread and putting it in bowls to rise, Mother began quiet preparations for Monday's washing and cooking.	Parents went to movie; younger son watched television (in company with two neighborhood children); older son went to a teen canteen; older daughter studied at home; younger daughter spent the evening at a friend's house.
8:30–9:00	Men, women, and children did final chores of the day and then sang the evening hymn.	There are few if any chores to be done. The two younger children put themselves to bed at nine; neither was tucked in by the parents, who were still at the movies.
9:15–9:30	Older children were in their own rooms studying Monday's lessons; younger children tucked in by parents.	

the easiest of needs for a community to fill—is often lacking and where available at all is limited mostly to boys and young men.

The lack of recreational facilities in many communities for those who have little or no money has been an outstanding point in all the studies made. The poverty of leisure on the part of many young people is shown by their answers when they are asked how they use their time.

"Just walk around, like the other girls do."
"Ride in a beer truck, ride in a car, loaf."
"Walk around and walk around and go home to bed. All my time is spare time."
"Lay under a shade tree in summer, nothing in winter."
"Gamble, shoot craps, read, and play pool."[5]

Unless youth has money in its pocket, there is not much to do during the hours left over from sleep and school or work. The two pictures in Figures 100 and 101 on pages 462 and 463 illustrate dramatically the aimlessness of much youthful leisure.

The war years brought into sharp relief the inadequacy of recreational opportunity for adolescents, either for those in school or for those who were working.[6] Such facilities as did exist were poorly distributed. The equipment needed for some of them wore out and could not be replaced, while others

[5] See C. G. Wrenn and D. L. Hartley, *Time on Their Hands,* American Council on Education, 1941, p. 3.
[6] H. Sorenson, "Wartime Recreation for Adolescents," in J. H. S. Bossard and E. S. Boll (eds.), "Adolescents in Wartime," *Annals of the American Academy of Political and Social Science,* 236:117–127, 1944.

(Photo by Vachon)

Fig. 100.   *Nonconstructive Leisure (1)*

From H. M. Bell, *Matching Youth and Jobs,* American Council on Education, 1940, 277 pp. Used by permission of the Council.

(Photo by R. W. Lee)

Fig. 101.   *Nonconstructive Leisure (2)*

From C. G. Wrenn and D. L. Hartley, *Time on Their Hands,* American Council on Education, 1941, p. 109. Used by permission of the Council.

had to be closed for lack of labor to keep them running. The majority were located in large cities and were available chiefly to white males. Small cities were virtually without public recreational agencies or even good commercial recreation. Negroes, adolescents in rural communities, adolescents who were employed, and girls were seriously neglected. Since girls of secondary school age are more mature socially, physically, and emotionally than boys, they were able to seek diversion in the servicemen's canteens—a poor place for them—and to compete with older girls for dates with the lads in uniform. These boys were usually from a group "just-older" than the girls, whom they would have ignored in normal times. That the adolescent girls were not mature enough to look after themselves was revealed by the great increases in delinquency among them during the war.

By the end of the war over two million adolescents were employed in full-time jobs. Most of them had plenty of money for the first time in their lives, they had emerged too early from both home and school control, they were too old for such public recreational facilities as playgrounds, and they were not eligible for servicemen's canteens. They diverted themselves as best they could during their leisure hours by using whatever commercial facilities were available, from skating rinks and swimming pools to cocktail bars and night clubs.

The typical embodiment of adolescent social drives to emerge from the war years was the "teen canteen," obviously modeled upon the gathering places maintained for servicemen. These canteens are open to all the boys and girls of a community. Usually their facilities extend only to dancing, loafing, and eating. Their adolescent patrons have given them such names as The Coop, the Coke Bar, Teen Town, The Rec, The Barn, El Dumpo, or the Campus Canteen. As far as they go, these informal social centers meet the needs of youngsters who want to spend long hours in their own society. Facilities and space for a greater variety of diversion are needed, and many teen canteens would be the better for a little unobtrusive adult guidance. Adolescents like to feel that they are mature enough to maintain their own clubs, but they have shown that they are not. Without the guidance and leadership of a sane, tactful adult, the founders of a teen canteen soon get themselves into managerial snarls, and they run out of interesting things to do. After an initial period of hectic activity the attendance gradually falls off, and the canteen dies from lack of patronage.

If a town or city wishes to provide better recreational facilities for its youth, it could hardly do better than to pursue the ten-point program shown in Figure 102 on page 465. Such plans cost money, but the expense of not having and carrying out a plan is greater.

III. Community Facilities

Thus far this chapter has presented the negative side of the community's contribution to adolescent development. There are certain positive elements as well. Many cities maintain a large number of playgrounds, municipal

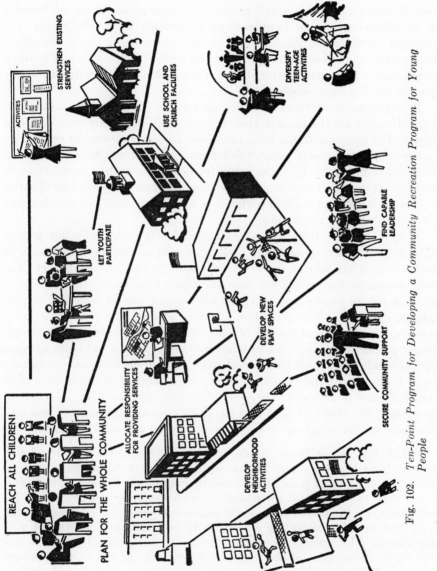

Fig. 102. *Ten-Point Program for Developing a Community Recreation Program for Young People*

M. W. Wells, "Youth and the Community," *Public Affairs Pamphlets*, No. 108, 1948, pp. 16-17.

swimming pools or beaches, skating rinks, a community theater, a sufficient number of good movie theaters, and a variety of clubhouses that offer numerous facilities. Wherever settlement houses or other kinds of clubs exist, the clubrooms are used almost continuously. If adults furnish the essential facilities, plus a small amount of supervision, most adolescents will amuse themselves in harmless and wholesome ways. Preferably, the expense of participation should be nil, so that out-of-work youth can afford the diversions they need so badly. More and more cities, towns, and country districts have taken constructive steps toward making communities healthier places in which young people may live.

In any community there are a certain number of educational influences. Most noticeable are the schools, churches, public libraries, art museums, and theaters. The influence of the school has been or will be discussed sufficiently in other chapters. Nobody denies the influence exerted by the other agencies just listed, but relatively little accurate measurement has been made to determine its extent. It is also generally conceded that museums and libraries are steadily increasing their importance in modern culture, but at what rate or to what degree is not known.

As a teacher of ethics, the average church has undeniably lost ground within the last three generations, but it is still a dominant influence. It remains also a stimulator of social development and social contact. The results shown in Figure 103 on page 467 come from three studies,[7] one of both high school pupils and college students, and two of men and women students, classified separately. For all three studies, the pattern is much the same: the commonest number of times in church is once a week, although a larger proportion of high school students than of college students go regularly on Sunday; the next commonest pattern is attendance once or twice a month. Failure to attend church at all is not as frequent as attendance more than four times in a month. There are differences also between the two college groups; the Harvard boys and Radcliffe girls are appreciably less religious than the mixed group of less highly selected university students.

Other interesting items, aside from mere frequency of attendance, emerged from these studies. In the second study those students who no longer attended church were asked when they had ceased to go. The answers showed that 18 per cent of the nonattenders had stopped by the end of the ninth grade; by the end of high school another 69 per cent had ceased to go; by the last year in college the remaining 13 per cent had lost contact with their church. The greatest loss was during the high school years. In the third study 68 per cent of the men and 82 per cent of the women thought they needed religion; 7 and 13 per cent, respectively, had passed through some kind of crisis or awakening in their religious development. These students were also asked to state their opinions as to what degree of contradiction they felt between religion and their work in science. Among the men,

---

[7] *Fortune* Survey, December, 1942; P. B. Horton, "Student Interest in the Church," *Religious Education*, 35:215–219, 1940; G. W. Allport, J. M. Gillespie, and J. Young, "Religion of the Post-War College Student," *Journal of Psychology*, 25:3–33, 1948.

53 per cent thought science and religion supported each other or that there was only negligible conflict between them; 30 per cent thought them almost or entirely irreconcilable; the remaining 17 per cent saw some conflict but

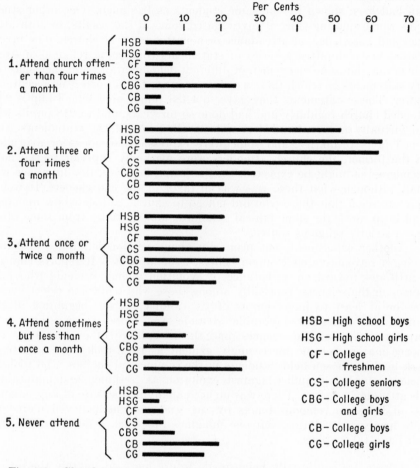

Fig. 103. *Church Attendance during Adolescence*

Based upon *Fortune* Survey, December, 1942, P. B. Horton, "Student Interest in the Church," *Religious Education,* 35:215–219, 1940; and G. W. Allport, J. M. Gillespie, and J. Young, "Religion of the Post War College Student," *Journal of Psychology*: 25: 3–33, 1948.

thought the differences could be reconciled. Seventy-three per cent of the Protestant men and 62 per cent of the Catholics had reacted at some time against their religious training.

Other studies shed a little more light upon the importance of religion among adolescents. For instance, of eleven colleges, nine still held chapel services in 1949, to which 75 per cent of the students came voluntarily.[8] Less

[8] D. S. Arbuckle, "Religious Services in College," *Journal of Higher Education,* 20:317–320, 1949.

than 5 per cent of the students said the services were without value. Three fourths of them selected courses in religion, and less than 4 per cent found these courses of no value to them. In another study, the ability of seniors to think about religious problems was found to be on a more mature level than had been shown by the same students as freshmen.[9] One other study seems worth quoting since it investigated some of the results, in both attitudes and knowledge, of attendance or nonattendance at church. The investigators first submitted a series of statements concerning religious matters to over one thousand clergymen of different denominations and then selected fifty statements on which there was agreement as to the correct or acceptable answer. These statements they gave to 1,483 junior high school pupils who attended church regularly and had done so for years, and to 218 pupils who had virtually never attended church at all. Some of the statements concerned facts primarily, and some were expressions of ideas or attitudes. On the former, the church attenders were markedly superior to the non-attenders—as might be expected. On the latter, however, the difference was small, although what there was was in favor of the churchgoers. It would therefore seem that those who did not go to church had somehow managed to pick up much the same ethical standards and attitudes from some other than a strictly religious source.[10]

Another experiment, not primarily about religion but quite probably having a retroactive effect upon beliefs, is of interest.[11] It reports changes in attitudes toward an acceptance of evolution among students who take courses in the sciences, especially among those who tended to reject evolution, or at least to have doubts of its validity, at the beginning of the courses. An unusually favorable attitude was found among those who majored in any of the sciences, and the acceptance of evolution by the science majors became increasingly evident as they took more and more work in their chosen field. Students in the commercial courses, who took no sciences, showed prejudice against evolution as freshmen and maintained this attitude as seniors. There was no accompanying measure of any possible loss of belief in religious tenets by the students who believed more and more firmly in evolution, but one imagines that such a development may well have taken place.

Efforts are continually being made to use more adequately the opportunities offered youth for instruction and development in art and music. Every year more children and adolescents visit museums and art galleries, and more go to concerts and to operas whenever these are presented. The average museum constantly tries to present displays which will be of such vital interest as to compete successfully with other types of diversion. Moreover, the museum staffs send circulating exhibits from school to school and

---

[9] H. K. Mull, "Comparison of Religious Thinking of Freshmen and Seniors in a Liberal Arts College," *Journal of Social Psychology*, 26:121–123, 1947.

[10] L. R. Wheeler and V. D. Wheeler, "Differences in Religious Ideas of Children Who Go to Church and Those Who Never Attend," *Religious Education*, 40:149–161, 1945.

[11] K. L. Barkley, "Influence of College Science Courses on the Development of Attitudes toward Evolution," *Journal of Applied Psychology*, 32:200–208, 1948.

from place to place, and teachers take or send entire classes to museums from time to time.

Education in music received its first great impetus with the invention of the phonograph. Progress has since been enormously accelerated by the radio. Knowledge of music and taste in musical appreciation have both been directly affected. In spite of some worthless musical programs heard over the radio, the average adolescent is hearing more good music and is receiving a better education in musical appreciation than any previous generation of adolescents has ever known. A generation ago, perhaps ten thousand people a year heard any one great Philharmonic orchestra; during the past year probably fifty million people heard the same group of artists. It is

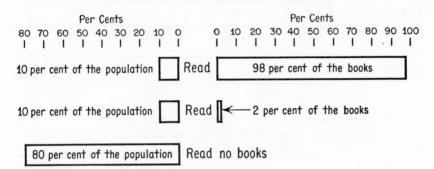

Fig. 104.   *Uneven Use of Library Facilities*

Based upon A. Campbell and C. A. Metzner, *Public Use of the Library and Other Sources of Information,* Institute of Social Research, University of Michigan, 1950, Fig. VIII.

not uncommon for a small boy to walk along his paper route whistling arias from grand opera. Such universal musical education is something new. Some adolescents have large collections of records, many of excellent quality, to which they listen for hours at a time.

In the entire country there are about seven thousand five hundred public libraries, with some twenty-five million registered users.[12] Many children and adolescents still do not have access to libraries, but most of those do who live in a community of five thousand or more adults. A fairly recent study has demonstrated the extent to which people of different ages and degrees of education use the libraries. The first point is that their use is very unevenly distributed. Ninety-eight per cent of all the books taken out in a single year were taken out by the 10 per cent of the population that individually read the most library books. Eighty per cent of the adult population did not use the library at all. The situation is pictured in Figure 104 on this page. Throughout the school years children and adolescents take out books with fair regularity, but use of the library drops off sharply after pupils leave school. The amount of schooling also has an effect upon reading

[12] A. Campbell and C. A. Metzer, *Public Use of the Library and Other Sources of Information,* Institute of Social Research, 1950, 75 pp.

habits. In the general population, 27 per cent of the adults never finished grammar school; they furnish only 5 per cent of the regular users of the library. The high school and college graduates make up only 38 per cent of the population but furnish 75 per cent of the library's steady customers. These facts are recorded in Figure 105 below. Either the amount of education has an effect in habituating pupils to the frequent use of books, or, what is more likely, those who already used and liked books were the ones who

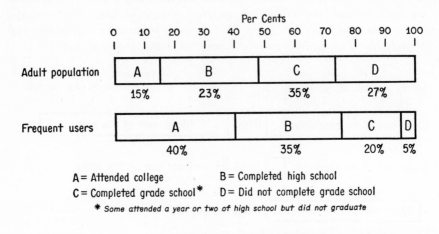

Per Cents

Adult population: A = 15%, B = 23%, C = 35%, D = 27%

Frequent users: A = 40%, B = 35%, C = 20%, D = 5%

A = Attended college
B = Completed high school
C = Completed grade school*
D = Did not complete grade school
* Some attended a year or two of high school but did not graduate

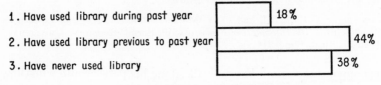

1. Have used library during past year — 18%
2. Have used library previous to past year — 44%
3. Have never used library — 38%

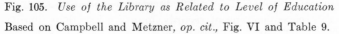

Fig. 105. *Use of the Library as Related to Level of Education*

Based on Campbell and Metzner, *op. cit.*, Fig. VI and Table 9.

extended their education beyond the minimum requirements. Of the entire adult population, only 18 per cent had been in the public library during the year before the investigation; 44 per cent had used it in previous years, and 38 per cent had never used it.

It remains to point out one further way in which the community is contributing more and more to adolescent development. Schools and teachers are using community resources as they never have before.[13] They are trying hard to relate education to life outside the school. One of the best techniques

---

[13] See, for example, H. Fields, "Making a School Community-Conscious," *Ninth Yearbook of the National Committee for the Social Studies,* 1940, pp. 164–169; G. M. Koor, "Utilizing Community Resources in an Integrated Program," *Educational Method,* 18:209–218, 1939; E. M. O'Connor, "Developing School and Community Relationships," *Teachers College Record,* 10:45–46, 1939; H. Harap, "The Community Survey in Curricular Development," in *Research in the Foundations of American Education,* 1939, pp. 54–56; N. M. Chambers, "Cooperation between Schools and Non-School Agencies," in *Research in the Foundations of American Education,* 1939, pp. 91–94.

thus far developed is to use the community as an original source. Thus if pupils are to be taught about trade unions, they go to members of local unions for interviews instead of merely reading a chapter in a textbook. The study of history is often vivified by visits to historical sites in the locality. An understanding of different countries may be heightened by having foreign residents come into the classroom and tell about their homeland. Vocational counselors often send pupils to visit local industries and to interview local businessmen. Pupils may learn mathematics by following construction work that is being done in the neighborhood. Excursions to police stations, courts, garbage disposal plants, or license bureaus throw light upon civic problems. In some towns the high school students take over the city government for a day, after going through all the processes of electing their officials. Such activities appeal to pupils as being "real" rather than just practice. Moreover, they help to integrate life in and out of the schoolroom.

Community surveys are now used as a basis for curricular developments. Teachers and students study the industries and the needs of their community and its environs. Committees on the course of study compare the results with the curricular offerings to find out if these are adequate to prepare pupils for the life of their locality. Such contacts between school and community are most helpful in adjusting education to life's needs.

During the writer's college years contacts between the college and community were relatively few; and when they occurred at all, their existence was due either to accident or to voluntary effort on the part of an individual student. The life of the college went on by itself, and the townspeople pursued whatever interests appealed to them; the only points of contact were the local churches (attended by a few of the students), the families and friends of students who lived in the community, and the various residents who worked in noninstructional positions at the college. In general, however, the college was a self-sufficient world that was tolerated by the community because of the business it brought. For the most part the two groups simply ignored each other, but if there was any feeling, it was usually one of hostility and distrust.

Recently, the writer had occasion to observe the college scene again. In the intervening forty years the community had become the laboratory of the college, and the college has become a means of self-expression for the community and a source of help in time of need. Students in the statistics classes obtain their material from the records in the city offices; students of political economy and economics make surveys of the city or county; psychology students test the school children; and youthful dietitians get their first practical training in the city hospitals. Little children from the community come to the college's nursery school; older ones come to Saturday morning classes in dancing, swimming, or other sports taught by college students, and high school pupils use the college library. Every few days a busload of youngsters arrives to look at the collections in the art museum. The community often asks members of the faculty to give lectures on their specialties, to serve on the school board, to assist the park commissioner, and to man the voting booths on election days. The play that was currently being rehearsed had this cast: four students from the college, some girl's boy friend who drove from a nearby technical school every week end for rehearsals, a druggist, a housewife, and a retired doctor from the community, plus one of the college gardeners and the college postmaster. The play, when given, would be open to the public. When a community committee was appointed by the mayor at the request of the local court to look into the causes of juvenile delinquency and to suggest possible preventive measures, the mayor selected five citizens and asked the college to select for him two students and two members of the faculty to join the townsmen. The college paper carries a column about what goes on in the city, and the city papers carry a column about affairs at the college.

In short, the college has learned to serve the community and at the same time to use it as a source of raw data for study. In one very popular class the students each year first meet with representatives from the community to plan a survey. They then make a house-to-house canvass, tabulate the results, and write a report to the original committee. At the end, the entire group meets two or three times to plan definite action on the basis of the report. As practical training for the students, nothing could be better. Incidentally, the community and the college have both been surprised and pleased to discover how much intelligence and skill were possessed by the other.

The relationship between school and community becomes steadily closer as the years roll on. It is one of the movements that is making both high school and college work less academic and better adapted to the requirements of the average pupil, who is not a scholar and who needs to have education made real and of practical significance in his daily living.

IV. Summary

The community is important in conditioning the development of adolescents, more especially those that have left school. Communities have both their defects and their merits; some of the former are perhaps unavoidable, and some of the latter are not always as conspicuous as they could be. As soon as boys and girls leave school they become dependent upon the community not only for work but for diversion. It is in the matter of providing for constructive uses of leisure that a community can have the most direct influence upon its young people. Communities are more and more contributing indirectly to adolescent happiness and security by their co-operation with schools in providing adolescents with a type of education best fitted to adapt them to community needs.

Since at the end of the adolescent period the individual has become an adult, he should gradually be emancipated from the shackles of childhood and should achieve freedom. At present this freedom is afforded so early that the average boy or girl cannot use it wisely. Adolescents need better protection than they usually get until they are old enough to protect themselves.

REFERENCES FOR FURTHER READING

BOOKS

1. Campbell, A., and C. A. Metzner, *Public Use of the Library and Other Sources of Information*, Institute for Social Research, University of Michigan, 1950, 75 pp.
2. Bernard, J., *American Community Behavior: An Analysis of Problems Confronting American Communities Today*, The Dryden Press, 1949, 688 pp. (Chaps. 2–5.)

3. Breckenridge and Vincent, *Child Development,* Chap. 6.
4. Butler, G. D., *Introduction to Community Recreation,* The Macmillan Company, 1940, 547 pp. (Chaps. 25, 27.)
5. Davis, Bredemeier, and Levy, *Modern American Society,* Chaps. 2–4, 16.
6. Garrison, *Psychology of Adolescence,* Chap. 13.
7. Havighurst and Taba, *Adolescent Character and Personality,* Chap. 6.
8. Landis, *Adolescence and Youth,* Chap. 4.
9. Malm and Jamison, *Adolescence,* Chap. 13.
10. McGill, N. P., and E. N. Matthews, *The Youth of New York City,* The Macmillan Company, 1941, 420 pp. (Chaps. 9–11.)
11. Neumeyer, *Juvenile Delinquency,* Chaps. 8, 14.
12. Sadler, *Adolescence Problems,* Chap. 20.
13. Tiegs and Katz, *Mental Hygiene in Education,* Chap. 12.
14. Wrenn, C. G., and D. L. Hartley, *Time on Their Hands,* American Council on Education, 1941, 266 pp. (Chaps. 1–6.)

MONOGRAPHS, BULLETINS, PROCEEDINGS, YEARBOOKS, ARTICLES

A. *Communities and Youth*

1. Bossard, J. H. S., "Social Changes in the United States," *Annals of the American Academy of Political and Social Science,* 265:69–79, 1949.
2. Keliher, A. V., "Community Neglect of Children," *Journal of Educational Psychology,* 20:259–263, 1947.
3. Sorenson, H., "Wartime Recreation for Adolescents," *Annals of the American Academy for Political and Social Science,* 236:145–151, 1940.
4. Wells, M. W., "Youth and the Community," *Public Affairs Pamphlet,* No. 108, 1948, 31 pp.

B. *Attitudes toward Religion*

1. Allport, G. W., J. M. Gillespie, and J. Young, "Religion of the Post-War College Student," *Journal of Psychology,* 25:3–33, 1948.
2. Braden, C. S., "Enrollment Trends in Religious Courses," *Religious Education,* 43:337–342, 1948.
3. Gragg, D. B., "Religious Attitudes of Denominational College Students," *Journal of Social Psychology,* 15:245–254, 1942.
4. Hicks, R. S., "Our Schools—Are They Godless?" *California Journal of Secondary Education,* 23:160–163, 1948.
5. Horne, E. B., and W. H. Stender, "Student Attitudes toward Religious Practices," *Journal of Social Psychology,* 22:215–218, 1945.
6. Horton, P. B., "Student Interest in the Church," *Religious Education,* 35:215–219, 1940.
7. Moreton, F. E., "Attitudes toward Religion among Adolescents and Adults," *British Journal of Educational Psychology,* 14:69–79, 1944.
8. Pullman, G. P., and E. E. Emme, "Changes in the Attitudes of College Students in Religion and Politics," *Proceedings of the Iowa Academy of Science,* 49:431–432, 1942.
9. Telford, C. W., "A Study of Religious Attitudes," *Journal of Social Psychology,* 31:217–230, 1950.
10. Vaughn, H., *et al.,* "Religious Practices in Teachers Colleges," *Twenty-sixth Yearbook of the American Association of College Teachers of Education,* 1947, pp. 114–118.

C. *Use of Community Resources in the Schools*

1. Benne, K. D., and A. F. Zander, "More Effective School-Community Projects," *National Education Association Journal,* 38:117–118, 1949.

2. Bottrell, H. R., "Community-Student Participation," *Journal of Higher Education,* 17:235–237, 1946.
3. Carlson, R. E., "Enrichment of the School Curriculum through Using the Immediate Environment," *Bulletin of the National Education Association of Secondary School Principals,* 31:83–86, 1947.
4. Fields, H., "Making a School Community-Conscious," *Ninth Yearbook of the National Committee for the Social Studies,* 1940, pp. 164–169.
5. Flood, G. F., "Cooperation of Secondary Schools with the Community in Furthering the Education of Students," *Proceedings of the National Catholic Education Association,* 1949, pp. 345–346.
6. Hinchey, C. E., "Community-School Partnership," *Education,* 69:216–219, 1948.
7. James, V. W., "On the Use of Community Resources," *Childhood Education,* 24:408–412, 1949.
8. Lucio, W. H., "Relating Curriculum Development to the Community," *Twentieth Yearbook of the Association of California Elementary School Principals,* 1948, pp. 57–69.
9. Mackenzie, G. N., "Community Co-operation in Curriculum Planning," *Teachers College Record,* 51:347–352, 1950.
10. Seay, M. F., "Community Resources Are Teaching Materials," *School Executive,* 67:33–35, 1948.
11. Stein, A. B., "Adolescent Participation in Community Co-ordinating Councils," *Journal of Educational Sociology,* 21:177–183, 1947.

PART FIVE

Intellectual
Development

CHAPTER FIFTEEN

Mental
Growth

Since the very earliest studies of adolescence, stress has been placed upon the characteristic intellectual development of the period. There is such an increase of mental power that subject matter too difficult for freshmen in high school or in college is easily learned by the same pupils when they become seniors. A high school teacher notes also marked increases in judgment, reasoning, comprehension, and memory. Some of the observed development in mental power comes from neural growth, but part of it is doubtless due to the piling up of experience and knowledge. By the end of the eighth grade a child has accumulated a considerable store of basic information and has reduced many simple skills to such an automatic level that he can use them in his thinking. He has, for instance, acquired meanings for about ten thousand words, and therefore has a vocabulary with which to think. Several mathematical skills are now habitual, many elementary scientific facts have been thoroughly absorbed, and there has been considerable experience with cause and effect relationships. The childhood years may thus represent a gradual development of sufficient experience to serve as a basis for more complicated thinking. In many curves of learning one finds long plateaus covering the periods during which basic skills are being acquired. At the end of such plateaus there is usually a sudden and marked rise in learning rate, presumably because of the co-ordination of simple skills without any known neurological development in the learner. This integration of experience, with childhood serving as a plateau, is perhaps one cause of the relatively rapid intellectual development during adolescence.

Tests of intelligence have been widely used for the last thirty years; literally millions of individuals have been tested at all levels from infancy to senescence. Several thousand children have been repeatedly retested. There have been investigations of the mental growth of brilliant, average, and dull children. The main evidence in regard to adolescent mental development has come through the use of objective tests. The first section of the present chapter will therefore deal with the adequacy of existing mental tests to measure the intellectual growth of the period. A second section will present data concerning normal mental growth and a third will deal with the distribution of mental ability in the high school population. The purpose of this presentation is to show the teacher what "pupil material" she may expect in her classes.

Adolescent growth is shown not only in general intellectual level but also in specific abilities. The ordinary intelligence test measures verbal capacity primarily; other tests have been used to investigate special abilities such as memory, imagination, or reasoning. Results of these researches will be presented in the fourth section of this chapter.

There will be no discussion of theories of intelligence. They are purposely avoided, partly because the whole matter is controversial and partly because such theories are of relatively little immediate value to the classroom teacher. The reader who is interested in general principles will find a theory implicit in the presentation; for others it may well be omitted.

I. Measurement of Adolescent Intelligence

Mental tests may be either verbal or nonverbal, and they may be given to one pupil at a time or to several pupils at once. For reliable individual scores it is necessary to test pupils one by one, but measurement of whole classes is possible by means of group tests. Most tests for use with adolescents are verbal—that is, they require the understanding of language, oral or written.

1. Types of Test: The most widely used individual test is the Binet examination, of which the most recent form is the Terman-Merrill revision.[1] The tests cover a range of mental ages from age two to a superior adult level. This revision gives the most reliable measures of intellectual ability. A few samples from various levels of the examination appear below:

1. How are wood and coal alike? an apple and a peach? a ship and an automobile? iron and silver?

2. What is wrong with this story? "They found a young man locked in his room with his hands and feet bound together. They think he locked himself in."

3. Rearrange the words below so that they make a sentence.

FOR THE STARTED AN WE COUNTRY EARLY AT HOUR

4. After a brief exposure, the pupil is to draw this diagram from memory:

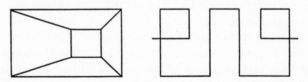

5. What is the difference between laziness and idleness? between poverty and misery? between character and reputation?[2]

The best of the nonverbal tests is the Arthur Performance Scale,[3] which

---

[1] L. M. Terman and M. A. Merrill, *Measuring Intelligence,* Houghton Mifflin Company, 1937, 481 pp.

[2] Quoted by permission of Houghton Mifflin Company, Form L, described on pp. 75–132.

[3] M. G. Arthur, *Point Scale of Performance Tests,* The Commonwealth Fund, rev. ed., 1943, 64 pp.

includes various puzzles and other problems that require few words from the examiner and none from the pupil. The scale yields mental ages from three to eighteen, but it has not been found generally reliable above twelve, although the tests are sometimes useful with adolescents who have language handicaps and therefore cannot show their capacity adequately by means of verbal tests. This test correlates 0.75 with the Binet.[4]

Group verbal tests are fairly numerous. In general nature they resemble the Binet examination, but the questions are given in written instead of oral form, and the pupil records his answers by selecting from an assortment the one that seems best. Among the best-known group tests are the Terman, the Otis, and the Pressey tests. A few sample items appear below:

DIRECTIONS: In each of the following series, four things are in some way alike, and one is different. You are to underline the one that is different from the other four.
1. snake bird elephant chair whale
2. taffeta vellum calico muslin serge
3. preface illustration title volume cabinet
4. vertical transverse sequential horizontal perpendicular
5. every about over until between

DIRECTIONS: Between the first two things in each of the following series there is a definite relationship. You are to select from the five words in the parentheses the one that has the same relationship to the third item of the series that the second item has to the first.
1. dog—puppy: cat— (chicken squirrel spawn kitten child)
2. black—white: evil— (green wicked generous good grey)
3. above—over: below— (above under between downwards into)
4. door—house: gate— (bungalow battleship desk office garden)
5. ancient—antiquity: new— (old modernity present yesterday modern)

DIRECTIONS: Answer each question by drawing a line under what you regard as the best answer.
1. What is the best thing to do if you want to go to college but have no money? stay at home forget about college and go to work go to work but attend evening school save some money and then go to college register at college and hope to get work
2. What would be the best thing to do if you were in a strange city and had only 10¢ in your pocket? telegraph home for money get a job write to a trusted friend for a loan buy a newspaper and read the ads apply to the nearest relief station
3. If you and your husband are both employed full-time, what is the best thing to do about your meals? eat all meals at a restaurant get all meals at home hire a full-time maid get breakfast at home, lunch at a restaurant, and hire someone to prepare dinner have your meals sent in from the nearest restaurant[5]

Table 36 shows the age norms from these three intelligence tests. The

[4] M. E. Hamilton, "Comparison of the Revised Arthur Performance Test, Form II, and the 1937 Binet," *Journal of Consulting Psychologists,* 13:44–49, 1949.
[5] These excerpts are from the Terman, Otis, and Pressey tests, respectively, and are used by permission of the World Book Company, Yonkers, N.Y.; and the Public School Publishing Company, Bloomington, Ill.

score is simply the average number of correct answers marked by the pupils of each age. The number of correct answers obviously increases more or less regularly from year to year throughout adolescence. If a child made a score of 30 on the Otis test, his mental age would be 13 years 6 months; on the Terman, 11 years, 2 months; and on the Pressey Classification, 13 years 1 month. There are, however, at least three important considerations in the interpretation of such results. These will be discussed in the next section.

Table 36

NORMS FOR THREE TESTS OF INTELLIGENCE

Ages	Otis Higher Examination	Terman Group Test	Pressey Senior Classification
10½	—	15	—
11½	—	40	15
12½	26	60	25
13½	30	80	33
14½	34	100	42
15½	38	125	50
16½	40	145	57
17½	42	167	64
18½	—	187	—
19½	—	210	—

2. Difficulties of Test Construction: The first point concerns the nature of the tests used and the difficulties of selecting appropriate material for them. Intelligence tests were originally supposed to measure innate ability. Everyone knows now, however, that they actually measure innate capacities plus experience and schooling to date. Theoretically, such a test should contain questions dealing only with things children have had a chance to learn but have not been taught. Naturally, a test involving schoolwork reflects the quality of the teaching quite as much as the ability of the children. Material specifically learned in school should therefore be eliminated from intelligence tests. Actually it cannot be, if group tests are used, because the pupils must read the items, and reading skill is a product of teaching. A question such as "At what point does the Missouri River flow into the Mississippi?" would not be at all appropriate for an intelligence test partly because it is likely to measure the results of teaching rather than the ability of the learner and partly because only those who live near the confluence of the two rivers can observe the phenomenon for themselves. Such a question as "What phrase is used in advertisements for ———— ————?"[6] is a better question, because all pupils have presumably had an opportunity to see or hear the slogan, and it is improbable that any teacher has taught them the answer. One trouble with tests of intelligence, so far as the measurement of adolescent abilities is concerned, is the lack of material that is independent of schoolteaching and still not too easy for high school pupils.

---

[6] Using any widely advertised product.

This problem becomes more difficult as soon as pupils have begun to diversify their work. Making a test for adolescents is far harder than making one for children. In the early years of childhood, for instance, one can assume that children have been taught to count from 1 to 20. On the basis of this common knowledge one can use as a test of intelligence the ability to continue with such series as:

9	8	7	6	5	—
11	13	15	17	19	—
5	6	8	11	15	—

These items call for a rearrangement of already known facts, and although the test is based somewhat on school achievement, it requires a mental manipulation of the material. By the time pupils reach high school, however, their course of study has become so varied there is no such common content as exists in the early years of elementary school. One cannot use a question requiring manipulation of positive and negative numbers because some pupils have not had algebra. One cannot present a question asking for judgment of some character in a story because there is no story that everyone has read. One cannot use anything but the simplest and most basic facts about history because the nucleus of information available to all pupils is so small. Items derived either from the general environment or from elementary school training are usually too easy to measure the upper limits of adolescent intelligence, and those based upon recent training and experience give an advantage to pupils who have had good preparation. A test of readiness to enter high school or college is easier to construct than a test of intelligence for pupils of the relevant ages, since a reasonable mastery of material taught in school is part of the "readiness" and may therefore quite legitimately be measured. Normally, tests of intelligence for older pupils include measurement of reading vocabulary, solution of problems, definitions of abstract terms, analogies, or rearrangements of concepts. Although these materials measure intelligence, they measure schooling too. The tests are therefore more nearly "classification" than "intelligence" tests.

Scores on tests of intelligence are unfortunately affected by the nature of the environment in which the individuals tested have lived and the nature of their experiences up to the time of the testing. It is only theoretically that tests of intelligence are independent of such environmental factors. Thus, a worker with Polynesian children reports complete uselessness of a test in the Binet scale that requires children to choose the prettier of two faces, one of which is very ugly. The Polynesian children refused point-blank to make any selection until they knew the social caste of each of the two individuals, and they then unerringly chose the one belonging to the higher caste. It made no difference whether the higher caste were assigned to the prettier or the uglier of the two faces. Workers with Indians are unanimous in testifying that intelligence tests with time limits cannot properly be used. Native Indian life puts no premium whatever upon time; in fact, one rarely succeeds in hurrying an Indian for any reason and certainly not for purposes of making a good score on a test. However, if they are allowed to complete a test at their own rate, Indian adolescents make scores closely approximating those of white children of the same age. Indian children score as inferior to whites on a test that requires them to "draw a man," but as superior to them if the test directions are changed to "draw a horse."[7] Children from rural backgrounds always score poorly on tests of intelligence. They, too, are in no particular hurry. Moreover, many items of the average intelligence test are based on experiences one has in a city but does not have in the country. Thus the answer to the question on the Binet scale, "What would you do if you were going some place and missed your train?" depends upon whether the trains run once an hour or twice a week. Norms for widely used intelligence tests are based almost exclusively upon results from urban children. The usual test automatically handicaps pupils coming from any other type of background, both in the nature of its content and in the basis for its norms. One of the clearest bits of evidence on this point is presented in a study of Negro children in a large city. When the scores at each age level were grouped in accordance with the length of time the children had been in the city, the average score correlated perfectly at every age with length of residence.[8] The latest arrivals scored lowest and those with the longest urban experience scored highest.

Tests of intelligence for use with adolescents are not measures of innate ability, but of ability plus training and experience to date. They are excellent in their ability to measure academic potentialities and are therefore extremely useful in classifying pupils for school purposes. The character of the ordinary intelligence test should never be forgotten in estimating the value of the results.

3. **Influence of Elimination on Norms:** Norms are usually based upon surveys of entire school populations. The results are then grouped by age, and a median or average is found for all pupils of a given age, regardless of their grade placement. However, with each passing year there is more and more elimination of children from school. Thus of all the seventeen-year-old girls, for instance, about 60 per cent are in high school, 3 per cent are still in junior high school, 8 per cent are married, 4 per cent are in college, 3 per cent are defective or in institutions of some kind, and the remaining 22 per cent are working or are living at home. If a test is used only in high school, not more than 60 per cent of the entire distribution is tested. Careful investigators determine the total number of children of a given age in a community; then they count as above the median those who are in college and as below the median all those who are defective, in grades below high school, or at work. Such a calculation, of course, assumes that all pupils eliminated from school are below average in mental capacity; some of them are not. A median found by using such scores as can be obtained and by assigning the missing scores to their probable half of the distribution is, however, more valid than a median that rests on only the 60 per cent, more or less, who happened to get tested. The investigator next plots a curve from the norms thus obtained for fourteen-, fifteen-, sixteen-,

---

[7] P. H. Du Bois, "A Test Standardized on Pueblo Indian Children," *Psychological Bulletin,* 36:523, 1939.

[8] O. Klineberg, *Negro Intelligence and Selective Migration,* Columbia University Press, 1935, 66 pp.

and seventeen-year-old children, and then projects the two ends of the curve to indicate the probable scores of twelve-, thirteen-, eighteen-, and nineteen-year-old pupils. In other words, there is no such thing as a really accurate age norm based on an entire distribution of any age above twelve. Recent investigators have been aware of this difficulty and have made attempts to correct the norms. In one case corrected norms are presented up to the age of forty.[9]

If, as is sometimes the case, the investigator does not take into consideration the missing pupils, the test norms reflect both increased intellectual ability *and* increased elimination. The effect may be considerable if promotion policies are strict and many children become so retarded that they drop out of school as soon as they legally can. If practically every child is promoted every year and if most children remain in school, the elimination becomes so small as to be negligible. Assuming, however, that some pupils will leave school each year and that these tend to come from the lower half of the distribution, the average score made by those remaining will rise whether there is an increase in intellectual capacity or not.

4. Methods of Expressing Scores: Finally, there is the manner in which the results of intelligence tests may be expressed. Individual tests commonly give a "mental age" and an "intelligence quotient," which are usually abbreviated to MA and IQ. The MA depends upon what tests a child passes; if he passes all those below the nine-year level, plus all tests for nine-year-olds but none of those for ten-year-old children, his MA is 10–0—that is, 10 years and 0 months. If he passes everything through the eleventh year and half the tests for the twelfth, his MA is 12–6 (or 12 years and 6 months). The IQ is the ratio between chronological and mental age. If a child's mental ability is exactly what would be expected for his age, his IQ is 100; if he is more advanced mentally than expected, it is over 100; if he is developing more slowly than others of his age, it is less than 100. A child with a CA of five and an MA of ten would have an IQ of 200; that is, he has twice as much ability as shown by other five-year-olds. A child with a CA of ten and an MA of five would have an IQ of 50; that is, his mental growth is only half the expected amount for his age. To get the IQ one simply divides the MA—reduced to months—by the CA—similarly reduced—as shown below.

$$CA = 10 \text{ years } 11 \text{ months } = 131 \text{ months}$$
$$MA = 13 \text{ years } 4 \text{ months } = 160 \text{ months}$$

$$131) \; 160 \; (\; 1.22 \; = IQ$$
$$\underline{131}$$
$$290$$
$$\underline{262}$$
$$280$$

---

[9] D. Wechsler, *The Measurement of Adult Intelligence,* Williams & Wilkins Company, 1939, 229 pp. Norms by Terman and Merrill are also corrected to take account of elimination.

This child has 22 per cent more mental ability than one expects from a child of his age. In actual practice the IQ is multiplied by 100 to get rid of the decimal point. The 1.22 above would therefore be read as 122.

The range of recorded IQ's is from about 15 to 195. The entire range is divided into levels as follows:

140 and above: brilliant
130–139: superior
116–129: bright
85–115: normal
80–84: dull normal
70–79: dull
69 or lower: defective

In theory, a person's IQ remains absolutely constant throughout life, but actually it does not do so. Either there are real changes in growth rate from time to time, perhaps because of variations in physical or emotional condition, or the variations from one test or one tester to another produce rather large differences. In any case, retests after a period of years show IQ's somewhat above or below the original ones, and a sufficient number of retests will produce quite a range of IQ's for the same child. Dull children vary least, brilliant children next, and those of average ability most. Three sample reports[10] show variations between the first and second IQ of −48 to +51 points, with an average of 9 points; of −43 to +47, with an average of 2.77; and of −16 to +20 with an average of 0. Another report presents quite detailed results upon the retest of 138 children after a lapse of ten years. These children were first tested at some age between two and five. Of the 138 children, 42 showed an IQ change of less than 5 points, 35 showed a change of less than 10; and 23, of less than 15. The remaining 38 varied in IQ by more than 15 points, plus or minus.[11] For two studies of superior children the average was only 7 points[12] and 3 points.[13] Although the extreme cases vary enormously, the averages are usually small and positive, the gain being due presumably to familiarity with the test. An excellent report covering retests of over seventeen hundred children of superior ability, first tested at the age of six and retested some years later, gives a standard deviation of between 12.3 and 18.5 for the eighteen different

[10] P. Cattell, "Stanford-Binet IQ Variations," *School and Society*, 45:615–618, 1937; H. C. O'Neill, "Variations in the Intelligence Quotient of 105 Children," *Child Development*, 8:357–363, 1937; M. C. Pritchard, K. M. Horan, and L. S. Hollingworth, "The Course of Mental Development in Slow Learners," *Thirty-ninth Yearbook of the National Society for the Study of Education*, 1940, Pt. II, pp. 245–253.

[11] K. P. Brodway, "IQ Constancy on the Revised Stanford-Binet from the Preschool to the Junior High School Level," *Journal of Genetic Psychology*, 65:197–217, 1944.

[12] E. A. Lincoln, "Stanford-Binet IQ Changes in the Harvard Growth Study," *Journal of Applied Psychology*, 20:236–242, 1936, and "The Stanford-Binet IQ Changes of Superior Children," *School and Society*, 41:519–520, 1935.

[13] R. L. Thorndike, "Retest Changes in the IQ of Certain Superior Students," *Thirty-ninth Yearbook of the National Society for the Study of Education*, 1940, Pt. II, pp. 351–361.

groups included in the study.[14] These figures mean that on the retest half the children showed a variation, plus or minus, of 12 to 18 points in IQ, while the other half showed a variation of more than these amounts.

An investigation by means of group tests of intelligence gives the following information about the variability of IQ's in high school.[15] The average IQ of 114 pupils rose from 104 in the freshman year to 106 in the senior year. For 7 per cent the IQ remained unchanged; for 22 per cent it increased 5 points or less; for 33 per cent it increased more than 5 points; for 22 per cent it decreased 5 points or less; and for 16 per cent it decreased more than 5 points.

It is interesting and enlightening to trace the variation in individual cases.[16] Figure 106 on page 486 gives results of repeated testings on eight children from two to eighteen years of age. Curves A, B, C, and D show relatively little variation. Any single testing would have diagnosed these four children respectively as brilliant, bright, average, and defective. Although Child C varied from a low of 87 to a high of 110—a total of 23 points—he was at no time outside the "normal" range of IQ's. The four curves in the second part of the figure, for children E, F, G, and H, present a different picture, however. Children E and F both started as low-normal and ended as bright (E) or normal (F), while Child G's IQ declined from 133 to 77, and Child F decreased from 120 to 64—in one case from superior to dull normal (G) and in the other from bright to defective (H). All four cases show steady trends. In the last two, one has to assume that the children really were deteriorating, since repeated tests demonstrated the same trend.

A single measure of intelligence is only an approximation, at best. It may be a child's best performance, his worst, or anything in between. It is not until one has enough repeated measurements to establish a *pattern of growth* that one is safe in making predictions. The inadequacy of any single point for this purpose is well demonstrated in Figure 107 on page 487. The individual results in the two halves of the figure come from repeated testing of the same children from eight years of age until they were sixteen. In the first half (A) appear the subsequent curves for the mental growth of 8 girls, all of whom made the same score when first tested. Eight years later 4 were slightly superior as compared to all the 256 girls included in the study, and 4 were somewhat inferior. In the second half of the figure (B) are the curves of 5 girls who at age sixteen made identical scores. Examination of their entire records showed this final score to be Girl E's best effort; it is quite typical of Girl B. It reflects the most recent trend for Girls A, C, and D, but it certainly gives no hint of their varied past performances.

Further light is thrown upon the causes of variability in the IQ by

---

[14] F. L. Goodenough, "Studies of the 1937 Revision of the Stanford-Binet Scale: I. Variability of the IQ at Successive Age Levels," *Journal of Educational Psychology*, 33:241–251, 1942.

[15] S. J. Knesevich, "The Constancy of the IQ of the Secondary School Pupil," *Journal of Educational Research*, 39:505–516, 1946.

[16] M. P. Honzik, J. W. MacFarlane, and L. Allen, "The Stability of Mental Test Performance between Two and Eighteen Years," *Journal of Experimental Education*, 17:309–324, 1948.

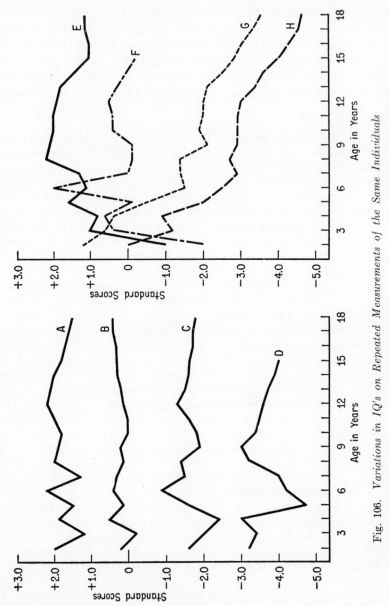

Fig. 106. *Variations in IQ's on Repeated Measurements of the Same Individuals*

From M. P. Honzik, L. W. MacFarlane, and L. Allen, "The Stability of Mental Test Performance between Two and Eighteen Years," *Journal of Experimental Education*, 17:317–318, 1948. Used by permission of the Journal.

following the case history of a single child and relating the IQ variations to nonintellectual factors in his life.[17] The boy whose record appears in Figure 108 on page 488 varied from 106 at a year and a half, to 123 at six years, to 163 at ten, to 122 at eighteen. This lad seems to have had a manic-

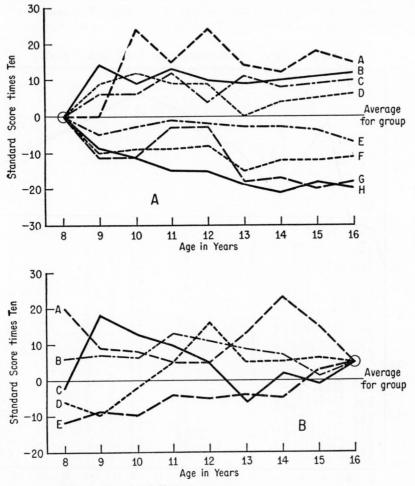

Fig. 107. *IQ's on Repeated Tests*

From C. M. Fleming, *Adolescence,* International Universities Press, 1949, pp. 105, 107. Based upon data from W. F. Dearborn, J. W. N. Rothney, and F. K. Shuttleworth, "Data on the Growth of Public School Children," *Monograph of the Society for Research in Child Development,* Vol. 3, No. 1, 1938, 136 pp.

depressive type of personality and was sometimes abnormally listless and shy, sometimes highly overactive. The examiners who gave him the tests at two, three, and four years reported that the scores were too low because the boy had no interest in the test and was unwilling to exert himself. He

---
[17] *Ibid.*

was also in poor physical condition. At age six, he had been in bed twelve weeks with episodic asthma (of possibly psychosomatic origin), his father was in a sanatorium with tuberculosis, and his mother had a full-time job. His highest IQ coincided with the return of his father to normal life, the recovery of his mother from an operation, and his own first reasonably healthy years and first favorable reports from school. The examiners who gave the tests at ages twelve and fourteen reported that the boy could not

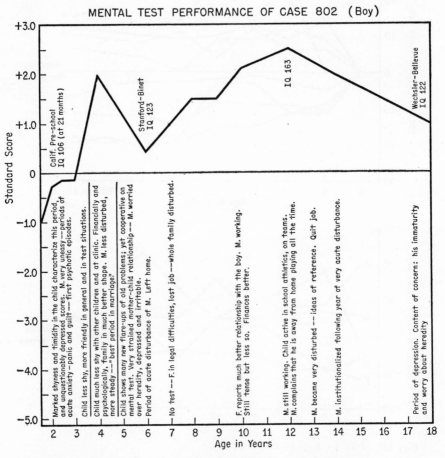

Fig. 108. *Variations in IQ as Related to Background Factors*

Honzik, MacFarlane, and Allen, "The Stability of Mental Test Performance," *loc. cit.*, p. 320. Used by permission of the *Journal of Experimental Education.*

be stimulated into really trying. The last score, at age eighteen, was preceded by a period of great excitement, overactivity, emotional preoccupation, and compulsive stealing. The personal disorganization shows in the lower IQ level. This boy's personality is of a type that interferes considerably with his mental functioning. Moreover, his home situation and pressures often combined to operate upon the already unstable child and depress his scores. Apparently, the date of the yearly test coincided just once with an optimum personal and social situation.

5. Environmental Influences: It is still a moot problem whether or not intelligence may be permanently increased or decreased by the effects of environment. Since environments cannot usually be changed at will, investigations have been largely of two types: those into the comparative development of identical twins who were reared in different surroundings, and those into the development of adopted or foster children who entered a home quite different from that of their true parents. In the former case, two people of similar heredity were exposed to different environmental pressures, while in the second the same children were exposed to two different kinds of environment.

There are two kinds of twins, identical and fraternal. The former come from the same fertilized egg and have therefore the same heredity, while the latter come from two eggs and differ in heredity as much as any other brothers or sisters. The twenty pairs of identical twins that have been studied most extensively had been separated from each other for periods varying from eleven to fifty-three years.[18] Twelve pairs were separated during the first year of life, five during the second year, one during the third, one during the fourth, and one during the seventh. For six pairs, separation was complete. In most of the other cases each twin knew the other existed but saw him or her only at rare intervals. These separated twins were compared with other identical twins who had been reared together. In standing height, the separated twins were as similar as the unseparated, the correlation in each case being 0.96. On the other hand, the correlation between the unseparated twins on Stanford-Binet IQ was 0.91, whereas that between the separated twins was 0.67—striking evidence that environment affects the growth of intelligence, either by supplying adequate stimulation or by withholding it. To be sure, the separated twins were still similar; but they were not as similar as they would have been had they been permitted to remain in close association throughout their lives. This study has been confirmed by others. One reviewer of the entire field makes the statement that ten years of research in twin resemblances in relation to environmental influences have shown clearly that there are moderate degrees of difference in the IQ of identical twins who have grown up in social and educational surroundings of a profoundly different nature.[19]

The influence of foster homes upon the IQ of adopted children has been investigated by a number of people, usually by correlating the intelligence of the children with that of both their true and their foster parents. For instance, the intelligence of 194 children, all adopted before they were six months old, showed a correlation with the intelligence of their true parents of 0.50, but with that of foster parents of about 0.25; since there was no blood relation, the latter coefficient should have been zero.[20] This suggestion of a

---

[18] H. H. Newman, F. N. Freeman, and K. J. Helzinger, *Twins: A Study of Heredity and Environment,* The University of Chicago Press, 1937, 369 pp.

[19] H. D. Carter, "Ten Years of Research on Twins," *Thirty-ninth Yearbook of the National Society for the Study of Education,* 1940, Pt. I, pp. 236–255.

[20] H. M. Skeels, "Some Iowa Studies of the Mental Growth of Children in Relation to Differentials of Environment: A Summary," *Thirty-ninth Yearbook of the National Society for the Study of Education,* 1940, Pt. II, pp. 281–308.

modest influence of foster parents upon a child's IQ was strengthened by another investigation[21] of 147 children who were placed for adoption in superior homes before they were six months of age. Practically no correlation was found between the intelligence of the children and that of their true mothers, but there was an appreciable relationship with that of their foster parents, indicating that environment had had more influence on their development than heredity. The average IQ of the true mothers was only 88, but the average for the children was 115. The difference, 27 points, is more than one would expect. These children continued to maintain their mental level during the eight years from 1940 to 1948. For 100 children from inferior backgrounds who were adopted into superior homes, the intellectual level is reported as being not only maintained but superior to that of "own" children of the same socioeconomic level.[22] Still another report of similar groups divided the children into (A) those whose mothers had IQ's of 70 or less (87 cases), (B) those whose fathers were casual laborers or unemployed (111 cases), and (C) those who came in both the above classes (31 cases).[23] The IQ's of the children, adopted at the age of about six months and tested at five years of age, were found to be as presented in Table 37.

Table 37

CHANGES IN IQ

Group	IQ Average	Above 120	Below 80
A	105.5	15	4
B	110.3	28	2
C	104.1	—	—

From H. M. Skeels and I. Harms, "Children with Inferior Social History: Their Mental Development in Adoptive Homes," *Journal of Genetic Psychology*, 72:283–294, 1948.

The general reaction to these studies, as to some that will be reported in a later chapter, has been one of resistance and unwillingness to believe. The thousands of studies already made concerning the inheritance and measurement of mental ability have convinced the general public that no one can add a cubit to his mental stature. It is possible that this basic assumption is not true; and if enough reputable investigators continue to present enough proof to the contrary, it will have to be modified. Assuming that a child develops in proportion to the amount of stimulation he gets, an adopted youngster who comes from an inferior economic level and is taken into a

[21] A. M. Leahy, "Nature-Nurture and Intelligence," *Genetic Psychology Monographs*, 17:236–308, 1935.

[22] M. Skodak and H. M. Skeels, "Final Follow-Up of 100 Adopted Children," *Journal of Genetic Psychology*, 75:85–125, 1949. See also M. L. Reymert and R. T. Hinton, "The Effect of Change to a Relatively Superior Environment upon the IQ of 100 Children," *Thirty-ninth Yearbook of the National Society for the Study of Education*, 1940, Pt. II, pp. 255–267.

[23] H. M. Skeels and I. Harms, "Children with Inferior Social History: Their Mental Development in Adoptive Homes," *Journal of Genetic Psychology*, 72:283–294, 1948.

superior home should develop faster and better than he would have done had he been left in his own family. Up to the point of developing to the maximum whatever ability is inherited, no one quarrels with this conclusion; the resistance begins when one assumes that the new environment has created a capacity that was not there before or has corrected a defective intelligence. At least, more proof is needed before such a point of view can be accepted as finally established.

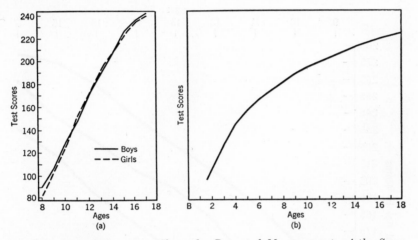

Fig. 109. *Mental Growth as Shown by Repeated Measurements of the Same Children*

From F. N. Freeman, "Intellectual Growth of Children as Indicated by Repeated Tests," *Psychological Monographs*, XLVII, Whole No. 212 (1936), 22, 24. Used by permission of the publisher.

(a) Curves for boys and girls, ages 8 to 17.
(b) A curve for 26 of the total group who were tested throughout their college years as well.

II. Normal Intellectual Growth

1. General Intelligence: As in the case of physical measurements, it is best to measure intelligence by means of longitudinal studies—that is, by repeated tests on the same children. Figure 109 on this page shows the mental growth of two groups of children. One set of records is based upon yearly examinations of the children between the ages of eight and seventeen, the other upon similar retests of another group between the ages of two and eighteen. The first curve is very nearly a straight line, the growth for all yearly intervals being approximately equal. For the second curve, the increase was greater in the earlier years than in the later. Both curves show continuing growth during adolescence.

Children develop intellectually at a rate that is directly proportional to their initial capacity. This growth, which seems hardly fair, is one more instance of "to him that hath shall be given." Figure 110 on page 492 shows the mental progress of three groups of children who had different degrees of intellectual ability to start with. It should be noted that each group retains its relative position from one age to another.

In mental development as in physical, there are wide individual variations. A few individual curves are shown in Figure 111 on page 493. Boys A, B, C, and E all had periods of growing alternately rapidly and slowly. The record of Boy D begins with a slight loss. Boy E started slowly, then

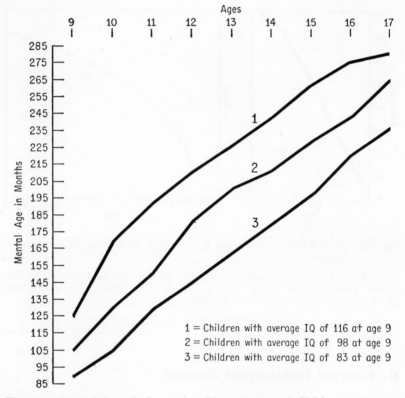

Fig. 110. *Mental Growth Curves for Three Groups of Children*

From Freeman, "Intellectual Growth of Children as Indicated by Repeated Tests," *loc. cit.*, p. 29.

entered a two-year plateau, with a marked rise for two subsequent years. Boys A and B developed more rapidly at first than later, while Boys D and E show concave curves; that of Boy C is convex up to age 13 and then tends to change. No curve crosses any other; that is, the duller children did not at any time overtake the brighter.

The curves for the girls show much the same phenomena, except for some crossing of the lines. Girl B, after an initial small loss, started off fast and grew rapidly up to age 14, when she entered a two-year plateau. At this point Girl A, who grew more evenly, overtook her. Curve C is almost

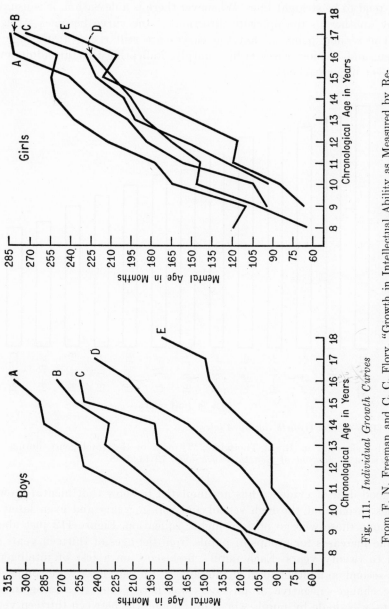

Fig. 111. *Individual Growth Curves*

From F. N. Freeman and C. C. Flory, "Growth in Intellectual Ability as Measured by Repeated Tests," *Monographs of the Society for Research in Child Development*, II, No. 7 (1937), 56–59. Used by permission of publisher.

straight. Girl D grew rapidly and evenly, except for one slight regression. Girl E shows two regressions.

Two points should be noted concerning these curves. The first is that they all tend to be straight lines. Whenever there is a deviation, it is usually offset by another in the opposite direction as the curve becomes straight again. The second point is that the curves are still rising at the age of seventeen, and in most cases rising sharply, indicating that an adult level has not yet been reached.

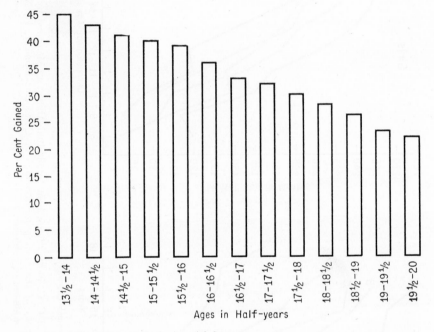

Fig. 112. *Mental Growth during Adolescence*

Based upon data in R. L. Thorndike, "Growth of the Intelligence during Adolescence," *Journal of Genetic Psychology,* 72:13, 1948.

A good deal of evidence has accumulated to show that mental growth continues throughout the high school and college years and even later, at least among those who go on into higher education. Figure 112 just above shows the increases for groups of pupils from the ages of thirteen years six months to twenty years. Each pupil's first score on a test of intelligence and his second on another form of the same test a year later were compared, and the change—negative or positive—was noted. The greatest gain—45 per cent—was made by pupils whose initial age was between thirteen years six months and fourteen years. The added increment became less with each successive age group, but even between the ages of nineteen years six months and twenty years, the students added 24 per cent to their previous scores. Some of the gain was undoubtedly due to mere familiarity with the test, but even after one has discounted this factor there is still a fairly marked gain throughout the adolescent period.

The superiority of college seniors over their own freshmen scores has also been reported. Thus, on one test, twenty-six students tested yearly increased from an average of 105 points as freshmen to 270 as seniors.[24] In another instance, the gain was from 48 to 79 points.[25]

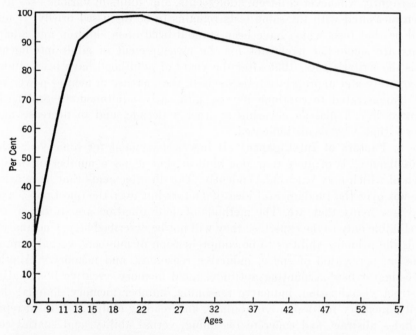

Fig. 113. *Mental Development from Childhood to Late Maturity*

Based upon D. Wechsler, *The Measurement of Adult Intelligence,* Williams & Williams Co., 1944, p. 118.

Mental development from an early age through maturity and into senescence has been traced more or less adequately. A typical curve appears in Figure 113 on this page. The rise is rapid from age 7 to age 13, then gradual until age 18. At that level mental ability remains fairly stable into the early twenties, but thereafter a slow decrease sets in, and continues up until about age 30. From this age on, the decline becomes more and more rapid. If people live long enough, their mental capacity declines until it is appreciably below the adolescent level. This curve does not wholly agree with one's observation that people certainly *seem* to acquire more ability at least through the early years of adult life—up until age 35 or 40. The

[24] F. N. Freeman, "Intellectual Growth of Children," *Psychological Monographs,* XLVII, No. 2, Whole No. 212 (1936), 20–34.
[25] A. M. Shuey, "Improvement in the Scores of the American Council Psychological Examination from Freshman to Senior Year," *Journal of Educational Psychology,* 39:417–426, 1948.

contradiction comes from the fact that between ages 18 and 22, when the mental capacities measure highest, adolescents do not have the experience to use them efficiently and are therefore at a disadvantage when compared with those who have a shade less capacity but are able to use more effectively a larger proportion of it.

One other explanation for the shape of the curve that has been found consistently whenever children, adolescents, and adults of various ages have been measured with the same tests remains to be discussed briefly. It may well be that tests which have been standardized upon children and adolescents are somewhat irrelevant for the measurement of adult intelligence. It is the writer's guess that after the years of adulthood have been studied adequately and appropriate tests devised, the increase in mental power will be demonstrated to continue its rise into early adulthood, to prolong its summit into a plateau covering at least a decade, and to decrease more slowly than now seems indicated.

2. Factors of Intelligence: It has been evident for some years that "intelligence" is of more than one kind or that it has a number of factors, each of which may vary independently. The disagreements that have arisen are not over the fundamental idea of factors but over the question of what and how many they are. The methods of determination are statistical and intelligible only to the expert, so they will not be described here. One analysis finds the primary abilities to be comprehension of numbers, verbal comprehension, perception of space, inductive reasoning, and memory.[26] Another investigator lists accounting aptitude, tonal memory, creative imagination, abstract visualization, inductive reasoning, number memory, manual dexterity, memory for design, vocabulary, and reading ability.[27] A third report includes abstract and concrete reasoning, verbal ability, and spatial concepts.[28] A fourth presents eight factors: verbal reasoning, mathematical ability, abstract reasoning, spatial relationships, reasoning about mechanical problems, clerical skills, and linguistic ability with both words and sentences.[29] Curves based upon the application of tests that measure this last series of factors appear in Figure 114 on page 497. A total of over 47,000 pupils in Grades 8 through 12, ranging from ages 13 through 18, took the tests. Since boys and girls differ a good deal in their specific abilities, the results have to be presented graphically for each sex separately. Curves 3, 6, and 2—respectively for verbal reasoning, number concepts, and abstract thinking—show a slight superiority for boys for seven of the fifteen recorded comparisons, a considerable superiority for two, a slight superiority for

[26] L. L. Thurstone, "Primary Abilities," *Occupations,* 27:527–529, 1949.

[27] J. O'Connor, *The Unique Individual,* Human Engineering Laboratory, Boston, 1948, 249 pp.

[28] J. J. Dempster, "An Investigation into the Use of Estimated Factor Scores in Describing and Comparing Groups of Secondary and Senior School Boys, of Eleven Plus," Unpublished Master's Thesis, University of London, 1944.

[29] J. E. Doppelt, "The Organization of Abilities in the Age Range from Thirteen to Seventeen, "*Teachers College Contributions to Education,* No. 962, 1950, 86 pp.

girls for two, and the same average for four. Curves 4 and 5—for ability to judge spatial relationships and to reason about mechanical problems— show a clear superiority for boys, especially in the latter ability. In contrast, the girls are markedly superior in Curves 1, 7, and 8—respectively clerical ability and ability to handle words and sentences. Probably their

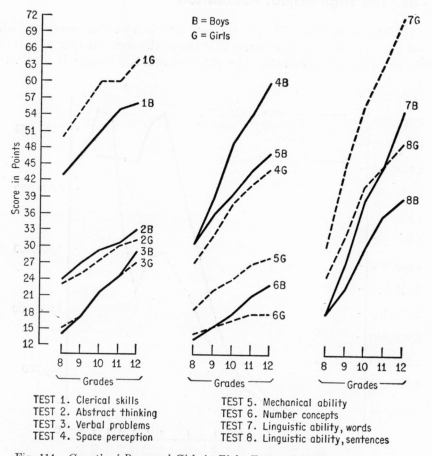

TEST 1. Clerical skills
TEST 2. Abstract thinking
TEST 3. Verbal problems
TEST 4. Space perception

TEST 5. Mechanical ability
TEST 6. Number concepts
TEST 7. Linguistic ability, words
TEST 8. Linguistic ability, sentences

Fig. 114.   *Growth of Boys and Girls in Eight Types of Ability*

Based on The Revised Norms for Form A of the Differential Aptitude Tests, as described in J. E. Doppelt, "The Organization of Abilities in the Age Range from Thirteen to Seventeen," *Teachers College Contributions to Education,* No. 962, 1950, 86 pp.

greater verbal gifts, rather than equal skill in inductive thinking, keep the girls' scores on Curve 3 identical with or close to those of the boys. It should be noted, however, that results for both sexes vary in accordance with the subject matter about which the reasoning is to be done. It might even turn out that some boys who reasoned well about gasoline engines reasoned with only moderate success about hydraulics and very poorly about television.

That is, "reasoning ability," which was formerly thought of as an abstract power which could be applied to anything, may turn out to be so specific and so dependent upon knowledge as to be almost a function of mastery rather than a separate skill that may be applied to the handling of facts.

III. The High School Population

1. Changes in Size: Within the last five decades the American high school has changed to such a degree that those who were familiar with it in 1900 can scarcely recognize it. The most outstanding change is the mere

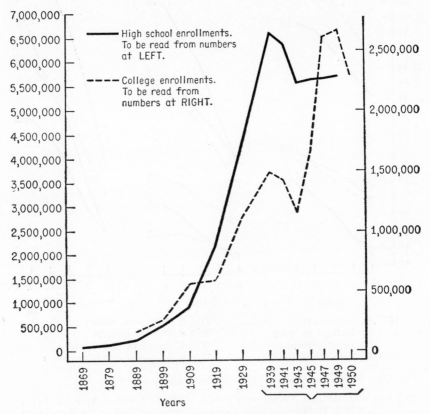

Fig. 115. *Enrollment in High Schools and Colleges*

Based upon the *Biennial Survey of Education in the United States, 1948–1950,* U. S. Office of Education, 1950, pp. 16, 35.

growth in numbers, which in turn has precipitated many alterations in both the curricular offerings and the methods of teaching. The numbers of students in public high schools and in colleges is shown in Figure 115 on this page. Up until 1889 the high schools were few and small. A growth began in the twenty years from 1889 through 1909, but the first spectacular increase occurred just after World War I, and continued until 1939. The enrollment between 1909 and 1939 registered an increase of 621 per cent. After 1940, enlistments in the armed forces began to cut down the numbers, as did employment in war industries. The figures in 1949 were almost a million less than in 1939. This decrease is, however, only temporary. Because of the high birth rate during and just after the war, forecasters estimate that there will be not far from 11,000,000 high school students when the bumper crop of war babies reaches Grade 9.

The enrollment in colleges and universities has also shown marked changes. The increase was gradual up until 1919. During the next twenty years, the number of students more than doubled. During World War II enrollment fell off, and would have decreased even further had not the Army sent many thousand men to college for various kinds of training. In 1947, however, came the deluge of returning soldiers, and the figures soared. The enrollment for 1947 was more than double that for 1943. By 1950, the veterans were through college, and the numbers began to shrink. When the war babies reach college level, the enrollments will again rise.

The developments just described reflect two tendencies that have offset each other to some extent—the diminishing size of the American family and the increasing demand for education. The interaction of decrease in num-

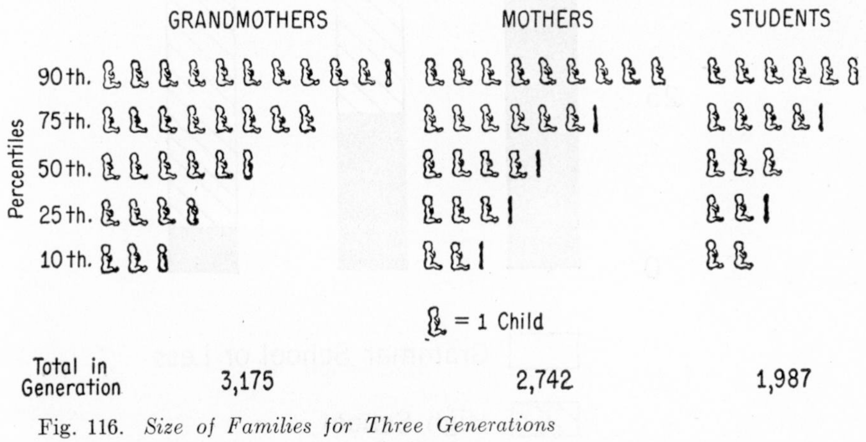

Fig. 116. *Size of Families for Three Generations*

Based on R. O. Truex, "The Size of the Families in Three Generations," *American Sociological Review,* 1:581–591, 1936.

bers and increase in level of education is well shown in miniature in one extremely interesting study[30] in which an investigator, by studying the size of families in 1935 and the family trees of 691 college students, traced the decline in birth rate through three generations in the same families. These results appear in Figure 116 just above. The median number of children per family (fiftieth percentile) in the students' generation was 2.9; for their

[30] R. O. Truex, "The Size of the Families in Three Generations," *American Sociological Review,* 1:581–591, 1936.

mothers' generation it was 4.2; and for their grandmothers', 5.8. The tenth percentile for the grandmothers' generation has become the median of the students', and the grandmothers' median is the students' ninetieth percentile. The

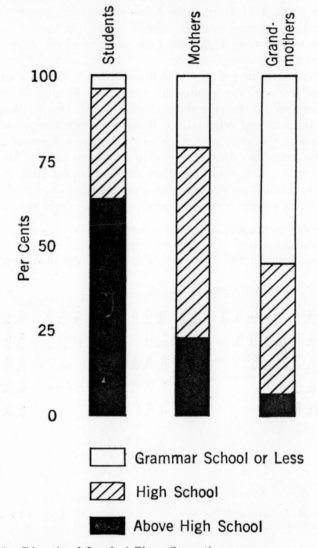

Fig. 117. *Educational Level of Three Generations*

Based on Truex, "The Size of the Families in Three Generations," *loc. cit.*

total number of persons per generation has shrunk from 3,175 to 2,742 to 1,987. The school enrollment above the elementary grades for these families, however, shows an opposite trend. It increased at first, in spite of the falling birth rate, as shown in Figure 117 on this page. In the grandmothers' generation, 54 per cent went only through elementary school, 39 per cent went to high school, and 7 per cent to college; in the mothers' generation 20 per cent went only through elementary school, 57 per cent went to high school, and 23 per cent to college; in the daughters' generation 5 per cent were still in elementary school, 33 per cent were attending high school, and 62 per cent were in college. Presumably, the 38 per cent consists of younger brothers and sisters. When all members of this generation finish school, the "gram-

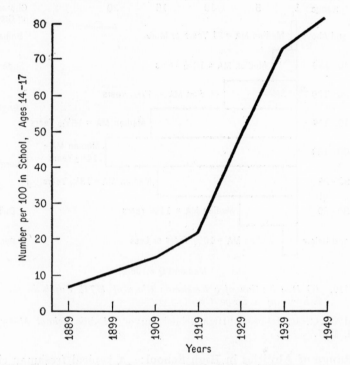

Fig. 118. *Proportion of Adolescents in High School, 1889–1949*

Based upon figures in the *Biennial Survey of Education in the United States, 1947–1948,* U. S. Office of Education, 1950, p. 25, and the *Statistical Abstracts of the United States, 1951,* Bureau of the Census, 1951, p. 107.

mar school or less" group will probably have vanished. In spite of the shrinkage in numbers from one generation to the next, the college enrollment from these families continued to grow, because 64 per cent of the 1,987 is larger than either 23 per cent or 2,742 or 7 per cent of 3,175.

The holding power of the schools has greatly increased since 1900 and accounts for the high enrollments after the compulsory school age has been reached. One method of demonstrating the extent to which schools are holding their pupils is to compare the number of adolescents in the total population with the number in high school. The more pupils there are between fourteen and eighteen in high school, the greater is the holding power. This relationship is shown in Figure 118 on this page. In 1889, only 7 adolescents out of each 100 were in school. Ten and twenty years later, the figures were 12 and 15, respectively. By 1939, the number had risen to 73. In 1949, it was 82. In short, the high schools are approaching a perfect record. The increase in holding power has been spectacular and is probably due to the great changes in the curriculum.

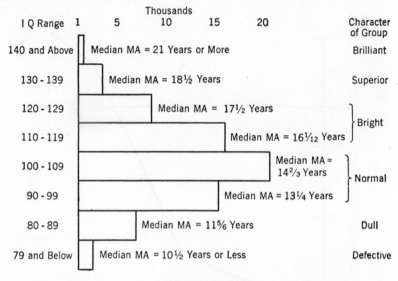

Median I Q = 106.2

Fig. 119. *IQ Distribution of a Freshman Class of 66,715 Pupils in the High Schools of a Large City*

Based on G. R. Johnson, "High School Survey," *Public School Messenger*, 35:14, 1937.

2. Range of Abilities in High School: A typical freshman class in a large city high school shows a range of intelligence quotients and mental ages about like that given in Figure 119 on this page. Here the mental age varies from that of the average fourth-grade child to that of the upper-classman in college. The IQ's show a range from brilliancy to defective intelligence. Thus the high school teacher does not have a selected group of pupils to teach but rather a cross section of almost as great variability as is found in the lower grades.

The question of what effect the increases in enrollments have had upon the average and the distribution of intellectual abilities was assumed until recently to have been settled, but upon logical rather than empirical grounds. The argument ran as follows: The pupils in private academies and such high schools as existed in 1890 were highly selected and highly intelligent; they were the children of people above the average in wealth, and since intelligence is related positively to income, they were presumed to be above average in intelligence; inasmuch as the secondary schools already enrolled pupils from the upper intellectual strata of society, any addition must have come from the lower levels, with a presumed lower general ability; the average for the enlarged secondary school group would, therefore, be reduced. This argument seems to have been fallacious, so far as one can judge from available proof. *observable*

What empirical evidence exists as to changes, if any, in the level of intelligence comes from the results of intelligence tests, which were not in use until about 1915. One is therefore limited to consideration of the past thirty to thirty-five years. The best single investigation presents evidence of two kinds. The first is shown in Figure 120, just below. Each dot rep-

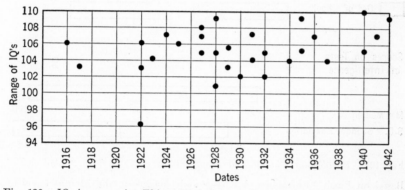

Fig. 120. *IQ Averages for Thirty High Schools Tested between 1916 and 1942*

From F. H. Finch, "Enrollment Increases and Changes in the Mental Level of the High School," *Applied Psychology Monographs,* No. 10, 1946, p. 10. Used by permission of the publisher.

resents the average IQ of an entire high school population measured by a recognized test of intelligence at some date between 1916 and 1942. There are thirty dots. The median of the first fifteen gives an IQ of 105; the median of the last fifteen is also 105. The "change" is therefore nonexistent. The second line of evidence consists of the comparison of results obtained in a city high school by the repetition in 1942 of a test given in 1923. The main facts are presented in Figure 121 on page 504. The increase in the general population of the school district for those between the ages of fourteen and eighteen was from 1,818 in 1920 to 3,022 in 1940, or 66 per cent. The high school enrollment, however, rose from 621 to 1,321, or 112 per cent, between the same two dates. The enrollments grew, therefore, nearly twice as fast as the population of the appropriate ages was increasing. If attendance were based on intelligence, then the earlier group would be the more highly selected. Test results, however, show a very slight increase in median from 65 to 69 points, and a slightly smaller range for the middle two thirds of the distribution, 51 to 87 (36 points) instead of 46 to 84 (38 points). The 1,321 pupils in 1940 were nearly two months younger than the 621 in 1920. Since intelligence scores rise with increasing age, the difference in favor of the 1940 group is actually a little more than it appears to be in Figure 121. In any case, there is not the slightest evidence that the inclusion of a higher percentage of the available population has resulted in an appreciable decrease in average intellectual capacity.

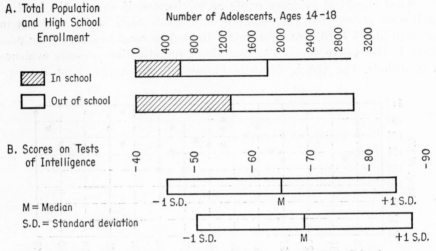

A. Total Population and High School Enrollment

Number of Adolescents, Ages 14–18

In school
Out of school

B. Scores on Tests of Intelligence

M = Median
S.D. = Standard deviation

−1 S.D.   M   +1 S.D.

−1 S.D.   M   +1 S.D.

Fig. 121. *Enrollment Change and Mental Level in One High School*

Based on Finch, "Enrollment Increases and Changes in the Mental Level of the High School Population," *loc. cit.,* pp. 42, 45.

Such evidence of developments since 1915 makes one suspicious of the assumptions concerning the high degree of selection in 1890, or at still earlier dates. Quite possibly the small enrollment at that time represented certain social classes containing children of all degrees of mental capacity rather than certain intellectual levels drawn from several social and occupational groups. Since the development of tests it has been demonstrated conclusively that while intelligence does show a rough correlation with family income, the total distribution of abilities from all income groups is almost the same, and that the overlapping from one such group to another is so great as to make the slight difference at the average of little significance. It was also shown many years ago that nearly half the children in a very large number of those with IQ's above 120 came from families in the lower occupational groups.[31] It is true that those pupils who remain in school make a higher average score than those who drop out, but the difference is small and the total distribution for both groups is practically identical. One investigation, typical of many others, gives an average IQ of 105 for those who left high school, as compared with 107 for those who remained.[32] Such a minor variation is not enough to account for elimination from school. It is therefore probable that in the decades from 1890 to 1920, the differences in intellectual level between in-school and out-of-school adolescents were

[31] S. M. Stoke and H. C. Lehman, "Intelligence Test Scores of Social and Occupational Groups," *School and Society,* 31:372–377, 1930. The data were collected in 1923.

[32] C. B. Smith, "A Study of Pupils Dropping Out of a Midwestern High School," *School Review,* 52:151–156, 1944.

greatly exaggerated. During these decades boys and girls could get good jobs if they left a school in which the curriculum was too narrow to be interesting for most adolescents. The proportion in each generation that can and will complete four years of Latin and three each of Greek and mathematics is very small and by no means coincides with the highest 10 per cent in the distribution of intelligence. Such a curriculum selects those of genuine scholarly tastes to whom such a curriculum is exciting, plus those to whom the prestige of a diploma is worth the hours of boredom necessary to obtain it. The group in 1890 was certainly "selected," but quite possibly upon social and economic rather than intellectual grounds. Indeed, in view of the curriculum, perhaps the brightest of the nonacademically minded pupils were the ones who left! One cannot produce objective evidence on this matter of selection before 1915 at the earliest, and arguments without data are notoriously fallacious. All one can say is that decreases in intelligence do not seem to have occurred since 1920, although the population of the high school has more than doubled since that time.

3. Withdrawal from School: There have been many competent investigations of why pupils leave high school without graduating, or at least of why pupils *say* they leave. In most schools a pupil who wants to withdraw after passing the legal age makes out a slip, upon which, among other things, he states his reasons. Analysis of withdrawal slips admittedly sheds only a dim light upon causes, but even a glimmer is better than nothing. The pupils give as their main reasons the need to earn money, a lack of interest, and poor health; girls may add two further reasons—getting married or being needed at home. A few students admit that the work is too hard for them or that they are in personal difficulties with school authorities. One is not at all sure, however, to what extent the reasons given are mere rationalizations of an underlying maladjustment which is not mentioned, assuming the student is aware of its existence.

When one compares the records of students who have dropped out of school with those of students who remained to graduate, three facts are at once apparent. First, the average intelligence is slightly lower, but it is not enough lower to account for the number of academic failures. In one investigation, nearly half the drop-outs had an IQ of 110 or above and were therefore capable of completing high school.[33] The average for pupils who voluntarily leave school is generally about 95, with the lower end of the distribution extending as low as 80. Second, the drop-outs tend to be academic failures irrespective of their fundamental ability. About half of them in a number of studies were failing one or more courses when they withdrew.[34]

[33] S. C. Karlan, "Failure in Secondary School as a Mental Hygiene Problem," *Mental Hygiene,* 18:611–620, 1934.

[34] See H. R. Douglass and I. Campbell, "Factors Related to Failure in a Minneapolis Junior High School," *Elementary School Journal,* 37:362–369, 1938; R. C. Fagan, "Why Pupils Fail," *Nation's Schools,* 27:58 ff., 1941; B. K. Farnsworth and J. B. Casper, "A Study of Pupil Failures in High School," *School Review,* 49:380–383, 1941; W. L. Gragg, "Some Factors Which Distinguish Drop-Outs from High School Graduates," *Occupations,* 27:457–459, 1949; H. M. Lafferty, "A Study of the Reasons for Pupil Failure in

On the other hand, about 10 per cent were doing definitely good work, and the remaining 40 per cent were getting average marks. Third, the drop-outs have records of persistent absence from school; some missed as many as half of their classes during the semester before they left school, and the majority missed a few of their classes. The typical drop-out is therefore a student of just sufficient intelligence to complete high school if he really wanted to, but he finds academic work uninteresting; he first absents himself from class and then finds a good pretext for separating himself permanently from the school.

A few investigators have followed the voluntary drop-out, talked with him, studied him, and tried to determine his real reason for leaving. One sample study of this sort will be briefly summarized.[35] During the first semester of 1948, a large city high school held 1,367 of its pupils but lost 96, or 6.6 per cent, through withdrawal. Of this number 60 were boys, and 36 were girls. This ratio of two to one is customary and suggests that there is more to the matter than variation in intelligence. Perhaps it is a reflection of the higher verbal ability among girls, but the writer is inclined to prefer a second explanation: a girl often feels that she can make a better marriage and can become more successful socially if she finishes high school, and so she tries harder than her brother and is far less willing than he to leave school, even though the classwork may bore her just as much. This motive is especially strong among girls from low socioeconomic backgrounds who hope to advance socially through marriage. Moreover, as long as a girl remains in school she has at least casual contact with dozens of boys; but if she leaves and goes to work, her main business contacts will be with other girls or with married men. The follow-up study of the 96 withdrawals included both analysis of their records and personal interviews with them. The average IQ of the group was 95, as compared with an average of 101 for pupils in the trade school and 105 for pupils in Grade 10 of the academic course.[36] The drop-outs showed, however, especially low scores on verbal parts of the intelligence tests, and they made markedly lower scores in reading than students of identical IQ who remained in school. Eighteen per cent of the drop-outs came from non-English-speaking homes, as compared with 10 per cent for the whole school, and the great majority of them came from inferior homes. The reasons given in the interviews are listed below. Some of them are repetitions of the familiar reasons, or excuses, but there are a few new ones.

1. Wages were needed at home.
2. Student had been working after school and liked the work better than school.

School," *Educational Administration and Supervision*, 24:260–267, 1938; C. L. Pitts, "A Partial Report of a Study of Failure in the First Year of High School," *Peabody Journal of Education*, 15:362–369, 1938; L. M. Snyder, "Why Do They Leave?" *Journal of Higher Education*, 11:26–32, 1940.

[35] J. A. Lanier, "A Guidance-Faculty Study of Student Withdrawals," *Journal of Educational Research*, 43:205–212, 1949.

[36] The average for Grades 11 and 12 of this course were 107 and 110, respectively.

3. Student was discouraged by making low test scores and by failing courses.

4. Student felt he did not "belong" in the high school group.

5. Sickness in home required presence of girl student there.

6. Student showed severe personal maladjustment to school life. Hated school. Felt rejected. No sense to studies, etc.

7. Student wanted to make money for self, as part of revolt from parental domination.

8. Student got such low grades he was ashamed.

9. Student felt tired all the time, could not get enough sleep.

10. Friends already out of school. No personal friends among classmates.

11. No fun in school any more.

12. Dislike for study; inability to prepare lessons or to read textbooks made school too difficult.

13. Student older than others in class.

14. Teachers not fair, picked on student, made no effort to help him.

15. Student unhappy both at home and at school; resentful toward parents and teachers.

These reasons make more sense than those thus far considered, mainly because they concern students' attitudes toward school. A pupil leaves primarily because he is discouraged, unhappy, socially isolated, and maladjusted. There is more than a suggestion that the drop-out has an abnormal personality structure, especially in his generous use of projection and in his hostile attitude toward his teachers and family.

By comparison with former decades the present number of withdrawals is small. In the modern high school one finds two different modes of attack upon the problem. On the one hand, courses are constantly being made easier, more varied, more useful and more practical, and less dependent upon purely verbal abilities. The modern high school has many courses that can be passed by pupils of low mental ability or low interest in academic material, and it makes an earnest effort to steer the potential academic failure into them. Second, careful attention is given to any pupil who does poor work. Often he is studied and the source of his difficulty found *before* he fails. As a result, the percentage of failures and eliminations becomes steadily less.

The figures above are about groups of pupils, and they leave out of account many problems of emotional and social maladjustment. The studies given below are included to show how such maladjustments operate in individual cases. One is from the high school level and one concerns elimination from college.

Justine entered high school at the age of sixteen, with a record of two retardations in elementary school. During the primary grades her work had been fair, but from the fourth grade on she had received poorer and poorer marks. The comments made by her successive teachers showed a progressive deterioration of personality, presumably the result of her chronic frustration. Her fourth-, fifth-, and sixth-grade teachers thought her a bit un-co-operative, but believed that she did really make an effort to learn her lessons. Outside class, they found her pleasant and willing to help by doing little chores about the school. Her seventh- and eighth-grade teachers were almost unanimous in labeling her sullen and lazy. In all grades, however, Justine had been fairly popular with the other children, although she was not a leader. At the end of the first semester in high school Justine failed every course she was taking. She was therefore sent to a counselor for an interview. At first, the girl was sullen and uncommunicative, but presently she began to tell about her difficulties, once she discovered that she had a sympathetic listener. She did not hate school, but she was most unhappy in class. She liked the teachers well enough and the other pupils very much. She enjoyed games and various co-curricular activities. Her vocational ambition was to become a cook. Justine did not seem to understand why she could not do the schoolwork that other pupils enjoyed—in fact, she appeared rather preoccupied with this problem. The counselor therefore gave the girl two tests of intelligence and let her score them herself. Then the counselor and Justine went over the results and compared them with the norms. One might have thought the girl would be discouraged by the findings, but actually she was greatly relieved. She exclaimed at once, "Then I'm *not* lazy!" She was reassured on this point and advised to elect a light program of courses that would lead directly to her vocational objective. Justine was co-operative and willing to be guided. She took only two courses —both in foods—plus classes in physical education, how to study, and remedial reading. She continued with her membership in three or four clubs. At the end of the year Justine passed her small amount of classwork, although by no great margin. At the beginning of her sophomore year the counselor found Justine a half-time position as assistant to the cook in a nearby bakery. Nothing was said about Justine's dropping out of school, but as the year progressed and she became more and more interested in her work at the bakery, she gradually stopped coming to class. As a means of keeping her social contacts, she continued to belong to one or two clubs and to play games with her former classmates. Instead of penalizing her for her nonattendance, the counselor let her drop the courses she did not finish. Justine's high school career petered out completely in the middle of what would have been her junior year if she had taken a normal schedule. By this time she had worked up to a responsible position in the bakery, she had many friends whom she had met through her work, and she had no more need for the high school. Justine has no sense of failure; she says that she went to high school as long as she wanted to do so and then left of her own accord. Her case was handled so wisely that she no longer feels frustrated or unhappy.

A rather good-looking but sulky girl came to her supervisor in a small college with the complaint that she simply did not like college and was unhappy there. It was evident after a few minutes of conversation that she had no interest in any of her courses. The counselor at first assumed that she wanted advice about further work in college, so he went through the catalogue, asking her if she would like to take this or that course that was open to freshmen. Nothing aroused the faintest spark. Indeed, as the possibilities for study were revealed to her, the girl grew more and more glum. Eventually, the counselor asked her what she intended to do after she was through college and received the surprising reply that she wanted to be a hostess in a night club. The counselor explained that college was no place to acquire whatever skills she might need, nor did he even know what the skills were, having always supposed that such positions were obtained mainly through being a friend of the owner of the club. He was also somewhat puzzled as to what helpful advice he could give. He told her he thought that she should withdraw from college, since the work offered had no bearing on her vocational objective, but this solution was not acceptable. The girl had got it into her head that at least a year or two of college was necessary for general social acceptance. She left the office still unhappy and even sulkier than before. A few weeks later she flunked out of college. At a final interview with her counselor she blamed her failure upon her teachers and complained bitterly about the unfairness of the marking system. The counselor tried to argue her into a better frame of mind but without much success. The next day she presumably left for home. The counselor was therefore not a little surprised to meet her on the street about three months later. She was wearing an air hostess's uniform and looked both pretty and happy. She voluntarily hailed the counselor and told him that she had been ashamed to go home, so she had registered at a training school for air hostesses. She was now working and was thrilled with her job.

This girl is an extreme case of a common type of drop-out. She had no interest in anything offered by higher education. She was not stupid, but her intellectual abilities were of too low an order for success in college without a great deal of application. She disliked studying, reading, or even thinking. She neither understood nor wanted to understand what her teachers were talking about. She had been swept along by the general exodus from her high school into college and had merely gone with her friends. Graduation from college had become for her a symbol of social success—an odd concept of the life academic. Many voluntary withdrawals are of this type. Such students do not belong in college, but it is often hard to convince them of this fact.

It is probable that there will always be withdrawals from schools and colleges. Sometimes the grounds are purely financial, sometimes the students are too dull to profit by further work, and sometimes they have no interests that could be served by the school. What is needed is a better "exit" service so that those who leave can do so without the feelings of disgrace and failure that often accompany the process. The counselor in many high schools tries to give this type of help, and in some places all pupils who want to withdraw have a series of talks with a counselor first. Some of them can—and should—be readjusted to school life, but others are definitely better off outside the school, provided the separation can be brought about without emotional shock.

IV. Development of Individual Mental Capacities

There was a time when memory, imagination, and reasoning were regarded as individual mental faculties more or less independent of each other. The popular conception postulated a mind divided off into areas, each of which functioned by itself and could be trained independently. Although this time-honored view has been abandoned in the light of modern research, such mental characteristics as imagination, memory, or reasoning still remain. These capacities are not, however, separate "mental functions." What differentiates reasoning from memory, for example, is the purpose toward which the integrated effort of the *entire intelligence* is directed. Presumably all these abilities involve use of one's total capacity, rather than any isolated portion of it. But the end in view varies from one "function" to another, as does a person's relative proficiency. It is thus possible, in spite of certain destructive criticism, to employ these terms with this somewhat changed meaning.

1. **Memory**: According to popular misconception, children have better memories than adolescents or adults. What is true is that they are much more willing to memorize; most adults do not like monotony and therefore prefer logical to rote learning. The typical adolescent distaste for memoriz-

ing is even more intense. Although children do not resent memorizing, they are not particularly efficient at it, as indicated alike by both observation and test results. For instance, one investigator studied recall of a moving picture that was seen but once.[37] Memory was measured three times—immediately after the movie, a month later, and three months later. The results appear in Figure 122 on this page. On all three occasions the children remembered least. The adolescents recalled more than the children but were clearly inferior to the adults.

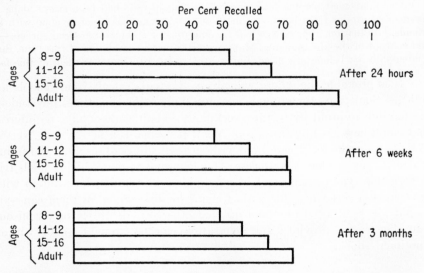

Fig. 122. *Memory for a Motion Picture*

Based on data in P. W. Holaday and G. D. Stoddard, *Getting Ideas from the Movies,* The Macmillan Company, 1933, Table XIII.

There is also evidence of growth of memory in the items of the Binet examination. A child of two and one half can repeat two digits after hearing them read aloud once; at three, he can repeat three digits; at four and one half, four digits; at seven years, five; at ten years, six; a superior adult can repeat eight. Memory appears, then, to increase with age instead of decreasing.

In bygone decades psychologists were greatly interested in memory and in the development of a greater capacity to memorize. Ebbinghaus invented the nonsense syllable[38] for the purpose of studying memory exactly and objectively and used it to determine the "laws" of rote learning. Since 1910, however, there has been less and less interest in the study of memory. The writers of books or pamphlets on how to study took over some of the general principles worked out earlier in the psychological laboratories, but the "laws" did not seem to work as well as expected, and some recent manuals

[37] P. W. Holaday and G. D. Stoddard, *Getting Ideas from the Movies,* The Macmillan Company, 1933, Table XIII.
[38] A nonsense syllable consists of two consonants with a vowel between them: tiv, mun, gok, pab, wef. The combination must not make a word and must be pronounceable.

on study omit the topic of memorizing altogether. In an imposing encyclopedia of psychology, published in 1946, there is no article whatever on

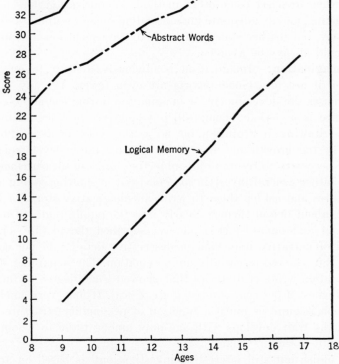

Fig. 123. *Growth in Memory*

Based upon figures in W. H. Pyle, *Nature and Development of Learning
Capacity,* Warwick & York, Inc., 1925, 119 pp.

memory.[39] In order, therefore, to find adequate studies of growth in the
ability to learn by rote during childhood and adolescence, it is necessary
to go back to work done in the opening decades of the present century.

[39] P. H. Harriman (ed.), *Encyclopedia of Psychology,* Philosophical Library, New
York, 1946, 897 pp.

The results of a sample study from an earlier period appear in Figure 123 on page 511. Between the ages of eight and eighteen the pupils showed increases in their ability to memorize words or to recall the meaning of a passage. Adolescents as a group do not like to memorize, but their ability to do so, when they wish to, increases from year to year.

It is not difficult to see why interest in memorizing has lagged. In former times memory was so overemphasized that the reaction against its use has been violent. The entire spirit of the progressive movement has been against rote learning. The essence of the reform has been to make school material so interesting and so meaningful to children that they will not need to memorize. After some years of going to an extreme in the matter, educationalists have realized that for some kinds of material memorization is a great timesaver. It should not be forced upon pupils, naturally, and they should learn when to select rote memory as an efficient means of learning and when to select some other method. Memorization does not lead to understanding, and an adequate understanding sometimes makes memorizing unnecessary, but neither statement leads to the conclusion that learning by heart should always be avoided.

2. Imagination: Imagination is obviously difficult to measure, and reports on it are few. Good reports are even fewer. Yet any high school teacher senses the development of imagination during the adolescent years. Adolescence is a period during which youngsters produce poems, stories, songs, and drawings in profusion, but no test has yet been devised to measure adequately the growth of imagination behind these developments. It is therefore necessary to resort to less objective forms of measurement.

One rather general investigation consisted in showing young adolescent girls pictures and asking them to write an imaginative story, of the fairy-tale type, about one of them.[40] Nearly half the pupils (ages 10 to 14) produced brief and banal stories, merely described the picture, or included only bits of narrative imbedded in descriptive details; 44 per cent of the "stories" thus showed essentially no imagination. The remaining 56 per cent of the children wrote real stories that showed some degree of imagination, and the highest 9 per cent showed a great deal. It may very likely be that imagination is quite as much a function of personality structure as of age and that the trait develops with age only among those to whom the gods have given it in the first place.

One oldish but still interesting investigation[41] is based on an analysis of compositions written by 2,642 boys and 2,138 girls between ages 9 and 18. The problem set them was to finish a story, the beginning of which was provided; given, also, were hints as to the nature of their compositions. The directions are reproduced on the opposite page.

---

[40] M. D. Vernon, "The Development of Imaginative Construction in Children," *British Journal of Psychology,* 39:102–111, 1948.

[41] Th. Valentiner, "Die Phantasie im freien Aufsatze der Kinder und Jugendlichen," *Beihefte zur Zeitschrift für Angewandte Psychologie,* 1916, 168 pp. These paragraphs are presented by permission of the *Zeitschrift für Angewandte Psychologie.*

This is the beginning of a story about the moon.

"On a recent night," narrated the moon, "I was sliding through heavy clouds of snow. My beams tried to pierce them in order to see what was happening on earth. Finally, the clouds parted before me and . . ."

You are to finish the story. You may choose any one of the five themes suggested below:

1. The moon sees a shipwreck.
2. The moon has a conversation with the giant, Roland, at the town hall of Bremen.
3. The moon comforts a sick man who is lying in bed.
4. The moon tells about a camp of hikers in the neighborhood of Bremen.
5. The moon talks with a pupil who cannot prepare his lessons.

By these directions, every pupil was led into a situation in which he had to use his imagination. He could, however, choose the topic around which his fancy played most readily; and he was free to introduce whatever embellishments and minor incidents might occur to him.

There were three outstanding differences between the themes of child and adolescent. The children represented the moon primarily as an acting being, while the adolescents described the moon's thoughts and emotions. The older pupils enlivened their stories with various minor episodes, droll happenings, and artistic touches, while the children clung to their central theme. The children's style was bald, but that of the adolescents showed numerous embellishments. The girls showed evidences of maturity earlier than the boys. The differences specifically in imagination are revealed in the two excerpts below, which are typical, respectively, of good childish and good adolescent imaginative power.

Child's Story

Because of the great distance the moon must sometimes use a spyglass, an opera glass, or glasses, or else send out his beams as messengers, for men appear to him as little ants and their lanterns as tiny glowworms. Up above in the heavens he flies through the clouds or in the clouds. Sometimes he allows a schoolboy to come up to him. Once he said, "Ah, my boy, can't you do your schoolwork well?"

"No, dear moon," answered the boy.

"Well, then, come up here to me."

The boy took his schoolbooks in his brief case and journeyed to the moon. Once he had arrived there, the moon indicated a room that looked exactly like a schoolroom. The moon then came into the room to the boy in order to help him with his lessons. The moon was willing to help him and sat down on a chair, took a pen, and did some arithmetic for him. Then he told the boy not to lose courage about his work. Later he picked up a book and read aloud from it.

Portion of Adolescent's Story

One evening I was making my usual round in the heavens. The little angels had polished me till I shone, so that I was quite satisfied with myself. The little stars, my courtiers, had been cleaned by the heavenly guards and filled with oil, for it would be a shame if these sources of light were ever to fail. Although I am an old man, my stride was very elastic, and in my joy I didn't notice at all that I came too near a little star. Suddenly! Crash! Bang! We had smashed into each other and a tiny piece of the star roared off in a wide, fiery arc. All at once we heard a wee, distant voice saying, "Oh, look! A shooting star! Shiver my timbers! Now I wish for myself a hundred thousand dollars." It was indisputably one of those tiny little men on the earth who call such a thing a "shooting star" and, when they see one, wish for themselves the most wonderful things. I was sunk deep in thought but was aroused by the complaints of the injured star that rubbed its head and wailed, "Oh, my lovely hat! Oh, my lovely hat!" I calmed him down and asked him what his name was and how long he had been in service as a guard in the sky. He answered, "My very respected Lord, I have not been very long in service here, only about eight hundred years." (All of this preceded the actual story told—an illustration of the adolescent tendency to introduce minor incidents.)

The child's composition shows certain elementary imaginative touches— the spyglass, the glowworms, the moonbeams used as messengers. But, on the whole, the story is prosaic; the tale would not have varied essentially if the boy had been helped by his uncle. The adolescent shows not only imaginative touches, but a truly fanciful situation in the concept of a heavenly collision, with its droll consequences. The effect of the mishap on human beings, moon, and star occupies more space than the description of the action.

The development of one girl in imagination from preadolescence into the earliest years of adulthood is well illustrated by the samples below. Although only one individual is involved, the study has at least the merit of being "longitudinal." The particular individual wrote much better poetry than the average, but its excellence does not prevent adolescent traits from appearing and disappearing with age. It is pleasant that the poems are of high intrinsic merit,[42] but their quality is irrelevant to the present discussion. The first poem is a description of a scene, presumably based upon pictures but involving some degree of imagination; it has a standard form, it displays no emotion, and it gives practically no interpretation. In its objectivity it is quite characteristic of late childhood. The second poem shows in its details the same descriptive tendencies as the first; it also expresses fancy and imagination in abundance but not much emotion, although it certainly does create a mood. The poem shows a breaking away from traditional form, a highly characteristic trait of adolescent work, and it makes repeated use of a word arrangement until it becomes almost a mannerism; that is, the author uses a noun, and immediately repeats it with an added adjective. This discovery of a new technique and its overuse are extremely adolescent. The theme of the third poem centers around love for an ideal mate, a typically adolescent topic. In thought, it is the most conventionalized of the series, it is rather sentimental, and it does not have the restraint of later productions, but its relative lack of clichés and its imaginative detail make it far better than most adolescent love poems. The fourth poem is again a lyric outpouring about youth and love, but on an appreciably more adult level. There is much emotion, the elation in the first two verses being in contrast to the desolation of the third. The feeling is so intense that it tends to swamp the meaning. The second, third, and fourth are all untraditional in form. They represent experiments and—in

[42] The writer is indebted to Ursula Kroeber for permission to quote these few samples of her many interesting poems.

all probability—revolt against convention. A period having these character-istics is likely to appear in the adolescent writings of those who accepted traditional forms as children and at least sometimes returned to them volun-tarily in adulthood. Revolt and experiment are an integral part of adoles-cence. The last example is a sonnet, a typically adult form of poetry. The theme shows a continuance of adolescent revolt against the idea of death, but there is the beginning of resignation. The poem is deeply emotional but shows great restraint.

Rite Primeval (Age 12)

Throb and thrum of native drum
Through the jungle booming,
Silhouettes seen through the nets
Of lianas, in the glooming.

Leap and dance, plunge and prance
From eve till break of day,
Through the night an age-old rite
Beats on its rhythmic way.

The Unicorns (Age 14)

Hush, oh hush, be silent now, be silent, hush, be silent, be still,
Hush, be still, and you shall hear, if you listen,
The slow low gallop of the unicorn herd,
Cantering slow, cantering soft, down to the silver stream
That sings as it flows and flows as it sings:
Hush, be still, you may hear the song.
Close your eyes in the dark, the dark, the sweet soft dark of the night or a dream,
And white in the dark you shall see the flanks, the sides and the necks,
The white arched necks of the unicorn herd,
Cantering down to the silver stream, the singing stream,
Arching their hoofs, their silver hoofs, flashing their horns, their spiral horns;
Be still in the dark, the gentle dark, you may hear the stream and the galloping hoofs.

Krasnovsky[a] (Age 16)

Here it is, here it is, it is like a hand on your eyelids, it is like a little bell in the rain,
It is like the little stem of a flower. . . .

Awaken, oh my soul: put forth your hands,
Take up the hills and the waters of day-break, breathe on the wide slopes and the
    mist on the sea,
Take up these things, that are love; find out your love's street and his hills, find out
    his sleep,
Sit at his table, bow your head with his, and find out all his dreams.
Take up these things, that are love, are forever love, but for you only an hour:
Arise, awake, awake to your love, that calls to you with the tender voice of the dawn,
With the tender voice of a dream. . . .

The Hunter (Age 19)

O your youngness is like a deer
stiff-legged: like the wind
now bright, now bleak.

---

[a] Krasniy means beautiful in Russian. Krasnovsky was an imaginary man, an ideal figure.

Rose and fire is love, fire in the wind,
the flute's voice of silence,
and the highness of the moon.

Skull-white, the moon: and the wind
dying: ash the rose, the fire,
fallen the flute's voice,
and the hunter is on the hills of Spring.

Sonnet (Age 22)

I am expert in youngness: all the days
Of verdure and of April have been mine.
And I have learnt the land where springs the vine
Splendid to summer; have I to change these ways?
Apprentice of mortality, to praise
The windless autumn, the regretful wine
That sucks its crimson from the year's decline,
And I learn November's land, who am of May's?
Immortal make the Spring those fortunate
Who gallantly the green-strown ways ascend
In youngness to their death, nor hesitate.
While I, though knowing where all seasons tend,
Yet cling to their obscure descent, and wait
As if for more than death, at seasons' end.

The entire series of poems shows a high degree of imagination and a strong tendency to word pictures. In childhood the latter tended to be so profuse as to obscure the meaning rather than illuminate it. In the last two poems it is well controlled and kept subordinate to the meaning. Emotion is at first lacking, then there is a deluge of it, but finally it is put under sufficient restraint to be highly effective.

In the course of years, objective tests of imagination will doubtless appear. In the meantime, one must be content with the indications of increased imaginative power as revealed by such evidence as that shown above.

3. Suggestibility: There has not been much recent research into the degree of suggestibility at different ages, but one investigation[43] seems worth reporting. It covers a wide range of years, from five to eighteen. The results are expressed in two ways: the percentage of pupils at each age who were suggestible and the percentage of responses of a suggestible character shown at each age. Both curves, which appear in Figure 124 on page 517, show children to be extremely suggestible. During late childhood and preadolescence the curves begin to fall and continue to do so steadily and quite evenly throughout the remaining years. At the age of eighteen only 18 per cent of the students and only 4 per cent of the responses were classified as suggestible. Teachers have long been aware that adolescents cannot be guided by suggestion as easily as children are. The common form of suggestion

---

[43] M. L. Reymert and H. A. Kohn, "An Objective Investigation of Suggestibility," *Character and Personality*, 9:44–48, 1940.

usually phrased as "Wouldn't you like to read another chapter?" has to be abandoned by the junior high school level, because many pupils have become too resistive to such simple means of suggestion. A few people remain suggestible to the end of their days, but as a trait it is characteristic of childhood and probably reflects both the child's dependence upon adults for guidance and his relative ignorance of the world. Adolescents often go through a period of being highly countersuggestible and react to the sug-

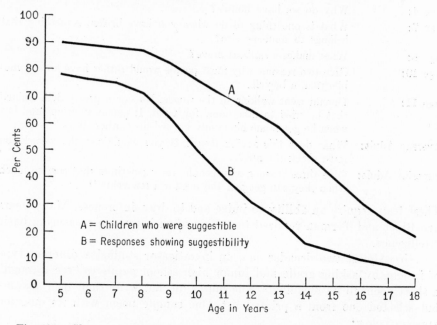

Fig. 124. *Changes in the Degree of Suggestibility with Age*

Based on Tables 3 and 4 of M. L. Reymert and H. A. Kohn, "An Objective Investigation of Suggestibility," *Character and Personality*, 9:44–48, 1940.

gestions of either parents or teachers by wanting to do the exact opposite. Such pupils are still immature, because they are still accepting suggestion, but in a negative rather than a positive manner.

4. Reasoning, Thinking, Judging, Obtaining Insights: It is probable that these words all refer to the same kind of ability to deal constructively with facts, to rearrange them, to draw conclusions, or to "see through" them. Investigations in this field are numerous, but only a few samples can be presented. The discussion will (a) begin with a listing of some "compre-hension" questions of the Stanford-Binet Scale, (b) continue with a sum-mary of an experiment in the ability to see through a poem by junior high school children, (c) go on to four studies of the ability of adolescents to give explanations, to reason about conclusions, to match specific illustrations with general principles, and to "see through" a parable or a cartoon to its meaning, (d) proceed to a discussion of the methods that college students use in solving problems, (e) continue with a few conclusions as to the improvement of reasoning skill by certain types of teaching, and (f) end with a brief suggestion as to the possible use of the ability to "see through" jokes as an indication of mental maturity.

(a) There is, first of all, the Binet examination with its series of "comprehension" questions. Growth is reflected by successive steps, as follows:

Age 3½:	What must you do when you are thirsty?
Age 4:	Why do we have houses?
Age 7:	What is one thing to do when you have broken something that belongs to someone else?
Age 8:	What makes a sailboat move?
Age 10:	Give two reasons why most people would rather have an automobile than a bicycle.
Age 11:	Donald went walking in the woods. He saw a pretty little animal that he tried to take home for a pet. It got away from him, but when he got home his family burned his clothes. Why?
Average Adult:	What does this saying mean: If you would eat the kernel you must crack the nut?
Superior Adult:	Give three reasons why people use typewriters that cost so much when they can get pen and ink for a few cents.[44]

These tests require an ability to judge and to draw inferences. Many years ago Binet and Terman realized the value of such tests in measuring basic intelligence.

(b) Almost two decades ago, an investigator studied a different type of insight by asking grade and junior high school pupils to "see through" a short poem to its meaning.[45] The pupils did not write their own answers but selected one from a printed list. One sample poem with its question appears below:

> I ate a small apple;
> It tasted good, and yet—
> I wish that small green apple
> And I had never met.

Why does he wish he had never met the apple?

> Because the apple made him sick.
> Because the apple was sour.
> Because the apple had worms.
> Because he was not hungry.
> Because green apples are not good for children.[46]

Figure 125 on page 519 gives the curve for growth in insight as measured by a total of five poems, also the curve for the poem quoted above. This form of thinking shows a steady gain throughout the grades.

---

[44] Terman and Merrill, *op. cit.*, Form L, pp. 75–132. Used by permission of Houghton Mifflin Company.

[45] W. H. Pyle, "An Experimental Study in the Development of Certain Aspects of Reasoning," *Journal of Educational Psychology*, 26:539–546, 1935.

[46] *Ibid.*, p. 544. Used by permission of the Journal.

(c) Investigations of how children and adolescents explain phenomena give evidence concerning the ability to generalize and reason.[47] Results from one study appear in Figure 126 on page 520. The pupils studied ranged in age from eight to sixteen. Their answers as to why pebbles sink in water, why water runs into a tube, why a windmill turns, why a bicycle goes,

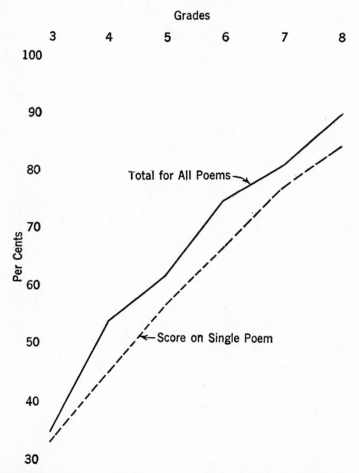

Fig. 125. *Growth in the Ability to Understand the Meaning of Poems*

From W. H. Pyle, "An Experimental Study in the Development of Certain Aspects of Reasoning," *Journal of Educational Psychology*, 26:546, 1935. Used by permission of the Journal.

and the like, were of three general types, which were designated as phenomenistic, logical, and mechanical. The first type of explanation includes such answers as "The pebble sinks in water because it is white"; the child has put together two phenomena that have no connection beyond mere con-

---

[47] J. M. Deutsche, "The Development of Children's Concepts of Causal Relations," *University of Minnesota Monographs in Child Welfare*, No. 13, 1937, 104 pp.

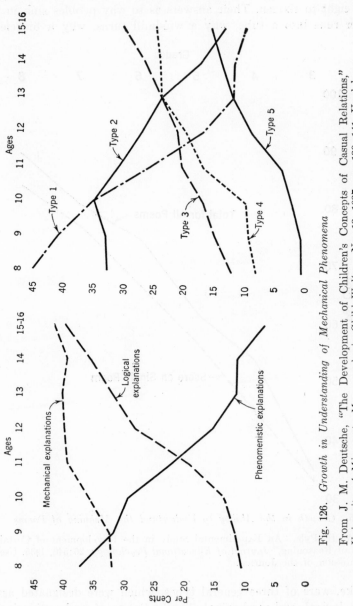

Fig. 126. *Growth in Understanding of Mechanical Phenomena*

From J. M. Deutsche, "The Development of Children's Concepts of Casual Relations," *University of Minnesota Monographs in Child Welfare*, No. 13, 1937, pp. 139, 141. Used by permission of the University of Minnesota Press.

tiguity in time or space. The logical type of answer gives an explanation of sorts, but it is incomplete: The pupil giving such an answer uses such concepts as weight, density, or gravity, and his explanation is sensible as far as it goes, but it is given in static terms. The third type of answer includes such explanations as: "A bicycle goes because, as the pedals are pushed, the chain makes the wheels turn." This explanation is made in terms of movement. The incidence of these three types of explanation, as given in the first part of Figure 139, shows a decrease in the phenomenistic and an increase in the other two during the years of preadolescence and the early years of adolescence.

The second part of Figure 139 shows results from a single question about what should be done to balance an uneven seesaw. The explanations were of five types, of which the following examples may be given:

To balance a seesaw, a bigger block is needed at one end than the other because:

1. One end is lower than the other, and the other end is higher.
2. The board is not even on its two ends.
3. The two sides do not balance.
4. One side is a good deal heavier than the other.
5. One side is longer and heavier, and needs a weight to balance it.[48]

At age 8, answers of Type 1 are commonest, and those of Type 5 are practically nonexistent; the types occur in frequency in order from 1 to 5. At ages 15 and 16, the order is almost exactly reversed. It seems curious that only 15 per cent of the oldest group marked answer Number 5.

Another investigator traced the ability among students in the ninth grade through the second year of college to match scientific illustrations with principles and to evaluate the correctness of explanations.[49] For the first part of the test, the students were provided with a short list of scientific principles and a longer one of illustrations and were asked to tell which items were examples of which principles, all of which might be used as many times as they seemed relevant. Incidentally, the investigator first designed his test by selecting principles from a report of those accepted by a dozen curricular studies as being appropriate for high school, but the resulting test was so hard that he had to reconstruct it, using the principles from a report that contained only those "suitable" for elementary school pupils. One wonders how suitable! The scores made in successive years appear in Figure 127 on page 522. For the second part of the test the investigator presented a short passage about common colds, followed by six questions concerning prevention, treatment, cause, value of current research,

---

[48] The first explanation lacks mechanical facts, general principle, and cause and effect relationships; the second contains a mechanical fact but is incomplete and gives no principle; the third mentions a principle but does not tie it in with the mechanical facts; the fourth gives the facts but lacks a principle; the last contains a fairly complete mechanical explanation, with the principle.

[49] T. B. Edwards, "Measurement of Some Aspects of Critical Thinking," *Journal of Experimental Education*, 18:263–278, 1950.

effect of vitamins, and need for medical attention. For each question there were four possible answers: (A) one was totally incorrect, (B) one was totally irrelevant, (C) one was fairly good but contained an inaccurate or irrelevant detail, and (D) one was correct. The students did not mark the right answer. They compared each answer with every other and stated, of each pair, which was the better. They compared, therefore, A with B, A with C, A with D, B with C, B with D, and C with D. Since there were

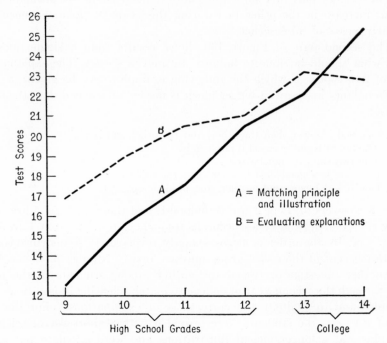

Fig. 127. *Growth (A) in the Ability to Match Principles with Illustrations and (B) in the Ability to Evaluate Explanations*

Based on T. B. Edwards, "Measurement of Some Aspects of Critical Thinking," *Journal of Experimental Education,* 18:268, 1950.

six such comparisons and six questions, the total possible score was 36. The highest actually made seems to have been 28. As shown in Figure 127 the average gain for the six years after entrance to high school was only from 16.8 to 23.5 points, a gain that could easily be due to mere elimination.

Adolescent ability to obtain insights, to judge, or to think is well measured by two distinctive and interesting experiments. The first of these presents results of a test designed to investigate comprehension of the sayings and parables of Jesus.[50] In this investigation, a series of objective tests was given to 637 children and adolescents, who were then classified on the basis of mental age. The study reports the percentage of children at each

---

[50] S. P. Franklin, "Comprehension of the Sayings of Jesus," *University of Iowa Studies in Character,* 2:1–63, 1928.

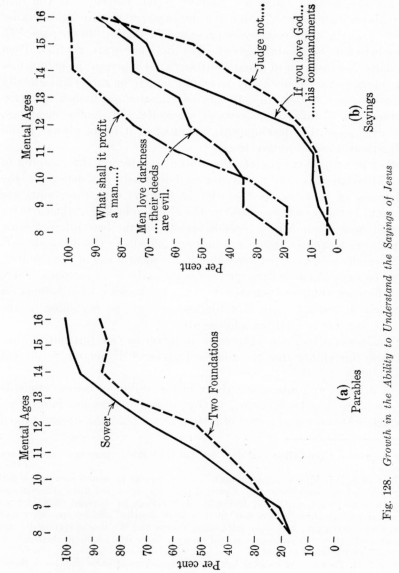

Fig. 128. *Growth in the Ability to Understand the Sayings of Jesus*

Based on S. P. Franklin, "Comprehension of the Sayings of Jesus," *University of Iowa Studies in Character*, 2:1-63, 1928.

mental age who were able to understand each saying or parable. As illustrations, results of two parables will be shown: "The Sower" and "The Two Foundations."[51] The development of comprehension for four famous sayings will also be presented: "What shall it profit a man if he gain the whole world but lose his own soul?" "Judge not, that ye be not judged," "If you love God, keep his commandments," "Men love darkness rather than light because their deeds are evil." The results are presented in Figure 128 on page 523. The gains between the mental ages of eight and eleven are gradual. Then there are large increases up to about fourteen; after fourteen the gain sometimes continues and sometimes not, depending largely on the height already reached by the curve at that time. In this investigation one finds a reflection of an increase in ability to understand allegories and double meanings. Teachers often sense this development, but proof of it is not always found in investigations using objective tests.

Another investigation concerns the ability to interpret the meaning of cartoons. Although this study was designed originally to determine the appropriateness of cartoons for inclusion in history texts, the results are equally useful in the present connection. The children looked at the cartoons and selected from a number of possible statements the best interpretation of each picture's meaning. Figure 129 on page 525 shows three sample cartoons. The results were grouped according to the mental age of the children. Figure 130 on page 526 shows the curves for the same three cartoons. There is some difference from one cartoon to another, because of difference in difficulty, but in general there is a marked rise at the beginning of the mental ages that are normal for adolescents.

The various studies show an increase in power to "see through" a situation. It is in this ability that the adolescent is most distinctively different from the child.

(d) A detailed and interesting study in the ability of college students to solve problems has been carried on by means of personal interviews, during which, after an initial period of getting acquainted, the student talked

---

[51] For the younger generation that does not know its Bible, these two parables are quoted below:

Matthew 13:3. Behold, a sower went forth to sow, and as he sowed some seeds fell by the wayside and the fowls came and devoured them up. Some fell upon stony places where they had not much earth and forthwith they sprung up because they had no deepness of earth; but when the sun was up they were scorched and because they had no root they withered away. And some fell among thorns and the thorns sprung up and choked them. But others fell on good soil and brought forth fruit, some a hundredfold, some sixtyfold, and some thirtyfold.

Matthew 7:24. Therefore whosoever heareth these sayings of mine and doeth them, I will liken him unto a wise man which built his house upon a rock; and the rain descended, and the floods came, and the winds blew and beat upon that house, and it fell not, for it was founded upon a rock. And everyone that heareth these sayings of mine and doeth them not shall be likened unto a foolish man which built his house upon the sand; and the rain descended, and the floods came, and the wind blew and beat upon that house: and it fell; and great was the fall thereof.

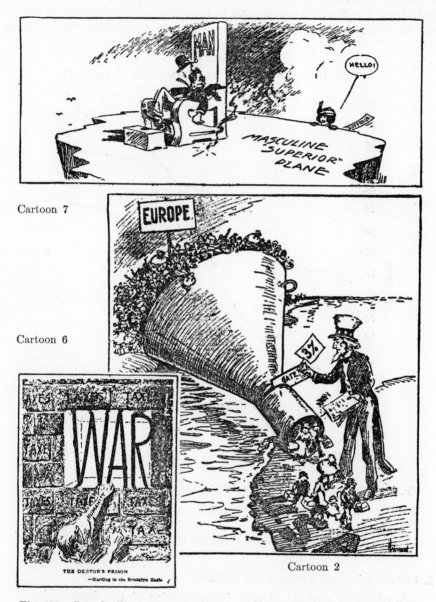

Cartoon 7

Cartoon 6

Cartoon 2

Fig. 129. *Sample Cartoons*

From L. Shaffer, "Children's Interpretation of Cartoons," *Teachers College Contributions to Education*, No. 429, 1930, pp. 24, 32, 34. By permission of Bureau of Publications of Teachers College, Columbia University. Cartoon 2 by Hallahan in the *Providence Evening Bulletin*; 6 by Harding in the *Brooklyn Daily Eagle*; 7 by Brown in the *Chicago Daily News*. All three are used by permission of their respective papers.

out loud as he thought through his answers.[52] The object of the investigation was to trace the thought process and to note where and why it went astray —not to determine how many problems a student could solve. As a student

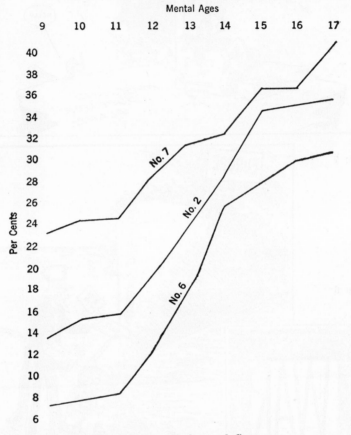

Fig. 130. *Growth in the Ability to Understand Cartoons*

Based on L. Shaffer, "Children's Interpretation of Cartoons," *loc. cit.*

thought aloud, the observer made a record of his errors and miscues, using the list below, of which only a few of the details are reproduced:

I. Understanding the nature of the problem

    A. Ability to start the problem (comprehension of directions)

        1. Rereads directions aimlessly—does not concentrate sufficiently to understand directions on first reading.

        2. Lacks understanding of the terms and phrases in the directions.

        3. Depends on the questions rather than the directions for an understanding of the nature of the problem.

---

[52] B. Bloom and L. J. Broder, "Problem-Solving Processes of College Students," *Supplementary Educational Monographs*, No. 73, The University of Chicago Press, 1950, 109 pp.

B. Ability to understand the specific problem . . .
   1. Has difficulty as a result of improper reading of directions. . . .
      a. Makes no attempt to read the directions. . . .
   2. Forgets or loses sight of the directions.

II. Understanding of the ideas contained in the problem

A. Ability to bring relevant knowledge to bear on the problem
   1. Possesses little or no knowledge about the ideas contained in the problem.
   2. Is unable to use whatever relevant knowledge is possessed because of the presence of unfamiliar terms and ideas.
B. Ability to comprehend the ideas in the form presented in the problem
   1. Is unable to translate the difficult and abstract terms of the problem into simple and more concrete terms or into more familiar terms. . . .

III. General approach to the solution of problems

A. Extent of thought about the problem
   1. Makes little or no use of hypotheses as to the correct solution.
   2. Makes little or no attempt to set up and use criteria which the solution must meet. . . .
B. Care and system in thinking about the problem
   1. Makes little or no attempt to reorganize the problem in order to gain an understanding of the material.
   2. Makes little or no attempt to delimit the possible answers or choices. . . .
C. Ability to follow through on a process of reasoning
   1. Carries reasoning part way through to completion, then gives up. . . .

IV. Attitude toward the solution of problems

A. Attitude toward reasoning
   1. Takes the attitude that reasoning is of little value—one either knows the answer or does not. . . .
B. Confidence in ability to solve problems
   1. Makes little attempt to attack the problems which appear to be complex and abstract.
   2. Makes only a superficial attempt to reason through a problem, then gives up and guesses. . . .
C. Introduction of personal considerations into problem-solving
   1. Has difficulty in maintaining an objective attitude in certain problems because personal opinions play an important part. . . .[53]

The above analysis breaks down the process of problem solving into four steps: understanding what is to be done, understanding the ideas contained in the problem, approaching the problem, and attitude toward the solution obtained. As illustration, the reports on two students are quoted below:

1. *Understanding the nature of the problem:* A major factor in [Louis's] lack of understanding of the problem is the fact that he misreads and misinterprets directions. This results, in many instances, in his attempting to solve an entirely different problem from the one posed. . . . He rarely focused attention on the essential parts of the directions, seemingly reading them as an unimportant part of his attack on the problem. . . .

---

[53] *Ibid.,* pp. 106 ff. Used by permission of The University of Chicago Press.

Nancy seems to have little difficulty understanding the nature of a problem. However, if the problem is exceedingly complex or if the solution is not immediately apparent, she becomes so involved in the details of the problem that she loses sight of the end she is seeking. As she reads the directions, she sometimes restates them in her own words, picking out the relevant ideas and determining exactly what she is to look for.

2. *Understanding the ideas contained in the problem:* Louis deals almost entirely with the terms as given in the problem, making no attempt to define these terms or to translate them into more familiar terms related to his own experience. He appears to have a somewhat limited technical vocabulary, and this proves to be a definite handicap to his problem-solving. . . . He is much disturbed by the fact that an addition or omission of one or two words in a problem changes its entire meaning. . . .

Nancy seems to have little difficulty understanding the ideas involved. When she is uncertain about a term used or has difficulty visualizing a situation, she seems to try to relate it to a concrete example or to establish a mental picture in order to clarify the situation for herself. She presents a particularly good example of one who can relate her knowledge and experience to the problem at hand.

3. *General approach to the solution of problems:* Louis seems to do little independent thinking in arriving at a solution, relying rather on the choices the examiner supplies. He selects an answer and attempts to justify it, rather than thinking through to the solution and *then* selecting an answer. Many times he does not know how or where to begin to attack the problem. . . .

Nancy is continually asking herself questions about the problem as she proceeds with the attack. She seems to answer these questions and then to go ahead on the basis of the answers and assumptions she has made. If she cannot attack the problem as a whole, she breaks it into parts and attacks each part separately. Her habit of questioning the various parts of a problem seems to be the directing influence in her ability to break down a problem.

4. *Attitude toward the solution of problems:* Louis feels that he does not have an adequate background with which to attack certain problems, and he refused to attempt the solution of these problems. He indicated that he believes it is unfair to guess at an answer. He will not select an answer unless he feels that he has a basis for his choice. (This basis may at times be quite flimsy.) When an answer is chosen, it is usually given in a rather positive and assured manner. He takes the attitude that one does or does not know the answer, and he makes little attempt to reason through to a solution. Another source of considerable difficulty for this student is that he cannot divorce his personal values from the problems he is solving and seems unable to maintain an objective attitude. Thus, he chooses an answer "that would be not only logic, but also uses my interpretation of equity.". . .

Nancy expresses some feelings of inferiority regarding her ability to attack certain problems. A typical reaction in a problem dealing with the laws of exponents was, "Wonder if I remember this. . . . What is given in the product when you first learn coefficients? Darn it, Nancy, you should know this. Coefficients. How did they do this? I can't remember at all." She usually makes some attempt to find an answer for each problem. She makes a great effort to explore her knowledge about a subject to determine what is relevant to each problem.[54]

It will be noted that there are two chief sources of difficulty: the student either does not find out just what he is to do before he starts or he does not know certain necessary facts.

---

[54] *Ibid.,* pp. 33–36. Used by permission of The University of Chicago Press.

(e) The main suggestion for improving whatever ability to think that pupils naturally have consists in giving them frequent and consistent practice in tracing cause and effect relationships, in making conclusions, and in solving problems. In short, one learns to think primarily by thinking. Experiments in high school science classes with teaching that emphasized causal relationships and the drawing of conclusions from data have shown a small but consistent advantage in favor of such teaching.[55] Of course, ability to think clearly is an evidence of intelligence, and some individuals do not learn to think well because they lack the necessary native ability. It is, however, possible to guide and develop the thinking of those who do have the basic intelligence.

(f) It is probable that an age scale could be made by using different kinds of jokes that seemed amusing to children of different ages. The Binet scale has one item of this sort in the "absurdities": "The police found the body of a man cut into 27 pieces, and they think he killed himself." Those children who "see through" this gruesome statement are greatly amused! Children who are too immature mentally do not see any contradiction in the two halves of the sentence. To see the point of any joke, the hearer must know whatever facts are needed for the interpretation, must have enough mental power to make associations among several elements all held in his mind at once, and must have had some experiences that are relevant to the situation portrayed in the joke.

For instance, the following colloquy is intelligible only to those who have sampled coffee in inferior restaurants:

WAITRESS *(setting down a cup of coffee)*: Well, sir, it looks like rain.
CUSTOMER: It certainly does but it may taste something like coffee.

Similarly, if one does not know that Dedham is about five miles from Boston or that one main artery south from Boston goes through it, and if one has never been acquainted with proper Bostonians, one fails to understand the joke about the Boston lady who traveled from her home to San Francisco; when asked by what route she had gone, she replied, "Via Dedham." The writer recalls clearly the use of a certain joke several times as a clinching argument to prove that she was still only a child—also at what moment and under what circumstances enlightenment finally arrived. One evening, her father read the following joke out of the paper:

NATIVE *(showing Bunker Hill Monument)*: This is where Warren fell.
VISITOR *(running his eye up and down the monument)*: Hurt him much?

In order to see through this joke one has to know that the monument is a tall shaft and who Warren was, and also to have two meanings for the verb "fall." In her childhood, the writer had only one of these necessary items. She often saw the monument and could easily understand that

---

[55] W. B. Reiner, "The Value of Cause and Effect Analysis in Developing Ability to Recognize Cause and Effect Relationships," *Journal of Experimental Education*, 15:324–330, 1947, and L. Teichman, "The Ability of Science Students to Make Conclusions," *Science Education*, 28:268–279, 1944.

Warren—whoever he was—might have been hurt had he fallen off it, but where was the joke? For some years whenever she thought herself old enough to do this or that, the joke was again presented and her inability to explain it used as evidence of immaturity. One day, however, in preparing a history lesson, she read, "At the battle of Bunker Hill, General Warren fell"—and all became clear.

Presumably a series of jokes would provide an excellent measure of maturity, because of the degree of insight involved. It is to be hoped that some day an earnest student will produce such a measure. It should reveal a facet of personality thus far measured only indirectly, if at all.

V. Summary

Teachers should always keep in mind the probable distribution of intelligence in high school, the probable direction of any changes in this distribution from year to year, and the undeniable presence of many definitely dull children in each entering class.

Throughout the average school system, intelligence tests are in constant use. A teacher needs to develop an understanding of them so that she can know what they will and what they will not do. A child's intellectual level is an important factor in conditioning his schoolwork, although it is by no means the only factor.

The teacher should change the nature of her assignments as the pupils mature. The growth in mental power is there; it merely awaits adequate stimulation by classwork. Readings that demand organization, experiments that require close reasoning, writing that calls for vivid imagination, and even assignments, properly presented, that demand memorizing, should be stressed. Opportunities for getting insight into social, scientific, aesthetic, moral, or practical problems should be numerous.

In the past the school has emphasized intellectual progress to the detriment of social and emotional development. The modern school has sometimes swung to the other extreme and has neglected intellectual development in order to concentrate the more heavily upon social and emotional adjustment. In such schools the classroom has become a side show, attached to the main tent where the co-curricular life of the school is in full swing. With all the intellectual growth and change that take place during this period, the relatively minor role played by classwork in the lives of many adolescents is deplorable. These vital powers are poured without stint into other kinds of work. It is the teacher's job so to utilize them in her daily assignments that her classwork stimulates eager interest and promotes growth in intellectual power.

REFERENCES FOR FURTHER READING

BOOKS

1. Anderson, *The Psychology of Development and Personal Adjustment*, Chaps. 8, 9.

2. Breckenridge and Vincent, *Child Development,* Chaps. 10–11.
3. Garrison, *Growth and Development,* Chaps. 8, 10.
4. Garrison, *Psychology of Adolescence,* Chap. 6.
5. Goodenough, F. L., *Mental Testing,* Rinehart & Company, 1949, 609 pp. (Chaps. 11, 12, 21.)
6. Kuhlen, *Psychology of Adolescent Development,* Chap. 3.
7. Rosenzweig, *Psychodiagnosis,* Chap. 3.
8. Schnell, D. M., *Mental Characteristics of Adolescence,* Burgess Publishing Company, 1947, 68 pp.
9. Segel, D., *Intellectual Abilities in the Adolescent Period: Their Growth and Development,* Federal Security Agency, United States Office of Education, 1948, 41 pp.
10. Terman, L. M., and M. A. Merrill, *Measuring Intelligence,* Houghton Mifflin Company, 1937, 461 pp. (Chaps. 2–4.)
11. Thurstone, L. L., and T. G. Thurstone, *Primary Mental Abilities,* Science Research Associates, 1951, 48 pp.
12. Travers, R. M. W., "Significant Research on the Prediction of Academic Success," in Donahue, *The Measurement of Student Adjustment and Achievement,* pp. 147–190.
13. Wechsler, D., *The Measurement of Adult Intelligence,* Williams & Wilkins Co., 1944, 229 pp. (Chaps. 1, 2, 3.)
14. Wile, *The Challenge of Adolescence,* Chap. 7.

MONOGRAPHS, BULLETINS, PROCEEDINGS, YEARBOOKS, ARTICLES

A. *Intellectual Growth in General*

1. Freeman, F. N., "Intellectual Growth of Children as Indicated by Repeated Tests," *Psychological Monographs,* XLVII, No. 2, Whole No. 212 (1936), 20–34.
2. Freeman, F. N., and C. D. Flory, "Growth in Intellectual Ability as Measured by Repeated Tests," *Monographs of the Society for Research in Child Development,* Vol. II, No. 7, 1937, 116 pp. (Chaps. 4, 6, 7.)
3. Goodenough, F. L., and K. M. Maurer, "Mental Growth of Children from 2 to 14 Years," *University of Minnesota Monographs,* No. 2, 1942, 130 pp.
4. Hilden, A. H., "A Longitudinal Study of Intellectual Development," *Journal of Psychology,* 28:187–214, 1949.
5. Jones, H. E., and N. Bayley, "Growth, Development, and Decline," *Annual Review of Psychology,* 1:1–8, 1950.

B. *Intellectual Growth during Adolescence*

1. Flory, C. D., "The Intellectual Growth of College Students," *Journal of Educational Research,* 33:430–441, 1940.
2. Hass, L., "Four-Year Studies of the Freshman Classes of 1936 and 1940 at the Eau Claire State Teachers College," *Journal of Educational Research,* 42:54–61, 1948.
3. Jones, H. E., and H. S. Conrad, "Mental Development in Adolescence," *Forty-third Yearbook of the National Society for the Study of Education,* 1944, Pt. I, pp. 146–163.
4. Shuey, A. M., "Improvement in the Scores on the American Council Psychological Examination from Freshman to Senior Year," *Journal of Educational Psychology,* 39:417–426, 1948.
5. Thorndike, R. L., "Growth of the Intelligence during Adolescence," *Journal of Genetic Psychology,* 72:11–15, 1948.

6. Vernon, P. E., "Changes in Abilities from 14 to 20 Years," *Advancement of Science,* 5:138–139, 1948.
7. Warbois, G. W., "Mental Development during the Preadolescent and Adolescent Periods," *Review of Educational Research,* 17:317–325, 1947.

C. *Changes in the IQ*

1. Baldwin, A. L., "Variation in Stanford-Binet IQ Resulting from an Artifact of the Test," *Journal of Personality,* 17:186–198, 1948.
2. Bayley, N., Consistency and Variability in the Growth of Intelligence from Birth to Eighteen Years," *Journal of Genetic Psychology,* 75:165–196, 1949.
3. Brodway, K. P., "IQ Constancy on the Revised Stanford-Binet from the Preschool to the Junior High School Level," *Journal of Genetic Psychology,* 65:197–217, 1944.
4. Goodenough, F. L., "Studies of the 1937 Revision of the Stanford-Binet Scale: I. Variability of the IQ at Successive Age Levels," *Journal of Educational Psychology,* 33:241–251, 1942.
5. Honzik, M. P., J. W. MacFarlane, and L. Allen, "The Stability of Mental Test Performance between Two and Eighteen Years," *Journal of Experimental Education,* 17:309–324, 1948.
6. Knesevich, S. J., "The Constancy of the IQ of the Secondary School Pupil," *Journal of Educational Research,* 39:506–516, 1946.
7. Sloan, W., and H. H. Harmon, "The Constancy of IQ in Mental Defectives," *Journal of Genetic Psychology,* 71:177–185, 1947.
8. Thorndike, R. L., "Retest Changes in the IQ of Certain Superior Students," *Thirty-ninth Yearbook of the National Society for the Study of Education,* 1940, Pt. II, pp. 351–361.

D. *Factors of Intelligence*

1. Chein, I., "An Empirical Study of Verbal, Numerical, and Spatial Factors in Mental Organization," *Psychological Record,* 3:71–94, 1939.
2. Clark, M. P., "Changes in Primary Mental Abilities with Age," *Archives of Psychology,* No. 291, 1945.
3. Doppelt, J. E., "The Organization of Abilities in the Age Range from Thirteen to Seventeen," *Teachers College Contributions to Education,* No. 962, 1950, 86 pp. (Chaps. 3–6.)
4. Freeman, F. N., H. S. Conrad, and H. E. Jones, "Differential Mental Growth," *Forty-third Yearbook of the National Society for the Study of Education,* 1944, Pt. I, pp. 164–184.
5. Swineford, F., "Growth in the General and Verbal Bi-Factors from Grade VII to Grade IX," *Journal of Educational Psychology,* 38: 257–272, 1947.
6. Swineford, F., "A Study in Factor Analysis: The Nature of the General, Verbal, and Spatial Bi-Factors," *Supplementary Educational Monographs,* 67:1–70, 1948.
7. Thurstone, L. L., "Primary Abilities," *Occupations,* 27:527–529, 1949.

E. *Nature and Nurture*

1. Carter, H. D., "Ten Years of Research on Twins," *Thirty-ninth Yearbook of the National Society for the Study of Education,* 1940, Pt. I, pp. 236–255.
2. Goodenough, F. L., "Some Evidence of Environmental Influence on Intelligence," *Thirty-ninth Yearbook of the National Society for the Study of Education,* 1940, Pt. I, pp. 307–365.
3. Reymert, M. V., and R. T. Hinton, "The Effect of Change to a Relatively

Superior Environment upon the IQ of 100 Children," *Thirty-ninth Yearbook of the National Society for the Study of Education*, 1940, Pt. II, pp. 255–267.

4. Skeels, H. M., "Some Iowa Studies of the Mental Growth of Children in Relation to Differentials of Environment," *Thirty-ninth Yearbook of the National Society for the Study of Education*, 1940, Pt. II, pp. 281–308.

5. Skeels, H. M., and I. Harms, "Children with Inferior Social Histories: Their Mental Development in Adoptive Homes," *Journal of Genetic Psychology*, 72:283–294, 1948.

6. Skodak, M., and H. M. Skeels, "Final Follow-up Study of One Hundred Adopted Children," *Journal of Genetic Psychology*, 75:85–125, 1949.

7. Thorndike, E. L., "The Resemblance of Siblings in Intelligence Test Scores," *Journal of Genetic Psychology*, 64:265–267, 1944.

F. *Special Mental Abilities*

1. Alpern, M. L., "Ability to Test Hypotheses," *Science Education*, 30:220–229, 1946.

2. Bloom, B., and L. J. Broder, "Problem-Solving Processes of College Students," *Supplementary Educational Monographs*, No. 73, The University of Chicago Press, 1950, 109 pp. (Chaps. 2, 3.)

3. Deutsche, J. M., "The Development of Children's Concepts of Causal Relations," *University of Minnesota Monographs in Child Welfare*, No. 13, 1937, 104 pp.

4. Edwards, T. B., "Measurement of Some Aspects of Critical Thinking," *Journal of Experimental Education*, 18:263–278, 1950.

5. Kilgore, W. A., "Identification of Ability to Apply Principles of Physics," *Teachers College Contributions to Education*, No. 840, 1941, 28 pp.

6. Oakes, M. E., "Children's Explanations of Natural Phenomena," *Teachers College Contributions to Education*, No. 926, 1949, 151 pp. (Chaps. 1–3.)

7. Reiner, W. B., "Value of Cause and Effect Analysis in Developing Ability to Recognize Cause and Effect Relationships," *Journal of Experimental Education*, 15:324–330, 1947.

8. Teichman, L., "The Ability of Science Students to Make Conclusions," *Science Education*, 28:268–279, 1944.

G. *Holding Power, School Enrollments, and Elimination*

1. Carrothers, G. E., "Why Do High School Pupils Fail?", *Bulletin of the National Association of Secondary School Principals*, 30:29–36, 1946.

2. Dillon, H. J., "Early School Leavers—A Major Educational Problem," *National Child Labor Publications*, No. 401, 1949, 94 pp.

3. Fagan, R. C., "Why Pupils Fail," *Nation's Schools*, 27:58–60, 1944.

4. Finch, F. H., "Enrollment Increases and Changes in the Mental Level of the High School Population," *Applied Psychology Monographs*, No. 10, 1946, 75 pp.

5. Gragg, W. L., "Some Factors Which Distinguish Drop-Outs from High School Graduates," *Occupations*, 27:457–459, 1949.

6. Johnson, E. S., and C. F. Legg, "Why Young People Leave School," *Bulletin of the National Association of Secondary School Principals*, 32:14–24, 1948.

7. Lanier, J. A., "A Guidance-Faculty Study of Student Withdrawals," *Journal of Educational Research*, 43:205–212, 1949.

8. Phearman, L. T., "Comparison of High School Graduates Who Go to College and Those Who Do Not," *Journal of Educational Psychology*, 40:405–414, 1949.

9. Truex, R. O., "The Size of the Families in Three Generations," *American Sociological Review*, 1:581–591, 1936.

H. *Intelligence and Social Status*

1. Havighurst, R. J., and F. H. Breeze, "Relation between Ability and Social Status in a Midwestern Community: III. Primary Mental Abilities," *Journal of Educational Psychology*, 38:241–247, 1947.
2. Schulman, M. J., and R. J. Havighurst, "Relations between Ability and Social Status in a Midwestern Community: IV. Size of Vocabulary," *Journal of Educational Psychology*, 38:437–442, 1947.

CHAPTER SIXTEEN

Intellectual-Cultural
Interests

The adolescent boy or girl has many interests. Some of them are con-tinuations of childhood pursuits, but many are new. High school pupils show their interests by their preferences for games or other diversions; by their choice of books, magazines, radio or television programs, and motion pictures; by their vocational ambitions; by the type of things they collect; by the kinds of books they read. The exact form that these interests take depends upon the environment. Because of the interrelation between adolescent drives and the environmental possibilities for their expression, the term "intellectual-cultural" has been used in describing these interests. The materials on this subject are diverse and numerous. If all relevant data were summarized, one would have a whole book. The writer has tried, therefore, to select a relatively few studies that illustrate the main trends. There will be an introductory section on the way in which adolescents spend their time and upon their comparative likes and dislikes for the various things they do. The next section deals with interest in the three main methods of mass communication and entertainment at present—television, radio, and motion pictures. There is a brief section on collecting, a longer one on play, and a closing section on interest in various types of reading—books, newspapers, magazines, and comics.

I. Adolescent Activities

Various investigators since 1945 have analyzed in more or less detail the usual occupations and diversions of the adolescent's day. Two summaries will be presented. Table 38 gives the results of one study[1] of over eight thousand high school boys and girls. It is at once obvious that while boys and girls spend their time in much the same pursuits, these activities are of varying degrees of interest for members of the two sexes. In general, girls did more work around the house than boys, read more, went to movies a little oftener, had more hobbies, took a greater part in religious activities, were more social, showed a greater interest in art and music, and took more lessons outside school—such as dancing, painting, music, and drama. Boys

---

[1] E. B. Olds, "How Do Young People Use Their Leisure Time?" *Recreation*, 42:458–463, 1949.

Table 38

USE OF LEISURE TIME

Boys who participated in each activity during sample week (%)	Activity	Girls who participated in each activity during sample week (%)
	A. Schoolwork	
87	1. Studying	94
	B. Commercial entertainment	
92	2. Radio listening	90
67	3. Movie attendance	72
27	4. Attendance at concerts, lectures	38 (+11)
	C. Games	
66	5. Playing games	60
68 (+21)	6. Watching games	47
40 (+13)	7. Supervised sports	27
57 (+30)	8. Unsupervised sports	27
	D. Social pursuits	
24	9. Chaperoned parties	42 (+18)
29	10. Unchaperoned parties	37
29	11. School activities	32
15 (+10)	12. Scout activities	5
85	13. Loafing with friends	90
40	14. Club meetings	52 (+12)
	E. Solitary pursuits	
82	15. Reading	91
33	16. Hobbies	42
43	17. Loafing alone	61 (+18)
	F. Lessons outside school	
23	18. Music	43 (+20)
5	19. Other classes	14
	G. Religious activities	
43	20. Church attendance, religious clubs, etc.	58 (+13)
	H. Homework	
73	21. Odd jobs around house and housework	86 (+13)

Numbers in parentheses indicate differences of 10 per cent or more.

From E. B. Olds, "How Do Young People Use Their Leisure Time?" *Recreation*, 42:458–463, 1949.

surpassed the girls in all activities having to do with sports and games. Members of the two sexes were alike in the time spent in study, in listening to the radio, and in loafing about with friends, although the girls spent more time in loafing alone.

Results concerning adolescent interests appear in Figure 131 just below. Boys and girls arranged the same twenty-three activities in order of interest, from greatest to least. The marked differences are indicated by lines; there are other small differences, but in the interest of clarity these are not shown in the figure. Boys are much more interested than girls in sports, television, pets, collecting, and the YMCA (as compared to YWCA

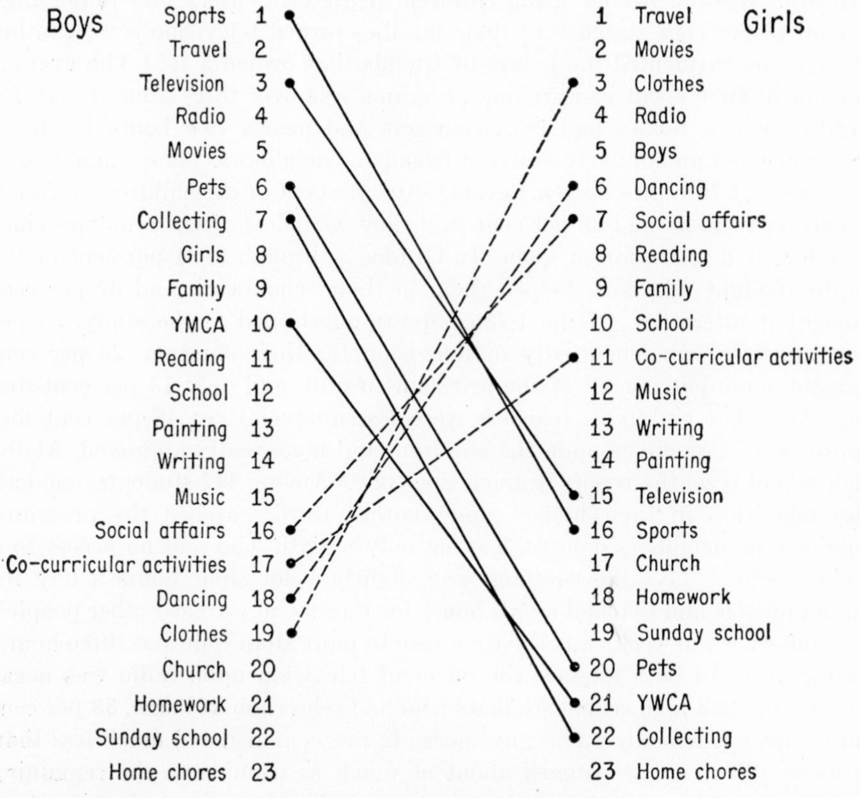

Boys				**Girls**
Sports	1	1	Travel	
Travel	2	2	Movies	
Television	3	3	Clothes	
Radio	4	4	Radio	
Movies	5	5	Boys	
Pets	6	6	Dancing	
Collecting	7	7	Social affairs	
Girls	8	8	Reading	
Family	9	9	Family	
YMCA	10	10	School	
Reading	11	11	Co-curricular activities	
School	12	12	Music	
Painting	13	13	Writing	
Writing	14	14	Painting	
Music	15	15	Television	
Social affairs	16	16	Sports	
Co-curricular activities	17	17	Church	
Dancing	18	18	Homework	
Clothes	19	19	Sunday school	
Church	20	20	Pets	
Homework	21	21	YWCA	
Sunday school	22	22	Collecting	
Home chores	23	23	Home chores	

Fig. 131. *Adolescent Interests*

for girls). Girls exceed boys markedly in their liking for clothes, dancing, social affairs, co-curricular activities, and boys (as compared to boys' rating of their interest in girls). Or perhaps the girls are only more willing to admit their liking! Members of the two sexes are both greatly interested in travel, the radio, the movies, and their families, rate their liking for painting and writing much the same but lower than the items just listed, and are unanimous in ranking household chores at the bottom. Girls rate reading, school, music, church, homework, and Sunday school a little higher than boys do.

II. Interest in Television, Radio, and Motion Pictures

1. **Television:**   The development of television is so recent that studies concerning it are just beginning to appear, and results are still tentative. It is already apparent, however, that children have taken television to their hearts, and it is probable that they are influenced a good deal by what they see and hear. In the absence of definitive studies, it is possible to quote only two brief reports. Among 2,135 children in the elementary and junior high school, 43 per cent stated that their families owned television sets; another 30 per cent frequented the homes of friends that owned a set.[2] The average amount of time spent in watching programs was over three hours a day for children whose homes had television sets and nearly two hours for those who depended on similarly situated friends or neighbors. These same homes also owned 1.76 radios apiece. Seventy-five per cent of the children preferred television to radio and 35 per cent said they went less often to movies since they had had television at home. In Grades 3 through 8, 31 per cent of the pupils thought television helped them in their schoolwork and 67 per cent thought it interfered. Of the 1,736 parents questioned in the study, 55 per cent approved wholeheartedly of television for their children, 25 per cent thought some but not all of the programs useful, and only 13 per cent disapproved. The children's teachers were less appreciative: 48 per cent disapproved of the effects upon the children, and none really approved. At the high school level the report is much the same.[3] Among 447 students, one half had television in their homes, and another third watched the programs regularly at neighbors' houses, leaving only a sixth who had no access to a set. On school days the listening was slightly below four hours a day for the set owners and two and a half hours for those who watched other people's sets, but over the week ends the time rose to more than four and three hours, respectively. In both studies, the effect of television upon radio was negative. Of the 223 high school students who had television at home, 33 per cent hardly ever listened to radio any more, 42 per cent listened much less than formerly, 20 per cent listened about as much as usual, and the remaining 5 per cent preferred radio to television and therefore listened at least as much as, if not more than, they had previously done. The time the students used for television was taken from time they had previously spent in reading, in playing games, in attending movies, in watching sports, and in going to church. One suspects that some of it also came from hours that should have been spent in sleep. The students reported relatively little interference

---

[2] P. A. Witty, "Children's, Parents', and Teachers' Reactions to Television," *Elementary English Review*, 27:349–355, 1950.

[3] Anon., "One High School Surveys Television's Effect on Pupils," *School and College Management*, 20:21–22, 1950.

with their studying because their parents took the precaution of making them finish their homework before they began to watch the programs, but no information was offered as to the comparative adequacy of their preparation. Although one cannot at this time assemble enough evidence to reach a definite conclusion as to the effect of television upon children and adolescents, two facts are already clear:[4] (a) the watching of an illuminated, flickering screen for three or four hours a day is putting undue strain upon children's eyes, and (b) the time devoted to watching has to be deducted from other activities that are probably more healthy. The data in regard to the type of program preferred are slight and may be summarized in a few words. Children voted heavily for Hopalong Cassidy, Howdy Doody, and the Lone Ranger, while adolescents liked best Milton Berle, Toast of the Town, Six-Gun Playhouse, and Captain Video.

2. Radio: The reactions to and interest in the radio have already been studied,[5] and there is no question as to the integral part the radio plays in the lives of both children and adolescents. More homes now have radios than have telephones; the percentage in the various studies ranged from 91 to 98. In a recent survey of the pupils in Grades 7 through 12, the students reported 3.5 radios per home, and almost half of them had radios in their own rooms.[6] Every fourth home in this study also had a television set. The students averaged two hours a day listening to the radio. Six per cent preferred listening to any other activity. There was little difference between boys and girls in the amount of time thus spent. Two thirds of the adolescents reported that they did other things while listening; they read, studied, ate, visited, or sewed. They rated their interest in the radio just below their liking for the movies, ahead of their interest in comics, and a good deal higher than their desire to read books.

Adolescent preferences run much the same in all studies. To be sure, pupils of all ages listen more or less to all kinds of programs, their choice being apparently determined more by the hour of a program than its nature, but when adolescents can choose—as over a week end—they concentrate on athletic contests, humorous programs, music, and drama. Boys and girls differ somewhat in their preferences, as shown in Table 39, but the differences are more in emphasis than in type of program. Girls rated drama and

[4] M. Harmon, "Television and the Leisure Time Activities of Children," *Education,* 71:126–128, 1950.

[5] The facts in the following paragraphs come from A. L. Chapman, "College-Level Students and Radio Listening," *University of Texas Publications,* No. 5016, 1950, 74 pp.; W. R. Clark, "Radio Listening Habits of Children," *Journal of Social Psychology,* 12:131–149, 1940; H. Gaudet, "High School Students Judge Radio Programs," *Education,* 60:639–646, 1940; F. C. Gruber, "Out-of-School Radio Listening Habits of High School Students," *English Journal,* 39:325–327, 1950; A. P. Sterner, "Radio, Motion Picture, and Reading Interests of High School Pupils," *Teachers College Contributions to Education,* No. 932, 1947, 102 pp.; P. A. Witty, *et al.,* "Interests of High School Students in Motion Pictures and the Radio," *Journal of Educational Psychology,* 32:176–185, 1941; P. Witty and A. Coomer, "Activities and Preferences of a Secondary School Group," *Journal of Educational Psychology,* 34:65–76, 1943.

[6] Gruber, "Out-of-School Radio Listening Habits of High School Students," *loc. cit.*

almost all types of musical programs higher than boys did and rated athletics, science, news, and humor lower. The girls reacted strongly to one type of radio personality that had little appeal for the boys—namely, the "crooner"; the audience to which the crooner sings is largely feminine and apparently of all ages. Presumably the high rating for familiar songs among the girls is due in some measure to the fact that a favorite crooner sings them. Adolescents of all intellectual and academic levels voted for the same programs; the main difference was that those who were given low ratings in character by either age-mates or teachers listened more than others to dance

Table 39

INTEREST IN RADIO PROGRAMS

Boys	Girls
1. Athletic contests	1. Swing music
2. Adult comedians	2. Familiar songs
3. News broadcasts	3. Band music
4. Swing music	4. Drama
5. Band music	5. Classical music
6. Melodrama	6. Adult comedians
7. Scientific topics	7. Melodrama
8. Classical music	8. News broadcasts
9. Drama	9. Athletic contests
10. Familiar songs	10. Church music
11. Hillbilly music	11. Hillbilly music
12. Church music	12. Scientific topics

E. B. Bolton and M. English, "Further Studies of the Attitudes of High School Seniors toward Problems of War and Peace," *Journal of Psychology*, 20:157–182, 1945.

music. For the most part, school pupils learned about new programs from each other. A few read the radio sheets and, presumably, spread the news about by word of mouth. Adult recommendation seems to be relatively ineffectual. Some students reported that they had learned many things from the radio and listed as evidence 285 new words—some of them doubtless of the "unlax yourself" variety—2,053 songs, 729 stories, 579 games, and 419 more or less desirable mannerisms. The parents felt that in general the effect of the radio was beneficial, although they wished the children would not listen so much in the evening. Interest in radio among these pupils was not limited to listening. For example, 19 per cent of them belonged to radio clubs, 13 per cent had taken part in contests, 15 per cent had been present at a broadcast, 21 per cent had written fan letters, and 11 per cent had heard their names read over the radio.[7]

There is some evidence that radio programs may have an undesirable emotional effect upon children. While they listen, their blood pressure goes up and their pulses beat more rapidly, especially during exciting

[7] A. L. Eisenberg, *Children and Radio Programs,* Columbia University Press, 1936, 237 pp.

episodes. Attendance at horror movies or addiction to crime stories over the radio have resulted in nervousness, fear of kidnaping, difficulty in sleeping, nightmares, disturbance of eating, nail biting, daydreaming, and development of an unusual interest in sex. The degree of addiction to these forms of entertainment correlated with the number and intensity of the symptoms.[8] Although the immediate symptoms of rapid heart beat and increased blood pressure soon disappear in most children, the indirect effects indicated above often persist.

One habit of most adolescents is to keep the radio going while they study. Many parents have been greatly distressed, and some forbid radio playing during study hours; but as soon as the adolescents were old enough to follow their own preferences, they promptly turned it on again. There has been some research into the effects of this habit upon studying. To the surprise of the investigators, those students who always studied with the radio on did better schoolwork than those who never played it while studying. The pupils themselves report only beneficial results. The writer has quizzed several adolescents to find out why they could study better with a distraction than without one and has found a reasonably good explanation. To begin with, youth of today loves noise and companionship and abhors silence and solitude. The emphasis upon socialization, beginning in nursery school, has had its influence, and by the years of adolescence children have become thoroughly socialized. They would prefer to study together, but since this arrangement is often impracticable, they compromise by turning on the radio. The nub of the matter is that they have been educated in the midst of social stimuli and cannot bear solitude. Silence is to them not a blessed relief from noise but an absence of all supporting human presence. Adolescent testimony is to the effect that they do not actually listen to the radio, but as long as it is going, they are not alone. Quiet and solitude are correlated in their minds with rejection and unpopularity, while noise and chatter mean acceptance and success. Hence they find silence unbearable, distracting, and frightening. Since they cannot have their peers with them every minute, they compromise by substituting the radio, which produces enough background commotion to let them relax. This unique point of view—unique to an older generation, certainly—is a logical result of the present intense socialization from the cradle to the grave, and those of us who grew up without such pressure will have to accept this curious by-product and let the radio run on and on. It comforts the adolescent and even helps him study.

3. Motion Pictures: Children and adolescents attend movies frequently and rate their interest in this form of entertainment even above the radio. One extensive study[9] involving over twenty thousand individuals

---

[8] These statements are based upon J. J. De Boer, "Radio and Children's Emotions," *School and Society,* 50:369–373, 1939; F. Frank, "Chills and Thrills in Radio, Movies, and Comics: A Psychiatric Opinion," *Childhood Education Monographs,* Vol. XXV, No. 2, 1948, 42 pp., and "Comics, Radio, Movies, and Children," *Public Affairs Pamphlets,* No. 148, 1949, 32 pp.; and M. I. Preston, "Children's Reactions to Movie Horror and Radio Crime," *Journal of Pediatrics,* 19:147–168, 1941.

[9] E. Dale, *Children's Attendance at Motion Pictures,* The Macmillan Company, 1935, 79 pp.

gives data on how frequent the attendance was during the sample week when the survey was made. This study is now nearly twenty years old, but

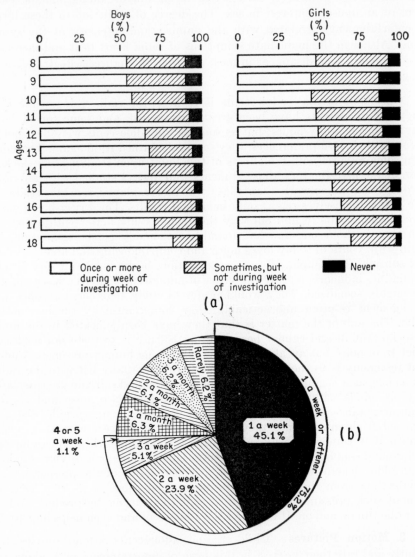

Fig. 132. *Attendance at Motion Pictures*

(a) Based on E. Dale, *Children's Attendance at Motion Pictures,* The Macmillan Company, 1935, p. 31.
(b) From U. H. Fleege, *Self-Revelation of the Adolescent Boy,* Bruce Publishing Company, 1944, p. 246.

such modern studies as touch at all upon attendance indicate little change. Two sets of results are shown in Figure 132 on this page. In (a) of the diagram is summarized the attendance by age from eight to eighteen for both boys and girls, from the older study. In general, attendance increased with age, but even at the lowest age, 50 per cent went once or more during the sample week. The proportion of children who never went to the movies varied at different ages from 8 to 2 per cent for the boys and from 12 to 2 per cent for the girls; from 3 to 6 per cent of the boys in this study went four times or more a week. The results in (b) are more recent but are limited to boys from fourteen to eighteen.[10] Of the two thousand boys included in the study, 75 per cent went once a week or oftener. Slightly over 6 per cent went more than twice a week. Nineteen per cent saw a movie from once to three times a month; the remaining 6 per cent went even less frequently. These results are similar to those for adults. Nearly 50 per cent of young adults go to the movies at least once a week.[11] There were no boys who never went to the movies, as compared to 2 to 8 per cent in the earlier study. The most frequent companions for both boys and girls were age-mates.[12] Nearly 15 per cent of the boys and 20 per cent of the girls went with their parents. Approximately 25 per cent of the boys went alone.

Adolescent preferences show several differences between the interests of boys and girls. The proportion of high school pupils expressing a liking for each of several types of movies is shown in Figure 133 on page 544. Members of both sexes like comedy best. Many more boys than girls vote for westerns, news, and gangster films, and boys show somewhat more interest in mysteries and cartoons, but the difference is not large. Nearly three times as many girls as boys voted for love stories, which rate at the very bottom of the boys' list.

When two thousand English adolescents thirteen to sixteen years of age were asked in 1949 to answer questions concerning the films they had seen during the previous week they showed preferences both as to the type of film and as to the outstanding characteristics they like.[13] Boys as usual preferred films dealing with war, drama, and adventure stories, while girls liked drama, stories of home life, and comedy, and rated adventure films quite low. The boys rated love stories and fantasies so low that these were not included among their first ten choices. When the results were tabulated by school grade, there were changes during the four years of secondary school; interest in westerns, gangster stories, and mysteries declined, while that in musical comedies rose somewhat for both sexes. The characteristics that appealed to adolescents were excitement, realism, and humor for members of both sexes, violence for the boys and both "star appeal" and senti-

---

[10] U. H. Fleege, *Self-Revelation of the Adolescent Boy,* Bruce Publishing Company, 1944, 384 pp.

[11] P. F. Lazarsfeld, "Motion Pictures, Radio Programs, and Youth," in F. Henne, A. Brooks, and R. Ersted (eds.), *Youth, Communication, and Libraries,* American Library Association, 1949, pp. 31–45.

[12] P. Lazarsfeld, "Audience Research in the Movie Field," *Annals of the American Academy of Political and Social Science,* 254:160–168, 1947.

[13] W. D. Wall and E. M. Smith, "Film Choices of Adolescents," and "Effects of Cinema Attendance on the Behavior of Adolescents as Seen by Their Contemporaries," *British Journal of Educational Psychology,* 19:121–136 and 53–61, 1949.

ment for the girls. In fact, girls seemed to choose their films more for the star than for the plot. The effects of the movies, as seen by age-mates, were principally in the imitation of superficial matters: ways of doing the hair, of walking, of talking, or of using make-up.

One investigator studied the 10 per cent of junior high school children who attended the movies most frequently and the 10 per cent who went least.[14] There were few differences between the two extremes, and those that

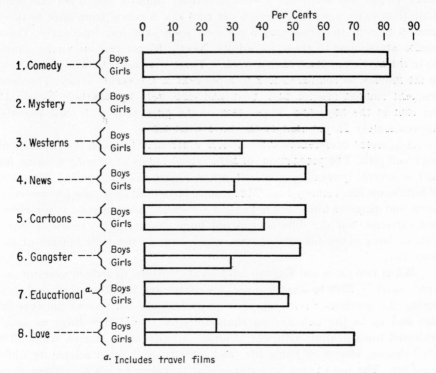

Fig. 133. *Adolescent Preferences in Motion Pictures*

Based upon P. A. Witty, S. Garfield, and W. Brink, "Interests of High School Students in Motion Pictures and the Radio," *Journal of Educational Psychology,* 32:176–185, 1941.

existed were mostly in favor of the movie-goers. As a group they were older, did better schoolwork, were more intelligent, and showed no larger proportion of maladjustment than those who went to the movies least. The one point against the former group was that they owned, and presumably read, fewer books. These results suggest that the movie-goers went because they had the time to do so; they did not take time that should have been spent in studying. Their failure to read may have been a contributing cause of their movie attendance rather than a result of it; that is, since they do not spend

14 F. Heisler, "Comparison of the Movie and Non-Movie Goers of the Elementary School," *Journal of Educational Research,* 41:541–546, 1948, and 42:182–190, 1948.

hours in voluntary reading, they have enough time to go often to the movies. The two facts are doubtless related, but one cannot be sure in precisely what manner. It is quite possible that the particular children would not read a great deal in any case and that, if they did not have movies to look at, they would spend their leisure in less desirable activities.

Recent literature has centered upon finding explanations for the universal appeal of the motion picture rather than upon statistics of attendance or other objective matters. The most widely held opinions would suggest the following explanations: (1) that the movies reflect the interests, needs, and anxieties of the audience, (2) that they present an intelligible interpretation of life, culled from the chaos of daily existence, (3) that they express the unconscious tendencies of all people and therefore serve as outlets for urges that would otherwise be suppressed and might develop into neuroses or psychoses, (4) that they furnish heroes and heroines, with whom members of the audience can identify themselves, and (5) that they provide an escape into fantasy.[15] Many of these explanations are of a psychoanalytic nature. However, many films of the last decade have dealt specifically with subject matter that can best be understood in psychoanalytic terms. Especially noteworthy have been the films dealing with insanity and with racial prejudice.

Table 40

INFLUENCE OF A SINGLE MOTION PICTURE
(*Average scores*)

	Experimental	Control
		Groups
Before seeing picture	23.55	26.54
Day after seeing picture	16.97	29.27
Three days later	16.40	27.06
Total gain or loss	—7.15	+0.52

Based on I. C. Rosen, "Effect of the Motion Picture 'Gentleman's Agreement' on Attitudes toward Jews," *Journal of Psychology*, 26:525–536, 1948.

Several investigations of the effect of a single motion picture upon attitudes have been made at one time or another, beginning three decades ago with the measurement of anti-Negro prejudice before and after seeing "The Birth of a Nation." Two recent studies give further evidence of modification of attitudes after seeing a single picture. In one instance, an experimental group of 50 non-Jewish, white college students and a control group of 90 students rated their feelings toward Jews on an attitude scale.[16] The members of the experimental group then saw the film, "Gentleman's Agreement." On the following day and again three days later, the 140 students repeated the test. The results appear in Table 40. The experimental group showed a somewhat more favorable attitude toward Jews than the control group even

[15] Lazarsfeld, "Motion Pictures, Radio Programs, and Youth," *loc. cit.*
[16] I. C. Rosen, "Effect of the Motion Picture 'Gentleman's Agreement' on Attitudes toward Jews," *Journal of Psychology*, 26:525–536, 1948.

before seeing the picture—in the test used, the lower the score, the less the prejudice. There was a marked lessening of prejudice after seeing the picture, and the new attitudes persisted and even improved a bit three days later. The scores of the control group went up and then came down, presumably reflecting the normal degree of variation inherent in the test.

A second study measured the effect of "Tomorrow the World"—the story of a Nazi youth (Emil) in America—upon such attitudes as the treatment of Jews, value of "youth" organizations, use of fear and force as bases of discipline, free expression of opinion in newspapers, radio, or books, treatment of a conquered enemy, and so on. About fifteen hundred pupils in Grades 7 through 12 took part in the experiment. A few sample results appear below:

The largest group of pupils recognized the basic problems of adjustment faced by a Nazi boy in America, and recommended severe discipline and re-education as means of solving his problems and improving his adjustment. The proportion expressing this view tended to be higher in the upper grades than in the lower. The next largest group did not see the problems clearly, felt the situation to be without a solution, and simply rejected Emil as an undesirable alien. The remaining students recommended kindness and re-education as the means of helping Emil, were quite sure he could become a good American, but did not clearly grasp the basic problems. That is, those who best understood the situation favored a firm treatment of Emil, while the advocates of kindness were inadequate in their thinking. The writers of the article purposely selected some schools enrolling children who belonged to minority groups—Jews, Mexicans, or Negroes—or to groups with points of view different from those of the general population—Mormon children and adolescents, for example. In general, the Jewish and Negro pupils showed greater condemnation and less mercy than others of the same age, while the Mormons tended to a greater degree of kindness and sympathy. The pupils in general showed an increased faith in American ideals—even though members of minorities were aware that these ideals are not always carried into practice—an increased condemnation for the use of force or fear, a greater sympathy toward the Jews, and a stronger tendency toward a merciful treatment of enemies,[17] as a result of seeing the film.

Perhaps the best way to see what effect movies have upon individual adolescents is to let them speak for themselves. Table 41 contains a list of the influences reported by two thousand adolescent boys. Although there are some undesirable effects, the benefits rather outweigh the unfavorable influences.

Nearly twenty years ago an investigator asked 458 high school students to write their motion-picture "autobiographies," telling what influence pictures in general or specific movies had had upon them.[18] Although the study is relatively old, the testimony given by the adolescents is still convincing. These pupils obtained help from the movies in selecting clothes, acquiring acceptable manners, developing better social adjustments, selecting love-

[17] M. J. Wiese and S. G. Cole, "A Study of Children's Attitudes and the Influence of a Commercial Motion Picture," *Journal of Psychology,* 21:151–171, 1946.

[18] H. Blumer, *Movies and Conduct,* The Macmillan Company, 1933, 254 pp.

Table 41

NATURE OF INFLUENCES EXERTED BY MOTION PICTURES

Rank	Manner of influence	Per cent
1.	Movies have caused me to imitate the hero and other characters; inspired me to do what they did, to try to live as they live	15.2
2.	Movies have influenced my actions, my behavior and conduct; I tried to be funny like the actors, to act tough like a gangster	14.6
3.	Movies changed my attitudes and gave me new viewpoints; affected my thinking on a number of things; set my imagination in motion..	9.9
4.	Movies taught me new ideas; gave me a broader view of life and people; influenced me educationally	9.6
5.	Movies have influenced my manners, my social relations; shown me how to act in public and in certain situations; made me more polite	9.2
6.	Movies influenced me in sex matters, morally; gave me impure ideas; drove me to impure actions	8.6
7.	I have imitated their talk and mannerisms; tried to talk more distinctly; imitated them in dress and appearance	8.4
8.	Movies gave me an ideal, a goal to aim at; stirred my ambitions vocationally. (10 per cent of these add: "But the ideal was false," or "Gave me impossible ambitions.")	8.2
9.	Movies gave me a desire to improve myself; to do better, to do good; showed that crime does not pay	7.5
10.	Movies affected my relations with girls; showed me love-making techniques; gave me a desire for pretty girls and more dates	7.4
11.	Movies gave me ambitions to do big things, to be a hero, to be rich, and to lead an easy life; a desire for popularity	6.2
12.	Movies have cleared up some of my problems, aroused my curiosity about things; "just a bad influence," have shown me how people get away with things	3.7

Adapted from U. H. Fleege, *Self-Revelation of the Adolescent Boy*, Bruce Publishing Company, 1944, p. 255. Used by permission of the publisher.

making techniques, acquiring a philosophy of life, getting a better idea of modern society, developing ambition, realizing the value of family affection and loyalty, and developing religious and moral attitudes. Various results of an emotional nature were also recorded. Movies led to daydreaming, terror, sorrow, romantic love, passionate love, general tenseness and excitement, longing to be "good," and resentment at social discrimination or at family interference with adolescent ambitions. Two thirds of the high school students reported the use of movie content in their daydreams. Definite statements of fright and terror occurred in 61 per cent of the high school autobiographies, and sorrow felt during pictures in 64 per cent. Of the 458 youngsters, 39 per cent admitted crying frequently. Reactions to romantic love were definitely mentioned in 55 per cent of the autobiographies. These adolescents spoke of having been thrilled or stirred by love stories; 30 per cent showed, either by statement or by indirect evidence, that they were unusually receptive to amorous advances after watching picture romances. Twenty per cent of these adolescents found dissatisfaction with their daily lives after observing the film life of a modern youth, and 12 per cent expressed this dissatisfaction in some form of rebellion against parental restraint. As a result of their attendance at the movies, 59 per cent had developed a desire for travel and 51 per cent a desire for more education.

A few excerpts from the autobiographies are revealing as to the specific influences exerted by motion pictures.

As I got into high school and into my sixteenth and seventeenth year I began to use the movies as a school of etiquette. I began to observe the table manners of the actors in the eating scenes. I watched for the proper way in which to conduct oneself at a night club, because I began to have ideas that way. The fact that the leading man's coat was single breasted or double breasted, the number of buttons on it, and the cut of its lapel all influenced me in the choice of my own suits.[19]

I remember once I had had trouble with my mother. I said that everything that was done in the house I had to do. I was very downhearted and thought how cruel they were to me. That night I went to the movies. I do not remember the name of the picture but it hit the nail on the head. It concerned one girl who did not get along with her family and one who did. The one girl was so good that everyone loved her, and her life was very happy. The other girl was not happy, and people did not like her because she was not sweet, good, and kind to her mother like the other girl. This made me think that I was just like the girl who was not good. I always wanted to be liked by everyone and to be happy, so I went home that night with the intention of being as good as possible to my mother and of trying to make family life as happy and pleasant as possible both for myself and mother and father. It has been a good many years since I saw this picture, and I am still trying to be that kind of a girl. I have succeeded some, but not enough yet.[20]

Movies have definitely formed part of my daydreams. Every girl, I think, must have the mental image of a man to idealize and build dreams about. Before she finds an actual person, she draws an imaginary figure. In any event that was made up mostly of movies stars. I spent much Latin-grammar time thinking up ways of becoming acquainted with my various heroes. Sometimes, though not often, I identified myself with the heroine of a picture I had seen. The role of the fragile, persecuted woman never appealed to me; it was always as the queen, the Joan of Arc, the woman who had power that I saw myself. These daydreams took up pretty much time, especially during my second year at high school, when I was in a strange environment; but I was always inwardly ashamed of them, and I do not believe that they ever carried over into action of any sort. I have never even sent for autographed pictures.[21]

During my last two years of high school, I did a lot of dating. That is, I had a date about once a week. My program or plan of campaign was, first, a movie, then a dance, then a slow drive home. When I first started taking girls out to the movies, I was impressed with the enormous number of fellows that put their arms around their date in the show and I became aware that heads already close got closer when love scenes were introduced. I tried the things I saw and was pleased with the results. A good love story was more inspiring on a date than a picture in which love was not the important element, and the girls seemed to enjoy themselves more under these circumstances. I didn't get a kick out of what appeared on the screen, but I did like the effect a love scene had on my dates. In "reel life" a boy usually does not go with a girl a long time before he kisses her. The average high school girl, it seems,

---

[19] Ibid., pp. 38–39. This excerpt and the following ones from this source are used by permission of The Macmillan Company.

[20] Ibid., p. 174.

[21] Ibid., p. 67.

follows this suggestion. The love scenes produce an emotional harmony that leads in some cases to kissing and necking.[22]

Sometimes movies make me think of myself as a criminal. I think of all the good times I could have with the money. I think of spending my proceeds of a criminal venture in an amusement park, at parties, in night clubs. Then my thought takes a different trend and I think that free spending of money and not working during the day might make the police suspicious. I then think of saving all the stolen money and working daytimes, so the police wouldn't be suspicious of me. Again I think that it wouldn't be fun robbing poor people like it sometimes shows in the movies because they work hard for their money. I then think of robbing rich people, but I think again that after all they work for their money also. The plan that springs into my mind is that of robbing a gambling establishment. If I succeeded the head of the establishment would not and could not tell the police because they would arrest him for operating a gambling den. I would then give part of the money to poor people and part of it I would keep for myself. But at the end of my thoughts I realized that no matter how skillful or how clever he may be or how much protection he has, the crook is always caught sometime or other. If he isn't caught he is killed by one of his associates. So I think that after all I might as well remain honest, try to make money in an honest way and spend it if and when I want to without the fear of being arrested or killed.[23]

Motion pictures are neither exclusively bad nor exclusively good influences, although they have been credited as being causes of crime, of maladjustment to home and school, and of dissatisfaction with life. It is far more probable that what adolescents—and adults, too, for that matter—get from the theater is mainly a crystallization of points of view, desires, or attitudes already in existence. Thus an already delinquent boy derives from the movies ideas about different techniques for bank robberies, holdups, or other criminal acts, but such details hardly register at all in the minds of the non-delinquents. The adolescent who is already sexually aroused obtains further excitement from the same pictures that furnish other boys and girls chiefly with ideas as to manners, customs, and styles of dress. A girl who has been puzzling about a possible vocation and hesitating between dancing and stenography sees a picture in which the heroine, after trials of various kinds, became a world-famous danseuse, and this picture leads to her firm decision that she too will select dancing as her vocation. To say, however, that the picture "caused" her to enter this profession would be inaccurate; the movie dramatized and crystallized a problem already in her mind. Any motion picture presents in dramatic form a large collection of ideas; each adolescent selects for himself what he wants to learn, just as he does from any other experience in life.

III. Interest in Collecting

The modern boy and girl make collections, but not to the extent that former generations did. The writer has an idea, not vouched for by anyone else, that the efficiency engineer has so eliminated the "wasted" space in the

---

[22] *Ibid.*, p. 115.
[23] H. Blumer and P. M. Hauser, *Movies, Delinquency and Crime,* The Macmillan Company, 1933, p. 151. Used by permission of the publisher.

modern house, and compressed the "functional" space, that there is no room for a small child to put a collection. For instance, the writer's brother gathered together perhaps a quarter of a ton of rocks, which were labeled and displayed on long shelves in his attic room, the walls of which he had decorated with a collection of wild-life scenes, perhaps a hundred of them tacked up, edge to edge. There was still plenty of room left for the necessary furniture, clothes, books, albums, skates, tennis rackets, and other impedimenta. But where in a modern house or apartment could one store a collection of rocks, or anything else bigger than a postage stamp? Every inch is "planned" and a space for children's "junk" is rarely included. Modern youngsters collect such costly things as phonograph records, model airplanes, or miniature figurines, but the expense prevents large assortments. Small boys still collect marbles (though not in such numbers as their fathers and grandfathers did), various kinds of pictures, and stamps. Little girls try to collect dolls, but the cost is prohibitive, and the interest in paper dolls is far less than it once was. They still assemble as many picture postal cards as they can, as well as coupons of all sorts. Modern life has had not only direct but indirect influences upon collecting. The small boy may still pick up bottle tops, with an idea of turning in a boxful to a junkman for a few pennies, but he can no longer get the tops flattened by putting them on the tracks and letting an electric car run over them. For one thing, there are few electrics left; for another, the modern car is so heavy that it smashes the bottle top to pieces instead of merely pressing it out evenly and neatly. Moreover, bottle tops are not the novelty they once were. One of the collections dearest to a small girl's heart in former generations was her assembly of hair ribbons; this collection has, of course, almost vanished.

To study the impulse to collect and to trace its development and expression, one has to go back about two decades in order to find relevant investigations. The things collected vary not only with age and sex, but also with the times, the environment, and the opportunities for storage. A group of 808 boys between the ages of nine and sixteen reported a total of 5,685 collections, or 7 per boy; 868 girls of the same ages reported 7,161 collections, or 8.2 per girl.[24] The percentage of children at each age who made collections varied from nearly 90 per cent at nine to 60 per cent at sixteen. The number of collections per age began with 1 for most six-year-olds, increased to 2 at seven years, and to 4 or 5 by eight. Between nine and thirteen the number of collections rose to some figure between 8 and 10; these are the ages when the collecting mania is normally in full force. At fifteen and sixteen the boys had from 4 to 5 and the girls from 4 to 6 collections, and at seventeen and eighteen about 4. At all ages girls make more different collections than boys do. Rural children far exceed urban children, although in adolescence the difference is not marked.

---

[24] P. A. Witty and H. C. Lehman, "Further Studies of Children's Interests in Collecting," *Journal of Educational Psychology,* 21:112–117, 1930, and "Collecting Interests of Town and Country Children," *Journal of Educational Psychology,* 24:170–184, 1933.

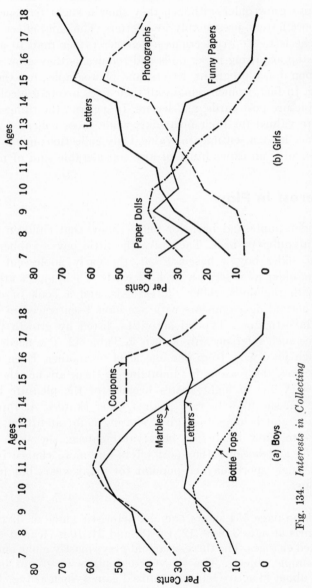

Fig. 134. *Interests in Collecting*

Based on M. T. Whitley, "Children's Interests in Collecting," *Journal of Educational Psychology*, 20:249–261, 1929.

The things that are collected at different age levels are more interesting than the mere numbers. Figure 134 on page 551 shows a few samples for both boys and girls. Boys collect marbles, coupons, and bottle tops less and less as they grow older. There is no type of collection that increases markedly with age as boys grow older, although they show a slight tendency to preserve a few more letters, presumably love letters. The chief effect of age on the male psyche is to stop collections altogether rather than to alter their nature. Girls stop acquiring paper dolls and funnies as they grow older and concentrate upon dance programs, letters, and photographs, but they do not stop collecting. In fact, women remain all their lives inveterate collectors of photographs, picture post cards, and letters. In general, the things collected by children are valued for their own sake, while those collected during or after adolescence have a sentimental value. Only collections made by adults are likely to involve an expenditure of any considerable sum of money.

IV. Interest in Play

Even maiden aunts and bachelor uncles know that children play different games at different ages. They give the little boy a rubber ball for Christmas, the older boy a baseball bat, the early adolescent a tennis racket, and the older adolescent a deck of cards. Their nieces are favored successively with rag dolls, roller skates, skis, and a book of crossword puzzles. Such normal developments with age have been traced in detail by a number of investigators. Typical activities, listed by growth period on the basis of one such reference, are shown in Table 42. The needs that are satisfied through play vary from one age level to another. Even when the same sports persist, the reasons for indulging in them are not the same at successive ages. A girl of eight skates because of the pleasure in bodily movement; at ten she likes to race against other skaters; at thirteen she plays ice hockey and belongs to a girls' skating club; at fifteen, she does figure skating—to show off before boys; at eighteen, she skates largely because boys do and because the sport offers one more chance to attract them. Thus, a single sport may be popular for many years but for vastly different reasons.

Figure 135 on page 554 shows one characteristic game or diversion for boys and for girls at ages 3, 6, 9, 12, 15, 18, and 21. It is clear at once that there are marked changes. The three-year-old plays mostly alone and amuses himself with simple objects. The six-year-old plays in groups of two or three and runs about in active but unorganized games, such as tag. The older boy spins tops, plays marbles, or flies a kite. There are also a number of popular group games that are usually called by the same names as those of the later years, but they are not played in the same way. For instance, what a small boy calls "baseball" is usually a game played by perhaps four boys against five others. His form of football involves an indeterminate number of urchins; after they have chosen sides, everyone runs and jumps on everyone else, without much regard to teamwork or to the progress of the game.

Table 42

PLAY ACTIVITIES AT DIFFERENT AGES

Period	Age	School	Activities	Characteristics
1. Early childhood	3–6	Preschool	Rolling, kicking, pushing, swinging, running, jumping; playing with blocks, swings, seesaws, slides; digging in sand, wading; many simple imitative plays	Need for action seems to be the main motivation; pleasure in the movement itself, rather than the results
2. Middle childhood (boys); middle and late (girls)	6–11	Elementary	*Boys:* (a) Imitative play—cowboys, Indians, soldiers, cops and robbers, etc.; (b) active play: wrestling, climbing, riding, bicycling, running, camping, hiking, skating, swimming; (c) group games: tag, hiding, marbles	Play is highly self-assertive; individualistic rather than social; continual self-testing; motivated by desire for individual prowess and for adventure; play often destructive
			Girls: (a) Imitative play: school, home, or nurse; dressing up like adults; (b) same as for boys except wrestling; (c) same, with the addition of singing games, hopscotch, and jumping rope	Play more socialized than among boys; less motivation from rivalry, personal prowess, or adventure; less destructiveness
3. Late childhood and preadolescence (boys); preadolescence and early adolescence (girls)	12–13	Junior high	*Boys:* (a) Games: baseball, football, basketball, and other team games; (b) sports: skating, swimming, skiing, etc., usually on competitive basis	Beginning of group spirit in teams and gangs; no interest in girls
			Girls: (a) Games: same as for boys; (b) sports: same but with less interest in competition; (c) parties, dances, etc.	Group spirit evident but less forceful than among boys
4. Early adolescence (boys); middle adolescence (girls)	14–18	High school	*Boys:* (a) Team games almost exclusively, except among boys too small for competition; (b) some interest in social activities	Dominance of group over individual
			Girls: (a) Games played less and less, but interest in sports continued; (b) main activities are dancing, having dates, making or remaking clothes, going to parties, personal grooming; (c) reading, especially of love stories	Girls acquire passive role as regards sports; their "adventures" are almost all social; strong motive to advance oneself to a higher status; emotional demands satisfied to some extent by reading and attending movies
5. Late adolescence	19–21	College	*Boys:* (a) Games: less participation in contact or vigorous games; substitution of golf or tennis for more strenuous sports; much spectator interest; (b) social activities: parties, dates, etc.	Lessening of competitive spirit and more playing just for fun; first real appreciation of social values
			Girls: (a) Some spectator interest in sports but little participation; (b) continued social activity; (c) reading and going to movies	Motivation toward relaxation and diversion; essentially no competition

Based upon E. D. Mitchell and B. S. Mason, *The Theory of Play*, A. S. Barnes & Company, rev. ed., 1948, 542 pp.

Fig. 135. *Typical Play Activities at Different Ages*

By the time a boy is twelve years old he prefers hiking, camping, and swimming. In early and middle adolescence, the favorite activities are highly organized group games, played with established rules. In late adolescence interest in games has become more passive than active; already the average boy has begun to develop the attitude of the average man, who derives pleasure from watching sports rather than from participating actively in them.

Among girls there are parallel developments. The little girl begins, as her brother does, by playing alone at such simple amusements as banging a pan with a spoon. By six, however, differences in interest between the sexes have begun to show. The six-year-old plays with her doll and also likes such group games as London Bridge, farmer in the dell, or drop the handkerchief. The nine-year-old likes to serve "afternoon tea," or to "dress up"; she also plays many active games such as run sheep run, or hare and hounds. At twelve her amusements are more like a boy's than they were earlier. Swimming, roller skating, and hiking are especially popular. So also is reading. By the age of fifteen practically all athletics are popular, and the average girl is more active in her amusements than she ever is again. Dances and parties vie with athletics, however, and are equally popular. The eighteen-year-old is strongly social in her interests—dates, parties, and dances engage most of her attention. She still likes sports—swimming or skating, for example—but organized games do not interest her much any longer. She reads, sews, looks in the shop windows, and talks interminably over the telephone. At twenty-one she is even less active, although she develops some degree of spectator interest in active games, but her real diversions are social gatherings of various kinds, reading, and above all the movies.

The transition from childish to adolescent interests in recreation takes place sometime between Grade 6 and Grade 10, with the girls leading the way. Since the process is gradual, teachers in the later junior high school and early high school grades find a mixture of attitudes and interests among their pupils. During the years the change in attitude from the absorption in violent physical activity that characterizes late childhood to the aversion for it that characterizes adulthood begins to take place.

In a ninth-grade gymnasium class for boys one finds the following types: *first,* the boys who still retain the enthusiasm of the twelve-year-old for team games but with the handicap of physique which keeps them from being able to compete for the school team; *second,* the boys whose interests in sports have become that of adult spectators as far as team games are concerned but who have an active interest in such sports as swimming, golf, tennis, or badminton, which they enjoy playing with either sex; *third,* the boys whose major interest is in participating in competitive school sports and whose ability enables them to do so; *fourth,* the boys who have never developed sufficient skill to take their places comfortably in any game and are always among the last to be chosen on teams; *fifth,* the boys who were not quite good enough for the school teams but who enjoy competitive games with others of like ability.

Among the girls who are enrolled in a ninth-grade gymnasium class one finds other types: *first,* those who complain of fatigue or pain whenever they are expected to take part in any physical activity except dancing; *second,* those who dislike team games but who enjoy learning individual games which could be played with either sex; *third,* those who have been so unsuccessful in team games that they had developed a resistance to learning any sport in which their prowess might be compared to that of others; *fourth,* those who are almost like boys in their skill in sports, but, in their desire to compete with the more feminine girls for dates, have denied their interest in games and concealed their abilities in this respect; *fifth,* those who are skilled and have retreated from competition for the interest of boys into a major interest in sports with like-minded girls. Frequently as wide an array of individuals as this is put through the same physical education program in an attempt to "round out" their physical development and without concern for the disastrous effects on their social development.[25]

The games children play and the intensity of their interest in games or exercise are thus indicative of their developmental age. It will be noted that girls mature earlier than boys in that their social interests appear sooner and their concentration upon organized group games disappears earlier. In general, also, girls are less active than boys, although there are a few years in early adolescence when this difference is not marked. These differences do not, of course, mean that girls and boys never engage in the same games. There is more or less overlapping in interests at all ages, and the fundamental drives are much the same for both sexes, but the forms of expression are somewhat different, partly at least because of environmental pressures. Thus boys are given carpentry sets and encouraged to build things, while a girl has to beg, borrow, or steal a hammer and saw if she wants to use them. On the other hand, girls are given dishes to play house with; any boy who uses them is likely to be called a sissy. The interests are not therefore purely spontaneous but are conditioned by social attitudes transmitted to children from previous generations.

Play among boys at least has a definite relation to size, health, and strength. An investigator who selected the highest and the lowest 10 per cent in strength and physical fitness among a group of young adolescent boys found that the high group greatly exceeded the low in all forms of active games, in their spectator interest, and in their social activities.[26] The 10 per cent with the lowest vitality exceeded the high group in reading and in making things—activities that demand relatively less strength and effort. There is no information as to whether the members of this latter group preferred such activities or indulged in them only because they were barred from successful competition with more vigorous age-mates.

Play is the child's outlet for his emotions and tensions, his chief means of self-expression, and his main form of social contact with his age-mates. It is by no means the aimless activity that adults of former generations have sometimes thought it to be. A teacher who watches her pupils at play will learn much about them that may escape her in their classroom behavior and reactions.

---

[25] L. H. Meek, *The Personal-Social Development of Boys and Girls,* Progressive Education Association, 1940, pp. 56–57. Used by permission of the Association.

[26] D. B. Van Dalen, "Differential Analysis of the Play of Adolescent Boys," *Journal of Educational Research,* 41:204–213, 1947.

V. Interests in Reading

It would be possible to list the books that were found most interesting last year to boys and girls of different ages, but because the turnover in new

B
O
Y
S

G
I
R
L
S

Fig. 136. *Reading Interests in Childhood*

books is so rapid, the lists would be of little value by the time this book was printed. Except for a few old favorites, like *Little Women* and *Treasure Island*, most of the titles on a current list would be unfamiliar to the average student reading this book, since his or her earlier favorites are already supplanted. It seems best, therefore, to limit the present discussion to types of books rather than to give specific titles. The types that appeal at different age levels are indicated by the sketches in Figures 136 through 140 on

Fig. 137. *Reading Interests in Preadolescence*

pages 557–561, which show book jackets of books for boys and girls from late childhood through late adolescence. Since the jacket of a book is supposed to indicate its nature, a series of jackets reflects interests at various ages.

The child of either sex who can just barely read likes a small-sized book with many pictures and a simple plot about animals or other children. Little girls like fairy stories better than small boys do, but it is not till middle childhood that the main sex differences appear. At the elementary

Fig. 138. *Reading Interests in Early Adolescence*

school level most boys like stories that deal with war, Boy Scouts, athletics, or strenuous adventure. In the preadolescent years many boys develop a craze for reading an entire series of books. The themes center mainly upon adventure and athletics. The plot is rather stereotyped; for instance, the poor but honest boy meets undeserved failure but triumphs in the end over his wicked enemies. The characters are also types rather than individuals.

It is not until the later years of adolescence that romantic novels make an appeal to the average boy, and some boys never care for them. Girls show a somewhat different development. During elementary school their

Fig. 139. *Reading Interests in Middle Adolescence*

interest is chiefly in fairy stories and tales of home or school life. They also read entire sets of books about the same main character. There is a short period during preadolescence when they like adventure stories, preferably of a romantic nature. With the beginning of adolescence, they become almost immediately interested in romantic literature; most girls of thirteen are already reading love stories. They also show great devotion to the continued story in popular magazines and a more pronounced liking than boys for detective stories, and they read more accounts of travel. Once the liking for adult fiction is established, it pushes out the juvenile forms.

Fig. 140.   *Reading Interests in Late Adolescence*

The figures from one typical investigation[27] of the reading interests of 14,324 pupils in Grades 7 through 12 are summarized in Table 43. The results are based upon the withdrawal of books from the school library and therefore do not show all the reading the pupils did, but presumably they

[27] P. S. McCarty, "Reading Interests as Shown by Choices of Books in School Libraries," *School Review,* 58:90–96, 1950.

Table 43

TYPES OF BOOKS WITHDRAWN FROM LIBRARIES BY ADOLESCENTS
(Figures are in per cents, which total 100 for each grade.)

Boys and Grade						Types of book	Girls and Grade					
7	8	9	10	11	12		7	8	9	10	11	12
29	33	29	28	20	17	1. Adventure	12	10	11	8	6	4
23	20	24	25	34	36	2. Romances	47	51	53	54	58	57
14	13	13	10	5	3	3. Animal stories	11	9	6	4	2	2
6	6	8	8	9	7	4. Biographies	5	5	7	7	9	6
6	8	8	7	5	5	5. Sports	1	1	1	1	1	1
5	6	7	6	5	7	6. War stories	1	1	1	2	1	2
8	6	4	4	3	2	7. Detective stories	11	7	6	4	1	1
2	2	2	2	3	3	8. Science	1	2	1	2	1	1
1	1		2	5	7	9. Arts	1	1	1	3	7	12
1	1	1	1	2	2	10. History	1	1	1	1	2	1
1	1					11. Mythology (fairy tales)	1	1		1		1
	1	1	1	2	1	12. Humorous stories	1		1	1	1	1
	1	1	1	1	1	13. Occupations				1	1	1
4	2	2	5	6	9	14. Miscellaneous	2	3	4	6	7	8
						15. Career stories (about women)	5	8	7	5	3	2

Average per year: 8.7 books   Average per year: 10.5 books

From P. S. McCarty, "Reading Interests as Shown by Choices of Books in School Libraries," *School Review*, 58:93–94, 1950. Used by permission of The University of Chicago Press.

do show a fair cross section. Boys concentrated upon stories of adventure, romances, and tales of animals—in the earlier grades—while girls put romance first, with adventure stories, mysteries, and animal tales considerably lower. For both sexes interest in adventure and animal stories decreased with age, while that in romances increased. Boys tend to spread their interests over more kinds of reading than girls, who concentrate upon romance.

Another investigator found that adventure stories which told of physical hardships and dangers were far more popular among boys than girls, while those that did not stress the physically grim showed much less difference.[28] That is, girls did not object to adventure per se, but they preferred to be spared the details of suffering. Boys showed a differential interest also in stories about wild animals and sports of all kinds. Girls had an excessive liking for biographies of women, mysteries, stories of home life, love stories, and tales that were sentimental though not involving a love theme. They liked essays better than boys did but readings in science less. In all studies girls read more than boys did. At all ages, for both sexes, fiction was from two to three times as popular as nonfiction.[29]

Reading has great value for adolescents because of its possible contribution to their development. It can provide relief from tension, opportunity for working out aggressive drives harmlessly, information for the resolution of conflicts, and characters for easy identification.[30] Reading can also

[28] G. W. Norvell, *Reading Interests of Young People*, D. C. Heath & Company, 1950, pp. 52, 56–57.

[29] McCarty, "Reading Interests as Shown by Choices of Books in School Libraries," *loc. cit.*

[30] B. Berelson, "Communication and Youth," in Henne, Brooks, and Ersted, *op. cit.*, pp. 14–30.

result in security and self-realization for an adolescent's inner life, better interpersonal relations with his family and peers, changes in behavior, new ideas, and increased appreciation of many life activities.[31] The crucial problem would seem to lie in getting the right books to the right adolescents. The values of reading are there, but boys and girls need help in finding them. In recent years, books have been used as a constructive form of treatment with delinquents because of their value in providing new identifications, new ideologies, new satisfactions, and new patterns of living.[32]

Members of both sexes used several media for obtaining news about current events, as shown in Table 44. Their main source was the radio. As

Table 44

MEDIA USED FOR OBTAINING NEWS OF CURRENT EVENTS

Source	*Grades*		
	7–8	9–10	11–12
	(389 pupils)	(394 pupils)	(394 pupils)
1. Radio	66%	69%	78%
2. Newspapers	50	54	70
3. News reels	15	27	36
4. School	10	17	34
5. Family	14	21	22
6. Magazines	5	11	26
7. Friends	7	14	17

From A. P. Sterner, "Radio, Motion Picture, and Reading Interests of High School Pupils," *Teachers College Contributions to Education*, No. 932, 1947, p. 192. Used by permission of the Bureau of Publications of Teachers College, Columbia University.

the 1,177 pupils involved in the study progressed through the grades they listened more to current events on the radio, they read more newspapers, and they obtained more information from news reels. In fact, all the sources listed contributed somewhat more in the upper as compared with the lower years.

Most adolescent boys read magazines that deal with mechanics, sports, athletics, and G men, while girls of the same age tend to concentrate upon magazines that contain "true life" stories, material about women's arts, stories of movie stars, and adult fiction of a sentimental character. During high school, boys and girls read an average of four magazines regularly, three others often, and another six sometimes.[33] At all ages the girls incline more than boys to love stories, while the boys read more than girls about current events.[34] The most widely read magazines are *Life, Reader's Digest, Time,*

---

[31] A. R. Brooks, "Developmental Value of Books," *ibid.*, pp. 49–61.

[32] J. Paulson, "Psychotherapeutic Value of Books in Treatment and Prevention of Delinquency," *American Journal of Psychotherapy*, 1:71–86, 1947.

[33] Witty and Coomer, "Activities and Preferences of a Secondary School Group," *loc. cit.*

[34] See M. I. Kramer, "Children's Interests in Magazines and Newspapers," *Catholic Educational Review*, 39:284–290, 1941; and W. G. Brink, "High School Pupils' Interests in Magazines and Newspapers," *School Review*, 48:40–48, 1940.

Saturday Evening Post, and *Collier's.*[35] Since high school girls are far more avid readers than are boys of the same ages, the fiction magazines that rate high in frequency have largely feminine appeal: *Cosmopolitan, American, Ladies' Home Journal, Good Housekeeping,* and *McCall's.* In one study of eleventh-grade students, the girls read a total of thirty-seven different magazines; the boys read thirty-one.[36] Two in every five students of both sexes read *Life,* and two in every five girls read *Seventeen.* As adolescents grow older, they often pass through a period of reading the pulps.

At all ages, the children of the millionaire, the university professor, the merchant, the butcher, the bricklayer, the teamster, the miner, and the day laborer read the comics. Every time one goes to the corner drugstore at least one small urchin may be seen sitting on the floor in front of the magazine rack completely absorbed in *Superman* or *Joe Palooka.* Disapproval of parents and teachers has had practically no effect upon this type of reading. Books of comics are favorites among children, even among those who also read good literature. The real mania for reading comics comes usually during late childhood, from eight or nine to eleven or twelve years of age, and is commonly more severe among boys. However, about two thirds of all high school pupils still read comics,[37] and not all adults scorn them. The IQ of students in Grades 11 and 12 who read books of comics was found to be 94 and 88, respectively,[38] as compared with an average of 108–110 for all the students in these grades. This fact suggests that a continuance of devotion to Dick Tracy *et al.* is a reflection of intellectual immaturity.

Since the comics are here to stay and since almost all children and adolescents read them, it is desirable to evaluate their nature as objectively as possible.[39] Their vocabulary is relatively easy. Each book of comics contains about ten thousand words, of which nine thousand are among the commonest in the language. There is some slang, but such words do not exceed 5 per cent of the reading matter. The chief appeal of the comics to children rests upon their love of excitement, adventure, mystery, sport, and humor—but the comics act also as a wish fulfillment for all the things children would like to do or to be.[40] Some children have been most unfortunately affected by the comics, usually by being frightened, and there have been tragedies because children based their imitative play upon what they had

---

[35] From E. B. Bolton and M. English, "Further Studies of the Attitudes of High School Seniors toward Problems of War and Peace," *Journal of Psychology,* 20:157–182, 1945.

[36] A. Shatter, "Survey of Student Reading," *English Journal,* 40:271–273, 1951.

[37] *Ibid.*

[38] L. Bender and R. Lowrie, "The Effect of Comic Books on the Ideology of Children," *American Journal of Orthopsychiatry,* 11:540–550, 1941.

[39] See G. E. Hill, "The Vocabulary of Comic Strips," *Journal of Educational Psychology,* 34:77–87, 1943; R. Strang, "Why Children Read the Comics," *Elementary School Journal,* 43:336–342, 1943; P. A. Witty, "Children's Interests in the Comics," *Journal of Experimental Education,* 10:100–104, 1941.

[40] F. C. Kinneman, "The Comics and Their Appeal to Youth of Today," *English Journal,* 32:331–335, 1943, and L. Bender, "The Psychology of Children's Reading and the Comics," *Journal of Educational Sociology,* 18:223–231, 1944.

read in the funnies. Perhaps someone with a talent for writing children's stories and a facility in drawing will be inspired to augment the comparatively slight number of imaginative stories in cartoon form, depicting incidents that interest children but omitting the brutality, bad manners, slang phrases, and coarseness often prevalent in the commercial offerings.[41] Since the cartoon form of presentation cannot be eliminated, perhaps it can be used constructively, as it already has been in presenting dramatic incidents from the Bible.

High school pupils read newspapers regularly. Unfortunately, they tend to concentrate upon the tabloids,[42] presumably because of the emphasis upon "human interest" and the greater detail about various forms of human endeavor. They also read the syndicated columns, perhaps to appear sophisticated. Like adults, they do not read evenly the different parts of the paper. Results from a study are shown in Table 45, which includes figures concern-

Table 45

ADOLESCENT INTEREST IN DIFFERENT PARTS OF THE NEWSPAPER

Parts of Paper	Grades		
	7–8 (%)	9–10 (%)	11–12 (%)
1. Comics	74	87	93
2. Sports	46	61	76
3. Foreign news	47	63	71
4. Movie news	43	57	67
5. Pictures	31	39	58
6. Crime	30	35	40
7. Advertisements	16	26	39
8. Local politics	8	22	36
9. Editorials	7	20	37
10. National politics	7	17	29
11. Society news	6	16	30
12. Continued stories	11	13	14
13. Columnists	2	11	15
14. Book reviews	5	6	13

From Sterner, "Radio, Motion Picture, and Reading Interests of High School Pupils," *loc. cit.*, p. 205. Used by permission of the Bureau of Publications of Teachers College, Columbia University.

ing the changes in reading habits from the seventh through the twelfth grades. It is to be regretted that the editorials do not rate higher; perhaps they would be read more if they were put on the same page with either the comics or the sporting news!

There is little doubt that the radio and more recently television have reduced the amount of reading done by children and adolescents. Radio

[41] See F. Wertham, "The Comics—Very Funny," *Saturday Review of Literature,* May 29, 1948; G. L. McIntyre, "Not So Funny Funnies," *Progressive Education,* 22:28–30, 1945; and Frank, "Comics, Radio, Movies, and Children," *loc. cit.*

[42] Shatter, "Survey of Student Reading," *loc. cit.*

listening begins long before children can read, and many of them develop the "radio habit" by the time they are able to read easily and therefore do not read as much outside school as they otherwise might. In any case, if a child listens to the radio or watches television for two or three hours a day, he has no time for reading. In fact, with the aid of the movies, radio, and television a child can almost avoid the printed page altogether, except when he is in school.

VI. Summary

Children's interests grow, alter, and wane; as the extent of these changes is realized, study of interests is being used to supplement other kinds of measurement. Adolescents are doubtless influenced a good deal by their interest in radio and motion pictures, and by their selection of reading matter. Many of these interests could obviously become the bases for lifelong hobbies; others could develop into occupations; some could furnish highly approved means for self-expression. If a school is wise, it encourages as many interests as possible and then guides them so that they may lead the adolescent into a happier and better-adjusted life.

REFERENCES FOR FURTHER READING

BOOKS

1. Dale, E., *Children's Attendance at Motion Pictures,* The Macmillan Company, 1935, 79 pp.
2. Dimock, *Rediscovering the Adolescent,* Chap. 2.
3. Fleege, *Self-Revelation of the Adolescent Boy,* Chaps. 13, 14.
4. Garrison, *Growth and Development,* Chap. 13.
5. Garrison, *Psychology of Adolescence,* Chap. 7.
6. Hartley, R. E., L. K. Frank, and R. M. Goldenson, *Understanding Children's Play,* Columbia University Press, 1952, 372 pp. (Chaps. 1–3.)
7. Henne, F., A. Brooks, and R. Ersted (eds.), *Youth Communication, and Libraries,* American Library Association, 1949, 233 pp. (Pp. 3–13, 31–49, 49–61, 69–77, 107–120, 134–146.)
8. Hurlock, *Adolescent Development,* Chaps. 8, 9.
9. Jackson, L., and K. M. Todd, *Child Treatment and the Therapy of Play,* The Ronald Press, 2d ed., 1950, 159 pp. (Chaps. 1, 5, 8.)
10. Jersild, A. T., and R. J. Tasch, *Children's Interests,* Bureau of Publications of Teachers College, Columbia University, 1950, 173 pp. (Chaps. 6, 10, 11.)
11. Jones, *Development in Adolescence,* Chap. 7.
12. Kuhlen, *The Psychology of Adolescent Development,* Chap. 5.
13. McGill, N. P., and E. N. Matthews, *The Youth of New York City,* The Macmillan Company, 1940, 420 pp. (Chaps. 11, 12.)
14. Merry and Merry, *The First Two Decades of Life,* Chap. 13.
15. Mitchell, E. D., and B. S. Mason, *The Theory of Play,* A. S. Barnes Company, rev. ed., 1948, 542 pp. (Chaps. 7, 10.)
16. Norvell, G. W., *Reading Interests of Young People,* D. C. Heath & Company, 1950, 262 pp. (Chaps. 3, 5–8.)
17. Sadler, *Adolescence Problems,* Chap. 3.

MONOGRAPHS, BULLETINS, PROCEEDINGS, YEARBOOKS, ARTICLES

A. *Play and Leisure Activities*

1. Erickson, E. H., "Sex Differences in the Play Configuration of Preadolescents," *American Journal of Orthopsychiatry,* 21:667–692, 1951.
2. McDonald, M., C. McGuire, and R. J. Havighurst, "Leisure Activities and the Sociometric Status of Children," *American Journal of Sociology,* 54:505–519, 1949.
3. Olds, E. B., "How Do Young People Use Their Leisure Time?" *Recreation,* 42:458–463, 1949.
4. Stewart, M., "The Leisure Activities of Grammar School Children." *British Journal of Educational Psychology,* 20:11–39, 1950.
5. Van Dalen, D. B., "Differential Analysis of the Play of Adolescent Boys," *Journal of Educational Research,* 41:204–213, 1947.
6. Volberding, E., "Out-of-School Behavior of Eleven-Year-Olds," *Elementary School Journal,* 48:432–441, 1948.
7. Witty, P., and A. Coomer, "Activities and Preferences of a Secondary School Group," *Journal of Educational Psychology,* 34:65–76, 1943.
8. Woody, G., "Similarities and Differences in the Play Activities of Children in Five Public Schools and Contrasting Environments," *Journal of Experimental Psychology,* 7:145–157, 1938.

B. *Reading Interests*

1. Bolton, E. B., and M. English, "Further Studies, of the Attitudes of High School Seniors toward Problems of War and Peace," *Journal of Psychology,* 20:157–182, 1945.
2. Brink, W. G., "High School Pupils' Interests in Magazines and Newspapers," *School Review,* 48:40–48, 1940.
3. Conant, J. V., and A. V. Davies, "A Measurement of the Number and Density of Periodicals in 92 American Cities," *Sociometry,* 11:117–120, 1948.
4. Feingold, G. A., "New Tastes of High School Students," *School and Society,* 59:316–319, 1944.
5. Johnson, J. B., "Books and the Five Adolescent Tasks," *Library Journal,* 68:35–53, 1943.
6. Kramer, M. I., "Children's Interests in Magazines and Newspapers," *Catholic Educational Review,* 39:284–290, 1941.
7. McCarty, P. S., "Reading Interests as Shown by Choices of Books in School Libraries," *School Review,* 58:90–96, 1950.
8. "Reading in High School and College," *Forty-seventh Yearbook of the National Society for the Study of Education,* 1948, Pt. II.
9. Shatter, A., "Survey of Student Reading," *English Journal,* 40:271–273, 1951.

C. *Interests in Movies*

1. Edman, M., "Attendance of School Pupils and Adults at Moving Pictures," *School Review,* 48:753–763, 1940.
2. Fearing, F., "The Effect of Radio and Motion Pictures on Children's Behavior," *Yearbook of the National Probation and Parole Association,* 1947, pp. 78–92.
3. Heisler, F., "Comparison of the Movie and Non-Movie Goers of the Elementary School," *Journal of Educational Research,* 41:541–546, 1948, and 42:182–190, 1948.
4. Jones, H. E., "Motion Pictures and Radio as Factors in Child Behavior," *Yearbook of the National Probation and Parole Association,* 1947, pp. 66–77.

5. Lazarsfeld, P., "Audience Research in the Movie Field," *Annals of the American Academy of Political and Social Science,* 254:160–168, 1947.
6. Wall, W. D., and E. M. Smith, "Effects of Cinema Attendance on the Behavior of Adolescents as Seen by Their Contemporaries," *British Journal of Educational Psychology,* 19:53–61, 1949.
7. Wall, W. D., and E. M. Smith, "Film Choices of Adolescents," *British Journal of Educational Psychology,* 19:121–136, 1949.
8. Weise, M. J., and S. G. Cole, "A Study of Children's Attitudes and the Influence of a Commercial Motion Picture," *Journal of Psychology,* 21:151–171, 1946.

D. *Interest in Comics*

1. Bender, L., and R. Lowrie, "The Effect of Comic Books on the Ideology of Children," *American Journal of Orthopsychiatry,* 11:540–550, 1941.
2. Frank, F., "Comics, Radio, Movies, and Children," *Public Affairs Pamphlets,* No. 148, 1949, 32 pp.
3. Hill, G. E., "The Vocabulary of Comic Strips," *Journal of Educational Psychology,* 34:77–87, 1943.
4. Kinneman, F. C., "The Comics and Their Appeal to Youth of Today," *English Journal,* 32:331–335, 1943.
5. "Reading the Comics: A Comparative Study," *Journal of Experimental Education,* 10:105–109, 1941.
6. Strang, R., "Why Children Read the Comics," *Elementary School Journal,* 43:336–342, 1943.
7. Witty, P. A., "Children's Interests in the Comics," *Journal of Experimental Education,* 10:100–104, 1941.

E. *Interest in Radio and Television*

1. Anon., "One High School Surveys Television's Effect on Pupils," *School and College Management,* 20:21–22, 1950.
2. Chapman, A. L., "College-Level Students and Radio Listening," *University of Texas Publications,* No. 5,016, 1950, 74 pp.
3. Clark, W. R., "Radio Listening Habits of Children," *Journal of Social Psychology,* 12:131–149, 1940.
4. De Boer, J. J., "Radio and Children's Emotions," *School and Society,* 50:369–373, 1939.
5. Frank, J., "Chills and Thrills in Radio, Movies, and Comics: A Psychiatric Opinion," *Childhood Education Monographs,* Vol. XXV, No. 2, 1948, 42 pp.
6. Gaudet, H., "High School Students Judge Radio Programs," *Education,* 60:639–646, 1940.
7. Gruber, F. C., "Out-of-School Radio Listening Habits of High School Students," *English Journal,* 39:325–327, 1950.
8. Harmon, M., "Television and the Leisure Time Activities of Children," *Education,* 71:126–128, 1950.
9. Preston, M. I., "Children's Reactions to Movie Horror and Radio Crime," *Journal of Pediatrics,* 19:147–168, 1941.
10. Sterner, A. P., "Radio, Motion Pictures, and Reading Interests of High School Pupils," *Teachers College Contributions to Education,* No. 932, 1947, 102 pp.
11. Witty, P. A., "Children's, Parents', and Teachers' Reactions to Television," *Elementary English Review,* 27:344–355, 1950.
12. Witty, P. A., *et al.,* "Interests of High School Students in Motion Pictures and the Radio," *Journal of Educational Psychology,* 32:176–185, 1941.

CHAPTER SEVENTEEN

Intellectual
Deviates

One of the most significant outcomes of the testing movement is the objective proof that children differ from each other in almost every intellectual trait. The total range of IQ's thus far determined varies from 15 to nearly 200[1]—that is, from an idiot whose capacity was only 15 per cent of what is normal for his age to a brilliant child with twice the average intellectual endowment. This entire range of IQ's forms an unbroken series from the lowest to the highest, but for purposes of convenience it is generally divided into a number of levels. It is usually assumed that those children with an IQ between 85 and 115 are of normal ability for their age; this group makes up about 65 per cent of the general population; approximately 30 per cent of children have mental ability that ranks them as slightly superior or slightly inferior—that is, as "bright" or "dull." The IQ's of the bright group run from 115 to 130 and those for the dull pupils from 70 to 85. The "dull" group, about 15 per cent of the school population, contains those children who learn slowly the basic facts of the elementary school curriculum, who generally lose at least one year in getting through elementary school, and who have great difficulty with high school if they attempt it. The "bright" group, again about 15 per cent of the school population, includes those who learn a little faster than the average and are a little more mentally alert. They usually complete their schoolwork in about a year less than the average pupil. While their work is uniformly good, it is only occasionally of outstanding merit. About 2.5 per cent of the school population is so superior in ability as to be termed "brilliant" (IQ above 130), while another 2.5 per cent is so inferior as to be termed "defective" (IQ below 70). With members of this latter group, the junior high school teacher has sometimes to deal but the high school teacher practically never, because the real mental defectives do not get beyond the elementary grades. The "brilliant" pupils, however, generally continue through high school.

The intellectual deviates in any school population are those who score in the extremes of the intelligence distribution for the school. Since the distribution changes as pupils proceed through the grades, the same children

---

[1] See, for instance, S. Goldberg, "Study of I., IQ 196," *Journal of Applied Psychology,* 18:550–560, 1934; and L. S. Hollingworth, "Growing up with Gifted Children," *Understanding the Child,* 17:45–49, 1948.

are not deviates at all levels. In high school the pupils in the "brilliant" group have IQ's from about 140 up to 190. At the other end of the distribution, the pupils in the "dull" group have IQ's that range from 95 downward. The differences between these approximate limits and those just given for the general school population are due to the elimination that has taken place during the first eight years of school. Because the lowest IQ's have already been weeded out, the extremes of the remaining distribution fall in a different place. The line of demarcation between these small, extreme groups and the rest of the high school population cannot, of course, be drawn in a hard-and-fast manner, and the limits suggested above are only approximate. The main thing to remember is that even these relative limits shift from one level of education to another, in terms of each fresh distribution.[2]

The remaining sections of the chapter will discuss the highest and the lowest groups at the high school level. What is said about them applies in reduced measure to those who are classified as a little above or a little below the average for their grade or age.

I. The Brilliant Adolescent

1. **Characteristics:** Brilliancy is not merely a state of mind. A brilliant individual is usually superior in all respects to those of less ability. The brilliant child is on the average slightly tall and heavy for his age; he grows faster than the average and matures earlier.[3] One group of fifty gifted children showed physical development as indicated in Table 46. This physical superiority is often obscured because brilliant children may be so accelerated in school that they are placed in grades with others from two to five years older than themselves. In comparison with these older pupils they almost always appear small. Hence the popular idea that intellectual superiority is associated with physical inferiority.

Superiority in size continues into adult life. In Terman's study of one thousand brilliant boys and girls, whom he has now followed for twenty-five years, the men averaged five feet eleven inches as compared with the national average of five feet seven and a half inches and the general average for college men of five feet eight and a half inches.[4] Twenty-eight per cent were six feet tall or over; not even the California sunshine can be held entirely responsible, since it did not shine exclusively upon them. The young

---

[2] For instance, the failing graduate student is typically a person who is well above the average of the general population in intelligence, but he is definitely inferior to the highest 5 per cent in verbal intelligence, from whom most graduate students are drawn. There is always a bottom to a distribution, no matter where it is cut off.

[3] See C. C. Miles, "Gifted Children," in L. Carmichael, *Manual of Child Psychology,* John Wiley & Sons, Inc., 1946, pp. 886–963; L. M. Terman, "Mental and Physical Traits of 1000 Gifted Children," in R. G. Barker, J. S. Kounin, and H. F. Wright, *Child Behavior and Development,* McGraw-Hill Book Company, 1932, pp. 279–306; and P. A. Witty, "A Genetic Study of Fifty Gifted Children," *Thirty-ninth Yearbook of the National Society for the Study of Education,* 1940, Pt. II, pp. 401–408.

[4] L. M. Terman and M. H. Oden, *The Gifted Child Grows Up,* Stanford University Press, 1947, p. 94.

Table 46

PHYSICAL GROWTH OF SUPERIOR CHILDREN

		Boys (%)	Girls (%)
Height	Above normal	62	56
	Normal	22	30
	Below normal	16	14
Weight	Above normal	61	70
	Normal	20	15
	Below normal	19	15
Health	Good	80	80
	Fair	17	8
	Poor	3	4

From P. A. Witty, "A Genetic Study of Fifty Gifted Children," *Thirty-ninth Yearbook of the National Society for the Study of Education*, 1940, Pt. II, pp. 403–404. Used by permission of the Public School Publishing Company.

women averaged five feet five and a half inches as against parallel averages of five feet three and a half inches and five feet four inches. At the time of the last investigation (1946), when the brilliant children of the 1920's had become men and women over thirty, the robust health they had shown in childhood was still with them; only 2 per cent of the men and 4 per cent of the women reported ill-health, and the death rate among them was approximately one third that of the general population.[5] Evidence from two other sources supports the above facts: The men who made the highest scores on the Army intelligence tests were taller and heavier than those who made low scores,[6] and winners in a national search for talent were heavier and taller than the average for their ages.[7]

Intellectually, the brilliant pupil stands out clearly and has done so from early childhood. He learns with unusual rapidity and retains what he learns. Usually he concentrates without effort and spontaneously uses economical methods of study. An outstanding mental characteristic is his ability to see relationships, to generalize, to distinguish the essential from the nonessential, and to see through facts to their logical conclusions. For the brilliant pupil ideas have a real fascination. He is vitally interested in both facts and theories. He wants to learn. From his earliest years he shows a liking for playing with ideas and for rearranging them in new combinations. This sort of mental exercise develops by the years of adolescence into real originality and resourcefulness. Indeed, the essence of brilliancy is probably a combination of the ability to make generalizations and this spontaneous originality in handling ideas. The merely bright child with a

[5] *Ibid.*, p. 79.
[6] W. D. Altus, "The Height and Weight of Soldiers as Associated with Scores on the Army General Classification Tests," *Journal of Social Psychology*, 29:201–210, 1949.
[7] H. A. Edgerton, S. H. Britt, and R. D. Norman, "Physical Differences between Ranking and Nonranking Contestants in the First Annual Science Talent Search," *American Journal of Physical Anthropology*, 5:435–452, 1949.

splendid memory and a quick reaction time has neither of these qualities in larger measure than the average person.

A comparison of bright and brilliant college students shows the two groups to be differentiated in quite recognizable fashion. The superior student shows his superiority in the ways indicated in Table 47.

Table 47

TRAITS OF THE INTELLECTUALLY MATURE PERSON

Trait	Number of Times Mentioned
1. Forms rational judgments uncolored by emotional tones	32
2. Can perceive relationships and correlate materials	19
3. Has a critical, evaluating attitude toward problems	19
4. Is independent	16
5. Has a wide background of information	15
6. Shows intellectual initiative	12
7. Is able to apply knowledge	11
8. Keeps an open mind	10
9. Assimilates new facts with the old	9
10. Has a good sense of values	7
11. Can separate the important from the unimportant	7
12. Shows tolerance toward those who differ in their opinions	6

From R. E. Eckert, "Intellectual Maturity," *Journal of Higher Education,* 5:478–484, 1934. Used by permission of the Journal.

The merely bright child learns a little faster and retains what he learns a little better than the average pupil, but he does not show to a marked degree the traits listed above.

Mental superiority, as measured by the Stanford-Binet Test at least, is permanent, although it does not seem to remain as high in later years as it was during childhood. Thus, Terman's 1,000 gifted children, twenty years after their original selection, were not as uniformly superior as they had been earlier,[8] but they still tested in the upper half of the general population. They were originally in the highest one percentile of their age group. As young adults their median was at the ninety-sixth percentile of the general population, and their tenth percentile was above the seventy-fifth for the normal distribution; that is, 90 per cent of them scored in the highest quarter. All but 2 of the 961 tested made scores above the general median. The results appear in Figure 141 on page 573. These adults were therefore still a markedly superior group, but they did not show the uniform superiority that had characterized them earlier. It is probable that a few of them were wrongly classified in the first place, since no test is infallible, and that they were bright but not brilliant children. It may also be that for a few members of the group the mental superiority was only transient. Others may have failed to receive in later years the amount and type of stimulation

---

[8] R. L. Thorndike, "An Evaluation of the Adult Intellectual Status of Terman's Gifted Children," *Journal of Genetic Psychology,* 72:17–27, 1948.

that would cause them to use their gifts and have therefore failed to develop in proportion to their original endowment. A few have doubtless actually deteriorated. In general, however, one can say that they are fulfilling the promise of their youth.

The brilliant student is an academic success. He is commonly accelerated one or two years and sometimes more. His school marks are high, especially in subjects demanding judgment, generalizing, and logical thinking. If a child of superior ability fails to do good schoolwork there is some-

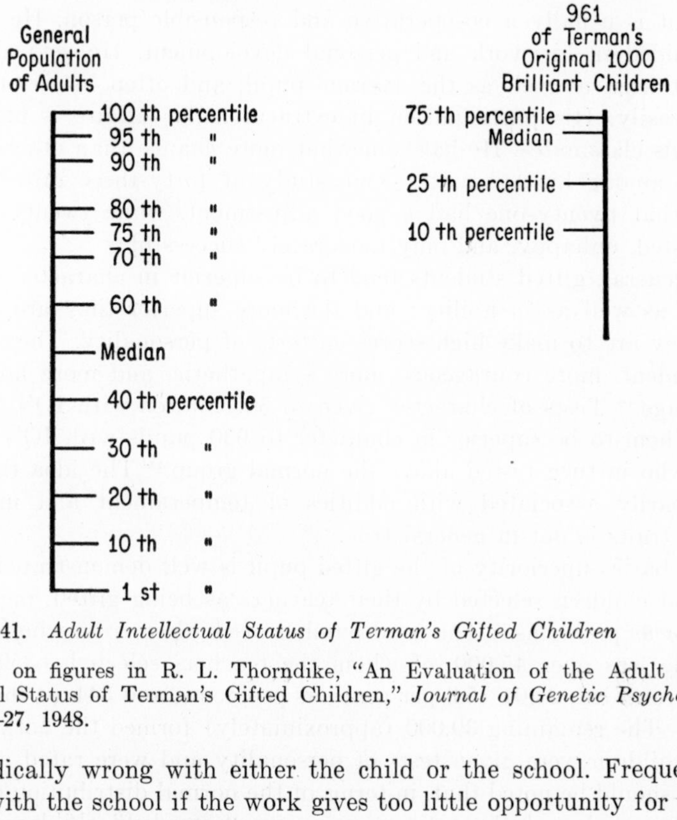

Fig. 141. *Adult Intellectual Status of Terman's Gifted Children*

Based on figures in R. L. Thorndike, "An Evaluation of the Adult Intellectual Status of Terman's Gifted Children," *Journal of Genetic Psychology,* 72:17–27, 1948.

thing radically wrong with either the child or the school. Frequently the fault is with the school if the work gives too little opportunity for the exercise of independent thinking and if teachers fail to recognize brilliancy. Because of the lack of challenge in most elementary school subjects, some brilliant children do not show their real ability until after they get into high school or even college and get their first taste of a type of teaching that requires them to think for themselves rather than to memorize what someone else has thought. Some brilliant pupils in high school are still unawakened from mere lack of intellectual stimulation, others work below their capacity because they are being forced into lines of work that are distasteful, and a few do so many things at once that nothing gets done well. Academic histories, while usually above average, are sometimes below the level that could have been reached. Society cannot afford to let superior students become mediocrities. There are altogether too few superior individuals born; none of them can be wasted.

Socially, the brilliant adolescent is—like everyone else—what his environment has made him. If he has been treated as a prodigy and has been a center of interest, he may have an unpleasant personality. If he has been allowed to concentrate upon academic work to the exclusion of social activities he may be markedly introverted. If he has had excessive parental protection because of his intellectual success, he may be spoiled and babyish. Unless environmental factors have been unfavorable, however, the brilliant adolescent is usually a co-operative and responsible person. He is willing to be guided in his work and personal development. He gets along with others at least as well as the average pupil, and often better. He makes friends easily. His participation in extracurricular affairs is higher than that of his classmates. He has somewhat more chance than others of being a leader among his age-mates. One study of forty-three gifted children showed that twenty-one had a good adjustment, while twenty-two were maladjusted, unhappy, and only moderately successful.[9]

In general, gifted students tend to be superior in character traits and interests as well as in ability; and the more superior they are, the more likely they are to make high scores on tests of personality. They are more self-confident, more courageous, more sympathetic, and more honest than the average.[10] Tests of character given to 50 children with IQ's above 145 showed them to be superior in character to 930 pupils with IQ's from 125 to 144, who in turn tested above the normal group.[11] The idea that genius is necessarily associated with oddities of temperament and undesirable personal traits is not in general true.

The basic superiority of the gifted pupil is well demonstrated by comparison of children selected by their teachers as being gifted, mentally retarded, or as problems.[12] The total number of children from whom selection was made was over 45,000, of whom the teachers selected 3,359 (7.4 per cent) as retarded, 2,401 (5.3 per cent) as problems, and 341 (0.76 per cent) as gifted. The remaining 39,000 (approximately) formed the normal group. All the children were given tests of personality and were rated on various traits. It should be noted that, in terms of the normal distribution of ability, the teachers selected three times as many "retarded" children and less than a third as many gifted children as would have been expected.[13] In the former group there must have been many who were "problems" and failed

---

[9] D. A. Thom and N. Newell, "Hazards of the High IQ," *Mental Hygiene*, 29:61–77, 1945.

[10] G. Lightfoot, *Characteristics of Bright and Dull Children,* Bureau of Publications of Teachers College, Columbia University, 1951, 136 pp.

[11] W. D. Lewis, "Some Characteristics of Very Superior Children," *Journal of Genetic Psychology*, 62:301–309, 1943.

[12] W. D. Lewis, "Some Characteristics of Children Designated as Mentally Retarded, as Problems, or as Geniuses by Teachers," *Journal of Genetic Psychology,* 70:29–51, 1947.

[13] See pp. 569–570.

to learn for other reasons than mental inadequacy; or else the curriculum was so difficult and the standards were so high that a disproportionate number of pupils were unable to meet the requirements. The children selected as gifted were undoubtedly very superior indeed, but many others with IQ's over 130 must have been regarded as only average. Assuming that the population contained the usual 2.5 per cent of brilliant children, the teachers recognized only one in four of them. The problem children were probably in the main those of the destructive-delinquent type who make trouble, the quiet problems being classed as defectives. Despite the presumed inaccu-

Table 48

CHARACTERISTIC TRAITS OF NORMAL, BRILLIANT, RETARDED, AND PROBLEM CHILDREN

Trait	Sex	Normal Pupils (%)	Brilliant Pupils (%)	Retarded Pupils (%)	Problem Pupils (%)
1. Dependability	Boys	31	61	11	6
	Girls	42	73	16	10
2. Friendliness	Boys	35	47	14	12
	Girls	36	59	12	12
3. Honesty	Boys	33	43	18	11
	Girls	37	51	22	13
4. Originality	Boys	10	46	1	5
	Girls	11	48	1	4
5. Self-reliance	Boys	8	21	1	3
	Girls	10	21	1	2
6. Ambition	Boys	22	66	5	6
	Girls	34	76	5	10
7. Happiness	Boys	38	50	23	17
	Girls	43	54	25	17

Based on W. D. Lewis, "Some Characteristics of Children Designated as Mentally Retarded, as Problems, or as Geniuses by Teachers," *Journal of Genetic Psychology*, 70:29–51, 1947.

racies of selection, which are understandable from a teacher's point of view, the comparisons of the groups are of interest, especially as showing the superiority of emotional and social adjustment on the part of the brilliant pupils. A few of the comparisons appear in Table 48, which gives the per cent of each group of pupils showing each character trait. The brilliant pupils were superior in every one. There is no suggestion that these outstandingly able pupils were queer or maladjusted. The dull children scored above the problem pupils in most of the traits reported.

When Terman's gifted children were in elementary and high school, they showed much the same range of social adjustment as other children of their age, but their average was higher and fewer of them suffered from extreme maladjustment. That is, they were a mentally healthy group when first identified. In 1940, 80 per cent of the young men and 82 per cent of the young women were still in good mental health, while 16 and 14 per cent, respectively, had some slight, but not serious, unsolved problems, and 4 per cent from each sex were seriously maladjusted. In 1947, the parallel figures for this group were 78 and 80 per cent, 17 and 15 per cent, and 5 per cent.[14]

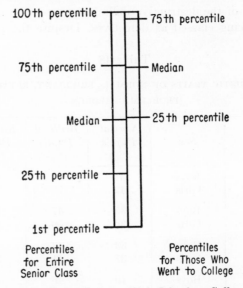

Fig. 142. *Continuance of Pupils from High School to College*

Based on L. T. Phearman, "Comparison of High School Graduates Who Go to College and Those Who Do Not," *Journal of Educational Psychology,* 40:405–414, 1949.

The actual numbers of insane people among the living men and women who could be located were 11 in 1940 and 18 in 1945—or 0.8 per cent and 1.3 per cent. The former figure is below the national average for the general population and the latter is just equal to expectation. In other words, insanity is no more common among the brilliant than among the nonbrilliant, and is actually far below the rates for dull people and defectives. Another evidence of their social acceptability is their marriage rate.[15] Whereas the general rate for persons of their age in 1946 was 67 per cent for men and 78 for women, the marriage rates for the brilliant students of both sexes were 84 per cent.

Gifted students go on to college and graduate work in greater proportion than any other group, presumably because the intellectual life of college or university is precisely what they want. For instance, in one city, 29 per cent of 2,616 recent high school graduates entered college.[16] The distribution

---

[14] Terman and Oden, *op. cit.,* p. 105.

[15] *Ibid.,* p. 225.

[16] L. T. Phearman, "Comparison of High School Graduates Who Go to College and Those Who Do Not," *Journal of Educational Psychology,* 40:405–414, 1949.

of their intelligence test scores, as compared with those graduates who did not go on to college, is shown in Figure 142. The median for the college-going group was at the seventy-fourth percentile of the group not college-bound. Of the 16 boys and girls who scored in the highest 2 per cent, 14 continued with their education. Terman's gifted pupils also showed a marked tendency to stay in school.[17] Ninety-three per cent of the boys entered college or an advanced technical school and 70 per cent graduated; 88 per cent of the girls continued beyond high school, and 67 per cent graduated. In the entire group there are 195 M.A.'s, 73 Ph.D.'s, 82 law degrees, 54 medical degrees, 21 in business administration, 16 in engineering, and 6 in theology.

2. Treatment: There are basically three adjustments that can be made to the presence of superior pupils in a school population: (1) they can be left where they are and allowed to proceed with their classmates without any change of curriculum, (2) they can be accelerated at the rate of a half grade or a grade each year until they get into a class where the work is a challenge to their minds, or (3) they can be "kept back" with their age-mates and given a greatly enriched curriculum, which may consist either of the same sort of thing studied by the others only more of it, or of new subject matter that they alone pursue. If either the first or the third method is selected, the brilliant child may remain in the same room as his age-mates, or he may be placed in a special room with other brilliant children. All these possible procedures have their advantages; what the proponents of each do not always realize is that all of them also have their disadvantages. The typical arguments are summarized in Table 49. The basic contrast is between academic adjustment and personal adjustment. The reader of articles on the matter of how brilliant children should be taught is likely to emerge with the conviction that the gifted can develop their minds only at the expense of their personalities, or vice versa, but that one or the other has to be at least partially sacrificed. The writer is not in agreement with this conclusion. There seems to be plenty of evidence that acceleration has a beneficial effect upon schoolwork and some evidence that it does not interfere with personal adjustment. Thus, in two recent studies of accelerated college students, the accelerated did better work than those of average age, more of them graduated, and more of them participated in student activities.[18] One cannot see that their acceleration did them any harm. In a most interesting follow-up of Amherst graduates between the years 1880 and 1900, the better adult achievements were found among the youngest graduates and the highest percentage of failures among those who graduated after they were twenty-five.[19] Table 50 tells the story. It is sug-

---

[17] Terman and Oden, *op. cit.,* pp. 149–150.

[18] O. C. England, "Comparing University Achievement of Students Having Eleven Year and Twelve Year Elementary–Secondary School Preparation," *Stanford University Abstracts of Dissertations,* 1948, pp. 246–253, and W. H. Harless, "A Study of Accelerated College Students," *Stanford University Abstracts of Dissertations,* 1948, pp. 26–32.

[19] S. L. Pressey, "Age of College Graduation and Success in Adult Life," *Journal of Applied Psychology,* 30:226–233, 1946.

Table 49

METHODS OF DEALING WITH SUPERIOR CHILDREN

Method	Advantages	Disadvantages
(1) Leaving child in regular room: (a) Same curriculum as for other children.	Child remains with his age-mates. Competes in games with those smaller than himself.	Child wastes his time, becomes bored, learns to loaf, often becomes a problem from idleness, does not acquire love of learning.
(b) Enriched curriculum: more of same subjects.	Same as above.	Child finds work somewhat more interesting, but much of what he learns is still too easy.
(c) Enriched curriculum: new subjects.	Same as above. Subjects are more likely to be challenging and to follow child's interests.	Child is aware that he gets special treatment. Administration is difficult for teacher.
(2) Putting child in special class with other brilliant children: (a) Enrichment but no acceleration.	Child learns more and competes with his peers. He also learns to work efficiently. He usually loves school. He gets better teaching.	Child is separated from his out-of-school friends. He may become conceited. His class group is probably of several chronological ages.
(b) Enrichment plus acceleration.	Same as for (a).	Same as for (a) but more so. Child may become quite isolated. New interests also erect a barrier. He gets little training in democracy or in adjusting to his mental inferiors.
(3) Accelerating child by either special class or double promotions, into a room with pupils from 2 to 3 years older than he.	Same as for 2(a) and 2(b) Years of productiveness increased.	Child cannot compete socially or in games with children who are more mature and bigger. He is likely to become a social outcast and to overconcentrate on books.
For high schools (4) Allowing elastic schedules that permit student to take as much as he can pass.	Pupil is interested in his work, he has enough to keep him busy, he is laying the foundation for college work.	Pupil may be overtrained or may take so much work that he has no time for social activities.

Based upon Education Policies Commission, *Education of the Gifted Child*, National Educational Association, 1950, 88 pp.

gested (a) that the older—not the younger—students were maladjusted to college work and college life and that they carried this handicap into the adult years, and (b) that their deferred graduation took too large a slice out of their most vigorous years, with a resulting failure to get really started upon a career before the waning of vitality overtook them. Before passing

Table 50

AGE IN COLLEGE AND SUBSEQUENT SUCCESS

Age at graduation	19	20	21	22	23	24	25	26	Over 26
(1) Per cent nationally known	29	22	15	12	10	3	2	3	—
(2) Per cent failures	4	6	6	5	2	3	6	11	15

From S. L. Pressey, "Age of College Graduation and Success in Adult Life," *Journal of Applied Psychology*, 30:228, 1946.

final judgment upon this vindication of acceleration, one would want to know what had become of the 67 per cent of nineteen-year-old graduates and the 72 per cent of twenty-year-old graduates who did not become nationally known and were not failures. If they are living lives that are just as normal as those of twenty-one-, twenty-two-, or twenty-three-year-old graduates, one has to grant the advantages of acceleration.

Those who favor enrichment have been alarmed by the indirect effects of too much acceleration. When superior children are allowed to move rapidly through the grades they lose the normal, close, daily contact with their age-mates and enter a group of children who are so big that the young accelerates cannot play with them and so mature in their interests that they cannot fit into their social groupings in or out of class.[20] With the coming of puberty the differences between the young brilliant child and his older classmates are exaggerated. Even though superior children mature earlier than children of average ability, their acceleration in school may be so great as to offset their maturity. Some of them enter high school before puberty. Consequently, the discrepancy in emotional reactions and social interests is brought into high relief. They do not fit readily into extracurricular activities at the high school level. They cannot get excited about dances and parties, they have little interest in members of the opposite sex, and they are not big enough to be successful in athletic competition. Their non-academic problems are therefore likely to be acute.

From a study[21] of fifty-seven students who were so far accelerated as to enter college at sixteen years of age, several important points emerged. These fifty-seven were matched with the same number of students two years older than they but having the same average high school grade, the same average on the Regents' examinations, and the same intelligence score on

[20] R. K. Boardman and G. Hildreth, "Adjustment Problems of the Gifted," *Understanding the Child*, 17:41–44, 1948.
[21] M. E. Sarbaugh, "The Young College Student," *University of Buffalo Studies in Administration*, 9:75–84, 1934.

their college intelligence test. In academic work the averages for the two groups were practically identical; in other words, these young brilliant students did just as good academic work, but no better. The proportion of students in the two groups receiving distinction at the end of their college course was also identical. The differences come in the field of personal adjustment. While less than 3 per cent of these unusually young students reported a feeling of intellectual inferiority, 32 per cent of them reported a feeling of social handicap in college; 46 per cent already had had a similar sense of social inferiority in high school. Since some of those who had earlier felt social handicaps had undoubtedly forgotten them and others were unwilling to admit them, it is safe to guess that over half of these young and brilliant college students were handicapped in their social relations during their high school years.

It is the writer's opinion that since the brilliant child is large and mature for his age, he may be somewhat accelerated without serious harm. The degree to which extra promotions are desirable depends upon the nonintellectual characteristics of each individual child. Some superior children are so babyish in their behavior that they become the butt of jokes if they are advanced into a grade with older and bigger children; others are so mature that they take their place more naturally with slightly older children than with those of their own age. The best solution lies in the individual approach.

Thus, in 1943, thirty-six high school students were allowed to enter the University of Illinois one or two semesters before they had finished high school.[22] These students were selected as being in the upper quarter academically of their classes, as having good recommendations from several teachers, as scoring above the seventy-fifth percentile in intelligence, and as showing satisfactory social and emotional maturity during interviews with a clinical psychologist. The group as a whole made higher than average freshman grades, no one in it showed signs of overstrain, and the personal adjustment of its members was satisfactory and normal. Such studies suggest that acceleration is safe if it is applied to the right students in the right way.

If any permanent damage had been done by acceleration, it ought to appear in the Terman follow-up studies. In their school days, over 4 per cent of these children were accelerated from three to four and a half years; 24 per cent were accelerated from two to two and a half years; 50 per cent were accelerated from one to one and a half years; and 12 per cent, one semester.[23] All but 10 per cent finished high school before they were eighteen. Ninety per cent were, therefore, accelerated more or less. It is a little hard to estimate the adult success of thirty to thirty-five-year-old women, because most of them are occupied with young children and housework, but the brilliant boys have made a more than satisfactory adult record, as indicated in Table 51. Since the harm supposedly done by acceleration does not show in their occupational level, their mental health, or in their divorce rate

---

[22] I. A. Berg and R. P. Larsen, "A Comparative Study of Students Entering College One or More Semesters before Graduation from High School," *Journal of Educational Research*, 39:33–41, 1945.

[23] Terman and Oden, *op. cit.*, p. 265.

Table 51

OCCUPATIONS OF TERMAN'S GIFTED CHILDREN AS YOUNG ADULTS

Type of Occupation	Men from Terman Study %	Employed Men in California %
Professions	45	6
Semiprofessions and Business Administration	26	8
Skilled clerical work or retail business	21	24
Farming	1	12
Semiskilled work	6	32
Unskilled work	1	18
Total	100	100

From L. M. Terman and M. H. Oden, *The Gifted Child Grows Up*, Stanford University Press, 1947, p. 172. Used by permission of the publishers.

(which is about one fifth of the average for the country), one wonders if the danger has not been exaggerated.

An improved course of study for superior students would, first of all, lead to a real mastery of the tools of learning. The brilliant adolescent should acquire at least one modern language and preferably two; he should read until he has made a start upon getting acquainted with his heritage of culture; he should develop a large general vocabulary and the beginning of several technical vocabularies; he should obtain a mastery of elementary facts in biological and nonbiological science; he should reduce elementary algebra to a technique he can use; he should know the outstanding facts in the history of the world and have some grasp of social and economic developments; he should be able to express himself correctly and easily in writing. These are the tools of the brilliant mind; without them, thinking on the higher levels cannot be done. The ordinary high school course fails to provide the superior student with those essentials which must act as a basis for his future development if he is to take the place in social evolution reserved for the talented. A fine social adjustment and agreeable personality will not atone for the lack of these elements of thought essential to the academic levels beyond high school.

3. Teaching: The successful handling of superior minds in secondary school and college consists of four basic steps, the first of which is to provide an adequate course of study. It should also be as elastic as practicable, but the main thing is that it should be adequate, exciting, and challenging.

It is not necessary to alter the essential nature of the curriculum, although minor adaptations to each group of gifted freshmen are desirable. There is nothing the matter with the traditional subjects, except that the students who would enjoy them are not given large enough amounts of such intellectual food to satisfy their hunger. The study of Greek grammar, for instance, even in the traditional manner, can be an exciting experience for a group of linguistically talented young people who already have the necessary background and training for the work. In fact, many of them will like it better than they like a highly "modernized" curriculum because it is more exacting and demands a more satisfying use of superior talents.

A second characteristic of high school education for the brilliant pupil is that it must give him training in self-discipline and hard work. Genius may not be an infinite capacity for taking pains, but it cannot grow without an infinite capacity for concentrated effort. The really superior student learns so rapidly and forgets so little that ordinary classwork calls for barely more than a casual glancing at assignments. Most people simply do not realize how little the burden is.

A few examples may illustrate this point. I have selected these from my own friends because I can vouch for their accuracy. One of my friends arrived at college five days before classes began. Not wanting to waste her time, she looked up her teachers to see if there were not some subject on which she could start work. The one professor she found in residence loaned her a copy of an Old English grammar and reader. The girl memorized the various word forms and read the stories in the back of the book in exactly five days, returned the book at the first class meeting, and made no preparation whatever during the following semester. In fact, she did not even buy a book, but she got an A. Another friend remained at college over the Thanksgiving holidays. Between Wednesday noon and the next Sunday night she did the necessary reading, planning, and writing for term papers in two courses. Each occupied about twenty typewritten pages, and both were retained by the professors as excellent examples to show subsequent classes. Another friend who was a brilliant freshman in chemistry—and has since become an outstanding research chemist—left twenty "unknowns" that she was supposed to solve one at a time during a whole semester, until a spring afternoon, when she ran the entire lot through the analysis at once. The work took her about seven hours, and she was the only student in the class who found every element in every unknown. Another friend was given two weeks in which to look up such materials as she needed to write a one-act play based upon some dramatic incident during a given period in history. She went home from class about three o'clock in the afternoon, wrote the play at once, typed it before dinner, put it away in her desk for two weeks, and did no work on the course during the next two weeks. The teacher gave the paper an A, and the other students selected it to present, practically without change, to the entire school.[24]

For such young people the usual assignment is so easy as to be a joke. It can be left till the last minute and then tossed off casually. The superior mind derives no training and little profit of any kind from it. Most certainly a superior mind will not be of much use to the world unless its possessor learns how to harness and drive it.

Third, the material to be learned should be presented in a stimulating manner and the student encouraged to use his initiative and originality to the greatest possible degree. Nothing is more fascinating to a person of alert mind than the process of thinking. The teacher of superior students should give them continual opportunity to demonstrate insights, to reason out problems, to make conclusions, to sense interrelationships, to handle

[24] L. Cole, *The Background of College Teaching*, Rinehart & Company, 1940, pp. 402–403.

ideas, to discuss theories, to see unity behind multiplicity. To provide for maximal stimulation, brilliant students should come into contact with the finest minds on the teaching staff. A successful teacher of brilliant students once gave the writer the following recipe for the proper instruction of superior students: "First, you demand the impossible, and then you keep out of the way while the youngsters deliver it." This capsule of methodology is useful for those who work with superior young minds.

Finally, a brilliant student's studies should be arranged so that he sometimes works with groups and so that some of his work is directed toward service to the school.[25] A superior student's first jobs are to master basic ideas, to learn how to work, and to develop his native talents, because by becoming himself he can best serve the world. That is, his immediate aim is self-development, but his ultimate aim is service. At the secondary school level, as at any other, he needs sometimes to work alone. However, there are always in progress several joint projects and some of immediate social usefulness, and in these he should do his share, like any other student. For instance, a few bright youngsters who are interested in botany can prepare a properly collected and labeled exhibit of local flora; if the project is well planned, they will learn a good many facts about botany, and they will develop social skills and ideals of service without which their talents cannot be put to the best use. Gifted adolescents need an ideal of service, and they need experience in joint undertakings, but not all their work should be "socialized." The solitary burning of the midnight oil is the natural way of genius.

So also is the passionate concentration on things that are of only moderate interest to children of average abilities. The resulting absorption marks off the talented from the merely bright as clearly as anything could. As the mother of a boy with high musical talent once said to the writer, "My son is a perfectly normal twelve-year-old boy, except that he practices the piano five hours a day." This boy played in the school orchestra and school band, he wrote school songs for various occasions, he played works of a different composer for two hours once a month in the school auditorium with the doors open for other students to come and listen, he was on the school swimming team, he took his part in preparing programs for school assembly, and he often played the hymns for the Christian Association meetings. He was accepted by his age-mates, although he was not especially popular. This boy's social adjustment was as good as one could expect. He was not isolated, he could get along with others on a common job, and he had a sense of service. But what twelve-year-old boy is "perfectly normal" when he willingly practices on the piano five hours a day and assiduously avoids any activity that might conceivably damage or even dirty his hands?

A few illustrative examples of work appropriate to bright pupils in

---

[25] M. V. Brown, "Teaching an Intellectually Gifted Group," *Elementary School Journal,* 49:380–388, 1949; and J. C. Seegers, "Teaching Bright Children," *Elementary School Journal,* 49:511–515, 1949.

various school grades are quoted below. Work of this type should be begun early, partly to keep the children interested in school, partly to prevent them from becoming loafers, and partly to lay the necessary foundation in independence for the relatively complex projects at the college level. The list below includes brief statements concerning a number of approaches that have been found useful.

A. Experiences in understanding citizenship

   1. A course in problems of democracy
     Submission of four reports at stated times during the semester. Participation was voluntary and any student was free to return to regular class at any time.
   2. A students' session of Congress
     An annual session of Congress was held in the high school class in American history. A speaker was elected, the class was divided into parties, committees were appointed, etc. Bills were presented. All engaged in much serious research into the issues at stake.
   3. An up-to-date course in American history
     Two hundred and fifty pupils of superior intelligence designed a course of study for themselves. It included units on the following topics relating to the period from 1830 to date:
     a. Democracy engages in social reform
     b. Democracy engages in social conflict
     c. Economic revolution overtakes democracy
     d. Democracy establishes a world power
     e. Reforming democracy: the progressive era
     f. Mobilization to make the world safe for democracy
     g. Democracy again engages in social reform
     h. A world-wide struggle for democracy

B. Experiences in intercultural relations

   1. A group looks into its own background
     In a city that contained several foreign colonies, the pupils studied the history, customs, and adjustment to American life of (a) Pennsylvania Germans (b) Hungarians, and (c) French Canadians.
   2. A high school group holds a Pan-American Conference
     Small groups of students represented each South and Central American country and met to discuss common problems.

C. Creative speech work in high school. In one school the superior students:

   1. Organized a speech institute which offered to every class and teacher in school well-prepared, factual, dynamic, and well-organized talks on eighteen different topics
   2. Organized a "Town Meeting of the Air" radio program
   3. Acted as judges for approximately twenty debates held in geography classes of the school
   4. Presented two open forums and two debates before the entire students' assembly, as well as before civic clubs
   5. Prepared for and competed in interscholastic contests in debate, oratory, and extemporaneous speaking[26]

[26] Summarized from E. H. Martens, "Curriculum Adjustments for Gifted Children," *United States Office of Education Bulletin*, No. 1, 1946, 82 pp.

D. Seminar for seniors[27]

The group was composed of twenty-three seniors, all of whom were honor students. Each pupil planned his term work around his scheduled program for that term, selecting a topic that would relate to several classes. A library corner was assigned to this group, and the librarian aided in the supervision. Some of the topics developed by members of the group are described below:

1. Postwar United States
   The pupil developing this project was a Spanish student who planned a study of Latin American and North American relationships after the war. He related his study to his twelfth-grade history by studying previous plans and their results throughout our history, as background for the present.
2. History as seen through literature
   One pupil prepared a bibliography of both fiction and nonfiction dealing with four periods: the American Revolution, the War of 1812, the Civil War, and the Period of Expansion. He read and evaluated the books himself.
3. Advancement of medicine in the United States from colonial period to the present time
   This pupil planned to enter some field of medical science later. History and science were correlated in this work as developments in medicine were paralleled with trends in American history.
4. A study of modern Russia: its people, and customs
   This pupil read two or three histories of Russia, a number of novels and plays, and several biographies of famous Russians, most of them from the modern period, and drew his own conclusions as to the nature of the Russian people.

In three respects, then, the treatment of brilliant students should differ from that given their classmates, and in one respect it should be parallel. In the nature of the material studied, in the amount studied, and in the manner of presentation their work should be different; but in its training for social participation and social responsibility, it should be the same. If such a program were adhered to, the awakening of the superior pupil would more frequently take place in high school, instead of being delayed till the last years of college and sometimes even later. The curriculum as taught in many present-day high school classes involves a tragic waste of the best intellects in each generation of students.

4. Characteristic Problems of Brilliant Pupils: The superior adolescent has problems of various kinds—intellectual, vocational, social, and emotional. His chief intellectual problem is to find something on which to sharpen his wits. A second problem in the same field is the delimitation of his interests. The brilliant adolescent is typically the person who sets out to master the entire universe. His intellectual interests need to be focused, not diffused. He often requires guidance into an extra-heavy load of those courses that will furnish a sound preparation for later work.

The main problems of the brilliant child are undoubtedly personal. Such an individual has certain abilities developed far beyond the normal for his age, and along these lines he is especially successful. Because he is suc-

[27] Summarized from A. M. Mosso, "An Experiment with and for Pupils of Superior Ability," *School Review,* 52:26–32, 1944. Used by permission of *School Review.*

cessful, he is likely to concentrate more and more upon his special interests. The things he likes best to do are precisely those that will further widen the gap between him and others of his own age group. By the time such a child reaches high school he may have become quite isolated and unsocial. He is therefore in need of personal help to assist him in making social adjustments.

The relatively few brilliant students who are seriously maladjusted show their condition clearly enough. Outside class they either stay by themselves or they fling out caustic remarks about the utter futility of all non-academic pursuits, or they publicly refuse to attend football games, dances, or other such activities for which social rather than intellectual maturity is necessary. They tend either to play with younger children or to hang around adults. In short, according to their degree of vitality and combativeness, they show either a humiliating acceptance of their social ineptitude or else a derisive attitude toward others—an overcompensation for their maladjustment. These attitudes are not typical of genius but they do exist, and quite unnecessarily.

5. Illustrative Case Studies: While reading the case studies below, the reader should note at what age unusual ability first appeared, how it was shown, and what adaptations to it were made by school or family.

Frank entered college at the age of sixteen. He was as big as the average boy of eighteen but did not have as good muscular co-ordination. In the gymnasium classes and intramural games he was always the boy who dropped the ball at critical moments or fell over his own feet. As soon as his required athletic participation was completed, he took no further part, although he would have liked to do so. By the time he had reached a normal muscular development he had lost contact with others who were interested in the athletic activities he liked. In his classes he was an outstanding scholar from the start. Ideas fascinated him. He exercised his mind in the same way that an athlete exercises his muscles. Frank went to summer school each year, took a heavy schedule at all times, and graduated from college before he was nineteen. At once he entered the graduate school, where he majored in Egyptian archaeology. He had already—to the mystification of his acquaintances—studied Latin and Greek. When he began Hebrew and Egyptian, he became simply incomprehensible to others of his age. He is now in his second year of graduate work and will presumably get his Ph.D. before his twenty-second birthday. He is a fine scholar, with a burning enthusiasm for his subject, and a thoroughly charming boy. He finds himself, however, greatly isolated. His age-mates are all so immature that their conversation bores him. Their thinking is not nearly as clear and concise as his own, and their efforts at discussion strike him as puerile. Many of his former friends he likes as personalities, but he wishes they would stop talking. Their interest in girls, social events, and "bull sessions" merely irritates him. The people with whom he can most easily and naturally make friends are about forty years old. They are as much too mature for him socially as he is for his classmates intellectually. His professors are almost the only people to whom he can really talk with satisfaction. For the next few years life will be relatively hard for this boy. He has the mental and scholarly development of a man and the social skills of a college sophomore. There is nothing abnormal about his personality, and he will probably settle down comfortably to academic life just as soon as he has time to grow up socially. Because he is at present something of a misfit, he seems seclusive and self-conscious, although he is not actually either—just a thoroughly nice boy with intellectual interests he cannot share with his age-mates.[28]

Leopold was the oldest son of a quite wealthy family. His IQ on several tests varied from 155 to 165. As soon as he entered the first grade of school it was at once evident that the work was far too easy. Leopold had been reading since he was four years old and hardly needed the word drills of the first grade. His facility with numbers was also extraordinary, and he was entirely fascinated by music.[29]

His parents' first adjustment to the problem of educating Leopold consisted in advancing him to the second grade at once and then sending him to school only for the morning session, during which he took part in all group activities and spent the rest of his time in helping slow readers or giving extra drill to children who did not know their number combinations. He also helped the teacher make and put up decorations. His penmanship and spelling were relatively poor, and he took a normal part in the classwork devoted to these subjects. During the afternoon he practiced the piano and flute, took music lessons, studied catalogues of phonograph records, selected what he wanted, rearranged his collection, listened to his records in various sequences, and generally amused himself until his age-mates were out of school. He would have remained absorbed in his music for hours if his mother had not interrupted him every day at three thirty and sent him out to play until dinnertime. On Saturdays he was not allowed to spend any time in musical pursuits, but on Sunday he sang in the church choir and spent most of the afternoon listening to records. This general routine continued throughout elementary school. Aside from his first advancement of one year, he was never accelerated. He did a great deal of outside reading, upon which he reported to the class, he helped slow pupils, and he generally made himself useful. The other pupils liked him, although most of them realized that he was "different." As one small boy explained to Leopold's mother, "He's so nice, you forget how bright he is." Leopold early acquired the attitude that because he could learn faster than others he had more time in which to be of some use in the world.

At the end of elementary school Leopold's parents felt that he was not learning as much as he easily could learn and that he was therefore wasting much of his time. On the other hand, they did not wish to interfere with his excellent social adjustment. During the year that Leopold was in the eighth grade they began to talk about spending some time in Europe. They brought home a number of travel books, many of which Leopold read. Gradually, they broached the idea of a year's schooling in France or Germany, where he could learn another language. Leopold himself proposed a school in Switzerland where he could learn two or three languages. He and his parents therefore spent a couple of months in Switzerland where he visited several schools and enrolled in the one he liked best. His parents remained near him for another six weeks, by which time he was so engrossed in learning French, German, and Italian, in going to concerts, in taking piano lessons, in practicing, and in participating in all sorts of school activities that he hardly knew when they left. The other boys at the school were of many nationalities, and Leopold learned to adjust to them. He remained there for three years, during which he completed enough courses for entrance to an American college. Each summer he came home and renewed his friendships. The first summer he went off to a camp, but the last two he spent at home, playing tennis, going to parties and picnics, swimming, and dancing. He was the first boy in his group to own a radio, and as a result his home became the rendezvous for the "crowd."

It will be noticed that Leopold gained another year in academic standing during secondary school, but he hardly realized it because he was in small, ungraded classes

---

[28] Adapted from Cole, *op. cit.*, pp. 396–397.

[29] This case should be compared with that of Oscar on pp. 143–145.

most of the time. Even though he learned three languages to the level of fluent use, added violin playing to his other accomplishments, took singing lessons, learned to ski and skate, and read three books for every one by other pupils, he finished the work of an American twelfth-grade class and entered college before his seventeenth birthday.

At this time he was average in height and above average in weight for his college group. He played ice hockey, basketball, and soccer, he made the freshman swimming team, he joined the band, the choir, the orchestra, the composers' club, the Deutscher Verein, the French club, and the Christian Association (this last mainly to play the organ for singing the hymns). His first year he carried a normal sixteen hours of work; the next year he was permitted to take twenty, and the last two years twenty-five and twenty-six respectively. In most classes he received A's and had no mark below a B. During his junior year he was elected as one of the judges of the student court and as a senior he was president of student government and of his own fraternity. He made Phi Beta Kappa but never wore his key until he was middle-aged. He was much prouder of the letter he won in basketball.

Leopold chose to complete his education by becoming a musicologist. He also studied composition and has done quite a little composing as an avocation. He is also a volunteer member of a well-known orchestra. Since taking his Ph.D. in musicology he has fitted out a yacht with the necessary recording instruments and spends part of his time doing valuable research at the ends of the earth. He specializes in such investigations as are too expensive for the average scholar to undertake, even with a moderate backing from national research funds. Leopold's work is first-class, his reputation is excellent, and he is a normal and delightful individual. There is nothing of the long-haired genius about him, and unless he is among other specialists he does not talk in an erudite manner. As his garage mechanic says, "That man may be a prof and a millionaire, but he's a regular guy, same like me."

During the war Leopold wanted active service, but he was assigned to Intelligence and spent most of his time listening to and translating foreign broadcasts. This man's parents were, of course, aided in their treatment of him by the fact that they were wealthy, but more important were their sanity and their understanding of his needs and problems. Leopold is now a normal, useful adult whose actions are governed by a strong sense of social responsibility.

Ruth T. is at present a successful writer of fiction. She is as well known as any woman writer in the United States, and her name is one of the few that are likely to be remembered fifty years from now. Ruth's history is of special interest, partly because it covers the years of fulfillment as well as those of promise and partly because she had the kind of difficulties that beset the brilliant child and adolescent.

Even as a baby Ruth was extraordinarily active. From her earliest days she showed a remarkable motor control and high verbal ability. She began to read before she was four years old; no one taught her, but she pestered her parents and older siblings until they told her what this or that word meant. In fact, she learned in spite of parental desire to have her wait until she was older. As soon as she entered the first grade Ruth began to have difficulties, chiefly because the work was so ridiculously easy. Since nothing in the work of the class challenged her attention she became impatient and tried to make a more interesting life for herself by bringing a copy of *Treasure Island* to school with her and reading it instead of the primer. This intelligent and mature reaction resulted in punishment. Ruth was told she must read what the other children did. When she persisted in bringing the book a second time, her teacher ordered her to read the assignment out of the primer before she went home, but this she refused to do on the grounds that it was nonsense. At five o'clock a small, stubborn child and an exasperated teacher still faced one another, the primer still unread. Ruth's father ended this particular deadlock by taking his daughter not only home but out of school altogether and enrolling her in a small private school in which the pupils received a good deal of individual attention. By the time she was eight years old Ruth had completed the first six grades of school. Her teachers wanted to slow down her rate of progress since she would otherwise be ready for high school before she was twelve. Ruth's own choice was to begin Latin. This subject was hard enough to prevent her from advancing more than one grade each year for the next three years. By then, however, she was again going too fast, so she learned first French and then German. With three languages acting as dragging anchors against too much speed she did not reach high school until she was a normal fourteen, but she had already mastered a sizable piece of secondary school work.

During her childhood years Ruth had two groups of friends. One consisted of the other pupils in her private school, most of whom did not live near her, and the second of the children of her age who lived in her neighborhood. With both groups Ruth was on excellent terms. There was not a great deal of social life at her school, but she took a normal part in whatever was going on. Usually she played two or three hours every afternoon with a small group of girls who were about a year older than she. Ruth differed from the other girls of her age in two ways: her extraordinary motor co-ordination made her successful at typical boys' games and she often played with boys rather than girls, and was accepted by them as an equal. The second difference was that her chum was a girl of very low social standing but possessed of a mind nearly as quick as her own. From the chum she obtained a degree of intellectual stimulation that she did not find among girls of her own social class, and even in childhood she was independent enough to do what gave her satisfaction. There were times when her various attachments and loyalties clashed with each other, but by the years of adolescence Ruth had become adept at maintaining several sets of social contacts at once. She was rarely a leader, but she was always reasonably popular.

Ruth entered the public high school, where she found herself a year behind most of her friends, since they were chronologically older than she and she had purposely been held back. With characteristic independence she went to the principal, arranged to take examinations in her languages, and to elect enough extra work to let her catch up with her friends. The heavy load kept her moderately busy for a year, but soon after her sophomore year began she again became bored from having nothing to do and started to get into mischief, to talk back to her teachers, to be a "smart-aleck" in class, and to do all manner of bizarre things. Punishment merely brought out her aggressiveness—often giving her a chance to be verbally cleverer than her teachers—and she was soon in conflict with the school. Again her parents withdrew her from public school and sent her to a private academy, where she found what she most needed—a heavy schedule, an active social life, a great many competitive games, and a stimulating faculty. She was given extra work in practically every class and especially in those in which she showed the slightest tendency to become troublesome, since her teachers realized that this superior student simply must be kept busy or her active and independent mind would soon lead her into defiance of authority. In the course of three years Ruth took almost every class offered in the school and carried out a number of extra reading and writing projects. She was in great demand as a writer of skits and songs and even entire plays. And she had to be firmly dissuaded from writing themes for her classmates. In her senior year she voluntarily read epics in Latin, Greek, French, German, and Old English—which she had studied by herself one summer—located what she regarded as roughly parallel passages, translated them into corresponding meters in English, and wrote a commentary of some thirty typewritten pages. This labor of love kept her busy for weeks but did not prevent her from winning the school's scholarship prize or from taking first place in the Regents' examinations. In both secondary school and college

Ruth was a member of many school athletic teams and belonged to a normal number of clubs. She was moderately popular and had many friends. After her first year in college she acquired a reputation of being something of a genius and was therefore permitted to show slight eccentricities.

By the end of her college career Ruth knew that she wanted to be a writer, but she also knew that she had nothing yet to say that the public might want to hear. After graduating she first got a small job on a newspaper, then a minor position with a publisher. In her free time she constantly wrote, but threw almost everything away. Then for two or three years she did library research for other writers, eventually becoming a steadily employed ghost writer because of her facility in imitating styles. At the age of thirty she married a surgeon somewhat older than herself and had two children. She was over thirty-five when she wrote her first novel, which was immediately successful. Since that time she has kept the home fires burning, brought up her children, been active in the political life of her city, and written a great many short stories and novels.

Ruth did not have a completely easy and comfortable childhood or adolescence. She had to learn to work with others who were slower than herself and to keep out of trouble. Her quickness often betrayed her into hurting the feelings of those she loved, and her independence of mind stimulated her into one revolt after another until she was mature enough to harness it. Her love of winning drove her into a good deal of senseless competition until she got it through her head that winning was not important. In short, she had many of the typical difficulties of the superior student.

II. The Adolescent with Inferior Mental Capacity

When the extent of individual differences was first realized it was tacitly assumed that mentally inferior individuals furnished the criminals, the paupers, the unemployed, and the unemployable. More has since been learned as to the nature of mental inferiority, and of late years much has been done in the way of adjusting dull people to their environment—and vice versa. It now appears that while delinquency and other forms of asocial behavior are more frequent in a group of dull adolescents than among average or bright youngsters, they are by no means necessary accompaniments of mental inferiority.

The individuals whose mental capacity is below the average of the population may be grouped roughly into four divisions. Lowest are the idiots, whose adult mental age does not exceed two years; they never go to school. Next come the imbeciles, with a mental age from three to seven or eight years; by the time they are adults they can complete about the first two grades of school, provided the methods of teaching are appropriate. Then come the morons, with an adult mental age from eight to eleven; few of them can finish elementary school with understanding and mastery of the material, but some of them do get into junior high school in these days of generous promotion policies. Finally come the dull children, with adult mental ages between eleven and thirteen and IQ's of 70 to 85. These pupils form the intellectual deviates at the lower end of the high school distribution. In considering high school pupils, the first three groups may be eliminated from consideration, except as results with them illustrate what may be done even more successfully with the fourth group.

It is necessary also to differentiate between feeblemindedness and mental retardation, between absolute and apparent feeblemindedness, and between true defect and social or educational impairment.[30] If a child is truly feebleminded, he is also socially incompetent; by the definition of former days, he is one "who cannot handle the ordinary affairs of life with prudence." The mentally retarded child may have no higher intelligence, but he is socially competent. That is, he cannot learn what is in books, but he can learn to lay bricks, or to play an oboe, or to mix sodas, or to work on a farm; and because he gets along well with other people, he can probably, after being properly trained, hold a job and stay out of trouble. It is easy for an inexperienced person to mistake such conditions as deafness, introversion, chronic illness, or emotional conflict for mental defect. Neurotic children often score low on tests through inattention, and they fail to learn in school for the same reason. They are so confused by their environment as to present sometimes a total picture of stupidity. The same impression is made by a child with undiagnosed deafness. The "problem" child may have any level of mental capacity, but his true ability is often concealed behind his numerous misdeeds and his constant hostility. As a result, he also may be diagnosed as feebleminded. Teachers are especially likely to fall into the error of mistaking educational impairment for defective intelligence.

In the last two decades there has been marked interest in following up the careers of defective or dull pupils who had been trained in the special classes of the public schools or in institutions for the feebleminded. In one instance, 102 feebleminded girls, all of whom had been in an institution, were sent out into various communities on parole. Fifty-two of them were living in their own homes; of these, 41 had made a good adjustment and were economically valuable in the home, leaving only 11 who were not getting along well. The other 50 girls were living at their places of employment. Only 1 was rated as doing poorly; 25 were doing well, and 24 were doing excellent work.[31] In another instance, a follow-up of 210 boys with IQ's from 52 to 83, who had been trained at a special-class center, revealed the following facts: 113 were on active duty with the Army or Navy, 76 were doing satisfactory industrial work of some kind, 7 were still in school, 8 were in institutions, 4 were dead, 1 was a discharged veteran, and 1 was a chronic invalid. Few of these boys had gone beyond the fourth grade in academic work. The average wage per week of the 76 who were employed was $48; a few earned as high as $72. A fifth of the entire group had never been without employment since leaving the center two to twelve years earlier.

---

[30] E. A. Doll, "Feeble-Mindedness vs. Intellectual Retardation," *Journal of Educational Research*, 40:569–573, 1947; W. H. Guertin, "Differential Characteristics of the Pseudo-Feebleminded," *American Journal of Mental Deficiency*, 54:394–398, 1950; R. Hartogs, "The Pseudo-Feebleminded Child and Adolescent in Court," *Nervous Child*, 7:425–431, 1949; L. Kanner, "Feeble-Mindedness: Absolute, Relative, and Apparent," *Nervous Child*, 7:416–420, 1949; D. Safian and E. Harms, "Social and Educational Impairment Wrongly Diagnosed as Feeble-Mindedness," *Nervous Child*, 7:416–420, 1949.

[31] E. Frankel, H. E. Heyer, *et al.*, "Institutional Education and Training for Community Release," *New Jersey State Board of Control of Institutions and Agencies*, No. 24, 1933, 28 pp.

Slightly less than a quarter of them had been haled into court, and slightly more than a tenth had at one time or another been committed to reform schools or prisons.[32] These last figures are high, but by comparison with untrained groups of similar mental inferiority during the war years, they are low.

Two reports within the past few years are of special interest. One covers the professional career of 1,000 boys who had been for at least six months in a trade school, sometimes from preference but more often because they did not profit by ordinary instruction and were creating more or less trouble in the regular classes.[33] The highest IQ in the group was 107. About 90 per cent had IQ's below 90, and 65 per cent had IQ's ranging from 80 down to 66. Most of these boys were not defective, but as a group they were dull, and with a few exceptions they did not have the capacity to do high school work. At the time of the follow-up 23 of the 1,000 had died, 270 were in the armed services, and 22 were unemployable. Of the remaining 685 graduates of the school, 38 per cent were making at least $30 a week and 20 per cent were earning as much as or more than the average industrial worker. Only 11 men (1.1 per cent) were in penal institutions. In the group there were 52 men with IQ's less than 60. Two thirds of these were self-supporting and a quarter of them had held their present job three years or longer; their average income was only a little over $20 a week, to be sure, but only 13 per cent of this lowly endowed group were unemployed.

One of the most hotly contested series of articles of recent years contains a follow-up report on 254 children who had been assigned at some age between twelve and fourteen to a special room for defectives in one public school system.[34] The selection of the children was based upon an average of several tests as well as upon their school record and the opinions of their teachers. The range of IQ's was from 27 to 69, with a median at 53. Moreover, 38 of the pupils had been behavior problems in school, 13 had court records, 8 had already been in institutions, and 6 were under treatment in behavior clinics. The physical condition of the group was below average: 62 per cent had some physical defect, 46 per cent had inadequate eyesight, and 16 per cent had subnormal hearing. The children came from economically substandard homes. Only 33 of the 254 were in the normal grade for their age; the remaining 221 were retarded from two to six years, the average being 4.2 grades. Each child remained in the remedial class for as long a period as seemed necessary to bring his work and conduct to a level that would permit a reassignment to some regular classroom. After a lapse of eight years, the follow-up study was made. Twenty-seven per cent of the entire group had graduated from high school, and 5 per cent were in college. Only 3 per cent were temporarily unemployed at the time of the follow-up, and they had been working regularly since leaving school. In fact, 80 per

[32] R. M. McKeen, "Mentally Retarded Boys in War Time," *Mental Hygiene*, 30:47–55, 1946.

[33] W. J. MacIntosh, "Follow-up Study of 1000 Nonacademic Boys," *Journal of Exceptional Children*, 15:166–170, 1949.

[34] B. G. Schmidt, "Development of Social Competence in Adolescents Originally Classified as Feeble-Minded," *American Journal of Orthopsychiatry*, 19:125–129, 1949, and "The Rehabilitation of Feeble-Minded Adolescents," *School and Society*, 62:409–412, 1945.

cent of those who had left school had regular jobs, about one third of them in skilled trades and one half in clerical occupations. Their IQ's had risen an average of 41 points, bringing the original 53 to 93; the total range of the variation in IQ was from −4 to +71. This report raised a storm of protest. Some people have refused to believe it, and some have explained the results by assuming that the children were not defectives in the first place. All the basic facts in the report are matters of record in the public school system, where any authorized person can check them. Since there has been so much protest against the findings, it is safe to assume that competent investigators have checked what children were assigned to the class, what their IQ's were, and what subsequent school progress they made. Thus far, the report has been discussed and criticized, but no one has yet proved in print that the basic facts were wrong. Subject to further evidence, one has to accept the facts, although one is still free to interpret them as one sees fit.

From these studies it can be seen that dull adolescents, high-grade morons, and even some imbeciles can be trained so that the majority of them make good social and vocational adjustments in the community. It would therefore seem inexcusable for the high school to fail, as it sometimes does, in preparing its dull and dull-normal pupils for successful work and adequate personal adjustment after they leave school. The education they receive in school should be modified if necessary until their success is at least as good as that shown by institutionally trained defectives.

1. **Characteristics:** The defective individual is, to start with, of inferior physical development. Comparisons of height and weight are shown in Figure 143 on page 594. The defective at twenty years of age is as tall and heavy as a schoolboy of fifteen or sixteen. His head is smaller in all dimensions, and his brain is lighter. In addition, defectives have more defects of eye, ear, nose, and teeth than normal children, and they have many more speech defects.[35] According to one authority, 10 per cent of normal children show a more or less serious defect of speech, as compared with 75 per cent of mental defectives.[36]

The defective shows his most severe defects, as one would expect, in the intellectual field. The dull pupil has especial difficulty with abstractions. He has little interest in ideas. He is typically a nonverbal, nonacademic person. He has difficulty in learning to read at all and rarely succeeds in achieving sixth-grade competency before he leaves school.[37] Quite often a dull pupil's inferiority does not become marked until the years of junior high school. He can learn the definite, factual material presented in the elementary grades, although perhaps a little more slowly than other pupils. It is not until the subject matter becomes too extensive and too theoretical for him that his defects stand out clearly.

---

[35] W. B. Featherstone, *Teaching the Slow Learner,* Bureau of Publications of Teachers College, Columbia University, rev. ed., 1951, 118 pp.

[36] G. W. Gens, "Speech Retardation in the Normal and Subnormal Child," *Training School Bulletin,* 47:32–36, 1950.

[37] R. H. Hungerford, C. J. De Prospo, and L. E. Rosenzweig, "The Non-Academic Pupil," *American Journal of Mental Deficiency,* 53:547–557, 1949.

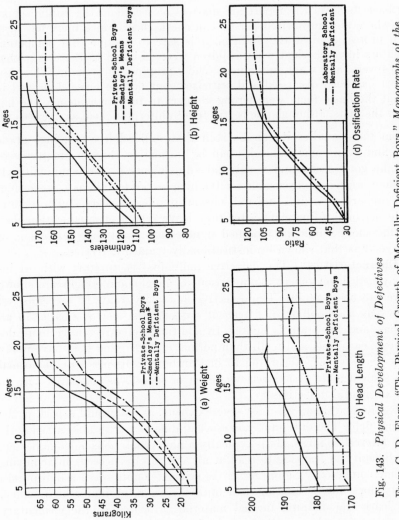

Fig. 143. *Physical Development of Defectives*

From C. D. Flory, "The Physical Growth of Mentally Deficient Boys," *Monographs of the Society for Research in Child Development*, I, No. 6 (1936), 18, 27, 33, 40. Used by permission of the publishers.

Socially and emotionally, dull adolescents are no different from other people. They can usually make and keep friends of their own or even superior ability. They can fit into the social milieu from which they come. Indeed, these dull children often get along well in nonacademic pursuits; they are willing to be led, they are delighted with any attention shown them, and they are devoted to their friends. There is no reason to suppose that social incompetence is inevitable in dull and low-normal individuals, although many of them have developed a deep-seated hostility to the world even before they enter school because they have already experienced rejection, aversion, and discrimination.

Naturally, however, many dull adolescents develop undesirable personal traits because too much is asked of them. They become discouraged, disillusioned, unhappy, truculent, and sometimes delinquent. Because good adjustment is made out of successes, not failures, such traits appear at any level of intelligence among those who believe themselves to be chronic misfits. If dull children show unfavorable traits more frequently than do those of average ability, it is because they have more reason for despair. In school they occupy an unenviable position at the bottom of the class. They soon learn that no matter how hard they try, their efforts will rarely be successful. Chronic academic failure arouses either profound feelings of inferiority, self-distrust, and physical timidity, or a defiant attitude toward the school.[38] Outside school, an environment of urban civilization may be too complex for them. They are called upon to render judgments involving the abstract thinking they are characteristically unable to do satisfactorily. It is all too probable that they are rejected by their parents, who often feel quite as frustrated, emotionally tense, and unhappy as the child.[39] In addition, many of the parents feel both ashamed and guilty. A defective child presents a tremendous problem, especially if there are other children in the family, and one cannot blame parents if they are unable to cope with the situation unaided. Their attitudes are, however, transmitted to their child, who reacts in one way or another to his inability to obtain normal emotional satisfaction and security in his home.

On the moral side, this inability to think in abstract terms is especially noticeable. The word "amoral" has been coined to describe the condition of a person who behaves contrary to accepted moral standards, not intentionally but because he is unable to grasp the underlying concepts. According to the Binet scale, a child must have a mental age of twelve before he develops even elementary concepts—such as an understanding of "pity," "sympathy," or other single virtues—and a considerably higher mentality seems needed for an adequate understanding of generalized principles of behavior. Since the dull adolescent does not have this degree of mental ability, he cannot do such thinking as is involved in solving a new situation.

---

[38] Lightfoot, op. cit.

[39] A. E. Heilman, "Parental Adjustment to the Dull Handicapped Child," *American Journal of Mental Deficiency,* 54:556–562, 1950.

For instance, a dull adolescent boy may know that stealing is wrong and may have no intention of stealing, but he can be easily persuaded to stand guard while a friend steals; the idea that he is an accomplice in the theft or that his behavior comes under the category of dishonesty may simply never occur to him. The unscrupulous adult often gets dull adolescents into trouble by such means.

The dull adolescent is, then, a nonintellectual person who has great difficulty with any kind of abstract thinking. His school standing is usually average or a little below average in elementary school, but becomes steadily lower thereafter. His social adjustment depends upon his particular experiences, but is more likely to be poor than not—unless he receives special training—because both in school and out his environment makes demands that cannot be met successfully by a person with his intellectual equipment.

2. Treatment: From the first days of compulsory education, schools have had to deal with the problem of what to do with the backward child. For many decades the routine treatment for dull boys was to beat them; dull girls also received punishment but of a less severe nature. The futility of this treatment eventually became evident, and teachers substituted the retardation of slow learners, holding them back for as many years as necessary until they met the academic requirements of each grade. As a result of this policy, a typical third-grade class would contain not only normal eight-year-olds but also dull and defective pupils ranging in age from ten to sixteen. The high school teacher was, however, not called upon to find a solution to the problem, because the grade school teachers retarded the dull pupils until these were over the compulsory age, after which they left school of their own accord.

For the last twenty years investigators have been proving that retardation is not the answer. The proof is of two sorts. The earlier type, in point of time, showed clearly that pupils who repeated grades knew no more at the end of the second or third time through than at the end of the first. That is, retardation had failed in its primary purpose—the better mastery of material that had not been learned earlier. Naturally, there are always a few cases in which an individual pupil does make progress, usually because he is a normal child who was for some reason absent a great deal, or because some inhibiting cause such as inadequate eyesight has been eliminated, or because he had been in violent conflict with his first teacher but liked the second one, and so on. In general, however, the causes which prevented pupils from learning on their first trip through the subject matter were still operative, and the second was just so much wasted time so far as educational achievement is concerned. A third and fourth trip were even less productive.

The second objection comes from the mental hygienist and concerns the effect of failure and retardation upon the pupil.[40] Nonpromoted pupils have

[40] See, for instance, R. D. Anfinson, "School Progress and Pupil Adjustment," *Elementary School Journal,* 41:507–514, 1941; W. W. Cook, "Some Effects of the Prac-

fewer friends, and they are definitely unpopular among their classmates, who are of course not their age-mates. In the last elementary school years and in junior high school the overage girls are mature and therefore inappropriately grouped with immature children. Retarded children are larger and stronger than their classmates, although they would be in the below-average group physically if compared with their age-mates. Their teachers

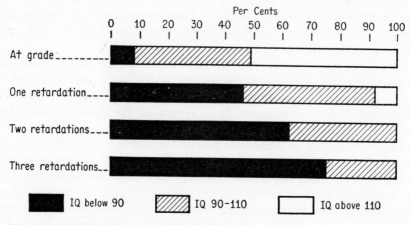

Fig. 144. *School Retardation and Intelligence*

Based on figures in A. A. Sandin, *Social and Emotional Adjustment of Regularly Promoted and Nonpromoted Children,* Bureau of Publications of Teachers College, Columbia University, 1944, p. 21.

rate them low on most traits of personality. At least a fourth of them are behavior problems. As a group they are mentally inferior, but by no means all of them can be so classed. For instance, the distribution of IQ's for 89 pupils who were one year retarded, 42 who were two years retarded, and 8 who had failed of promotion three times was found to be, in comparison with the normal distribution, as indicated in Figure 144 on this page. Even in the slowest group there are some children of normal intelligence, and among those having only one retardation, over half had IQ's above 90. The net result of retardation for most children is, thus, a failure to profit academically and a more serious personal maladjustment than existed earlier.[41]

During the last decade or more, these facts about the futility of nonpromotion have found their way into school policies. In many schools every pupil is promoted every year, regardless of achievement. As a result, the

---

tice of Non-Promotion of Pupils of Low Achievement," National Education Association, Official Report of the 1940 Meeting, pp. 150–154; E. S. Farley, "Regarding Repeaters: The Sad Effects of Failure upon the Child," *Nation's Schools,* 18:37–39, 1936; C. Saunders, *Promotion or Failure for the Elementary School Pupil,* Bureau of Publications of Teachers College, Columbia University, 1941, 77 pp.

[41] A. R. Mangus, "Effect of Mental and Educational Retardation on Personality Development of Children," *American Journal of Mental Deficiency,* 55:208–212, 1950.

high school teacher now finds in her classes those dull and nonacademic students who would never have reached high school in any earlier period. The situation has precipitated a profound reorganization of work and a change in educational objectives at the high school level in order to make possible a profitable use of time for either average or dull students. Teachers may regret the changes, but American education is dedicated to teaching all the children of all the people, to developing each pupil in any way that is of profit to him, and to preparing the members of each generation for a contented and adequate adulthood. This theory includes the dull, who, like the poor, are always with us.

A constructive program for dull adolescents in high school would start by abandoning the traditional curriculum, which is not only too hard but largely irrelevant. A program having several different elements should be substituted. First, there should be a review of the essential skills from elementary schoolwork, with direct application to common adult problems. Second, there should be immediate preparation for earning one's living. For girls, this phase of training would include such courses as typing, office work, sewing, cooking, domestic service, buying, child care, and so on. For boys, the vocational training would require courses leading to the skilled and semiskilled trades—bricklaying, carpentry, cement work, tile setting, printing, shoe repairing, upholstering, and the like. A third element in the high school program would give direct preparation for daily life; this training would consist mainly of courses dealing with problems of mental hygiene, social adjustment, and homemaking. Extracurricular activities to give experience in social contacts would also be needed. Fourth, there would be an adequate amount of training in good uses of leisure time: experience in games, in various avocational forms of handiwork, in reading whatever books or magazines will be read at all, and so on. Finally there would be what, for lack of a better term, might be called "moral training."

It should be noted that in this proposed program there is no inclusion of the subjects typically taught in high school. Some small bits and pieces of the traditional subjects may be added for individual boys or girls who display an interest in them. For instance, the writer once spent a half hour or so a day for a semester teaching Latin word roots to a dull adolescent girl who had a curiosity about where words came from and how they were put together. The work was prefaced with stories of Roman life and examination of many pictures. Then about twenty word roots and prefixes were presented, one by one. The first was "port-." The girl looked in the dictionary and was delighted to find such words as "porter," and "portable"—in the meaning of a typewriter like her own that could be carried. She then progressed to "transport," "report," and so on. The girl derived great pleasure from the mere playing with words, she enlarged her vocabulary, and she was overheard telling her friends that she too was learning Latin! This sort of skittering over the surface of a subject is precisely what dull adolescents can do and often like to do. One cannot say in advance just what topics beyond the obvious essentials should be taught, but one should be prepared to follow for a little way any interest a pupil shows but at the same time one must be careful not to go beyond what can be grasped. This "extensive" learning of a little about many things is far better suited to dull mentalities than the "intensive" learning of many facts about a few things. The main thing to remember in planning a curriculum for these pupils is that it should be *different*, not merely a diluted form of what already exists.[42]

The dull adolescent needs careful vocational guidance. If left to himself he is likely either to have no objective at all or to select an inappropriate one. Many occupations are closed to him, but he may not realize it. If he makes no vocational plans he is practically certain to drift into dead-end jobs, at best, because he is unprepared for anything else and is not bright enough to pick up skills on the job. He may join the ranks of the unemployed, since his untrained abilities are of too low an order to be easily marketable, or he may enter the criminal ranks because he has little success in earning a living otherwise. If a dull adolescent fixes his imagination upon a vocation that is quite beyond his abilities, he meets with discouragement, failure, disillusionment, and frustration. Early and frequent help in selecting a vocation is therefore essential.

3. Educational Programs: The scope of the programs now in use varies from small but sometimes effective efforts by a few teachers and parents to systematic state-wide plans. Often, a committee surveys the local working scene to determine what kinds of jobs are available and then introduces into the curriculum for the duller children and adolescents the training that is needed for doing the work.[43] It is customary to begin the partial segregation of the children as low as the third grade so as to give them basic training in hand dexterity and to withdraw them from the competitive pressure of the usual curriculum. The state schedules are more ambitious, and they are often more concerned with such matters as the size of class (fifteen is a common number), certification of teachers, keeping of records, and selection of pupils than with what is to be taught after the class is organized.[44]

A good though generalized program for dealing with dull children is quoted in Table 52. In this plan, which runs from Grade 1 to Grade 12, seven points are to be noted as significant: (1) The academic skills included are those that can be learned by a dull child during his elementary school years.

---

[42] For further suggestions see Anon., "High School Methods with Slow Learners," *National Education Association Research Bulletin,* 21:59–87, 1943; W. H. Bristow and R. H. Hungerford, "Slower-Learning Pupils—Problems and Issues," *High Points,* 27:10–16, 1945; L. Mones, "Experimenting with Mentally Retarded Pupils in High School," *American Journal of Mental Defectives,* 46:89–93, 1941; B. McAdow, "Ten Years with Slow Readers," *English Journal,* 30:73–79, 1941; G. D. Stevens, "Some Problems Related to the Education of the Slow-Learning Adolescent," *School Review,* 51:550–554, 1943.

[43] C. Lovell, "Educational-Occupational Programs for Special Class Girls," *American Journal of Mental Deficiency,* 51:452–455, 1947; and M. M. Birmingham, "Organizing a Special Class for Slow-Learning Children," *Understanding the Child,* 18:140–160, 1949.

[44] See, for instance, R. Graham, "The Illinois Program of Special Education in Public Schools for the Educable Mentally Handicapped Children," *American Journal of Mental Deficiency,* 51:460–466, 1947.

Table 52

A PLAN FOR THE EDUCATION OF DEFECTIVES

Grades 1–3   Ages 7–11   IQ's 50–79
a. Such academic skills as the child can acquire b. Such mechanical skills as they can develop c. Such social skills as their social ages permit

Grades 4–6   Ages 11–14   IQ's 50–79
a. Some additional academic skills but less emphasis on this phase b. Additional mechanical skills c. Increasing emphasis on social skills and understanding of social developments, insofar as may be possible

Grades 7–9 Ages 14–17 IQ's 50–89 *Junior Prevocational School*	Grades 7–9 Ages 14–17 IQ's 70–89 *Junior High School*
a. A minimum program of social studies b. Main emphasis upon manipulative skills developed in routine manual tasks	a. Continued work in social studies b. Shopwork c. Individualized instruction by special homeroom teacher

Grades 10–12 Ages 17–19 IQ's 65–89	Ages 17–19 IQ's 70–89
a. Increased emphasis upon social studies and development of social skills b. Increased mechanical skills	a. Main emphasis on shopwork b. Continued instruction and guidance by homeroom teacher

From E. M. Kelly, "Organization of Special Classes to Fit the Needs of Different Ability Groupings," *American Journal of Mental Deficiency*, 48:80–86, 1943. Used by permission of the Journal.

(2) There is constant emphasis upon the development of social skills and whatever understanding of social drives, pressures, and developments as may be possible at each level. (3) Manipulative skills are stressed from the first and receive increasing emphasis as the children grow older, until these skills lead to appropriate vocations. On the side of organization three further points should be mentioned. (4) Children with IQ's from 50 to 79 form the "dull" group in the elementary grades, but by the years of senior high school the "dull" children are those with IQ's from 70 to 89. (5) At the end of the sixth grade, the dullest children and those with a preference for such work are sent to a prevocational school, which parallels the high school, insofar as its grade level is concerned. Its main purpose, however, is to prepare adolescents to enter the simpler occupations and to give them whatever social understanding they can acquire. The brighter children go into the regular high school, where they concentrate upon shopwork that will lead into some of the skilled trades. Such academic work as they pursue is confined to the social sciences, and, since they cannot unaided keep up with brighter pupils, they receive individual help from a specially trained teacher, who also gives them aid in their personal or vocational problems if they want it. (6) It should be noted that a retardation of two years for this dull group has occurred during elementary school. One year is accounted for by entrance into school at seven instead of at six. The children spend a semester or a year in kindergarten or in a "developmental" class before they are

mature enough to do first-grade work. During elementary school they are to lose another year, but since the class they are in will be ungraded, there will be no definite moment of nonpromotion. The work will merely be spread out over an additional year. Pupils with IQ's from 50 to 89 at age 14 would enter junior high school with a range of mental ages from 7 to $12\frac{1}{2}$, and senior high school at age 17 (Grade 10) with mental ages from 11 to 15 for the vocational school and 12 to 15 for the high school. The amount of retardation is not therefore sufficient to compensate for the dullness, but a higher degree would, as already shown, do little to improve their academic standing and much to mar their personalities. Finally (7) the children would, if this plan were used, be selected within the first few weeks after their entrance to school and separated then from the others. Presumably, a return to the regular classes by any pupils wrongly classified would be provided. This early start is highly desirable. The high school would also do well to initiate a sorting of its entrants and to get as many of its dull freshmen as possible out of the academic courses. But it will need to prepare a number of courses that these dull youngsters can take with profit and will want to take.

Table 53

A PROPOSED PROGRAM FOR SLOW PUPILS IN HIGH SCHOOL

Period	Monday	Tuesday	Wednesday	Thursday	Friday
1	Physical and mental health; societal interrelationships: boys and girls				
2	Woodworking: boys Homemaking: girls	Physical education: boys and girls	Woodworking: boys Homemaking: girls	Physical education: boys and girls	Woodworking: boys Homemaking: girls
3 (In homeroom)	Group guidance: boys and girls	Clubs	Group guidance: boys and girls	Clubs	Group guidance: boys and girls
4	Remedial reading: boys and girls	Physical education: boys and girls	Remedial reading: boys and girls	Physical education: boys and girls	Guidance in reading: boys and girls
5	Occupational guidance and training. Individual guidance and training in tool subjects				
6	Home economics: girls Home mechanics: boys				
7	Language development; socialization; free activities for boys and girls				Attendance at Youth Center

From S. A. Kirk, *et al.*, "Educating the Mentally Handicapped in the Secondary Schools," *Illinois Circular*, Series A, No. 51, Bulletin No. 12, 1951, 53 pp. Used by permission of the Superintendent of Public Instruction of the State of Illinois.

A course of study specifically designed for dull pupils in high school has recently appeared. As one can see by examining Table 53, the traditional curriculum of secondary education has been completely abandoned.[45]

[45] S. A. Kirk, *et al.*, "Educating the Mentally Handicapped in the Secondary Schools," *Illinois Circular*, Series A, No. 51, Bulletin No. 12, 1951. 53 pp.

The proposed plan contains four main divisions of subject matter: physical and mental health, homemaking, societal relationships, and occupational training. The authors of the plan have evidently as their objective the education of dull students to be useful, normal individuals, and they make not the slightest effort to turn these laggards into scholars. One should note also the individualization of such schoolwork as is included.

4. Outstanding Problems of Dull Adolescents: The dull adolescent's first problem is to learn how to live contentedly in a social and vocational milieu to which he can adjust. A solution to this problem requires that he achieve a pleasant emotional tone toward the things he can do successfully.

One of the unfortunate effects of efforts at universal education has been a tendency to look down upon honest labor with one's hands. There are many causes for this attitude. Perhaps the most important is the over-bookish type of education given in many schools—a survival of the time when education was a gentleman's privilege rather than a universal possession. Second, teachers themselves belong to a "white-collar" occupation; they are therefore likely to convey to the pupils their own attitude toward other types of work. Practically all teachers in the elementary schools and the majority of those in high school are women; they do not know much about masculine trades and are inclined to look down upon what they do not understand. Finally, there is the widespread opinion—which may or may not be justified by facts—that the longer a student pursues the typical academic curriculum the higher type of job he is likely to get after he leaves school. As a result of all these tendencies there has developed a general attitude that "handwork" is degrading. This attitude must be overcome and supplanted with a feeling of pride in a job well done, no matter what it is. If the dull adolescent can be so conditioned as to feel a warm glow of satisfaction over success in such work as he can do well, half his troubles are over because he will have learned to be content with "that state of life into which it has pleased God to call him."

The dull adolescent's second personal problem is the acquisition of acceptable social and moral behavior. For his own safety, he must have achieved the necessary habits before he leaves school. Before him lie the usual stresses and strains incident to adult life. He will be called upon to make decisions, and he will not have the mental capacity to reason out for himself what decision he should make. Only habits so ingrained as to be an integral part of himself will bring him safely through danger. If he leaves high school as a thoroughly happy individual, well adjusted to his social group, equipped with what vocational and academic skills he will need to earn a living, enthusiastic about his work, and well grounded in fundamental habits of honesty, responsibility, and decency, the dull adolescent is hardly more likely to err than the rest of mankind.

5. Illustrative Case Studies: The two histories below have been selected because they show successful treatment of dull junior high and high school pupils.

Wallace is at present in the ninth grade, although his ability and scores in achievement tests place him at about the sixth-grade level. He has had difficulty with his schcolwork since his second year, when he began to fall behind the rest of the class in his reading. This subject has remained especially hard for him. His work in other subjects is usually just barely passing. Since every child in his school is promoted every year, without respect to achievement, Wallace has now appeared as a freshman in high school, but he is unable to read well enough to pass any of the courses. His IQ is 81—about twenty points too low for success in high school.

Wallace has always liked school, even though he knew that he stood near the bottom of the class. He gets on well with his teachers, likes and is liked by his age-mates, and is an obedient, docile pupil. He is good-natured and emotionally quite mature. As far as known, he has no bad habits and has never been in disciplinary difficulties. He does not seem to feel inferior to the other pupils, although he admits freely that they learn faster than he does. At the moment he is somewhat bewildered by the assignments given him, but he has evidently been in this state of mind a good many times before and therefore supposes that things will soon begin to clear up for him.

Wallace has two older sisters, who graduated from high school with average records. His father is dead. His mother works as a clerk in a store and seems to be a well-meaning but not very intelligent woman. Wallace is happy at home. One of the sisters works; the other is married. The visiting teacher who went to the home one evening found only harmony and affection between the members of the little family.

During the last two summers Wallace has worked as delivery boy for a neighborhood grocery. This store does not have regular deliveries, but if customers want to pay an extra quarter, Wallace will bring their groceries to their homes in a little cart hitched tc his bicycle. In the summertime he earned $3 to $4 a day in this work. The grocer found him reliable and honest. At present the grocer needs another clerk in his store during the afternoon hours to help him wait on customers. Wallace has been around the store so much during the past two years that he knows where everything in it is kept, and he has such a gracious manner that customers like him. His arithmetic would be inadequate if he had to add long columns of figures, but with the adding machine he does well enough.

Since there seems little likelihood that Wallace will be able to pass much if any of his high school work, the personnel officer has arranged for the boy to take on the afternoon work as a form of "applied mathematics," for which he will get school credit, and to restrict his schedule to a class in swimming, one in arithmetic—a review course for freshmen who are not ready for algebra—and one in composition. He has eight scheduled classes for which he has to make preparation, two swimming periods each week, and thirteen free periods during which he can make whatever preparation he is capable of making. The boy is now fifteen years old and will not need to continue in school after this year unless he wishes to do so. It is probable that he will begin next year to work full time in the grocery. If he continues at all in school, it will be on a part-time basis. This arrangement appears to be satisfactory to all concerned.

Natalie was nearly sixteen when she reached high school. She had twice been retarded in the lower grades and still felt unhappy over her failures to be promoted. Since she was a small girl she could pass for fourteen and usually did so. Although her retardations had given her an emotional scar, they had at least deposited her on the high school's doorstep with more maturity of mind than would otherwise have been the case.

Upon entrance to high school Natalie elected a college preparatory course, although she was advised not to because her recorded IQ's on three tests of intelligence were 82, 87, and 91. When the "warning" lists reached the counselor's office in November, Natalie's name appeared on four of them. The counselor sent for the girl to talk over the situation with her and found the child frightened out of what wits she possessed by her own conviction of prospective failure and by her inability to make sense out of her assignments. She was passing her social studies course, and such work as she had handed in in English was good enough but she was badly behind in it. It was arranged that for immediate relief Natalie should drop three of her five courses, should make up her back work in English, and should come to the counselor again before she made out her schedule for the next semester. Natalie received C's in both courses. When she visited the counselor she stated that she wanted to go on with both history and English, but she did not know what else to take. Her out-of-school interests were chiefly confined to sewing, embroidery, crocheting, knitting, and simple forms of painting—coloring, putting geometrical designs onto glass, block-printing cloth, copying Christmas cards, and the like. She showed some of her work to the counselor. It was evident that Natalie was a painstaking, accurate, unimaginative, neat copyist in whatever she did. The counselor enrolled her in a class in design and one in leatherwork. At the end of the second semester Natalie received a B, two C's, and a D. She has continued in high school, taking one or two academic and two or three vocational courses each semester. She gets mostly C's and D's and an occasional B, but she has never failed anything. She is proceeding so slowly that she will need five years to graduate, at which time she will be nearly twenty-one. Her parents are glad to have her keep on in school, and Natalie herself is as young in spirit as she is in mind. In earlier generations Natalie would certainly have been eliminated. Under present conditions she will probably graduate. Her presence in school has harmed no one, and her continued success in such work as she can master at all has given her a sense of adequacy and confidence in her ability to earn her own living. She will probably be a useful citizen in some humble task, and she will be the happier for having the satisfaction of graduating from the local high school—"just like everyone else."

III. Summary

The high school contains a small number of extreme deviates at each end of the distribution of intelligence and a considerably larger group of those who vary slightly from the average. The extremely bright and the dull both have their characteristic traits and are distinguishable from the average and from each other by their physical, social, and emotional development quite as much as by their intellectual deviation. For neither extreme group is the usual high school curriculum appropriate. The brilliant need more and harder work that is presented in the most stimulating manner possible. The dull need less that is academic and more that is immediately applicable to life. Similar but less extensive changes are needed if work is to be adjusted to the needs of those who vary to a lesser degree above or below the average.

REFERENCES FOR FURTHER READING

BOOKS
1. Carroll, H., *Genius in the Making*, McGraw-Hill Book Company, 1940, 307 pp. (Chaps. 4–6, 9–11.)
2. Doll, E. A., "The Feebleminded Child," in Carmichael, *Manual of Child Psychology*, pp. 875–885.

3. Educational Policies Association, *Education of the Gifted Child,* National Education Association, 1950, 88 pp.
4. Featherstone, W. B., *Teaching the Slow Learner,* Bureau of Publications of Teachers College, Columbia University, rev. ed., 1951, 118 pp. (Chaps. 1, 3, 6, 7.)
5. Fleming, *Adolescence: Its Social Psychology,* Chap. 9.
6. Garrison, *The Psychology of Exceptional Children,* Chaps. 6–9, 10–13.
7. Heck, A. O., *Exceptional Children,* McGraw-Hill Book Company, 1940, 536 pp. (Chaps. 26–29, 23–25.)
8. Hollingworth, L. S., *Children above 180 IQ,* World Book Company, 1942, 332 pp. (Chaps. 16–17, and any two of Chapters 4–15.)
9. Lightfoot, C., *Characteristics of Bright and Dull Children,* Bureau of Publications of Teachers College, Columbia University, 1951, 136 pp. (Chaps. 2, 3, 5, 6.)
10. Louttit, *Clinical Psychology of Children's Behavior,* Chaps. 6–9.
11. Miles, C. C., "Gifted Children," in Carmichael, *Manual of Child Psychology,* pp. 886–953.
12. Sandin, A. A., *Social and Emotional Adjustment of Regularly Promoted and Non-Promoted Pupils,* Columbia University Press, 1944, 142 pp. (Chaps. 3, 4, 5.)
13. Sarason, S. B., *Psychological Problems in Mental Deficiency,* Harper & Brothers, 1949, 366 pp. (Chaps. 1, 4, 5, 6.)
14. Terman, L. M., and M. H. Oden, *The Gifted Child Grows Up,* Vol. IV of the Genetic Studies of Genius Series, Stanford University Press, 1947, 448 pp. (Chaps. 2–5, 9–12, 20, 21.)
15. Tyler, L. E., *The Psychology of Human Differences,* Appleton-Century-Crofts, Inc., 1947, 420 pp. (Chaps. 6–9.)
16. Wallin, J. E. W., *Children with Mental and Physical Handicaps,* Prentice-Hall, Inc., 1949, 527 pp. (Chaps. 5–9.)
17. Witty, P., *The Gifted Child,* D. C. Heath & Company, 1951, 338 pp. (Chaps. 3–5, 7, 9–10.)

MONOGRAPHS, BULLETINS, PROCEEDINGS, YEARBOOKS, ARTICLES

A. *General Summaries*

1. Conference of Education of the Exceptional Child, "The Emotional Climate of the Exceptional Child," *Proceedings of the Spring Conference of the Child Research Clinic of the Woods School,* 1949, 50 pp.
2. Witty, P., "Thirty Years of Research upon Gifted Children," *Understanding the Child,* 17:35–40, 1948.

B. *Characteristics of Brilliant Children*

1. Altus, W. D., "The Height and Weight of Soldiers as Associated with Scores on the Army General Classification Tests," *Journal of Social Psychology,* 29:201–210, 1949.
2. Carroll, H. C., "Intellectually Gifted Children: Their Characteristics and Problems," *Teachers College Record,* 42:212–221, 1940.
3. Edgerton, H. A., S. H. Britt, and R. D. Norman, "Physical Differences between Ranking and Nonranking Contestants in the First Annual Science Talent Search," *American Journal of Physical Anthropology,* 5:435–452, 1947.
4. Jenkins, M. L., "Case Studies of Negro Children on Binet IQ 160 and Above," *Journal of Negro Education,* 12:154–166, 1943.
5. Lewis, W. D., "Some Characteristics of Children Designated as Mentally

Retarded, as Problems, or as Geniuses by Teachers," *Journal of Genetic Psychology,* 70:29–51, 1947.

6. Lewis, W. D., "Some Characteristics of Very Superior Children," *Journal of Genetic Psychology,* 62:301–309, 1943.

7. Thorndike, R. L., "An Evaluation of the Adult Intellectual Status of Terman's Gifted Children," *Journal of Genetic Psychology,* 72:17–27, 1948.

8. Witty, P. A., "A Genetic Study of 100 Gifted Children," *Thirty-ninth Yearbook of the National Society for the Study of Education,* 1940, Pt. I, pp. 401–408.

9. Witty, P. A., "The Gifted Child in the Secondary School," *Bulletin of the National Association of Secondary School Principals,* 33:259–264, 1949.

10. Woods, E. L., "The Mentally Gifted," *Review of Educational Research,* 14:224–230, 1944.

C. *Problems of Brilliant Children*

1. Berg, I. A., and R. P. Larsen, "A Comparative Study of Students Entering College One or More Semesters before Graduation from High School," *Journal of Educational Research,* 39:33–41, 1945.

2. Boardman, R. K., and G. Hildreth, "Adjustment Problems of the Gifted," *Understanding the Child,* 17:41–44, 51, 1948.

3. Burns, C. L. C., "Maladjusted Children of High Intelligence," *British Journal of Educational Psychology,* 19:137–141, 1949.

4. Hollingworth, L. S., "Growing up with Gifted Children," *Understanding the Child,* 17:45–49, 1948.

5. Pressey, S. L., "Educational Acceleration: Appraisal and Basic Problems," *Bureau of Educational Research Monographs,* No. 31, Ohio State University, 1949, 153 pp.

6. Pressey, S. L., "Age of College Graduation and Success in Adult Life," *Journal of Applied Psychology,* 30:226–233, 1946.

7. Thom, D. A., and N. Newell, "Hazards of the High IQ," *Mental Hygiene,* 29:61–77, 1945.

8. Wells, F. L., "Adjustment Problems at the Upper Extremities of Test Intelligence: Cases 19–28," *Journal of Genetic Psychology,* 74:61–84, 1949.

9. Wells, F. L., "Adjustment Problems at the Upper Extremities of Test Intelligence: Cases 39–54," *Journal of Genetic Psychology,* 76:3–37, 1950.

D. *Teaching the Brilliant Pupil*

1. Alpern, H., "How Can Schools Meet the Needs of Gifted and Superior Children?" *Bulletin of the National Association of Secondary School Principals,* 36:110–117, 1952.

2. Baker, H. P., "An Experiment in the Education of Gifted Children," *Journal of Exceptional Children,* 9:112–114, 1943.

3. Brown, M. V., "Teaching an Intellectually Gifted Group," *Elementary School Journal,* 49:380–388, 1949.

4. Burnside, L. H., "An Experimental Program in the Education of the Intellectually Gifted Adolescent," *School Review,* 50:274–285, 1942.

5. Flesher, M. A., "Did They Graduate Too Young?" *Educational Research Bulletin,* 24:218–221, 1945.

6. Martens, E. H., "Curriculum Adjustments for Gifted Children," *United States Office of Education Bulletin,* No. 1, 1946, 82 pp.

7. Moskowitz, F., "Educating Superior Children," *High Points,* 28:5–9, 1946.

8. Mosso, A. M., "An Experiment with and for Pupils of Superior Ability," *School Review,* 52:26–32, 1944.

9. Scharer, N. B., "How Can Schools Meet the Needs of Gifted and Superior Children?" *Bulletin of the National Association of Secondary School Principals*, 36:99–109, 1952.
10. Seegers, J. C., "Teaching Bright Children," *Elementary School Journal*, 49:511–515, 1949.
11. Strang, R., "The Inner World of Gifted Adolescents," *Journal of Exceptional Children*, 16:97–101, 1950.

E. *The Recognition of Mental Defect*
1. Doll, E. A., "Feeble-Mindedness *vs.* Intellectual Retardation," *Journal of Educational Research*, 40:569–573, 1947.
2. Guertin, W. H., "Differential Characteristics of the Pseudo-Feebleminded," *American Journal of Mental Deficiency*, 54:394–398, 1950.
3. Guertin, W. H., "Mental Growth in Pseudo-Feeblemindedness," *Journal of Clinical Psychology*, 5:414–418, 1949.
4. Kanner, L., "Feeble Mindedness: Absolute, Relative, and Apparent," *Nervous Child*, 7:365–397, 1949.

F. *Characteristics of the Dull Pupil*
1. Flory, C. D., "The Physical Growth of Mentally Deficient Boys," *Monographs of the Society for Research in Child Development*, Vol. I, No. 6, 1936, 119 pp.
2. Hungerford, R. H., C. J. Del Prospo, and L. E. Rosenzweig, "The Non-Academic Pupil," *American Journal of Mental Deficiency*, 53:547–557, 1949.
3. Kingsley, L. V., and R. W. Hyde, "The Health and Occupational Adequacy of the Mental Defective," *Journal of Abnormal Psychology*, 40:37–46, 1945.
4. Safian, D., and E. Harms, "Social and Educational Impairment Wrongly Diagnosed as Feeblemindedness," *Nervous Child*, 4:416–420, 1949.

G. *Results of Teaching Adapted to Dull Pupils*
1. Hill, A., "Does Special Education Result in Improved Intelligence for the Slow Learner?" *Journal of Exceptional Children*, 14:207–213, 1948.
2. Kirk, S. A., "An Evaluation of the Study by Bernadine G. Schmidt Entitled: 'Changes in Personal, Social, and Intellectual Behavior of Children Originally Classified as Feeble-Minded,'" *Psychological Bulletin*, 45:321–333, 1948.
3. MacIntosh, W. J., "Follow-Up Study of 1000 Nonacademic Boys," *Journal of Exceptional Children*, 15:166–170, 1949.
4. McKeen, R. M., "Mentally Retarded Boys in War Time," *Mental Hygiene*, 30:47–55, 1946.
5. Schmidt, B. G., "Changes in Behavior of Originally Feeble-Minded Children," *Journal of Exceptional Children*, 14:67–72, 94, 1947.
6. Schmidt, B. G., "Changes in the Personal, Social, and Intellectual Behavior of Children Originally Classified as Feeble-Minded," *Psychological Monographs*, Vol. LX, No. 5, 1946, 144 pp.
7. Schmidt, B. G., "Development of Social Competence in Adolescents Originally Classified as Feeble-Minded," *American Journal of Orthopsychiatry*, 19:125–129, 1949.
8. Schmidt, B. G., "A Reply," *Psychological Bulletin*, 45:334–343, 1948.

H. *Problems of Dull Pupils*
1. Heilman, A. E., "Parental Adjustment to the Dull Handicapped Child," *American Journal of Mental Deficiency*, 54:556–562, 1950.
2. Richards, E. L., "Relationships of Declining Intelligence Quotients to Maladjustment of School Children," *Archives of Neurology and Psychiatry*, 37:817–838, 1937.

I. *The Teaching of Dull Pupils*

1. Anon., "High School Methods with Slow Learners," *National Education Association Research Bulletin,* 21:59–87, 1943.

2. Birmingham, M. M., "Organizing a Special Class for Slow-Learning Children," *Understanding the Child,* 18:140–160, 1949.

3. California State Committee on the Secondary School, "Reading Instruction for Slow Learners in the Secondary School," *Bulletin of the National Association of Secondary School Principals,* 35:8–55, 1951.

4. Candless, E. M., "A Study of Educative Methods Used in the Treatment of the Feeble-Minded," *Training School Bulletin,* 41:22–29, 1944.

5. Gibbs, E. F., "The Slow Learner in Secondary School," *California Journal of Secondary Education,* 24:199–202, 1949.

6. Graham, R., "The Illinois Program of Special Education in Public Schools for the Educable Mentally Handicapped Children," *American Journal of Mental Deficiency,* 51:460–466, 1947.

7. Hegge, T. G., "Education for the Mentally Retarded Pupils of High School Age," *American Journal of Mental Deficiency,* 54:190–191, 1949.

8. Kelly, E. M., "Organization of Special Classes to Fit the Needs of Different Ability Groupings," *American Journal of Mental Deficiency,* 48:80–86, 1943.

9. Kirk, S. A., *et al.*, "Educating the Mentally Handicapped in the Secondary Schools," *Illinois Circular,* Ser. A, No. 51, Bulletin No. 12, 1951, 53 pp.

10. Lewis, W. D., "The Relative Intellectual Achievements of Mentally Gifted and Mentally Retarded Children," *Journal of Experiments in Education,* 13:98–109, 1945.

11. Lovell, C., "Educational-Occupational Programs for Special Class Girls," *American Journal of Mental Deficiency,* 51:452–455, 1947.

12. Lovell, C., and C. P. Ingram, "High School Program for Mentally Retarded Girls," *Journal of Educational Research,* 40:574–582, 1947.

13. Mones, L., "High School Methods with Slow Learners," *National Education Association Research Bulletin,* 21:59–87, 1943.

14. Patterson, R. M., "Evaluation of a Prolonged Preacademic Program for High School Mentally Deficient Children in Terms of Subsequent Progress," *Journal of Experiments in Education,* 13:86–91, 1945.

15. Shotwell, A. M., "The Effect of Institutional Training for Mentally Defective Girls," *American Journal of Mental Deficiency,* 53:432–437, 1949.

16. Stevens, G. D., "Some Problems Related to the Education of Slow-Learning Adolescents," *School Review,* 51:550–554, 1943.

17. Willenberg, E. P., "A County Program of Public Education for Mentally Retarded Children," *Journal of Exceptional Children,* 16:129–135, 1950.

CHAPTER EIGHTEEN

Personnel Work in the High School

The personnel department of a high school has many functions. It collects data, it gives courses, it administers tests, it does research, it gives interviews, it provides guidance, it finds jobs for students, it helps them with whatever problems arise. Not all these functions will be discussed in this chapter, which will be restricted mainly to two topics—the general purpose of the guidance program and the specific work in vocational guidance.

I. The Personnel Movement

The guidance program of the high school started in a modest way as a means of advising adolescents about future occupations. As the movement grew, its objectives and methods both changed. The counselors are now expected to furnish guidance in any phase of a pupil's development. This broadening of the objective was more or less forced upon counselors, partly because the choice of vocation involved measurement of each pupil's personal traits and consideration of his entire history and partly because the pupils continually pestered the guidance personnel for help in all sorts of difficulties. A good definition of counseling at the present time is as follows: Student counseling is a purposeful, face-to-face relationship between a counselor and a student with focus upon the student's growth in self-understanding and self-decision, to which the counselor contributes careful understanding and skillful assistance.[1] From the first there were a few writers on guidance who emphasized the supplying of information rather than the giving of advice, but in the early days the counselors—at best untrained teachers who seemed to have a flair for getting along with adolescents—were somewhat too eager to advise and too reluctant to provide data and let the pupils make up their own minds. In recent years the "nondirective" type of counseling has come into use. The counselor's part in the conferences is mainly to keep the pupil talking, to recall him to the subject in hand in case he strays too far away from it, and to suggest books or reports that he might read. Essentially, however, the adolescent works out his own salvation, guided and occasionally prodded but not advised by the coun-

---

[1] C. G. Wrenn and W. E. Dugan, *Guidance Procedures in High School,* University of Minnesota Press, 1950, p. 28.

selor. As he talks and reads and talks again, he gradually begins to see what his problems are, and his own discovery of them convinces him of their reality and importance. Then he asks about possible solutions and, again gradually, works his way to an acceptable adjustment. This procedure takes far longer than the giving of advice, but its advantages are obvious. The adolescent comes to the counselor of his own volition and as many times as he thinks he needs to, he talks about whatever is puzzling him, he finds the counselor an excellent and sympathetic listener who will really hear him out, he discharges a considerable proportion of his emotional difficulties by mere talking, and he solves or at least adjusts his own problems largely by his own efforts.

More and more schools are setting up or expanding guidance facilities. In 1932, only 28 per cent of high schools with an enrollment of 1,000 or over had counselors.[2] In 1940, the percentage had grown to 44.[3] In 1949, reports from 447 secondary schools throughout the country showed 79 per cent.[4] The chief methods of providing guidance were through the use of counselors (79 per cent), through the homeroom teachers (65 per cent), through school assemblies (61 per cent), through orientation courses (30 per cent), or through occupation courses (29 per cent). The last three means are forms of group rather than individual guidance.

The objective of counseling was generally reported to be the educational, vocational, and personal adjustment of pupils through the solution of whatever problems may exist. This diversity of problems is perhaps not of the counselor's own choosing. It arose as soon as the counselors stopped talking and began to listen, stopped leading and began to follow, stopped advising and began to guide. Since the pupil holds the initiative and in the permissive atmosphere of the counselor's room can direct the conversation as he wishes, the number of problems a counselor has to deal with is limited only by the number brought up by the pupils for discussion. One writer has classified under the following headings the motives that brought students to the counselor: lack of assurance, information, or skill; excessive dependence on others; cultural conflict (as between an American-born student and his foreign-born parents); conflict between student and age-mates, family, or teachers; conflict within the individual from divergent urges; and anxiety over his choice of courses, future occupation, or both.[5] One can see that a counselor is forced into providing guidance in many fields. A list of counseling activities in 447 high schools appears in Table 54.

---

[2] T. V. Koos and G. N. Kefauver, *Guidance in Secondary Schools*, The Macmillan Company, 1932, 610 pp.

[3] C. E. Erickson and S. A. Hamrin, "Trends in Guidance and Personnel," *School Activities*, 11:187–188, 1940.

[4] N. E. Wimmer, "Guidance in Secondary Schools," *School Review*, 56:343–349, 1948.

[5] H. B. Pepinsky, "The Selection and Use of Diagnostic Categories in Clinical Counseling," *Applied Psychology Monographs*, 1948, No. 15, 140 pp.

Table 54

NATURE AND FREQUENCY OF COUNSELING ACTIVITIES AMONG COUNSELORS
IN 447 HIGH SCHOOLS

		Per cent
Information	about school	34
	about courses	48
	about occupations	61
	about activities	35
	about hobbies and uses of leisure	35
Help	in choosing career	64
	in getting along with other people	50
	in preparing for a career	58
	in selecting courses	58
	in improving relationships with family	39
	in boy-and-girl relationships	35
	in learning better methods of study	64
	in getting part-time work	40
	in getting a job after graduation	48
	in developing better manners	30
Testing	for abilities and interests	56
	of personality	42
	for special aptitudes	52
Counseling	on personal problems	67
	on vocational problems	70

From N. E. Wimmer, "Guidance in Secondary Schools," *School Review*, 56:346, 1948. Used by permission of the University of Chicago Press.

In order to carry out his or her part in the personal interviews with students a counselor needs to have a good deal of information about each student. For this purpose, the personnel office usually amasses data covering the following topics:

Areas of Information	Means of Appraisal
1. Scholastic aptitude	Previous grades, psychological tests of ability and achievement
2. Scholastic achievement and basic skills	Previous grades, standardized and teacher-made achievement tests, survey and diagnositic tests of basic skills, school activities, and work experience
3. Special abilities: clerical, mathematical, artistic, and the like	Special aptitude tests, interviews, evaluation of previous achievement or performance (work experience, hobbies, extracurricular activities)
4. Interests and plans	Autobiographies, interest inventories or tests, stated interests, interviews, previous achievement, and both work and leisure activities
5. Health and physical status	Physical examination, health history, observation, attendance record and nurse follow-up, and family consultation

Areas of Information	Means of Appraisal
6. Home and family relationships	Observation, anecdotes, rating scales, interviews, autobiographies, themes, check lists and adjustment inventories, reports from employers, group workers, or group leaders, and parent conferences
7. Emotional stability and adjustment	
8. Attitudes	Student questionnaires, home contacts, interviews, themes, autobiographies and other documentary information, and standardized rating scales
9. Work experience	Record of employer, reports of vocational counselor, interviews, and student questionnaires.[6]

Without this background, counselors are unable to furnish the necessary guidance because they are not sufficiently acquainted with the students to whom they talk.

The success of a guidance program may be measured in a number of ways, many of which are indirect. If guidance actually helps students, they will stay in school longer, change their schedules less frequently, pass more of their courses, and get into fewer difficulties of adjustment. A few of the possible criteria are listed below:

1. Reduction in the number of academic failures
2. Reduction in the number of disciplinary problems
3. Reduction in the number of requests for program changes
4. Increase in the use of the counseling service
5. Increase in the relationship between vocational choice and ability
6. Increase in the holding power of the school
7. Increase in the number of students who participate in school activities
8. Increase in the use of service by former students
9. Increase in successful job placement.[7]

Naturally, other forces operating in the school also affect these criteria. One must therefore use caution and, in an investigation, control carefully such factors as changes in promotion policy, in curricular offerings, and so on.

II. Vocational Guidance

An adult's chief business is to work, and many of his chief joys come from his successes in the world of practical accomplishment—whether his achievement consists in selling real estate, composing operas, laying sewers, or designing hats. Because success on the job is so important in adult life, it is a terrible blow to fail—either actually or in relation to one's expectations. In addition, an individual who has failed—now handicapped by an exhausting emotional experience—must start all over in some new line of work, which must obviously be no better than a second choice. Not all

---

[6] From C. G. Wrenn and W. E. Dugan, *Guidance Procedures in High School*, copyright 1950, University of Minnesota Press, pp. 18–19. Used by permission of the University of Minnesota Press.

[7] *Ibid.*, p. 60.

debacles can be either foreseen or prevented, but much agony of spirit and loss of confidence can be avoided if pupils in school are steered toward vocations for which they are adequately fitted.

The making of a vocational choice is an outstanding problem of adolescence. The ambitions of children have too little relationship to reality to be used as a basis in selecting a career, and after the days of adolescence are over there is no time left. The typical development of vocational interest is

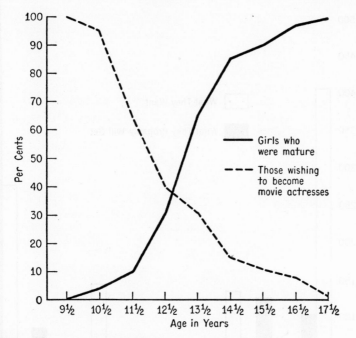

Fig. 145.   *Glamour and Maturity*

Based upon H. C. Lehman and P. A. Witty, "A Study of Vocational Attitude in Relation to Puberty," *American Journal of Psychology,* 43:93–101, 1931.

from active, exciting occupations of low prestige value—e.g., being a cowboy—to emotionalized ambitions having great prestige—i.e., being a famous trial lawyer—and finally to some occupation that represents a compromise between what a person would like to do and what he thinks he can do. One report demonstrates the interest of girls in occupations having glamour. The study covers the years from eight—before any of the girls had matured —to eighteen, at which age all of them were mature.[8] The proportion at each age interested in becoming a movie actress and the proportion that had passed through puberty make two curves of almost reverse shape, which are shown in Figure 145 on this page. The older the girls were, the less were they attracted by glamour. Since girls develop in all ways faster than boys, more

[8] H. C. Lehman and P. A. Witty, "A Study of Vocational Attitude in Relation to Puberty," *American Journal of Psychology,* 43:93–101, 1931.

of them at entrance to high school have emerged from their interest in glamour. Most freshmen boys have grown out of the cowboy stage, to be sure, but they are not as close to a compromise with reality as the freshmen girls are.

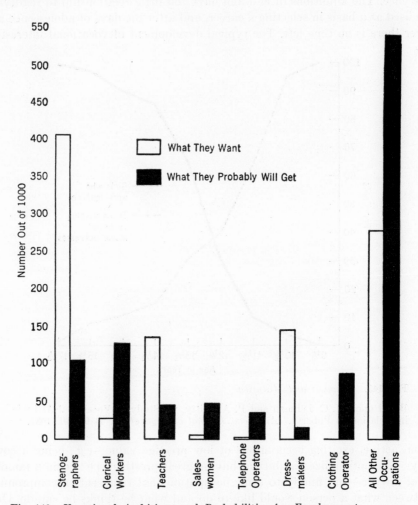

Fig. 146. *Vocational Ambitions and Probabilities for Employment*

From Bell, *Matching Youth and Jobs,* p. 107. Used by permission of the American Council on Education.

1. Need for Guidance: The need for guidance is especially well demonstrated by two studies, one concerning the relation between the occupations that pupils hoped to enter and those needed by society, and the second concerning the relation between vocational choice and ability. In the first study, 1,000 girls in the seventh grade of New York's junior high schools expressed their vocational hopes, as recorded by the white columns in Figure

146 on page 614. The choices made by these girls were compared with the figures on the occupations of women in New York City, as given in the census. As shown in Figure 146, four times as many girls wanted to be stenographers as could probably be employed, three times as many wanted to be teachers as there were openings for teachers, and ten times as many wanted to be dressmakers as could probably find jobs. The great majority of the girls centered upon these three types of work. All other occupations made an insufficient appeal. Although 34 in every 1,000 employed women in New York City were telephone operators, only 2 of the 1,000 girls wanted to enter this occupation; 128 women were clerical workers, but only 28 girls had vocational ambitions in that direction. Unless a considerable proportion of these girls changed their objectives, there was probably much disappointment and hardship in store for them.

The second study confirms the facts of the first insofar as the inappropriateness of the choices is concerned, but adds a further item. Of 533 boys and girls in Grades 7 through 12 of one school system, 50 per cent had selected occupations that were clearly beyond their mental capacities.[9] Their motives for choosing one occupation rather than another seemed to be casual, selfish, and incidental, definitely not based upon information about either jobs or themselves and quite without consideration of the number of people per occupation that could be used by society.

2. **The Traditional Bases for Selection of an Occupation:** There are three traditional bases for the selection of a lifework: the following of one's father, the following of familial ambitions, and the following of interest. The first two are sometimes the same and sometimes not. It is probably rash for parents to destine a child from birth to any one type of work because they cannot know his potentialities, but by the time he is sixteen his parents may know him better than anyone else and can often therefore select a suitable line of work. Parents are not always wrong! One rather interesting investigation touched upon the relationship of the father's occupation to the work the son hoped for and the work be actually expected to do.[10] All the boys in a union high school (165 cases) made out statements as to their grandfather's and father's occupations, and their own desired and expected jobs. The investigator first classified into a seven-point scale all male occupations reported in the census. He then tabulated the occupations of the pupils' grandfathers and fathers and both the desired and expected occupations of the boys. The grandfathers' work averaged at 3.6, the fathers' at 3.7, the boys' hoped-for occupation at 4.9, and their expected one at 4.0. That is, the boys would probably enter a line of work of a type similar to that of their immediate male ancestors, although they *hoped* for something a little better. In individual cases, however, the objec-

9 U. H. Fleege and H. J. Malone, "Motivation in Occupational Choice among Junior–Senior High School Students," *Journal of Educational Psychology,* 37:77–86, 1946.
10 F. M. Carp, "High School Boys Are Realistic about Occupations," *Occupations,* 28:97–99, 1949.

tives were not so realistic. Some sons of fathers in Groups 6 and 7 (professional men and business officials) wanted to enter work classified in Groups 1 or 2 (unskilled or semiskilled labor) while some sons of unskilled laborers wanted to enter the professions. Before one can venture an opinion on these cases one would have to know the individual. If one of the first boys mentioned above is the almost defective son of a business executive and one of the second is the intelligent son of a Negro janitor, there is nothing basically wrong with their choices.

The use of interest as a main basis for the selection of an occupation is a matter that has received much attention. The first point to consider is the permanence of vocational interests. If they are continually changing, they are obviously unsuitable as bases for guidance. The bulk of the evidence seems to be that after the age of fifteen or sixteen interests remain reasonably stable. For instance, coefficients of correlation for stated interests among 58 girls in the eleventh grade and the same girls a year later in the twelfth was 0.89.[11] It was 0.84 for 223 college graduates between their stated interests in college and five years after graduation; and in another study, it varied for different groups from 0.48 to 0.66 between sophomore and senior years in high school.[12] Choices expressed by over 1,000 students in 1933 as freshmen and in 1937 as seniors were the same in 64 per cent of the cases; four years later, in 1941, 62 per cent made the same choices they had made in 1937.[13] These various results indicate an adequate stability after the junior year in high school, but not before.[14]

An interesting reflection of stability or its absence is shown by the profiles in Figure 147 on page 617. High school girls and boys estimated twice or more their degree of interest in each of several occupations. The extent of the variation from one year to the next indicates the stability of each pupil's interests. The girls expressed their attitudes toward twelve possible vocations, the boys toward seven. Girl A shows a quite consistent set of interests; she wants to be a doctor, but she has a secondary leaning toward teaching. Girl B is also fairly consistent, but her major and minor interests in salesmanship and teaching change places in the two sets of results. Girl C flatly contradicts herself on many of the ratings; she does not even know what she dislikes. Boy A shows a consistent desire to be a sales-

---

[11] K. Taylor and H. D. Carter, "Retest Consistency of Vocational Interest Patterns of High School Girls," *Journal of Consulting Psychology*, 6:95–101, 1942.

[12] E. K. Strong, "The Permanence of Vocational Interests," *Journal of Educational Psychology*, 25:336–344, 1934; and L. Canning, *et al.*, "Permanence of Vocational Interests of High School Boys," *Journal of Educational Psychology*, 32:481–494, 1946.

[13] M. I. Wightwick, "Vocational Interest Patterns," *Teachers College Record*, 46:460–461, 1945.

[14] Canning, *et al.*, "Permanence of Vocational Interests of High School Boys," *loc. cit.*; L. Angus, "A Comparative Study of the Methods of Measuring Interest in Science and Its Relation to Ability and Achievement," *British Journal of Educational Psychology*, 20:63–65, 1950; S. F. Klugman, "Permanence of Clerical Interests in Relation to Age and Various Abilities," *Journal of Social Psychology*, 21:115–120, 1945; and A. C. Van Dusen, "Permanence of Vocational Interests," *Journal of Educational Psychology*, 31:401–424, 1940.

man, but he has some interest in office and secretrial work. Boy B wants to be a chemist, but he could be satisfied with teaching or working as an accountant. The two measurements give quite similar ratings. Boy C re-

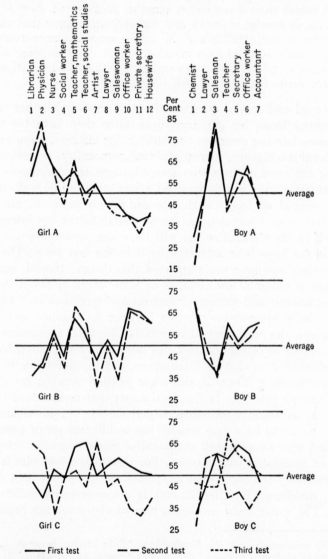

Fig. 147. *Profiles of Vocational Interests*

From H. D. Carter, "The Development of Interest in Vocations," *Forty-third Yearbook of the National Society for the Study of Education,* 1944, Pt. I, pp. 262, 263, 264, 265, 266, 268. Used by permission of the publishers.

corded his interests three times, with widely different results. All one can be fairly sure of is that he does not want to be a chemist. Girl A is highly intelligent and comes from a home that is well above average in its socioeconomic level. Whether or not her ability is high enough for the long grind of medical school is a question. Girl B has average intelligence and comes from an average home. She might perhaps better be guided toward office work than toward teaching. Girl C scores a bit below average in ability, but comes from a somewhat superior background. Boy A is slightly below average in mental capacity and comes from a home that rates rather low. Boy B has a high intelligence and comes from an above-average home; he would probably succeed as a chemist. Boy C is of average ability, but his home ranks very low. Both boys and girls with settled vocational choices seem to have made reasonably good selections.

The second and crucial question about interests is whether or not they are trustworthy bases for guidance, even after they have become stable. That is, does a burning desire to be a doctor, for instance, have a fixed relation to general intelligence, special abilities, personality, or adequate preparation? The argument of those who accept interest as a main basis for selecting an occupation runs in this wise: If a boy wants to be a doctor, he will read everything about medicine that he can get his hands on, ask questions, find out what courses to take, and be so stimulated by his interest that he will do well in his work. Also, he will have the personality for doctoring, or he would not have been attracted by it in the first place. The results of many investigations have not supported this theory. Indeed, quite the reverse. There is either a low relation or none at all between interest and intelligence, interest and success, or interest and special skills.[15] On the other hand, there is an appreciable relation between intelligence and success. In some instances, the coefficient of correlation between a measure of intelligence and marks in college courses has been somewhat raised by adding a measure of interest to that of intelligence, but the difference in prediction was not spectacular.[16] There is also some relation between personality and interest, although this may be due to the fact that measures of interest are often used as subtests in measures of personality, on the assumption that a boy who wants to be a lens grinder has a different set of personal traits from the lad who wants to sell automobiles. Some degree of special ability is also often associated with interest. For instance, a boy who is interested in music probably has some kind of special ability, which may or may not have been developed, but the amount is not necessarily sufficient for his ambitions. The writer knew one young man of above average musical talents

---

[15] R. W. Edminston and W. Vordenberg, "Relationship between Interests and School Marks of College Freshmen," *School and Society,* 64:153–154, 1946; E. S. Jones, "Relation of Ability to Preferred and Probable Occupations," *Educational Administration and Supervision,* 26:220–226, 1940; T. Kapp and L. Tussig, "The Vocational Choices of High School Students as Related to Scores on a Vocational Interest Inventory," *Occupations,* 25:334–339, 1947; R. M. Dorcus and K. Dunlap, "Aspiration, Interest, and Achievement," *Business Education,* 21:287–291, 1940; and Van Dusen, "Permanence of Vocational Interests," *loc. cit.* E. K. Strong, "The Role of Interest in Guidance," *Occupations,* 27:517–522, 1949.

[16] Angus, "A Comparative Study of the Methods of Measuring Interest in Science and Its Relation to Ability and Achievement," *loc. cit.*

who wanted to enter the field of musicology, but he lacked absolute pitch, which is considered essential.

3. Measures of Fitness for Different Types of Work: The usual method of expressing the results from a group of measurements is to construct a profile. Often a single set of tests will yield many different profiles, depending upon whether a given pupil does well or poorly. The general prin-

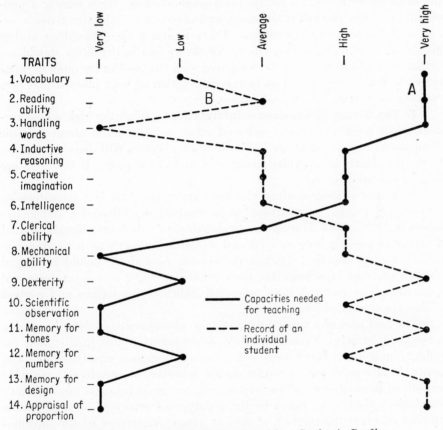

Fig. 148. *Comparison of an "Ideal" Profile with a Student's Profile*

Based on figures in J. O'Connor, *The Unique Individual*, Human Engineering Laboratory, 1948, p. 13.

ciple underlying the use of the profile, aside from its mere convenience, is that there exists an "ideal" combination of traits for each occupation, and hence an "ideal" profile. If one can measure enough essential skills accurately and can obtain test results from successful men and women in each occupation, then one would need only to measure an applicant and to match his profile against that which is most desired. This utopian state of affairs has not yet been reached, but several investigators have taken at least some steps in the right direction. For instance, the basic intellectual abilities needed for teaching are fairly well known, as indicated in Figure 148 on page 619. What a teacher needs most is a large vocabulary, a high degree of reading skill, and an ability to handle words; a teacher also needs a better than average creative imagination, ability to reason with abstract ideas, and good general intelligence. Average clerical skill is sufficient. The other abilities on the list are not essential, although their possession does no harm and may serve as the basis for the teaching of special subjects. On the same figure there is a profile for a single student. He is clearly a non-verbal type. His clerical, mechanical, and scientific abilities are above average, and his dexterity is excellent. There is also a suggestion that he has artistic and musical abilities. His profile shows that he definitely should not teach; it should presumably be compared with the profiles for other occupations. A final choice would include consideration of both interest and personality as well as intellectual fitness.

4. The Giving of Vocational Information: What the high school student needs most from the vocational office is information about possible occupations and about himself. The following section will discuss what information should be provided about jobs and about people if the facts are to help the adolescent.

In a later chapter dealing with the curriculum there is a recommendation for a course on "occupations" to be required of all freshmen and sophomores in high school. During the freshman year this course should present a survey of possible lines of work and should include at least a rough measure of various abilities. During the second year there should be actual observation and experience for each pupil according to his interests and capacities. The material here presented indicates the nature and content of this recommended program.

The first part of a general course on occupations should describe a large assortment of jobs. Naturally, there is neither time nor justification for telling pupils about every possible job any of them may sometime hold. The person in charge of such a course should, however, be sure to select a wide variety of occupations and to present, without prejudices, *all* lines of adult economic activity. In regard to the occupations presented, a considerable amount of exact information should be given. An outline of the information needed is presented below:

EMPLOYMENT PROSPECTS: Are workers in demand today? Is employment in this occupation expected to increase or decrease?

NATURE OF THE WORK: What is the work of a typical day, week, month, year? What are all the things a worker may have to do in this occupation, the pleasant things, the unpleasant things, the big and little tasks, the important responsibilities and the less glamorous details?

QUALIFICATIONS: *Age.* What are the upper and lower age limits for entrance and retirement?

Sex. Is this predominantly a male or a female occupation? Are there reasonable opportunities for both? Is there any more active demand for one than for the other?

Height and weight. Are there any minimum or maximum requirements? What are they?

Other physical requirements. Are there any other measurable physical requirements, e.g., 20/20 vision, freedom from color-blindness, average or superior hearing, physical strength, etc.?

Aptitudes. Has there been any research on aptitudes required, e.g., minimum or maximum intelligence quotient, percentile, rank on specific tests of mechanical aptitude, clerical aptitude, finger dexterity, pitch discrimination, reaction time, etc.?

Interests. Have any vocational interest tests been validated against workers in this occupation?

Tools and equipment. Must these be supplied to the worker at his own expense? What is the average cost?

Legal requirements. Is a license or certificate required? What are the requirements for getting it?

UNIONS: Is the closed shop common or predominant? If so, what are the requirements for entrance to the union? Initiation fees? Dues? Does the union limit the number admitted?

DISCRIMINATION: Do employees, unions, or training institutions discriminate against Negroes, Jews, others?

PREPARATION: Distinguish clearly between what is desirable and what is indispensable.

How much and what kind of preparation is required to meet legal requirements and employers' standards?

How long does it take? What does it cost? What does it include? How much elimination is there during the training?

Where can one get a list of approved schools?

What kind of high school or college program should precede entrance into the professional schools? What subjects must or should be chosen?

What provisions, if any, are made for apprenticeship or other training on the job?

Is experience of some kind prerequisite to entrance? Is the completion of a part of the course of any value, or must one finish the training in order to derive benefit from it?

ENTRANCE: How does one get his first job? By taking an examination? By applying to employers? By joining a union? By registering with employment agencies? By saving to acquire capital and opening his own business? How much capital is required?

ADVANCEMENT: What proportion of workers advance? To what? After how long and after what additional preparation or experience?

What are the related occupations to which this may lead, if any?

EARNINGS: What are the most dependable average figures on earnings by week, month, or year?

What is the range of the middle 50 per cent?

Are earnings higher or lower in certain parts of the United States, or in certain branches of the occupation?

NUMBER AND DISTRIBUTION OF WORKERS: Are the workers evenly distributed over the U.S. in proportion to population, or concentrated in certain areas? Where? Why?

Can a person practice this occupation anywhere he may wish to live?

Do conditions in small towns and rural areas differ materially from those in urban centers? How?

ADVANTAGES AND DISADVANTAGES: What do workers say they like best and dislike most about their jobs?

Are hours regular or irregular, long or short? Is there frequent overtime or night work? Sunday and holiday work?

What about vacations?

Is employment steady, seasonal, or irregular? Does one earn more or less with advancing age?

Is the working lifetime shorter than average, e.g., professional athletics?

Are the skills acquired transferable to other occupations?

Is the work hazardous? What about accidents, occupational diseases?

In comparison with other occupations requiring about the same level of ability and training, in what ways is this one more or less attractive?[17]

The need for this type of information, even in college, is well shown by a study made some years ago.[18] Out of **888** university students, **70** per cent were planning to enter teaching, medicine, or law—at that time the three most overcrowded vocations in the country. The students were asked to state also how much they expected to earn per annum; **80** per cent of them expected to earn more than the average worker in these fields. Sixty-six per cent had intelligence scores below the level needed for the work they had chosen, and **37** per cent did not have good enough marks to enter the special training that would prepare them for their chosen lifework. This situation seems to have improved somewhat since the above study was made. In an investigation of the objectives of **1,283** men and **1,450** women freshmen in the municipal colleges of New York, **89** per cent of the men wanted to become physical scientists; **31** per cent, businessmen, public school teachers, doctors, or government agents of some sort.[19] Of the women, **54** per cent expected to enter public school teaching, **10** per cent wanted to become social workers, and another **10** per cent businesswomen. These ambitions are definitely more realistic than those reported in the previous study.

Because of the need for a balanced investigation of personal fitness, the second section of a course on occupations should present opportunities for adolescents to find out about themselves; and the more objective such information is, the better. Students need to know where they stand in regard to the entire distribution on each of a number of traits. Fortunately, the technique of testing has advanced to such a stage that objective self-estimation is possible. A plan like that suggested below might well be followed.

During the second semester of the freshman year in the course on occupations, the instructor might devote a week's work to a general discussion of the relationship between types of individuals and types of work, with illustrations of how some people fail to achieve their ambitions because of

---

[17] R. Hoppock, "A Check List of Factors about Jobs for Use in Vocational Guidance," *American Psychologist*, 8:417–418, 1948. Used by permission of the American Psychological Association.

[18] E. J. Sparling, "Do College Students Choose Vocations Wisely?" *Teachers College Contributions to Education*, No. 561, 1933, 110 pp. See also R. P. Fischer, "Need for Vocational Information," *Journal of Higher Education*, 16:33–36, 1945.

[19] R. M. W. Travers and H. Niebuhr, "Vocational Choices of Freshmen Attending the City Colleges," *Research Publication No. 6*, Office of Research and Evaluation, College of the City of New York, 1950, 8 pp.

their personal characteristics. If this line of thought is well presented, the students will spontaneously want to know something about themselves so that they may select occupations as wisely as possible. This interest leads quite naturally to the administration of perhaps a half-dozen objective, standardized tests; two tests of intelligence, two or three tests of academic preparation, two or three questionnaires about personality traits, and several tests of vocational aptitude should be included. Naturally, the clerical burden from such extensive testing of the entire freshman class is considerable, but the use to which the tests are to be put suggests a solution of the clerical problem. These tests are being given to inform students about themselves; they should therefore score their own tests. If they realize these tests are not being given as examinations, will not be used to prejudice their schoolwork, and will not be shown to other people, adolescents can be trusted to score their own tests. However, if precaution against cheating is regarded as essential, all tests can be marked with indelible pencils, which are collected immediately after the tests are finished. Alterations and additions will not then usually be made, and if made are easily detected. From these test scores a total distribution should be made, and each pupil should see where he stands.

Objections are always made to letting pupils know what scores they make on tests of intelligence. Two such tests have been recommended as a means of avoiding chance errors in a single score. If a pupil stands third from the bottom of a class on one test and eighth from the bottom on the second, the sooner he appreciates his comparative ability the better. In the course of time he will inevitably learn of his deficiencies. The only choice lies between informing him at the beginning of his secondary school course and allowing successive blows of fate to reveal the situation to him—probably producing a series of emotional storms in the process. If the instructor has reasonable tact, he will make clear that the possession of inferior ability is nothing to be ashamed of, but rather an unavoidable fact with which one must deal. In a similar manner the results of tests of schooling and personality should be interpreted for the pupil. Each pupil should be encouraged to make a graph showing his standing in terms of total distributions in the three important elements of intelligence, previous school achievement, and personality. He is then ready to make a summary of his available talents.

The second year of vocational work should be devoted to actual observations of various occupations, and to a certain amount of apprenticeship on the job. The arrangements for such observation will naturally vary from one community to another, depending upon a variety of factors. There is, however, no substitute for direct study. An adolescent will learn more about a job during a week's observation of some individual at work than he will from reading innumerable descriptions.

In this connection, the writer would like to suggest the establishment of a "Work Week" during the sophomore year of high school, preferably at the close of the first semester, after the final examinations in academic courses have been given. During this Work Week each sophomore in the school would be assigned to some worker, through arrangements already made with various individuals and concerns. Thus the girl who wanted to be a salesclerk would be assigned to observe

624   INTELLECTUAL DEVELOPMENT

and, if possible, to assist a saleswoman in some store. The girl who wanted to be a teacher could spend each school day in some teacher's room observing what is actually done. The boy who wanted to be a mechanic would seek work in a garage, while the prospective lawyer would spend some days in court watching cases being tried and other days in a lawyer's office observing the preparation of cases for trial. Exploratory work of this sort already done by various vocational counselors has shown that plenty of adults can be found who will take under their tutelage for a week an adolescent boy or girl who wishes to observe a given type of work. Naturally not all phases of a particular job could be demonstrated, but some degree of practical acquaintance with various activities could be obtained, thus substituting direct knowledge for the adolescent's own imaginative notions. Such a system of apprenticeship would do a great deal toward clarifying the problem of vocational choice.

5. Vocational Satisfaction: Satisfaction with one's work is the product of many factors. This phase of vocational guidance has received relatively little attention, but is of undoubted importance. In a one-year follow-up study of 1,080 high school graduates, the 665 (62 per cent) who were doing the kind of work they had planned to do were reasonably well satisfied.[20] The other 415 were not following their high school plans. Their deviation had affected their satisfaction with their work, but not their efficiency.

In another study workers in several fields were asked to express their satisfaction with several different phases of their employment.[21] A few sample results appear in Figure 149 on page 625. Dissatisfaction with pay, with opportunities for advancement, and with the general nature of their work was lowest among business men and skilled laborers, average in the professions and among office workers, and highest among semi-skilled and unskilled laborers. The workers also estimated the degree of self-expression and security in their jobs. The results suggest that one cannot hope for both these features. The more opportunity there was for self-expression, the less the feeling of security, and vice versa. This relationship might well be brought to the attention of young people as one factor to be considered in the selection of an occupation.

The high school population must furnish the individuals who will in the next generation occupy every kind of job above the level of the day laborer, who is recruited mostly from those who do not reach high school; therefore any consideration of occupations should stress equally and without prejudice the entire range of jobs into which high school students will go. It is essential that work of all types should be presented and that no work at any level should be labeled, openly or by implication, as being menial or unworthy. The work of the world has to be done, and it will be much better done if every worker is proud of his work. The desirable attitude toward one's work, no matter what it is, is shown in the following brief accounts:

Mr. H. is almost an institution in the small city where he lives. As nearly as his occupation could be classified, he would be called a "handy man." He mows

[20] Wightwick, "Vocational Interest Patterns," *loc. cit.*
[21] R. Centers, "Motivational Aspects of Occupational Stratification," *Journal of Social Psychology,* 28:187–217, 1948.

lawns, weeds gardens, and washes windows in the summer; in the winter he fixes electrical gadgets that refuse to work, tends the furnaces, and shovels snow. In addition to these routine activities, he builds almost anything from a birdhouse to a bookcase, or from a flagstone walk to a brick wall. His work is not especially ingenious, but it is well done. He tends to minutiae with loving care, measures from all angles, planes and sandpapers each board before using it, and spends hours in getting each detail exactly right. The remarkable thing about Mr. H. is not, however, his workmanship but his pride in each thing he finishes. If it is portable, he

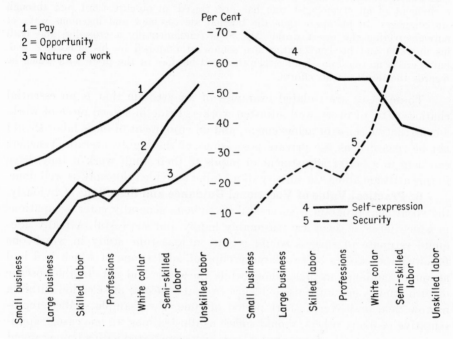

Fig. 149. *Dissatisfaction, Self-Expression, and Security*

Based on R. Centers, "Motivational Aspects of Occupational Stratification," *Journal of Social Psychology,* 28:198–211, 1948.

carries it around the neighborhood and shows it to families for whom he works. If it is not portable, he persuades his numerous employers to come and see what he has done. He does not want to be praised or complimented; what he wants is to have others enjoy the perfection of the thing he has built. He once escorted the writer for a distance of six blocks to show her three brick steps he had built to replace some wooden ones that had fallen into decay. The point he wanted admired was the absolute evenness and straightness of the steps from any angle whatever; the fact that he had made them was not as important as the accuracy of the work. Throughout one section of the city there are lawns Mr. H. has planted and tended, garages he has built or rebuilt, roofs he has shingled, shrubs he has transplanted, fences he has put up, and houses he has painted. His progress through the neighborhood is rather deliberate, because he stops in front of every fourth or fifth house to enjoy the fruits of his labors. Mr. H. is neither conceited nor boastful; he has only an honest pride in simple work that is carefully done. In his humble way he has left more of an imprint upon the life of the community than many a man of more spectacular talents.

Mr. S. is known in the city where he works simply as the "bugman." It is doubtful if many of the people who send for him when ants, termites, fleas, or other undesirable guests invade their houses know him by any other name. The distinguishing thing about him is not his efficiency in routing the pests, but his delight in his success. There is more joy in his heart over the wresting of one oldish wooden house from the termites than over the rescue of twenty new cement houses. There is little that he does not know about insects and their habits, and he is a tireless worker in saving the world from being eaten alive by them. His cheerfulness and enthusiasm are neither sales patter nor surface mannerisms; they are as real as the excitement of an etymologist who has just traced an obscure word root through six languages. In his spare time the bugman devises new and ingenious ways of outmaneuvering the insect world. Mr. S. is fundamentally a crusader, and both his interests and his conversation are somewhat cramped by his crusader's zeal, but there is no question about either the good he does or the pride with which he regards the results of his efforts.

These cases are isolated examples of an attitude that is an essential characteristic of every well-adjusted worker. Pride in a good piece of work, a constructive sense of achievement, and an enjoyment of one's labor should not be regarded as the private possessions of the highly literate. Teachers can help in a better adjustment of pupils to their adult work if they drive in this attitude about the dignity of all labor provided the work is well done.

6. Practical Value of Vocational Guidance and Selection: Obviously, the vocational program is successful if students generally enter occupations in which most of them are reasonably happy and successful. A really adequate estimate of success would require a long-time study in which one followed the careers of two large groups of adults, one of which had had adequate guidance in high school while the other had not. In the absence of such studies one must use evidence from the success of selection within a narrow field and over a short period of time. Two sample studies, representative of many others, should suffice as illustrations. In one case,[22] applicants to the police department of a large city were tested with a temperament scale, which correlated with the appraisal of success on the job with a coefficient of 0.72. Of the original 621 applicants, 233 were discharged and 79 resigned. Only 2 per cent of the discharged men made high scores on the scale; 26 per cent made average scores, and 72 per cent made low or very low scores. The corresponding percentages for the 79 who resigned were 11, 39, and 50. The second report dealt with the success of placement by various tests of the women in one of the English military services.[23] The follow-up of the personnel showed a sufficient degree of satisfaction and efficiency to permit continuance of the work in 95 per cent of the cases. One cannot say what the proportion would have been without the test selection, but one suspects it would have been appreciably lower.

Perhaps the most convincing proof of the value of guidance is still the

[22] D. G. Humm and K. A. Humm, "The Humm-Wadsworth Temperament Scale Appraisals Compared with Criteria of Job Success in the Los Angeles Police Department," *Journal of Psychology*, 30:63–75, 1950.

[23] M. Wickham, "Follow-Up of Personnel Selection in the ATS," *Occupational Psychology*, 23:153–169, 1949.

success of the individual case. The three studies that follow tell the histories of three misfits. Such stories almost always involve misfits, since they are the ones who ask for help and for whom a case-study exists. One of these three was of low intelligence, one was quite introverted, and a third was a victim of well-intentioned parental misguidance.

Alfred was a freshman in high school and a complete failure in all academic work. He had never done satisfactory schoolwork in any grade, but he went to a progressive school in which every pupil was promoted every year. Since Alfred's IQ was 78, it is unlikely that he ever really understood much of his work. He arrived at high school when he was fourteen. At this time his mental age was 11 years, much too low for high school. At the end of the first semester he was sent to the counselor to see what might be done for him during the remaining two years that the law required him to remain in school.

Alfred's motor co-ordination was so poor and his mentality so low that it did not seem wise to enroll him in a trade school, at least not at once. The one ability he had was along musical lines. He had a good ear and sang well, but he was unable to read music. He had learned to pick out tunes on the piano and greatly enjoyed doing so. The music teacher suggested that the boy might try to learn to play an oboe or a bass viol, for both of which the score is relatively easy to read, since neither instrument has a wide range of tones. Alfred took one lesson every day on the oboe, practiced faithfully, and spent two hours a day in a remedial reading class. He was assigned several hours a week on the playground, mostly with younger children since the organized games of adolescence were too difficult for him. He helped the playground teacher with the little children, with whom he played willingly and well. This regime was followed for a year. During his next year, he obtained a part-time job as a playground assistant and worked mornings, helping little children build sand castles and supervising them on the swings and slides. He was always kind and considerate, and the children were fond of him. Each afternoon he practiced on the oboe, which he was by now playing quite well. He had, to be sure, no dash and no imagination, but an oboe player is not a solo artist. He still did not read a score well, but he was improving in this respect. At the end of his second year he did not want to drop out of school, so he was allowed to take a special reading course with some of the slower freshmen and to enter a current events class. During this year he became a regularly assigned assistant on the playground where he had worked the year before and was paid a small sum for his time there. He was also given an opportunity to practice with a local orchestra and was able to give a satisfactory performance by getting the scores ahead of time and practicing them under supervision at school during the afternoons. At the present time Alfred is a regular member of the orchestra and receives a small salary. His life is quiet and uneventful. In the mornings he works on the playground, in the afternoons he practices—sometimes at the school—and two evenings a week he plays or practices with the orchestra. He has never shown any inclination to become a delinquent. Alfred is a living demonstration of the value of guidance.

Hazel was a quiet, serious girl who had a good record in the elementary grades and an average record in high school. Over the years she had taken five group tests of intelligence and had scored between the median and the seventy-fifth percentile on all of them. She had never been in disciplinary difficulties. Her teachers reported her as being too withdrawn and too quiet. Efforts to interest her in various activities had not been especially effective, although she seemed to get some enjoyment out of her leather working club and out of singing in the school chorus. As a sophomore in high school, Hazel came voluntarily to the guidance office because she lacked adequate self-confidence. Subsequent interviews revealed a home situation that accounted in large measure for Hazel's reticence. Her parents were both repressed people who rejected with horror any show of emotion. They were never affectionate with her or with each other. They were both sensitive to social approval and determined to be decorous and correct at all costs. Hazel learned at an early age to be quiet, reserved, industrious, sober, conscientious, and conventional, since such behavior met with approval. She had accepted her parents' standards and had molded herself accordingly.

With assistance the girl managed to develop a moderate degree of self-confidence in her schoolwork and to obtain better marks, but she continued to be abnormally quiet and self-effacing in social relationships, although the number of her social contacts was increased by membership in two more school clubs. In her junior year Hazel began to think about what kind of work she could do after leaving school. She had no desire to go on to college, and her counselor felt that the girl's abilities, though average, were not high enough to compensate for her negative personality and that she would not be successful in college. In talking with Hazel about the matter it became evident that Hazel wanted work that had two characteristics—permanency and monotony. She disliked change of any kind—even a change to something better—and she wanted the support of routine to bolster her courage. She was therefore advised to elect courses in office routine. After a little training Hazel decided she would like to be a filing clerk or some kind of record keeper. She felt that such work was within her capacities and that she could perform her duties without strain. At first the counselor was inclined to think that Hazel had more ability than was needed for such simple work and would therefore soon become discontented and bored, but eventually she realized that the girl needed security above everything else and that she would be happy only in work that was far below her capacity and would not frighten her. The counselor therefore encouraged Hazel to take such further training as she needed for obtaining a clerical position. After graduation from high school Hazel went to work as a filing clerk in the records room of a large hospital. She liked the work from the first day, and she liked the courtesy with which she was treated. She has remained in the records office of the same hospital for four years now and is still contented and does not want to change her job.

Earl S. was a freshman in engineering who had just failed both mathematics and mechanical drawing. By contrast, his work in English had been outstandingly good. When Earl first talked with the counselor he refused to so much as consider changing from engineering into some other course of study. He refused to take any aptitude tests although the counselor suggested that the results might be useful to him. He was quite unable to accept the idea that he might actually need help.

About a week before the end of the following semester Earl returned to the counselor in a state bordering upon panic. It appeared that he was now failing everything, even his English. Gradually Earl was able to bring out the main outlines of his difficulties. He had always done well in linguistic studies and badly in both mathematics and science. He was, however, convinced that he "ought" to take things that were hard for him in order to improve his mind. He had entered engineering at the urging of his father, who had always regretted that he had not taken an engineering course. Earl had a great admiration for his father but at the same time stood somewhat in awe of him, and he did not see how he could face him after the complete failure of his second semester's work. The counselor tried to talk the lad into a more cheerful mood and managed to relieve his worst apprehensions by offering to break the news to the father and to discuss with him a possible future for Earl, now that the engineering school was about to dismiss him. The father turned out to be a man who was deeply devoted to his son, but he was an extroverted, overactive, talkative individual who expressed his own ideas so continually that he never did learn what other people thought or felt. He was genuinely surprised to discover that Earl did not like engineering. Apparently it had never crossed his mind that his son was not merely a younger edition of himself. It was also clear to the counselor that all the talk about the fascination of engineering was merely an outlet for the father whenever he happened to be bored with his work as a lawyer—an occupation to which he was far better adapted than to engineering. As a fantasy it did no harm, but when he tried to influence his son into living out his own fantasy, the trouble began. The man was bright enough to see the situation and perfectly willing to take the major blame for his son's academic maladjustment. His devotion seemed genuine, and he did not even resent the advice to talk less and listen more!

The following year Earl transferred to a small arts college, where he majored in English literature. Since his early failure in engineering seemed still to rankle a bit, he returned to the university from which he had been dismissed and took his Ph.D. there, doing most of his work in Old English. Earl is now a professor in a small college, and his father is extremely proud of him.

III. Summary

Personnel work in the high schools has become a permanent part of the services rendered to students. Each year more schools introduce counseling, and the many that already have it expand the activities of the counselors. Recent years have seen a decided trend toward the student-centered type of counseling, which merely guides the student's own thinking and helps him to find a solution to his problems after he has identified them. The main problems center around the selection of courses, the selection of a vocation, and the attainment of a good social adjustment, but many others appear from time to time.

The selection of a vocation is a matter of vital importance to the adolescent because of the influence it will have upon his future. Adolescents often concentrate upon a comparatively few occupations, without much respect to either the demands of the work or their own abilities to meet the requirements. They need therefore to be guided, not so much by advice as by information. Boys and girls should, of course, take their interests into consideration as one element in the situation, but they need to see that interest is not the only factor. At entrance to high school many young adolescents still have glamorous notions about the work they want to do, and they need help in outgrowing these childish attitudes. Many adolescents come to the counselor's office voluntarily to obtain an appraisal of themselves so that they may know what their strong and weak points are. This development is highly desirable, since the students come in a frame of mind that permits the most valuable types of guidance.

REFERENCES TO FURTHER READING

BOOKS

1. Alexander and Saylor, *Secondary Education,* Chap. 20.
2. Bell, H. M., *Matching Youth and Jobs,* American Council on Education, 1940, 247 pp. (Pt. I.)
3. Belting, P. E., and A. W. Clevenger, *The High School at Work,* Rand McNally & Company, 1939, 441 pp. (Chap. 2.)

4. Blum, M. L., and B. Balinsky, *Counseling and Psychology*, Prentice-Hall, Inc., 1951, 586 pp. (Chaps. 4–5, 7–11, 13–14.)
5. Brewer, J. M., and E. Landy, *Occupations Today*, Ginn and Company, 1949, 383 pp. (Chaps. 1–4.)
6. Cox, P. W. L., *et al.*, *Basic Principles of Guidance*, Prentice-Hall, Inc., 2d ed., 1948, 439 pp. (Chaps. 5–7, 10, 11, 16, 18, 19.)
7. Crow and Crow, *Our Teen-Age Boys and Girls*, Chaps. 7, 8.
8. Darley, J. G., *Testing and Counseling in the High School Guidance Program*, Science Research Associates, 1943, 222 pp. (Chaps. 1–2, 6–7.)
9. Fleming, *Adolescence: Its Social Psychology*, Chap. 15.
10. Garrison, *Psychology of Adolescence*, Chaps. 19, 20.
11. Ginsberg, E., *Occupational Choice*, Columbia University Press, 1951, 271 pp. (Chaps. 7–10, 14.)
12. Goodenough, F. L., *Developmental Psychology*, Chap. 28.
13. Hahn, M. E., and M. S. MacLean, *General Clinical Counseling in Educational Institutions*, McGraw-Hill Book Company, 1950, 375 pp. (Chaps. 3–5, 8.)
14. Hamrin, I. A., and B. B. Paulson, *Counseling Adolescents*, Science Research Associates, 1950, 371 pp. (Chaps. 3, 6, 10 or Chaps. 7, 8, 9.)
15. Havighurst and Taba, *Adolescent Character and Personality*, Chaps. 6, 8, 9.
16. Hunt, M. L., "Projective Techniques in Guidance," in Donahue, *Student Adjustment*, pp. 54–70.
17. Kuhlen, *Psychology of Adolescent Development*, Chap. 11.
18. Landis, *Adolescence and Youth*, Chaps. 16, 17.
19. Malm and Jamison, *Adolescence*, Chap. 10.
20. McGill and Matthews, *The Youth of New York City*, Chaps. 6–8.
21. O'Connor, J., *The Unique Individual*, Human Engineering Laboratory, 1948, 249 pp. (Chaps. 1, 2, 6–9, 11, 12, 16.)
22. Paulson, B., "The Pattern of My Tomorrows," *Self-Appraisal and Careers Pamphlet Series*, No. 1, Board of Education, Chicago, 1946, 61 pp.
23. Rogers, C. R., *Client-Centered Therapy*, Houghton Mifflin Company, 1951, 560 pp.
24. Rogers, C. R., *Counseling and Psychotherapy*, Houghton Mifflin Company, 1942, 450 pp. (Chaps. 1–5 and any one chapter in Pt. II.)
25. Rothney, J. W. M., and B. A. Roems, *Counseling the Individual Student*, The Dryden Press, 1949, 364 pp. (Chaps. 1–3, 5.)
26. Snyder, W. V., *A Case Book of Non-Directive Counseling*, Houghton Mifflin Company, 1947, 339 pp. (Any one case.)
27. Steckle, *Problems of Human Adjustment*, Chap. 10.
28. Super, D. E., *Appraising Vocational Fitness by Means of Psychological Tests*, Harper & Brothers, 1949, 727 pp. (Chaps. 1, 2, 4, 16, 17, 20.)
29. Super, D. E., *Avocational Interest Patterns*, Stanford University Press, 1940, 148 pp. (Chaps. 5, 7, 8, 9.)
30. Valentine, *Twentieth Century Education*, Chaps. 15, 30.
31. Warters, J., *High School Personnel Work*, McGraw-Hill Book Company, 1946, 277 pp. (Chaps. 1–2, 5–6, 7–9.)
32. Warters, *Achieving Maturity*, Chaps. 12, 13.
33. Williamson, E. G., *Counseling Adolescents*, McGraw-Hill Book Company, rev. ed., 1950, 548 pp. (Chaps. 3–5, 9, and any one case from the Appendix.)
34. Williamson, E. G., *Trends in Student Personnel Work*, University of Minnesota Press, 417 pp. (Pp. 52–61, 62–72, 80–95, 120–128.)
35. Williamson, E. G., and J. D. Foley, *Counseling and Discipline*, McGraw-Hill Book Company, 1949, 387 pp. (Chaps. 1–4, and any case study from the Appendix.)

36. Wrenn, C. G., *Student Personnel Work in College, with Emphasis on Counseling and Group Experience.* The Ronald Press, 1951, 589 pp. (Chaps. 3–7.)
37. Wrenn, C. G., and W. E. Dugan, *Guidance Procedures in High School,* University of Minnesota Press, 1950, 71 pp.
38. Wright, B. H., *Practical Handbook for Group Guidance,* Science Research Associates, 1948, 225 pp. (Chaps. 9–15.)
39. Zachry and Lighty, *Emotions and Conduct in Adolescence,* Chap. 12.

MONOGRAPHS, BULLETINS, PROCEEDINGS, YEARBOOKS, ARTICLES

A. *Procedures in Counseling*

1. Bixler, R. H., and V. H. Bixler, "Clinical Counseling in Vocational Counseling," *Journal of Clinical Psychology,* 1:186–192, 1945.
2. Combs, A. W., "Vocational Counseling and Non-Directive Therapy," *Occupations,* 26:261–267, 1947.
3. Kilby, R. W., "Some Vocational Counseling Methods," *Educational and Psychological Measurement,* 9:173–191, 1949.
4. Muench, G. A., "An Evaluation of Non-Directive Psychotherapy," *Applied Psychology Monographs,* No. 13, 1947, 163 pp.
5. Rogers, C. R., "Development of Nondirective Therapy," *Journal of Consulting Psychology,* 12:92–110, 1948.
6. Rogers, C. R., "Some Implications of Client-Centered Counseling for College Personnel Work," *College and University,* 24:59–67, 1948.
7. Rothney, J. W. M., and P. J. Danielson, "Counseling," *Review of Educational Research,* 21:132–139, 1951.
8. Schloerb, L. J., "Guidance Programs and Problems at the Secondary School Level," *School Review,* 51:202–207, 1946.
9. Warters, J., "Guidance through Groups," *Review of Educational Research,* 21:140–148, 1951.
10. Wimmer, N. E., "Guidance in Secondary Schools," *School Review,* 56:343–349, 1948.
11. Wrenn, C. G., "Client-Centered Counseling," *Educational and Psychological Measurement,* 6:439–444, 1946.

B. *Vocations*

1. Bateman, R. M., and H. H. Remmers, "Attitudes of High School Freshmen toward the Occupations of Their Choice before and after Studying the Occupations by Means of a Career Book," *Journal of Educational Psychology,* 30:657–666, 1939.
2. Carp, F. M., "High School Boys Are Realistic about Occupations," *Occupations,* 28:97–99, 1949.
3. Centers, R., "Motivational Aspects of Occupational Stratification," *Journal of Social Psychology,* 28:187–217, 1948.
4. Greenleaf, W. J., "Educational and Vocational Information," *Review of Educational Research,* 21:149–158, 1951.
5. Hoppock, R., "A Check List of Factors about Jobs for Use in Vocational Guidance," *American Psychologist,* 3:417–418, 1948.
6. Jones, E. S., "Relation of Ability to Preferred and Probable Occupations," *Educational Administration and Supervision,* 26:220–226, 1940.
7. Kroger, R., and C. M. Louttit, "The Influence of Fathers' Occupations on Vocational Choices of High School Boys," *Journal of Applied Psychology,* 19:205–212, 1935.

8. Recktenwald, L. N., "Attitudes toward Occupations before and after Vocational Information," *Occupations*, 24:220–223, 1946.

C. *Interests*

1. Angus, L., "A Comparative Study of the Methods of Measuring Interest in Science and Its Relation to Ability and Achievement," *British Journal of Educational Psychology*, 20:63–65, 1950.
2. Canning, L., *et al.*, "Permanence of Vocational Interests of High School Boys," *Journal of Educational Psychology*, 32:481–494, 1941.
3. Carter, H. D., "Development of Interest in Vocations," *Forty-third Yearbook of the National Society for the Study of Education*, 1944, Pt. I, pp. 255–276.
4. Daniels, E. E., and W. A. Hunter, "MMPI Personality Patterns for Various Occupations," *Journal of Applied Psychology*, 33:559–565, 1949.
5. Fleege, U. H., and H. J. Malone, "Motivation in Occupational Choice among Junior–Senior High School Students," *Journal of Educational Psychology*, 37:77–86, 1946.
6. Jacobs, R., "Stability of Interests at the Secondary School Level," *Educational Research Bulletin*, 52:83–87, 1949.
7. Strong, E. K., "The Role of Interests in Guidance," *Occupations*, 27:517–522, 1949.
8. Taylor, K., and H. D. Carter, "Retest Consistency of Vocational Interest Patterns of High School Girls," *Journal of Consulting Psychology*, 6:95–101, 1942.
9. Wightwick, M. I., "Vocational Interest Patterns," *Teachers College Record*, 46:460–461, 1945.
10. Witty, P. A., *et al.*, "Comparison of the Vocational Interests of Negro and White High School Students," *Journal of Educational Psychology*, 32:124–132, 1941.

D. *Tests and Predictions*

1. Bradford, E. L., "Selection for Technical Education," *British Journal of Educational Psychology*, XVI, Pt. II (1946), 69–81.
2. Cooprider, H. A., and H. R. Laslett, "Predictive Values of the Stanford Scientific Aptitude Factors," *Occupations*, 26:683–687, 1948.
3. Krathworth, W. C., "Predictions of Average Class Achievement by Means of Aptitude Tests," *Journal of Engineering Education*, 37:234–243, 1946.
4. Segel, D., "Validity of a Multiple Aptitude Test at the Secondary School Level," *Educational and Psychological Measurements*, 7:695–705, 1947.
5. Shoemaker, H. A., and J. H. Rohrer, "Relationship between Success in the Study of Medicine and Certain Psychological and Personal Data," *Journal of the Association of American Medical Colleges*, 23:190–200, 1948.
6. Super, D. E., "The Place of Aptitude Testing in the Public Schools," *Educational and Psychological Measurement*, 2:267–278, 1942.
7. Traxler, A. E., "Evaluation of Aptitude and Achievement in a Guidance Program," *Educational and Psychological Measurement*, 6:3–16, 1946.

E. *Counselors, Problems, and Programs*

1. Arnold, D. L., "Qualifications of a Guidance Counselor," *Purdue University Studies in Higher Education*, 55:8–19, 1946.
2. Pepinsky, H. B., "The Selection and Use of Diagnostic Categories in Clinical Counseling," *Applied Psychology Monographs*, No. 15, 1948, 140 pp.
3. Polmentier, P. C., and F. McKinney, "Programs of Personnel Work," *Review of Educational Research*, 18:150–156, 1948.
4. Wimmer, N. E., "Guidance in Secondary Schools," *School Review*, 56:343–349, 1948.

CHAPTER NINETEEN

The High School Curriculum

Since the high school is a public institution, it should serve the needs of all the adolescents who attend it. It must concern itself with social adjustment, growth of personality, development of moral attitudes, vocational choice, and physical development, as well as with mastery of academic subjects. Some of these points have been discussed in other chapters, but there remain a few topics that require further consideration.

The secondary school curriculum in the United States has a fairly long history, dating from the early eighteenth century. Certain of the elements still contained in it and certain of the attitudes toward it are survivals of an earlier day. It therefore seems desirable to begin the present chapter with a brief summary of developments in the American secondary school. Various investigators have stressed the need for a general reorganization of the high school curriculum. The curricular offerings—both required and elective—of the high school will therefore be discussed in a second section. The third section will deal with the work of the teacher. If a high school is to serve the needs of youth, it must offer an appropriate course of study and teach it by methods that stimulate growth and mastery.

I. Growth of the High School Curriculum

The curriculum of secondary education in America was borrowed originally from the schools of England. This model was aristocratic, cloistered, humanistic, disciplinary, and masculine. The training given was intended for a selected group of boys, who were to be molded into gentlemen. Girls were given smaller doses of the same course of study, without respect to its appropriateness for them. The studies were strongly humanistic; that is, the heaviest concentration of work was in Greek and Latin. The school was not supposed to be closely related to life or to contribute directly to an understanding of the practical world. The boys led a cloistered existence for several years, during which their minds were supposed to be disciplined by their study of ancient languages and mathematics. This curriculum was transplanted to American soil, where it grew and changed only slowly up until the time of the Revolution. After that upheaval the desire to break away from everything English led to some modifications, but the main

633

changes were at the elementary level. The country already knew what kind of basic education it wanted, but it was not yet ready to develop a secondary school especially adapted to its needs. The English model for secondary schools, plus some accretions from German secondary education, lingered on into modern times, in spite of its inappropriateness to the American way of life. It was not, indeed, until the very end of the nineteenth century that the high school began to be "Americanized" into the unique institution it is today.

During most of the nineteenth century the curriculum of the secondary school consisted of Latin, Greek, algebra, geometry, rhetoric, a little history, a little elementary work in the physical sciences, and sometimes German or French—subjects demanded as a basis for the education of a scholar and a gentleman. They still remain subjects that are necessary for a scholar, but they are not and never were intended as subjects for the average adolescent boy or girl.

It was not until after 1890 that the high school began to grow, and then it grew slowly for two decades, as shown in Figure 115 on page 498. In 1890, only 7 adolescents in every 100 between the ages of fourteen and eighteen were in school. By 1910 the number had risen to a modest 11 in every 100. During the following decade came World War I and a great upsurge in secondary education. By 1940, 68 adolescents in every 100 were in school, and in some cities where the offerings were exceptionally good the proportion had risen to over 80 in every 100.

During World War II the number of adolescents in school decreased markedly, while the number employed rose by more than 300 per cent. The enrollment figures—minus the eighteen-year-olds who were not included in the totals for either school or work[1]—sank from an all-time high of 6,713,913 in 1940 to 5,761,000 in 1943. Among the nearly 3,000,000 employed adolescents in 1943, not counting domestic servants and farm laborers, over 1,280,000 were under sixteen years of age.[2] The normal trends were therefore interrupted by the war, partly by military service, partly by the need for workers, and partly by mere restlessness from the general tension. After 1943 there was another rise in the number of students in secondary education as the ex-soldiers returned to school. Since the birth rate rose markedly during the war years, a greatly increased enrollment can be expected in high school from 1958 to 1962. It has been estimated that 11,000,000 students will be enrolled, a number almost double the enrollment at present.[3] After the "war babies" graduate, it is probable that the falling birth rate will again begin to offset the increased holding power of the high school, and the enrollments will go down.[4]

---

[1] Since most of the boys and some of the girls were in the Army or the Navy, and many others were postponing the finishing of their high school work.

[2] J. H. S. Bossard and E. S. Boll (eds.), "Adolescents in Wartime," *Annals of the American Academy of Political and Social Science*, 236:83–91, 101–109, 1944.

[3] *Biennial Survey of Education in the United States, 1949–1950*, 1952, Chap. 4.

[4] See pp. 498–502.

2. Number and Type of Curricular Offerings: The curriculum that was originally imported from England may or may not have been appropriate for a small and highly selected group of English adolescents, but it has proved undesirable for the larger and more heterogeneous groups that even from the first attended the American secondary school. By the middle of the nineteenth century there was much criticism of the schools, but reform came slowly and in the main only after the rising enrollments had emphasized the situation. After some minor adaptations, three liberalizing developments took place during the decade between 1910 and 1920: (1) different courses of instruction were introduced—college preparatory, scientific, vocational, and commercial; (2) a small number of vocational and industrial classes made their appearance; and (3) pupils were allowed to take a few electives.

A good example of conservative and cautious change is given in Table 55. This curriculum contained only two courses of study. The difference

Table 55

A CONSERVATIVE CURRICULUM IN 1914

Latin Course	*Scientific Course*
FIRST YEAR	
Arithmetic $\frac{1}{2}$	Arithmetic $\frac{1}{2}$
Algebra $\frac{1}{2}$	Algebra $\frac{1}{2}$
English history	English history
English	English
Latin	Physical geography $\frac{1}{2}$
	Civil government $\frac{1}{2}$
SECOND YEAR	
Algebra	Algebra
Ancient history	Ancient history
English	English
Latin	Chemistry
THIRD YEAR	
Algebra $\frac{1}{2}$	Algebra $\frac{1}{2}$
Geometry $\frac{1}{2}$	Geometry $\frac{1}{2}$
English	English
Latin	Physics or medieval or
German	French history
	German
FOURTH YEAR	
Geometry	Geometry
English	English
Latin	Physics or United
German	States history
	German

From J. P. Leonard, *Developing the Secondary School Curriculum*, Rinehart & Company, 1946, pp. 34–35.

between them consisted of the substitution of science or history for Latin. Once a pupil had made his choice between the two courses, all his work was prescribed. At the radical end of developments in 1914, one finds such differentiation as that shown in Table 56, which includes the subjects in six courses of study for the first and last years of high school.

English was required in every course in every year, although the assignments presumably varied somewhat from one class to another. In the senior year, a course in American history and one in vocations were also required. The electives within each course consisted chiefly of the required subjects from other courses. Students in the classical subjects could branch out into history, modern languages, or a little science, while those in the scientific course could lean toward either the classics or the manual arts. In the four vocational courses, the students might elect either technical or semitechnical classes from other vocations or a smattering of modern language, history, or mathematics. This curriculum has in it the germ of those that developed in the following ten to fifteen years.

As soon as differentiation and liberalization were accepted as basic principles in the preparation of a curriculum, many new courses were introduced, usually as electives but sometimes as requirements in one or two courses of study and elective in others. A few classes such as moral philosophy or natural science were dropped because they were either overdifficult or outdated, in name at least. In 1906 a group of typical schools offered an average of 24 subjects and a total of 53 different courses; in 1930, the average in the same schools had risen to 48 and the total to 306.[5] At present in one large city high school the number of courses in the catalogue is 574. The most frequent arrangement was for all courses of study to have a small, common core—usually English, history, or science, in different years—plus a few units of required work each semester for those in each course, with the remaining hours to be chosen from an array of electives. The new classes that were introduced during the period from 1900 to 1920 were of five types: further subdivisions or extensions of traditional subject matter, new material drawn from the growing social sciences, additions of a vocational and utilitarian nature, classes in the appreciation of music and art, and expanded work in physical education. As will shortly appear, these sundry additions represent variant points of view as to the desirable nature of a high school curriculum.

As a result of the onslaught of students just after and since World War I, the high school curriculum sprang new leaks that were plugged up as well as seemed possible with a variety of temporary corks, but it was soon clear that the curriculum needed a thorough re-evaluation in terms of modern objectives, a complete overhauling of courses, and the establishment of a much closer relationship between what was taught and the characteristics of both the learner and the environment in which he lived. The overhauling is still in progress, and the proposed curricula are

---

[5] J. P. Leonard, *Developing the Secondary School Curriculum,* rev. ed., Rinehart & Company, 1953, p. 36.

Table 56

A LIBERAL CURRICULUM IN 1914

Classical	Scientific	Commercial	Manual Arts	Agriculture	Home Economics
		FIRST YEAR			
Required:					
English	English	English	English	English	English
Algebra	Algebra	Physical	Commercial	Physical	Elementary
	Physical	geography	arithmetic	geography	cooking
	geography	Commercial	Mechanical	Commercial	Cleaning
	Commercial	geography	drawing	geography	Handwork
	geography	Spelling and	Manual	Agriculture	Physiology
		word	training	Soils	and
		analysis		Breeds of	hygiene
		Penmanship		livestock	
Elective:					
Ancient	Latin	Algebra	Algebra	Algebra	Algebra
history	German	Ancient	Physical	Commercial	Physical
Physical	Ancient	history	geography	arithmetic	geography
geography	history	German	Commercial	Manual	Commercial
Commercial	Manual		geography	training	geography
geography	training		Ancient	Domestic	Ancient
	Domestic		history	science	history
	science		German		German
		FOURTH YEAR			
Required:					
English	English	English	English	English	English
American	American	American	American	American	American
history	history	history	history	history	history
and civics	and civics	and civics	and civics	and civics	and civics
Vocational	Vocational	Vocational	Vocational	Vocational	Vocational
direction	direction	direction	direction	direction	direction
Virgil	Physics		Architectural	Feeds	Dressmaking
			drafting	Farm	Millinery
				management	
				Insect pests	
				Fungus	
				diseases	
				Farm law	
Elective:					
German	French	French	French	Physics	French
French	Trigonometry	Physics	Physics	Breeding	Physics
Trigonometry	Political	Chemistry	Trigonometry	Farm	Psychology
Political	economy	History of	Agriculture	surveying	Home
economy	Psychology	commerce		Marketing	sanitation
Psychology	Principles	Advertising		farm prod-	Home
Principles	of teaching	and sales-		ucts	planning
of teaching		manship		Manual	
Physics		Stenography		training	
		Typewriting		Domestic	
				science	

From J. E. Stout, *The High School: Its Function, Organization and Administration*, D. C. Heath and Company, 1914, pp. 305, 309–311. Used by permission of the publisher. See also J. E. Stout, "The Development of High School Curricula in the North Central States, 1860–1918," *University of Chicago Supplementary Education Monographs*, No. 15, 1921; and G. E. Van Dyke, "Trends in the Development of High School Offerings I and II," *School Review*, 39 :657–664, 737–747, 1931.

for the most part still in terms of objectives, but some hints as to their eventual nature are already apparent. The basis will be sociological: i.e., the gradual adaptation of each pupil to the increasingly complex and widening environment to which he must adjust himself. The methods of teaching will be psychological; that is, the teachers will stimulate each pupil to feel definite needs and interests, by placing before him the means best adapted to his abilities and by organizing the material he will learn into units, each of which is drawn from the daily life about him and will illuminate that life with new understanding.

As a summary of the newer point of view concerning the aims and nature of secondary education, the conclusions from three studies will be briefly presented.

One recent report characterizes certain necessary features of the modern curriculum in the following way.[6] It should be so designed and so administered that it is an excellent illustration of democratic living. That is, it should serve as many pupils as possible as well as possible, it should be the result of a co-operative effort of all whom it affects, and it should express the will of the majority. It should also help the student to formulate a social philosophy for his own guidance. It should emphasize the study of contemporary life, especially as it affects youth. It should provide adequate training in health. It should furnish opportunity for improvement in the skills that are necessary for participation in a democracy. And it should include guidance, both personal and vocational, for all students. Teachers might find it illuminating to check the curriculum of their school against these criteria.

Another typical investigation into the curricular offerings of a single school as related to the characteristics of the student population, the nature of student activities and attitudes, the stated objectives of the school, and the characteristics both of the community in which the school was situated and of modern society as a whole concludes with the following statements:[7] (1) That the survival of the democratic society depends upon the development of a school curriculum and procedure that are appropriate to the best social, personal, and intellectual development of adolescents, (2) that the present curricula of secondary education consist mainly of traditional subject matter taught with the object of training the mind, and (3) that the content and methods of education need not only to be brought into line with modern knowledge but also to be more closely related than at present both to the characteristics and needs of adolescents and to the requirements of modern living.

A third study presents the list given below as points of emphasis and guidance in the construction of the curriculum for the secondary school.

1. The object is the preparation of young people for the common life of their time.

2. There should be no concern with the specialized knowledge of the scholar.

---

[6] V. E. Herrick and R. W. Tyler, "Toward Improved Curricular Theory," *Supplementary Educational Monographs*, University of Chicago, No. 71, 1950, 124 pp.

[7] W. H. Quins, W. H. Fox, and D. Segel, "A Study of a Secondary School Program in the Light of the Characteristics and Needs of Youth," *Bulletin of the School of Education*, Indiana University, XXV, No. 6 (1949), 1–69.

3. There should be no effort at specialization.

4. There should be no vocationalism.

5. Subject matter from allied fields should be integrated.

6. There should be more prescription.

7. All work should be related to the vital needs and problems of human beings.

8. Teaching should be altered and improved.

9. The curriculum should lead to an acquisition of information, understandings, skills, ideals, and attitudes which meet the present and future needs of all young people.

10. The specific areas to be covered are the home life, the vocational life, the civic life, the leisure life, and the physical and mental health of youth.[8]

One can see that the underlying philosophy of secondary education has changed markedly. Whether for better or for worse depends upon one's point of view, but in any event the changes are here to stay. The clock runs in only one direction.

2. The Various Theoretical Bases of the Curriculum: Any high school offers courses that are reflections of numerous attitudes on the part of past administrators as well as of circumstances. The most obvious of these are the size and the financial support of the school. A high school with no more than fifty pupils can offer only one main course of study because its teaching staff of perhaps four or five teachers will be inadequate for anything more. Such a school does not have the funds with which to install equipment for certain types of vocational training or for laboratory work. These limitations are mainly responsible for the appearance of consolidated or union high schools, each serving a district that previously would have supported a half-dozen smaller schools.

In addition to these practical considerations, certain well-established points of view have exerted great influence upon the growth of the curriculum. First in historical sequence comes the theory that high school courses should prepare students for college. For those who go on to college this preparatory function is still vital. The concepts and skills learned in algebra, geometry, English composition, and elementary work in languages, history, and science are the tools of scholarship: without them one can be a respectable, useful, God-fearing, honest citizen and workman, but one cannot be a scholar. Objections arise therefore only when the preparatory function is applied to the wrong pupils. Not over 30 to 40 per cent of high school graduates enter college, of whom considerably less than half will graduate. For the bulk of the pupils the years in secondary school are the end of formal schooling, and for them the traditional subjects are irrelevant, since they lead the learner into paths that at least two thirds of the freshmen in Grade 9 have neither desire nor ability to enter.

A second theory instrumental in forming and sustaining the traditional curriculum was the concept of mental discipline—the idea of training the mind by means of proper mental exercises just as one trains the body. In

---

[8] Educational Policies Commission, *Education for All American Youth,* National Education Association, 1944, 421 pp.; and Douglas, "Education for All Youth in Life Adjustment," *loc. cit.*

the words of a modern exponent of this point of view, "An intellect properly disciplined, an intellect properly habituated is an intellect able to operate well in any field. An education that consists of the cultivation of intellectual virtues therefore is the most useful education, whether the student is destined for a life of contemplation or a life of action."[9]

From the first, Latin and geometry were thought of as subjects that would teach the pupil to memorize quickly, to reason accurately, and to think closely, thus producing mental powers that could be directed against any new problem. If this assumption were only true, education could be greatly simplified! One would need only to determine which courses gave the greatest mental discipline and then require all pupils to take them. The content, since it would be merely for purposes of exercise, would not need to be relevant to anything. Unfortunately, no such short cut exists. Modern experimentation has shown that those who study geometry surpass others of equal intelligence who do not study the subject only in their ability to reason in geometry, but not in their capacity to think out problems involving data drawn from chemistry, politics, literature, aesthetics, or any other field of thought that impinges little upon geometry. The students of any given subject do learn how to reason within their subject, and they do acquire skills and ideas which can be transferred to other subjects. What they do not get is an ability to think that transcends the data by means of which it has been nourished. Courses cannot therefore be included in a curriculum merely as sources of mental discipline, because all courses give a certain amount of discipline so far as the data studied are concerned, all provide facts and skills that can be transferred to other schoolwork and to life outside school, all provide more or less training in habits of study or techniques of thought and procedure, and all give the learner a basic vocabulary by means of which he can think, but no course is better than any other, except as there may be variations in difficulty, which in turn produce variations in effort on the part of the learner. A course must, therefore, stand or fall upon the value of its content for some other end than mental discipline.

As soon as high schools began to grow rapidly and to enroll students of widely varying interests, it became evident that what many pupils needed was vocational education. There have been enthusiasts who wanted to turn practically all higher education into vocational training. The vocational motif certainly has its place in the total plan of secondary education, but it would not appear to be adequate as a sole basis for the selection of courses.

Up until the last three decades the curriculum rested mainly upon its preparatory, its disciplinary, or its vocational justification. During the recent period, several groups of individuals have made determined assaults upon the existing curriculum. One group wanted to do away with traditional, scholarly training, another wanted to do away with specialization, a third wanted to base high school courses exclusively upon the present needs of pupils, and a fourth wanted to prepare students for their daily lives as future

[9] R. M. Hutchins, *The Higher Learning in America*, Yale University Press, 1936, p. 64. Quoted by permission of the Yale University Press.

American citizens. In actual practice, the last two groups often joined forces. There have been, then, in recent decades, three main kinds of rebels: the antitraditionists, the antispecializationists, and the education-related-to-life progressivists. The curriculum of today is a direct result of these attacks.

In the days when only 5 to 8 per cent of adolescents continued their education into secondary school, the curriculum was quite rightly devoted to the producing of scholars, since that proportion is needed in each generation. Preparation for scholarship is just as specialized as preparation for carpentry, only there is more of it and therefore it takes longer. The scholar serves an eight-year apprenticeship—roughly from the ninth grade through college; then he enters a six-to-ten-year advanced training period parallel to that of a journeyman—from the beginning of graduate work to the achievement of permanent tenure as an associate professor—at which time he becomes a "master" of his trade, is authorized to vote in his guild, and may participate in the training of successive generations of journeymen. An academic education is certainly irrelevant to the needs of the youthful army now enrolled in high school, nor could society absorb such a large number of scholars even if they could be trained. Presumably every high school graduate should know something about scholarly pursuits, just as he should know something about plumbing or salesmanship or modern art. The revolt against the traditional curriculum, which began about 1910, has been gathering momentum ever since and will eventually succeed in eliminating from the curriculum such traditional elements as still survive, except as these may be desired as electives or as necessary parts of a preparation of some pupils for college.

Along with the revolt against tradition has gone an equally violent rebellion against specialization of all sorts, not only against the dividing off of subject matter into a hundred sharply differentiated compartments but also against highly concentrated vocational training, which was just as narrow as any other restricted type of education. The object of these particular rebels was to break down the artificial barriers between fields of learning, to integrate allied fields on the lower levels at least, and to present learning as a single picture instead of as a mosaic. One outcome of this movement has been the substitution of survey courses for the required work of previous decades. Thus, instead of taking five hours of modern history, three of ancient history, and three of civics, every student took one five-hour survey course in the social studies, in which he was given an integrated presentation of whatever material from these allied subjects seemed most vital for the future citizen. It should be noted that the basis of selection was general usefulness to the student who was *not* going to take further work in the social sciences rather than general usefulness in building a firm foundation for the student who was.

Members of the modern, progressive school of thought wanted to base the curriculum upon either the present or the future needs and interests of the pupils. The resulting program is supposed to provide for the acquisition of such information, skills, understandings, ideals, attitudes, and interests as are demanded by the different areas of living in which all people must make some adjustment—notably home life, vocational life, civic life, leisure life, and healthy survival, both mental and physical.[10] Some of the investigators who wished to remake the curriculum along these lines began by studying the average day of many thousands of adults, to determine what was needed that had not already been supplied by the years below secondary school, while other investigators began to study the here-and-now needs of high school students, often by asking them to list questions to which they needed answers. The resulting lists are long and heterogeneous. A few samples appear below:

Personal Problems

1. How can I become more attractive and popular?
2. Am I normal?
3. Is God a person?
4. I'd like to know how my mind works.
5. How can I find a goal in life?
6. What should my attitude toward alcohol, smoking, profanity be?
7. Why can't I have dates like other students?
8. How can I get a summer job?
9. When should a person get married?

Home Problems

10. How many dates should I have a week?
11. What should be my share of the housework?
12. How long should I let my parents dominate me?

School Problems

13. Why do teachers have favorites?
14. Should I join a school secret society if invited?
15. Why doesn't the school do more to prepare me for a job?
16. Why do we have to study Latin (algebra, grammar, etc.)?
17. Why do so many boys stand around when there are girls who want to dance?
18. How can I learn to concentrate?

Community Problems

19. How can I find out the difference between religions?
20. How can I learn not to be fooled by radio and newspapers?
21. What causes war?
22. How important is marriage to success in life?
23. How can the world organize for peace?
24. Why are taxes so high?
25. How can I find out which political candidate is telling the truth?[11]

Any such accumulation of questions runs the entire gamut from an inquiry by some child who wants to know if she is old enough yet to use lipstick to a mature question as to whether or not a good citizen is bound to obey a law he knows is unjust and, if he does obey it, how he can register his disapproval. If one follows this approach to its logical conclusion, one establishes courses in acceptable social usages, in effective methods of study, in

---

[10] H. R. Douglass, "Education of All Youth for Life Adjustment," *Annals of the American Academy of Political and Social Science,* 265:108–114, 1949.

[11] C. B. Mendenhall and K. J. Arisman, *Secondary Education,* The Dryden Press, 1951, pp. 123–129.

courtship and marriage, in the concepts of morals and religion, in modern social problems, in mental hygiene, and so on, because such subject matter contains whatever answers may be given to the questions that are most commonly asked. That is, the curriculum is "adolescent-centered."

It is not difficult to find objections to any of these theories of curriculum construction. The preparation-for-college approach by itself produces a course of study quite inappropriate for most people because it stresses the technical preparation needed by a scholar, and most people will not become scholars. The mental-discipline theory has been shown to be false in its main contentions. The sociological approach, if used alone, would produce a curriculum that crystallizes things-as-they-are rather than things-as-they-should-be and would, if adhered to strictly, eliminate some of the courses that adolescents like best. A purely vocational basis is no better than any of the others, since it produces a course of study that is extremely narrow and does not prepare a pupil for the American custom of changing jobs at frequent intervals, nor for the wise use of leisure, nor for the business of being a good citizen and an intelligent voter. The basing of the curriculum exclusively upon the needs and drives of youth produces a curious and unbalanced course of study. It is, of course, not necessary that the student-centered curriculum should be superficial or trivial, but it sometimes turns out to be. Yet all of these bases contribute something to the determination of what the curriculum should contain. A high school has to prepare some pupils for college, it has to furnish as much transfer of training as possible, it has to help students to live in the world of today and tomorrow, it has to meet at least some of the students' more pressing needs and solve some of their more pressing problems, and it has to prepare for earning their living those who will go no further. In an effort to meet all these demands, many high schools present a curriculum without unity or coherence, and leave it to each student to find his way through the numerous offerings to whatever goal he seeks.

3. The Old and the New: The revolution in secondary education has been extensive and fundamental. It has affected every phase of high school work. In this book it is not possible to discuss the changes in more detail, but a brief case study might serve to illustrate the contrast between curricular offerings and the methods of presenting them in 1910 and 1950.

The writer attended a secondary school in which the college preparatory course followed strictly traditional lines. In four years of Latin, four of English literature, three of French, two of German, one each of algebra and plane geometry, one of ancient history, and one of chemistry there was no slightest effort to relate the material taught to daily living. Much of the work happened to be extremely interesting to the writer, but the demarcation between what happened in class and what happened outside was clear and sharply defined. The students never discovered, except through their own spontaneous observation, that English and Latin were related languages. The work in English, French, and German was mostly grammatical, and what readings were assigned were from classics written before 1800. Topics for composition were usually based on the readings. Skills and ideas in mathematics operated in a vacuum, and ancient history stayed decently dead. Having elected a preparatory course, one had no further choice as to what one studied. The teaching was often excellent, but the notion that schoolwork might be related either to the student or to life did not penetrate the classroom. There was nothing intrinsically wrong with the material itself; at present, in many schools, the same topics are so presented that they make a vital contribution to the life of adolescent boys and girls.

Nothing reflects changing modes of thought better than the accepted and popular materials of instruction. Beginning on this page are excerpts from the introductory lessons in two beginning books in Latin, one that was popular in the first decade of this century and a second that is in use today. First to be noted is the approach. The older book threw the lesson at the student, who usually reacted by memorizing it, since he could rarely make much sense out of it. The newer text makes a more gradual approach, with illustrations and explanations. The writers of the older book clearly intended the student to learn Latin. This intent appears in the emphasis upon grammar, in the selection of words for the vocabulary (which was undoubtedly based upon Caesar's *Gallic Wars*), by the meaning of the illustrative sentences, and by the immediate introduction into Latin prose. The modern book concentrates upon the relation of Latin to English; it provides only a homeopathic dose of grammar; it minimizes the need for translation; and it uses only common words. Its vocabulary load is less than half that of the earlier book, and all terms are defined and illustrated. The immediate objective of the later book is clearly not the mastery of Latin or of prose style, but rather the development of an interest in what was Roman and an understanding of the relation of Roman culture and language to the student's own. These descriptions illustrate in condensed form the changes that have taken place in the secondary school curriculum.

The modern text begins with some introductory material on what a student can expect to get from a study of Latin, a brief discourse on the position of the Romans in world history, and a section giving direct quotations of Latin often heard in English speech—such as *veni, vidi, vici; magna charta; persona non grata;* or *quid pro quo*—with translations and explanations, plus two samples of English material translated into Latin—"My Country 'tis of Thee" and the nursery rhyme, "Twinkle, twinkle, little star." The first grammatical lesson begins with the following sentences:

> Britannia* est īnsula. Eurōpa nōn est īnsula. Italia paene* est īnsula. Italia paenīnsula* est. Sicilia et Italia īnsula et paenīnsula in Eurōpā sunt. Silvae et viae in īnsulā Britanniā sunt.

The directions to the student for reading the Latin sentences come next:

> Read through a Latin sentence, trying to get the meaning of each word as you come to it. Sometimes an English word derived from a Latin one will give you a clue, and sometimes you will have to guess the meaning of a word

---

* Translations of these words are given, or explanations, or questions about them.

from the rest of the sentence. Some words are purposely used in the Latin passages which are not explained in the vocabulary lists. If you cannot guess their meanings, look them up in the back of the book. Pay careful attention to the endings. When you understand the passage, answer the thought questions; then translate the sentences into good English.

These directions are essentially the same as those usually given for reading French or Spanish. This introductory work on translation is followed by a section on grammar, one on English words derived or borrowed from Latin, and a third on vocabulary. The grammar is presented as quoted below:

The Latin and English passages above are made up of sentences—that is, groups of words that express thoughts. Each sentence consists of two parts: the subject, about which something is said, and the predicate, which says something about the subject.

The boy	sees his sister
subject	predicate

Nouns: (a) a noun is a word that names a person, place, or thing. In the Latin passage you have just studied, the subject of each sentence is a noun. (b) Nouns are singular in number when they mean one person or thing: *island, insula.* They are plural when they mean more than one: *islands, insulae.* Note that Latin nouns, like English ones, are changed to show plural number. Pick out the singular and plural nouns in the Latin passage.

(c) The use of a noun in a sentence determines its case. In English we sometimes change the ending of a noun to show the case: the boy's *hat.* In Latin the cases are distinguished by their endings.

Use of Cases: (a) In Latin, as in English, the subject of a sentence is in the nominative case. The nominative case-endings of some Latin words are -a for the singular and -ae for the plural: *insula, insulae.*

(b) A noun used in the predicate after *is, was, are, were,* or *seems,* to complete its meaning is in the nominative.

Britannia	est	insula		Britain	is	an island
subject in nominative case	predicate nominative			subject		predicate nominative

English Word Study: Below are some English words, borrowed from Latin, which have kept their Latin endings, both singular and plural. Consult your dictionary for the English pronunciation and meaning of these "loan words": *alumna, alumnae, antenna, antennae, larva, larvae, minutiae* (plural only), *amoeba, amoebae, vertebra, vertebrae.* From what Latin word is *insular* derived? Explain this sentence: *Puerto Rico is an insular possession of the United States. Insulation* and *isolation* are both derived from the same word. Can you explain what is meant by an *insulated wire* or a *policy of isolation?*

The vocabulary consists of three nouns, two forms of the verb *to be,* and one negative. After the English meaning appears an English word that is derived from the Latin *one:*

insula: island (insulate)
via: way, road (viaduct)
silva: forest, woods (Pennsylvania)
est: is
sunt: are
non: not (non-playing, non-essential)

The student is told to make sure he knows the meaning of the derivatives and can use them in English sentences. He is then to enter the vocabulary words into his notebook and try to find more English words derived from them.

Up to this point, there have been six illustrations of Roman scenes, four of them colored. Throughout the book, there are more pages with pictures than without them. In every way the writers have made use of the pupils' daily experiences and have made provision for direct transfer of what is learned in class to daily life outside of class. For instance, instead of stating baldly that "place to which" (*ad urbem*) takes the accusative, place "in which" (*in ūrbe*) takes the ablative, and place "from which" (*ex ūrbe*) takes the ablative, and leaving the student to make any sense out of it he can, the writers use a picture showing one lad treading water in a lake, another diving into the water from a springboard, and a third just emerging from the lake after his swim. These lads are labeled as *in aquā, ad aquam,* and *ex aquā.* Humor is frequently introduced. For instance, in a series of cartoon-like sketches, used in explaining indirect objects, there is one that shows a policeman writing out a ticket for a motorist who was shown speeding in an earlier picture; the policeman is saying, "Ubi ignis est?"[12] Another series of illustrations, sprinkled through the book, shows pictures of modern postage stamps that have Roman statues, boats, temples, ruins, or individuals on them, and it is suggested to the student that he collect other stamps of similar character. Some attention is also paid to the feminine half of the student population—a feature sadly lacking in earlier texts—by such devices as a conversation between a mother and her two daughters, pictures of toys used by Roman girls, and descriptions of Roman houses, rooms, cooking utensils, and so on.

In the first lesson, the authors introduce eleven technical words: sentence, subject, predicate, noun, singular, plural, number, case, nominative, case-endings, and predicate nominative. All these words are explained. The student progresses to the thirteenth lesson before he meets any nouns that are not in the first declension. Far more space is given to the transfer of Latin to English than to grammar.[13]

In marked contrast to the modern text is the one studied by the writer in about the year 1900. The introductory matter was concerned mainly with how Latin words were pronounced. The first lesson occupied two facing pages. It began, without preamble, with three rules:

The subject of a transitive verb is in the nominative case.

---

[12] Where's the fire?
[13] B. L. Ullman and N. E. Henry, *Latin for Americans,* The Macmillan Company, copyright 1941, 422 pp. Illustrative excerpts are used by permission of The Macmillan Company.

The object of a transitive verb is in the accusative case.
A predicate noun is in the nominative case.

There was no explanation of the technical terms. There followed the statement that Latin nouns belonged to one of five declensions and that those
of the first declension ended in -a. Then came a paradigm of the word
"hasta" (meaning *spear*). At the top of the second page was a vocabulary
of twenty-two words, of which eight referred to military matters—presumably as a preparation for reading Caesar. Next came about a dozen
sentences to be translated from Latin into English, and then a similar
number to be written by the student from English into Latin. There were
no pictures or illustrations. At the very end of the lesson was a sentence in
Latin to be memorized: *Cathāgō delenda est*. There was no explanation as
to what this remark meant, who said it, or why it was important enough
to be memorized.

The total load of technical words, all used without explanation, was as
follows: subject, transitive, verb, nominative, case, object, sentence, predicate nominative, genitive, dative, accusative, ablative, vocative, number,
singular, plural, inflection, declension, ending, gender, masculine, feminine,
neuter, common gender (which appeared in a footnote), stem, noun. The
total is twenty-six words, many of which a pupil would almost certainly
not know the meaning of.

It will be noted that the approach was wholly grammatical and that no
attempt was made either to interest the student or to relate the work to the
student's interests, activities, or abilities. There was one short section, just
before the vocabularies at the back of the book, that listed English derivatives from Latin words, but few students ever had time to look at this section. In any case, it appeared to have been an afterthought on the part of
the textbook writers and was clearly of no great importance to them.[14]

II. The Curriculum of Today and Tomorrow

1. The Core Curriculum: The core curriculum has a number of advantages over the former plan of required, individual courses. (1) It cuts
across subject matter boundaries and draws upon material from all fields
for the solution of specific problems, thus tending to prevent the division of
knowledge into compartments. (2) It leaves free a number of elective hours
for meeting the needs and interests of each individual pupil. (3) It forces
teachers from all areas to work co-operatively in planning the educational
experience of students. (4) It encourages co-operation between students
and teachers in planning the curriculum. (5) It provides for great flexibility.
(6) It assures the setting aside of adequate blocks of time for the consideration of current problems. (7) It provides an exceptionally good opportunity
for guidance because of the emphasis upon pupils' needs. (8) It prevents
much of the overlapping between courses. (9) It emphasizes the development of the whole personality and is as much concerned with the growth

---

[14] The name of the text has been omitted at the request of the publishers, since
a few schools are still using it.

of attitudes, critical thinking, social sensitivity, and interests as with the acquisition of skills or information.[15]

Such a curriculum is well illustrated by the course of study outlined in Table 57. The material for the "core" has obviously been drawn from many

Table 57

PROBLEM AREAS

I. Immediate Personal-Social Problems

Grades 7, 8, 9:

Orientation to School, Living in the Home, Making and Holding Friends, Sex Relationships

Grades 10, 11, 12:

Education in American Democracy, The Family in Civilization, Improving Home Life, Boy-Girl Relationships

II. Immediate and Wider Community Problems

Grades 7, 8, 9:

Living in the Community, Community Agencies and Services, Community Recreation, Community Citizenship, Transportation, Beautifying the Community, The Air Age, How People in Other Lands Live, Our Latin-American Neighbors

Grades 10, 11, 12:

Community Survey, Community Health, Community and National Planning, War, International Organization, Role of America among the Nations, Role of Government, The American Tradition, Contemporary Cultures, Contemporary Religions, Propaganda Analysis, Public Opinion, Races, Ethnic and Class Groups

III. Wider Socioeconomic Problems

Grades 7, 8, 9:

How People Make a Living, Community Industries, Science in Our Daily Lives, Earning Money and Budgeting an Allowance

Grades 10, 11, 12:

Selecting a Vocation and Getting a Job, Getting Your Money's Worth, How Technology Is Changing Our Way of Living, Conservation of Resources, Competing Economic Systems

IV. Personal Development Problems

Grades 7, 8, 9:

Life and Growth, Maintaining Good Health, How We Get Our Beliefs, Personal Planning, Personal Appearance and Grooming, Developing Intellectual, Aesthetic, and Practical Interests

Grades 10, 11, 12:

Personality Development, Developing Intellectual, Aesthetic, and Practical Interests, Building a Social Outlook, Competing Philosophies of Life, Intelligence and Learning

From H. Alberty, *Reorganizing the High School Curriculum,* The Macmillan Company, copyright 1947, pp. 174–175. Used by permission of The Macmillan Company.

---

[15] Leonard, rev. ed., *op. cit.,* p. 400.

fields. Every pupil takes this one unit of social science during each of his four years, without respect to what else he studies, because the core contains material that he as a citizen will need to know.

The courses that are to be required of all students should be selected with care on the basis of extended research into the needs of adults, the drives and problems of adolescents, and the needs of society in a democracy. The following paragraphs contain the writer's own analysis of adult needs that form the basis for the curriculum.

Perhaps the most evident adjustment that all people must learn to make is to get along with their families, friends, and neighbors. Everyone is a member of society, and everyone's social value depends upon his ability to adapt to his group. To get along peaceably in a community a student needs information along two main lines: he must understand something of how society is organized and controlled, and something of how human nature reacts to stimuli. Translated into terms of the curriculum, this statement means that the adolescent should study the social sciences and psychology, but neither of these subjects as it is traditionally taught.

A second need of every adult is the ability to recognize the common symptoms of either physical or mental abnormality. Physical diseases often exist for some time without arousing suspicion, and mental abnormalities are even less well recognized. When a psychiatrist studies a patient, he usually finds a long history of what, to him, appears as abnormal conduct; yet the person may not have been considered as more than mildly unusual, if that, by his friends, parents, or teachers. Every pupil in high school needs, therefore, to learn how to maintain physical and mental health. These two subjects are particularly appropriate to high school because they concern matters directly related to adolescent problems and interests.

The need of mankind for literacy is so obvious that it is sometimes forgotten. All children, adolescents, and adults need to read well enough to get meaning from newspapers and magazines and easily enough to enjoy reading books during leisure hours. The basic skills are usually mastered in elementary school, but a few pupils reach high school without them. For these youngsters, work in learning to read more easily and more efficiently is desirable. A similar situation exists in regard to the universal need to write well enough to produce an intelligible letter.

Boys and girls of high school age will soon want to establish homes and families of their own. It is therefore essential for them to learn all they can about these matters. Generally, such information is available only to girls. To be sure, they have the major need for technical information in regard to housekeeping, but in the social and emotional development of a home the father is quite as important as the mother. A course designed especially to fit adolescent boys and girls for their responsibility as members of a home and as parents of children should be required of all students toward the end of their high school career.

Adolescents, like everyone else, need outlets for their emotional interests and for self-expression. Their schoolwork and the constantly shifting social adjustments inevitably put considerable strain upon them. They have a real need for such subjects as music, art, dramatics, writing, physical education, and for participation in all kinds of extracurricular activities. The object of the required work in these fields should be to provide for such enjoyable self-expression as can be indulged in by the untalented. The games in physical education should be those that can be played with enjoyment even by the clumsiest, rather than those demanding expert coordination. These activities should contribute greatly to a wise use of leisure time in later years.

The modern world is based upon scientific discoveries in both biological and physical fields. A person with a low comprehension of scientific principles and an inadequate knowledge of scientific facts not only is unable to adjust to modern life but is actually in danger from the necessary use of modern appliances. Modern industry, modern daily life, and modern warfare all require a mastery of elementary physical facts. The core course in science should be designed for those pupils who have no intention of taking more than one year of work and want to get from it whatever items of information will be most useful to them in their daily lives. They want to understand something about electrical fixtures, automobiles and airplanes, and household mechanics. Physics and chemistry both have an enormous number of facts that are of constant usefulness in everyday living. There is no dearth of practical subject matter; the difficulty is rather one of selection.

In the field of biological science there have also been great developments. Matters of diet, effects of drugs, causes and prevention of disease come at once to mind as common problems. It is presumably in this field that information about sex and reproduction should be given. A course in biological science of essential value to every pupil in high school could be devised, but it would not contain the same subject matter as the traditional introductory course.

Young people are interested in the age-old questions of what life is for, what values are best, what is right, what is wrong, what is worth while, and so on. In former days the various churches were supposed to deal with these problems of value for the majority of adolescents. Even those who did not belong to a church received guidance by advice and precept from parents, teachers, and other adults. Not all adults were "good," any more than they are now, but they had fairly uniform standards as to what goodness consisted of. At the present time, the morals of the world are chaotic and complex, and it is no wonder that adolescents fail to find stable values by which they can guide their own behavior. As they grow older they will lose their fine eagerness to save themselves and the world; hence they should be helped in their groping toward a philosophy of life at a time when such help is desired.

Finally, one must add the two courses on vocations, already discussed in the previous chapter—a descriptive course for freshmen and an apprenticeship course for sophomores—since all adults should work, and most of them have to.

The core of the curriculum, if one were to follow to their logical conclusions this analysis of social needs and adolescent drives, would consist of such courses as the following:

Social science
Biological science
Physical science (including mathematics)
Hygiene, physical and mental
Psychology

Homemaking
Philosophy of life
Expressive arts
Games
Occupations

Reading (if necessary)

The above curriculum contains courses of six types: those that prepare a pupil for his civic responsibilities; those that teach him about the modern physical world; those that help him to develop himself; those that teach him to understand people—either singly or in social groups; those that contribute to a sensible use of leisure; and those that prepare him to earn his living—or in the case of students who go to college, those that prepare him for entrance.

It is almost certain that high school pupils would appreciate a core of material such as is represented by the courses listed above. The extent to which high school work, as traditionally organized, fails to meet the needs of the pupils is well revealed by the results of a questionnaire given to a large number of adolescents. A few items are quoted in Table 58. It would

Table 58

STUDENTS' OPINION CONCERNING THE CURRICULUM

	Yes (%)	Uncertain (%)	No (%)
1. Should or should not work experience be a requirement for high school graduation?	48	9	43
a. Is work experience required in your school?	12	15	73
2. Should or should not the school be required to give a thorough physical examination to each pupil each year?	79	5	16
a. Does your school give such an examination?	23	10	67
3. Should or should not each pupil be required to participate in at least one activity other than required courses?	72	4	24
a. Are you required to do this in your school?	25	8	67
4. Should or should not high schools require class visits to industrial establishments, prisons, museums, etc.?	85	5	10
a. Does your school require such class visits?	25	12	63
5. Should or should not high schools attempt to help pupils solve their personal problems?	60	7	33
a. Does your school attempt to do so?	25	8	67
6. Do or do not high schools provide enough opportunities for pupil discussion of school problems?	38	7	55
a. Does your school provide enough opportunities?	33	7	60
7. Is or is there not enough cooperation in high schools between parents and school authorities?	38	9	53
a. Is there enough cooperation in your schools?	38	11	51

From H. H. Remmers and K. S. Davenport, "Youth Looks at Education," *American School Board Journal*, 113:19–20, 1946.

seem as if a core curriculum designed to meet the immediate and future needs of high school pupils would satisfy many of the demands by the students who recorded the answers.

2. Elective Work: Theoretically, there is no limit to the number or nature of electives. All that is needed for establishing an elective course is a group of interested students and an adequately prepared instructor. The interests of both students and teachers should be allowed full play. If there are in a high school pupils who have the desire and the ability to study Sanskrit, calculus, plant pathology, or pre-Shakespearean drama, and if there are teachers who have the desire and the ability to present such material, there should be no objection to the inclusion of relevant courses in the high school curriculum. In fact, elective courses should purposely be designed to serve and develop adolescent interests in as many fields as possible. The limits of knowledge, interest, and ability are the only limits to elective offerings.

There are, however, many practical reasons why elective work cannot be expanded indefinitely. If a high school employs thirty-five teachers, some of whose time must be given to required courses, there can be only the number and type of electives which can be given during the remaining class periods by these teachers. Therefore, the courses offered must be those that will serve the greatest number of pupils. Whatever electives are to be offered within a department and whatever topics are to be covered should be decided by the mature and balanced judgment of its most experienced teachers. It is only the required work that need be concerned with the practical question of the average individual's everyday needs.

Many of the elective courses will be vocational or prevocational in nature.[16] Some of them should lead directly into occupations. For many pupils the years of high school mark the end of formal training. These students must not be neglected. The number and type of strictly vocational courses are naturally limited by the available equipment and instructional force. Every pupil who is not reasonably certain of succeeding in college should complete some type of vocational training before he leaves high school.

No attempt will be made to list electives of any kind, vocational or otherwise. The number and character of elective courses depend upon local needs, interest of pupils, equipment, and available personnel. Naturally, as many and as varied electives as possible should be offered, since their major purpose is to awaken, broaden, and intensify adolescent interests. In the

---

[16] The same course may be vocational for some pupils and a free elective for others. The future carpenter may take a course in woodworking as a preparation for his job, while a future philosopher may elect it because he likes to build things in his spare time. A girl in the commercial course takes stenography as part of her vocational training, another pupil may elect shorthand merely because she wants to learn it. For students in the college preparatory course, algebra is a "tool" subject because it presents facts they will need to use in college courses; yet elementary algebra may be an elective for students who do not plan for college. One cannot, therefore, draw a sharp line between vocational and elective courses.

case of the vocational courses, care should be taken not only to offer a variety but also to make the courses practical and to enroll in them those pupils who most need them.

3. A Suggested Schedule: It is, of course, necessary to show how the core curriculum, the required work within each course of study, and a student's electives can be integrated into a coherent plan of work. The schedule given in Table 59 presents the general scheme. The assignment of hours is

Table 59

A PROPOSED CURRICULUM

First Year	Semester 1	Semester 2	Second Year	Semester 1	Semester 2
Core subjects:	*1*	*2*	Core subjects:	*1*	*2*
Social science	3[a]	3	Biological science	3	...
Hygiene			Physical science	...	3
Physical	2	...	Expressive arts	2	2
Mental	...	2	Occupations	2	2
Occupations	2	2	Clubs[b]	2	...
Clubs[b]	2	2	Physical education	2	2
Physical education	2	2		—	—
	—	—	Total	11	9
Total	11	11	Unassigned	5–8	7–9
Unassigned: including classes required for a given course of study, free electives and remedial work	5–8	5–8			

Third Year	Semester 1	Semester 2	Fourth Year	Semester 1	Semester 2
Core subjects:	*1*	*2*	Core subject:	*1*	*2*
Homemaking	2	2	Philosophy of life	3	...
Psychology	2	2		—	—
	—	—	Total	3	...
Total	4	4	Unassigned	12–15	12–18
Unassigned	11–14	11–14			

[a] The hours per course are only approximations.
[b] Each pupil should select a minimum of two hours a week of practice in games or attendance at clubs, the arrangement being adapted to each one's interests and needs. Additional hours devoted to activities should be voluntary. After the first three semesters, all are voluntary.

based on an assumption of six fifty-minute periods a day. An average pupil would have fourteen or fifteen classes a week for which preparation was needed, three to four unprepared classes, and eleven to thirteen hours for study during school time. The number of unprepared hours is diminished from year to year. It is assumed that pupils will, through the earlier requirements, be guided into appropriate extracurricular activities. Thus if a boy elects music during one semester, dramatics during the other, soccer in the fall term, swimming during the winter, tennis in the spring, and uses his "club" hour to visit (in the course of the year) the literary, radio, carpentry, mechanical drawing, French, auto mechanics, and printing clubs, he should have made enough contacts to continue his own interests without further requirements. The majority of the required hours are placed in the first two years. Those students who drop out after one or two years remain in high school too short a time to receive much vocational training in any case, but they can be given a maximum of preparation for normal living. Moreover, by postponing specialization, transfer from one course to another is greatly facilitated.

The above schedule represents a compromise between the new and the old. It may well be that like most compromises it will suit no one. It is intended as the best plan the writer can suggest that might actually be used, not as an ideal to be dreamed of but never reached.

In Figure 150 on page 655 are two diagrams showing proposed arrangements of the curriculum, from the seventh grade through the sophomore year in college. Both show a general plan for a six-period school day. The first plan allows two hours a day, in Grades 7, 8, and 9, for the exploration of personal interests, three for the "Common Learnings" or the required core taken by everyone, and one hour for games or physical education classes. By the tenth grade the pupil is presumed to have made a choice of vocation and applies one hour a day to preparation for it. If he wants to be a court stenographer, he takes shorthand during his "preparation" hour; if he expects to enter college, he takes algebra; if he wants to become a carpenter, he takes woodworking; and so on. The number of specifically "preparation" hours becomes larger as the student advances, but is at no level over half the total. Presumably the hour for "individual interests" could in case of necessity be added, unless it is assumed that a student cannot be interested in his main work. Part (b) of the figure gives a schematic representation of the writer's own idea on planning. Aside from differences in vocabulary, the main difference between the two lies in the greater proportion of time devoted to preparation in (b); there are more hours, and they begin sooner. Also, the core curriculum occupies somewhat less space in (b) than in (a), and there is one less elective hour.

It would be hard to overrate the importance of the curriculum. It furnishes pupils with many of the basic ideas they are going to use throughout their lives. It influences and often determines their future vocational level. It keeps them in school or drives them out of it. And, unfortunately, it is sometimes the source of frustration. If the curriculum becomes either a source of frustration or a drag, the students will devote their energies to extracurricular activities or leave school. It takes the combined efforts of philosophers, sociologists, psychologists, research experts, school administrators, teachers, and students to keep a curriculum up-to-date, vital, and healthy, but with such co-operation it can give adolescents the nourishment they need.

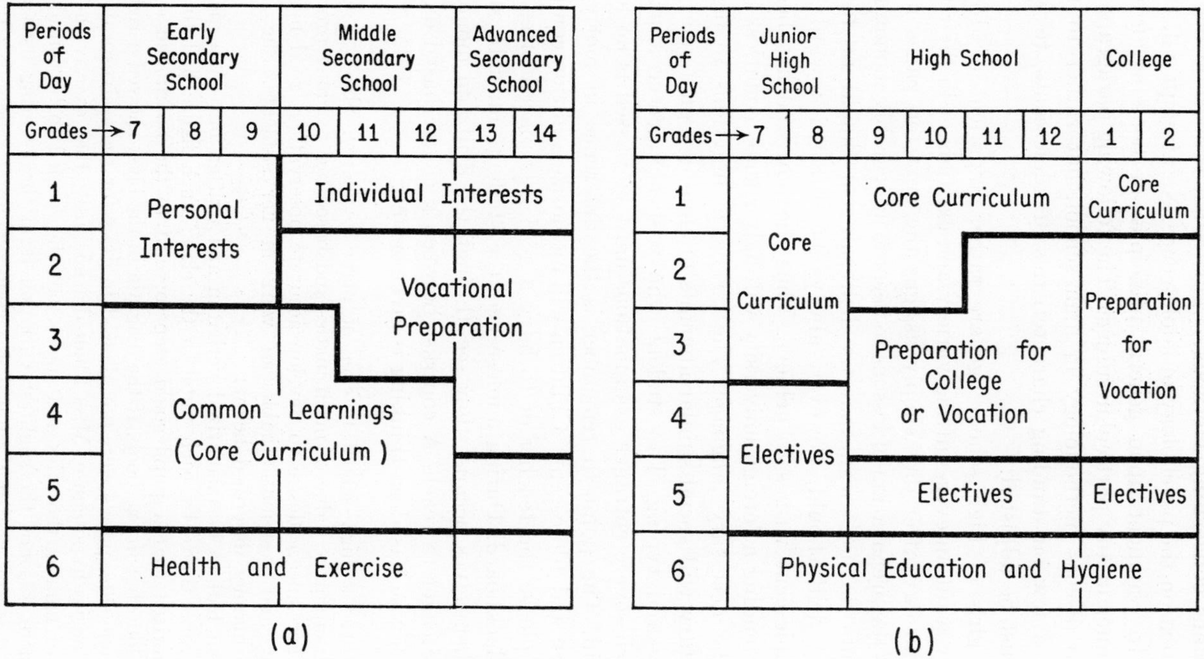

(a)

(b)

Fig. 150. *Two Diagrams of a Curriculum*

From H. Alberty, *Reorganization of the High School Curriculum*, copyright, 1948, The Macmillan Company, p. 170. Used by permission of The Macmillan Company, publishers.

656 INTELLECTUAL DEVELOPMENT

III. The High School Teacher

1. **Suggestions concerning Methods:** This is not a book on teaching methods but a text on the psychology of adolescence. No attempt will therefore be made to comment upon general principles of teaching or upon teaching techniques in any particular subject. The following paragraphs are not intended to discuss methodology in high school, but rather to focus attention upon a few outstanding characteristics of adolescents, to whom the teaching must be adjusted.

Boys and girls of high school age are rather impatient of drill or monotony. They want an ever-shifting variety and excitement in their lives. The teacher who day after day simply assigns the next ten pages in the textbook allows the preparation of lessons to become unbearably monotonous. These statements do not mean that no drill subjects should be taught. Work involving drill should, however, always be directed toward some purpose the adolescent wishes to achieve. Thus the boy who has become interested in attending a foreign university willingly spends countless hours in mastering the necessary language. The girl with ambitions to become a private secretary will spend similar amounts of time in monotonous drill on stenography and typing. The student who wishes to enter a private college for which severe entrance examinations must be passed is no longer resistive to drill. The point to remember is the difference in motivation between children and adolescents. Children will memorize addition combinations either to please the teacher or to have a gold star placed after their name on the blackboard. During adolescence, the students must be stimulated to drill themselves because they see, through the drill and monotony, a goal they are eager to reach. A contrast between a course based on drill and a parallel course based on thinking is given below:

Miss Elliot was a high school teacher of plane geometry. She was a firm believer in the disciplinary value of mathematics and based her teaching procedure primarily upon her sincere desire to develop accurate observation, good memory, logical reasoning, and systematic habits of work in her students. She taught geometry in the manner described below:

Each theorem had to be memorized verbatim and written out from memory, not once but several times, by each pupil in the class. Each figure had to be so completely memorized that a pupil could step forward to the board and draw a diagram exactly like that in the book. If the diagram in the book showed a right triangle sitting on one side, pupils were not allowed to draw for themselves a diagram showing it lying on its hypotenuse. Miss Elliot did not insist that exactly the same letters be used for naming the sides and angles, but she seemed to be considerably happier when there was not the slightest variation from the lettering used in the text. When the theorem was first studied a certain amount of inductive thinking was done by the pupils as a group, but at an early point the thinking stopped and the memorizing began. The entire proof had to be given exactly as it appeared in the text. Moreover, Miss Elliott required each pupil to keep a notebook. In this notebook each theorem was written as it was being studied, the diagram placed on the board was copied—which was the same as the diagram in the textbook—

and the successive steps in the proof were written down on the day the proof was worked out, these successive steps forming an exact replica of the proof already available in much more legible form in the text. Since the pupils knew by the end of the first month that a new theorem would be treated in this way, most of them simply copied the demonstration in the text verbatim and did not bother to do any inductive reasoning whatever.

This performance went on for the entire year, being varied only by work with original propositions, the demonstrations for which had to be written out and memorized as for the regular theorems. The real work of the course was the continual memorizing of figures for propositions, of the letters used in the figures, and of demonstrations leading to a proof. The class was hopelessly dull; hardly a student in it did constructive thinking about geometry during the entire year, and disciplinary difficulties were of daily occurrence. Miss Elliot did not succeed in developing the power to reason, and whatever increase in efficiency of memorizing she might have brought about was more than offset by the violent distaste for memorizing developed by her students.

Miss Jones taught solid geometry to freshmen in a small arts college that required this course of all its students. The pupils in Miss Jones's classes varied all the way from excellent to failing in geometry. Miss Jones did not trouble with a textbook. She dictated theorems two or three at a time, each such unit serving for at least a week's work. Every pupil brought to class some pieces of cardboard, some old pencils, and some pieces of string; with this equipment the students constructed figures that would serve to illustrate each theorem. Thus for a particular theorem a piece of cardboard would serve for a plane; a pencil pushed through it and projecting several inches on either side would represent a line perpendicular to the plane; and a piece of string knotted around one end of the pencil, drawn through a hole in the cardboard and attached to the other end of the pencil, would serve to show a line dropped from the perpendicular line to the plane surface. The first step in reasoning out a proof was to construct an acceptable figure. Miss Jones encouraged the construction of many different figures, all of which would fulfill the requirements of the theorem. When everyone had an acceptable model, the students sat and turned these figures over and over, looking at them from all angles, until some facts about the interrelationships of lines and planes occurred to somebody. Anyone who thought he or she had an idea simply went to the blackboard and started writing out a proof. About two thirds of these efforts were abortive, but at least everyone was trying to think how to get from the facts given to the one fact to be proved. This performance would sometimes go on for two or three days before the combined efforts of the class produced a correct proof. If, in the course of events, two correct but different proofs were developed, Miss Jones was delighted. In fact, the only type of assistance she regularly gave was to encourage the work of a pupil who had started off on an unusual type of proof which could still be made to work. She would not allow such a line of argument to be dropped but would encourage its use until someone in the class had seen how to reach the desired conclusion from the start already made. All correct beginnings were left on the board from day to day. By this technique, the poorer students in the class got some help in getting started on their proofs. Miss Jones did not believe in socialized work and allowed no conversation in the classroom, but she was entirely willing to have her students make use of each others' ideas as expressed on the blackboard.

Once a proof or series of proofs had been arrived at, Miss Jones gave some advice in regard to impressing these proofs upon one's mind. She frankly advised the poor students in the class to copy the shortest, easiest, and most obvious proof into a notebook and then to memorize it. She advised the most capable pupils in the class to memorize nothing at all but rather to direct their attention toward the techniques by which one moved from the given facts to the beginning of a proof. As the end of the semester approached, she classified the pupils into groups according to the amount of original work she would expect from them on the final examination. Her final test consisted usually of seven familiar and seven unfamiliar theorems, although no student in the class was asked to solve more than six out of the fourteen. On each student's examination paper was a statement of how many theorems of each type he or she must solve. These assignments varied all the way from one or two students who were required to solve six out of the seven original problems to one or two who were required to reproduce proofs for the six already familiar. Miss Jones gauged the abilities of her students so well that little complaint against this system was ever heard.

To be sure, Miss Jones varied her standard of performance in terms of the abilities of her students. She stated frankly that there was nothing sacred about solid geometry; she regarded the subject rather as an opportunity for a pupil to learn to think as well as his ability would let him. If an individual came up to her estimate of his or her ability, that student passed the course. The total number of theorems one could demonstrate was a matter of indifference to Miss Jones. As a result of her procedure, solid geometry, which is usually a difficult and uninteresting subject, was one of the most fascinating classes on the campus; everyone in the class, even those at the tail end, had a good time—partly through the informality of the class and partly through the adjustment of the work to each pupil's ability. The obtaining of sudden insights was a frequent occurrence, although some pupils experienced this intellectual excitement more frequently than others. But everyone in the class sometimes derived pleasure from the thrill which comes from suddenly seeing through a matter which has previously been obscure. Miss Jones got plenty of work out of both the most unlikely and the most promising students because she adjusted her requirements to each student's ability, insisting only that everyone think.

The work in high school must be interesting. This statement is not made in defense of a painless education. Classroom work must compete with all the other things a boy or girl likes to do. The adolescent will spend time in studying only if the work is as interesting as the other things to which the same time might be put. If classwork is not interesting it will be neglected in favor of athletics, extracurricular activities, individual schemes of various sorts, money-making tasks, reading of light fiction, dances, or other such diversions. The adolescent can no longer be controlled, as the child can be, by mere authority, and he is not yet old enough to be controlled by economic pressure. In the intervening years he will therefore follow his interests. It is part of the teacher's business to capitalize on them.

Classroom work must furnish adolescents with an opportunity to exercise their minds. Naturally, the assignments appropriate for the more capable are too difficult for the dull, but for pupils of all levels of ability there must be a real opportunity for mental effort. Boys and girls of this age spontaneously spend hours in solving all kinds of puzzles or in playing games that demand quick thinking and cleverness in outwitting one's opponent. Assignments therefore need to present puzzles that will intrigue the adolescent into thinking.

Whenever possible, subject matter should be approached through the emotions and imagination rather than through impersonal logic. Adolescents are stimulated by anything in which there is a bit of romance. They show this inclination clearly in their choice of movies or reading matter and in their hero worship of some idealized historic or fictional character. The chemistry teacher might bring about more learning of chemistry if he would start his course with the reading of *Crucibles;* the biologist would be well advised to begin his elementary classes with the reading of *The Microbe Hunters.* Such reading is stimulating to the imagination and ideals of youth and serves to maintain adolescent effort through the hours of drill necessary in the first year of any science. Naturally, a profound arousal of the emotions is undesirable, but too little stimulation is equally fatal to schoolwork.

One of the adolescent's favorite illusions is his conviction that he is now an adult. He therefore insists upon his ability to manage his own affairs and resents having his work arranged for him. Instead of regarding detailed directions for preparing an assignment as a help, he is likely to regard them as an unwarranted intrusion upon his sense of independence. Pupils in high school should be allowed, within reasonable limits, to plan their own work and the means of getting it done. Some guidance must, of course, be given—but primarily when asked for. Arranging his own work not only gives an adolescent a feeling of independence but arouses responsibility for getting the work done. If he has planned a particular task, he is working for himself, not the teacher. Decisions made in relatively unimportant matters often bring about a quite disproportionate conviction of self-direction. Thus if an English teacher wants pupils to read part or whole of an epic, she may either assign a particular epic or she may tell the pupil to find out what epics there are and then to select for himself which one he will read. The second type or assignment is decidedly preferable.

Whenever possible a pupil should be allowed to tell his classmates what he has found out about a given topic and to discuss it with them. The traditional recitation, during which the student talks to the teacher, is not a desirable method for socialization—aside from being a poor method for other reasons. The strong drives for social approval and prestige make socialization especially desirable.

The material that goes into a course has to be selected upon one basis or another from the total data available in a given field. It is best to select those items that have the greatest immediate practical usefulness to the adolescent, in school or out. Pupils have many problems of their own, to the solving of which schoolwork should contribute. Whenever teachers see a chance, they should make such applications and give such examples as will be of greatest service to the pupils in their daily living.

Finally, teaching should emphasize, insofar as the particular group being taught can appreciate, the general implications, conclusions, and theories inherent in the facts under consideration. For the first time in his life, the high school pupil is able to regard a general principle as something more than a series of words to be memorized. When he discovers that theories give him an explanation of otherwise puzzling facts, he is eager

660 INTELLECTUAL DEVELOPMENT

to have more of them and thus achieve further enlightenment. Most adolescents want explanations of *why* things happen. In contrast, the child is content to know *what* happens. As will be pointed out in the last chapter, an adolescent has not become an adult until he has achieved some integrated attitude toward himself and the world about him. Although too much theory leads to bewilderment, too little leads to failure in achieving an adult point of view.

Teaching in high school should, then, have the following eight characteristics if it is to motivate the learner into getting his work done: it must relate drill to some desired purpose and must eliminate sheer monotony as much as possible; it must be interesting; it must give the adolescent mental exercise; it must stir his imagination; it must allow him to feel and develop his independence; it must socialize him; it must give him insight into his daily life; and it must provide him with as many explanations as he can understand. Work that lacks these characteristics simply does not get done because learning cannot be brought about without the earnest cooperation of the learner.

2. The Duties of the Modern Teacher: The extent of the changes in the objectives and methods of the secondary school is well reflected in an excellent analysis of the modern teacher's duties.[17] She is (a) to study her pupils as individuals and as members of groups; (b) to study group processes to determine what leads to acceptance, rejection, leadership, values, participation; (c) to create an environment in which the emotional atmosphere, the feeling of belonging, and the security will lead to learning; (d) to establish the best possible personal relationship with her class; (e) to organize classroom situations so that learning will take place, largely by using the interests of the pupils; (f) to observe needs and diagnose frustrations; (g) to help pupils organize themselves in groups for carrying on the activities of the classroom; (h) to aid pupils in the selection of the most worth-while experiences; (i) to apply such therapy as may be needed to remove fear, insecurity, prejudice, and so forth; (j) to record the progress of each pupil in health and in social and emotional adjustment; and (k) to help the pupil to interpret the facts relative to his own growth and adjustment. Conspicuously absent from this long list is any direct mention of subject-matter, of "teaching" in the conventional sense, or of discipline. The fundamental theory is that all children will learn spontaneously and will behave themselves acceptably if their surroundings furnish them with security and if their personal frustrations can be eliminated. The teachers therefore concentrate upon the pupil and the social situation and let the learning look after itself. Perhaps this procedure is better adapted to the present generation of high school students than the traditional methods, but one sometimes wonders if the modern emphasis upon socialization and integration is not so extreme as to precipitate a partial return to earlier instructional precedures, with an eventual blending of what is best in both.

---

[17] Based upon Mendenhall and Arisman, *op. cit.,* pp. 76–81.

IV. Summary

The curriculum of the high school is a heritage from former days, both remote and recent. It represents many trends and many points of view. It is not as well adapted to the needs of adolescents as it could be. The writer is still old-fashioned enough to believe that the center of school life ought to be its classwork and that a school is no better than its curriculum. Many people would not agree with either notion. The details of curricular development are, however, not as important as the conviction that what is taught in class really matters. The methods of presentation also matter. Both content and method should be adapted to the nature of adolescent needs, adolescent abilities, and adolescent attitudes. Classwork ought to be about something that boys and girls want to learn because it is important to them, either immediately or in their plans for the future. And classes ought to be fun. When these two conditions are met, the curriculum has a chance to be a vital force in adolescent life.

REFERENCES FOR FURTHER READING

BOOKS

1. Alberty, H., *Reorganizing the High School Curriculum*, The Macmillan Company, 1947, 458 pp. (Chaps. 2–6, 15.)
2. Belting and Clevenger, *The High School at Work*, Chap. 15.
3. Faunce, R. C., and N. L. Bossing, *Developing the Core Curriculum*, Prentice-Hall, Inc., 1951, 311 pp. (Chaps. 1–4, 6, 12.)
4. Featherstone, W. B., *Functional Curriculum for Youth*, American Book Company, 1950, 276 pp. (Chaps. 4, 6–9.)
5. Giles, H. H., *Teacher-Pupil Planning*, Harper & Brothers, 1941, 395 pp. (Chaps. 1, 2, 3.)
6. Jersild, A. T., *et al.*, *Child Development and the Curriculum*, Columbia University Press, 1946, 274 pp. (Chap. 6, pp. 166–236.)
7. Landis, *Adolescence and Youth*, Chaps. 19, 20.
8. Leonard, J. P., *Developing the Secondary School Curriculum*, Rinehart & Company, 1946, 560 pp. (Chaps. 2, 11, 12.)
9. Malm and Jamison, *Adolescence*, Chap. 14.
10. Mendenhall, C. B., and K. J. Arisman, *Secondary Education*, The Dryden Press, 1951, 424 pp. (Chaps. 3, 5, 6, 8.)
11. Roucek, J. S., "Social Foundations of Education," in P. F. Valentine, *Twentieth Century Education*, Philosophical Library, 1946, 655 pp. (Pp. 414–432.)
12. *Thirty Schools Tell Their Story*, Harper & Brothers, 1943, Vol. V, 802 pp. (Any one report on any one school.)
13. Valentine, *Twentieth Century Education*, Chaps. 13, 24, 25.

MONOGRAPHS, BULLETINS, PROCEEDINGS, YEARBOOKS, ARTICLES

A. *Curriculum Construction*

1. Alberty, H., "Development of the Core Curriculum," *Educational Research Bulletin*, 17:222–230, 1938.
2. "American Education in the Post War Period: Curriculum Construction," *Forty-fourth Yearbook of the National Society for the Study of Education*, 1945, Pt. I, 292 pp.

3. Bristow, W. H., "Curriculum Foundations," *Review of Educational Research,* 18:221–259, 1948.

4. Douglass, H. R., "Education for All Youth in Life Adjustment," *Annals of the American Academy of Political and Social Science,* 265:108–114, 1949.

5. Douglass, H. R., *Education for Life Adjustment,* The Ronald Press, 1950, 491 pp. (Chaps. 1, 3, 4, 15, 19, and any one from Chaps. 5 to 14.)

6. Douglass, H. R., H. J. Otto, and S. Romine, "Curriculum: Status and Description," *Review of Educational Research,* 18:231–248, 1948.

7. Educational Policies Commission, *Education for All American Youth,* National Education Association, 1944, 421 pp. (Chaps. 2, 6, and any one of Chaps. 3–5.)

8. Herrick, V. E., and R. W. Tyler, "Toward Improved Curricular Theory," *Supplementary Educational Monographs,* No. 71, University of Chicago, 1950, 124 pp. (Chaps. 1–4, 9, 12.)

9. Kubie, L. S., "The Psychiatrist Considers Curricular Development," *Teachers College Record,* 50:241–246, 1949.

10. McKenzie, G. W., and M. R. Lawler, "Curriculum: Change and Improvement," *Review of Educational Research,* 18:273–281, 1948.

11. Taba, H., "General Technique of Curriculum Planning," *Forty-fourth Yearbook of the National Society for the Study of Education,* 1945, Pt. I, pp. 209–228.

B. *The Needs of Youth and the Curriculum*

1. Anderson, H. A., "Study of Youth as a Basis for Curriculum Construction," *School Review,* 55:383–394, 1947.

2. Anfinson, R. D., "School Progress and Pupil Adjustment," *Elementary School Journal,* 41:507–514, 1941.

3. Bailey, D. W., "The Student Is the Curriculum," *Progressive Education,* 16:38–43, 1939.

4. Corey, S. M., "Designing a Curriculum for Student Adjustment," *Bulletin of the National Association of Secondary School Principals,* 32:101–110, 1948.

5. "Life Adjustment Education for Every Youth," Federal Security Agency, Office of Education, 1948, 122 pp.

6. Low, C. M., "Neglect of the Personal-Social Needs of Youth," *Progressive Education,* 28:52–56, 1950.

7. Lyman, H. B., "Differentiation Attitudes of Students in Two High Schools by Use of a School Attitude Inventory," *Educational and Psychological Measurement,* 9:227–232, 1949.

8. Morgan, M. I., "Teaching Family Relationships in High School," *Marriage and Family Living,* 11:43–44, 1949.

9. Perry, W. D., "Some Approaches to Education for Family Living for Secondary Schools," *Marriage and Family Living,* 11:41, 1949.

10. Quins, W. H., W. H. Fox, and D. Segel, "A Study of a Secondary School Program in the Light of the Characteristics and Needs of Youth," *Bulletin of the School of Education,* Indiana University, XXV, No. 6 (1949), 1–69.

11. Remmers, H. H., and K. S. Davenport, "Youth Looks at Education," *American School Board Journal,* 13:19–20, 1949.

12. "University High School Study of Adolescence," *University High School Journal,* 19:177–219, 1941.

Conclusion

CHAPTER TWENTY

The End of
Adolescence

Adolescence is an interesting period to the teacher and an exciting period to the individual who is in the midst of it, but eventually it must end and make way for the emergence of adulthood. It seems, therefore, useful to consider of what maturity consists, as reported by several people competent to judge. Although these excerpts do not say all there is to be said on the matter, they contain food for thought.

1. An adult is (a) one who is able to see objects, persons, and facts (reality) in terms of what they are, cleansed of all infantile symbolic investiture; (b) one who is under no compulsion to do or not to do, but who is free to act in accordance with the reality of any given situation; (c) one who is able to adjust to an unalterable situation with a minimum of conflict.[1]

2. An adult is a person who is successful (a) in functioning as an independent unit with gratification of his desires in terms of the culture in which he lives; (b) in establishing satisfactory and acceptable biologic and social interaction with other people; and (c) in finding self-expression, self-extension, and self-objectivation in his social milieu.[2]

3. An adult is one who (a) has an integrated personality; (b) has sublimated or socialized his basic impulses and drives; (c) can accept reality, tolerate frustration, inhibit his impulses, accept his own inadequacies and unavoidable pains, humiliations, and losses, and is free from excessive anxieties, worries, or fears; (d) can solve the common problems of living; (e) is happy in his work; (f) accepts responsibility for his own actions; (g) can establish and maintain satisfactory and lasting relationships with other people; and (h) is able to feel strong emotions but also able to control their expression.[3]

These authors are referring primarily to emotional and social maturity. An adult faces reality, estimates it objectively, and adjusts himself to it. To be sure, the standards above are set so high that most people will not reach all of them. The child that each individual once was remains within him, and from that child he never quite escapes.

Some of the criteria by which one may know that adolescence has come to an end are more definite and more easily recognizable than others. The measures of maturity to be discussed in the following section have been derived partly from analysis of adults who failed to grow out of childish

---

[1] F. E. Williams, *Adolescence*, Rinehart & Company, 1930, p. 15.

[2] J. Ruesch, "The Infantile Personality," *Psychosomatic Medicine*, 10:134–144, 1948.

[3] P. M. Symonds, *The Dynamics of Personal Adjustment*, Appleton-Century-Crofts, Inc., 1946, 666 pp.

or adolescent points of view, partly from experimental results in the longitudinal studies already referred to at various times, and partly from a consideration of the essential problems of adolescence—as summarized from many sources in the first chapter of this book.

I. Adult Levels

1. Physical Maturity: For physical adolescence, the end of the period may be seen most objectively. A high school pupil is physically an adult when he has reached his final height, when his body has assumed adult proportions, when his heart and other organs are of adult size, when his bones have reached their final size and density, when his sexual functions have become established, and when all secondary sexual characteristics are in evidence. Skeletal growth and establishment of primary and secondary sexual functions are usually complete by the age of eighteen, but internal growth is still in progress. Some people hold that all gains in weight after the age of twenty-five are abnormal and consist of unnecessary deposits of fat; others think that small increases of weight should take place until the later years of adult life.

Physical adulthood is almost certain to arrive; indeed, it can be prevented only by extreme deprivation or deficiency. It is one type of maturity that is not appreciably affected even by the greatest coddling or the most ardent wishes to remain a child.

2. Emotional Maturity: This type of maturity is more difficult to estimate. As long as people become angry over superficial social situations, are dependent upon older people or members of their own sex for happiness, are inclined to take things personally, or continue to run away from reality, they are not yet adults emotionally. It is at once clear that some people never grow up and that others do not become mature until long after they have passed beyond the age of legal responsibility.

The homosexual adult, the promiscuous adult, and the person who falls in love with much older people are showing behavior appropriate to an earlier period and inappropriate to mature life. The true adult has selected what he or she believes to be a permanent mate, has left experimentation behind, and has settled down to normal sexual restrictions. Not all people—especially not all women—marry. The unmarried adult has special problems of maturity. He, or more likely she, learns to substitute other drives and interests for those that are sexual. Most unmarried people have at one time or another intended to marry and have gone through the preparatory emotional stages of increasing heterosexual interests and concentration upon one person. They were therefore adults at one time. The chief danger for them is that, having failed in their first major emotional venture, they will retrogress to the earlier levels of dependency upon older people or upon homosexual attachments for emotional satisfaction. Such a regression not only is undesirable in itself but may prevent a second marital attempt.

Adolescents tend to take everything personally, to get their feelings hurt if they are criticized, and to be quite unwilling to face unpleasant situations—especially of their own making. As long as these reactions persist, an adult is still an emotional adolescent, no matter if he is the head of a corporation or the president of a bank. The businessman who tells his secretary to get him out of an appointment he does not want to keep—although he may have made it himself—so that he can keep some other engagement that appeals to him more is showing no more mature behavior than the adolescent who, on the ground that he now likes some other girl better, wants his mother to get him out of going to a party with the girl he has already asked. Facing reality is admittedly a tough job, but it has to be done if one is to grow up.

The child knows he has limitations, but generally he does not care a great deal, and the adolescent likes to hide his shortcomings even from himself. The adult, however, has to admit to himself at least that there are things he cannot do and that he is not the genius he may once have believed himself to be. If he evaluates himself objectively and plans his life to suit his capacities, he has entered emotional adulthood. Thus, for instance, the drugstore proprietor in a small town who says, "I'd be a failure in a big city, but I'm doing fine here; I've a nice home and family, and I'm happy," has made his compromise with life and is now a true adult. The hectic rushing about, the sowing of wild oats, the search for a thrill belong to the years of adolescence. The adult who still shows these symptoms has not completely grown up.

The small child inhibits his emotions hardly at all; whatever he feels is translated into action. If he does not like a new acquaintance, he pushes him away. An adolescent has somewhat more self-control and can inhibit his expression well enough to observe common courtesies to those whom he does not like, although he soon regresses to childish levels if he is forced to work with or to be frequently with a disliked person. It takes an adult with well-developed powers of inhibition to work day after day in moderately close contact with someone he dislikes and neither wear out under the strain nor precipitate scenes.

The typical causes of emotional behavior among adolescents and the reactions commonly made to these stimuli have already been discussed in an earlier chapter.[4] As long as these stimuli produce these results, an individual is emotionally adolescent—not emotionally mature. Naturally adults have emotions that can be just as violent as those produced at any earlier age. The exhausting ones are, however, not as easily aroused, and when aroused they are better controlled and more readily diverted into relatively harmless channels. Experience with sundry forms of escape has

---

[4] See pp. 122–139.

provided means for resolving minor conflicts. Even the pleasant emotions are not as easily aroused as they once were, nor are they quite as enjoyable.

In order to illustrate the points made concerning each type of maturity, a few case histories are presented from time to time. These persons were all within the limits of normality, and in many respects they were delightful individuals, but each showed more or less serious and pervasive forms of immaturity.

Miss R. is a brilliant woman of forty-eight. She has for ten years been an excellent high school teacher, one of the best in a large system. Since her adolescent days she has had three different bosom friends. The first was a childhood acquaintance with whom Miss R. roomed in both boarding school and college. Both taught in the same school and continued to live together. Miss R. was dominant and most attractive. Many boys and men fell in love with her, but none awakened an ounce of interest. About five years after graduation Miss R.'s friend met a young man to whom she became engaged. Miss R. appeared to have no objections, but managed subtly to keep the marriage postponed until the man lost interest. She and her friend had a terrific row and separated—the friend to remain single all her life. Miss R. was despondent for a month or two, until she found another companion— a woman ten years younger than herself. Then she again became radiant and fascinating. Eventually the second friend also fell in love. This engagement was broken three or four times, but in the end the friend married and went away. Again Miss R. was disconsolate for some time. During this period she herself finally yielded to her most persistent suitor and married. She and her husband are good friends; he is deeply in love with her and has apparently decided to be content with whatever she sees fit to give him. In the second year of her marriage Miss R. became interested in a girl nearly twenty years her junior. Eventually the girl came to live with her married friend. The strangely assorted trio is still together, but the girl—now a woman—is trying to break away. Miss R. is again indulging in her skillful machinations, and the husband is trying to be deaf, dumb, and blind to the strain. There has never been any suspicion of actual sexual relations between Miss R. and any of her three intimate friends; the relationship is rather what one finds between two inseparable chums twelve or thirteen years old. Miss R. is not so much homosexual as preadolescent. If she were homosexual she would probably not have married, and she almost certainly would not form attachments with perfectly normal girls and women. It is to be noted that with each shift in companion Miss R. is forced into selecting as her new chum a person whose age is further and further below her own. Those of her own age are by now too mature to be interested. If the present chum leaves, Miss R.—now nearly fifty years old—will have to attract some girl thirty to thirty-five years younger than herself, or else finally grow up—which is unlikely.

Millie is a woman, now in her seventies, with most of her life behind her. She is an odd creature in many ways, most of which are attributable to her extreme emotional childishness.

As an only child, Millie was the center of her parents' devotion. They had little money, but whatever they could save they spent on Millie, who always had more hair ribbons, prettier clothes, and more playthings than her friends. Her mother waited on her, dressed her, washed her, and guarded her. A princess could hardly have had a more devoted slave. Millie was not very happy with other children because she did not know how to adjust herself to them; in fact, it probably never occurred to her that there was any adjusting for her to do. She always wanted the leading role in every game, but since she was timid, hesitant in speech, deliberate in thought, and pathologically afraid of being hurt or of soiling her lovely clothes, she was not exactly equipped by nature for being a leader. Actually she trailed along with the other girls in the neighborhood, never popular, but over-looked rather than disliked. In school, Millie was docile and applied herself with moderate success to her lessons. Throughout her childhood she continued her dependence upon her parents and her avoidance of anything that was dirty, noisy, dangerous, or unfamiliar. She disliked all small boys on principle. With small girls she was not especially happy either, but she developed very early a habit of day-dreaming about her daily experiences, assigning to herself a dominating role. As a result, the childhood that she now recalls was a golden age. Most of what she recalls either never happened at all or is so distorted as to be barely recognizable.

After she graduated from high school Millie remained at home. She read a good many books and magazines, spent hours in selecting materials for her dresses, and even more time in idle daydreaming. She changed all her clothes twice every day; she stepped out of whatever she was wearing, leaving everything on the floor while her mother prepared a bath and then redressed her in clean clothes and combed her hair. Millie never washed or ironed her own clothes or prepared a meal or washed a dish or sewed on a button. Once in a while she helped her father in his store by playing cashier for a few hours. She was willing also to take orders over the telephone, and she quite enjoyed adding up the monthly accounts and making out the bills.

When Millie was about twenty-five, her father died, and she inherited his small grocery store. Millie left most of the waiting on customers to an elderly clerk who had worked in the store for years, and applied herself to the ordering of sup-plies and the handling of finances. She was quite successful at both. In the course of time she even helped somewhat in the store by waiting on such customers as she had known as a child, since she could in this way maintain a semblance of social life. Millie continued to live with her mother. She often complained because her acquaintances married and moved away, whereas she had to stay in one place and never had a chance to meet any eligible men. This latter statement was not true, for Millie had as many "chances" as any other girl in her group, but she regarded men and boys as ogres and would have nothing to do with them. She has never been to a party or a dance or to the movies with a boy or man in her entire life.

When Millie was about forty-five, her mother died, chiefly from overwork. This death left Millie not only alone but quite helpless in regard to the daily routine of eating, bathing, dressing, and so on. For instance, Millie had never combed her own hair or drawn the water for a bath or boiled the eggs for her breakfast. For some weeks her life was chaotic, as she slowly learned to meet her own personal require-ments. Her mother's death was the one really bad shock of Millie's life. She reacted to it in two ways: by wailing hopelessly like a three-year-old and by becoming in-furiated in the manner of small children who are too young to understand why any-thing they want should be denied them.

Gradually, Millie made sufficient adjustment for continued survival, chiefly through the hiring of a colored woman to whom she turned over all household matters. Millie then devoted her full time to the store, of which she has made a modest success. She was never lacking in intelligence, and after reading many books on how to manage a store, she developed enough confidence in herself to earn her own living.

Millie has now retired from active participation, although she is still a partner in the store and derives an income from it. She can hardly be said to have retired from social life also, because one cannot retire from what one has never entered. Millie sometimes sees an old acquaintance, but otherwise she talks only with her housekeeper. She could presumably talk intelligently about the management of a small store, but actually her only topics are her mother (whom she still calls "Mamma"), her childhood memories, and her resentment against the world because she has no parents, no husband, and practically no friends. Her only regular human contact, except with the housekeeper, occurs at noon when she goes to a nearby, small cafeteria for her dinner—a habit she developed in the period after her mother's death. There her performance is always the same: she cannot decide what she wants, so she takes a helping of everything she sees that appeals to her; as a result she arrives at the checker's desk with two kinds of soup, four different rolls, both tea and coffee, three salads, and four desserts. An assistant then carries her tray or trays to a table, gently but firmly removes two thirds to three fourths of the servings, collects the money for the balance, and settles Millie at her favorite table. This procedure has been going on for two decades. Millie prefers young men to young women, falls in love with each successive one (occasionally making so bold as to bring him a bag of candy), and talks endlessly about him to her housekeeper. The managers of the cafeteria rather foster these innocent attachments, since Millie's pleasure in her few "intimate" moments with her latest young man are sufficient stimulus to keep her from blocking the line, as will otherwise certainly happen.

Millie is not insane, merely extremely childish in all personal matters. She has never had an intimate friend, and it is improbable that she ever will. Whatever value she had for her community has already been contributed. From now on she will have to be looked after by hired guardians—and no matter how much attention she gets from them, it will never be enough.

3. Social Maturity: The socially adequate adult is also difficult to describe, although the experienced clinician can recognize both social maturity and social immaturity without too much trouble. Blind loyalty to one's friends and blind prejudice against anyone who is different are adolescent characteristics; a person of adult years who shows them is still socially an adolescent. The true adult is able to get along in casual business relationships with practically any other normal adult. One naturally cannot be expected to like everyone in the world, or to approve of everyone, but the grown man who can work only under a friend's direction is on a social par with the adolescent who can do laboratory work only if paired with his chum.

Complete emancipation from home must take place, or adolescence is not yet over. No matter how old individuals are, they remain children emotionally if they must run continually to their parents for understanding or assistance. One should not suppose, however, that callous indifference to parents is a sign of maturity. Quite the opposite! Revolt and indifference are normal in adolescence because they are often necessary in order to break familial ties, but they are indicative of immaturity thereafter. The need for revolt should be over. If it nevertheless continues, or if the scars of previous antagonisms have culminated in either indifference or hatred, childhood and adolescence linger on. The true adult loves his parents and is willing to take their desires into consideration, but he makes his own decisions and lives his own life.

The adolescent is typically a person who feels insecure because he does not know what to do or how to act in various social relationships. Of course, an older person who finds himself in a quite new social situation—in a foreign country, for instance—may be as lost as an adolescent, but an adult is characteristically able to adjust himself easily and naturally to ordinary and recurrent social situations. The grown person who is still embarrassed and distressed by the customary daily contacts with people has not yet reached the end of his adolescence.

The adolescent is abnormally dependent upon his own small group of friends. He must have precisely the same clothes that they have, must enjoy the same things, must use the same catchwords, must hold the same opinions. Otherwise he will be considered "queer"—a terrible fate. A person is not an adult until he is free from such slavish imitation. Those of mature years who expend time, energy, and money in "keeping up with the Joneses" are showing a typically adolescent trait that has persisted after its period of usefulness.

The two individuals described in the following histories had not yet reached an adult level of social competence. The first was still a child and the second had prolonged her adolescent enthusiasms and attitudes into her mature years.

Mr. B. is a young man of thirty-two, the only child of a widowed mother. When Mr. B. graduated from high school he entered his father's business as a book-keeper. A year later his father died. Mr. B. had always been abnormally attached to his mother, upon whom he depended for all kinds of help. His mother kept his clothes in order, bought everything for him, was his constant companion, read aloud to him in the evening, cooked his favorite foods, adjusted her time to suit his, helped him with extra work when necessary, read and abstracted professional books, kept his bank account, wrote his checks, made his appointments, sent him at intervals to the dentist, chose the few acquaintances she allowed him, and was the center of his life. The young man had never had a girl, nor had he felt the need of feminine friends except his mother. Two years ago the mother died. The emotional shock was severe, but the practical results were even worse. Mr. B. could not tie his own necktie, shine his shoes, or even find his belongings. He did not know how much razor blades, soap, or toothpaste cost because he had never bought them. He had no idea what his current expenses were. He had no friends to whom he could turn. Without his mother's constant supervision he got behind in his office work and soon lost his job. His clothes became shabby, but he did not know where to get more or how much he should pay for them. The childishness of this man's behavior is too obvious to require comment.

Mrs. W. is now over fifty. Her husband is dead, and she never had any children. In her youth she went to a small school, where she did only mediocre classwork but had a glorious time. Mrs. W. was not a popular student in her own right, but she basked in the reflected glory of a sister who had been a great leader in school affairs. After graduation Mrs. W. had married one of her sister's cast-off beaux. He was a wealthy man upon whom she prevailed to make large donations to her former school. Eventually he became a trustee. Mrs. W. never missed a reunion or other gathering of alumnae. In addition she frequently returned to school for a visit, often remaining for several weeks. She knew almost every girl in every class, entertained students in her rooms, and was entranced by their chatter. After her husband's death she rented a house near the school grounds and has lived there ever since. The girls stream in and out of her house, accepting her hospitality but making slurring comments about her among themselves. Since she will probably leave her considerable fortune to the school, the authorities do not care to interfere with her harmless but rather silly contacts with the students. When she is with them, nothing but her gray hair and matronly figure distinguishes her from them. Her conversation consists chiefly of anecdotes about students—past or present. She giggles at their witticisms, admires their talents, and follows their careers. To her age-mates she is an utter bore. She never tires of telling how she was once caught eating bread and jam in the chemistry laboratory or how her sister held three important student offices at once. Mrs. W. is by no means a fool, in spite of her obsessions about student life. She handles her own investments shrewdly, makes excellent addresses before clubs when the school wants to raise money, dresses well, and manages her house with taste and skill. It is in her social development that she is retarded. In the midst of adolescent chaff and humor she is at home; in an adult conversation she is confused and uncomfortable. She has no friends of her own age—but many adolescent girls find in her a person who is comfortably older in worldly wisdom and comfortably adolescent in interests and enthusiasm.

4. Moral Maturity: The end of moral adolescence is extremely difficult to define. It consists probably in the development of a relatively stable and relatively satisfying attitude toward life and the establishment of ideals by which one's own conduct is guided. The adult who is still perplexed and emotionally searching for an answer to the universe—and expecting to find one—is showing typical adolescent behavior. An adult does not accept unthinkingly the existing code of morals or current social situations, but he does regard such matters as facts which exist and to which one must make some reasonable adjustment. The adult who is still in a state of flaming revolt against the world has not outgrown his moral adolescence. The desire to reform the world before tomorrow is an attitude of youth, not of maturity. Deep-set racial prejudices, bigoted religious beliefs, and uncompromising ethical standards are all typical of the adolescent period. The tendency from the days of childhood into the adult years is from conservation and rigid belief toward liberalism and tolerance. The change is so gradual that the exact moment when the adolescent becomes an adult is impossible to determine, but a grown person who still carries the burden of uncompromising intolerance around with him has not yet reached his moral and ethical maturity.

The writer first knew Miss N. during their common childhood and has seen her at intervals ever since. Even as a child Miss N. was a rather timorous creature who clung to older people and wanted someone else to tell her what she ought to do in each small emergency. Just what gave Miss N. the idea that she could be successful in social service is not known, but after she had completed high school and a year in a teachers college, she entered a school for social work, eventually graduating from it. For a few years she worked for various charitable organizations, but never held a position for long. When she was nearly thirty, she took on a quite routine job in the psychiatric ward of a large hospital taking brief case histories of the patients at their entrance into the hospital. Much of the information she obtained from whoever accompanied the patient at the time of entrance; she sent for any other person who might add data, and had to leave the hospital only if an informant whom she needed to question could not come to her. The histories she took went to the medical staff and eventually into the records. Miss N. usually never saw the patient. Once she had written something in every space on the blank used for recording the admission history, her work was done. She was conscientious and meticulous about filling every space on every blank. As a form of social work Miss N.'s job was deadly dull, but it suited her excellently, and she has held it for over thirty years. Her only complaint has been that from time to time the upper echelon of authority in the hospital saw fit to modify the blank, thus forcing her to omit a few questions she had been asking and add a few new on s.

In her life outside the hospital Miss N. always leaned on someone who would make decisions for her. Until she was nearly forty, her mother told her what was right or wrong. After her mother's death, Miss N. tried to attach herself to various people whom she admired, but without success. After some five years of failure in personal relations she became a devout Catholic, agreeing willingly with whatever doctrines she was told were true. Moreover, she began to live with a domineering, elderly woman, who told her what she should do and think. With her problems thus settled, Miss N. was completely content with her life. Not long ago she explained to the writer her method of attack upon a new problem. She said she asked herself two questions: Would my mother want me to do this? Would the Church want me to do this? If both answers were affirmative, or both were negative, she acted accordingly; if there were a tie score, she asked her housemate for an opinion, thus having someone else cast the deciding vote. Miss N. seems to have no concepts of right and wrong for her guidance. She leans on others for their opinions just as she leans on an unfilled case-study blank for guidance in asking questions.

Mrs. C. is an elderly woman who has supported herself by renting rooms to college students. Her advertisement in the college newspaper always stated that she would not accept Negroes, Orientals, Jews, or foreigners. Last year she discovered in the middle of the semester that one of the boys was Jewish, though neither his appearance nor his name suggested it. She immediately ordered him to leave and upbraided him for deceiving her. He answered that he had not seen her advertisement and had been sent to her house by a Gentile friend, who had told him nothing about her prejudices. He offered to leave at the end of the semester but pointed out that all rooms near the campus were already taken and if he left at once he would have to move to the outskirts of the city and spend one to two hours a day on busses. Mrs. C. would hear of no compromise. The boy did not move, and the next evening he found his door locked when he returned. He spent the night with friends and the next day talked with the dean of men to find out if his landlady had the right to put him out of his room in the middle of the semester. The dean called Mrs. C. on the telephone, but she remained adamant and refused to let the boy stay for the remaining weeks of the semester. Finally the dean sent the lad with a campus policeman to the address, where the policeman's uniform and authority made a great impression upon Mrs. C. Under protest she unlocked the door and agreed to let the student remain for two or three days until some other arrangement could be made. In the meantime, the dean located and telephoned to Mrs. C.'s married daughter, who was greatly upset when she learned that a policeman had been sent to the house. The daughter offered to accept the boy in her own home for the balance of the year and to keep her mother away during that time if the authorities would let her mother alone. Since her house was as near the campus as her mother's the student willingly moved. The dean agreed to take no further action, except to cross Mrs. C.'s house off the approved list and to order the student paper to reject any further advertisements from her. Upon being informed of these measures, Mrs. C. visited the dean to lodge a protest. He expected to find her generally deteriorated and childish, but such was not the case. She was rigid in her thinking, to be sure, but her wits were sharp and she constantly outmaneuvered him in conversation. She seemed in most ways rather more mature than the average. Her aversion to various minority groups she attributed to once sitting for a semester in school next to a foreign boy who smelled of garlic. The rationalization and the prejudice were about equally childish, and she reverted to an almost infantile peevishness when she was finally convinced that in the future she would have to rent her rooms to businessmen and not to students. She still nurses her grievance against the college and expatiates upon it to anyone who will listen, but the more she talks, the more she demonstrates her underlying immaturity.

5. Intellectual Maturity: Mature thinking is indicated by a number of more or less related developments. Unless an individual is a defective or a lunatic, he will achieve at least the minimum level of adult intelligence— that is, in objective figures, he will eventually have a mental age of at least thirteen. Mental, like physical, development takes place with age, and is prevented only by extreme deprivation. From present data one can reasonably assume that an adult mental level is reached at some time between the ages of sixteen and twenty-five. In the course of time it may be possible to tell when an individual has reached a mature level in judgment, reasoning, imagination, or other intellectual qualities, although such measurements are not as yet adequate for purposes of establishing the level of maturity. Nor have tests succeeded in tracing the growth of intellectual independence, or the ability to substitute the independent evaluation of evidence for dependence upon authority.

At the same time that a person's mental capacities are growing, his interests are changing. The man who continues to play strenuous team games and the woman who dotes on parties are both showing adolescent traits. So also is the adult for whom the sentimental love story and movie still have a fascination, or the one who hangs over the radio or television set by the hour. The true adult may have a keen spectator interest in games, but sports are not meat and drink to him—unless they are a legitimate part of his business. He occasionally listens for a few minutes to some catchy dance tune on the radio and is amused by the cowboy on the television screen, but he soon turns to something else. He goes to parties now and then, but they are no longer the high points in his life. He reads current-events magazines, a few short stories, and more or less technical material concerning his work. When he has become fully mature he discovers that the typical interests of adolescence not only fail to thrill him but actually bore him. Not all people, however, succeed in developing mature intellectual interests and attitudes, even though their basic ability has reached an adult level.

Miss M. is a teacher of art in a girls' boarding school. She has been there for many years. The girls like her well enough, when they think about her at all— which is not often. If a student states to a newcomer that there are nine resident teachers in the school and then starts to enumerate them, she almost always leaves out Miss M. and cannot even think who is missing. In appearance Miss M. is a roundish, rubicund, bustling sort of person, with a constantly smiling face and a girlish giggle, which is, however, only a mannerism and not the result of having a sense of humor. The giggle and the smile are as empty as they are indiscriminate. Together they form Miss M.'s defense against a world that she does not in the least understand. The woman does no harm so far as the casual observer can make out, but it is doubtful if she does much good either.

Conversation with Miss M. is difficult, not because she does not try to be pleasant but because she has nothing to say. She has no opinion on any topic, even in her own field, although she is an industrious reader of books on art. Her class-work is based upon what she has read, and she does not encourage deviations from her plans for the day's lesson. If a pupil brings up a new point, Miss M. smiles pleasantly and says, "Yes there may be a lot of truth in what you say" or some-thing else equally vague, and goes right on with what she had planned. She constantly quotes authorities, often verbatim, both in class and in conversation.

Miss M.'s most irritating trait is a tendency to quote the sayings of her students. Aside from the fact that teachers in a boarding school become very tired of listening to the outpourings of adolescents, either directly or in quoted form, Miss M.'s anecdotes are only slightly amusing at the best and are often quite pointless. The writer remembers one exchange of remarks between two other teachers in the presence of Miss M. because the latter repeated it several times to others during the next few days as a sample of sparkling wit.

TEACHER NO. 1: Those shoes of yours are just what I want. Where did you buy them?

TEACHER NO. 2: In Belgium last summer.

TEACHER NO. 1: In that case, I guess I'll have to go on wearing my old ones.

Miss M. laughed uproariously at the time of this exchange and was still referring to it a dozen years later.

Except in intellectual maturity Miss M. is not a silly woman. She manages the practical affairs of life quite as well as the next person. Her manners are excellent, and she is entirely at ease in all kinds of gatherings. She is never awkward or at a loss for something gracious to say. She does not get embarrassed or upset. She is not moody. As a cheerful, laughing, healthy child of ten she would be a great success, and it is a pity that she could not have an adequate adult life in a feminine version of Peter Pan. She can get along well enough in adult social life, but adult intellectual life baffles her completely.

Finally, a fully grown-up person has found work that he likes and can do satisfactorily. The selection of an occupation, the preliminary training, the search for a job, and the early adaptations to the conditions of employ-ment are all problems of middle and late adolescence. A person is not eco-nomically adult until he is free of them. Sometimes, to be sure, an individual gets into and continues in the wrong kind of work for several years and then has a chance to take the training needed for another job. He therefore re-turns to his adolescence for a short period. Such interludes are often neces-sary and, if not repeated, constitute only a temporary and recognized immaturity. The vocationally childish people are those who hate either all work or their particular work, those who change jobs constantly, those who have no interest in what they are doing, and those who are never satisfied with their working conditions, hours, or salaries. The adolescent frequently considers steady employment as an imposition—once the thrill has worn off. When he gets bored with some chore he is supposed to do, no one is sur-prised if he simply quits. Until boys and girls find their places in the world, one can expect unrest, boredom, and revolt. They become adults when they settle down to a job that appeals to them and exchange adolescent rebellion for adult dependability and interest in their work.

Mr. J. is a charming man of twenty-four. He is good-looking in a rather boyish way and has pleasant manners, especially toward older people. He has been earning his own living, mostly in dead-end occupations, since he was seventeen. Mr. J. has plenty of ambition, but he attaches his enthusiasm to quite unreachable goals. At seventeen he decided to be a singer, left school, and got a small job that left him some hours free each day for practice. For two years he worked hard and faithfully, but he simply did not have the necessary native talents. Thus far the story is not remarkable. Most adolescents have one or more episodes of this sort. Upon being disillusioned about his voice, Mr. J. took up ballet dancing— although friends told him he was already much too old. Again he plunged into his training, working at a job only enough to support himself and spending the rest of his time in training. For two years he was heart and soul for the ballet. He made some progress, but not sufficient to meet competition in an overcrowded market. He next became fascinated by radio work. He got a job as messenger boy in a large broadcasting station, spent his earnings in taking voice training and courses in radio announcing. He was given a few chances on small programs, but was too colorless to attract attention. Eventually he decided to forsake broadcasting, but he still wanted to do something in radio, so he learned to play a trombone moderately well and got a job with a small band that played once in a while on some program. He became the band's business manager, secured a few bookings, and struggled along for about six months before admitting failure. While he was out of work he took a job as scene shifter in a theater. He was delighted with the stir and excitement behind the scenes. Within a week he was enrolled in an extension course in dramatics. His enthusiasm again ran high as he began to train himself to be an actor. He is still at it and is extremely annoyed over the likelihood of being drafted within a few weeks. His teachers agree that he is a pleasant, capable young man with an agreeable speaking voice, but no particular talent for the stage. Mr. J. has never outgrown his adolescence. Occupations that seem to him glamorous continue to arouse his enthusiasm. At twenty-four he has not yet shown an interest in any work for which he has adequate ability. He has never faced the fact that he is an ordinary young man who has an appreciation of the aesthetic but no specific talent. He is content with dead-end jobs that leave him free time for pursuing his most recent enthusiasm. He lives in a tiny room, eats little, works at tasks below his mental level, and eschews all vices. Thus far his life has been utterly harmless— and utterly impractical.

5. Summary: A true adult is, then, a person of adequate physical and mental development, controlled emotional reactions, and tolerant attitudes; he has the ability to treat others objectively; he is independent of parental control, reasonably satisfied with his point of view toward life, and reasonably happy in his job; he is economically independent; he is not dominated by the opinions of those about him, nor is he in revolt against social conventions; he can get along in ordinary social situations without attracting unfavorable attention; and, above all, he has learned to accept the truth about himself and to face reality instead of either running away from it or making believe it is not there.

II. The Adult World

The world is conducted primarily by and for adults. Recent emphasis upon childhood and adolescence has made many people forget that about 65 per cent of the population is over twenty and only 35 per cent under. Modern concentration upon infancy, childhood, and adolescence as interesting and important levels of development has sometimes distracted attention from the function of these stages in preparing an individual to live a normal adult life. The increasing need for such preparation may be demonstrated by consideration of the proportional age distribution of the general population, past and present.

Census figures have now been collected for approximately a century, although the early results contain data on only a few points. One can, however, trace changes in the proportional distribution of the population by ages. This distribution has been influenced by three main factors: the rate of immigration, the birth rate, and the death rate. Since middle-aged and elderly people leave their homes only in cases of catastrophe, most of the

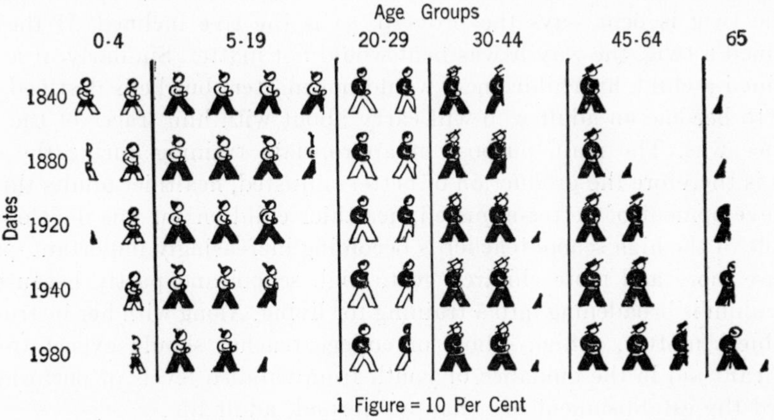

1 Figure = 10 Per Cent

Fig. 151. *Population Changes*

Based upon figures in W. S. Thompson and P. K. Whelpton, *Estimates of the Future Population of the United States,* Government Printing Office, 1945, 137 pp.

immigrants to America have been young people, often with babies and little children and capable of having further offspring. During the decades from 1920 to 1950 immigration was restricted to a mere trickle. The birth rate has been falling for the last fifty years, with the exception of a five-year period during and just after each of the world wars. Over the same period the death rate was also falling because of better medical care, better nutrition, better living conditions, and better education. Figure 151 on this page shows the proportion of the population in each of several major age groups in 1840, 1880, 1920, and 1940, together with the probable distribution in 1980. In 1840 the average age of the entire population was sixteen; in 1880 it was twenty; in 1940 it was twenty-seven; by 1980 it will presumably have risen to thirty-one. In 1840 the country was decidedly a young man's country. Only twenty-eight people in a hundred were over thirty years old and not over three in a hundred were over sixty-five. By 1980 it will be a middle-aged man's country, unless present trends reverse themselves. By then, sixty people in a hundred will presumably be over thirty, and twelve in a hundred over sixty-five; nearly seventy-five will be over twenty years of age. In 1840 there was less than one adult for every child or adolescent. Now there are about three adults to every child. With every passing decade since 1840, therefore, the need for a good adjustment to the adult world has become a little greater. If present trends continue, the future will require an even better adjustment.

III. Summary

People sometimes forget that adulthood is a far longer period than childhood and adolescence combined. The latter periods are of vital importance, not in themselves, but because of their influence upon later life. As the twig is bent, says the proverb, so is the tree inclined. If the twig remained a twig, the way it was bent would not matter. Similarly, if a child remained a child, his childishness would not matter; but he is destined from birth to become an adult who will carry about with him traces of the child he once was. The main purpose of appropriate training during the early years is therefore the production of better-adjusted, healthier adults through the development of better-adjusted, healthier children. In this development the role of the high school teacher is becoming increasingly important, partly because more and more children go to high school and partly because the curriculum is broadening into a training for living. Along with her instruction in subject matter, a high school or college teacher should expect to give significant aid in the guidance of youth from childish levels of performance toward the establishment of a happy, normal, adult life.

REFERENCES FOR FURTHER READING

BOOKS

1. Cole, L., *Attaining Maturity*, Rinehart & Company, 1944, 212 pp. (Chaps. 3–6, 14–17.)
2. Dublin, L. I., and M. Spiegelman, *The Facts of Life*, The Macmillan Company, 1951, 461 pp. (Chaps. 7, 15.)
3. Garrison, *Growth and Development*, Chap. 18.
4. Hurlock, *Adolescent Development*, Chap. 15.
5. Overstreet, H. A., *The Mature Mind*, W. W. Norton & Company, 1949, 292 pp. (Chap. 2.)
6. Preston, *The Substance of Mental Health*, Chap. 8.
7. Taylor, *Do Adolescents Need Parents?*, Chap. 12.
8. Van Waters, *Parents on Probation*, Chap. 11.
9. Zachry and Lighty, *Emotion and Conduct in Adolescence*, Chaps. 13, 14.

YEARBOOKS AND ARTICLES

1. Ruesch, J., "The Infantile Personality," *Psychosomatic Medicine*, 10:134–144, 1948.
2. Zachry, C. B., "Preparing Adolescents to Be Adults," *Forty-third Yearbook of the National Society for the Study of Education*, 1944, Pt. I, pp. 332–346.

APPENDIX A

List of Novels

The following references have been included because, even though the stories are pure fiction, they describe phases of development. The list by no means exhausts the full range of creative literature on the subject. Because they give a more detailed and more lifelike interpretation than the impersonal presentation of a text, novels are useful in connection with the study of adolescence. The instructor is urged to assign as many novels as the students can be expected to read. It is best to ask students to relate what they find in the novels to topics in the course—not to ask them to write a book review. Many students who have little interest in an abstract presentation learn the same principles when these are illustrated, vitalized, and simplified in an interesting narrative. Improperly used, novels may be misleading, but with reasonable safeguards, they form a valuable adjunct to a systematic text.

The list here presented is long and contains novels of many types. No effort has been made to classify the titles. A few of the books deal directly and almost exclusively with the adolescent period—Tarkington's *Seventeen,* for example. Others trace the growth of a personality from childhood into the adult years, as in Parrish, *The Perennial Bachelor.* Still others deal with a single problem of the adolescent years—for instance, Ferber, *Mother Knows Best.* There is also an occasional study of college life—Marks, *The Plastic Age,* for example. From all these varieties of presentation a student should be able to find a reasonable number that are interesting and valuable in illustrating some of the basic facts about adolescence.

Booklist of Fiction and Biography

√Asch, S., *East River,* Putnam, 1946.
Barbellion, W. N. P., *The Journal of a Disappointed Man,* Doran, 1919.
Becker, M. L., *Under Twenty,* Harcourt, Brace, 1932.
Bellamann, H., *King's Row,* Simon and Schuster, 1940.
Bennett, Arnold, *The Clayhanger Family,* Methuen Press, 1925.
Bennett, Mrs. Arnold, *Arnold Bennett,*[1] Adelphi Press, 1925, and "On Arnold Bennett," from the introduction to the *Old Wives' Tale.*
Beresford-Howe, C., *The Unreasoning Heart,* Dodd, Mead, 1946.
Björkman, Edwin, *Gates of Life,* Knopf, 1923.
  Soul of a Child, Knopf, 1922.
Bowen, Elizabeth, *Death of the Heart,* Knopf, 1939.
  The Hotel, Dial, 1928.
Bromfield, L., *The Louis Bromfield Trilogy* (3 vols.), Halcyon House, 1933 (*The Green Bay Tree, Possession, Early Autumn*).

---

[1] About a stammerer.

Brontë, E., *Wuthering Heights*, Dodd, Mead, 1939.

Broun, Heywood, *The Boy Grew Older*, Putnam, 1922.

Byrne, D., *O'Malley of Shanganagh*, Century, 1924.

Canby, H. S., *Alma Mater*, Rinehart, 1936.

✓Canfield, D., *The Bent Twig*, Grosset & Dunlap, 1934.

Cather, Willa, *Lucy Gayheart*, Knopf, 1935.

Celine, L. F., *Journey to the End of the Night*, McClelland, 1934.

Clark, W., *City of Trembling Leaves*, Random House, 1945.

Cronin, A. T., *Hatter's Castle*, Little, Brown, 1931.
   The Green Years, Little, Brown, 1944.

Davenport, M., *The Valley of Decision*, Scribner, 1942.

Delafield, E. M., *The Chip and the Block*, Hutchinson, 1930.

De la Roche, Mazo, *Growth of a Man*, Little, Brown, 1938.

Dell, Floyd, *Moon-Calf*, Knopf, 1920.
   Janet Marsh, Doran, 1927.

Dostoevski, F., *The Brothers Karamazov*, translated by C. Garnett. Modern Library, 1929.

Dreiser, Theodore, *An American Tragedy*, Simon and Schuster, 1929.

Eliot, George, *Mill on the Floss*, Harper, 1932.

Ertz, Susan, *The Story of Julian*, Appleton-Century, 1931.

Farrell, J. T., *Father and Son*, Vanguard, 1940.
   Studs Lonigan (Vol. 1, Trilogy), Vanguard, 1932.

Faulkner, William, *Absalom, Absalom!*, Random House, 1929.
   Sanctuary, Modern Library, 1931.

Ferber, Edna, *The Girls*, Grosset & Dunlap, 1924.
   Mother Knows Best, Grosset & Dunlap, 1928.
   One Basket, Simon and Schuster, 1946.
   So Big, Heinemann, 1932.

Forbes, E., *Johnny Tremain*, Houghton Mifflin, 1943.

Fournier, Alain, *The Wanderer*, Houghton Mifflin, 1928.

Frost, Frances M., *Yoke of Stars*, Rinehart, 1939.

Gale, Zona, *Preface to a Life*, Grosset & Dunlap, 1929.

Galsworthy, J., *Dark Flower*, Scribner, 1919.
   To Let, Scribner, 1921.

Gilfillan, L. W., *I Went to Pit College*, Viking, 1934.

Girling, Zoe, *Polonaise*, Macmillan, 1940.

Glasgow, Ellen, *Barren Grounds*, Doubleday, 1935.
   They Stooped to Folly, Doubleday, 1929.

Glaspell, Susan, *Brook Evans*, Stokes, 1928.
   Judd Rankin's Daughter, Lippincott, 1945.

Godden, Rumer, *The River*, Little, Brown, 1946.
   Take Three Tenses, Little, Brown, 1945.

Goldman, Emma, *Living My Life*, Knopf, 1934.

Gorky, Maxine, *The Bystander*, Appleton, 1930.

Green, Julian, *The Closed Garden*, Harper, 1928.
   The Dark Journey, Harper, 1929.

Gunnarsson, Gunnar, *The Night and the Dream*, Bobbs-Merrill, 1938.

Hackett, Francis, *Green Lion*, Doubleday, 1936.

Haines, W. W., *Slim*, Little, Brown, 1923.

Hall Radclyffe, *The Unlit Lamp*, Cape, 1933.
   The Well of Loneliness, Covici-Friede, 1932.

Halper, Albert, *The Chute*, Viking, 1937.

Hamsun, Knut, *August*, Grosset & Dunlap, 1933.
   Vagabonds, Cassell, 1931.

Hathaway, Katherine, *The Little Locksmith,* Coward McCann, 1943.
Herbert, A. P., *Water Gipsies, Methuen,* 1934.
Hillyer, Laurine, *Time Remembered,* Macmillan, 1945.
Hull, Helen, *Morning Shows the Day,* Coward McCann, 1934.
Hurst, Fannie, *Five and Ten,* Cape, 1934.
    Humoresque, Peter Smith, 1934.
Hutchinson, A. S., *If Winter Comes,* Hodder & Stoughton, 1933.
Hutchinson, R. C., *Interim,* Rinehart, 1945.
Huxley, Aldous, *Eyeless in Gaza,* Harper, 1936.
Jacobsen, Jens, *Nils Lyhne,* American Scandinavian Foundation, 1919.
James, Henry, *The Ambassadors,* Harper, 1904.
    The Turn of the Screw, Modern Library, 1930.
Jenkins, Elizabeth, *Harriet,* Doubleday, 1934.
Johnson, Josephine, *Wildwood,* Harper, 1946.
Johnson, O., *Stover at Yale,* Stokes, 1912.
    The Varmint, Baker & Taylor, 1910.
Joseph, Donald, *October's Child,* Stokes, 1929.
Keller, Helen, *Story of My Life,* Doubleday, 1929.
Kingsley, C., *Charles Kingsley—His Letters and Memories of His Life,*[2] Macmillan, 1890.
Kipling, R., *Stalky and Company,* Doubleday, 1930.
Koestler, Arthur, *Thieves in the Night,* Macmillan, 1946.
Lehmann, Rosamond, *The Ballad and the Source,* Reynal & Hitchcock, 1945.
Lewis, Eiluned, *Dew on the Grass,* Macmillan, 1934.
Liepmann, Heinz, *Nights of an Old Child,* Lippincott, 1937.
Lincoln, Victoria, *February Hill,* Rinehart, 1934.
Linder, R., *Stone Walls and Men,* Odyssey, 1946.
Lothar, Ernst, *The Prisoner,* Doubleday, 1945.
Lowe, F., *Somebody Else's Shoes,* Rinehart, 1948.
Lunn, A., *The Harrovians,* Methuen, 1919.
Mackenzie, C., *Youth's Encounter,* Appleton, 1913.
Mackinley, Helen, *Angel Mo' and Her Son, Roland Hayes,* Little, Brown, 1942.
Mann, Thomas, *Stories of Three Decades,* Knopf, 1936.
Mansfield, K., *The Short Stories of Katherine Mansfield,* Knopf, 1937.
Marks, Percy, *The Plastic Age,* Grosset & Dunlap, 1924.
    A Tree Grown Straight, Stokes, 1936.
Marquand, John P., *Warning Hill,* Little, Brown, 1930.
    B.F.'s Daughter, Little, Brown, 1946.
Marsh, Ellen, *Drink to the Hunted,* Dutton, 1945.
    Dull the Sharp Edge, Dutton, 1947.
Martin du Gard, Roger, *The Thibaults,* Viking, 1939.
Matthiessen, F. O., *The James Family,* Knopf, 1947.
Maugham, Somerset, *Of Human Bondage,* Doubleday, 1929.
    The Razor's Edge, Doubleday, 1944.
    The Summing Up,[3] Doubleday, Doran, 1938.
Maxwell, William, *The Folded Leaf,* Harper, 1945.
Meredith, George, *The Ordeal of Richard Feverel,* Scribner, 1926.
Millay, Kathleen, *Against the Wall,* Macaulay, 1929.
Millin, S. G., *God's Stepchildren,* Constable, 1929.
Mitchell, M., *Gone with the Wind,* Macmillan, 1936.
Moore, George, *Confessions of a Young Man,* Heinemann, 1933.
Mumford, Lewis, *Green Memories,* Harcourt, Brace, 1947.

---

[2] About a stammerer.
[3] About a stammerer.

O'Higgins, Harry J., *Julie Cane*, Harper, 1924.

O'Sullivan, *Twenty Years A-Growing*, Viking, 1933.

Pach, W., *Vincent Van Gogh*, New York Art Museum, 1936.

Papashvily, G. and H., *Anything Can Happen*, Pocket Books, 1948.

Parrish, Anne, *All Kneeling*, Harper, 1928.

 The Perennial Bachelor, Grosset & Dunlap, 1929.

Powys, J. C., *Wolf Solent*, Cape, 1933.

Priestley, J. B., *Angel Pavement*, Harper, 1930.

Proust, M., *Remembrances of Things Past*, Random House, 1934.

Rolland, Romain, *Jean Christophe*, Holt, 1928.

Rölvaag, O. E., *Peder Victorius*, Harper, 1928.

Salinger, J. D., *The Catcher in the Rye*, Little, Brown, 1951.

Scott, N. A., *The Story of Mrs. Murphy*, Dutton, 1947.

Sedgwick, A. D., *Dark Hester*, Houghton Mifflin, 1929.

Sinclair, Jo, *Wasteland*, Harper, 1946.

Sinclair, May, *Life and Death of Harriet Freem*, Macmillan, 1922.

 Mary Olivier, Macmillan, 1910.

 Three Sisters, Macmillan, 1933.

Stern, G. B. S., *The Reasonable Shores*, Macmillan, 1946.

Stone, Irving, *Lust for Life*, Longmans, Green, 1934.

Tarkington, Booth, *Alice Adams*, Doubleday, 1922.

 The Fighting Littles, Doubleday, 1941.

 Seventeen, Harper, 1916.

Thurstone, E. T., *Millennium*, Doubleday, 1930.

Tolstoi, *Anna Karenina*, Crowell, 1886.

Undset, Sigrid, *Kristin Lavransdatter*, Knopf, 1929.

Van Ammers-Küller, *The Rebel Generation*, Dutton, 1928.

Vidal, G., *The City and the Pillar*, Dutton, 1948.

Walker, Mildred, *The Quarry*, Harcourt, Brace, 1947.

 Winter Wheat, Harcourt, Brace, 1944.

Walpole, Hugh, *Fortitude*, Modern Library, 1930.

 Jeremy at Crale, Doran, 1927.

Ward, M. J., *The Snake Pit*, Random House, 1946.

Waugh, Evelyn, *Brideshead Revisited*, Little, Brown, 1946.

 The Loved One, Little, Brown, 1948.

 Vile Bodies, Little, Brown, 1946.

Weaver, John, *Her Knight Comes Riding*, Knopf, 1928.

Webster, B., *Mrs. Heriot's House*, Scribner, 1945.

Wells, H. G., *Ann Veronica*, Smith, 1909.

 Joan and Peter, Macmillan, 1918.

West, Rebecca, *The Judge*, Hutchinson, 1933.

Wharton, Edith, *The Children*, Appleton, 1928.

 Ethan Frome, Scribner, 1911.

 The Old Maid, Appleton, 1921.

White, Victor, *Peter Domanig: Morning in Vienna*, Bobbs-Merrill, 1944.

Williams, R. A., *The Strange Woman*, Houghton Mifflin, 1941.

Wilson, Margaret, *The Kenworthys*, Grosset & Dunlap, 1930.

Wolfe, Thomas, *Look Homeward, Angel*, Scribner, 1924.

 Of Time and the River, Scribner, 1935.

Woodbury, Helen, *The Misty Flats*, Little, Brown, 1925.

Woolf, Virginia, *The Waves*, Harcourt, Brace, 1931.

Worth, K., *The Middle Button*, Doubleday, 1946.

Wunsch, W. R. & Albers, E. (eds.), *Thicker Than Water*, Appleton-Century, 1939.

Zugsmith, Leona, *The Reckoning*, McLeod, 1934.

Zweig, Stefan, *World of Yesterday*, Viking, 1943.

APPENDIX B

Problems and

Projects

It is not expected that any student will be assigned more than one or two of the questions for each chapter. A number have been offered in order that both instructor and student may have a choice.

Chapter Two: Growth in Tissue, Muscle, and Bone

1. Compare records of individual children with the norms for height and weight at various ages.
2. Make a collection of nicknames applied to members of the class and their friends. What percentage is based on physical characteristics?
3. What are the advantages and disadvantages of being unusually tall or unusually short?
4. Write a brief account of a school acquaintance who, for lack of size or stamina, could not compete in sports and therefore turned his or her energies into other channels.
5. How many different types of build are recognizable among members of the class?
6. What reasons are there for the differences in strength between men and women?
7. What explanations are there for the results in Figure 16, page 36?
8. What would you consider the differential characteristics other than mere size that give babies, children, adolescents, and adults their differences in proportion?
9. Collect a series of photographs of the same person from infancy to maturity and trace the growth of the face.
10. Write a history of someone you know who is very fat. Can you see what the causes are? Is eating being used as a defense or escape?
11. If you know any families that have been in this country for one or two generations, measure those who were born elsewhere and those who were born here and compare each group with norms for sex and age. Are the children and grandchildren taller and heavier than the parents and grandparents?
12. If your college keeps records of height and weight (either in the medical examiner's office or in the physical education department) tabulate the first fifty cases from the earliest year of the records for height and weight and the first fifty cases of the current year. Is there any difference? (It is best to have twenty-five girls and twenty-five boys in a coeducational college; to get this number, you may have to examine more than a hundred records.)
13. If you can find a family in which each child's height on successive birthdays has been marked on the wall, make a record of the heights and plot a growth curve for each child. Compare curves thus obtained with the norms.

Chapter Three: Physiological Growth

1. Enumerate the indirect effects of physiological maturity upon as many other phases of growth as you can.

2. Make a chart, with a list of the endocrines down the left margin, and fill in columns headed "position," "secretion," "normal function," "results of excessive activity," "results of insufficient activity."
3. What reactions to sexual maturity did you observe among your classmates in junior high and high school?
4. Find out at what age each girl in your dormitory, sorority, or rooming house began to menstruate. Make a chart of the results and compare with Figure 43, page 69.
5. Collect information from both the boys and the girls in the class concerning the age at which they first obtained information on the topics listed in Figure 48, page 78. At the same time determine the source of the information and compare the results with Figure 50, page 104.

Chapter Four: Health and Hygiene

1. What proportion of the members of the class wears glasses? Have each student count the number in at least one other class (also the total enrollment) and then put all the results together.
2. At what age did you start wearing glasses? What symptoms did you have? Were they connected with schoolwork?
3. Write a brief case history of some acquaintance of high school age who had a chronic physical condition that prevented normal adjustment.
4. What do you consider the basic requirements of good personal hygiene? To what extent do you adhere to these principles in your daily life?
5. Hold a debate on the question of whether or not the school should be responsible for giving sex information.
6. Write a case study of a stammerer, a stutterer, or a partially deaf student whom you have known.
7. Have each member of the class list what he or she has eaten during the last twenty-four hours—including whatever has been taken between meals. Are there differences between the sexes? Among members of the same sex?

Chapter Five: Emotional Growth

1. Make a chart of a typical emotional reaction, beginning with the secretion of adrenalin, and showing a series of chain reactions by which the adrenalin affects various organs, and the changes that occur.
2. Describe two or three occasions in which you were "frustrated." What fundamental drive were you expressing? What blocked you? What reaction did you make to the blocking?
3. From novels you have read or movies you have seen or people you have known, write a brief history of someone whose fundamental drives were blocked but who succeeded in finding satisfaction through some substitute. The story on pages 115–116 may be used as a starting point.
4. List the situations that have caused you to become angry within the past week. How would you classify these situations? What reactions did you make? Were they direct or indirect?
5. To what extent are emotions necessary or useful in one's daily life?
6. Defend or attack the hypothesis that a modern environment makes normal expression of the emotions difficult if not impossible.
7. Make a list of the things you are now afraid of, worried about, or anxious about. What proportion of your fears do you consider childish, adolescent, adult?
8. In previous wars soldiers were taught to be ashamed of fear. In the last war they were taught to admit it. What differences in reaction might result?
9. Have you ever recovered from a specific fear? How did you do it?
10. Why is fear regarded as destructive?

11. You have probably been in love a dozen times since your infancy. With whom? How old were you when you were attracted to each person? What was the age and sex of each? Does your history conform to the summary on page 139 or is it different?
12. [For girls] Write a brief account of a "crush" that you have observed. What behavior did the girl show? How did the older girl or woman treat her? What reasons can you give for this fixation on the part of this particular girl?
13. Describe briefly someone you know whose development seems to have stopped short of maturity. Can you give any explanation for the failure to attain adult attitudes?
14. Rate yourself as very strong, strong, average, weak, very weak in each of the drives listed in Table 3, page 112.
15. Should an individual enjoy his emotions or should his goal be their elimination or sublimation?
16. Describe the various levels indicated by the psychoanalysts as oral, anal, Oedipal, latent, and genital. What are the characteristics of each? The normal age limits? Do these concepts help you in understanding emotional growth?
17. Which mechanisms of escape from conflict do you use? What methods have you observed in other people? Write an account of one or two incidents that seem to you to illustrate one or more of the escapes listed.
18. What have you wanted most for Christmas at different ages?

Chapter Six: Personality: Measurement and Types

1. Collect as many different kinds of projective tests as you can. What do you consider the strengths and weaknesses of each?
2. Rate at least a half-dozen people whom you know well on the Guilford-Zimmerman rating scale shown on page 160 and in Figure 58, page 160. Do you get significant differences of profile?
3. Before beginning the work of this chapter the instructor might give a sentence-completion test of the type described on pages 161 ff., either using a standard form or making up his or her own list of items. The answers, typed without names or other identification, can be assigned to students to work over. What different kinds of response are shown? Can the completions be classified as intrapunitive, extrapunitive, or impunitive?
4. Assume that you are going to give a TAT test in either a girls' or a boys' secondary school in which the pupils are fifteen to eighteen years of age. Collect from magazines a series of pictures that you think would be appropriate.
5. Make a list of the friends whom you know well enough to classify as to personality. Using the categories given in Table 7, pages 176–177, classify as many as you can. What proportion do you have left over?
6. Cut about one hundred geometrical forms out of colored paper, using the types shown in Figures 63 and 64, pages 170, 171, as models. Then ask a dozen different students to arrange them into diagrams. Are there differences? What do you think they mean?
7. Make an ink blot of irregular outline, such as that shown in Figure 65, page 172. Show it to a number of people and ask what it makes them think of. How many different responses do you get? Can you explain any of the differences?

Chapter Seven: Emotional Deviates

1. Write a brief history of someone you have known who fits into each of the main categories discussed in this chapter. (Different members of the class should take different categories, so that each person writes only one or two histories.)
2. Find in the library one or two illustrative studies for each classification.
3. It has been said that neuroses and psychoses are outgrowths or exaggerations

of particular types of personality. To what extent does this hypothesis seem to you to be true?

4. Everyone has feelings of inferiority, which may or may not have a basis in reality. List the sources of inferiority you have noticed among your friends.

5. Do you know a student who might be classified as a braggart, a show-off, an exhibitionist, or a pompous ass? What is he or she trying to cover up? Or compensate for?

6. What symptoms (a) of inferiority and (b) of overcompensation are shown by groups that are in the minority in your neighborhood? (Negroes, Orientals, foreigners, Jews, Catholics, or any other group that is in the minority.)

7. Over half the medical discharges given soldiers in the recent war and over a third of the rejections were due to neuropsychiatric conditions. What conclusions do you draw from these facts?

8. Some children who have autocratic, cold, repressive parents or overprotective, indulgent ones grow up to be perfectly normal adults. What explanations can you give? Do you know of such an instance?

9. Do you know anyone who seems to you to have an illness of psychosomatic origin? What makes you think so?

10. List all the times you can remember when you have been ill at just the right time to avoid doing something you did not want to do. Can you group these episodes into purely imaginary illnesses, illnesses of psychosomatic origin, and illnesses of physiological origin?

11. Read any of the published diaries of adolescents or any series of published poems by adolescents. What moods do you find reflected in these writings?

12. You must know at least one fanatic. What are his or her symptoms? What purposes does the fanaticism serve and what drives does it satisfy?

Chapter Eight: Emotions and the School

1. Can you recall any requirements or administrative procedures in high school that aroused anger or other emotion among the students? Was this result inevitable? Were the procedures necessary?

2. How can a school best protect a dull child, a Negro, or a foreign pupil from being avoided, becoming isolated, and developing undesirable personal traits?

3. Did you ever have a teacher you were afraid of? What characteristics aroused this attitude on your part?

4. Take a census among your friends to determine what proportion really fear examinations. What reasons are given? What symptoms do they have? How would you propose re-educating them?

5. Consider the teachers you have known who have aroused fear or anger among their students. What types of treatment or reactions, what character traits did they show? Make a single list for all such teachers you have known.

6. Thinking back to your own high school days, how many of the problems listed in Table 12 (page 248 ff.) did you have? How many and what ones are still unsolved?

7. You must have known at least one peculiar, abnormal, or eccentric pupil in school. What symptoms from those listed on page 255 did he or she show? Were there other symptoms? In about what grades did the unusual behavior appear? Was anything done to help the pupil?

8. Did the teachers and administrators in your high school discriminate against any pupils or groups of pupils? In what way?

9. Write a brief description of the best and the worst teacher you have had to date and compare your descriptions with Table 9, page 232. How many and what characteristics did each teacher show? Do you have any new ones to add to the list?

Chapter Nine: Social Growth

1. Make a sociogram to show the interrelations among members of the "crowd" you went with in high school.
2. Make a similar diagram for some small group of college students, in your own clique or in another.
3. Why is social isolation an especially serious problem during adolescence?
4. Make a list of a dozen socially isolated people you have known. Then, for each one, list the reasons for the isolation. What environmental causes and what traits of personality do you find?
5. Most secondary schools in the United States are coeducational. What effect may this situation have upon the establishment of heterosexual friendships?
6. If an unpopular boy (or girl) came to you for advice about how to improve his (or her) social standing, what advice would you give?
7. List three student leaders whom you have known. What traits or complex of traits caused them to be leaders?
8. List the traits of the most popular and the least popular student whom you know. Compare your list of traits with that given in Table 16, page 288.
9. Do you believe in education for leadership? Why or why not?
10. Analyze a love affair—your own, a friend's, or one out of a novel—that waxed and waned. Use the analysis given in Figure 68, page 275.
11. Describe your own high school crowd. Of whom did it consist? What was its relation to other crowds? What were its advantages and disadvantages?
12. What social classes were represented in your own high school? If you still have your senior yearbook, go through it and group the members of your class into three or five classes as to social status. Then compare the extent to which members of your highest and lowest classes participated in various school activities.
13. Who were the leaders in your high school? What traits did they have? Compare them with the list on page 295 and with the subsequent discussion.

Chapter Ten: The Adolescent and His Home

1. Why is emancipation from home (a) necessary and (b) a problem of adolescence?
2. Classify your own home and that of your best friend according to the scheme presented on pages 313–316. Can you see a relationship between home treatment and the personality of the children?
3. Can you give instances of homes in which the children received the same treatment but turned out quite differently?
4. Make a list of the specific problems you and your friends have encountered in trying to emancipate yourselves from your homes.
5. Do you know any adolescent who seems to lack the usual desire to get away from home? Can you give an explanation?
6. Give a half-dozen short illustrations of difficulties of any type into which you or your friends have gotten, at one time or another. Did you get yourselves out, or did some older person help you?
7. Give an instance from your own observation of parental maladjustment that has been passed along to the children.
8. In your adolescence did you go through the usual experience of being ashamed of your home? On what grounds?
9. Describe some "insecure" homes that you have observed.
10. Describe briefly some "incomplete" homes and indicate what each lacked, and why.
11. In high school and college you must have known at least one unemancipated

adolescent. Describe him or her, making clear what traits or reactions showed his failure to become independent.

12. Suppose that a mothers' club asked you to write five or six rules for them to follow in dealing with their adolescent children, what would you give them? Can you rewrite them for the use of a high school teacher in dealing with her pupils?

13. Was your home mother-dominated, mother-led, father-dominated, or father-led? Give explicit incidents to prove your conclusion.

14. Do you have any friends who were homesick when they first came to college? Can you give any reasons for this manifestation?

15. Hold a debate on the question of whether American society is becoming more and more matriarchal.

Chapter Eleven: Delinquency

1. Look up an article that gives results about a group of delinquents. What mental, physical, social, emotional, and moral traits are they reported as having?

2. How do you account for the extreme educational retardation of delinquents?

3. What useful social traits do many delinquents possess? What constructive use might be made of them?

4. Delinquency has been regarded (a) as a result of inherited traits within the child, (b) as the result of maladjustment between child and environment, (c) as the result of frustration of fundamental drives, and (d) as the product of unwholesome environment. What point or points of view seem to you most tenable?

5. What are the characteristics of a "delinquent" home?

6. Do you know, or can you find out, if in your own home town juvenile delinquency varies with different areas? If possible, get some results, by wards or other local units, and make such a map as appears in Figure 85, page 363.

7. How would you characterize a delinquent district? (Before answering this question, you would do well to find out where there is such a district and then walk through it—but do not go alone.)

8. Think back to your own days in junior high and high school. What elements in school work and life do you think might have been undesirable when applied to delinquents?

9. Why is delinquency so difficult to "cure"?

10. Suppose you, as a teacher, have observed minor delinquency in Johnnie, aged twelve, and that you discover upon inquiry that he has shown similar behavior off and on for a couple of years. What recommendations would you make for dealing constructively with him?

11. What reasons can you give for the increase of delinquency during World War II?

12. What drives are most important to the delinquent? (Use the list given in Table 3, page 112.) Wherein does he differ from other people?

13. Follow the reports of one or two cases of juvenile delinquents as reported in the newspapers. Can you isolate any factors that might have influenced the boy or girl to become delinquent?

14. What steps could a community take if it wishes to reduce the amount of delinquency among its children and adolescents?

Chapter Twelve: The Social Life of the School

1. Make a list of the co-curricular activities in either your high school or your college. Mark those in which you participated. Check your list against that given on pages 400–401. Do you think the range of activities adequate?

2. Suppose you were asked to justify the existence and prominence of school activities. What arguments would you use?

3. Give an instance in which some activity was of definite value to you.

4. Have all members of the class—and of other classes, if possible—turn in (a) a statement of what clubs or groups they belong to and (b) the number of hours they have spent in these activities during some previous period, such as three days or at most a week. Make a figure to compare with Figure 92, page 405.

5. What should be the relation of the teaching staff to the school activities?

6. What should be the relation between activities and curriculum?

7. Make a sociogram of a small college class.

8. Suppose that you are a teacher in high school and that you have made a sociogram of your class. You find (a) two or three small cliques, (b) three pair of mutual friends, (c) six isolates, (d) three rival leaders, (e) two pupils who are generally disliked, and (f) one who is greatly admired. What steps could you take to improve the social relationships?

9. Select in your own mind an isolated student whom you have noticed in your classes. Do not tell anyone what you are doing or whom you have selected. Bring the student's name into a number of conversations as naturally as you can, and listen to the reactions you get. Then make a diagram of him or her, like that shown in Figure 69 or 91, pages 277 and 395. Do not approach the isolate in any way; be content with what you can deduce from observation. You might, however, make a list of suggestions as to what measures you think might be taken to bring about a better adjustment.

Chapter Thirteen: Growth in Attitudes

1. Rate yourself in your attitude toward other races, other nationalities, other religions. (Thus, if you are white, American, and Protestant, rate your attitude toward Negroes, Japanese, English, Germans, Italians, Jews, and Catholics.) Can you account for your prejudices?

2. After reading the material on the stereotypes of the Negro and Jew on page 419, outline a stereotype for any other racial, national, or religious group with which you may be familiar.

3. Read one or more articles on race riots. Do you think the theory of "group frustration" tenable?

4. Do you really believe that "all men are created equal"?

5. If you belong to a minority group, list a few incidents in which you have been rejected by the majority. What reaction did you make to the rejection?

6. In case you still go to church at least every other Sunday, make a brief statement as to what values you derive from your attendance. If you no longer go to church—or not oftener than once or twice a year, perhaps under parental pressure—give a brief explanation of why the church failed to hold you.

7. Prepare a list of statements of a nature similar to those in Figure 94, page 430, and have them checked by members of the class or of any other group. Make a chart of the results.

8. Write a brief description of a Sunday school you have attended. State your own age at the time. Mention procedures, methods, and personal traits of your teacher or teachers. What values did you derive? What recommendations for improvement can you make?

9. Make a list of what seem to you to be typical adolescent ideals.

10. Hold a debate on the topic: Ideals are based upon habits.

11. Do you think the direct teaching of ideals, as reported on page 444, the best approach? If not, can you suggest another?

12. Write an account of an incident in which you have observed cheating. If possible, give the reasons behind the behavior.

13. Write in not over a page—a paragraph is enough—a simple and direct statement of your own philosophy of life, insofar as you have evolved one.
14. If you are in the habit of praying, compare your prayers with those reported on pages 431–432.
15. With whom have you identified yourself at different ages? Whom did you wish to be like?
16. What recommendations can you make for changing the attitude of prejudiced people toward a minority race or an ethnic group?
17. Select any minority group with which you are familiar. Then make two lists, one showing what you consider to be actual and demonstrable differences between it and the majority group and a second containing the imputed differences. For example, Negroes differ from white people in their skin color—an actual difference—and are often said to be lazy—an imputed but not proven difference. How do your two lists compare?
18. From what sources did you derive your own philosophy of life?
19. Write a case history of (a) a strongly prejudiced person and (b) a highly religious individual. These should be people whom you know well. Bring out their traits of personality and whatever you know about their childhood and youth.
20. The Jews have been persecuted in many countries for many centuries. Can you give any reasons why they have been the recipients of so much aggression?

Chapter Fourteen: Community Influences

1. Think of the town or section of a city that you know best. In parallel columns list, with brief descriptions or comments, the positive and the negative influences.
2. Give instances from your own experience of the use of community facilities by the school as a part of its curricular activities.
3. If you have attended a teen canteen (by whatever name it was called) describe it and give reasons for its success or failure as a center for adolescent social life.
4. What possibilities for diversion are offered by your home and by your community to young people?
5. Give evidence that the modern family (a) has retained its solidarity and (b) has lost its former solidarity.

Chapter Fifteen: Mental Growth

1. Try constructing a half-dozen items for an intelligence test to be used with high school pupils.
2. Figure the IQ's for the following results:

| MA | 6–4 * | MA | 14–2 | MA | 8–0 | MA | 5–1 |
| CA | 7–1 | CA | 12–6 | CA | 8–3 | CA | 4–1 |

* These numbers are to be read "6 years 4 months."

3. In the *Biennial Survey of Education* (for whatever year is most recent) look up the number of pupils ages 14 to 18 who are in high school in your state; also the number in college. Then find the total population at these ages from the most recent census. What proportions between ages 14 and 22 are in school?
4. If possible, obtain intelligence test results from a nearby school and tabulate the results, as in Figure 119, page 502. Can you explain any discrepancies?
5. If you have any stories, letters, or other writing from your elementary and high school years, get them out and compare them for evidences of growth.
6. Children like comics but not cartoons. Can you give an explanation for this preference?
7. Compare some of the poems written for children (by Stevenson or Riley, for example) and consider whether or not children would be likely to understand them.

8. Do you memorize as well as you did five years ago, assuming an equal desire in both cases?
9. Each student should write on a slip the number of his own siblings, the number for his father and his mother, and—if possible—that for each of his four grandparents. A comparison may be made with the results in Figure 116.
10. If you teach a Sunday school class, read the children one of the less familiar parables and ask them to interpret its meaning.
11. Collect about a dozen cartoons dealing with events of the present or the very recent past. Submit them to as many people of different ages as you can. What responses do you get?
12. If you can, get from the high school you attended the enrollment figures for every five or ten years since it opened. Make a curve such as that shown in Figure 115, page 498.
13. Obtain similar figures from the college in which you are enrolled.
14. You certainly have some friends who have dropped out of school at some time since your freshman year in high school. What reasons did they give? Are there other reasons that you think were operative?
15. If the administration of a high school wants to keep every adolescent in school until he graduates, what changes would have to be made in the materials and methods of instruction?
16. How many different kinds of "ages" have been mentioned? What is the value of such concepts?

Chapter Sixteen: Intellectual-Cultural Interests

1. What games or amusements interested you most when you were at ages 10–11, 14–15, 19–20 years? Can you explain any shifts of interest?
2. As you have observed them in your own home or in the homes of your friends, what are the differences in the radio programs listened to by the adults, the adolescents, and the children?
3. How often has each member of the class attended the movies during the past week?
4. Describe one or two instances in which you have gotten ideas from the movies. (See pages 548–549.)
5. Debate the statement that movies do adolescents more harm than good.
6. What kinds of collections have you made? At, roughly, what ages?
7. What are the characteristic play activities of adolescence? Of childhood? Of adulthood?
8. Can you remember a half-dozen books that made so great an impression upon you that you read and reread and daydreamed about them? What books? And at what ages did they have this effect? Does your experience agree with the results on pages 557 ff.
9. During the summer vacation, how often did you use the public or the loan libraries?
10. Keep track of how much time you spend listening to the radio or watching television. Do you keep your radio going while you study? Why?
11. Through what media do you get information on current events?

Chapter Seventeen: Intellectual Deviates

1. Several children have IQ's as follows:

Mary	— 107	Paul	— 157
James	— 86	Ellen	— 59
Betty	— 117	Donald	— 92
David	— 122	Doris	— 64
Amos	— 98	Polly	— 171
Grace	— 74	Carl	— 104

How would you classify these children? Which ones would be "average" for elementary school but "dull" for high school?

2. Why do teachers often think that brilliant children are small for their age?
3. From the material thus far given on physical and emotional growth, how do you feel about the following problems: (a) Should a bright child be kept back with children his own age or allowed to go faster? (b) Should a dull child be promoted every semester, regardless of his academic progress?
4. You have probably known a bright boy or girl who concentrated upon academic work, became a "grind," and was scorned by other students. Can you give any explanation for this behavior?
5. Did your high school make any arrangements that you know of for pupils of exceptional ability in any given field? Does your college?
6. Take any small unit of subject matter from any course and write out (a) a half-dozen assignments for bright and for dull students in the same course and (b) one or two questions for a final exam for each extreme. Use the same material but vary the approach.
7. Write a description of some brilliant student whom you have known. .
8. What conclusions do you draw from the reports summarized on pages 591–593?
9. Is it inevitable that a dull pupil will become unhappy and discouraged in high school?
10. Write a history of a definitely dull or defective classmate of yours in junior high or high school, noting especially his reactions to his incapacities.
11. Both very bright and very dull pupils develop feelings of inferiority. How do you explain them? What could you do to help the pupil recover from them?
12. Describe two or three dull individuals whom you have known who have made a satisfactory adjustment to life.
13. Hold a debate on this question: Should every child be promoted every year, without respect to his mastery of subject matter?

Chapter Eighteen: Personnel Work in the High School

1. If possible, obtain data from the local high schools concerning the vocational choices of their pupils—especially their freshmen. Then find out through the Chamber of Commerce what the needs of the community are. Compare these two results as in Figure 146, page 614.
2. What are the advantages and disadvantages in following the occupation of one's father?
3. What vocational ambitions have you had at different ages?
4. Every year the arts colleges graduate students who have no training (given in their regular classwork) for earning their living. What do you think of this situation?
5. What is your own vocational objective? What proportion of the facts you should know about it—as given on pages 620–622—do you actually know?
6. Give an example from your own experience of a person with the "wrong disposition" for his job.
7. Were there counselors in your high school? What did they do?
8. You must know at least one student who is preparing to enter a vocation that seems to you unsuited to his abilities and personality. Write a brief description of such a student, making clear why you think he will not succeed.
9. Make a profile of yourself, such as are shown in Figure 147, page 617. If possible, make similar profiles of your friends.
10. Consider the extent to which your prospective vocation will give you (a) chances for self-expression, (b) financial returns, and (c) security. See Figure 149, page 625. Next, consider your own needs, using the list given in Table 3, page 112. How are your data interrelated?

Chapter Nineteen: The High School Curriculum

1. If possible, have your parents list the courses they took in high school. List your own courses. Compare the two. Was your own curriculum "modern"?
2. Debate the value of the various objectives discussed on pages 639–643 in the selection of material for the high school curriculum.
3. Compare your college curriculum with the criteria given on pages 638–639. What differences do you note? Should there be such differences between high school and college?
4. What courses are you required to take? Why?
5. During the eight years of high school and college what proportion of work each year do you think should be selective?
6. Describe your best and your worst high school teacher.
7. Get a copy of the local high school's curriculum. To what extent do you think it is adapted to adolescent needs?
8. List the subjects you took in high school and classify them according to Figure 150, page 655.
9. Hold a debate on this topic: The present high school curriculum is better than that in vogue in 1915. (For a rough idea of the curriculum in 1915, see Tables 55 and 56.)

Index

Index

A

Abnormal mental conditions, 182ff.
  anxiety neuroses, 190–193
  in army and navy, 184–185
  in college, 183–184
  fanaticism, 211–214
  hysteria, 209–211
  incidence, 182–185
  inferiority, 197–202
  moodiness, 202–205
  neurasthenia, 205–208, 209
  phobias, 186–190
  psychopathic personality, 214–219
  psychosomatic conditions, 193–197
  schizophrenia, 219–226
Abstractions, 9, 522–524, 549, 595–596, 602, 659–660
Academic success as compensation, 36, 143, 586
Acceleration of brilliant children, 437, 577–581
Acceptance, by age mates, 394, 395–396
  in classroom, 237–239
  parental, 313–315
Acceptant parents, 314–315
Acne, 61
Activities (*see* Co-curricular activities; Interests)
Adjustment, difficulties of, 5ff., 247ff., 610–611, 642
  nature of, 145–146
Adolescence as a period of life, 1–3
Adolescent centered high school, 643
Adolescent interests as basis for curriculum, 642
Adolescents, problems of, 5–9, 247ff., 610–611, 642
Adrenalin, 117, 119–120
Adult, intelligence, 495–496
  needs as basis of curriculum, 641–642
  role in adolescent social life, 267–268
  world, 676–678

Adulthood, definitions of, 665
Adventure stories, 559, 562
Age, and emotional drives, 113–114
  of first delinquency, 375–376
  of graduation from college, 575
  and interests, 542–613
  and mental development, 485, 491–496
  of mental maturity, 491–495
  and moral development, 142, 430, 442–445
  and physical development, 16–17, 20, 30, 31, 32–34, 49, 50–52, 70ff.
  social, 305
Aggression, and intolerance, 422, 428
  analysis of, 122–126
  as escape mechanism, 147, 150–151
  levels of, 420–421
  release through reading, 562
  scapegoating, 420
  symptoms of, 256
Agility, 29–32
Aiming test, 30–31
Allowance, 328–329
Androgen, 72
Anger, 122ff.
  causes of, 123–124
  diaries, 122–123
  duration of, 125–126
  reactions to, 125
Anxiety neuroses, 190–193
Anxieties (*see* Problems)
Appetite, 60–61
Armed forces, abnormality in, 184–185
Arteries, 56
Arthur Performance Scale, 478–479
Athletics, interest in, 552–556
  in school program, 402
  skill and success in, 34–38
Attendance at movies, 542–543
Attention-getting behavior, 317
  See also Exhibitionism; Overcompensation

697